About the Author

Lean'tin Bracks, is Associate Professor of African American Literature, Chair of the Department of Arts and Languages, and Discipline Coordinator for English at Fisk University in Nashville, Tennessee. She is the author of *Writings on Black Women of the Diaspora: History Language and Identity,* and editor of the university text *The Black Arts Movement of the 1960's.* She has made numerous contributions to historical, biographical, and critical texts such as *Children of the Changing South: Accounts of Growing Up During and After Integration, Freedom Facts and Firsts, African American National Biography, Encyclopedia of African American Popular Culture, African American Almanac* 11th edition, *Notable African American Men,* and *Contemporary African-American Novelists: A Bio-Bibliographical Critical Sourcebook.* Bracks has also contributed to scholarly journals such as *The Black Scholar* and *Nineteenth-Century Prose.* Her many awards include an Honorary Degree from her undergraduate institution, Kenyon College in Gambier, Ohio; Outstanding Teaching Awards in the Humanities; and an Excellence in Service Award from her university. Dr. Bracks is a native of Texas City, Texas, and completed her graduate work at the University of Nebraska, Lincoln, where she earned her M.A. and Ph.D.

ALSO FROM VISIBLE INK PRESS

Black Firsts: 4,000 Ground-Breaking and Pioneering Events, 2nd Edition
by Jessie Carney Smith
ISBN: 978-1-57859-142-8

Black Heroes
by Jessie Carney Smith
ISBN: 978-1-57859-136-7

Freedom Facts and Firsts:
400 Years of the African American Civil Rights Experience
by Jessie Carney Smith and Linda T. Wynn
ISBN: 978-1-57859-192-3

Please visit us at VisibleInkPress.com

African American Almanac

400 Years of Triumph, Courage and Excellence

Visible Ink Press®
43311 Joy Rd., #414
Canton, MI 48187-2075

Visible Ink Press is a registered trademark of Visible Ink Press LLC.

Most Visible Ink Press books are available at special quantity discounts when purchased in bulk by corporations, organizations, or groups. Customized printings, special imprints, messages, and excerpts can be produced to meet your needs. For more information, contact Special Markets Director, Visible Ink Press, www.visibleinkpress.com, or 734-667-3211.

Managing Editor: Kevin S. Hile
Art Director: Mary Claire Krzewinski
Typesetting: Marco Di Vita
Proofreaders: Sarah Hermsen, Sharon Malinowski
Indexing: Shoshana Hurwitz

ISBN 978-1-57859-323-1

Cover images: iStock.

Library of Congress Cataloguing-in-Publication Data

Bracks, Lean'tin L.
  African American almanac : 400 years of triumph, courage and excellence / Lean'tin Bracks.
      p. cm. ISBN 978-1-57859-323-1 (pbk.)
    1. African Americans—History. 2. African Americans—Social life and customs. 3. African Americans—Intellectual life. 4. African Americans—Biography. I. Title.
  E185.B8127 2012
  973'.0496073—dc23   2011038636

Printed in the United States of America

10 9 8 7 6 5 4 3 2 1

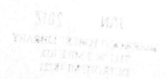

African American Almanac

400 Years of Triumph, Courage and Excellence

Lean'tin Bracks

Foreword by Jessie Carney Smith

Detroit

Contents

Foreword

African American history continues to be recorded in various sources and in many formats. To paraphrase on old expression, "we cannot count the ways." These works tell a story—an African American story—often arranged under a variety of main topics and subheadings. When the story is incomplete, as it often is, the reason may be that someone in America's past failed to search for all the pieces of our puzzled lives, considered the life and work of our ancestors irrelevant, or deliberately failed to record the whole truth. As a long-time librarian in one of America's Historically Black Colleges and Universities—one that concentrates its sources of information on African Americans in a special collection—time consistently proves that, thus far, we are still in need of sources. Our people continue to achieve, historians and writers continue to record, and users continue to seek accounts of our past and present.

Like any work regarding our culture that intends to be historically comprehensive, publications such as this almanac cover America's early settlers, when Africans arrived in America, and then fill in the years between 1619 and the present. It follows that discussions of slavery will occupy a portion of this work. However it is recorded, the cruelties of the slavery period can-

not be overshadowed, yet we marvel over the craftiness of our ancestors: the scientists and inventors (Elijah McCoy, Garrett A. Morgan, Onesimus, and Norbert Rillieux); the preachers (Richard Allen and Henry McNeal Turner); the abolitionists (Martin Delany, Frederick Douglass, Josiah Henson, William Still, Harriet Tubman, and Sojourner Truth); the slave insurgents (Gabriel Prosser, Nat Turner, and Denmark Vesey); the musicians (Elizabeth Taylor Greenfield, Francis Johnson, and Blind Tom); and the poets and writers (William Wells Brown, Jupiter Hammon, and Phillis Wheatley). These people and others like them left a lasting impact on our culture.

In *The African American Almanac: 400 Years of Triumph, Courage and Excellence* the work of these early leaders, especially the civil rights pioneers, is balanced by more contemporary American counterparts—men like W.E.B. Du Bois, Louis Farrakhan, Marcus Garvey, Martin Luther King Jr., Malcolm X, Thurgood Marshall, Al Sharpton, and Booker T. Washington; or by women leaders such as Daisy Bates, Ella Baker, Fannie Lou Hamer, Rosa Parks, Constance Baker Motley, Mary Church Terrell, and many, many more. Similarly, the mutinies, insurrections, and the early civil rights movement are balanced by the marches, demonstrations, and protests of the twentieth century.

Like other repositories of information on African Americans and their culture, we note the continuing and increasing interest in the story of the civil rights activities—the work of the abolitionists, the events of the late 1800s and the modern movement of the 1960s. We see a still-surging interest in the work of women, whether in civil rights, education, politics, arts and entertainment, organizations, or elsewhere. Names like Maya Angelou, Ida Wells-Barnett, Zora Neale Hurston, Nikki Giovanni, Barbara Jordan, Toni Morrison, and Alice Walker continue to pique the interest of student researchers whose needs our libraries appropriately address. At the same time, we do not disregard the work of our leading educators, people like Mary McLeod Bethune, Nannie Helen Burroughs, Johnnetta Cole, John Hope Franklin, Benjamin Mayes, and Carter G. Woodson, or the Historically Black Colleges and Universities (HBCUs). Neither do we ignore the media for its coverage of our history, nor the achievements of those popular personalities whose names we read about almost daily—Tom Joyner, Tavis Smiley, and Oprah Winfrey, for example. We shine as well in the arts, music, on stage and on screen.

While so many recent political, biographical, and other works on African Americans illustrate their covers and include a biography or essay on President Barack Obama, in the view of black America this attention is not too much. Arguably, his achievement is regarded as one of the most noteworthy accomplishments of our race and our time. In another view, it may be the most significant achievement of a singular African American in the history of our nation. As we see in *African American Almanac*, an almanac is a good source of information on currently popular issues and topics, from the No Child Left Behind Act, which President George W. Bush signed into law on January 8, 2002, to Race to the Top, a program that President Obama's administration conceived in 2010, almanacs can give an overview of federal interest and involvement in improving education.

Reflecting on my educational experiences, I realize now how fortunate I am to have been exposed to African American literature, beginning with my elementary school and continuing through college, but unfortunately less so in my graduate school experiences. To spend most of my professional life guiding the development of a major research resource on African American culture is an experience that I would never want to change. Nor would I change the influence of my predecessor, Arna Bontemps, a luminary from the Harlem Renaissance whose vision for collecting and preserving African Americana I share and cherish. I am able to share the fruits of my labor with others, however, as I continue to work with those who write the almanacs, as well as in the biographical and encyclopedic works that I have published. My colleague Dr. Lean'tin Bracks, who edited this almanac, and I also have a common bond when it comes to preserving and interpreting the works of our ancestors. Her platform is in the classroom, while mine is in the library. We share the desire of historical recognition of the African American experience and devote ourselves to preservation, research, and accuracy in our work. Her scholarship, already demonstrated in the articles and books on African American themes that she has published, are testimonies to her ability to produce a good product. In this almanac, she has wrought well.

As libraries strive to remain a vital research resource for a variety of users—from undergraduate students to doctoral students, to writers of histories and literary works—we are challenged to ensure that our clientele has access to the almanacs, biographical works, histories, and the myriad of information sources that will fill this audience's needs, as well as lead people to other sources that are well worth exploration. This almanac will add to the needed resources that will expand the scope of information available to all learners.

Jessie Carney Smith
Dean of the Library and
William and Camille Cosby
Professor in the Humanities,
Fisk University

Introduction

The *African American Almanac: 400 Years of Triumph, Courage and Excellence* is a thoughtful and focused book that is based on the premise of sharing knowledge, history, and inspiration regarding the African American experience, building on that knowledge with the biographies of individuals who have made progress and positive change possible. Africans in America have endured and excelled during a unique and extraordinary journey that spans well over 400 years, and that lends itself to an understanding of struggle and survival worthy of acclaim and respect.

This almanac was first realized as *African America: Portrait of a People* and was published as a work that condensed the wealth of information and inspiration of the award-winning text *The African-American Almanac,* formerly *The Negro Almanac*, thus creating a unique and valuable reader devoted to illustrating and demystifying the moving, difficult, and often lost history of black life in America. This text sets about to further emphasize that objective and has moved into the role of a repository of history and history makers.

The African American community has come a long way in creating, designing, and redesigning "the portrait of a people," and has continued to succeed against generations of inhumanity and denied citizenship. As the generations have moved forward, African Americans have removed the barriers of enslavement, lynching, segregation, and legal discrimination and have transformed the arts, music, science, and medicine. An awareness of the journey to accomplish these goals is a powerful tool and resource in understanding the African American story, as well as the story of this nation. Although in the twenty-first century there continues to be areas where African Americans break new ground by being the first in accessing areas of American society, their continued contributions to the reinvention and creativity of many other aspects of the national and global scene are quite profound. With the nation having elected the first African American president in 2008, the idea of a post-racial society only flickered for a moment as the true issues of political, social, and economic parity in America are yet to be fully realized.

The African American Almanac is broken down into twelve chapters consisting of Africans in America, Civil Rights, Politics, Education, Religion, Literature, Business, Visual and Performing Arts, Music, Science & Medicine, Sports, and the Military. Each chapter begins with an historical accounting of the evolution of the chapter's focus and discusses the influences that impacted the move toward change and progress through to the twenty-first century.

The biographies offer a view of individuals who have contributed to the growth and change in each chapter, as well as those who have established a level of influence and those who serve as role models. They also provide insight into the lives and accomplishments of African Americans inclusive of notables such as the first African American president, Barack H. Obama; the only black billionaire in America, Oprah Winfrey; the youngest president of the NAACP, Ben Jealous; an artist considered the greatest entertainer of all time, Michael Jackson; the recipient of the Pulitzer Prize for Literature, Toni Morrison; rapper, artist, and music mogul Jay Z; the Queen of Soul, Aretha Franklin; and the first female bishop in the African Methodist Episcopal (AME) church, Vashti McKenzie.

While vigorously seeking to recognize those persons from the past who have sacrificed greatly, and those who have opened doors of opportunity so that others may pass through, I have done my best to share with you as many histories and stories as possible of "triumph, courage and excellence."

Acknowledgements

As an editor, scholar, and teacher, I accepted this project as a means to further promote the African American story and subsequently the story of our nation. No work can ever be successful without the help of publishers who understand the purpose as well as the product, all while being flexible and patient. Many thanks to my publisher, Roger Jänecke, and managing editor, Kevin Hile, for their guidance and commitment. I also wish to gratefully acknowledge Dr. Jessie Carney Smith for her encouragement and support while I tackled this project as the singular researcher, and Bobby Bracks, who helped make possible the hours and days of research needed to maintain an uninterrupted focus. The contributions of those writers and researchers who provided the original manuscript for this project created a solid foundation from which to build and move forward. Others who made invaluable contributions to the success of this project include typesetter Marco DiVita and page and cover designer Mary Claire Krzewinski.

Lean'tin Bracks, Ph.D.
Editor

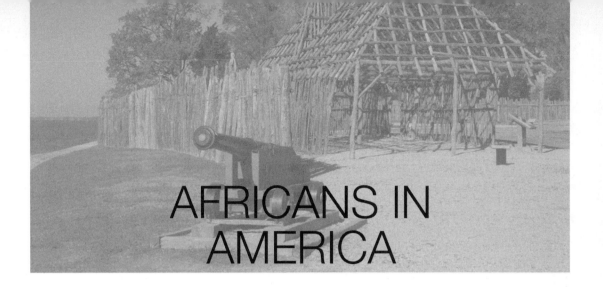

AFRICANS IN AMERICA

The exact date of the arrival of Africans in the Americas has been a point of contention for historians. Although the year 1619 serves as the first recorded date of twenty Ndongan Africans' forced arrival in North America, the presence of thirty-two Africans who were already among the settlers remains unresolved. Scholars such as Ivan Van Sertima argue from archeological, anthropological, botanical, and linguistic evidence that Africans were present in pre-Columbian America. Others mark the advent of the African presence as coinciding with the arrival of the Europeans.

Pedro Alonzo Niño, an explorer and companion to Christopher Columbus on his exploratory journey of 1492, was of African descent and the African named Estevanico accompanied the Spanish explorers Panfilo de Narvaez and Alvar Nuñez Cabeza de Vaca on trips throughout the American Southwest during the 1500s. Vasco Nuñez de Balboa and Hernán Cortés also had African members in their parties.

In 1496 Santo Domingo was established as the first permanent European settlement in the Americas. Indigenous Carib Indians were at first used as laborers; however, they were ill-suited for the dehumanizing rigors of the European system of slavery and died in large numbers from either disease or the constant pressure of forced labor. Portuguese explorers first visited the west coast of Africa in the fifteenth century and found that slave trading was an established institution. West Africans had for some time sold each other to Arabic traders from North Africa. By the early sixteenth century the Portuguese and Spanish were supplying newly established colonies in the Americas with African slave labor, and by the seventeenth century several other European nations had entered the trade. African slaves proved to be a relatively cheap and inexhaustible source of labor, and from about 1501 they were increasingly used as slaves, replacing the dwindling Indian labor pool.

As the opportunities for increased production and economic gain were further realized through forced African slave labor, the traditional meaning of slavery as practiced in Africa took on a vastly different meaning when Europeans incorporated it. The almost inexhaustible supply of Africans practically eliminated the acknowledgement of them by Europeans as human beings, in deference to Africans as "other." This forced migration of millions of Africans has been called by African American activists and historians as Maafa, a Kiswahili word meaning "disaster," which is defined as the Black Holocaust. People of African descent who have been separated from their homeland and placed among other cultures have become a Diaspora people. Africans in North America have struggled to overcome the challenges of their new homeland while maintaining, protecting, and still discovering their cultural roots, as well as forging their identity as African Americans.

In 1619 twenty Ndongans, originally headed for Mexico, were rerouted to North America, and landed in Jamestown, Virginia. As captives they were sold for supplies and became indentured servants who worked for a contracted period of time. Some Africans were contracted for life and others died before their contracts expired. Those who survived their contract time were freed and thus able to claim the liberties and privileges of a "free laboring class." By 1650 there were about three hundred Africans in the American colonies, most of whom were indentured servants and some of whom eventually became property holders and active citizens. The first African American born in the colonies, William Tucker in 1624,

shared with the other settlers the common birthright of freedom. The slave Anthony Johnson became free in 1622 and had by 1651 amassed enough wealth to import five servants of his own, for which he obtained two hundred and fifty acres from the colonial government; the African American carpenter Richard Johnson imported two white servants in 1654 and received one hundred acres.

It is unclear when the very first African slaves arrived in the North American colonies. A census taken in Virginia in 1619 included thirty-two Africans but no other notations regarding their arrival or their life in the New World were recorded. From the 1640s Africans were increasingly regarded as chattel (or persons regarded as fixed items of personal property). In 1641 Massachusetts became the first state to make perpetual bondage legal, and the institution gradually spread among the original thirteen colonies. Rhode Island had an anti-slavery ordinance, but this was openly violated, and

Visitors to the Jamestown National Historic Site view artifacts of the preserved town where, in 1619, twenty Ndongans from Africa were brought and worked as indentured servants.

only Pennsylvania maintained a sustained opposition to slavery. By the 1650s Africans were commonly sold for life, and in 1661 the Virginia House of Burgesses formally recognized the institution of black slavery. The erosion of African indentured servitude in Maryland was finalized with the slave law of 1663, which stated specifically that "all negroes or other slaves within the province, [and] all negroes to be hereafter imported, shall serve durante vita."

As white indentured servitude gradually disappeared from the colonial labor market, the flow of African labor into the colonies was accelerated, and planters rigidly institutionalized the perpetual servitude of Africans. One practical reason for this system was that slaves of African origin could be more easily detected than whites should they escape. And among the common rationalizations for the enslavement of Africans was reference to their non-Christian status; it was asserted that Africans were primitive and savage, and fit for nothing better than a life of unbroken labor. Even after African Americans became Christianized, their slave status was not altered; in 1667 the Virginia legislature enacted a statute that proclaimed that "baptism doth not alter the condition of the person as to his bondage or freedom."

The Dutch West India Company began to provide slave labor to the American colonies in 1621. By the late seventeenth century the Royal African Company, an English company whose most profitable commodity was slaves, began to exert powerful influence within the English court and parliament. The British government in turn exerted great pressure upon the American colonies to develop attitudes and laws that would support a slave economy. The influence of the Royal African Company contributed to William Penn's decision to overrule the objections of fellow Quakers and permit slavery in Pennsylvania. The company also drew the shipping industry of New England into the slave trade. By the time the Royal African Company lost its monopoly on the West African slave trade in 1696, the sea captains of New England were participating in the massive slave incursions into Africa.

African slaves being transported on the slave ship *Wildfire* in 1860.

The majority of Africans who were transported to the Americas as slaves came from the area comprising the modern nations of Senegal, Gambia, Guinea, Sierra Leone, Liberia, Upper Volta, Ivory Coast, Ghana, Togo, Benin, Nigeria, Cameroon, Gabon, and the Republic of the Congo. The number of Africans who reached the Americas is estimated at between ten and twenty million. About six hundred thousand Africans were brought during the sixteenth century, two million in the seventeenth century, five million in the eighteenth century, and three million in the nineteenth century. In addition to those who reached the Americas must be added the enormous number who died in passage. It is estimated that 15 percent of those who were shipped to the Americas died of disease on the overcrowded boats of the "Middle Passage," and that another 30 percent died during the brutal training period faced in the West Indies before shipment to the American mainland.

The colonies of New England played a principal role in the slave trade, despite their having little local need for slave labor. By 1700 African Americans of New England numbered only one thousand among a population of ninety thousand. In the mid-Atlantic colonies the population comprised a larger percentage, as small slaveholdings employed slaves as farm laborers, domestics, and craftsmen. In New York slaves comprised 12 percent of the population during the mid-eighteenth century. The Quakers of Pennsylvania protested that slavery violated the principles of Christianity and the rights of man, and passed laws prohibiting the slave trade in 1688, 1693, and 1696, but the British parliament overruled these statutes in 1712. Most slaves lived in the South. The southern colonies were divided between the tobacco-producing provinces of Virginia, Maryland, and North Carolina, and the huge rice and indigo plantations now comprising South Carolina and Georgia. Tobacco tended to be grown on family farms around the Chesapeake Bay area, and because of this the slave population was not as concentrated as it was on the plantations farther to the south.

The growth of a plantation economy and the concentration of a large number of African Americans in the southern states led first Virginia (1636) and then the other states to form all-white militias. The fear of slave uprisings led the slaveholders to institute ever harsher slave codes. Ultimately, a slave could not own anything, carry a weapon, or even leave the plantation without a written pass. Murder, rape, arson, and even lesser offenses were punishable by death; small offenses were commonly punished by whipping, maiming, and branding. In the area where 90 percent of colonial African Americans lived, a slave had no rights to defend himself against a white, and as far north as Virginia it was impossible for a white to be convicted for the murder of a slave.

The large slave revolt in New York City in 1712 and the public paranoia over an alleged slave conspiracy of 1741 led to the development of slave codes that were in some cases as severe as those in the South, but in general the North was a relatively less oppressive environment. In Pennsylvania the Quakers allowed African Americans a relative degree of freedom, and in New England the slave codes tended to reflect Old Testament law, maintaining the legal status of slaves as persons with certain limited rights.

Records of King William's War (1689–1697) relate that the first to fall in Massachusetts was "an Naygro of Colo. Tyng," slain at Falmouth. During Queen Anne's War (1702–1713), African Americans were drafted and sent to fight the French and the Indians when white colonists failed to provide the number of requisitioned men. Many armed African Americans fought at Fort William Henry in New York. Slaves sought freedom as their payment for fighting, and those who were already free sought the wider benefits of land and cash payments. The colony of Virginia ended its policy of excluding African Americans from the militia by 1723, and in 1747 the South Carolina Company made slaves eligible for enlistment in the territorial militia according to a quota system in which a 3:1 ratio was maintained between whites and blacks, thus abating the whites' fears of insurrection. African Americans also fought for the British in the French and Indian War.

In the years leading up to the Revolutionary War it became apparent that, despite the growth of slavery, at least some African Americans were willing to fight alongside white Americans. On March 5, 1770, an African American named Crispus Attucks was one of the first men killed in the Revolutionary War, when British troops fired on a crowd of protesters in the Boston Massacre. Many African American Minutemen fought at the defense of Concord Bridge: among them were Lemuel Haynes, a gifted speaker and later a prominent Congregationalist minister, and Peter Salem, who had received his freedom to enlist. Other figures of the Revolutionary War include Pomp Blackman, Caesar Ferrit and his son John, Prince Estabrook (who was wounded at Lexington), Samuel Craft, and Primas Black and Epheram Blackman (who were members of Ethan Allen's Green Mountain Boys, an army against territorial expansion for New York).

With the enormous slave populations of certain southern states many whites lived in perpetual fear of slave uprisings. As a result, a major

A depiction of a scene from the American Revolution by artist Percy Moran. One would be hard pressed to find a drawing or work of art from the period showing African American soldiers, though many did fight for their new country.

issue during the Revolutionary War was whether African slaves, and even freemen of African descent (African Americans), should be permitted to bear arms. In South Carolina slaves outnumbered whites, and in Georgia the population was over 40 percent slaves. On May 29, 1775, the Massachusetts Committee of Safety, in a move that reflected their desire to strengthen ties with southern states, proclaimed that the enlistment of slaves "was inconsistent with the principles that were to be supported, and reflect[ed] dishonor on the colony." On July 9, 1775, Horatio Gates, the adjutant general of the Continental Army, issued from General Washington's headquarters the order that recruiting officers should not accept "any stroller, Negro, or vagabond."

To minimize the risk of slaves arming themselves, Edward Rutledge of South Carolina introduced a measure in Congress to discharge all African Americans (whether free or enslaved) from the Continental Army. Although the proposal was rejected, General George Washington's own council of war decided to terminate all

African American enlistment two weeks later, and on October 13, 1775, Congress passed the law. Colonial generals like John Thomas argued that African Americans soldiered as well as whites and had already "proved themselves brave" in action, but their protests went unheeded. At the close of 1775 it was extremely difficult for African Americans to join the revolutionary forces at any level.

As the leaders of the Revolution realized that there were inadequate numbers of white troops, they brought an end to their racially exclusionary policy. Local militias that were unable to fill their muster rolls won the quiet agreement of recruiting boards and the reluctant acceptance of slave owners as slaves were substituted for those white men who bought their way out of service. As the war progressed slave owners were compensated for the enlistment of slaves, who were then made free. During the course of the Revolution many colonies granted freedom to slaves in return for military service. Rhode Island passed the first slave enlistment act on February 2, 1778, raising a regiment that participated gallantly in many important battles. In 1780 Maryland became the only southern colony to enroll slave troops, while South Carolina and Georgia refused altogether to even arm their slaves. While slave conscripts were at first assigned to combat support, in the heat of battle they were often armed. African Americans were often enlisted for longer terms than whites, and by the later years of the war many of the most seasoned veterans were African American troops.

At the end of the war about five thousand African Americans had been emancipated through military service. In the following years the northern states abolished slavery: Vermont in 1777, Massachusetts in 1783, Connecticut and Rhode Island in 1784, New York in 1785, New Jersey in 1786, and Pennsylvania in 1789. In the mid-Atlantic state of Virginia, Thomas Jefferson convinced the state legislature to allow slave owners to free their slaves in 1783. In 1790 there were 757,208 African Americans comprising 19 percent of the population of the United States: 697,681 were slaves, and 59,527 were free. During this time the free population faced many of the same restrictions as the slave population: they could not walk on the streets after dark, travel between towns without a pass, or own weapons. There was also the danger of being captured and enslaved, whether one was free or not.

The U.S. Constitution, drafted in 1787 and ratified in 1788, provided fundamental political principles for the nation. Key among these principles was the belief that all people share a fundamental equality, that they possess certain unalienable rights, and that government derives its power from the people. But African Americans were not afforded the rights and privileges of the Constitution. At the time, it was generally believed by whites that people of African descent were racially inferior and incapable of being assimilated into society. It was also widely believed that they were not citizens of the new republic. Article I, section 2 of the Constitution specifies that all persons who are not free shall be counted as three-fifths a person for the sake of tax pur-

poses, and article I, section 9 authorizes the continued importation of slaves until 1808.

In 1793 Eli Whitney invented the cotton gin, which separated cotton from cotton fiber; this led to a subsequent increase in the consumption of cotton and heightened the demand for slaves in the cotton-producing states. In 1800 there were more than 893,600 African slaves in the United States; by 1810 there were 1,191,300. Although the slave trade was technically discontinued in 1808, it is estimated that from that date until 1860 more than 250,000 slaves were illegally imported; furthermore, nothing prohibited slaves from being bartered, and the breeding of slaves for sale became a specialized business. Some of the largest slave-trading firms in the nation were located in Maryland, Virginia, and the District of Columbia. Such was the expansion of slavery that, between 1800 and 1859, the population of Mississippi grew from 3,489 slaves and 5,179 whites to 309,878 slaves and 295,718 whites.

By the mid-eighteenth century, three-fourths of the cotton produced in the world came from the United States, and profits from cotton were so great that vast plantations were hacked from the wilderness, allowing armies of slaves to work the fields. By mid-century the states of Georgia, Alabama, Mississippi, and Louisiana annually produced 1,726,349 bales of cotton, 48 million pounds of rice, and 226,098,000 pounds of sugar. With the outbreak of the Civil War in 1861 there were nearly four million slaves in the United States, and nearly three-fourths of them worked in cotton agriculture.

The mistreatment of slaves in the years after the Revolution led to an atmosphere of suspicion and terror. Masters lived in constant fear of uprisings, and much time was given over to surveillance. Although organized rebellions were rare, there were many instances of angry slaves burning dwellings and murdering their masters. Slave codes became increasingly strict, but no amount of regulation could dissipate the anger of the slaves nor the guilt and unease that many slave owners experienced.

In 1800 an African American named Denmark Vesey purchased his freedom and around

1817 began to plan a slave revolt in Charleston, South Carolina. The revolt was scheduled to begin on July 14, 1822. With the help of five other African Americans as many as nine thousand slaves were recruited before their plans were uncovered. As word of the revolt began to leak out, Vesey was forced to move the date to June 16; again word was leaked. The state militia was mustered, and an intense investigation of the plot was begun. One hundred and thirty-five slaves were arrested during the course of the investigation; ninety-seven were bound over for trial; forty-five were transported out of the country; and Vesey and thirty-four others were hanged. As news of the conspiracy spread, southern states further tightened their slave codes.

In the early seventeenth century the French began to settle in what comprises present-day Illinois, Indiana, Michigan, Ohio, Wisconsin, and part of Minnesota. The British began to settle in the area during the mid-eighteenth century; and in July 1787 Congress passed the Northwest Ordinance, which established a government for the Northwest Territory and provided terms under which states could be formed for entrance into the Union. The ordinance also contained controversial provisions: one prohibited slavery and involuntary servitude in the territory, and the other provided for the return of fugitive slaves to the states from which they had escaped. The European farmers who had brought slaves into the territory were angered by the clause prohibiting slavery, and Congress was petitioned for its repeal. The prohibition against slavery was practically circumvented when the Illinois and Indiana territories established a system of indentured servitude under which any person owning slaves could bring them into the region and place them under lifetime indenture. The restrictions placed on these servants were much like the slave codes of the southern colonies: indentured servants could not travel alone without a pass or attend public gatherings independently.

In April 1803 the United States paid $15 million for the Louisiana Territory, an area comprising the entire Mississippi drainage basin, which had been settled by the French in the late seventeenth century. Many southerners hoped to extend slavery into the vast new territory, and it was widely expected that Missouri would be admitted to the Union as a slave state. A series of heated debates erupted over the extension of slavery in the region, and in 1819 the House of Representatives introduced legislation authorizing statehood for Missouri while prohibiting the further introduction of slavery into the new state. This drew angry protest from pro-slavery supporters. The controversy was further escalated by two events: Alabama was admitted to the Union as a slave state in 1819, making the total number of slave and free states equal, and Maine applied for statehood in 1820. In 1820 the Missouri Compromise was reached, admitting Missouri to the Union as a slave state with a slave population of almost 10,000, and Maine as a free state, with the understanding that the future expansion of slavery would be prohibited above the latitude of 36° 33'N.

The territory comprising Texas was part of the Louisiana Territory when the United States purchased it in 1803, but by 1819 it had become part of Mexico. Mexico provided land grants to American settlers (many of whom brought their slaves with them), and soon Americans outnumbered the Mexicans of the region. In 1836 Texas declared its independence from Mexico and requested annexation to the United States. The possibility of another slave state entering the Union stirred fresh debate. On March 1, 1845, President John Tyler signed the joint resolution of Congress to admit Texas as a slave state; the voters of Texas supported the action, and Texas became a slave state on December 29, 1845. In 1846 Mexican and American troops clashed in Texas, and the United States declared war on the Republic of Mexico. The war ended in 1848, with Mexico relinquishing its claims to Texas, and with the United States having acquired the entire region extending to the Pacific Ocean.

In 1846 David Wilmot, a Democrat from Pennsylvania, introduced an amendment to a bill appropriating $2 million for President James Polk to use in negotiating a territorial settlement with Mexico; the amendment stipulated that none of

Cartoon showing Abolitionists vying against supporters of the 1850 Fugitive Slave Act such as Secretary of State Daniel Webster.

the newly acquired land would be open to slavery. Although the amendment received strong support from northern Democrats and was passed by the House of Representatives, the Senate adjourned without voting on it. During the next session of Congress a new bill providing $3 million for territorial settlement was introduced. Wilmot again proposed an amendment prohibiting the expansion of slavery into the newly acquired territory. The bill was passed by the House of Representatives, but the Senate drew up a new bill excluding the Wilmot proviso.

Tensions between northern and southern politicians continued to mount over the issue of fugitive slaves. Article IV, Section 2 of the Constitution authorized the return of fugitive slaves and provided procedures for recovery, and in 1793 the Fugitive Slave Act was passed. In northern states that strongly opposed slavery, "personal liberty" laws were passed in order to undermine federal law; liberty laws placed the burden of proof on masters in cases concerning alleged fugitive slaves. Such a law was enacted in Pennsylvania in 1826, requiring state certification before alleged fugitives could be returned. When Edward Prigg, a professional slave catcher, attempted to capture a fugitive slave residing in the state, he was arrested on kidnapping charges for failing to acquire necessary certification. The Supreme Court ruled in Prigg v. Pennsylvania (1842) that the state's law could not interfere with federal action regarding fugitives and the right of slaveholders to recover property; it also found that states would not be obligated to enforce federal fugitive slave statutes. This led abolitionists to seize upon the idea of not enforcing federal statutes. Following the Court's decision several northern states enacted even more radical personal liberty laws prohibiting the enforcement of the Fugitive Slave Act.

The early opposition to slavery was generally based on religious beliefs; Christian ethics were seen as incompatible with slavery. Quakers (or the Society of Friends) and Mennonites were two of the first groups to oppose the practice in the United States. Quakers and Mennonites settled mainly in Pennsylvania, though also in the South, and advocated simple living, modest dress, and nonviolence. In 1652 the Quakers passed a resolution against lifetime indenture, and in 1688 the Mennonites did the same. With the continued rise of slavery in the South, many Quakers protested and moved north into Indiana and Ohio.

In 1787 the Free African Society was organized in Philadelphia by two African Americans, the Reverends Richard Allen and Absalom Jones; Allen later founded the Bethel African Methodist Church, and Jones became the rector of a Protestant Episcopal Church. The society was an important model for political consciousness and economic organization for African Americans throughout the country. It provided economic and medical aid, advocated abolition, and maintained channels of communication with African Americans in the South. Like the many other African American organizations that followed, the society was rooted in religious principles. Throughout the nineteenth century a number of mutual aid societies also sprang up in African American communities of the eastern seaboard, providing loans, insurance, and various other economic and social services to their members and the larger community.

In 1816 the American Colonization Society was organized in Washington, D.C., with the objective of encouraging the repatriation of African Americans to Africa. While the idea of returning free African Americans was motivated in part by humanitarian intent, the society was rather moderate in its opposition to slavery. Support for the society came in part from those who feared the possibility of a large free African American population in the United States.

Congress issued a charter to the society for the transportation of freed slaves to the west coast of Africa, provided funds, and assisted in negotiations with African chiefs who ceded the land that comprised what became Liberia. While northerners contributed support and donations to the society, southern patrols threatened freedmen into emigrating. In 1822 the first settlers landed at the site on the western coast of Africa which was later named Monrovia after President James Monroe. In 1838 the Commonwealth of Liberia was formed and placed under the administration of a governor appointed by the society.

The earliest abolition societies were the Pennsylvania Society for Promoting the Abolition of Slavery, formed in Philadelphia in 1775, and the New York Manumission Society, formed in the city in 1785. Prior to the 1830s a number of anti-slavery societies arose in both the North and the South, and during the 1830s and 1840s numerous abolitionist organizations arose alongside the women's rights organizations as part of the general social reform movement. The American Anti-Slavery Society was formed in Philadelphia in 1833, and after attending one of its meetings, the Quaker abolitionist Lucretia Coffin Mott formed the Philadelphia Female Anti-Slavery Society with the assistance of Elizabeth Cady Stanton. Mott and her husband, James, were active in the Underground Railroad and various other anti-slavery activities, and James served as a delegate to the World Anti-Slavery Convention.

The primary tool of the anti-slavery movement was the press. It was through the press that abolitionists both black and white were made aware of different events that affected the movement on local and national levels: warnings of legal issues such as the Fugitive Slave Laws, notices of speakers and groups that would inspire such as Frederick Douglass or Sojourner Truth, and a means to create a more organized group toward abolitishing slavery. In 1827 the journalists Samuel Cornish and John Russwurn launched *Freedom's Journal,* the first African American-owned and edited newspaper; in 1831 William Lloyd Garrison published the first issue of the *Liberator;* and other anti-slavery papers followed, including *Anti-Slavery Record,* the *Emancipator,*

An 1893 painting by Charles Webber depicts the hardships slaves faced as they fled the South on the Underground Railroad.

Human Rights, and the *North Star*, launched by Frederick Douglass.

While many of the anti-slavery organizations were dominated by whites, African American leaders played an important role in the abolition movement. Some of the most notable leaders were Alexander Crummell, Frederick Douglass, Sarah Mapp Douglass, Charlotte Forten, Henry Highland Garnet, Sojourner Truth, and David Walker. Most of these leaders were committed to cooperative relations with whites and opposed separatist doctrines, while some of the more militant abolitionists (like Garnet and Walker) stressed the conditional necessity of violence in the struggle against slavery.

Early Black Nationalism in the United States is associated with the activities of two enterprising capitalists in the maritime industries, Paul Cuffee, a New Bedford sea captain, and James Forten, a Philadelphia sailmaker. These two fig-

ures combined a bourgeois economic nationalism with a Christian thrust, and hoped to develop Christianity, commerce, and civilization in Africa while providing a homeland for African Americans. Their repatriationist activities were brought to a halt in 1817, when Henry Clay, Andrew Jackson, and other white Americans formed the American Society for Colonizing the Free People of Color in the United States, usually called the American Colonization Society. The American Colonization Society had other prominent slaveholders among its leadership, and expressly denied any sympathy for abolition; large numbers of blacks reacted by demonstrating a marked hostility to the society and its aims. Cuffee died shortly after the society's founding, and Forten felt constrained to silence, although he continued to believe that Black Americans would "never become a people until they come out from amongst the white people." Those who continued to support repatriation, or who migrated under the auspices of the American Colonization Society, became the objects of extreme vituperation.

Black Nationalism, in its nineteenth-century form, consisted of efforts by African American groups and individuals to create a sovereign nation-state. The quest for a national homeland expressed a perceived need to demonstrate the capacity of black people for self-government but often it has simply implied moral support for decolonizing Africa and advancing the material and spiritual interests of African peoples everywhere.

Black Nationalism and repatriationism were not always the same thing, however, and hostility to the American Colonization Society did not always lead to the abandonment of nationalist rhetoric. Maria Stewart referred to herself as an African, but was hostile to the colonization movement. She insisted on her rights as an American, but at the same time denounced the United States with strident jeremiadic rhetoric. Stewart clearly viewed black America as a captive nation, existing in a type of Babylonian captivity, and conceived of African Americans as a people with a national destiny without advocating political separatism or the desire to form a nation-state. In a similar vein, David Walker denounced colonization and emigration with the religious fervor of an Old Testament prophet. Curiously, he insisted on the separate mission and destiny of African Americans as colored citizens of the world, while simultaneously maintaining that black and white Americans could be "a united and happy people."

Black Nationalist motivations have been attributed to the major slave conspiracies of Gabriel Prosser and Denmark Vesey, who were inspired by the Haitian revolt, and both seem to have had as their goal the creation of a black nation with ties to the Caribbean. For the most part, however, evidence of Black Nationalism in the United States was found among the free black population of the North. It was in the so-called Free African Societies, which sprang up in the black communities of New York, Boston, and Philadelphia, that a conception of black historical identity and destiny was strongest. During the 1830s and 1840s,

Black Nationalist thinking was associated with religious leadership such as that provided by the bishop of the African Methodist Episcopal Church, Richard Allen, who believed in a special God-given mission for Black Americans as a people but steadfastly opposed the American Colonization Society. Peter Williams, leader of the Afro-American Group of the Episcopal Church in New York, took a more tolerant view of colonization. He eulogized Paul Cuffee and remained friendly with John Russwurm, even after the latter immigrated to Liberia and was burned in effigy by anti-colonization activists.

President Andrew Jackson was one of the founders of the American Colonization Society, an anti-abolitionist organization.

The flourishing of Black Nationalism occurred during the 1850s and 1860s. To some degree, the movement owed its rebirth to the passage of the Fugitive Slave Act (1850) which legalized the return of slaves to their owners regardless of whether they were captured in a slave or free state, and the *Dred Scott v. Sandford* decision (1857) which declared that blacks had no rights that a white man was bound to respect. The decision also went so far as to deny citizenships to blacks.

In the South the activities of the abolition movement only hardened the resolve of the slave-holding class to maintain the system of slavery. Depending on the circumstances, southern justification of slavery continued along several lines: it was an economic necessity, a means of converting African pagans to Christianity, and a means of controlling a supposedly inferior race.

A vast network of individuals and groups developed throughout the country to help African Americans escape from slavery. Abolitionists provided "stations," food, shelter, and financial assistance, while experienced "conductors," who were often themselves runaway slaves, led thousands of "passengers" to freedom in the North, Canada, and the Caribbean. Most of the movement occurred at night, with passengers hiding in the barns and homes of sympathetic whites and African Americans during the day. Two of the most famous conductors were Josiah Henson and Harriet Tubman.

In February 1831 Nat Turner, a slave in Southampton County, Virginia, began to plan a slave revolt, and on August 22 Turner and his co-conspirators killed Turner's master and family. Within twenty-four hours about sixty whites in the county had been killed. Turner was captured on October 30 and hanged on November 11. The incident contributed to the increasing paranoia of southern society.

Radical Democrats and members of the Whig party who opposed slavery united to form a new political party in Buffalo, New York, in 1848. The party adopted a platform supporting free labor and free soil in response to feelings among northerners that slavery restricted the freedom of northern workers to contract for work and should

therefore be excluded from the developing regions of the West. Southerners wanted the freedom to expand westward and take their slaves with them. Senator John C. Calhoun of South Carolina and other southern delegates maintained that both Congress and the territorial legislatures lacked the authority to restrict the expansion of slavery into the territories. The control of northern states over the national government led these men to consider secession from the Union.

As the debate over the admission of new western states continued, southerners argued that the South should be given guarantees of equal positioning in the territories. In 1850 Senator Henry Clay proposed a compromise in which California would be admitted as a free state, the new territories of New Mexico and Utah would be organized, slavery would be abolished in the District of Columbia, more forceful fugitive slave legislation would be enacted, and the Texas war debt would be resolved. At the time the compromise was hailed by many as the solution to the debate over slavery.

The slavery debate presented supporters and opponents of the institution with two very important questions: how should fugitives from slavery be treated in jurisdictions where slavery was illegal, and should a slave brought into a free state by his master be viewed as free? The first question was partially addressed by Article IV, Section 2 of the Constitution and by the Fugitive Slave Acts of 1793 and 1850, but the second question had not yet been addressed. During the 1830s and 1840s a slave by the name of Dred Scott accompanied his master, a surgeon in the U.S. Army, on numerous trips to military posts around the country, including the free states of Illinois and the territory of Wisconsin. In 1846 Scott sued his master for his freedom, asserting that his sojourns in free jurisdictions made him free. After numerous delays, trials, and retrials, the case reached the Supreme Court in 1856. The Court responded with nine separate opinions, and Chief Justice Roger Brook Taney delivered the deciding opinion. The ruling was both complex and controversial: the Missouri Compromise of 1820 was ruled unconstitutional on the grounds that Congress did not have authority to limit the expansion of slavery; slavery was found to be legal in the territories until the citizens voted for or against it; and Africans and their descendants were found to be ineligible for citizenship in the United States as the framers of the Constitution had not viewed Africans as citizens. Since African Americans were not viewed by the Court as citizens, they could not file suit. Despite the finality of the Court's decision, the issue of slavery remained unresolved.

On October 16, 1859, a white, visionary abolitionist named John Brown led a band of twenty-one men (five of whom were African Americans) in the seizure of the federal arsenal at Harpers Ferry. After holding the site for several hours, Brown and his followers were captured by federal troops under the command of Robert E. Lee. Southerners were outraged by Brown's actions, interpreting them as symptomatic of a willingness among northerners to attempt the forcible overthrow of slavery. In December 1859 Brown was hanged alongside Dangerfield Newby, a runaway slave; John A. Copeland of Carolina; Sheridan Leary, a harness maker and freedman; and Shields Gree, a sailor from South Carolina.

In 1860 Abraham Lincoln, a northern Republican, was elected president amid continuing polarization over the issue of slavery. Lincoln had voiced opposition to the expansion of slavery in the past, and with his election southerners became even more fearful of an ideological assault on states' rights and the abolition of slavery nationwide. In 1860 a delegation from South Carolina voted unanimously for the repeal of the state's 1788 ratification of the Constitution and the severing of all relations with the Union; Georgia, Florida, Alabama, Mississippi, Louisiana, and Texas soon followed. In February 1861 the seven states drew up a constitution and elected Jefferson Davis as president of the Confederate States of America. As northern leaders sought a means of preserving the nation, southern troops seized federal installations, post offices, and customs houses, and in April 1861 Confederate forces took one of the last Union holds in the South, Fort Sumter in Charleston Harbor, South Carolina. Lincoln was forced to retaliate.

Sometimes called "The Great Emancipator," President Abraham Lincoln opposed expansion of slavery before being elected to high office. As president, he was in favor of abolition as a means to win the war, resulting in the Emancipation Proclamation.

From the beginning of the war African Americans engaged in the fighting, although Lincoln at first refused to officially employ them in the Union army. By 1862 Lincoln concluded that the use of African American soldiers was a necessity. An estimated 180,000 black soldiers served in the Union army and another 20,000 served in its navy. But not all of those African Americans who participated in the war fought on the Union side; although there are no accurate records of how many fought for the South, the numbers grew as white southerners became more desperate.

Lincoln faced a dilemma in that if he issued an order of universal emancipation, as the abolitionists encouraged him to do, he risked alienating the border states that remained supportive of the Union: these were Delaware, Maryland, Kentucky, and Missouri. In a letter to Horace Greely, Lincoln stated:

> If I could save the Union without freeing any slave, I would do it; if I could save it by freeing all the slaves, I would do it; and if I could save it by freeing some and leaving others alone, I would also do that. What I do about slavery and the colored race, I do because I believe it helps save the Union.

During the summer of 1862 Lincoln began to feel that the emancipation of the slaves would be necessary to realizing victory over the South, and on January 1, 1863, he issued the Emancipation Proclamation, freeing slaves in those states that had seceded from the Union. Because the proclamation did not apply to the areas under occupation by Union forces, 800,000 slaves remained unaffected by its provisions. He dared not alienate the slave-owning states on the Union side, especially in light of the growing antipathy toward African Americans in many northern cities. In the Draft Riots of July 13–16, 1863, huge mobs of whites in New York City (angry over the provisions of the Conscription Act which required quotas of volunteers) attacked blacks and abolitionists, destroying property and viciously beating many to death.

The Civil War lasted from April 1861 to April 1865, and at the end more than 360,000 Union soldiers and 258,000 Confederate soldiers were dead. By the end of the war twenty-one African Americans had received the Medal of Honor, and indeterminate numbers of others had made sacrifices for the cause. On December 18, 1865, the Thirteenth Amendment of the Constitution was ratified, formally abolishing slavery in the United States.

On March 3, 1865, Congress enacted the first of several acts that set up and empowered the Bureau of Refugees, Freedmen and Abandoned Lands (or the Freedmen's Bureau). The organization provided former slaves with basic health and educational services, and adminis-

tered land which had been abandoned during the war. In 1866 Congress passed the Civil Rights Act, in which a number of personal liberties were outlined, including the right to make contracts, sue or be sued, own and sell property, and receive the equal benefit of the law. The Reconstruction Act of March 2, 1867, outlined the terms under which the southern states might re-enter the Union; one of these terms required the drafting of a new state constitution with the guarantee of voting rights for all races. President Andrew Johnson vetoed this bill, but radical Republicans in Congress were able to muster the necessary two-thirds majority needed to override the veto.

On July 23, 1868, the Fourteenth Amendment was ratified, providing definitions of national and state citizenship, effectively overriding the Supreme Court's decision in *Dred Scott v. Sandford 1857,* and providing for equal privileges of citizenship and protection of the law. On March 30, 1870, the Fifteenth Amendment was ratified to ensure the right to vote. But the amendment proved unsuccessful in its aims, since many state and local governments created voting regulations that ensured African Americans would not vote: these included grandfather clauses, requiring that one's grandfather had voted; literacy tests; poll taxes; and "white primaries," which were held prior to general elections and permitted only whites to vote. In addition, southern states enacted many laws (known as black codes) that curbed the new rights of the freed slaves: South Carolina made it illegal for African Americans to possess firearms, and other states restricted their right to make and enforce contracts; to marry and intermarry; and even to assemble, "wander," or be "idle."

In 1875 Congress attempted to establish a semblance of racial equality by enacting a law that made it illegal to deprive another person of the "full and equal enjoyment of the accommodations, advantages, facilities, and privileges of inns, public conveyance, … and other places of public amusement" on account of race. In a number of cases (known as the Civil Rights Cases) the Supreme Court ruled that the Fourteenth Amendment did not authorize Congress to legislate against discriminatory state action, while disregarding discrimination by private individuals, including the owners of hotels, theaters, and restaurants. This point led to an end of federal efforts to protect the civil rights of African Americans until the mid-twentieth century.

In *Hall v. DeCuir* (1878) the Supreme Court decided that states could not outlaw segregation on common carriers such as streetcars and railroads, and in 1896 the Court again faced the issue of segregation on public transportation in the case of *Plessy v. Ferguson*. The case concerned Homer Adolph Plessy, an African American who was arrested for refusing to ride in the "colored" railway coach while traveling by train from New Orleans to Covington, Louisiana. The law in Louisiana required that "equal but separate" accommodations for blacks and whites be maintained in public facilities, but Plessy challenged this. Justice Billings Brown delivered the majority opinion that separate but equal accommodations constituted a reasonable use of state police power and that the Fourteenth Amendment could not have been an effort to abolish social or racial distinctions or to force a co-mingling of the races. In his dissenting opinion, Justice John Marshall Harlen remarked:

> The judgement, this day rendered will, in time, prove to be quite as pernicious as the decision made by this tribunal in the Dred Scott case. The thin disguise of equal accommodation for passengers in railroad coaches will not mislead anyone nor atone for the wrong this day done.

The ruling paved the way for the doctrine of separate but equal in all walks of life, and not until the case of *Brown v. Board of Education of Topeka* (1954) would the constitutionality of segregation be seriously challenged. As a result of the successful *Brown v. Board* case and the desegregation of schools, Freedom Riders and the desegregation of transportation, and acts that removed contrived barriers for African Americans, the nation moved toward implementing equal access to citizenship rights previously guaranteed to African Americans in the Fourteenth Amendment.

As Black Nationalism continued through the efforts of organizers such as Marcus Garvey in the mid-twentieth century, one key aspect that has gained support into the twenty-first century is the issue of reparations for people of African descent all over the globe. In 2001 Black Nationalists from all over the world attended the United Nations World Conference. As a result of their efforts the United Nations announced that the trans-Atlantic Slave Trade was a crime against humanity and that reparations should be one of the major issues for the conference. In October 2002, the Global Afrikan Congress was formed, which represented thirty-five nations and became the largest Pan-African Black Nationalist group in the world.

In 2005 restitutions were made by J.P. Morgan and Wachovia Bank, who apologized for slavery. They established scholarships, and contributed to African American organizations. In 2006 the U.S. Court of Appeals in Chicago ruled that any corporation that hid the fact that they were participants in the slave trade were guilty of consumer fraud. On June 13, 2009, the U.S. Congress passed a resolution apologizing for slavery, but the Senate held the resolution for almost a year ultimately attaching a statement barring the use of the apology as legal grounds for reparations. No systemic form of compensation has ever been presented to African Americans as a way to repay the debt owed for generations of economic, political, and social exploitation and disenfranchisement.

BIOGRAPHIES

Crispus Attucks (c. 1723–1770)
Slave

Attucks, a runaway slave who lived in Boston, was the first of five men killed on March 5, 1770, when British troops fired on a crowd of colonial protesters in the Boston Massacre. The most widely accepted account of the incident is that of John Adams, who said at the subsequent trial of the British soldiers that Attucks undertook "to be the hero of the night; and to lead this army with banners, to form them in the first place in Dock Square, and march them up to King Street with their clubs." When the crowd reached the soldiers it was Attucks who "had hardiness enough to fall in upon them, and with one hand took hold of a bayonet, and with the other knocked the man down." At that point the panicked soldiers fired, and in the echoes of their volley, five men lay dying; the seeds of the Revolution were sown. Attucks is remembered as "the first to defy, the first to die."

Joseph Cinqué (c. 1814–1849)
Slave

Purchased by Spaniards in Havana, Cuba, in 1839, he was placed aboard the *Amistad* bound for Puerto Principe. When the crew became exhausted from battling a storm, Cinqué led the slaves in seizing the ship and killing all but two of the crew, who were kept alive to navigate a course back to Africa. The captive pilots headed north, against the slaves' knowledge, and when the ship was sighted off the coast of Long Island the slaves were taken to Connecticut and placed in prison. Abolitionists took up the cause of the men and enabled Cinqué to raise funds for judicial appeals by speaking on their lecture circuit; his words were translated from Mende, and he became known as an excellent speaker. In 1841 attorney and future president John Quincy Adams won the slaves' case, and they were released. Missionaries and other supporters raised funds so that Cinqué and the remaining Africans were returned to West Africa.

William Craft (1842–1900) and Ellen Smith Craft (1826–1891)
Abolitionists

Ellen Smith was born to a slave mother and her master. The family resemblance to her master was so great that she was sent to live with her master's daughter as a housemaid in nearby Macon, Georgia. It was there in 1846 that she met William Craft, a carpenter.

The Crafts wanted to escape from slavery and procure a Christian marriage so they decided that during Christmas 1848 Ellen Craft would pose as a sickly young man and William Craft would pose as her slave accompanying him to Philadelphia. Because slaves are given some time off during the holiday the couple hoped that would not be missed. Traveling by train and boat they arrived safely in Philadelphia. They became popular speakers for the abolitionist cause in several cities in the North and settled for a while in Boston. With the Fugitive Slave Law of 1859 the Crafts decided to go to England. While there, in 1860 they published the book, *Running a Thousand Miles for Freedom.* During their time in England they were active in benevolent societies. Their family had grown and included four boys and a girl. After nineteen years in England, the family returned to the United States and in 1871 they opened a school for black children in Georgia. The school closed in 1878. Ellen Craft died in 1891 and William Craft in 1900 in Charleston, South Carolina.

Ayuba Suleiman Diallo (1701–1773)
Slave

Diallo, known as Job ben Solomon, was born in Bondu, Senegal, West Africa, and was a member of the Diallo Muslim merchant clan. In 1730 Diallo, a trader, traveled over 300 miles and succeeded in selling two people and buying paper. While resting at the home of a friend he was captured after removing his weapons. Diallo was taken by Mandingoes and sold into the increasing traffic of the Atlantic slave trade.

While enslaved it was discovered that Diallo was not a common slave as he wrote Arabic and carried his aristocratic behavior. He was finally purchased, freed, and in July 1734 returned to

Gambia, his home region. Ayuba's story, *Some Memoirs of the Life of Job, the Son of Solomon the High Priest of Boonda in Africa, 1734,* was a first-person account of the slave trade reported by Thomas Bluett, a lawyer who recognized Diallo's qualities. The narrative was printed several times in French and also in English.

Frederick Douglass (1817–1895)
Abolitionist

 Frederick Douglass was born Frederick August Washington Bailey in 1817 in Talbot County, Maryland. Douglas was sent to Baltimore as a house servant at the age of eight, where his mistress taught him to read and write. Upon the death of his master he was sent to the country to work as a field hand. During his time in the South he was severely flogged for his resistance to slavery. In his early teens he began to teach in a Sunday school that was later forcibly shut down by hostile whites. After an unsuccessful attempt to escape from slavery, he succeeded in making his way to New York disguised as a sailor in 1838. He found work as a day laborer in New Bedford, Massachusetts, and after an extemporaneous speech before the Massachusetts Anti-Slavery Society became one of its agents.

Douglass quickly became a nationally recognized figure among abolitionists. In 1845 he bravely published his *Narrative of the Life of Frederick Douglass,* which related his experiences as a slave, revealed his fugitive status, and further exposed him to the danger of re-enslavement. In the same year he went to England and Ireland, where he remained until 1847, speaking on slavery and women's rights, and ultimately raising sufficient funds to purchase his freedom. Upon returning to the United States he founded the *North Star* journal. In the tense years before the Civil War he was forced to flee to Canada when the governor of Virginia swore out a warrant for his arrest.

Douglass returned to the United States before the beginning of the Civil War, and after meeting with President Abraham Lincoln he assisted in the formation of the 54th and 55th Negro regiments of Massachusetts. During Reconstruction he became deeply involved in the civil rights movement, and in 1871 he was appointed to the territorial legislature of the District of Columbia. He served as one of the presidential electors-at-large for New York in 1872 and shortly thereafter became the secretary of the Santo Domingo Commission. After serving for a short time as the police commissioner of the District of Columbia, he was appointed marshal in 1871 and held the post until he was appointed the recorder of deeds in 1881. In 1890 his support of the presidential campaign of Benjamin Harrison won him his most important federal post: he became minister resident and consul general to the Republic of Haiti and later, the chargé d'affaires of Santo Domingo. In 1891 he resigned the position in protest of the unscrupulous business practices of American businessmen. Douglass died at his home in Washington, D.C., on February 20, 1895.

Estevanico (c. 1503–c. 1539)
Explorer

Born in Azemmour, Morocco, Estevanico is thought to have been captured and placed in slavery between 1513 and 1521. Estevanico, also known as Estebanico, Esteban, Estevanico the Moor, Black Stephen, and Esteban de Dorantes, accompanied his master, Spanish explorer Andres de Dorantes, in 1528. The expedition of some three hundred men was led by conquistador Panfilo de Narvaez. They traveled in territories of North America including the Florida Panhandle and the Mississippi River, and became shipwrecked on what is now Galveston Island in Texas. Almost the entire group died with the exception of four members, including Estevanico.

The surviving members of the expedition were captured and placed in slavery with different tribes. After years of being immersed in the culture Estevanico learned many languages and became known as a healer. He was eventually killed for reasons unknown. Estevanico is considered the first black man to set foot on what is now the United States.

Sally Hemings (1773–1835)
Slave, Mistress of Thomas Jefferson

Hemings, known as Sally, Yellow Sally, Dusky Sally, or Monticellian Sally, was born on the Forest Plantation in Virginia. She was the daughter of Elizabeth Hemings, a slave and the concubine of John Wayles, who was Sally's father. Sally Hemings, who was a mulatto and racially determined to be a quadroon, was physically very light with long hair. In 1774, with the death of Wayles and the settlement of his estate, Hemings, her mother, and her five siblings were sent to Monticello as slaves. Hemings became the servant to Martha Wayles Jeffers, her half-sister, who was married to Thomas Jefferson.

With the death of Martha Jefferson, and her desire that Thomas Jefferson not remarry, Hemings eventually became Jefferson's concubine. In 1790, while living in Paris and two years after Martha Jefferson's death, Hemings, just fifteen, became pregnant with her first child by Jefferson, but the child did not survive. Over the next eighteen years Hemings had seven children by Jefferson but only four survived. She came to the attention of nineteenth-century America because of a newspaper story in 1802 about her role as Jefferson's longtime slave mistress. The article was written as a means to derail Jefferson's campaign for president.

With the death of Jefferson in 1826 all of Hemings's children were freed and two of them chose to pass as white. Four years later Hemings and her two sons were listed on the census as free whites. Hemings died in Charlottesville, Virginia, in 1835.

Josiah Henson (1789–1883)
Slave, Abolitionist

Born a slave in Charles County, Maryland, Henson grew up with the experience of his family being cruelly treated by his master. By the time he was eighteen he was supervising the master's farm. In 1825 he and his wife and children were moved to Kentucky, where conditions were greatly improved, and in 1828 he became a preacher in a Methodist Episcopal Church. Under the threat of being sold, he and his family escaped to Ohio in 1830, and in the following year entered Canada by way of Buffalo, New York. In Canada he learned to read and write from one of his sons, and he soon began preaching in Dresden, Ontario.

While in Canada he became active in the Underground Railroad, helping nearly two hundred slaves escape to freedom. In 1842 he and several others attempted to start the British-American Manual Labor Institute, but the industrial school proved unsuccessful. Henson related his story to Harriet Beecher Stowe (the author of *Uncle Tom's Cabin*), and it has been disputed whether or not her story is based in part on aspects of his life. He traveled to England three times, where he met distinguished people, was honored for his abolitionist activities and personal escape from slavery, and was offered a number of positions which he turned down in order to return to Canada. He published his autobiography in 1849 and rewrote and reissued it in 1858 and 1879. Henson died in Ontario.

James Armistead Lafayette (c. 1760–1830)
Slave

Born a slave, he risked his life behind enemy lines collecting information for the Continental Army. He furnished valuable information to the Marquis de Lafayette and enabled the French commander to check the troop advances of British general Cornwallis; this set the stage for General George Washington's victory at Yorktown in 1781 and for the end of the Revolutionary War. In recognition of his services, he was granted his freedom by the Virginia legislature in 1786, although it was not until 1819 that Virginia awarded him a pension of $40 a year and a grant of $100. He adopted the surname "Lafayette" in honor of his former commander, who visited him during a trip to the United States in 1824.

Onesimus (1706–1770)
Slave, Medical Innovator

Onesimus, who was born in Africa, was a slave in Boston in the 1700s. He was one of approximately a thousand people of African descent in Boston who were either slaves, indentured servants, or free. Onesimus was purchased for Cotton Mather, a prominent New England minister, by his congregation. The transaction was noted in Mather's diary dated December 13, 1706.

Mather wanted to Christianize Onesimus but diary entries suggest that he was not successful in the way he hoped. Onesimus did marry and had one son who died in 1714. In 1716 Onesimus attempted to purchase his freedom by giving Mather money to purchase another servant in his place. Mather signed a document that freed Onesimus, but the document still required Onesimus to provide some services for Mather. Little is known of Onesimus after he purchased his freedom.

When the smallpox epidemic of 1721 hit Boston, Mather used the method of inoculation that Onesimus had taught Mather while in his service. This old African tradition used material from the pustile of an infected person and with the use of a twig or thorn, the material was scratched onto the skin of a person who was not infected. Mather tested the practice on his son and two slaves. The procedure of infecting a person to inoculate them was not well received as African knowledge was not respected. For the six hundred who were inoculated by Mather and another local doctor, only two percent caught the disease and died. Without Onesimus's recollection of traditional African medicine, many people would have perished.

François Dominique Toussaint L'Ouverture (1743–1803)
Slave, Revolutionary

Born Francois Dominique Toussaint L'Ouverture, a slave on the island of Hispaniola (now Haiti and the Dominican Republic), he learned to read and write under a benevolent master. When he was fifty, a violent revolt erupted on the island. White French planters, African slaves, and free mulattoes (some of whom owned slaves) clashed over issues of rights, land, and labor, as the forces of France, Britain, and Spain manipulated the conflict. At first the slaves and mulattoes shared the goals of the French Revolution in opposition to the Royalist French planters, but with time a coalition of planters and mulattoes arose in opposition to the slaves.

Toussaint became the leader of the revolutionary slave forces, which by 1794 consisted of a disciplined group of four thousand mostly exslaves. He successfully waged various campaigns, first against the French and then against the British, and was at the height of his power and influence when in 1796 General Rigaud (who led the mulatto forces) sought to re-impose slavery on the black islanders. Rigaud quickly achieved victory, captured Santo Domingo, and by 1801 had virtual control of the Spanish part of the island. In 1802 a French expeditionary force was sent to re-establish French control of the island. Toussaint was tricked, captured, and sent to France where he died on April 7, 1803, under inhumane conditions.

Gabriel Prosser (1775–1800)
Slave

The coachman of Thomas Prosser of Henrico County, Virginia, Gabriel Prosser planned a large, highly organized revolt to take place on the last night of August 1800 around Richmond, Virginia. There were about 32,000 slaves and only 8,000 whites in the area, and it was his intention to kill all of the whites except for the French, Quakers, elderly women, and children. The ultimate goal was that the remaining 300,000 slaves in the state would follow his lead and seize the entire state. The revolt was set to coincide with the harvest so that his followers would be spared any shortage of food, and it was decided that the conspirators would meet at the Old Brook Swamp outside of Richmond and marshal forces to attack the city.

The insurrection fell apart when a severe rainstorm made it impossible for many of the slaves to assemble and a pair of house slaves who did not wish their master killed revealed the plot. Panic swept through the city, martial law was declared, and those suspected of involvement were rounded up and hanged; when it became clear that the slave population would be devastated if all of those implicated were dealt with in like fashion, the courts began to mete out less severe sentences. Prosser was apprehended in the hold of a schooner that docked in Norfolk, Virginia, and was brought back in chains, interrogated by the governor (though he refused to divulge details of the conspiracy), and hanged.

Dred Scott (1795–1858)
Slave

Born in Southampton, Virginia, his first name was simply "Sam." He worked as a farmhand, handyman, and dockworker, and moved with his master to Huntsville, Alabama, and later to St. Louis, Missouri. In 1831 his owner, Peter Blow, died, and he was bought by John Emerson, a surgeon in the U.S. Army. Sam accompanied his new master to Illinois (a free state) and Wisconsin (a territory). Sometime after 1836 he received permission to marry, and by 1848 he had changed his name to Dred Scott. At various times he attempted to buy his freedom or escape but was unsuccessful. In 1843 Emerson died and left his estate to his widow Irene Emerson, who also refused Scott his freedom. He then obtained the assistance of two attorneys who helped him to sue for his freedom in county court.

Scott lost this case, but the verdict was set aside, and in 1847 he won a second trial on the grounds that his slave status had been nullified upon entering into a free state. Scott received financial backing and legal representation through

the sons of Peter Blow, Irene Emerson's brother John Sanford, and her second husband Dr. C.C. Chaffee, all of whom apparently saw the case as an important challenge to slavery. In 1857 the U.S. Supreme Court ruled against Scott, stating that slaves were not legally citizens of the United States and therefore had no standing in the courts. Shortly after the decision was handed down Mrs. Emerson freed Scott. The case led to the nullification of the Missouri Compromise of 1820, allowing the expansion of slavery into formerly free territories. Scott died from tuberculosis in 1858.

William Still (1821–1902)
Underground Railroad Conductor

Still was born in New Jersey in 1821, the son of a former slave. He left home in 1844 for Philadelphia and in 1847 he became a clerk at the office of the Pennsylvania Society for the Abolition of Slavery. Still rose through the ranks of the Society and became the premier person of the secretive Underground Railroad. He also became chairman of the organization's Vigilance Committee.

With the passage of the Fugitive Slave Act in 1850 more and more runaways needed aid in escaping to freedom. The Vigilance Committee helped nearly five hundred fugitives between 1852 and 1857. Many of the fugitives were interview by Still and their stories recorded. He used these stories to document the history of the Underground Railroad and in 1872 published a book, over six hundred pages, titled *The Underground Rail Road: A Record of Facts, Authentic Narratives, Letters, etc., Narrating the Hardships, Hair-breadth Escape, and Death Struggles of the Slaves In their Efforts for Freedom, as Related by Themselves and Others, or Witnessed by the Author, Together with Sketches of Some of the Largest Stockholders, and Most Liberal Aiders and Advisers, of the Road.* His book, sold on a subscription basis, recounts many stories, letters, and news articles while thanking "conductors" like Harriet Tubman for her bravery and commitment to the Underground Railroad. The book sold thousands of copies, went through three editions, and several printings.

Still devoted much of his life to improving the condition of the black community in Philadelphia, and was a member of the Freedmen's Aid Commission and several charitable institutions. He worked to establish the first Young Men's Christian Association (YMCA) in Philadelphia. Still died on July 14, 1902.

Sojourner Truth (c. 1797–1883)
Abolitionist

Born Isabella Baumfree in Ulster County, New York, she was freed by the New York State Emancipation Act of 1827 and lived in New York City for a time. After taking the name Sojourner Truth, which she felt God had given her, she assumed the "mission" of spreading "the Truth" across the country. She became famous as an itinerant preacher, drawing huge crowds with her oratorical (and some said "mystical") gifts wherever she appeared. She became one of an active group of black women abolitionists, lectured before numerous abolitionist audiences, and was friends with such leading white abolitionists as James and Lucretia Mott and Harriet Beecher Stowe. With the outbreak of the Civil War she raised money to purchase gifts for the soldiers, distributing them herself in the camps. She also helped African Americans who had escaped to the North to find habitation and shelter. Age and ill health caused her to retire from the lecture circuit, and she spent her last days in a sanatorium in Battle Creek, Michigan, passing away on November 26, 1883.

Harriet Tubman (c. 1820–1913)
Abolitionist

Born about 1820 in Dorchester County, Maryland, Harriet Tubman lived the hard childhood of a slave: much work, little schooling, and severe punishment. In 1848 she escaped, leaving behind

her husband John Tubman, who threatened to report her to their master. As a free woman, she began to devise practical ways of helping other slaves escape. Over the following ten years she made about twenty trips from the North into the South and rescued more than three hundred slaves. Her reputation spread rapidly, and she won the admiration of leading abolitionists (some of whom sheltered her passengers). Eventually a reward of $40,000 was posted for her capture.

Tubman met and aided John Brown in recruiting soldiers for his raid on Harpers Ferry—Brown referred to her as "General Tubman." One of her major disappointments was the failure of the raid, and she is said to have regarded Brown as the true emancipator of her people, not President Abraham Lincoln. In 1860 she began to canvass the nation, appearing at anti-slavery meetings and speaking on women's rights. Shortly before the outbreak of the Civil War she was forced to leave for Canada, but she returned to the United States and served the Union as a nurse, soldier, and spy; she was particularly valuable to the army as a scout because of the knowledge of the terrain she had gained as a conductor on the Underground Railroad.

Tubman's biography (from which she received the proceeds) was written by Sarah Bradford in 1868. Tubman's husband, John, died two years after the end of the war, and in 1869 she married war veteran Nelson Davis. Despite receiving many honors and tributes (including a medal from Queen Victoria), she spent her last days in poverty, not receiving a pension until thirty years after the Civil War. With the $20 dollars a month that she finally received, she helped to found a home for the aged and needy, which was later renamed the Harriet Tubman Home. She died in Auburn, New York, March 10, 1913.

Nat Turner (1800–1831)
Slave

Born October 2, 1800, Nat Turner was a slave from Southampton County, Virginia. He was an

Discovery of Nat Turner.

This wood engraving by Benjamin Phipps depicts the capture of Nat Turner in 1831.

avid reader of the Bible who prayed, fasted, and experienced "voices," ultimately becoming a visionary mystic with a belief that God had given him the special destiny of conquering Southampton County. After recruiting a handful of conspirators, he struck at isolated homes in his immediate area, and within forty-eight hours the band of insurrectionists had reached sixty armed men. They killed fifty-five whites before deciding to attack the county seat in Jerusalem, but while en route they were overtaken by a posse

and dispersed. Turner took refuge in the Dismal Swamp and remained there for six weeks before he was captured, brought to trial, and hanged, along with sixteen other African Americans, on November 11, 1831.

Denmark Vesey (c. 1767–1822)
Slave

Sold by his master at an early age and later bought back because of epilepsy, Denmark Vesey sailed with his master, Captain Vesey, to the Virgin Islands and Haiti for twenty years. He enjoyed a considerable degree of mobility in his home port of Charleston, South Carolina, and eventually purchased his freedom from his master for $600; he had won $1,500 in a lottery. He became a Methodist minister and used his church as a base to recruit supporters to take over Charleston. The revolt was planned for the second Sunday in July 1822.

Vesey's plans were betrayed when a slave alerted the white authorities of the city. Hundreds of African Americans were rounded up, though some of Vesey's collaborators most likely escaped to the Carolinas where they fought as maroons. After a twenty-two-day search, Vesey was apprehended and stood trial. During the trial he adeptly cross-examined witnesses but ultimately could not deny his intention to overthrow the city, and he was hanged on July 2, along with several collaborators.

David Walker (1796–1830)
Revolutionary Abolitionist, Author

Walker was born in Wilmington, North Carolina, in 1796 to a free black mother and a father who was a slave. At the time, the child followed the condition of the mother, making Walker a free man. Whether in the South or the North, Walker witnessed the brutality of slavery as well as the injustices and degradation that blacks endured. Walker settled in Boston in the 1820s and opened a used-clothing store. He became an activist and a contributor to the first African American newspaper, *Freedom's Journal*. By 1828 Walker was a leading spokesman against slavery and had also married. He had a daughter who died of tuberculosis a few days before his death, and a son born after his death.

On September 28, 1829, Walker published his *Appeal, in Four Articles, Together with a Preamble, to the Colored Citizens of the World, But in Particular, and Very Expressly to Those of the United States of America*. The appeal was distributed throughout the region by ship and by individuals, which resulted in the printing of three editions by 1830. Walker's *Appeal* inspired pride and hope for the slaves, and horrified slave owners to the point that laws were passed to forbid slaves from learning to read or write, and making the distribution of anti-slavery material illegal. A reward of $3,000 was offered for Walker and $10,000 for anyone who could deliver him to the South. As a Christian, Walker was willing to die for this heavenly cause of abolition.

On August 30, 1830, two months after the third edition of the *Appeal*, Walker was found dead. Although there is no evidence that supports exactly how he died, it is said that he died from poisoning, while some scholars say he died of tuberculosis, which was the same disease his daughter died from.

BIOGRAPHIES: BLACK NATIONALISTS

John Henrik Clarke (1915–1998)
Educator

Clarke was born on January 1, 1915, in Union Springs, Alabama. His family moved to Columbus, Georgia, when Clarke was four. Clarke, who had become a part-time student, farmer, and worker, only completed the first half of the seventh grade. When told by a white attorney that blacks had no history, Clarke became interested in finding the history of black people. In 1932 at the age of seventeen, Clarke went to Harlem to pursue a career as a writer. He took classes at Columbia University and found a mentor in Arthur Schomburg of the New York Harlem branch of the public library. Clarke continued to take classes, travel to Ghana and West Africa, teach, and do research on the history of black people.

In 1964 Clarke was licensed to teach at People's College on Long Island. He was an advocate for African-centered, or Afrocentric, scholarship and a supporter of the Black Power movement. In 1970 he was appointed professor of Black and

Puerto Rican Studies. He retired in 1985. Clarke published six books and helped to create several quarterlies that focused on black people. Clarke died in 1998 of a heart attack.

Paul Cuffee (1759–1817)
Sailor, Sea Captain, Activist

Cuffee was born January 17, 1759, on Cuttyhunk Island near New Bedford, Massachusetts. He was the son of Cuffee Slocum, a freed slave, and Ruth Moses, a Wampanoag Indian.

By the time Cuffee was sixteen he was earning a living as a sailor on a whaling vessel. After making numerous voyages he was captured by the British but later released. He studied arithmetic and navigation but soon returned to the sea. In 1795 he had his own ship, *Ranger*, and in eleven years he had become a landholder and owner of numerous other sailing vessels.

An 1812 engraving shows a silhouette of Paul Cuffee with his ship docked in Sierra Leone.

Besides being a merchant seaman Cuffee was also a civil rights activist. He discarded his father's slave surname and took his father's Christian first name in its place. He filed suffrage complaints in the Massachusetts court and, although unsuccessful, his court actions laid the groundwork for later civil rights legislation.

Cuffee was also a believer in free blacks voluntarily returning to Africa. In 1811 aboard his ship *Traveller* he sailed to Sierra Leone where he founded the Friendly Society, which helped blacks return to Africa. In 1815 he sailed with thirty-eight colonists for Africa. It was to be his last voyage, however, for he died September 9, 1817.

Martin Delany (1812–1885)
Physician, Journalist, Author, Abolitionist

Born May 6, 1812, in Charles Town, West Virginia, editor, author, physician, abolitionist, and Black Nationalist Martin Delany received his first education from a book peddler who also served as an itinerant teacher. Since blacks in the South were forbidden to learn to read, when others found out he could read, the family was forced to flee north to Pennsylvania so that their children could continue to study. At the age of nineteen, Delany left home to seek further education. He studied with a young divinity student and a white doctor for a time.

As an adult, he became involved in anti-slavery reform and the literacy movement. He began to publish *The Mystery*, a weekly newspaper devoted to news of the anti-slavery movement. When it folded after only a year of publication, Delany became co-editor of the *North Star*, a newspaper started by Frederick Douglass.

In 1848 Delany quit the *North Star* to pursue his medical studies. After being rejected on account of his race from several prominent Pennsylvania medical schools, he was able to attend the Harvard Medical School for a year before he was expelled from there because of his race. While he did not receive his degree, he did learn enough to practice medicine the rest of his life. In the 1850s, he became something of a local legend when he saved many lives during a fierce cholera epidemic in Pittsburgh.

The years following medical school were a grave disappointment to Delany, for blacks in America continued to be treated inhumanely no matter how hard he worked against slavery. He became an ardent Black Nationalist and recommended emigration to establish an independent colony for African Americans in South America or Africa. He wrote prolifically on the subject, held several national conventions, and set out on an exploratory expedition to Africa.

After the Emancipation Proclamation of 1863, Delany met with President Abraham Lincoln to discuss the establishment of black regiments in the army. Lincoln commissioned him as the first black major in the U.S. Army. He passed away on January 24, 1885.

After the Civil War, Delany continued to work with reconstructionists trying to get fair treatment for newly freed slaves, still advocating emigration. He continued to pursue his scholarship, and in 1879 published his *Principal of Ethnology: The Origin of Races and Color,* in which he discussed the role of black people in the world's civilization. He died in 1885, before he was able to actually move to Africa himself.

Louis Farrakhan (1933–)
Religious Leader

 Born May 11, 1933, in New York City, Louis Farrakhan (then known as Louis Eugene Walcott) was an outstanding student at Boston English High School and then attended Winston-Salem Teacher's College. Farrakhan was an excellent musician; he played the violin and was a calypso singer. It was as a singer that he earned his livelihood prior to converting to Elijah Muhammad's Nation of Islam in the 1950s. He quickly worked his way up to a leadership position, becoming the minister of the Boston mosque. He loudly denounced Malcolm X after the latter split with Elijah Muhammad in

1963. He soon assumed leadership of the Harlem mosque, which Malcolm had previously led. After Elijah Muhammad's death in 1975, he briefly supported Muhammad's son and designated successor, Warith Muhammad, as leader of the Nation of Islam. Shortly after Warith Muhammad began accepting whites as members within the Nation of Islam, now renamed the World Community of Al-Islam in the West, Farrakhan split from him and established a rival organization with about ten thousand members.

Farrakhan's vigorous support for Jesse Jackson's presidential candidacy in 1984 quickly became an issue after Farrakhan made several controversial statements, most notably calling Judaism a "gutter religion." Overshadowed in the controversy was the involvement of Nation of Islam leaders in American electoral politics for the first time. Previously, Black Muslims had generally followed Elijah Muhammad's counsel not to vote or to take part in political campaigns.

In early 1995 Farrakhan, once aware that Malcolm X's daughter Qubilah Bahiyah Shabazz had been arrested for hiring an FBI agent to kill him, declared the situation an FBI trap. Farrakhan was believed to have been involved in Malcolm X's murder.

On October 16, 1995, The Million Man March/Day of Absence, proposed by Farrakhan, took place at the Lincoln Memorial in Washington, D.C. Although the park services in D.C. reported four hundred thousand in attendance, organizers claimed a million participants. African American men came from all over the country and were given the charge, once returning home, to improve themselves, their families, and their communities.

International travel has often drawn criticism for Farrakhan. In 1996, during an eighteen nation tour of Africa and the Middle East, he visited countries suspected of supporting terrorism. In 2001 the fifteen-year ban placed on his travel by the British High Court was removed but, because of his views regarding Osama bin Laden and the bombing of Afghanistan, the ban was reinstated in 2002.

Farrakhan was diagnosed with prostate cancer in 1999 but recovered and in 2000 was able to continue his vigorous participation in the betterment of the world community.

James Forten (1766–1842)
Abolitionist

Forten was born of free African American parents in Philadelphia on September 2, 1766. He studied at a Quaker school but quit at the age of fifteen to serve as a powder boy aboard the privateer *Royal Louis* during the Revolutionary War. He was captured by the British and held prisoner for seven months. He eventually spent a year in England where he was introduced to abolitionist philosophy.

Upon returning to America he was apprentice to a sailmaker, and by 1786 he was foreman and in 1798 became owner of the company. The business prospered and in 1832 employed forty white and African American workers.

By the 1830s Forten had become active in the abolitionist movement and was a strong opponent of African colonization. He became a noted pamphleteer, a nineteenth-century form of social activism, and was an early fund-raiser for William Lloyd Garrison's *The Liberator.*

Forten was president and founder of the American Moral Reform Society and was active in the American Anti-Slavery Society. He was a vigorous opponent of northern implementation of the 1793 Fugitive Slave Act. Forten died in Philadelphia on March 4, 1842.

Henry Highland Garnet (1815–1882)
Religious Leader

Garnet was born into slavery on December 23, 1815, near New Market, Kent County, Maryland. His family escaped slavery in 1824 and Garnet began school in New Hope, Pennsylvania. The family moved to New York and Garnet began attending the African Free School. It was here in the company of future leaders such as celebrated abolitionists Samuel Ringgold Ward and Episcopal Priest Alexander Crummell that Garnet found his purpose. Garnet attended the Oneida Institute in Whitesboro, New York, and graduated with honors in 1840.

Garnet became an important figure among abolitionists. He was an independent thinker and felt that blacks should control their own destiny. He believed in taking direct action and became a member of the American Colonization Society. At the end of the Civil War on February 12, 1865, he became the first African American to deliver a sermon in the House of Representatives in the U.S. Capitol. Garnet lobbied for the position of minister to Liberia and was given the post. After landing in Monrovia on December 28, 1881, he died a short time later on February 12, 1882.

Marcus Garvey (1887–1940)
Journalist, Activist

Born August 17, 1887, in St. Ann's Bay, Jamaica, Garvey was the youngest of eleven children. Garvey moved to Kingston at the age of fourteen, found work in a print shop, and became acquainted with the abysmal living conditions of the laboring class. He quickly involved himself in social reform, participating in the first Printers' Union strike in Jamaica in 1907 and in setting up the newspaper *The Watchman.* Leaving the island to earn money to finance his projects, he visited Central and South America, amassing evidence that black people everywhere were victims of discrimination.

Garvey returned to Jamaica in 1911 and began to lay the groundwork of the Universal Negro Improvement Association, to which he devoted his life. Undaunted by lack of enthusiasm for his plans, Garvey left for England in 1912 in search of additional financial backing. While there, he met a Sudanese-Egyptian journalist, Duse Mo-hammed Ali. While working for Ali's publication, *African Times* and *Oriental Review*, Garvey began to study the history of Africa—particularly the exploitation of black peoples by colonial powers—and he read Booker T. Washington's *Up From Slavery*, which advocated black self-help.

In 1914 Garvey organized the Universal Negro Improvement Association (UNIA) and its coordinating body, the African Communities League. In 1920 the organization held its first convention in New York. The convention opened with a parade down Harlem's Lenox Avenue. That evening, before a crowd of 25,000, Garvey outlined his plan to build an African nation-state. In New York City his ideas attracted popular support, and thousands enrolled in the UNIA. He began publishing the newspaper *The Negro World* and toured the United States preaching Black Nationalism. In a matter of months, he had founded over thirty UNIA branches and launched some ambitious business ventures, notably the Black Star Shipping Line.

In the years following the organization's first convention, the UNIA began to decline in popularity. With the Black Star Line in serious financial difficulties, Garvey promoted two new business organizations—the African Communities League and the Negro Factories Corporation. He also tried to salvage his colonization scheme by sending a delegation to appeal to the League of Nations for transfer to the UNIA of the African colonies taken from Germany during World War I.

Financial betrayal by trusted aides and a host of legal entanglements (based on charges that he had used the U.S. mail system to defraud prospective investors) eventually led to Garvey's imprisonment in Atlanta Federal Penitentiary for a five-year term. In 1927 his half-served sentence was commuted, and he was deported to Jamaica by order of President Calvin Coolidge.

Garvey then turned his energies to Jamaican politics, campaigning on a platform of self-government, minimum wage laws, and land and judicial reform. He was soundly defeated at the polls, however, because most of his followers did not have the necessary voting qualifications.

In 1935 Garvey left for England where, in near obscurity, he died on June 10, 1940, in a cottage in West Kensington.

Malcolm X (1925–1965)
Civil Rights Leader

Born Malcolm Little in Omaha, Nebraska, on May 19, 1925, Malcolm X was the son of a Baptist minister who was an avid supporter of Marcus Garvey's United Negro Improvement Association. While living in Omaha, the family was often harassed—at one point the family's house was set afire. In 1929 the family moved to Lansing, Michigan. While in Michigan, Malcolm's father was killed—his body severed in two by a streetcar and his head smashed. In his autobiography, written with Alex Haley, Malcolm asserted that his father may have been killed by members of the Ku Klux Klan. His mother, stricken by the death of her husband and the demands of providing for the family, was committed to a mental institution.

Leaving school after the eighth grade, Malcolm made his way to New York, working for a time as a waiter at Smalls Paradise in Harlem. Malcolm began selling and using drugs, turned to burglary and, in 1946, was sentenced to a ten-year prison term on burglary charges.

While in prison Malcolm became acquainted with the Black Muslim sect headed by Elijah Muhammad, and was quickly converted. Following his parole in 1952, he soon became an outspoken defender of Muslim doctrines, accepting the basic argument that evil was an inherent characteristic of the "white man's Christian world."

Unlike Muhammad, Malcolm sought publicity, making provocative and inflammatory statements to predominantly white civic groups and college campus audiences. Branding white people "devils," he spoke bitterly of a philosophy of vengeance and "an eye for an eye." When, in 1963, he characterized the Kennedy assassination as a case of "chickens coming home to roost," he was suspended from the Black Muslim movement by Elijah Muhammad.

Disillusioned with Elijah Muhammad's teachings, Malcolm formed his own organizations, the Organization of Afro-American Unity and the Muslim Mosque Inc. In 1964 he made a pilgrimage to Islam's holy city, Mecca, and adopted the name El-Hajj Malik El-Shabazz. He also adopted views that were not popular with other Black Nationalists, including the idea that not all whites were evil and that blacks could make gains by working through established channels.

As a result of his new views, Malcolm became the victim of death threats. On February 14, 1965, his home was firebombed; his wife and children escaped unharmed. A week later, Malcolm was shot and killed at the Audubon Ballroom in Harlem, while preparing to speak. Three of the men arrested were later identified as members of the Nation of Islam, but there still remains controversy over who conspired to kill Malcolm X.

Malcolm X had a profound influence on both blacks and whites. Many blacks responded to a feeling that he was a man of the people, experienced in the ways of the street rather than the pulpit or the college campus, which traditionally had provided the preponderance of black leaders. Many young whites responded to Malcolm's blunt, colorful language and unwillingness to retreat in the face of hostility. His emphasis on black pride and self determination along with a sharp and intelligent analysis of American policies and practices created both anger and respect.

The memory and image of Malcolm X has changed as much after his death as his own philosophies changed during his life. At first thought to be a violent fanatic, he is now thought to be an advocate of self-help, self-defense, and education; as a philosopher and pedagogue, he succeeded in integrating history, religion, and mythology to establish a framework for his ultimate belief in world brotherhood and human justice. Faith, in his view, was a prelude to action; ideas were reckless without policy. At least three books published since his death effectively present his most enduring thoughts. In 1992 a monumental film by Spike Lee based on Malcolm's autobiography renewed interest and understanding in the meaning of the life and death of Malcolm X.

Elijah Muhammad (1897–1975)
Religious Leader, Activist

Elijah Muhammad was born Elijah Poole in Sandersville, Georgia, on October 10, 1897. His father, a Baptist preacher, had been a slave.

As a boy, Elijah worked at various jobs involving manual labor. At the age of twenty-six, he moved with his wife and two children (he was to have eight children in all) to Detroit. There in 1930, Poole met Fard Muhammad, also known as W.D. Fard, who had founded the Lost-Found Nation of Islam. Poole soon became Fard's chief assistant and in 1932 went to Chicago, where he established the Nation of Islam's Temple, Number Two, which soon became the largest. In 1934 he returned to Detroit. When Fard disappeared in that year, political and theological rivals accused Poole of foul play. He returned to Chicago where he organized his own movement in which Fard was deified as Allah, and Elijah (Poole) Muhammad became known as Allah's Messenger. This movement soon became known as the Black Muslims.

During World War II, Elijah Muhammad expressed support for Japan, on the basis of its being a nonwhite country, and was jailed for sedition. The time Muhammad served in prison was probably significant in his later, successful attempts to convert large numbers of black prison inmates, including Malcolm X, to the Nation of Islam. During the 1950s and 1960s, the Nation grew under Muhammad's leadership. Internal differences between Muhammad and Malcolm X, followed by the break between the two men and Malcolm's assassination, for which three Black Muslim gunmen were convicted, provided a great deal of unfavorable media coverage, but this did not slow the growth of the movement. In the late

1960s and early 1970s, Elijah Muhammad moderated the Nation's criticism of whites without compromising its message of black integrity. When Muhammad died in 1975, the Nation was an important religious, political, and economic force among America's blacks, especially in the country's major cities.

Elijah Muhammad was not original in his rejection of Christianity as the religion of the oppressor. Noble Drew Ali and the Black Jews had arrived at this conclusion well before him. But Muhammad was the most successful salesman for this brand of African American religion. Thus he was able to build the first strong, black religious group in the United States that appealed primarily to the unemployed and underemployed city dweller, and ultimately to some in the black middle class. In addition, his message on the virtues of being black was explicit and uncompromising, and he sought, with at least a little success, to bolster the economic independence of African Americans by establishing schools and businesses under the auspices of the Nation of Islam.

Henry McNeal Turner (1834–1915)
Religious Leader

Henry McNeal Turner was born near Abbeville, South Carolina, of free parents. He was ordained a minister in the African Methodist Episcopal Church in 1853 and bishop in 1880. In 1863 Turner became the first African American Army chaplain. He was also president of Morris Brown College for twelve years.

Turner was a leading advocate of repatriation. In 1876 he was elected vice president of the American Colonization Society. He made several trips to Africa and lectured throughout the world.

Turner was convinced that blacks had no future in America. Instead, he felt that God had brought blacks to the New World as a means of spreading Christianity and preparing them to redeem Africa. Turner edited and published several papers, including *Voice of Missions and Voice of the People,* in which he advocated black colonization of Africa.

CIVIL RIGHTS

Throughout the history of the United States, African Americans have struggled to obtain basic civil rights. It is a struggle that has spanned several centuries—from the mutinies by Africans during the Atlantic crossing, to the insurrections organized by slaves in the New World, to the founding of such organizations as the Free African Society, to the abolition movement, to the civil rights marches and demonstrations of the twentieth century, to the campaigns for America to acknowledge injustice and to maintain laws and acts that protect citizenship rights in the twenty-first century.

As a result of segregation and discriminatory practices within the Methodist Church, the Free African Society was organized in 1787 in Philadelphia by the Reverends Richard Allen and Absalom Jones. As the Philadelphia organization grew, other Free African societies formed in such places as Boston, New York, and Newport. Like many black movements to follow, the Free African Society provided spiritual guidance and religious instruction, while providing economic aid, burial assistance, and relief to widows and orphans. The society also helped to facilitate communications between free blacks throughout the country.

The press and the pulpit served as important tools in the anti-slavery movement. In 1827 in

New York, Samuel Cornish and John Russwurm founded *Freedom's Journal*, the first black-owned and operated newspaper in the United States. *Freedom's Journal*, which ceased publication after only three years, was concerned not only with eradicating slavery but also with the growing discrimination and cruelty against free blacks in both the South and North.

In 1847 abolitionist Frederick Douglass published the first edition of the *North Star*, which eventually became one of most successful black newspapers in America prior to the outbreak of the Civil War. Douglass, an escaped slave from Maryland, became one of the best-known black abolitionists in the country. He lectured extensively throughout the United States and England. In 1845 he published his autobiography, *Narrative of Frederick Douglass*.

Although the abolition movement was dominated by whites, numerous black leaders played a major role in the movement, including such figures as Henry Highland Garnet, Harriet Tubman, and Sojourner Truth.

Following the war, Republicans, who controlled the U.S. Congress, took up the cause of the newly freed African Americans. Between 1865 and 1875, three amendments to the Con-

Frederick Douglass

acted the Ku Klux Klan Act as an effort to end intimidation and violence directed at blacks. The act failed, however, to exterminate the Klan and other terrorist organizations.

The civil rights and Reconstruction legislation were difficult for many whites to accept and did little to change their attitudes. The last of the civil rights acts passed by Congress in 1875 prohibited discrimination in public accommodations. However, by the 1880s the debate as to the constitutionality of such legislation had reached the U.S. Supreme Court. Ruling in a group of five cases in 1883, which became known as the Civil Rights Cases, the U.S. Supreme Court concluded that the 1875 Civil Rights Act was unconstitutional on the grounds that the Fourteenth Amendment authorized Congress to legislate only against discriminatory state action, and not discrimination by private individuals. The Court's ruling brought about an end to federal efforts to protect the civil rights of African Americans until the mid-twentieth century.

By the late nineteenth and early twentieth centuries, lynching had become a weapon used by whites against blacks throughout the country. Between 1882 and 1890 approximately 1,750 African Americans were lynched in the United States. Victims, who included women, had been accused of a variety of "offenses" ranging from testifying in court against a white man to failing to use the word "mister" when addressing a white person. Ida B. Wells Barnett, a journalist and social activist, became one of the leading voices in the anti-lynching crusade by writing and lecturing throughout the United States against the practice of lynching.

In 1896 the U.S. Supreme Court was faced with the issue of segregation on public transportation. At the time, as was the case in many parts of the South, a Louisiana state law was enacted requiring that "separate but equal" accommodations for blacks and whites be maintained in all public facilities. When Homer Adolph Plessy, a black man traveling by train from New Orleans to Covington, Louisiana, refused to ride in the "colored" railway coach, he was arrested.

stitution and a string of civil rights and Reconstruction legislation was passed by Congress. The Thirteenth Amendment, ratified December 18, 1865, abolished slavery and involuntary servitude. The Fourteenth Amendment, ratified July 28, 1868, guaranteed citizenship and provided equal protection under the law. Ratified March 30, 1870, the Fifteenth Amendment was designed to protect the right of all citizens to vote. In 1866, 1870, 1871, and 1875 Congress passed civil rights legislation outlining and protecting basic rights, including the right to purchase and sell property and access to public accommodations. The Reconstruction Acts, passed between 1867 and 1869, called for new state constitutional conventions in those states that had seceded from the Union prior to the Civil War.

Reconstruction eventually produced a wave of anti-African sentiment. White organizations like the Ku Klux Klan, which were aimed at intimidating blacks and preventing them from taking their place in society, sprang up throughout the North and the South. In 1871 Congress en-

Prior to the case of *Plessy v. Ferguson*, the Court had started to build a platform upon which the doctrine of separate but equal would be based. In 1878, ruling in the case *Hall v. DeCuir*, the Court declared that states could not outlaw segregation on common carriers, such as street-cars and railroads. Segregation laws sprang up throughout the South.

With Justice Billings Brown delivering the majority opinion in the Plessy case, the Court declared that "separate but equal" accommodations constituted a reasonable use of state police power and that the Fourteenth Amendment of the Constitution could not be used to abolish social or racial distinctions or to force a co-mingling of the two races.

The Supreme Court had effectively reduced the significance of the Fourteenth Amendment, which was designed to give blacks specific rights and protections. The Plessy ruling, which was termed the "separate but equal" doctrine, paved the way for the segregation of African Americans in all walks of life.

During the late nineteenth and early twentieth centuries, two figures—Booker T. Washington and William Edward Burghardt DuBois—emerged as leaders in the struggle for black political and civil rights.

Washington, an educator and founder of the Tuskegee Normal and Industrial Institute, was a strong advocate of practical, utilitarian education and manual training as a means for developing African Americans. Tuskegee Normal and Industrial Institute, which was founded in 1881 and based on a program at Hampton Institute, provided vocational training and prepared its students to survive economically in a segregated society. In Washington's opinion, education was to provide African Americans with the means to become economically self-supporting. Speaking at the Cotton States International Exposition in Atlanta in 1895, Washington outlined his philosophy of self-help and cooperation between blacks and whites.

To those of my race who depend on bettering their condition in a foreign land,

or who underestimate the importance of cultivating friendly relations with the Southern white man, who is their next door neighbor, I would say: "Cast down your bucket where you are"—cast it down in making friends in every manly way of the people of all races by whom we are surrounded.

W.E.B. DuBois, a young historian and Harvard graduate, challenged Washington's passive policies in a series of stinging essays and speeches. DuBois advocated the uplifting of African Americans through an educated black elite, which he referred to as the "Talented Tenth," or roughly a tenth of the African American population. He believed that these African Americans must become proficient in education and culture, which would eventually benefit all.

In 1905 DuBois, along with a group of other black intellectuals, formed the Niagara Movement. The group drew up a platform that called for full citizenship rights for blacks and public

W. E. B. DuBois

recognition of their contributions to America's stability and progress. The movement eventually evolved into what became known as the National Association for the Advancement of Colored People.

The civil rights movement suffered many defeats in the first half of the twentieth century. Repeated efforts to obtain passage of federal anti-lynching bills failed. The all-white primary system, which effectively disenfranchised southern blacks, resisted numerous court challenges. The Depression worsened conditions on farms and in ghettos. On the positive side, the growing political power of blacks in northern cities and an increasingly liberal trend in the Supreme Court portended the legal and legislative victories of the 1950s and 1960s.

A great deal of the civil rights struggle throughout this period was carried on by the National Association for the Advancement of Colored People, which had begun chipping away at the roots of legalized segregation in a series of successful lawsuits. A major breakthrough for the NAACP came in 1954 when the Supreme Court ruled in *Brown v. Board of Education of Topeka* that discrimination in education was unconstitutional. This decision was as momentous as the Supreme Court's ruling in *Plessy v. Ferguson* in 1896, which legalized the doctrine of "separate but equal" treatment for blacks.

The Brown case involved the practice of denying black children equal access to state public schools due to state laws requiring or permitting racial segregation. The U.S. Supreme Court unanimously held that segregation deprived the children of equal protection under the Fourteenth Amendment to the U.S. Constitution, overturning the "separate but equal" doctrine established in Plessy.

In 1941 A. Philip Randolph, organizer of an employment bureau for untrained blacks and founder the Brotherhood of Sleeping Car Porters, came up with the idea of leading a protest march of blacks in Washington, D.C., to protest discrimination. On July 25, less than a week before the scheduled demonstration, President Franklin D. Roosevelt issued Executive Order No. 8802, which banned discrimination in the defense industry and led to the creation of the Fair Employment Practices Committee.

Rosa Parks was one of the major catalysts of the 1960s' civil rights movement. On December 1, 1955, Parks refused to give up her seat on a Montgomery bus to a white man, as the law required, and was arrested and sent to jail. As a result of Parks's arrest, blacks throughout Montgomery refused to ride city buses. Because blacks were the majority riders on the city buses, their absence had a manjor impact on the local economy. The Montgomery bus boycott led by Martin Luther King Jr. was highly successful and ultimately led to the integration of all Montgomery city buses.

The eventual success of the Montgomery bus boycott encouraged a wave of massive demonstrations that swept across the South. In 1960 a group of students who were denied service at a Greensboro, North Carolina, lunch counter started the "sit-in" movement. That same year, the Student Nonviolent Coordinating Committee was created and would include among its members Julian Bond, H. Rap Brown, Stokely Carmichael, and John Lewis.

The civil rights movement of the 1960s galvanized blacks and sympathetic whites as nothing had ever done before, but it was not without cost. Thousands of people were jailed because they defied Jim Crow laws. Jim Crow laws legalized racial segregation and discrimination and denied equal access to all citizens. Others involved in the movement were murdered, and homes and churches were bombed. People lost their jobs and their homes because they supported the movement.

On August 28, 1963, nearly 250,000 blacks and whites marched in Washington, D.C., to awaken the nation's consciousness regarding civil rights and to encourage the passage of civil rights legislation pending in Congress. The march was a cooperative effort of several civil rights organizations, including the Southern Christian Leadership Conference, the Congress of Racial Equality, the NAACP, the Negro American Labor

The 1963 March on Washington.

Council, and the National Urban League. It was during this demonstration that Dr. Martin Luther King Jr., in the shadow of the Lincoln Memorial, gave his "I Have a Dream" speech.

At its zenith, the civil rights movement was the most important event taking place in America. Through demonstrations, sit-ins, marches, and soaring rhetoric, the movement aroused widespread public indignation, thus creating an atmosphere in which it was possible to make positive changes in American society.

Although the civil rights movement of the 1950s and 1960s produced significant gains for African Americans, progress continues today. This progress is evident in the passage of the most recent civil rights legislation. In June 1989 the U.S. Supreme Court delivered opinions in several cases dealing with seniority systems and racial discrimination in employment. Ruling in the cases *Lorance v. AT&T Technologies Inc., Martin v. Wilks,*

Patterson v. McLean Credit Union, and *Wards Cove Packing Co. v. Antonio*, the Court appeared to reverse earlier civil rights rulings.

Prior to the Court's ruling in *Wards Cove*, the burden of proof in job discrimination suits had been placed on employers, requiring businesses to prove that there was a legitimate business reason for alleged discriminatory practices. With the *Wards Cove* decision, the Court made it more difficult for groups to win such suits by requiring workers to prove that there was no clear business reason for an employer's use of practices that result in discrimination.

Civil rights organizations were quick to protest the ruling; opponents of the ruling, including the NAACP Legal Defense and Educational Fund and the Leadership Conference on Civil Rights, argued that the Court had undermined the protection granted by federal civil rights and equal employment legislation.

On October 16 and 17, 1990, both houses of Congress approved a bill designed to reverse the Court's ruling. The proposed legislation not only reversed the Court's ruling in *Wards Cove*, but strengthened provisions of the 1964 Civil Rights Act. On October 22 President George H.W. Bush vetoed the bill, claiming that the bill's provisions would encourage employers to establish hiring quotas.

This was not the first time that Congress moved to reverse a Court action in the area of civil rights—in 1987 Congress passed the Civil Rights Restoration Act of 1988, which reversed the Court's ruling in *Grove City College v. Bell* (1984). In the *Grove City College* case, the Supreme Court ruled that not all programs and activities of an institution were covered by Title IX of the Education Amendments of 1972 (Public Law 89–10, 79 Stat. 27), which prohibits discrimination in educational programs receiving federal financial assistance.

After vetoing Congress's 1990 civil rights legislation, the Bush administration joined both houses of Congress in working on alternative bills. On October 30, following months of negotiation, the Senate passed a bill designed to provide additional remedies to deter harassment and intentional discrimination in the workplace, provide guidelines for the adjudication of cases arising under Title VII of the Civil Rights Act of 1964, and expand the scope of civil rights legislation weakened by Supreme Court decisions. The House of Representatives passed the bill on November 7, and on November 21 President Bush signed the Civil Rights Act of 1991. Also in 1991, the Glass Ceiling Act was established to study the underrepresentation of women and minorities in upper level management and decision-making positions in the workforce.

On June 23, 2003, the Supreme Court ruled on their first affirmative action cases in higher education in twenty-five years. The pivotal case in the decisions was *Grutter v. Bollinger* filed in 1997 against the University of Michigan law school. The suit challenged the University's affirmative action proviso using race as a criteria in the admissions process. The ruling of 6-3 declared that the criteria for the law school would be upheld, but the undergraduate criteria were deemed unconstitutional. This decision along with California's Proposition 209, championed by businessman Ward Connerly in 1996, and Washington's Initiative 200 in 1998 were among the states' efforts to eradicate affirmative action. As a result of these actions, the number of African American students in public universities in those states dramatically decreased.

On February 7, 2005, the U.S. Senate passed Resolution 39 which apologized for lynching in the United States. The lack of prior action by the Senate, which rejected three anti-lynching measures presented by the U.S. House of Representatives between 1920 and 1940, resulted in denied civil rights and the deaths of numerous African Americans. The Resolution acknowledges lynching as the ultimate act of racism and apologizes to not only the victims but to the families. As a result of Resolution 39, the Emmett Till Unsolved Civil Rights Crime Act was made into law. This legislation established within the U.S. Department of Justice an office to investigate and prosecute Civil Rights Era murders.

The Voting Rights Act of 1965 and all amendments were reauthorized on July 27, 2006, for twenty-five years. The Reauthorization Act, which was named in honor of civil rights activists Fanny Lou Hamer, Rosa Parks, and Coretta Scott King, was delayed due to efforts by Republicans to amend or defeat the bill. The bill was signed by President George W. Bush a year before the 2007 expiration date.

As the new generation of civil rights leaders inherit the struggle of equality, they become the first generation not to have experienced segregation, lynch mobs, Jim Crow, and the enforcement of denied citizenship. The previous generation, referred to by the first African American president, Baraka Obama, as the Moses generation, sees that the new generation has challenges that require new weapons to maintain and further establish civil rights. This newer generation has known failed schools, urban violence, increased numbers of both African American men and women being incarcerated, and an economy that has further decreased opportunities.

BIOGRAPHIES: CIVIL RIGHTS

Ralph David Abernathy (1926–1990)
Minister

Born March 11, 1926, in Linden, Alabama, the Reverend Ralph David Abernathy was ordained a minister in 1948. He received his bachelor's degree from Alabama State College (now Alabama State University) in 1950 and his master's degree from Atlanta University in 1951.

The alliance between Abernathy and Martin Luther King Jr., stretched back to the mid-1950s. While attending Atlanta University, Abernathy had the opportunity to hear King preach at Ebenezer Baptist Church. After obtaining his master's degree, Abernathy returned to Alabama to serve as a part-time minister at the Eastern Star Baptist Church in Demopolis. In 1951 Abernathy moved to First Baptist Church in Montgomery. Around this time King accepted a position at Montgomery's Dexter Avenue Baptist Church; Abernathy and King became close friends.

In 1955 Abernathy and King organized the Montgomery Improvement Association to coordinate a citywide bus boycott. The success of the boycott led to the creation of the Southern Negro Leaders Conference; the organization's name was later changed to the Southern Leadership Conference and finally the Southern Christian Leadership Conference. In January 1957 King was elected the organization's first president.

From the time of King's death in 1968 until 1977, Abernathy served as president of the Southern Christian Leadership Conference. Abernathy continued as a leading figure in the movement until his resignation in 1977.

In 1977 Abernathy made an unsuccessful bid for a U.S. congressional seat. In 1989 he published his autobiography, *And the Walls Came Tumbling Down*, which was criticized by some black leaders for Abernathy's inclusion of details regarding King's extramarital affairs. Abernathy died of cardiac arrest on April 17, 1990.

Ella Baker (1903–1986)
Activist

Ella Baker was born on December 19, 1903, in Norfolk, Virginia, to Blake and Georgiana Ross Baker, both educated people who worked hard to educate their children. The family and community in which she grew up instilled in her a sense of sharing and community cooperation.

When she was fifteen, Baker was sent to the Shaw Boarding School in Raleigh. The Shaw school was both a high school and college, and she graduated with a bachelor's degree as valedictorian in 1927. After graduation, she moved to New York City. She quickly became involved in progressive politics and attended as many meetings and discussions as she could find.

In the 1940s Baker began to work for the NAACP. Between 1940 and 1943 she was a field secretary, traveling all over the country setting up branch offices and teaching people to fight for their own rights; her traveling gave her the opportunity to develop a vast network of contacts in the South that she later relied on when working for the Student Nonviolent Coordinating Committee and Southern Christian Leadership Conference. In 1943 she became the director of branches for the NAACP. During the 1950s she started fund-raising activities in New York for the civil rights struggles in the South, and in 1958 moved to Atlanta to work with the SCLC.

Working for the SCLC, Baker became disillusioned with the top-heavy, male-dominated organizational structure of the group. In 1960 she quit the SCLC and took a job with the Young

Women's Christian Association instead. When students began leading sit-ins, she shifted her focus to the development of the Student Nonviolent Coordinating Committee. She acted as an unofficial adviser for the group, counseling them to set up their own student-run organization rather than be subsumed under the SCLC or the NAACP. She helped launch the Mississippi Freedom Democratic Party that challenged the all-white Democratic delegation at the 1964 presidential convention. She also acted as staff consultant for the interracial SCLC educational fund.

Baker returned to New York City in 1965 but kept working with national and international civil rights organizations. Baker's belief in the power of communal action and reliance on the workers rather than the leaders had an enormous impact. She worked for all of the major civil rights organizations at their time of greatest need. By the time the SCLC and the SNCC were formed, she had almost thirty years of civil rights and community organizing experience to offer. She continually strove to keep the movement people oriented, and she succeeded in helping the SNCC remain a student group. Through her philosophy and actions, she motivated hundreds to act to help themselves and their neighbors as she had learned to do as a child.

Daisy Bates (1914–1999)
Publisher, Author, Activist

After attending segregated schools where all of the new equipment and up-to-date texts were reserved for whites only, Daisy Bates spent much of her energy as an adult successfully integrating the schools of Little Rock, Arkansas.

Shortly after their marriage in 1941, Daisy and her husband, Lucius Christopher Bates, a journalist, started to publish a newspaper, the *Arkansas State Press*. They made it a point in their paper to report incidents of police brutality and other racially-motivated violence; their newspaper became known throughout the state for its campaign to improve the social and economic circumstances of African Americans. Because of

their work, the city of Little Rock began to hire black police officers, and the number of racial incidents lessened.

In 1952 Daisy Bates became the Arkansas president of the NAACP; after the 1954 court decision in the *Brown v. Board of Education of Topeka* case, she became very active in school desegregation. She began taking black children to white schools to be registered, and if the school refused to register the children, she would report it in her paper. In 1957, the superintendent of schools in Little Rock decided to try to integrate the schools and chose nine students, now called the Little Rock Nine, to be the first black children to attend Central High, a white school. Most white citizens of Little Rock objected. Bates organized the Little Rock Nine, accompanied them to Central High, and stood with them against the state troopers that Governor Orval Faubus had sent in to prevent the integration. For days she escorted the children to school, only to be turned away by an angry mob. On September 25, 1957, Daisy Bates entered Central High in Little Rock with the nine children, escorted by 1,000 paratroopers that President Dwight Eisenhower had sent in; the first steps toward integration were successful. For the rest of their years at Central High, Bates kept track of the students and acted as their advocate when problems arose, frequently accompanying them and their parents to meetings with school officials.

In October 1957 one month after she marched into Central High, Daisy Bates was arrested on charges of failing to provide membership information on the NAACP to city officials. The charges were later overturned. Two years later, the *Arkansas State Press* folded, but Bates kept active in the civil rights fight, touring and speaking, and working with the Student Nonviolent Coordinating Committee to register voters. In 1985 the *State Press* began to publish again, and it has continued to serve the needs of the African American community in Little Rock. Bates continued her service to the community until her death on November 4, 1999. President Bill Clinton honored her service by allowing her body to lie in state at the Capital.

Stokely Carmichael (1941–1998)
Activist

If there was one individual during the 1960s who stood at the forefront of the Black Power movement, it was Stokely Carmichael. He soared to fame by popularizing the dynamic phrase "black power" and as one of the most powerful and influential leaders of the Student Nonviolent Coordinating Committee.

He was born in Trinidad on June 29, 1941, and moved to the United States with his family when he was eleven. As a teenager, Carmichael was jolted by ghetto life in which "black" and "impotent" seemed to be synonymous terms. He was not reassured later when he was admitted to the Bronx High School of Science, encountered white liberals, and felt he had been adopted by them as a mascot. Although he was offered good scholarships to white universities, Carmichael opted to attend Howard University. During his first year there, 1960, he joined the Congress of Racial Equality in its efforts to integrate public accommodations in the South. After graduation in 1964, he rejected scholarship opportunities for graduate school and went south to join the SNCC. As one of their finest organizers, he worked ceaselessly, registering and educating voters in the South. In 1966, he was elected chairman of the SNCC, but as the group's youngest chair he espoused views that were considered too radical by some members.

Carmichael's cry for "black power" thrilled many disenfranchised young African Americans but troubled others, who thought it sounded too violent. He was labeled as potentially violent by the media and the legal authorities. Disagreement with SNCC members arose over the issues of self-defense versus nonviolence, and the participation of whites in black grass-roots organizations. In 1967 he resigned as chairman and was later expelled from the SNCC.

Carmichael spent much of 1968 traveling around the world, speaking to many organizations, including some in Communist countries. His travels included Ghana, where he joined the Pan-African movement. After returning to the United States, he went to work for the Black Panther Party. In this country, however, he was subject to almost constant harassment from the FBI because of his connection with the Panthers, and because he had visited Communist countries while traveling. In 1969 he resigned from the Black Panthers and moved to Guinea, where he had been offered political asylum.

In Guinea, Carmichael turned his efforts to supporting Pan-Africanism; he organized many local chapters throughout the world of the All African Peoples Revolutionary Party. In 1978, to honor the two men who most influenced his Pan-African philosophical education, SeKou Toure and Kwame Nkrumah, he changed his name to Kwame Toure. Toure traveled throughout the world, working toward a united African people. In 1994 Toure was awarded an L.L.D. from Shaw University for his lifelong efforts to liberate African American people. He died on November 15, 1998, from prostate cancer. In 2003 Scribner published Toure's autobiography, *Ready for a Revolution: The Life and Struggles of Stokely Carmichael.*

Angela Davis (1944–)
Author, Scholar, Activist

Angela Davis was born in Birmingham, Alabama, on January 26, 1944, to middle-class parents who stressed both academic excellence and political awareness and activism. Her mother, Sally E. Davis, had been politically active since her college days, and Angela participated in demonstrations with her mother from the time she was in elementary school. To ensure a better education than she could receive in the segregated schools of the South, her parents sent her to Elizabeth Irwin High School, a private progressive school in New York. The school had many radical teachers and students, and Angela soon joined a Marxist study group there.

After graduation, Davis continued to seek high-quality education. She majored in French at

Brandeis College, studying at the Sorbonne in Paris her junior year. She then pursued graduate studies in philosophy at the Goethe University in Frankfurt, and in 1967 she returned to the United States to study with the well-known philosopher Herbert Marcuse at the University of California at San Diego. When she was almost done with her degree, she took a teaching job at the University of California at Los Angeles.

In 1969 Davis joined the Communist Party; the regents of UCLA tried to fire her, but she fought them in court. The following year she became involved with the Black Panther Party. Guns she had bought for self-defense were used by a member of the Black Panthers in a courtroom shooting. Believing she was involved, the FBI sought her arrest, so she went underground to avoid them. She was put on the FBI's most-wanted list and later arrested. In 1972 she was acquitted of all charges, but was not hired back by the university. California Governor Ronald Reagan and the regents of the university decreed that she would never teach in California again.

Since her trial, Davis has served as co-chair of the National Alliance against Racism and Political Repression, a legal group providing defense of minority prisoners. A writer and philosopher, she has written several books, including *If They Come in the Morning* (1971), *Women, Race and Class* (1983), *Angela Davis: An Autobiography* (1988), and *Women, Culture and Politics* (1989). She continues to write and lecture and remains politically active. In 1995 Davis was appointed presidential chair for the development of new ethnic courses for the University of California—Santa Cruz. In spite of opposition from the Republican legislature regarding her Communist affiliations, Davis took this position and continues to be in the forefront regarding women's rights, health care, and nuclear disarmament.

W.E.B. DuBois (1868–1963)
Scholar, Critic, Editor, Author, Activist

An outstanding critic, editor, scholar, author, and civil rights leader, W.E.B. DuBois is certainly among the most influential blacks of the twentieth century.

Born in Great Barrington, Massachusetts, on February 23, 1868, DuBois received a bachelor's degree from Fisk University and went on to win a second bachelor's, as well as a Ph.D., from Harvard. He was professor of Latin and Greek at Wilberforce and the University of Pennsylvania, and also served as a professor of economics and history at Atlanta University.

One of the founders of the National Association for the Advancement of Colored People in 1909, DuBois served as that organization's director of publications and editor of *Crisis* magazine until 1934. In 1944 he returned from Atlanta University to become head of the NAACP's special research department, a post he held until 1948. DuBois immigrated to Africa in 1961 and became editor in chief of the *Encyclopedia Africana*, an enormous publishing venture that had been planned by Kwame Nkrumah, since then deposed as president of Ghana. DuBois died in Ghana in 1963 at the age of ninety-five.

His numerous books include *The Suppression of the Slave Trade* (1896), *The Philadelphia Negro* (1899), *The Souls of Black Folk* (1903), *John Brown* (1909), *Quest of the Silver Fleece* (1911), *The Negro* (1915), *Darkwater* (1920), *The Gift of Black Folk* (1924), *Dark Princess* (1928), *Black Folk: Then and Now* (1939), *Dusk of Dawn* (1940), *Color and Democracy* (1945), *The World and Africa* (1947), *In Battle for Peace* (1952), and a trilogy, *Black Flame* (1957–1961).

It is this enormous literary output on such a wide variety of themes that offers the most convincing testimony to DuBois's lifetime position that it was vital for blacks to cultivate their own aesthetic and cultural values even as they made valuable strides toward social emancipation. In this he was opposed by Booker T. Washington, who felt that black people should concentrate on developing technical and mechanical skills before all else.

DuBois was one of the first male civil rights leaders to recognize the problems of gender discrimination. He was among the first men to understand the unique problems of black women, and to value their contributions. He supported the women's suffrage movement and strove to integrate this mostly white struggle. He encouraged many black female writers, artists, poets, and novelists, featuring their works in *Crisis* and sometimes providing personal financial assistance to them. Several of his novels feature women as prominently as men, an unusual approach for any author of his day. DuBois spent his life working not just for the equality of all men, but for the equality of all people.

Medgar Evers (1925–1963)
Civil Rights Leader

Medgar Evers, field secretary for the NAACP, was one of the first martyrs of the civil rights movement. On June 13, 1963, he drove home from a meeting, stepped out of his car, and was shot in the back.

Evers was born in 1925 in Decatur, Mississippi, to James and Jessie Evers. After a short stint in the army, he enrolled in Alcorn A&M College, graduating in 1952. His first job out of college was traveling around rural Mississippi selling insurance. He soon grew enraged at the despicable conditions of poor black families in his state and joined the NAACP. In 1954 he was appointed Mississippi's first field secretary.

Evers was outspoken, and his demands were radical for his rigidly segregated state. He fought for the enforcement of the 1954 court decision of *Brown v. Board of Education of Topeka*, which outlawed school segregation; he fought for the right to vote; and he advocated boycotting merchants who discriminated. He worked unceasingly despite the threats of violence that his speeches engendered. He gave much of himself to this struggle, and in 1963, he gave his life.

Immediately after his death, the shotgun that was used to kill him was found in bushes nearby, with the owner's fingerprints still fresh. Byron de la Beckwith, a vocal member of a local white supremacist group, was arrested. Despite the evidence against him, which included an earlier statement that he wanted to kill Evers, two trials with all-white juries ended in deadlock and Beckwith walked free.

Twenty years later, in 1989, information surfaced that suggested the jury in both trials had been tampered with. The assistant district attorney, with the help of Evers's widow, began putting together a new case. In 1990 the case reopened and Beckwith was arrested. On February 4, 1994, Beckwith at the age of 74 was found guilty and sentenced to life in prison by a jury of eight African Americans and four whites. Beckwith died in prison in 2001.

Evers's death changed the tenor of the civil rights struggle. Anger replaced fear in the South, as hundreds of demonstrators marched in protest. His death prompted President John F. Kennedy to ask Congress for a comprehensive civil rights bill, which President Lyndon Johnson signed into law the following year. Evers's death, and his life, contributed much to the struggle for equality.

Fannie Lou Hamer (1917–1977)
Activist

 As a poor sharecropper, she had only an elementary education, yet Fannie Lou Hamer was one of the most eloquent speakers for the civil rights movement in the South. She worked for political, social, and economic equality for herself and all African Americans; she fought to integrate the national Democratic Party; and she became one of the party's first black delegates to a presidential convention.

Hamer, the youngest of twenty siblings, was born to Jim and Ella Townsend on October 6, 1917, in Montgomery County, Mississippi. She began picking cotton when she was six and attended school until she had to drop out in the sixth grade to work full time. She worked first as a sharecropper, and then as a timekeeper on the same plantation in Mississippi for almost forty years. In 1962, because she tried to exercise her right to vote, she lost her job and, frightened by threats of violent reprisals, was forced to move away from her home and her family. Angered into action, she went to work for the Student Nonviolent Coordinating Committee, helping many blacks register to vote.

Because the Democratic Party refused to send blacks as delegates to the national presidential convention, in 1964 Hamer and others formed the Mississippi Freedom Democratic Party (MFDP) to send black delegates to the convention. They challenged the Democratic delegates from Mississippi for their seats at the convention, arguing that the all-white delegation could not adequately represent their state, which had a large black population. Hamer's own speech on their behalf frightened the incumbent President Lyndon Johnson so much so that he tried to block the televised coverage of her. The MFDP lost its bid that year, but their actions did result in a pledge from the national party not to seat delegations excluding blacks in the 1968 convention. In 1968 Fannie Lou Hamer was among the first black delegates to the Democratic National Convention.

For the next decade, Hamer remained active in the struggle for civil and economic rights. In 1969 she founded the Freedom Farms Corporation to help needy families raise food and livestock. They also provided basic social services, scholarships and grants for education, and helped fund minority business opportunities. She became a sought-after speaker, and in the 1970s, even as her health was failing from cancer, she still toured the country speaking about civil rights for all. Hamer died on March 14, 1977, after being hospitalized. Before her death she was honored by the Congressional Black Caucus for her dedication to the U.S. Constitution's principles of justice.

A. Leon Higginbotham Jr. (1928–1998)
Attorney, Judge, Civil Rights Leader

A. Leon Higginbotham Jr. was appointed on October 13, 1977, by President Jimmy Carter to the U.S. Circuit Judge's position. Just prior to this appointment, he had served on the Federal Trade Commission—the first black and the youngest person ever to hold the post of commissioner.

 Born in Trenton, New Jersey, on February 25, 1928, Higginbotham began as an engineering student at Purdue University but later went to Antioch College to study liberal arts. He received his LL.B. in 1952 from Yale School of Law. This was quite a step for a man who started out as a shoe store porter.

After graduation, Higginbotham became an assistant district attorney in Philadelphia and later moved into private practice. He was sought out by Pennsylvania Governor David Lawrence to become a member of the Pennsylvania Human Rights Commission. Elected president of the Philadelphia chapter of the NAACP, Higginbotham later earned the honor of "One of the 10 Outstanding Young Men in America" by the United States Junior Chamber of Commerce. He was made district judge in 1964, where he served until his appointment to the U.S. Circuit Court in 1977. Higginbotham was also a lecturer at Harvard Law School and an adjunct professor at the University of Pennsylvania.

Higginbotham is well known for his prolific writing. He authored more than one hundred articles as well as an acclaimed book, *In the Matter of Color: Race and the American Legal Process; The Colonial Period published in 1978*. He has also been praised for his unusual competency in logic and language. In his esteemed career, he won over forty honorary degrees and received the Presidential Medal of Freedom from President Bill Clinton in 1995. He died in 1998 of a stroke.

Anita Hill (1956–)
Attorney, Educator

Born on July 30, 1956, in Morns, Oklahoma, Anita Hill was a relatively unknown law professor at the University of Oklahoma when her name became a household word virtually overnight. It was during the Senate confirmation hearings in October 1991 for U.S. Supreme Court Justice Clarence Thomas that Hill became famous. She came forward with sexual harassment charges against Judge Thomas that shocked the nation, and many watched as she poured out painful details of Thomas's alleged sexual harassment, purportedly committed when both had worked for the Equal Employment Opportunities Commission. Hill claimed that Thomas repeatedly pressured her to date him, told her plots of pornographic movies, and bragged about his sexual exploits. When asked why she didn't quit her job or report Thomas when the incidents occurred during the early 1980s, Hill answered that she feared she wouldn't be able to get another job.

Following the hearings, Hill continued to be hounded by the press. Her experience with the hearings changed her life, as well as her career direction. She had been a professor of commercial law. She decided to take a year-long sabbatical in order to look at the possibility of founding an institute with the purpose of researching racism and sexism. Hill also made many speeches around the country about her experience.

Controversy didn't escape her on campus either. Several lawmakers made news when they asked that Hill be fired. Nonetheless, her dean and other members of the faculty supported her. In spite of opposition, the endowed Anita Faye Hill Professorship was established in 1995. The position was to support research regarding women's rights in the workplace. Although Hill considered resigning from the university in 1995, she remained in the post until 1997 when she joined the faculty of Brandeis University as a professor of social policy, law, and women's studies. Hill co-authored the book *Race, Gender, and Power in America* in 1995, and in 1998 wrote her autobiography, *Speaking Truth to Power.*

Jesse Jackson Sr. (1941–)
Activist, Minister

Jesse Louis Jackson Sr. was born October 8, 1941, in Greenville, South Carolina. In 1959 Jackson

left South Carolina to attend the University of Illinois. He became dissatisfied with his treatment on campus, however, and decided to transfer to North Carolina Agricultural and Technical College. After receiving his B.A. in sociology he went on to attend the Chicago Theological Seminary. He was ordained a Baptist minister in 1968.

 Jackson joined the Southern Christian Leadership Conference in 1965. It was also in 1965 that Jackson met the Rev. Dr. Martin Luther King Jr. during the Selma to Montgomery, Alabama, march against the violation of African Americans' civil rights. Jackson was with King and other organizers in Memphis, Tennessee, when King was assassinated on April 4, 1968. In 1966 Jackson became involved with the SCLC's Operation Breadbasket, the goal of which was to increase opportunities for blacks in the business community of Chicago, and from 1967 to 1971 he served as the program's executive director and expanded the goal to a national focus. Jackson resigned from the SCLC in 1971 to found his own organization, Operation PUSH (People United to Save Humanity). Through PUSH Jackson continued to pursue the economic objectives of Operation Breadbasket and expanded into areas of social and political development. Of all the civil rights leaders, Jackson seemed to have the best ability to relate to the young. He was possessed with a gift of being able to summon out the best in them, in a phrase that became his trademark, "I am somebody." Out of this came Jackson's program, PUSHEXCEL, which sought to motivate young school children to do better academically. With funding from President Jimmy Carter's administration, the PUSHEXCEL program was placed in five other cities.

The Jesse Jackson of the 1980s is best remembered for his two runs for the Democratic nomination for president of the United States. In 1983 many, but not all, black political leaders endorsed the idea of a black presidential candidate to create a "people's" platform, increase voter registration, and establish a power base from which there could be greater input into the political process. His 1984 campaign was launched under the aegis of the National Rainbow Coalition, Inc., an umbrella organization of minority groups. Black support was divided, however, between Jackson and former vice president Walter Mondale. During this campaign Jackson attracted considerable media coverage with controversial remarks and actions, demonstrating a lack of familiarity with national politics. Over the course of the campaign Jackson demonstrated enormous personal and political growth; his candidacy was no longer a symbolic gesture but was a real and compelling demonstration of his effectiveness as a candidate.

In 1989 Jackson moved with his Rainbow Coalition from Chicago to Washington, D.C.; he believed that the coalition could be more effective working in the nation's capital. He traveled throughout the world to meet with leaders of other nations and used his fame and influence to help Americans in trouble abroad. In 1991 he traveled to Iraq and convinced Saddam Hussein to begin releasing Americans held hostage after Hussein's invasion of Kuwait, and in 1999 he secured the release of three U.S. soldiers who were prisoners in the Kosovo crisis.

Although many expected him to run for president again in 1992, Jackson decided against it, saying that he was too tired, and the strain on his family too severe. While still continuing his activism, Jackson supported his son, Jessie Jackson Jr.'s political aspiration. In January 2001 personal turmoil ensued for Jackson as an extramarital affair with the former head of the Rainbow/PUSH coalition was revealed. The relationship also acknowledged that Jackson fathered a daughter. Still moving forward, Jackson and the Rainbow/PUSH Coalition celebrated thirty years of service to the community in August 2001.

In honor of Jackson's continued service, he received in 1993 the Martin Luther King Jr. Nonviolent Peace Prize, and on August 9, 2000, he received the Presidential Medal of Honor presented by President Bill Clinton.

Coretta Scott King (1927–2006)
Civil Rights Leader

As the wife of civil rights leader Martin Luther King Jr., Coretta Scott King was ready to continue his work and perpetuate his ideals after his 1968 assassination. While her primary role in the early years of marriage was to raise her four children, she became increasingly involved in the struggle for civil rights through her husband's activities. After his death, she quickly became a dynamic activist and peace crusader.

Born one of three children on April 27, 1927, King is a native of Heilberger, Alabama. During the Depression she was forced to contribute to the family income by hoeing and picking cotton, but she resolved early to overcome adversity, seek treatment as an equal, and struggle to achieve a sound education. After graduating from the private Lincoln High School in 1945, she entered Antioch College in Yellow Springs, Ohio, on a scholarship, majoring in education and music. A teaching career appealed to her, but she became disillusioned when she was not allowed to do her practice teaching in the public schools of the town. No black had ever taught there, and she was not destined to be the first to break the tradition.

Musical training in voice and piano absorbed much of her time with the result that, upon graduation, she decided to continue her studies at the New England Conservatory of Music in Boston, attending on a modest fellowship that covered tuition but made part-time work a necessity. Her meeting with Martin Luther King thrust her into a whirlwind romance, and also presented her with the opportunity to marry an exceptional young minister whose intense convictions and concern for humanity brought her a measure of rare self-realization early in life. Sensing his incredible charisma, she suffered no regrets at the prospect of relinquishing her own possible career.

Completing her studies in 1954, King moved back south with her husband, who became pastor of Drexel Avenue Baptist Church in Montgomery, Alabama. Within a year, Martin Luther King had led the Montgomery bus boycott and inaugurated a new era of civil rights agitation. Two years later, he was the head of the Southern Christian Leadership Conference (SCLC).

Over the years Coretta Scott King became gradually more involved in her husband's work. In 1962 she served as a Woman's Strike for Peace delegate to the seventeen-nation Disarmament Conference in Geneva, Switzerland. In the mid-1960s, she sang in the multi-arts Freedom Concerts that raised money for the SCLC. As demands on Martin became too much, she began to fill the speaking engagements he could not. After his assassination, she filled many of the commitments his death left empty, but she soon became sought-after in her own right.

Her speech on Solidarity Day, June 19, 1968, is often identified as a prime example of her emergence from the shadow of her husband's memory. In it, she called upon American women to "unite and form a solid block of women power" to fight the three great evils of racism, poverty, and war. Much of her subsequent activity revolved around building plans for the creation of the Martin Luther King Jr. Memorial in Atlanta, which she began to work on in 1969, and it was established under the care of the National Park Service in 1980. She also published a book of reminiscences, *My Life with Martin Luther King, Jr.*

Coretta Scott King joined with many others who lobbied for a holiday in celebration of her late husband's life. In November 1983 their efforts were rewarded and the holiday was signed into existence. King became chair of the Martin Luther King Jr. Federal Holiday Commission whose sole purpose was to formalize plans for the first King Holiday celebration.

King's sense of justice and her eloquence in negotiating matters extended to issues both at home and abroad. In 1986, after protesting against South Africa's regime in previous years, she met with anti-apartheid leaders. In 1993 she urged the United Nations to impose sanctions against Haiti because of human rights violations. Her work at the King Center for Social change saw her negotiating a disagreement with the National Park Services about the use of space in the area of the King memorial in historic Atlanta, to regaining control over her husband's legacy regarding documents previously given to Boston University.

King was a tireless advocate for African Americans, human rights, and the philosophy of nonviolence. She received numerous honorary degrees from colleges and universities all over the country, and in September 1995 King, along with Myrlie Evers-Williams and Betty Shabazz, were honored for her commitment to change by the National Political Congress of Black Women. King's tireless efforts were only dimmed by a stroke and a mild myocardial infarction in 2005. Her last public appearance before her death was at a Martin Luther King Jr. celebration in Atlanta, Georgia. The occasion, a Salute to Greatness, resulted in a standing ovation given to King by her children and the audience.

In 2006 King received treatment for advanced ovarian cancer at a holistic health clinic in Rosarito Beach, Mexico. On January 30, at the age of seventy-eight, Coretta Scott King died in her sleep. Although many remember her as the wife of Martin Luther King Jr., Coretta Scott King was in her own right a tireless advocate for nonviolence and for human rights.

Martin Luther King Jr. (1929–1968)
Civil Rights Leader, Minister

Any number of historic moments in the civil rights struggle have been used to identify Martin Luther King Jr.—prime mover of the Montgomery bus boycott (1956), keynote speaker at the March on Washington (1963), youngest Nobel Peace Prize laureate (1964). But in retrospect, single events are less important than the fact that King, with his policy of nonviolent protest, was the dominant force in the civil rights movement during its decade of greatest achievement, from 1957 to 1968.

King was born Michael Luther King in Atlanta on January 15, 1929—one of the three children of Martin Luther King Sr., pastor of Ebenezer Baptist Church, and Alberta (Williams) King, a former schoolteacher. (He did not receive the name of "Martin" until he was about six years of age.)

After attending grammar and high schools locally, King enrolled in Morehouse College (also in Atlanta) in 1944. At this time he was not inclined to enter the ministry, but while there he came under the influence of Dr. Benjamin Mays, a scholar whose manner and bearing convinced him that a religious career could have its intellectual satisfactions as well. After receiving his B.A. in 1948, King attended Crozer Theological Seminary in Chester, Pennsylvania, winning the Plafker Award as the outstanding student of the graduating class, and the J. Lewis Crozer Fellowship as well. King completed the course work for his doctorate in 1953 and was granted the degree two years later upon completion of his dissertation.

Married by then, King returned south, accepting the pastorate of the Dexter Avenue Baptist Church in Montgomery, Alabama. It was here that he made his first mark on the civil rights movement, by mobilizing the black community during a 382-day boycott of the city's bus lines. Working through the Montgomery Improvement Association, King overcame arrest and other violent harassment, including the bombing of his home. Ultimately, the U.S. Supreme Court declared the Alabama laws requiring bus segregation unconstitutional, with the result that blacks were allowed to ride Montgomery buses on equal footing with whites.

A national hero and a civil rights figure of growing importance, King summoned together a number of black leaders in 1957 and laid the groundwork for the organization now known as the Southern Christian Leadership Conference (SCLC). Elected its president, he soon sought to assist other communities in the organization of protest campaigns against discrimination and in voter registration activities as well.

After completing his first book and making a trip to India, King returned to the United States in 1960 to become co-pastor, with his father, of Ebenezer Baptist Church. Three years later, in 1963, King's nonviolent tactics were put to their most severe test in Birmingham, Alabama, during a mass protest for fair hiring practices, the establishment of a biracial committee, and the desegregation of department store facilities. Police brutality used against the marchers dramatized the plight of blacks to the nation at large with enormous impact. King was arrested, but his voice was not silenced as he issued his classic "Letter from a Birmingham Jail" to refute his critics.

Later that year King was a principal speaker at the historic March on Washington, where he delivered one of the most passionate addresses of his career, his "I Have a Dream" speech. At the beginning of the following year *Time* magazine designated him as its Man of the Year for 1963. A few months later he was named recipient of the 1964 Nobel Peace Prize.

Upon his return from Oslo, where he had gone to accept the award, King entered a new battle, this time in Selma, Alabama, where he led a voter registration campaign that culminated in the Selma-to-Montgomery Freedom March. King next brought his crusade to Chicago where he launched a slum-rehabilitation and open-housing program.

In the North, however, King soon discovered that young and angry blacks cared little for his pulpit oratory and even less for his solemn pleas for peaceful protest. Their disenchantment was clearly one of the factors influencing his decision to rally behind a new cause and stake out a fresh battleground: the war in Vietnam. Although his aim was to fuse a new coalition of dissent based on equal support for the peace crusade and the civil rights movement, King antagonized many civil rights leaders by declaring the United States to be "the greatest purveyor of violence in the world."

The rift was immediate. The NAACP saw King's shift of emphasis as "a serious tactical mistake"; the Urban League warned that the "limited resources" of the civil rights movement would be spread too thin; Bayard Rustin claimed black support of the peace movement would be negligible; Ralph Bunche felt King was undertaking an impossible mission in trying to bring the campaign for peace in step with the goals of the civil rights movement.

From the vantage point of history, King's timing could only be regarded as superb. In announcing his opposition to the war, and in characterizing it as a "tragic adventure" that was playing "havoc with the destiny of the entire world," King again forced the white middle class to concede that no movement could dramatically affect the course of government in the United States unless it involved deliberate and restrained aggressiveness, persistent dissent, and even militant confrontation. These were precisely the ingredients of the civil rights struggle in the South in the early 1960s.

As students, professors, intellectuals, clergymen, and reformers of every stripe rushed into the movement (in a sense forcing fiery black militants like Stokely Carmichael and Floyd McKissick to surrender their control over anti-war polemics), King turned his attention to the domestic issue that, in his view, was directly related to the Vietnam struggle: the war on poverty.

At one point, he called for a guaranteed family income, threatened national boycotts, and spoke of disrupting entire cities by nonviolent "camp-ins." With this in mind, he began to draw up plans for a massive march of the poor on Washington, D.C., itself, envisioning a popular demonstration of unsurpassed intensity and magnitude designed to force Congress and the political parties to recognize and deal with the unseen and ignored masses of desperate and downtrodden Americans.

King's decision to interrupt these plans to lend his support to the Memphis sanitation men's strike was based in part on his desire to discourage violence, as well as to focus national attention on the plight of the poor, unorganized workers of the city. The men were bargaining for little else beyond basic union representation and long overdue salary considerations. Though he was unable to eliminate the violence that had re-

sulted in the summoning and subsequent departure of the National Guard, King stayed on in Memphis and was in the process of planning for a march, which he vowed to carry out in defiance of a federal court injunction if necessary.

On the night of April 3, 1968, he told a church congregation: "Well I don't know what will happen now.... But it really doesn't matter...." (At other times, musing over the possibility that he might be killed, King had assured his colleagues that he had "the advantage over most people" because he had "conquered the fear of death.")

Death came for King on the balcony of the black-owned Lorraine Motel just off Beale Street on the evening of April 4. While King was standing outside with Jesse Jackson and Ralph Abernathy, a shot rang out. King fell over, struck in the neck by a rifle bullet that left him dying. At 7:05 P.M. he was pronounced dead at St. Joseph's Hospital.

King's death caused a wave of violence in major cities across the country. King's legacy, however, has lasted much longer than the memories of those post-assassination riots. In 1969 his widow, Coretta Scott King, organized the Martin Luther King Jr. Center for Nonviolent Social Change. Today it stands next to his beloved Ebenezer Baptist Church in Atlanta, and with the surrounding buildings it is a national historic landmark under the administration of the National Park Service. King's birthday, January 15, is a national holiday, celebrated each year with educational programs, artistic displays, and concerts throughout the United States. The Lorraine Motel where he was shot is now the National Civil Rights Museum.

Thurgood Marshall (1908–1993)
U.S. Supreme Court Justice

Thurgood Marshall's long and illustrious career was capped by his 1967 nomination to the highest court in the land—the U.S. Supreme Court —where he became the first African American to hold the coveted position of Supreme Court Justice. At fifty-nine, the son of a sleeping-car porter and the great-grandson of a slave became a sign of progress for many. He was viewed with the utmost respect for all of his years on the bench, retiring June 27, 1991. Marshall died at the age of eighty-four in 1993. He lay in state in the Great Hall of the Supreme Court of the United States on the same bier where Abraham Lincoln once rested. Over 20,000 mourners paid their last respects to Justice Marshall.

Born in Baltimore, Maryland, on July 2, 1908, Marshall earned a B.A. from Lincoln University, hoping to become a dentist. He changed his mind, however, and instead went to Howard University's law school, graduating in 1933 at the top of his class. He immediately went into private practice in Baltimore, where he remained for five years.

In 1936 he entered into what was going to be a long and illustrious career with the NAACP, starting as an assistant special counsel. In 1938, as a national special counsel, he handled all cases involving the constitutional rights of African Americans. Then, in 1950, he was named director-counsel of the organization's eleven-year-old Legal Defense and Education Fund, a position he held until 1961. In 1954, as part of an imposing team of lawyers, he played a key role in the now-historic Supreme Court decision on school de-segregation, *Brown v. Board of Education of Topeka*, which overruled the "separate but equal" doctrine in public education. He also figured prominently in such important cases as *Sweatt v. Painter* (requiring the admission of a qualified black student to the law school of Texas University), and *Smith v. Allwright* (establishing the right of Texas blacks to vote in Democratic primaries). Of the thirty-two cases that he argued before the Supreme Court, Marshall won twenty-nine.

Marshall was also known for his lifelong support of rights for women. Constance Baker Motley commented that Marshall hired her for an NAACP counsel position when virtually every other employer had turned her down. He also encouraged her when she argued cases before the

Supreme Court, and made certain he pointed out other African American women role models.

In 1961 Marshall became a federal circuit judge for the second circuit. In 1946 he was awarded the prestigious Spingarn Medal for his many achievements. He had over twenty honorary degrees to his credit. Marshall was the first recipient of the American Bar Association's Thurgood Marshall Award in 1992. The award recognizes those who fought for personal liberty and civil rights. Because of declining health, Marshall resigned from the court in 1991 and died on January 24, 1993.

Constance Baker Motley (1921–2005)
Attorney, Judge, Politician, Activist

Born September 14, 1921, in New Haven, Connecticut, Constance Baker Motley became the first African American woman to become a federal judge. The child of West Indian parents was appointed in 1966 by President Johnson to the U.S. District Court for Southern New York. The appointment marked the high point of her long career in politics and civic affairs.

While still a law student at Columbia University, Motley began working with the NAACP Legal Defense and Educational Fund, beginning an association that would make her famous as a defender of civil rights. In 1946 she was awarded her LL.B. and began to work full time with the NAACP, eventually becoming an associate counsel. During her twenty-year career with the organization, Motley argued nine successful NAACP cases before the U.S. Supreme Court, and participated in almost every important civil rights case that had passed through the courts since 1954—from Autherine Lucy in Alabama to James Meredith in Mississippi.

In 1964 Motley decided to make a run for the New York State Senate, and was successful. She became the first African American woman to hold that position. After only a year in the Senate, Motley ran for the position of Manhattan borough president, emerging the victor by the unanimous final vote of the city council. She thus became the first woman to serve as a city borough president and, therefore, also the first woman on the Board of Estimate.

Motley was appointed to the U.S. District Court in 1966. In 1982 she was named chief judge of the federal district court that covers Manhattan, the Bronx, and six counties north of New York City. She became senior judge of the federal district court in 1986. Motley was presented with more than twenty honorary degrees and was inducted into the National Women's Hall of Fame in 1993. She died on September 28, 2005.

Rosa Parks (1913–2005)
Activist

Rosa Parks has been called the spark that lit the fire, and the mother of the movement. Her courage to defy custom and law to uphold her personal rights and dignity inspired the African Americans in Montgomery, Alabama, to fight for their rights by staging one of the longest boycotts in history.

Born Rosa Louise McCauley on February 4, 1913, she was raised by her mother and grandparents in Tuskegee and Montgomery, Alabama. After attending segregated schools, she went to the all-black Alabama State College. In 1932 she married Raymond Parks, a barber. Both of them worked for the local NAACP chapter, and Rosa became local NAACP secretary in the 1950s.

On December 1, 1955, as she was riding home from work, she was ordered by the bus driver to give up her seat so that a white man might sit. She refused. She was arrested and fined $14. Her case was the last straw for the blacks of Montgomery, who were tired of being treated as underclass citizens, as Parks was. A city-wide boycott was organized to force the city to desegregate public transportation. A young, little-known minister by the name of Martin Luther King Jr. became involved and lectured the nation on the injustice of segregation. Blacks, and a few whites, organized peacefully together to transport boycotters to and from work, and they continued, despite opposition from the city and state governments, for 382 days.

When the boycott ended on December 21, 1956, both Parks and King were national heroes, and the Supreme Court had ruled that segregation on city buses was unconstitutional. The mass movement of nonviolent social change that was started lasted more than a decade, culminating in the Civil Rights Act of 1964 and the Voter's Rights Act of 1965.

Because of the harassment Rosa Parks and her family received during and after the boycott, they moved to Detroit, Michigan, in 1957. She began working with Congressman John Conyers and continued to be involved in the civil rights struggle. She marched on Washington in 1963, and into Montgomery in 1965. Even as her life had quieted down, she received tributes for her dedication and inspiration; in 1980 she received the Martin Luther King Jr. Nonviolent Peace Prize. As she headed toward retirement from John Conyers's office in 1988, she became involved in other activities, like the Rosa and Raymond Parks Institute of Self Development in Detroit, founded in 1987.

Once retired, in the years that followed, Parks' courage and commitment to justice was honored with numerous accolades. In 1990 her birthday was celebrated in the Kennedy Center in Washington D.C.; in April 1999 she was awarded the Presidential Medal of Freedom and the inaugural International Freedom Conductor Award; and Congressed authorized President Bill Clinton to bestow on Parks the Congressional Gold Medal, which is the country's highest civilian honor.

In the state of Alabama, Parks was awarded the Alabama Academy of Honor and the first Governor's Medal of Honor in 2000, and in 2001 Troy State University in Montgomery dedicated the Rosa Parks Library and Museum. The Museum featured a statue of Parks and an exhibit featuring her conversation with the bus driver in 1955 when she was told to give up her seat. In 2001 her home was placed on the Nation Registry of Historic Places, and in 2002 her life story was portrayed in the television movie *Mine Eyes Have Seen the Glory*. In the midst of positives in her life, Parks did have some challenges. In 2000 she went to court to challenge the use of her name in the title of a song by the group Outkast that she saw as offensive. The case was initially dismissed but in 2001 it was brought before an appeals court. The court ruled in her favor.

In 2004 Parks was diagnosed with dementia, which diminishes the cognitive skills. On October 25, 2005, at the age of ninety-two, Rosa Louise Mc-Cauley Parks died in Detroit, Michigan. Parks's body lay in state at the African Methodist Church and later was moved to the Capitol Rotunda in Washington, D.C., as decreed by a resolution and vote by the U.S. Congress. This honor is only given to those citizens who have given extraordinary service to the nation. Her body was later taken back to Detroit to the Charles H. Wright Museum of African American History where it lay in state until her funeral on November 2. On the fiftieth anniversary of Parks's arrest, President George W. Bush signed a resolution that called for a statue of Parks to be placed in the U.S. Capitol's National Statuary Hall. Rosa Parks, known as the Mother of the Modern Civil Rights Movement, dedicated her life to freedom, justice, and equality for all citizens.

Al Sharpton (1954–)
Minister, Activist

Sharpton was born in 1954 in Brooklyn, New York. He went to public schools, graduated from Tilden High School, and briefly attended Brooklyn College. At the age of thirteen he was ordained a Pentecostal minister. Sharpton was soon befriended by a number of well-known and influential African Americans, including Congressman Adam Clayton Powell Jr., Jesse Jackson, and singer James Brown. In 1969 Jackson appointed Sharpton youth director of Operation Breadbasket.

Around this time James Brown made Sharpton one of his bodyguards, and soon he was doing promotions for the singer. In 1983 Sharpton married singer Kathy Jordan and soon became involved with fight promoter Don King.

Even though Sharpton was promoting boxers and entertainers, he had long before put himself in the public spotlight in the role of social activist. In 1971 he founded the National Youth Movement (later called the United African Movement) ostensibly to combat drug use. The movement, however, soon became known as a vehicle for Sharpton to draw attention to himself.

Sharpton made himself part of the publicity surrounding the Bernard Goetz murder trial (1984), the Howard Beach racial killing (1986), the Twana Brawley debacle (1987), and the Yusef Hawkins-Bensonhurst killing (1989). In 1988 Sharpton was accused of being an FBI informant and passing on information about Don King, reputed organized-crime figures, and various African American leaders. These accusations stemmed from a 1983 FBI surveillance tape shown on television by HBO Real Sports with Brian Gumbel. Sharpton was shown discussing a cocaine deal. The accusations were never substantiated and no charges were ever filed. Sharpton sued HBO but no action has ever been taken. In 1989 and 1990 he was acquitted on charges of income tax evasion and embezzling National Youth Movement funds. In 1991 Sharpton was briefly hospitalized after being stabbed by a man wielding a pocket knife.

Sharpton published *Go Tell Pharaoh* (1996) and *Al on America* (2002). He continued to be active in community injustices that were claiming racism, police brutality, and racial profiling. In 1999 Sharpton led community efforts toward pursuing the arresting officer accused of the sodomy and arrest of Haitian immigrant Abner Louima. Sharpton became involved in the cases of West African immigrant Amadou Diallo in 1999 who was unarmed, yet shot to death by a New York policeman, and again in 2003 regarding another West African immigrant Ousmane Zongo who was killed under similar circumstances. Sharpton brought these cases to the attention of the media and demanded justice for the victims and their families.

Sharpton used his visibility in the political arena by running for the office of U.S. senator. He ran on the newly formed Freedom Party established on August 2, 1994. The Freedom Party, established by Sharpton, reached out to those African Americans who had been economically, socially, and politically disenfranchised by other mainstream political parties. Although Sharpton was unsuccessful in his Senate race, his political aspirations were not diminished.

On May 1, 2001, Sharpton was arrested after protesting the U.S. Navy's use of the island of Vieques, Puerto Rico, for a bombing site. He was given a ninety-day prison sentence and later went on a hunger strike. This event and his overall activism boosted his visibility to a national scale. On January 5, 2003, Sharpton announced his candidacy for president of the United States on the Democratic Party ticket. He took the opportunity to keep the issues regarding the underserved in the forefront of the campaign and remained in the race until March 2004. He was not successful in the bid for president, but he did make the concerns of the average American a key part of political agendas. Many tried to use Sharpton's past activities to detract from his speeches, but he overshadowed their efforts with well developed, powerful, and thoughtful issues of concern regarding all Americans and particularly African Americans.

Mary E. Church Terrell (1863–1954)
Civil Rights Activist, Women's Rights Leader

Terrell was born on September 23, 1863, in Memphis, Tennessee. Because of limited educational opportunities, her family sent her to live with friends in Ohio. She received her early education in Yellow Springs, Ohio, and earned her college degree from Oberlin College in Oberlin, Ohio, in 1884. She also spent two years abroad studying French, German, and Italian. After graduation and a short stay at home in Memphis, Terrell accepted a position at Wilberforce College. She later moved to Washington, D.C., for a teaching position at M Street High School. While in D.C. Terrell met and married Robert Heberton Terrell on October 18, 1891.

While in Washington, D.C., she also became very active in women's rights. She founded the Colored Woman's League in 1892, which merged with the National Federation of Afro-American Women in 1896. The organization was renamed the National Association of Colored Women and elected Terrell as their first president. In 1895 Terrell was appointed to the Washington, D.C., School Board, making her the first woman of color ever to receive such a position. She remained on the board until 1901, was reappointed in 1906, and served until 1911.

Terrell became a popular lecturer and speaker who denounced segregation. She wrote numerous articles that reached the national and international media using the pseudonym Euphemia Kirk, which she later dropped. Terrell and another Memphis native, Ida B. Wells-Barnett, were the only women who signed the "Call," a declaration of principles that called for an end to legal, economic, educational, and social discrimination, and became charter members of the National Association for the Advancement of Colored People. In 1914 she helped in the formation of Delta Sigma Theta Sorority at Howard University, and in 1920 she worked with other women in securing the ratification of the Nineteenth Amendment of the Constitution for women's suffrage.

Terrell campaigned for civil rights throughout her life and was highly respected by her community. She received recognition for her role as speaker at the Quinquennial International Peace Conference in Zurich, Germany, in 1937, and in 1940 she wrote her autobiography, *A Colored Woman in a White World*. On July 24, 1954, after a brief illness, Mary Church Terrell died at the Anne Arrundel General Hospital, Annapolis, Maryland.

Booker T. Washington (1856–1915)
Educator, Author, Civil Rights Leader

Booker T. Washington was born a slave in Hale's Ford, Virginia, reportedly in April 1856. After

Booker T. Washington

dented honor for a black man. His speech explained his major thesis that blacks could secure their constitutional rights through their own economic and moral advancement rather than through legal and political changes. Although his conciliatory stand angered some blacks who feared it would encourage the foes of equal rights, many whites approved of his views. Thus his major achievement was to win over diverse elements among southern whites, without whose support the programs he envisioned and brought into being would have been impossible.

BIOGRAPHIES: NATIONAL ORGANIZATION LEADERS

emancipation, his family was so poverty stricken that he worked in salt furnaces and coal mines from age nine. Always an intelligent and curious child, he yearned for an education and was frustrated when he could not receive good schooling locally. When he was sixteen, his parents allowed him to quit work to go to school. They had no money to help him, so he walked 200 miles to attend the Hampton Institute in Virginia and paid his tuition and board there by working as the janitor.

Dedicating himself to the idea that education would raise his people to equality in this country, Washington became a teacher. He taught first in his hometown and then at the Hampton Institute, and in 1881 he founded the Tuskegee Normal and Industrial Institute in Tuskegee, Alabama. As head of the Institute, Washington traveled the country unceasingly to raise funds from blacks and whites both; soon he became a well-known speaker.

In 1895 he was asked to speak at the opening of the Cotton States Exposition, an unprece-

Roslyn M. Brock (1965–)
Civil Rights Leader, Health Care Activist

Born in Pierce, Florida, on May 30, 1965, Roslyn Brock became the fourth woman and the youngest ever to become chairperson of the National Board of Directors for the National Association for the Advancement of Colored People (NAACP).

Brock earned her B.A. from Virginia Union University, magna cum laude, in 1987, and three master's degrees: in healthcare administration from George Washington University in 1989; business administration from Kellogg School of Management at Northwestern University in 1999; and a divinity degree from the Samuel DeWitt Proctor School of Theology at Virginia Union in 2009. Her 1989 thesis "Developing a NAACP Health Outreach Program for Minorities" was supervised by the executive director of the NAACP at the time, the Rev. Dr. Benjamin Hooks. Brock spent ten years in the health care management arena and in 2001 was an executive for Bon Secours Health Systems in Marriottsville, Maryland.

In 1989, while a freshman at Virginia Union University, Brock joined the NAACP and took on many leadership roles in the years that followed. In February 2001 Brock was unanimously elected as vice chair of the NAACP National Board of Directors. She was the youngest person and the first woman to have this position. When Julian Bond's tenure as chairman, from 1998 to 2009, ended Brock was selected as the new chairman on February 20, 2010.

Marian Wright Edelman (1939–)
Civil Rights Activist,
Children's Rights Activist

Born June 6, 1939, in Bennettsville, South Carolina, Marian Wright Edelman understood early on the need for education and the rights of children. She completed her undergraduate degree from Spelman College in 1960 and her law degree from Yale in 1963. That same year she joined the NAACP Legal Defense and Education Fund as staff attorney. A year later she organized the Jackson, Mississippi, branch of the NAACP Legal Defense and Educational Fund, serving as its director until 1968. That year, she founded the Washington Research Project of the Southern Center for Public Policy, which later developed into the Children's Defense Fund.

Wright has served as director of the Harvard University Center for Law and Education, chairperson of the Spelman College board of trustees, a member of the Yale University Corporation and the National Commission on Children, and on the boards of the Center on Budget and Policy Priorities, the U.S. Committee for UNICEF, and the Joint Center for Political and Economic Studies.

As Children's Defense Fund president, Edelman has become the nation's most effective lobbyist on behalf of children. Even while social spending was being cut, she managed to score some victories. In 1986 nine federal programs known as "the Children's Initiative" received a $500 million increase in their $36 billion budget for families and children's health care, nutrition, and early education.

The most visible focus of CDF is its teen pregnancy prevention program. Through Edelman's efforts, Medicaid coverage for expectant mothers and children was boosted in 1984. In 1985 Edelman began holding an annual Pregnancy Prevention Conference, bringing thousands of religious leaders, social and health workers, and community organizations to Washington to discuss ways of dealing with the problem.

In her 1987 book, *Families in Peril: An Agenda for Social Change,* Edelman wrote, "As adults, we are responsible for meeting the needs of children. It is our moral obligation. We brought about their births and their lives, and they cannot fend for themselves." Her other books include *Children Out of School in America, School Suspensions: Are They Helping Children?, Portrait of Inequality: Black and White Children in America,* and *The Measure of Our Success: A Letter to My Children.*

In 2000 Edelman received the Presidential Medal of Freedom from President Bill Clinton for her work on the Children's Defense Fund.

Myrlie Evers-Williams (1933–)
Civil Rights Leader

In 1995 Myrlie Evers-Williams became the first female chairperson of the NAACP Board of Directors. She brought to the organization years of personal and community commitment to the cause of civil rights.

Evers-Williams was born on March 17, 1933, in Vicksburg, Mississippi, as Myrlie Beasley. She was raised by her grandmother, Annie McCain Beasley, and an aunt, Myrlie Beasley Polk, who were both schoolteachers. Inspired by their example, Evers-Williams entered Alcorn A&M College in 1950. She left in her second year of college to marry Medgar Evers, an Army veteran, an upperclassman, and a member of the football team. Medgar Evers graduated in 1952 and, after realizing his commitment to civil rights, became a field secretary for the NAACP in Mississippi. This often placed him in dangerous situations. On June 12, 1963, Myrlie Evers found her husband shot on their driveway, and he later died. She was persistent over the years to bring to justice the person who murdered her husband. In 1967 Evers wrote a book about Medgar Evers, *For us, the Living*. In 1994 Byron de la Beckwith, who was then seventy-three years old, was convicted and sentenced to life in prison for the murder. He died in prison in 2001.

Evers moved to Claremont, California, a town east of Los Angeles, in 1967. She later graduated from Pomona College with a degree in sociology. After serving as assistant director of planning development for the Claremont College system and consumer affairs director for the Atlantic Richfield Company, Evers-Williams moved to Los Angeles, in 1988 and was appointed a member of the Los Angeles Board of Public Works by mayor Tom Bradley. In 1995 Myrlie Evers-Williams lost her second husband Walter Williams, whom she had been married to since 1975, to prostate cancer.

As a long time member of the NAACP, Evers-Williams was selected for a leadership role in the organization. She successfully served as chairperson of the Board of Directors of the NAACP from 1995 to 1998. In 1999 she published her memoirs: *Watch Me FLY: What I Learned on the Way to Becoming the Woman I Was Meant to Be*. Evers-Williams has received many awards, including the Spingarn Medal awarded in 1998. She continues to lecture and appear on television and radio programs across the country.

Prince Hall (c. 1735–1807)
Minister, Abolitionist, Religious Leader

Prince Hall is believed to have been born in Bridge Town, Barbados, and to have migrated to the United States in 1765; other records claim that during the late 1740s he had been a slave to

William Hall of Boston, Massachusetts, and freed by Hall on April 9, 1770.

In March 1775 Hall and fifteen other blacks were initiated into a lodge of British army Freemasons stationed in Boston. The group of black masons was issued a permit to meet at a lodge on March 17, 1775, and on July 3, 1775; they organized the African Lodge No. 1, with Hall as master of the lodge. The lodge received official recognition from England as a regular Lodge of Free and Accepted Masons in 1784 and was designated the African Lodge 459.

Hall, in addition to leading the organization of Black Freemasonry, was active as an abolitionist. In January 1777 he was the prime force behind a black petition sent to the Massachusetts state legislature requesting the abolition of slavery in the state. Another important petition drawn up under his leadership in 1788 called for an end to the kidnapping and sale of free blacks into slavery. He also actively lobbied for the organization of schools for black children in Boston. Prince Hall died on December 4, 1807, in Boston.

Dorothy Height (1912–2010)
Educator, Activist

Born in 1912 in Richmond, Virginia, Dorothy Height holds a master's degree from New York University and has studied at the New York School of Social Work. In the fall of 1952, she served as a visiting professor at the Delhi School of Social Work in New Delhi, India. Six years later, she was appointed to the Social Welfare Board of New York by Governor Averell Harriman, and was reappointed by Governor Nelson Rockefeller in 1961. Since 1957 she has been president of the National Council of Negro Women, an organization founded by Mary McLeod Bethune in 1935.

Before becoming the fourth president of the National Council of Negro Women, Height served on the organization's board of directors. She also served as associate director for leadership training services for the Young Women's Christian Association; as a member of the Defense Advisory Committee on Women in the Services; as president of Delta Sigma Theta sorority; as vice president of the National Council of Women; as president of Women in Community Services, Inc.; and founder of the Black Family Reunion, which seeks to combat negative images of African American families in the media.

Height served a long and illustrious career as a civil rights leader. She served as counsel to Eleanor Roosevelt, wife of President Franklin Roosevelt, and was advisor to U.S. presidents from Dwight D. Eisenhower to Barack Obama. She received over thirty-five honorary doctorates and was awarded the nation's highest civilian awards, the Presidential Medal of Freedom in 1994 and the Congressional Gold Medal in 2004. Height continued her mission of activism well into her nineties. She died on April 20, 2010, twenty-seven days after her ninety-eighth birthday.

Benjamin Hooks (1925–2010)
Minister, Attorney, Civil Rights Leader

Hooks, who was born on January 31, 1925, in Memphis, Tennessee, and attended Le Moyne College and Howard University. He received his J.D. from DePaul University College of Law in 1948. During World War II he served in the 92nd Infantry Division in Italy.

From 1949 to 1965, and again from 1968 to 1972, Hooks worked as a lawyer in Memphis. In 1966 Hooks became the first black judge to serve in the Shelby County (Tennessee) criminal court. As an ordained minister, he preached at Middle Baptist Church in Memphis and the Greater New Mount Moriah Baptist Church in Detroit. As a prominent local businessman, he was the co-founder and vice president of the Mutual Federal Savings and Loan Association in Memphis.

On January 10, 1977, Hooks was unanimously elected executive director of the NAACP by its board of directors, succeeding the retiring Roy Wilkins.

Under his progressive leadership, the association took an aggressive posture on U.S. policy toward African nations. Among his many battles on Capitol Hill, Hooks led the historic prayer vigil in Washington, D.C., in 1979 against the Mott anti-busing amendment, which was eventually defeated in Congress; led in the fight for passage of the District of Columbia Home Rule Bill; and was instrumental in gathering important Senate and House votes on the Humphrey–Hawkins Full Employment Bill.

At the NAACP's national convention in 1986, Hooks was awarded the association's highest honor, the Spingarn Medal. Hooks retired as executive director of the NAACP in March 1993 and returned to the pulpit as minister of Greater Middle Baptist Church in Memphis. He became senior vice president of the Chapman Brokerage Co., a minority business, and served as president of the National Civil Rights Museum, both in Memphis. Hooks was also named professor of social justice at Fisk University in Nashville, Tennessee. On April 15, 2010, Hooks died after a long illness.

Vernon Eulion Jordan Jr. (1935–)
Attorney, Civil Rights Leader

Vernon Eulion Jordan, Jr. was born in Atlanta in 1935. After graduating from DePauw University in 1957 and from Howard Law School in 1960, he returned to Georgia.

From 1962 to 1964 Jordan served as field secretary for the Georgia branch of the NAACP. Between 1964 and 1968 Jordan served as director of the Voter Education Project of the Southern Regional Council and led its successful drives to register nearly two million blacks in the South. In 1970 Jordan moved to New York to become executive director of the United Negro College Fund, helping to raise record sums for its member colleges, until he was tapped by the Urban League to become the successor to the late Whitney Young.

Taking over as National Urban League executive director in January 1972, Jordan moved the organization into new arenas, including voter registration in northern and western cities, while continuing to strengthen the League's traditional social service programs. An outspoken advocate of the cause of the black and the poor, Jordan has taken strong stands in favor of busing, an income maintenance system that ends poverty, scatter-site housing, and a federally financed and administered national health system. Maintaining that the "issues have changed" since the 1960s, Jordan has called for "equal access and employment up to and including top policy-making jobs."

The nation was stunned on May 29, 1980, when Jordan, who had just delivered an address to the Fort Wayne Urban League, was shot by a sniper as he returned to his motel; Jordan was confined to the hospital, first in Fort Wayne, Indiana, and later in New York City, for ninety days.

On September 9, 1981, Jordan announced his retirement after ten years as head of the National Urban League. During Jordan's tenure, the League increased its number of affiliates from 99 to 118, its staff from 2,100 to 4,200, and its overall budget from $40 million annually to $150 million.

As a member of President Bill Clinton's transition team in January 1993, Jordan was appointed in April to the Foreign Intelligence Advisory Board. Although successful in that position, Jordan became infamous for his role in securing a position for Monica Lewinsky. Lewinsky and President Clinton were involved in a sex scandal.

After stepping down from his government post in 2000 Jordan returned to practicing law full time. In December 2001 he published his memoir, *Vernon Can Read!: A Memoir.*

Joseph E. Lowery (1921–)
Minister, Civil Rights Leader

The Reverend Joseph Echols Lowery was born in Huntsville, Alabama. He holds a doctor of divinity degree, among others, and has attended numerous educational institutions, including Clark College,

the Chicago Ecumenical Institute, Garrett Theological Seminary, Payne College and Theological Seminary, and Morehouse University. Reverend Lowery's ministry began in 1952 at the Warren Street Church in Birmingham, where he served until 1961. From there he moved on to become pastor of St. Paul Church from 1964 to 1968.

 Lowery was one of the co-founders of the Southern Negro Leaders Conference (which later became the Southern Christian Leadership Conference); the Reverend Martin Luther King Jr. served as the organization's first president, with Lowery serving as vice-president.

In 1977 Lowery succeeded the Reverend Ralph David Abernathy as president of the SCLC. Under his leadership, the SCLC has broadened its activities to include the reinstitution of its Operation Breadbasket to encourage businesses that earn substantial profits in the black community to reinvest equitably and employ blacks in equitable numbers; involvement in the plight of Haitian refugees jailed by the American government; and a march from Selma to Washington, D.C., in connection with the renewal of the Voting Rights Act of 1982. Since 1986, Lowery has served as pastor of the Cascade United Methodist Church in Atlanta, Georgia.

In 1992 Lowery retired from the Southern Christian Leadership Conference and was succeeded by Martin Luther King III. In celebration of Lowery's eightieth birthday in October 2001, the city of Atlanta renamed Ashby Street the Joseph E. Lowery Boulevard. Also in celebration, Clark Atlanta University honored Lowery by establishing the Institute for Justice and Human Rights.

Marc H. Morial (1958–)
Civic Leader, Attorney, Politician

Morial was born on January 3, 1958, to Ernest N. "Dutch" Morial, a lawyer and the first African American mayor of New Orleans, and Sybil Haydel Morial, a schoolteacher. Morial graduated from Jesuit High School in 1976 and went on to get a B.A. in Economics in 1980 from the University of Pennsylvania and a law degree in 1983 from Georgetown University Law Center.

Morial operated a private practice from 1986 to 1988. He was successfully elected to the Louisiana State Senate and served from 1992 to 1994. Morial, following in his father's footsteps, ran for mayor of New Orleans and won the position in 1994. He served two terms with his tenure ending in 2002. On May 15, 2003, he was selected as president and CEO of the Urban League and continues in that position.

Huey Newton (1942–1989)
Political Activist

The youngest of seven children, Huey Percy Newton was born in Monroe, Louisiana, on February 17, 1942. He attended Oakland City College, where he founded the Afro-American Society, and later studied at San Francisco Law School. In 1966 Newton joined forces with Bobby Seale and established the Black Panther Party for Self-Defense.

Newton and his partner almost immediately became targets of sharp police resentment and uneasiness. The hostility came to a climax in 1967 when Newton allegedly killed an Oakland police officer. Newton was convicted of voluntary manslaughter and sent to the California Men's Colony. His conviction was later overturned by the California Court of Appeals.

By the 1970s the Black Panther Party became a potent political force in California. In 1977 the Panthers helped to elect the city's first black mayor, Lionel Wilson. Meanwhile, Newton continued to have problems with the law.

In 1980 Newton earned his Ph.D. in philosophy from the University of California. However, this achievement was followed by further problems. He was charged with embezzling state and federal funds from an educational and nutritional program he headed in 1985, and in 1987 he was convicted of illegal possession of guns. In 1989 he was fatally shot by a small-time drug dealer.

Asa Philip Randolph (1889–1979)
Civil Rights Leader

Asa Philip Randolph was born in Crescent City, Florida, on April 15, 1889. He attended Cookman Institute in Jacksonville, Florida, before moving to New York City.

In New York Randolph worked as a porter, railroad waiter, and elevator operator. While attending the College of the City of New York, he was exposed to the socialist movement, and in 1917 he organized *The Messenger*, a socialist newspaper. In 1925 Randolph founded the Brotherhood of Sleeping Car Porters to help black railway car attendants working for the Pullman Palace Car Company. In 1935, after a ten-year struggle, Randolph and the union negotiated a contract with Pullman.

Randolph served as a member of New York City's Commission on Race and as president of the National Negro Congress. In 1941 he organized a march on Washington, D.C., to bring attention to discrimination in employment. In 1942 Randolph was appointed to the New York Housing Authority and, in 1955 he was appointed to the AFL-CIO executive council.

In 1960 Randolph organized the Negro American Labor Council. He was also one of the organizers of the 1963 March on Washington. In 1964 he founded the A. Philip Randolph Institute in New York City to eradicate discrimination and to defend human and civil rights. After fifteen years of service through his institute, A. Philip Randolph died on May 16, 1979.

Randall Robinson (1941–)
Attorney, Activist

Randall Robinson, brother to the late news anchor Max Robinson, was born in Richmond, Virginia, and is a graduate of Virginia Union University and Harvard Law School. In 1977 Robinson founded TransAfrica to lobby Congress and the White House on foreign policy matters involving Africa and the Caribbean. Since its creation, the organization has grown from two thousand to over fifteen thousand members.

In 1984 and 1985, in protest of the policy of apartheid in South Africa, TransAfrica organized demonstrations in front of the South African embassy in Washington, D.C.; Robinson and other protesters, including singer Stevie Wonder, were arrested. In addition to its opposition to apartheid, the organization has been active in the cessation of aid to countries with human rights problems. In 1981 TransAfrica Forum, an educational and research arm of TransAfrica, was organized to collect and disseminate information on foreign policy affecting Africa and the Caribbean and to encourage public participation in policy debates.

In 1994, as a result of the denial of asylum hearings for Haitian refugees, Robinson began a liquid-fast diet on April 12. His goal of influencing the Clinton administration toward policy change for refugees was accomplished on May 8 when hearings were announced. Robinson again challenged governmental forces in 1995 by protesting Nigerian military leaders for brutality and the execution of a prominent Nigerian writer and eight other activists. His efforts were supported by TransAfrica and South African Bishop Desmond Tutu among others.

Robinson published his memoirs, *Defending the Spirit: A Black Life in America*, in 1997. In 1999 he wrote *The Debt: What America Owes to Blacks*. Robinson wanted to focus on the responsibility of the role of government to its African American citizens. He followed this work in 2002 with *The Reckoning: What Blacks Owe to Each Other*, which focuses on what the African American community must do to be effective citizens and to be taken seriously by the government.

Bayard Rustin (1912–1987)
Activist, Civil Rights Leader

Bayard Rustin was born in West Chester, Pennsylvania. While in school, he was an honor student and a star athlete, experiencing his first act of public discrimination when he was refused restaurant service in Pennsylvania while on tour with the football team. He attended Wilberforce University, Cheyney State Normal School (now Cheyney State College), and the City College of New York.

Rustin was active in various peace organizations, efforts to restrict nuclear armaments, and movements toward African independence. Between 1936 and 1941 Rustin worked as an organizer of the Young Communist League. In 1941 he joined the Fellowship of Reconciliation, a nonviolent antiwar group, and later served as its director of race relations. In 1942 Rustin, along with James Farmer, became active in the Chicago Committee of Racial Equality, out of which the Congress of Racial Equality (CORE) grew.

Rustin was one of the founding members of the Southern Christian Leadership Conference (SCLC). In 1963 he was named chief logistics expert and organizational coordinator of the march on Washington. From 1964 to 1979, Rustin served as executive director of the A. Philip Randolph Institute in New York City. In 1975 he founded the Organization for Black Americans to Support Israel.

Throughout the 1960s Rustin was hardpressed to maintain support for the nonviolent philosophy to which he had dedicated his life. Nonviolence, he argued, was not outdated; it was a necessary and inexorable plan called for by the blacks' condition in the United States. Guerrilla warfare and armed insurrection, Rustin explained, required friendly border sanctuaries, a steady source of arms and equipment, and the support of the majority of a country's inhabitants. Rustin continued to be active in the civil rights movement until his death in August 1987 at the age of seventy-seven.

Faye Wattleton (1943–)
Women's Rights Activist

Born on July 8, 1943, Faye Wattleton became part of a family that believed in helping others who were in need. Wattleton graduated from Ohio State University in 1964, spent two years as a maternity nursing instructor for the Miami Valley Hospital School of Nursing in Dayton, and earned an M.S. degree in maternal and infant health care from Columbia University on full scholarship in 1967. While interning at Harlem Hospital, Wattleton saw firsthand the dangers of abortions done by untrained persons.

In 1967 Wattleton became assistant director of Public Health Nursing services in Dayton, Ohio. After joining the board of the local Planned Parenthood board in Dayton, Wattleton became the director of a council that represented Planned Parenthood locations and their affiliates around the country. Due to this high-profile position, in 1978 Wattleton became the first African American woman and the youngest person to head Planned Parenthood.

Wattleton advocated for women's rights and full access to a range of health services. She was successful in uniting the organization's mostly white, middle-class members and the clients who were primarily poor. Her efforts brought the organization into a position of influence and brought attention to women's reproductive and health issues.

Walter White (1893–1955)
Civil Rights Leader

Walter Francis White was born July 1, 1893, into a middle class family in Atlanta, Georgia. He attended Atlanta University and in 1918 began to work for the NAACP. Because of his very light complexion and the texture of his hair, White was able to access places, particularly in the South, that other African Americans could not. In the 1920s White did undercover investigations about lynching, which became the basis for his book *The Fire in the Flint*. White's book brought both controversy and attention to him.

In 1931 White was selected as executive secretary of the NAACP. Under White's leadership the organization gained prominence and was seen as influential in the African American community. The NAACP's perspective and participation were sought by various entities, including U.S. presidents. The organization fought for full voting rights, admission to graduate and professional schools, and equal pay for African American teachers.

White died on March 21, 1955, of a heart attack. Over three thousand people attended his funeral.

Whitney Moore Young Jr. (1921–1971)
Civil Rights Leader

Whitney Moore Young Jr. was born in Lincoln Ridge, Kentucky. He received his B.A. from Kentucky State College in 1941, then went on to attend the Massachusetts Institute of Technology. In 1947 he earned an M.A. in social work from the University of Minnesota.

In 1947 Young was made director of industrial relations and vocational guidance for the St. Paul, Minnesota, Urban League. In 1950 he moved on to become executive secretary of the St. Paul chapter. Between 1954 and 1961 Young served as dean of the Atlanta University School of Social Work. He also served as a visiting scholar at Harvard University under a Rockefeller Foundation grant.

In 1961 the National Urban League's board of directors elected Young as president of the organization. Young instituted new programs like the National Skills Bank, the Broadcast Skills Bank, the Secretarial Training Project, and an on-the-job training program with the U.S. Department of Labor. Between 1961 and 1971 the organization grew from sixty-three to ninety-eight affiliates.

In addition to his work with the National Urban League, Young served as president of the National Association of Social Workers and the National Conference on Social Welfare, and on the boards and advisory committees of the Rockefeller Foundation, Urban Coalition, and Urban Institute, and on seven presidential commissions. In 1969 Young was selected by President Lyndon Johnson to receive the Medal of Freedom, the nation's highest civilian award. Young authored two books, *To Be Equal* (1964) and *Beyond Racism: Building an Open Society* (1969), and co-authored *A Second Look* (1958).

Young died in 1971 while attending a conference in Africa.

POLITICS

It was not until after the Civil War (1861–1865) that America made possible the full participation of African Americans as citizens with the passage of the Fifteenth Amendment in 1870, which provided the right to vote for all citizens (men only). African Americans stepped into the political arena and through the power of the vote helped to change the face of government. The period of political progress known as Reconstruction (1865–1877) reflects both the presidential and congressional policies of reconstructing the South while the larger view of Reconstruction extends into the 1890s as African Americans created institutions to support citizenship rights.

More than six hundred black men were elected to serve in state legislatures in the South during Reconstruction, and by the 1870s seven black men were serving in the 41st and 42nd Congresses of the United States. Congressional members included one senator, Hiram R. Revels (Mississippi), and six Representatives, Benjamin S. Turner (Alabama), Robert C. De Large (South Carolina), Josiah Walls (Florida), Jefferson R. Long (Georgia), Joseph H. Rainey (South Carolina), and Robert Brown Elliott (South Carolina). South Carolina's Reconstruction legislature had a black majority in the House of Representatives, but not in the Senate. In spite of

black representation, at no point did blacks rule. By the end of the 1870s various white groups, such as the Ku Klux Klan and other white militia groups, used intimidation, terrorism, and violence to take back their monopoly of power.

With the Supreme Court ruling of *Plessy v. Ferguson* in 1896, which condoned racial segregation, Black Americans were barred from political, social, and economic opportunities. This set the tone of disenfranchisement and racial degradation that inundated the South and much of the North well into the middle of the twentieth century.

Associations are among the largest and most influential forces in the United States and have played an important part in the economic, social, and educational development of African Americans. Organizations have been crucial in developing and disseminating information, ensuring representation for private interests, and promoting social and policy objectives.

The Free African Society, organized in Philadelphia in 1787, has been generally accepted as the first African American organization in the United States. Founded by Methodist ministers Richard Allen and Absalom Jones, the Free African Society served as an important source of political consciousness and welfare for blacks throughout the country, combining economic and medical aid for poor blacks with the support of abolition and sub-rosa communication with blacks in the South.

The abolitionist movement of the nineteenth century produced numerous organizations concerned with issues of importance to African Americans, including the American Colonization Society (founded in 1816), the New England Anti-Slavery Society (founded in 1832), and the American Anti-Slavery Society (founded in 1833). Although most of these organizations were dominated by whites, some black leaders, including Paul Cuffee and Frederick Douglass, played an active role in the movement and in anti-slavery organizations of the time.

During the late nineteenth and early twentieth centuries many black organizations came into existence; the thrust of most of these groups was toward education, betterment, and religious training. In 1895 the National Medical Association was founded to further the interests of black physicians, pharmacists, and nurses; Mary McLeod Bethune organized the National Association of Colored Women in 1896; and in 1900 the National Negro Business League was formed to promote commercial development. In 1909 the Niagara Movement was succeeded by a new organization—one that would later become the National Association for the Advancement of Colored People.

The Niagara Movement of 1905 marked a turning point in African American history. This new organization, founded by a group of black intellectuals and headed by W.E.B. DuBois, a professor at Atlanta University, met from July 11 to 13, 1905, in Buffalo, New York. The organization represented a formal renunciation of Booker T. Washington's program of manual and industrial training for the black as a means of gaining economic security, and conciliation as a means of gaining social equality.

Over the years, many organizations have been organized to better the condition of African Americans through litigation, legislation, and education. Perhaps the most significant victory was

in 1954 when the historic *Brown v. Board of Education of Topeka* case threw out the "separate but equal" doctrine established by the Supreme Court in *Plessy v. Ferguson* in 1896, and eliminated segregation in public education.

The most important gain to the political system by an African American, in politics, was realized in the twenty-first century with the successful campaign of Barack Hussein Obama as the 44th president of the United States of America and the first African American president. Obama, who was sworn in on January 20, 2009, won the election with 365 of the electoral votes and 52.9 percent of the popular votes. Voter turnout was 64.1 percent of the national population, which is the highest percentage since the turnout of 65.7 percent in 1908. Of the turnout, statistics show that 95 percent of African Americans, 66 percent of Latinos, and 61 percent of Asian Americans voted for Obama. Although

Barack Obama campaigning for the presidency. Many felt the then-senator from Illinois had little chance of winning because of his relatively short political resume.

many white Americans voted for Obama, it was the overall minority vote that secured the election for him. Obama embraced and utilized the advanced technology of the day, the Internet, and communicated with Americans of all ages and races regarding their desire for change from the policies that had frustrated an immense portion of America's citizens.

Obama, with his "Yes We Can" slogan during his presidential campaign, had already created change in the political arena for African Americans by his election in 2005 as the fifth African American senator in U.S. history and only the third since Reconstruction (1865–1877). When Obama resigned from his Illinois senate seat, once being elected president, Roland W. Burris was appointed by the governor of Illinois as his replacement. Surrounded by controversy, Burris took the junior senate seat in January 2009. Only one woman is among the five elected senators; Carol Moseley-Braun from Illinois, who served from 1993 to 1998. In the 110th Congress (2007–2009), in the House of Representatives, African American elected officials seated totaled forty-two, the largest number since Reconstruction. Black elected officials consisting of governors, mayors, and state and local officers have increased steadily over the decades. Between 1970 and 2002 the numbers increased six times with 34 percent of the increase being women.

Obama's political career began with his successful election in 1996 as state senator of Illinois. He made his first campaign for the U.S. Congress in 2000 when he challenged Democrat Bobby Rush for a seat in the House of Representatives. Obama was unsuccessful having received only 30 percent of the votes. Obama's entry into the national political scene came during 2004 when he again ran for a seat in the U.S. Congress, but this campaign was for the seat as U.S. Senator from Illinois. His campaign was for the open seat vacated by Peter Fitzgerald. With the withdrawal of the Republican primary winner from the campaign due to allegations of sexual misconduct, Obama initially ran unopposed. Three months before the election, the Republican Party backed Alan Keyes, an African American, as their candidate. Obama won the election with over 70 percent of the votes and became the junior senator from Illinois and one of the youngest U.S. Senators at forty-three. The historic nature of his campaign as the fifth African American to be elected to the U.S. Senate and the third since Reconstruction, combined with his gifts of putting others at ease and using his superb intellect to unite people, resulted in national recognition.

Obama was invited to deliver the keynote address at the Democratic National Convention in July 2004. His stirring speech titled "The Audacity of Hope," which focused on uniting the American political scene, caused many to see Obama as a viable candidate for the office of president of the United States. On February 10, 2007, prepared with a successful record of public service; the release of his autobiography *Dreams from My Father* (1995) and *The Audacity of Hope* (2006), which showed personal transparency and intellectual savvy; and the support of his family, Barack Hussein Obama announced his candidacy for president of the United States.

Because of obvious danger and the fears expressed by other African Americans and other colleagues, the Secret Service was lobbied to put Obama under their protection while campaigning for president. In May 2007, approximately eight months before the first primary, the Secret Service was assigned to Obama making this the earliest that any candidate has been extended such services in the election process.

Obama was accused of being distant because of his focus and disciplined nature. In trying to address this issue, he would watch tapes of his campaign and find ways to "loosen up a bit." Thanks to a single black woman in a crowd in Greenwood, South Carolina, his connection was found. "Fired up"! "Ready to go!" became his campaign call to reach his audience throughout the campaign. In January 2008 Obama won the Iowa caucus against Hillary Clinton, his Democratic rival. Obama had many important supporters such as Oprah Winfrey and Ted and Caroline Kennedy. Former pastor and Obama supporter, Reverend Jeremiah Wright, sparked controversy because of his sermons that often focused on historical inequities in America and the anger they generated. As a result of this, Obama gave a speech on March 18, 2008, acknowledging the anger that has been part of the relationship between blacks and whites. His speech, which was open and honest, lacked the divisiveness that often ensues with the discussion of race in America.

On June 3, 2008, Obama defeated Hilary Clinton and became the Democratic nominee for president. On November 3, 2008, Barack Hussein Obama won the presidential election with 365 electoral votes while Republican candidate John McCain received only 173 votes. Obama became the forty-fourth president of the United States of America and the first president of African descent.

Obama's inauguration on January 20, 2009, was the day after the national celebration of Rev. Dr. Martin Luther King Jr., a renowned and revered civil rights leader, and the year marked the 200-year anniversary of Abraham Lincoln's birth, the sixteenth president of the United States. For the swearing in ceremony Obama used the same Bible that Lincoln used in 1861 when he was sworn in. The inauguration was watched by the nation and as many as two million people traveled to Washington, D.C., a city of 600,000, to witness the swearing in. The National Mall was opened for the first time in U.S. history and massive viewing screens were set up for the crowd. Obama's inaugural address, which he began writing in November, reflected the optimism and hope of America as a diverse nation, and the recognition of challenges that only collective change can resolve.

Only twelve days after Obama was elected to office, he was selected for the Nobel Peace Prize. This honor was unexpected but received by Obama as a "call to action." The Nobel committee chair Thorbjorn Jagland stated that the unanimous selection of Obama was because of his efforts to "strengthen international diplomacy and cooperation between peoples." As a U.S. president, Obama became the fourth president to receive the Nobel Prize and the third president to receive it while in office.

Obama came into the White House with African Americans and the nation as a whole still recovering from Hurricane Katrina, one of the worst natural disasters, which hit New Orleans, Louisiana, and other coastal cities on August 28, 2005. Over 1,700 people were killed and the destruction directly impacted the 68 percent African American population of New Orleans. Recovery for New Orleans continues as an ongoing concern regarding the inequities perceived in the process of rescue and recovery for African Americans and governmental parity in aiding all of its citizens.

Many of the gains in representation, as seen in the mid-1990s, can be attributed to an increasing acceptance of African Americans as viable political candidates. Also, the process of redistricting has benefited minority political candidates. Redistricting occurs every ten years and involves the reapportionment of all 435 seats in the U.S. House of Representatives according to population shifts among the fifty states.

The 1992 national elections increased the number of African American representatives in Congress. Thirty-nine African Americans were seated in the 103rd Congress, compared with only twenty-five African American representatives in the 102nd Congress. The largest number of representatives so far was in the 110th Congress with forty-three African American members, forty-two in the House of Representatives and one in the Senate.

The 111th Congress, in session under President Barack Obama, seated forty-two African Americans or 7.8 percent of the total membership. Forty-one of those seated are in the House of Representatives and one in the Senate, the one senator from the state of Illinois who replaced Obama when he won the presidency. Of the forty-two seated, fourteen are African American women with voting rights and two with non-voting rights, all serving in the House of Representatives. Non-voting members are from the District of Columbia and the Virgin Islands. The Obama administration has key positions held by African Americans, including Eric Holder Jr., attorney general; Lisa P. Jackson, administrator of the Environmental Protection Agency; Ronald Kirk, trade representative; Susan E. Rice, ambassador and permanent representative to the United Nations; and Regina Benjamin as surgeon general.

BIOGRAPHIES

Regina Benjamin (1956–)
U.S. Surgeon General, Physician

Benjamin was born on October 26, 1956, in Mobile, Alabama. After graduating from Fairhope High School, she received her undergraduate degree from Xavier University of Louisiana in 1979 and went on to be among the second graduating class of the Morehouse School of Medicine. In 1984 Benjamin received her M.D. from the University of Alabama at Birmingham.

In 1990 Benjamin founded the Bayou La Batre Rural Health Clinic and has since rebuilt it after damage by hurricanes Georges in 1988 and Katrina in 2005. From 2002 to 2003 Benjamin served as associate dean for rural health at the University of South Alabama's College of Medicine and as president of the State of Alabama Medical Association. She was nominated by President Obama as surgeon general of the United States and as a medical director in the regular corps of the Public Health Service. She was confirmed on October 29, 2009. Benjamin's dissatisfaction with the current health care system is influenced by her experiences with the death of family members due to lack of access and cost.

Julian Bond (1940–)
Politician, Educator, Author, Civil Rights Leader

Throughout his successful career and personal and political adversity, Julian Bond has been labeled everything from a national hero to a national traitor. He has faced violent segregationists and his own political failures and scandals. In spite of everything, he has remained an influential voice in politics, education, and the media.

Bond was born on January 14, 1940. His father, an eminent scholar and president of Lincoln University in Pennsylvania, wanted Julian to follow him into the world of academia. In 1960 Bond attended Morehouse College in Atlanta. While at Morehouse, Bond developed an interest in civil rights activism. He and several other students formed the Atlanta Committee on Appeal for Human Rights (COAHR). Along with other members, Bond participated in several sit-ins at segregated lunch counters in downtown Atlanta. The activities of Bond and his cohorts attracted the attention of Martin Luther King Jr. and the Southern Christian Leadership Conference (SCLC). King invited Bond and other COAHR members to Shaw University in North Carolina to help devise new civil rights strategies. At this conference, the Student Nonviolent Coordinating Committee (SNCC) was created. The SNCC eventually absorbed COAHR, and Bond accepted a position as the SNCC director of communications. By 1966 Bond had grown tired of the SNCC and decided to embark on a new career in politics.

In 1966 Bond campaigned for a seat in the Georgia House of Representatives. He won the election and prepared to take his seat in the Georgia legislature. However, Bond was soon embroiled in a bitter controversy when he publicly announced that he opposed U.S. involvement in Vietnam and supported students who burned their draft cards to protest against the Vietnam War. These statements outraged many conservative members of the Georgia House of Representatives and, on January 10, 1966, they voted to prevent Bond's admission to the legislature. On December 5, 1966, the Court ruled that the Georgia vote was a violation of Bond's First Amendment right of free speech and ordered that he be admitted to the legislature. The members of the Georgia House of Representatives reluctantly allowed Bond to take his seat, but treated him as an outcast.

Bond's battle with the Georgia House of Representatives was not his last experience as the center of controversy. In 1968 Bond and several other members of the Georgia Democratic Party Forum protested Governor Lester Maddox's decision to send only six African American delegates out of 107 to the Democratic National Convention. Bond and his supporters arrived at the convention and set up a rival delegation. After several bitter arguments with Georgia's official delegation, Bond's delegation had captured nearly half of Georgia's delegate votes. Bond's actions made him a national hero to many African Americans. He became the Democratic Party's first black candidate for the U.S. vice presidency, a position he declined.

Throughout the 1970s Bond was no longer in the national spotlight. In 1974 he became president of the Atlanta branch of the NAACP and served until 1989. Also, Bond was elected to the Georgia Senate in 1975 and remained a member until 1987. In 1976 he refused a cabinet position in the Carter administration. Although Bond continued to express his political views as a writer and lecturer, his popularity plummeted dramatically.

The 1980s proved to be difficult for Bond on both a professional and personal level. Bond ran for a seat in the U.S. Congress in 1986 but lost the election. In 1989 he divorced his wife after twenty-eight years of marriage. Shortly thereafter he became embroiled in a paternity suit. He initially denied the allegations but admitted in May 1990 to fathering the child and was ordered to pay child support. Bond remarried in March 1990.

Although Bond retired from political life, he remained active regarding issues of the community. He was a popular lecturer and writer and was often called upon to comment on political and social issues. Bond hosted a popular television program, *America's Black Forum*, and narrated the highly acclaimed public television series *Eyes on the Prize*. He has written syndicated newspaper columns and narrated the documentaries *The American Experience: Duke Ellington Reminiscing in Tempo* (1992) and *A Time for Justice,* which won an Academy Award. He has written several books, including *Mose T's Slapout Family Album* (1996)

and *Lift Every Voice and Sing: A Celebration of the Negro National Anthem* (2000).

In 1998 Bond was elected as chairman of the Board of Directors for the NAACP. He maintained this office until 2009. Bond is a distinguished professor in residence at American University and is a professor of history and African-American studies at the University of Virginia.

Tom Bradley (1917–1998)
Politician, Former Mayor of Washington, D.C.

Bradley was born on December 29, 1917, in Calvert, Texas. In 1924 he moved with his family to Los Angeles. Bradley graduated from Polytechnic High School in 1937 and attended the University of California at Los Angeles on an athletic scholarship. He excelled at track before quitting college in 1940 and joining the Los Angeles Police Department.

As a member of the police force, Bradley worked as a detective, as a community relations officer, and in the department's juvenile division. In the early 1950s Bradley began studying law at two Los Angeles colleges, Loyola University and later Southwestern University, where he earned an LL.B. in 1956. Bradley stayed with the LAPD until 1961 when he entered private law practice.

In 1963 Bradley became the first African American elected to the Los Angeles City Council and was re-elected in 1967 and 1971. In a hotly contested 1973 election Bradley became mayor of Los Angeles, winning 56 percent of the vote. Bradley retired as mayor of Los Angeles in 1993.

Bradley served as president of the National League of Cities and the Southern California Association of Governments. He belonged to the Urban League of Los Angeles and was a founding member of the NAACP's Black Achievers Committee. On the national level he served on President Gerald Ford's National Committee on Productivity and Work Quality and on the National Energy Advisory Council. Bradley received many accolades which included the Thurgood

Marshall Award in 1974, the Award of Merit given by the National Council of Women in 1978, and the NAACP's Spingarn Medal awarded in 1985. Bradley died in 1998.

Carol Moseley Braun (1947–)
Attorney, U.S. Senator

Carol Moseley Braun was born in Chicago on August 16, 1947. She received her B.A. from the University of Illinois in 1969 and her J.D. from the University of Chicago Law School in 1972.

After graduating from law school, Braun was an assistant U.S. attorney for the northern district of Illinois from 1973 until 1977. In 1979 she was elected an Illinois state representative from the 25th district, where she became known as an ardent supporter of civil rights legislation. She was later elected Cook County recorder of deeds in 1986.

In 1992 Braun became the nation's first African American woman elected to the U.S. Senate. Her term in the Senate was overshadowed by allegations of missing campaign funds. After a five-year investigation by the Federal Election Commission, no wrongdoing was uncovered. Even though Braun had received numerous awards and garnered much positive attention throughout the nation, she was defeated in her bid for re-election in 1998.

Braun remained active in politics and was appointed by President Bill Clinton in 1999 as special consultant to the Department of Education. She was nominated and approved as ambassador to New Zealand in 2001. She briefly became a candidate for the Democratic presidential nomination in 2006, but withdrew her candidacy four days later and endorsed Howard Dean. Braun returned to the practice of law full time at a private firm in Chicago, Illinois.

Edward W. Brooke (1919–)
U.S. Senator

During his two terms in the U.S. Senate, Edward W. Brooke, the first black to be elected to that body since 1881, defied conventional political wisdom. In Massachusetts, a state that was overwhelmingly Democratic and in which blacks constituted only three percent of the population, he was one of its most popular political figures and a Republican.

Born October 26, 1919, into a middle-class Washington, D.C., environment, Brooke attended public schools locally and went on to graduate from Howard University. Inducted into an all-black infantry unit during World War II, Brooke rose to the rank of captain and was ultimately given a Bronze Star for his work in intelligence.

Brooke was later nominated for the attorney general's office, encountering stiff opposition within his own party. He eventually won both the Republican primary and the general election against his Democratic opponent. Upon entering the national political scene, Brooke espoused the notion that the Great Society could not become a reality until it was preceded by the "Responsible Society." He called this a society in which "it's more profitable to work than not to work. You don't help a man by constantly giving him more handouts."

When first elected, Brooke strongly supported U.S. participation in the Vietnam War, though most black leaders were opposing it. However, in 1971 Brooke supported the McGovern-Hatfield Amendment, which called for withdrawal of the United States from Vietnam.

Matters of race rather than foreign affairs were to become Brooke's area of expertise. Reluctant and subdued, Brooke proceeded carefully at first, waiting to be consulted by President Richard Nixon and loyally accepting the latter's apparent indifference to his views. As pressure mounted from the established civil rights groups and impatient black militants, however, he decided to attack the Nixon policies. Brooke was roused into a more active role by the administration's vacillating school desegregation guidelines; its firing of Health, Education, and Welfare official Leon Panetta; and the nominations to the

Supreme Court of judicial conservatives Clement Haynsworth and G. Harrold Carswell.

In 1972 Brooke was re-elected to the Senate overwhelmingly, even though Massachusetts was the only state not won by his party in the presidential election. While Brooke seconded the nomination of President Nixon at the 1972 Republican Convention, he became increasingly critical of the Nixon administration. He also began to appear publicly at meetings of the Congressional Black Caucus, a group he had avoided in the past. Brooke was considered a member of the moderate-to-liberal wing of the Republican Party.

In 1978 Brooke's bid for a third term in the Senate was defeated by Democrat Paul Tsongas. Brooke has received over thirty honorary degrees as well as the Spingarn Medal from the NAACP for his distinguished service. Even after returning to private practice as a lawyer, his meritorious service was again recognized with the Presidential Medal of Freedom in 2004.

Brooke, after being diagnosed with breast cancer in 2002, remains active and serves as a spokesman regarding this disease in men. He also is chairman emeritus of the fraternity Alpha Phi Alpha's World Policy Council. As the first ever chairman of the Council, the group continues to expand its involvement in global issues through Brooke's leadership.

Ron Brown (1941–1996)

Former U.S. Secretary of Commerce

Born in Washington, D.C., on August 1, 1941, Ronald Harmon Brown was raised in Harlem and attended White Plains High School and Rhodes and Walden Preparatory Schools in New York. He graduated from Middlebury College in Middlebury, Vermont, with a B.A. in political science in 1962. Upon graduating he enlisted in the army and achieved the rank of captain while serving in West Germany and Korea. Brown then graduated from New York City's St. John's University Law School in 1970.

While attending law school Brown began working for the National Urban League's job training center in the Bronx, New York, in 1968. He continued with them until 1979, working as general counsel, Washington spokesperson, deputy executive director, and vice president of Washington operations. In 1980 he resigned to become chief counsel of the U.S. Senate judiciary committee and in 1981 general counsel and staff coordinator for Senator Edward Kennedy. In that year he also became a partner in the Washington law firm of Patton, Boggs & Blow. In 1989 Brown became the first African American to head a major American political party when he was appointed chairman of the Democratic National Committee. In 1993 President Bill Clinton appointed Brown commerce secretary, making him the first African American to hold this post.

Although Brown's tenure was marked by controversy, he opened doors for minorities and women to be more involved in opportunities throughout the Commerce Department. During one of Brown's trips to promote trade and encourage investments to rebuild war-torn Croatia, his plane crashed near the Croatian coast. The crash, which occurred on April 3, 1996, killed Brown and all aboard the flight.

Blanche Kelso Bruce (1841–1898)

Slave, U.S. Senator

Blanche Kelso Bruce was born a slave in Farmville, Prince Edward County, Virginia, on March 1, 1841. He received his early formal education in Missouri, where his parents had moved while he was still quite young, and later studied at Oberlin College in Ohio. In 1868 Bruce settled in Floreyville, Mississippi. He worked as a planter and eventually built up a considerable fortune in property.

In 1870 Bruce entered politics and was elected sergeant-at-arms of the Mississippi Senate. A year later he was named assessor of taxes in Bolivar County. In 1872 he served as sheriff of that county and as a member of the Board of Levee Commissioners of Mississippi.

Bruce was nominated to the U.S. Senate from Mississippi in February 1874. Upon his election he became the first black person to serve a full term in the U.S. Senate. Bruce became an outspoken defender of the rights of minority groups, including the Chinese and Indians. He also investigated alleged bank and election frauds and worked for the improvement of navigation on the Mississippi River in the hope of increasing interstate and foreign commerce. Bruce also supported legislation aimed at eliminating reprisals against those who had opposed Negro emancipation.

After Bruce completed his term in the Senate, he was named register of the U.S. Treasury Department by President James A. Garfield. Bruce held this position until 1885. In 1889 President Benjamin Harrison appointed him recorder of deeds for the District of Columbia. Bruce served as recorder of deeds until 1893, when he became a trustee for the District of Columbia public schools. In 1897 President William McKinley reappointed him to his former post as register of the Treasury. Bruce died on March 17, 1898.

Ralph Bunche (1904–1971)
Educator, Diplomat

The first African American to win the Nobel Peace Prize, Ralph Bunche was an internationally acclaimed statesman whose record of achievement places him among the most significant American diplomats of the twentieth century. Bunche received the coveted award in 1950 for his role in effecting a ceasefire in the Arab-Israeli dispute that threatened to engulf the entire Middle East in armed conflict.

Born in Detroit, Michigan, on August 7, 1904, Bunche graduated from UCLA in 1927, summa cum laude, and with Phi Beta Kappa hon-

ors. A year later he received his M.A. in government from Harvard. Soon thereafter he was named head of the Department of Political Science at Howard University, remaining there until 1932, when he was able to resume work toward his doctorate from Harvard. He later studied at Northwestern University, the London School of Economics, and Capetown University.

The single event that brought the name of Ralph Bunche into the international spotlight occurred soon after his appointment in 1948 as chief assistant to Count Folke Bernadotte, the United Nations' mediator in the Palestine crisis. With the latter's assassination, Bunche was faced with the great challenge of somehow continuing ceasefire talks between Egypt and Israel. After six weeks of intensive negotiations, Bunche worked out the now famous "Four Armistice Agreements," which brokered an immediate cessation of the hostilities between the two combatants. Once the actual ceasefire was signed, Bunche received numerous congratulatory letters and telegrams from many heads of state and was given a hero's welcome upon his return to the United States.

Bunche served as undersecretary of Special Political Affairs from 1957 to 1967. By 1968 Bunche had attained the rank of undersecretary general, the highest position ever held by an American at the United Nations.

Bunche retired in October 1971 and died on December 9, 1971.

Yvonne Brathwaite Burke (1932–)
U.S. Congresswoman

Attorney and former California State Assemblywoman Yvonne Brathwaite Burke became the first black woman from California to be elected to the House of Representatives in November 1972.

Congresswoman Burke served in the state assembly for six years prior to her election to Congress. During her final two years there, she was chair of the Committee on Urban Development and Housing and a member of the Health, Finance, and Insurance committees.

During Burke's first term in Congress, she proved to be an ardent spokesperson for the downtrodden. She became a member of the Committee on Appropriations in December 1974 and used her position on this committee to advocate an increase in funding for senior citizen services and community nutrition and food programs. Although her proposal for increased spending was defeated by the House of Representatives, Burke's efforts earned the respect of the African American community. In January 1977 Burke worked diligently for the passage of the Displaced Homemakers Act, which proposed the creation of counseling programs and job training centers for women entering the workforce for the first time.

In 1978 Burke resigned to run for attorney general in California. She lost that race but, in 1979 she was appointed to the Los Angeles County Board of Supervisors. She resigned from the board in December 1980 and returned to her private law practice. Although she no longer holds public office, Burke remains a prominent figure in California politics. She has also taken on a number of civic responsibilities, including serving as a member of the University of California Board of Regents. Burke also serves on the Los Angeles County Board and functioned as the board chairperson in 1992.

Shirley Chisholm (1924–2005)
Educator, U.S. Congresswoman

Chisholm was born on November 30, 1924, in New York City. She graduated cum laude from Brooklyn College in 1946 with a B.A. in sociology and with an M.A. in elementary education from Columbia University in 1952. She had an early career in child care and preschool education culminating in her directorship of the Hamilton-Madison Child Care Center in New York. Leaving

that position in 1959, she served until 1964 as a consultant to the Day Care Division of New York City's Bureau of Child Welfare.

In 1964 she was elected New York State Assemblywoman representing the 55th district in New York City. In 1968 she became the first African American woman elected to the U.S. House of Representatives. Chisholm represented the twelfth district after defeating James Farmer. She served on several House committees but the most powerful was the Education and Labor Committee. In 1969 Chisholm was among the founding members of the Congressional Black Caucus. In 1972 Chisholm ran for the Democratic presidential nomination garnering 152 first ballots. Throughout her political career Chisholm was a staunch Democrat in her elected positions, as a delegate to the Democratic National Mid-Term Conference in 1974, and as a Democratic National Committeewoman.

Chisholm retired from politics in 1982. In 1984 she co-founded the National Political Congress of Black Women and was named as the Purington chair at Mount Holyoke College teaching political science. A year later she became a visiting scholar at Spelman College. Chisholm wrote two books, *Unbossed & Unbought* (1970) and *The Good Fight* (1973). In 1993 Chisholm was inducted into the National Women's Hall of Fame and was nominated by President Bill Clinton as the ambassador to Jamaica, but she declined due to poor health. She received numerous awards for her national service and community activism. Chisholm died on January 1, 2005, in Florida.

Cardiss Collins (1931–)
U.S. Congresswoman

Collins was born Cardiss Robertson on September 24, 1931, in St. Louis, Missouri, and by the time she was ten years old her family had moved to Detroit. After graduating from Detroit's Commerce High School, Collins moved to Chicago, where she worked as a secretary for the state's Department of Revenue. She began studying accounting at Northwestern University and was promoted first to accountant, then auditor.

In 1973 Collins was elected U.S. Representative from Illinois's seventh district. She was elected to fill the seat vacated by her husband, George Collins, who was killed in an airplane crash. She soon became the first African American and the first woman to hold the position of Democratic whip-at-large. Collins served on congressional subcommittees dealing with consumer protection, national security, hazardous materials, and narcotic abuse and control. Between 1989 and 1991 Collins, as chair of the Government and Activities and Transportation Subcommittee, worked toward laws that limited the exposure of minority communities from the transport and placement of hazardous materials. She sought to correct discrimination toward minority agencies and, through Title IX, helped to create legislation that required institutions of higher education to report on gender-based activities and participation. She also was a proponent of universal health care.

After serving one year as chair of the Congressional Black Caucus and winning her bid for re-election in 1995, Collins decided to retire after twenty-four years in Congress. Her service made her the longest serving African American female in congressional history. Collins has received many awards and belongs to numerous organizations, including the NAACP, National Women's Political Caucus, the National Council of Negro Women, and the Chicago Urban League. Collins remains a strong advocate for civil rights.

John Conyers (1929–)

U.S. Congressman

Conyers was born in Detroit on May 16, 1929, and graduated from Northwestern High School in 1947. In 1950 he enlisted in the U.S. Army as a private and served in Korea before being honorably discharged as a second lieutenant in 1957. He then attended Wayne State University in De-

troit, and after studying in a dual program he received a B.A. in 1957 and a law degree in 1958.

Conyers served as a legislative assistant to Congressman John Dingell Jr. from 1958 to 1961 and was a senior partner in the law firm of Conyers, Bell & Townsend from 1959 to 1961. In that year he took a referee position with the Michigan Workman's Compensation Department and stayed until 1963. In 1964 he won election as a democrat to the U.S. House of Representatives for the 14th District. Conyers has long been active in the Democratic Party, belonging to the Young Democrats and the University Democrats and serving as a precinct delegate to the Democratic Party.

After his election Conyers was assigned to the powerful House Judiciary Committee. From that position he worked for legislation dealing with civil rights, Medicare, immigration reform, and truth-in-packaging laws. He was an early opponent of U.S. involvement in Vietnam and an early proponent of the Voting Rights Act of 1965. Conyers is one of the founding members of the Congressional Black Caucus and introduced the bill to make Martin Luther King Jr.'s birthday a national holiday. In 1994, as the senior African American member of Congress, Conyers led a movement seeking reparations from the government on behalf of those whose ancestors were slaves. In the wake of the 2004 presidential election and the disenfranchisement of minority voters, Conyers issued the report *What Went Wrong in Ohio: The Conyers Report on the 2004 Presidential Election* and in 2007, when Democrats had majority control over Congress, Conyers became chair of the powerful House Judiciary Committee.

Conyers has been vice-chairman of the National Board of Americans for Democratic Action and the American Civil Liberties Union. He is on the executive board of the Detroit Chapter of the NAACP and belongs to the Wolverine Bar Association. Conyers has the longest tenure of any African American who has served in the U.S. Congress.

Ronald V. Dellums (1935–)

U.S. Congressman

Dellums was born in Oakland, California on November 24, 1935. After attending McClymonds and Oakland Technical High Schools, Dellums joined the U.S. Marine Corps in 1954 and was discharged after two years of service. He returned to school, receiving an associate of arts degree from Oakland City College (1958), a bachelor's degree from San Francisco State College (1960), and a master's degree in social work from the University of California at Berkeley (1962).

After graduation Dellums was involved in numerous social work positions from 1962 to 1970. He was a psychiatric social worker with the Berkeley Department of Mental Hygiene, program director of the Bayview Community Center, director of the Hunters Point Youth Opportunity Center, consultant to the Bay Area Social Planning Council, and program director for the San Francisco Economic Opportunity Council. From 1968 to 1970 Dellums lectured at San Francisco State College and the University of California's School of Social Work. He also served as a consultant to Social Dynamics, Inc.

Dellums was elected to the Berkeley City Council in 1967 and served until his election as a Democrat to the U.S. House of Representatives in 1971. As a representative he chaired the House Committee on the District of Columbia and served on the House Armed Services Subcommittee on Military Facilities and Installations as well as the Subcommittee on Military Research and Development. He has been the chairman of the Defense Policy Panel and in 1983 authored *Defense Sense: The Search for a Rational Military Policy*.

As chair of the Armed Service Committee in 1993, Dellums advocated the removal of a block against gays in the military. Dellums was disappointed with President Bill Clinton's lack of action and follow-through on this prior promise of removing the block. In 1998, after twenty-seven years of service, Dellums retired and became president of Healthcare International Management Company. Dellums also became an advocate for AIDS programs and served on President Clinton's Advisory Council on AIDS and HIV.

David Dinkins (1927–)

Mayor

In September 1989 David Dinkins surprised political observers by defeating incumbent mayor Edward I. Koch in New York's Democratic mayoral primary. In the November election of that year he defeated Rudolph Giuliani, a popular district attorney. Dinkins's victory marked the first time an African American was elected as mayor of New York City.

David Dinkins was born in Trenton, New Jersey, in 1927. His parents separated when he was quite young and he moved to Harlem with his mother and sister. He returned to Trenton to attend high school and later graduated from Howard University in Washington, D.C., in 1950. In 1953 Dinkins enrolled at Brooklyn Law School and graduated in 1956. He became an attorney and, eventually, a partner in the law firm of Dyett, Alexander, Dinkins, Patterson, Michael, Dinkins & Jones.

Dinkins's first foray into the world of politics occurred in 1965 when he won an election to the New York State Assembly. He served until 1967 but did not seek re-election after his district was redrawn. In 1972 Dinkins was appointed president of elections for the City of New York and served for one year. In 1975 he was appointed city clerk and served until 1985. Dinkins ran for the office of Manhattan borough president in 1977 and 1981. He lost both elections by a wide margin. Dinkins ran again in 1985 and was elected. As Manhattan borough president, Dinkins was viewed as a mediator who tried to address a myriad of community concerns, such as school decentralization, AIDS treatment and prevention services, and pedestrian safety.

In November 1993 Dinkins lost the mayoral election to the opponent he had triumphed over in the 1989 campaign, Republican Rudolph Giuliani. In 1994 Dinkins began teaching at Columbia University. After recovering from a triple bypass in 1995 he went on to serve as a senior fellow in the area of public affairs at the Barnard-Columbia Center for Urban Policy.

Mike Espy (1953–)
U.S. Congressman, Secretary of Agriculture

Espy was born on November 30, 1953. He received a B.A. from Howard University in 1975 and a J.D. from the Santa Clara School of Law in 1978.

After graduation Espy practiced law in Yazoo City, Mississippi, and managed Central Mississippi Legal Services. From 1980 until 1984 he was director of Public Lands and Elections, which is a division of the Mississippi State Secretary's Office. In 1984 Espy left the directorship to become chief of the Consumer Protection Division of the State Attorney General's Office. Espy was then elected to the U.S. House of Representatives, and in 1993 President Bill Clinton appointed Espy secretary of agriculture, the first African American to hold this post.

During Espy's tenure he became the subject of controversy. Espy was investigated by the federal ethics committee which divulged that he had taken gifts from companies that his office regulated. Although admitting no wrongdoings, Espy resigned his post on December 31, 1994. Fueled by further allegations of corruption during his time in the cabinet, Espy was the subject of a four-year investigation. With over thirty counts of corruption levied against Espy, the investigation and the jury trial resulted in his exoneration. On December 1998 he was determined to be not guilty on all counts.

Espy currently practices laws in Mississippi and is affiliated with the American Bar Association and the National Conference of Black Leaders.

Chaka Fattah (1956–)
U.S. Congressman

Born on November 21, 1956, Arthur Davenport, later renamed by his mother as Chaka Fattah, grew up in a socially active family. His father was a sergeant in the U.S. Army and his mother was the editor of the *Philadelphia Tribune,* the oldest black newspaper in America. Although Fattah dropped out of high school in 1974 he later received his GED and went on to received an M.A. in governmental administration from the University of Pennsylvania.

In 1982 Fattah ran a successful campaign and was elected to the House of Representatives for the state of Pennsylvania. At twenty-five years old, he became the youngest man elected to the state General Assembly of Pennsylvania. In 1988 he was elected to the state Senate.

Fattah's first bid for a seat in the U.S. House of Representatives was in 1991 when William H. Gray III retired. Although he was initially unsuccessful, he campaigned again in 1994 and won with 58 percent of the votes. Fattah's focus in Congress has centered on equal access to higher education, housing reform, and urban renewal.

Walter E. Fauntroy (1933–)
Pastor, Activist, U.S. Congressman

Delegate Walter Edward Fauntroy, pastor of New Bethel Baptist Church in Washington, D.C., represents the District of Columbia. A Yale Divinity School alumnus, he was chairman of the Caucus task force for the 1972 Democratic National Committee and chairman of the platform committee of the National Black Political Convention. Fauntroy was Washington, D.C., coordinator for the March on Washington for Jobs and Freedom in 1963, coordinator for the Selma-to-

Montgomery march in 1965, and national coordinator for the Poor People's Campaign in 1969. He was also a chairman of the board of directors of the Southern Christian Leadership Conference. Fauntroy was the chief architect of legislation in 1973 that permitted the District of Columbia to elect its own mayor and city council and engineered the passage by both the House and Senate of a constitutional amendment calling for full congressional representation for District of Columbia residents in the U.S. Congress. He has strong support from the city's majority black population, especially the large population of black civil servants.

Once elected to the House of Representatives in 1971, Fauntroy continued to build a record of achievement by playing key roles in the mobilization of black political power from the National Black Political Convention in 1972 to the presidential elections of 1972 and 1976. He is a member of the House Select Committee on Narcotics Abuse and Control and cosponsored the 1988 $2.7 billion anti-drug bill. On Thanksgiving Eve in 1984 Fauntroy and two prominent national leaders launched the Free South Africa Movement (FSAM) with their arrest at the South African embassy. He serves as cochair of the steering committee of the FSAM.

In 1990 Fauntroy retired from Congress and ran for mayor of Washington, D.C. He lost the race but continued in his political pursuits. He began Walter E. Fauntroy & Associates, as a lobbying service for organizations.

Fauntroy was diagnosed in 1993 with tuberculosis and was treated and subsequently cured. He became a spokesman regarding the illness so that others would understand there is hope and a cure. His contributions as a politician and his ongoing fight for human rights have earned him honorary degrees from his alma maters, Virginia Union University, Yale Divinity School, Howard University, and Georgetown University Law Center. Fauntroy also is honorary chairman of the Sudan campaign, which he co-founded in 2001, that seeks to provide aid to poverty stricken countries in Africa.

Harold E. Ford Jr. (1970–)
U.S. Congressman

Harold E. Ford Jr. comes from a family immersed in politics and public service, and the owners of a mortuary service. As a longstanding prominent African American family in Memphis, Tennessee, the Ford family is led by Harold Eugene Ford Sr. and Dorothy Bowles Ford. Ford Jr.'s father, who served for eleven terms as a congressman, inspired Ford Jr. to enter politics.

Harold Ford Jr. was born on May 11, 1970, in Memphis and moved with his family in 1974 to Washington, D.C. when his father was elected to the U.S. House of Representatives. Ford Jr. spent his younger years in Washington, D.C., and after attending the elite school St. Albans School for Boys he went on to earn his B.A. in history from the University of Pennsylvania in 1992. In 1996, when his father decided not to run for a twelfth term, Ford Jr. ran to succeed his father. He was successful in his campaign and was reelected four times. Harold Ford Jr.'s national recognition came when he was the keynote speaker for the 2000 Democratic Convention, which selected Vice President Al Gore as the Democratic Party's presidential nominee.

In 2005 Ford Jr. announced his candidacy for the U.S. senator from Tennessee when the senior senator, Bill Frist, decided not to run for another term. Ford Jr. had a strong and well-organized staff and was successful in raising funds. The name recognition as a Ford also gave him access to many votes. The election was very close at times, but Harold Ford Jr. lost by three percent of the vote. Upon leaving Congress in 2007 Ford Jr. became a visiting professor of public policy at Vanderbilt University and at the University of Texas-Austin for the Lyndon B. Johnson School of Public Affairs. Later that year he was named vice chairman at Merrill Lynch & Company and became a commentator and analyst in the 2008 elections. In 2010 Ford became a visiting professor at New York University's Wagner School of Public Service.

Shirley C. Franklin (1945–)
Mayor, Business Executive

In 2002 Shirley C. Franklin became the mayor of Atlanta, Georgia. She thus became the first African American woman and first woman to be the mayor of a major city in the South.

Franklin, born in Philadelphia in 1945, did her undergraduate studies at Howard University earning a degree in sociology in 1968 and later earning an M.A. in 1969 from the University of Pennsylvania. In 1978 Franklin began her career in Atlanta as the director and commissioner of cultural affairs during the administration of Maynard Jackson. She later became executive officer for operations during Jackson's third term. During her time in the administration of Mayor Andrew Young, Franklin was responsible for some of the major projects for the city, such as the construction of a new city hall, the municipal court building, and the expansion of the Hartsfield International Airport.

From 1991 to 1996 Franklin left city government and worked as the senior vice president for external relations of the Atlanta Committee for the Olympic Games. In 2000 Franklin ran for the mayor of Atlanta and won in a very close race. She defeated two opponents and succeeded Bill Campbell whose administration was under federal investigation.

Franklin's campaign promised to make Atlanta city government more effective and transparent. Under her administration the city developed five balanced budgets and presented a government that has emphasized integrity. Her administration also led the initiative that secured the Martin Luther King Jr. papers, for $32 million with corporate and community partners for display in the city of Atlanta.

Patricia Harris (1924–1985)
U.S. Secretary of Housing and Urban Development, U.S. Secretary of Health, Education, and Welfare

As U.S. ambassador to Luxembourg, Patricia Harris was the first black woman to hold this diplomatic rank. Until President Ronald Reagan won the election in 1980, Harris served as secretary of the Department of Health and Human Services and also as secretary of Housing and Urban Development under President Jimmy Carter.

Born in Mattoon, Illinois, Harris attended elementary school in Chicago and received her undergraduate degree from Howard University in 1945. While at Howard, Harris also served as vice-chairman of a student branch of the NAACP and was involved in early nonviolent demonstrations against racial discrimination. After completing postgraduate work at the University of Chicago and at American University, she earned her doctorate in jurisprudence from George Washington University Law School in 1960.

An attorney and professor before she entered politics, Harris was appointed co-chair of the National Women's Committee on Civil Rights by President John F. Kennedy and was later named to the Commission on the Status of Puerto Rico. In 1965 Harris was chosen by President Lyndon Johnson to become U.S. ambassador to Luxembourg, the first black woman ever to be named an American envoy.

In 1977 Harris was chosen by President Jimmy Carter to serve as secretary of Housing and Urban Development. She was also selected as secretary of the Department of Health and Human Services in 1979. Harris remained in these positions until the inauguration of President Ronald Reagan in 1981.

Harris ran an unsuccessful campaign for mayor of Washington, D.C., in 1982. She became a law professor at George Washington University in 1983 and remained there until her death from cancer in 1985.

Alexis Herman (1947–)
U.S. Secretary of Labor

Alexis Herman was born in Mobile, Alabama, on July 16, 1947. She attended Edgewood College and Spring Hill College before completing her

B.A. at Xavier University in 1969. That same year she took a position with Catholic Charities as a social worker developing employment and training opportunities for youth and women. She developed plans that helped black women in the rural Southeast to gain employment and be trained with new skills.

 In 1976 Herman was appointed by President Jimmy Carter as director of the Department of the Women's Labor Bureau. She became the youngest person to hold this position and the highest ranking African American in the Labor Department. With the election of Ronald Reagan, Herman returned to the private sector and started the A.M. Herman and Associates marketing and management firm.

In 1989 Herman was selected by longtime friend and chair of the Democratic National Committee, Ron Brown, as chief of staff and by 1992 she was selected as CEO of the Democratic National Convention. During President Bill Clinton's second term Herman was named secretary of labor. Although her appointment was initially opposed by Republicans in Congress she won confirmation. Herman became the first African American to hold this post. During her tenure she developed a standard for child labor on a global level, launched an aggressive plan for employing youths, and looked for initiatives that would prepare and create access for minorities and women into the workforce. Herman was investigated by authorities regarding misuse of funds and kickbacks, but she was exonerated from all accusations.

Herman continues to serve on the board of corporations, such as Metro Goldwyn Mayer and Prudential, among others. She is chair and chief executive officer of New Ventures, Inc. and chair of the Coca-Cola company.

Eric Holder (1951–)
U.S. Attorney General

Eric Himpton Holder Jr., born January 21, 1951, grew up in East Elmhurst Queens, New York, with strong ties to Barbados. His father Eric

Himpton Holder Sr. was born in Barbados and became a real estate broker, and his mother Miriam was from New Jersey but her parents had emigrated from Saint Philip Barbados. Holder graduated from Stuyvesant High School in 1969. He attended Columbia University and earned his B.A. in American history and received his J.D. in 1976 from Columbia Law School.

 After serving in the U.S. Justice Department from 1976 to 1988, Holder was appointed by President Ronald Reagan to serve as a justice of the Superior Court of the District of Columbia. In 1993 he was appointed by President Bill Clinton as U.S. attorney for the District of Columbia, the first African American to hold this position. In 1997 Holder was appointed as deputy attorney, serving until 2001. Holder was appointed as acting attorney general for a two-month period during the George W. Bush administration. In his role he prosecuted Democratic Congressman John Jenrette for bribery as a result of the Abscam sting and he oversaw the corruption case against Dan Rostenkowski in the congressional post office scandal.

In 2001 Holder was an attorney for the firm Covington and Burling. He handled many high-profile cases, including representing the National Football League (NFL) regarding the Michael Vick dog-fighting case, and he was part of the Janet Reno lead initiative regarding the Second Amendment and the right to bear arms in Washington, D.C. In 2007 Holder became senior advisor for the presidential campaign of Barack Obama.

On February 3, 2009, Holder, after having been nominated by President Barack Obama for attorney general, and approved by the Senate, assumed the office as the 82nd U.S. attorney general. He is the first African American to hold this position.

Jessie Jackson Jr. (1965–)
U.S. Congressman

Jessie Jackson Jr., born on March 11, 1965, in Greenville, South Carolina, is the second of five children born to Jessie Jackson Sr., one of the foremost civil rights activist of the twenty-first century, and Jacqueline Davis Jackson. Jackson earned his secondary and college education in North Carolina, culminating in a B.S in business management, magna cum laude, from North Carolina Agricultural and Technical University in Greensboro. He also earned a master of arts degree in theology from Chicago Theological Seminary and a J.D. from the University of Illinois College of Law in 1993.

In 1995 Jackson ran for the U.S. House seat vacated by incumbent Mel Reynolds from the Second Congressional District. Jackson won the seat with 48 percent of the votes. Jackson has supported and introduced legislation related to health care, the right to vote, funding for historically black colleges, and humanitarian aid for sub-Saharan African countries.

Lisa P. Jackson (1962–)
Chemical Engineer, Head of
U.S. Environmental Protection Agency

Jackson was born on February 8, 1962, in Philadelphia, Pennsylvania. She was adopted and grew up in Pontchartrain Park, a predominately African American neighborhood in New Orleans, Louisiana. Jackson graduated as valedictorian from Saint Mary's Dominican High School in 1979. She graduated in 1983, summa cum laude, with a B.S. degree in chemical engineering from Tulane University, and an M.S. in 1986 from Princeton University.

Jackson began her career with the Environmental Protection Agency in 1986 and continued there until March 2002. During her tenure she served as deputy director and acting director of the agency. In 2002 Jackson served as assistant commissioner of compliance and enforcement and in 2005 was named assistant commissioner for land

use management for the New Jersey Department of Environmental Protection. Jackson developed standards for implementing the historic Highland Water Protection and Planning Act.

In 2006 Jackson became commissioner of Environmental Protection in New Jersey. She was responsible for the preservation and enhancement of the natural resources of the state. Jackson was nominated as the administrator of the Environmental Protection Agency by President Barack Obama. She was confirmed on January 22, 2009, and became the first African American to hold this position.

Barbara Jordan (1936–1996)
U.S. Congresswoman, Civil Rights Leader

Jordan was born on February 21, 1936, in Houston, Texas. She attended Phillis Wheatley High School, where she graduated as a member of the honor society in 1952. In 1956 Jordan received a B.A. from Texas Southern University in history and political science. She went on to Boston University, where she earned a J.D. in 1959.

After teaching at Tuskegee Institute for a year, Jordan returned to Houston, where she practiced law and was appointed administrative assistant to a Harris County judge. In 1966 Jordan was elected to the Texas Senate. She was the first African American to serve as president pro tem of that body and to chair the important Labor and Management Relations Committee. In 1972 Jordan was elected to the U.S. House of Representatives, where she stayed until 1978. During her terms in both the Texas Senate and the U.S. House, Jordan was known as a champion of civil rights, minorities, and the poor.

From 1979 to 1982 she was a professor at the Lyndon Baines Johnson School of Public Affairs at the Austin campus of the University of Texas. In 1982 she was named recipient of the Lyndon Baines Johnson Centennial Chair of National Policy. In 1993 Jordan was named chair of the U.S.

Commission on Immigration Reform by President Bill Clinton. Jordan, who had suffered from multiple sclerosis and leukemia, died due to complications of pneumonia on January 17, 1996.

Jordan co-authored two books, *Barbara Jordan: A Self-Portrait* (1979) and *The Great Society: A Twenty Year Critique* (1986). She served on the Democratic Caucus Steering and Policy Committee, and in 1976 and 1992 she was the keynote speaker at the Democratic National Convention. Jordan was an accomplished politician and humanitarian. She received over twenty-seven honorary degrees and had an endowed chair in the LBJ School of Public Affairs. She was listed in the 1976 *Ladies Home Journal*'s 100 Most Influential Women in America and *Time* magazine's Ten Women of the Year. She was awarded the Eleanor Roosevelt Humanities Award and membership in the Texas Women's Hall of Fame in 1984. Jordan received the Presidential Medal of Freedom, the highest civilian honor, in 1994, presented by President Bill Clinton.

Ron Kirk (1954–)
Mayor, U.S. Trade Representative

Kirk was born in Austin, Texas, on June 27, 1954. Kirk graduated from the Austin's Public School System and held the position as president of the student council. In 1976 Kirk graduated from Austin College with a degree in political science and sociology and went on to earn his J.D. in 1979 from the University of Texas. After practicing law for several years, working in the office of Senator Lloyd Bentsen, and lobbing in the state legislature, Kirk ran for mayor of Dallas in 1994. He was successful and became the first African American mayor of Dallas.

As mayor, Kirk proved himself to be a coalition builder while developing a long-term plan for the growth and development of the city. Kirk was re-elected for a second term as mayor in 1999 but resigned in 2001 to run for a Senate

seat. He lost the election and returned to the law firm of Gardere Wynne Sewell in Dallas.

Many speculated that Kirk would be nominated for secretary of transportation but instead was nominated for trade representative. In reviewing his nomination, issues of Kirk's tax return were under scrutiny. Kirk was confirmed as U.S trade representative on March 18, 2009.

John Mercer Langston (1829–1897)
Abolitionist, Educator, University President, U.S. Congressman

John Mercer Langston was born in Virginia in 1829. Upon the death of his father, Ralph Quarles, an estate owner, young Langston was emancipated and sent to Ohio, where he was given over to the care of a friend of his father. Langston spent his childhood there, attending private school in Cincinnati before graduating from Oberlin College in 1849. Four years later, after getting his degree from the theological department of Oberlin, he studied law and was admitted to the Ohio bar in 1854.

Langston began his practice in Brownhelm, Ohio. He was chosen in 1855 to serve as clerk of this township by the Liberty Party. During the Civil War, he was a recruiting agent for Negro servicemen, helping to organize such famed regiments as the 54th and 55th Massachusetts, and the 5th Ohio.

In 1867 Langston served as inspector general of the Freedmen's Bureau, and he served as dean and vice president of Howard University from 1868 to 1875. In 1877 he was named minister resident to Haiti and chargé d'affaires to Santo Domingo, remaining in diplomatic service until 1885.

Soon after his return to the United States and to his law practice, he was named president of the Virginia Normal and Collegiate Institute. In 1888 he was elected to Congress from Virginia, but he was not seated for two years until vote-counting irregularities had been investigated. He was defeated in his bid for a second term. In 1894 Langston wrote an autobiography, *From the Virginia Plantation to the National Capital*. Eleven years earlier he had published a volume of his speeches, *Freedom and Citizenship*. Langston died in 1897.

Sheila Jackson Lee (1950–)
Judge, U.S. Congresswoman

Born in Queens, New York, on January 12, 1950, Sheila Jackson Lee received her undergraduate degree from Yale University in 1972 and a J.D. in 1975 from the University of Virginia Law School. After serving as associate judge in the Houston municipal courts for three years, Lee was elected in 1990 to an at-large position on the city council.

In 1994 Lee entered the congressional primary for the Houston area representative against incumbent Craig Washington. She won the election to the U.S. House of Representatives with 63 percent of the votes in the primary and 73 percent of the votes in the general election. Lee has been an outspoken advocate for civil rights and against racism in South Africa. As a member of the Congressional Black Caucus, Lee was the first vice-chairwoman for the caucus.

John Lewis (1940–)
U.S. Congressman

Lewis was born in Troy, Alabama, on February 21, 1940. He received a B.S. in 1961 from the American Baptist Theological Seminary, and in 1967 he earned another B.A. from Fisk University.

Lewis, while attending the American Baptist Theological Seminary in Nashville, was involved in the civil rights movement and participated in sit-ins and worked with the Freedom Riders. He was arrested over forty times and was attacked and beaten by an angry mob. Lewis was associated with several social activist organizations, including the Student Nonviolent Coordinating Committee; he served as associate director of the Field Foundation, project director of the Southern Regional Council, and executive director of the Voter Education Project, Inc.

After an unsuccessful first run in politics in 1977 for a seat in Georgia's Fifth Congressional District, Lewis was elected Atlanta City councilman-at-large in 1982, and in 1986 voters sent him to the U.S. House of Representatives as a Democrat. Lewis has served on committees such as the powerful House Ways and Means Committee, the Select Committee on Aging, and Public Works. Lewis has also championed an African American history museum as a part of the Smithsonian.

Lewis is a recipient of the Martin Luther King Jr. Nonviolent Peace Prize awarded in 1975 and belongs to the Martin Luther King Jr. Center for Social Change. In 2001 Lewis was awarded the John F. Kennedy Profile in Courage Award for Lifetime Achievement. The award marked the fortieth anniversary of the Freedom Rides. Lewis published his autobiography, *Walking with the Wind: A Memoir of the Movement*, in 1998 with Michael D'Orso.

C. Ray Nagin (1956–)
Mayor

Clarence Ray Nagin was born in New Orleans and has spent most of his childhood and adult life there. He received his B.A. from Tuskegee University in 1978 but returned to Louisiana to attend Tulane University earning an M.B.A. in 1994.

With most of Nagin's experience in the private sector, he still decided to enter politics in 2002. He saw a need to address political corruption in the city of New Orleans and to transform the city's image into a more positive one. In the primary Nagin ended up in a runoff with the chief of police, Richard Pennington. Nagin won the election.

The real test of Nagin's ability to manage the city came on August 28, 2005, when a hurricane, which was named Katrina, became a Category 4. On August 29 when Hurricane Katrina touched down on land, 80 percent of the city was flooded. The slow execution of the evacuation of citizens by the city, state, and federal governments resulted in many being displaced. Recovery continues.

Because of Katrina the mayoral election was postponed until April. In spite of criticism, the dispersion of New Orleans citizens to over forty-four states, and some controversial statements by Nagin, he was re-elected for a second term in 2006. Ineligible for a third term, Nagin left his role as mayor of New Orleans on May 3, 2010.

Eleanor Holmes Norton (1938–)
U.S. Congresswoman

Norton was born Eleanor Holmes on April 8, 1938, in Washington, D.C. She attended Antioch College in Ohio, but transferred to Yale University and received an M.A. in American studies in 1963 and a J.D. from Yale's law school in 1964.

After graduating from law school Norton clerked for a federal judge in Philadelphia before joining the American Civil Liberties Union in 1965 as a litigator, specializing in free-speech issues. She stayed with the ACLU until 1970, reaching the position of assistant legal director and successfully arguing a First Amendment case before the U.S. Supreme Court. In 1970 she became chairwoman of the New York City Commission on Human Rights, a post she held until 1977 when she headed the Equal Employment Opportunity Commission. In 1981 she was a senior fellow at the Urban Institute, and in 1982 she accepted the position of professor of law at Georgetown University. Norton had previously

taught black history at Pratt Institute in Brooklyn, New York, and law at New York City University Law School.

In 1990 Norton was elected congressional delegate to the U.S. House of Representatives for the District of Columbia, a non-voting position. Norton, who is allowed to vote in committee but not on floor votes, continued to campaign for equal voting rights for citizens of the district. In 1993 she was allowed to cast a vote in the House as the legislation she sponsored for voting rights for Washington, D.C., was under review, but it was rejected. Norton continues her campaign for full congressional voting rights and representation for the citizens of Washington, D.C.

Norton has received numerous honorary degrees from over fifty institutions which recognize her service as a congresswoman, her national role in civil rights, and her activism regarding feminist issues. Norton was named in 1989 as one of the One Hundred Most Powerful Women in Washington by the *Washington Magazine*, and she received the Distinguished Public Service Award in 1985 from the Center for National Policy.

Barack H. Obama (1961–)
President of the United States

Ann Dunham from Wichita, Kansas, and Barack Hussein Obama from Kenya, Africa (with family ties to the Luo tribe), saw the birth of their first child, Barack Hussein Obama Jr., on August 4, 1961, in Honolulu, Oahu, Hawaii. After completing his Ph.D. at Harvard, Barack's father returned to Kenya and took a job as an economic planner. The couple later decided to divorce. Barack's father died in an automobile accident in Kenya in 1982.

In the years after his parents' divorce Obama's mother remarried and they moved to Jakarta, Indonesia. In 1967 Obama returned to Honolulu and was raised by his maternal grandparents. After graduating high school Obama left Hawaii in 1979 and moved to Los Angeles. In

1983 he graduated from Columbia University with a degree in political science with specialization in international relations. Wanting to be involved in community-based organizations, Obama moved to Chicago in 1985 and went to work with a church-based group that focused on the city's poor neighborhoods. He became a community organizer in the Altgeld Gardens housing project on the south side of Chicago.

After spending time in Chicago, Obama entered Harvard Law School in 1988. He became the first African American editor of the *Harvard Law Review* in 1990. After graduating, magna cum laude, in 1991, Obama wrote his autobiography, *Dreams from My Father: A Story of Race and Inheritance*. It was published in 1995 and re-released in 2004. In 1992 while working in a corporate law firm in Chicago, Obama met Michelle Robinson, a Harvard Law School graduate from Chicago. Robinson and Obama were married in 1992. Obama practiced civil rights law with a public interest law firm, Miner, Barnhill and Galland, P.C. He also became a lecturer of constitutional law at the University of Chicago.

In 2000 Obama ran against incumbent, Bobby Rush, a former Black Panther for the First Congressional District and lost. He ran again in 2004 for the seat as U.S. senator from Illinois, vacated by Peter Fitzgerald. Obama won the Democratic primary. The Republican Party selected Alan Keyes, a former ambassador and African American conservative residing in Maryland, to oppose Obama. In spite of these efforts, Obama became the third African American to be elected in the U.S. Senate since Reconstruction and the fifth African American to be elected in the history of the entire country. Obama also became the only African American Senator in the 109th Congress.

Obama's campaign was so successful that he was invited to give the keynote address at the 2004 Democratic National Convention in Boston, Massachusetts. As only the third African American to give this keynote convention speech, he was preceded only by Barbara Jordan in 1976 and Harold Ford Jr. in 2000. In 2006 Obama published the book *The Audacity of Hope*, paying homage to the legacy of America as a place of possibilities.

In February 2007 Barack Obama announced his intentions to run as a candidate for the Democratic presidential nomination. On June 3, 2008, Obama won the Democratic nomination and on November 3, 2008, he was elected president of the United States of America. Barack Hussein Obama, an African American, a husband to Michelle Obama, and father of two girls, Sasha and Malia, became the forty-fourth president of the United States of America and the first African American to achieve this office.

Hazel R. O'Leary (1937–)
U.S. Secretary of Energy

O'Leary was born Hazel Reid on May 17, 1937, in Newport News, Virginia. She received a B.A. from Fisk College in 1959 and a J.D. from Rutgers University School of Law in 1966.

Hazel O'Leary was a utilities regulator under Presidents Gerald Ford and Jimmy Carter and an executive vice-president of the Northern States Power Co., where she functioned as a Washington lobbyist. O'Leary has been a proponent of energy conservation and alternate energy sources. She is a certified financial planner and a member of the New Jersey and Washington bars, and has been vice-president and general counsel of O'Leary Associates in Washington, D.C.

In January 1993 O'Leary was confirmed as President Bill Clinton's secretary of energy. She not only developed policies that would regulate energy usage, but she also worked to reveal secret atomic laboratories and weapons storage and encourage the development of domestic energy sources. O'Leary came under fire regarding her spending. Her overseas travel expenses were considered excessive but Vice President Al Gore challenged the criticism. In 1993 O'Leary was honored for her work by the Congressional Black Caucus. She served as secretary of energy until 1997 when she resigned. O'Leary became president of Blaylock & Partners and remained in the private sector until she was named president of her alma mater, Fisk University in Nashville, Tennessee, in 2004.

P.B.S. Pinchback (1837–1921)
Governor

Pinchback was born in Macon, Georgia, on May 10, 1837. Although his mother had been a slave, by the time Pinchback was born she had been emancipated by Pinchback's father. Moving to Ohio with his mother, Pinchback attended high school in Cincinnati in 1847, but in 1848 he began working on riverboats, first as a cabin boy and then as a steward.

At the outbreak of the Civil War Pinchback went to Louisiana and in 1862 he enlisted in the Union Army. He soon began recruiting soldiers for an African American troop variously known as the Louisiana Native Guards and the Corps d'Afrique. Racial problems soon arose with the military hierarchy and Pinchback resigned his commission in protest.

After the war Pinchback became active in Louisiana politics. He organized a Republican Club in 1867 and in 1868 was a delegate to a state constitutional convention. In that year he was also elected to the state senate and in 1871 he became president pro tem of that body. He soon became lieutenant governor of Louisiana through the line of succession. For five weeks in late 1872 and early 1873 Pinchback was governor of Louisiana while the elected official underwent impeachment proceedings. In 1872 and 1873 Pinchback was elected to the U.S. Senate and the U.S. House of Representatives. He was refused seating both times when the elections were contested and ruled in favor of his Democratic opponent. He did, however, receive what would have been his salary as an elected official.

In 1877 Pinchback switched his allegiance to the Democratic Party and in 1882 was appointed surveyor of customs for New Orleans. In 1887 he began attending law school at Straight University in New Orleans and was later admitted to the bar. In 1890 Pinchback moved to Washington, D.C., where he died December 21, 1921.

Adam Clayton Powell Jr. (1908–1972)
Pastor, U.S. Congressman

Born in November 29, 1908, in New Haven, Connecticut, to Mattie Fletcher and Adam Clayton Powell Sr., Adam Powell was raised in New York City, attended high school there, and then went to Colgate University, where he earned a bachelor's degree in 1930. In 1931 Powell graduated from Columbia University with a master's degree in religious education.

The young Powell launched his career as a crusader for reform during the Depression. He forced several large corporations to drop their unofficial bans on employing blacks and directed a kitchen and relief operation which fed, clothed, and provided fuel for thousands of Harlem's needy and destitute. He was instrumental in persuading officials of Harlem Hospital to integrate their medical and nursing staffs, helped many blacks find employment along Harlem's "main stem," 125th Street, and campaigned against the city's bus lines, which were discriminating against black drivers and mechanics.

When Powell Sr. retired from Abyssinian Baptist Church in 1936, his son, who had already served as manager and assistant pastor there, was named his successor.

Powell won a seat on the New York City Council in 1941 with the third highest number of votes ever cast for a candidate in municipal elections. In 1942 he turned to journalism for a second time (he had already been on the staff of the *New York Evening Post* in 1934), and published and edited the weekly *People's Voice*, which he called "the largest Negro tabloid in the world." He became a member of the New York State Office of Price Administration in 1942 and served until 1944.

In 1944 Powell was elected to Congress and represented a constituency of three hundred thousand, 89 percent of whom were black. Identified at once as "Mr. Civil Rights," he encountered a host of discriminatory procedures upon his arrival in the nation's capital. He could not rent a room or attend a movie in downtown Washington. Within Congress itself, he was not allowed to use such communal facilities as dining rooms, steam baths, showers, and barbershops. Powell defied such rebuffs head-on by making use of all such facilities and insisting that his entire staff follow his lead.

As a freshman legislator, Powell engaged in fiery debates with segregationists, fought for the abolition of discriminatory practices at U.S. military installations, and sought—through the controversial Powell Amendment—to deny federal funds to any project where discrimination existed. This amendment eventually became part of the Flanagan School Lunch Bill, making Powell the first black congressman since Reconstruction to have legislation passed by both houses.

Powell also sponsored legislation advocating federal aid to education, a minimum-wage scale, and greater benefits for the chronically unemployed. He also drew attention to certain discriminatory practices on Capitol Hill and worked toward their elimination. It was Powell who first demanded that a black journalist be allowed to sit in the Senate and House press galleries, introduced the first Jim Crow transportation legislation, and introduced the first bill to prohibit segregation in the Armed Forces. At one point in his career, the congressional record reported that the House Committee on Education and Labor had processed more important legislation than any other major committee. In 1960 Powell, as senior member of this committee, became its chairman. He had a hand in the development and passage of such significant legislation as the Minimum Wage Bill of 1961, the Manpower Development and Training Act, the Anti-Poverty Bill, the Juvenile Delinquency Act, the Voca-

tional Education Act, and the National Defense Education Act. In all, the Powell committee helped pass forty-eight laws involving a total outlay of $14 billion.

The flamboyant congressman, however, was accused of putting an excessive number of friends on the congressional payroll, of having a high rate of absenteeism from congressional votes, and of excessive zeal for the "playboy's" life.

In 1967 the controversies and irregularities surrounding him led to censure in the House and a vote to exclude him from his seat in the 90th Congress. The House based its decision on the allegation that he had misused public funds and was in contempt of the New York courts due to a lengthy and involved defamation case that had resulted in a trial for civil and criminal contempt. Despite his exclusion, Powell was readmitted to the 91st Congress in 1968. In mid-1969, the Supreme Court ruled that the House had violated the Constitution by excluding him from membership but left open the questions of his loss of twenty-two years' seniority and the chairmanship of the Education and Labor Committee. Also unresolved were the $25,000 fine levied against him and the matter of back pay.

However, rather than return to Congress, Powell spent most of his time on the West Indian island of Bimini, where process servers could not reach him. But photographers did, and the ensuing photos of Powell vacationing on his boat while crucial votes were taken in Congress began to affect Powell in his home district. In 1970 he lost the Democratic congressional primary to Charles Rangel by 150 votes. Powell retired from public office and worked as a minister at the Abyssinian Baptist Church. On April 4, 1972, Powell died in Miami.

Charles Rangel (1930–)
U.S. Congressman

Harlem-born Charles Rangel vaulted into the national spotlight in 1970, when he defeated Adam Clayton Powell Jr. for the Democratic nomination in New York's Eighteenth Congressional District. Rangel's upset victory stirred hopes among black leaders that a grassroots political movement that was generated from within Harlem, rather than stemming from beyond the community, might result in the grooming of an energetic, capable, and untainted successor to the volatile and unpredictable Powell.

Born on June 11, 1930, Rangel attended Harlem elementary and secondary schools before volunteering to serve in the U.S. Army during the Korean War. While stationed in Korea with the 2nd Infantry, he saw heavy combat and received the Purple Heart and the Bronze Star Medal for Valor, as well as U.S. and Korean presidential citations. Discharged honorably as a staff sergeant, Rangel returned to finish high school and to study at New York University's School of Commerce, from which he graduated in 1957. The recipient of a scholarship, Rangel then attended St. John's Law School, graduating in 1960.

After being admitted to the bar, Rangel earned a key appointment as assistant U.S. attorney in the southern district of New York in 1961. For the next five years, he acquired legal experience as legal counsel to the New York City Housing and Redevelopment Board, as legal assistant to Judge James L. Watson, as associate counsel to the speaker of the New York State Assembly, and as general counsel to the National Advisory Commission on Selective Service. In 1966 Rangel was chosen to represent the 72nd District, Central Harlem, in the State Assembly. Since then, he has served as a member of, and secretary to, the New York State Commission on Revision of the Penal Law and Criminal Code.

In 1972 Rangel easily defeated Livingston Wingate in the Democratic congressional primary and went on to an overwhelming victory in November. In 1974 he was elected chairman of the Congressional Black Caucus. Rangel served as chairman of the Congressional Black Caucus in 1974–1975 and was a member of the Judiciary Committee when it voted to impeach President Nixon. In 1975 he moved to the Ways and Means Committee, becoming the first African American to serve on this committee.

Rangel's service makes him the fourth longest serving Democratic member of the U.S. House of Representatives. In 2008 Rangel was investigated on charges of failing to comply with tax laws. He was convicted of eleven counts of ethics misconduct in 2010 and later censured. Rangel, nevertheless, was re-elected and continues to serve in Congress.

Hiram Rhodes Revels (1827–1901)
U.S. Senator

Hiram Rhodes Revels, a native of North Carolina, was the first black man to serve in the U.S. Senate. Revels was elected from his adopted state of Mississippi and served for approximately one year.

Born in 1827, Revels was educated in Indiana and attended Knox College in Illinois. Ordained a minister in the African Methodist Church, he worked among black settlers in Kansas, Maryland, Illinois, Indiana, Tennessee, Kentucky, and Missouri before settling in Baltimore in 1860. There he served as a church pastor and school principal.

During the Civil War, Revels helped organize a pair of Negro regiments in Maryland, and in 1863 he went to St. Louis to establish a freedmen school and to carry on his work as a recruiter. For a year he served as chaplain of a Mississippi regiment before becoming provost marshal of Vicksburg.

Revels settled in Natchez, Mississippi, in 1866 and was appointed alderman by the Union military governor of the state. In 1870 Revels was elected to the U.S. Senate to replace Jefferson Davis, the former president of the Confederacy. Revels' appointment caused a storm of protest from white southerners. Nonetheless, Revels was allowed to take his seat in the Senate.

As a U.S. senator, Revels quickly won the respect of many of his constituents for his alert grasp of important state issues and for his courageous support of legislation that would have restored voting and officeholding privileges to disenfranchised southerners. He believed that the best way for blacks to gain their rightful place in American society was not through violent means, but by obtaining an education and leading an exemplary life of courage and moral fortitude. He spoke out against the segregation of the Washington, D.C., public school system and defended the rights of black men who were denied work at the Washington Navy Yard because of their race.

Revels left the Senate in 1871 after serving one full term. He was named president of Alcorn University near Lorman, Mississippi. He left Alcorn in 1873 to serve as Mississippi's secretary of state on an interim basis. He returned to Alcorn in 1876 and became editor of the *SouthWestern Christian Advocate*, a religious journal. He retired from Alcorn University in 1882.

Revels lived in Holly Springs, Mississippi, during his later years and taught theology at Shaw University. He died on January 16, 1901.

Condoleezza Rice (1954–)
U.S. Secretary of State, University Professor

Condoleezza Rice, a native of Birmingham, Alabama, was born November 14, 1954. She earned a B.A. in political science in 1974 from the University of Denver and graduated Phi Beta Kappa and cum laude. Rice later earned her master's degree from the University of Notre Dame, and in 1981 a Ph.D. from the University of Denver's Graduate School of International Studies.

Rice served on the faculty of Stanford University from 1981 to 1993 before accepting the position of university provost from 1993 to 1999. During this time Rice accepted the position of advisor to the Joint Chiefs of Staff on nuclear policy and was named in 1989 as director of Soviet and East European affairs on the National Security Council, which advised then President George H.W. Bush.

During the presidential campaign for George W. Bush, Rice left Stanford and served as Bush's advisor on foreign policy. After Bush was elected in November 2000, Rice was appointed as national security advisor. She was the first woman and the first African American to hold this position. In her efforts to combat terrorism and threats to America both home and abroad, Rice became a key spokesperson during the attacks on September 11, 2001; she addressed the issue that Afghanistan was harboring Saudi exile, Osama bin Laden, the founder of Al Qaeda, who took responsibility of the 9/11 attacks; and she confronted the controversy of weapons of mass destruction by Iraqi leader Saddam Hussein. The United States invaded Iraq in 2003. In 2005 during Bush's second term Rice was appointed secretary of state. She represented the United States regarding all areas of global concern and national interest.

With the election of Barack Obama as president in 2009, Rice planned to return to academia. She continues to serve on numerous boards and is the author of several books.

Susan E. Rice (1964–)
Government Official, Ambassador

Ambassador Susan Elizabeth Rice was confirmed on January 22, 2009, as the U.S. permanent representative to the United Nations.

Rice was born on November 17, 1964, in Washington, D.C. Her father, Emmett J. Rice, was an economics professor at Cornell University and former governor of the Federal Reserve System; and her mother, Lois Dickson Fitt, was an education policy scholar at the Brookings Instituttion. Rice graduated as valedictorian from the

National Cathedral School, a private day girl's school in D.C. In college Rice, a Truman Scholar, received her B.A. in history with honors, including the prestigious academic designation of Phi Beta Kappa from Stanford University. As a Rhodes Scholar she later received her M.Phil. and D.Phil. in international relations from New College, Oxford University, England.

From 1993 to 1997 Rice served in the White House as director for International Organizations and Peacekeeping on the National Security Council, special assistant to President Clinton, and senior director for African affairs on the National Security Council. From 1997 to 2001 she became assistant secretary of state for African affairs. From 2002 to 2009 she was a senior fellow at the Brookings Institution, focusing on issues such as U.S. foreign policy and global poverty and development.

Rice served on Obama's election campaign as senior advisor for national security affairs. Her experience and overall performance as a spokesperson on global and national concerns made her nomination and subsequently her confirmation as permanent representative to the United Nations a unanimous one by the U.S. Senate.

Edith Sampson (c. 1901–1979)
Judge, United Nations Delegate

The first black woman to be named an official representative to the United Nations, Edith Sampson served in this body from 1950 until 1953, first as an appointee of President Harry S. Truman and later during a portion of the Eisenhower administration.

A native of Pittsburgh, Sampson acquired a bachelor of laws degree from the John Marshall Law School in Chicago in 1925, and two years later she joined the Illinois bar and became the first woman to receive a master of laws from Loyola University.

One of Sampson's cases took her all the way to the Supreme Court in 1934. During the 1930s she maintained her own private practice specializing particularly in domestic relations and criminal law.

After her U.N. appointment Sampson traveled around the world, often as a lecturer under State Department auspices. She was elected associate judge of the Municipal Court of Chicago in 1962, becoming the first black woman ever to sit as a circuit court judge. She gained acclaim for her superior mediating powers, her heartfelt sincerity, and her humanistic approach to rendering judgments. In 1978 she retired from Cook County Circuit Court.

Sampson died on October 7, 1979, at Northwestern Hospital in Chicago, Illinois.

Carl B. Stokes (1927–1996)
Mayor

In 1967 Carl B. Stokes became the first African American mayor of a major U.S. city. Stokes was born in Cleveland, Ohio, on June 21, 1927. Soon after returning from fighting in World War II, Stokes entered the University of Minnesota and earned a B.S. in law in 1954. He received his J.D. from the Cleveland Marshall School of Law.

Stokes entered the political scene for the city of Cleveland in 1957, the same year he and his brother started a law practice. Stokes was appointed assistant city prosecutor in 1958 and became actively involved in the civil rights movement, served on the board of the NAACP, and was a member of the Urban League. He won a seat in the Ohio General Assembly in 1962 and served until his run for mayor in 1967. Stokes won the election with 50 percent of the total vote and 37 percent of the African American vote. Stokes's administration tried to increase services to the inner city while addressing shootouts during urban riots. In spite of difficulties in his first term, Stokes won a second term in 1969. He did not seek a third term.

In 1972 Stokes moved to New York and became the first African American news anchor in the New York City area working for WNBC television station. In 1983 he returned to Cleveland and was elected to municipal judge. In 1994 Stokes was appointed as ambassador to the Seychelles by President Clinton, but had to take a leave of absence due to medical issues. He was diagnosed with cancer of the esophagus in 1995 and died on April 3, 1996, in his hometown of Cleveland.

Louis Stokes (1925–)
U.S. Congressman

Louis Stokes was born in Cleveland, Ohio, on February 23, 1925. He served in the U.S. Army from 1943 until 1946, then attended Case Western Reserve University from 1946 to 1948. In 1953 he received a J.D. from Cleveland Marshall Law School. After fourteen years in private practice with the law firm of Stokes, Character, Terry & Perry he was elected as a Democrat to the U.S. House of Representatives in 1969.

As Ohio's first African American representative, Stokes has served on a number of committees, including the House Assassination Committee, which investigated the deaths of Martin Luther King Jr. and President John F. Kennedy, and he was the first African American to serve on the House of Representatives Intelligence Committee and the Iran-Contra Committee. In 1972 and 1973 Stokes chaired the Congressional Black Caucus and in 1972, 1976, and 1980 he was a delegate to the Democratic National Convention.

Stokes retired in 1999 after thirty years, making him the first African American to have completed such a long career of service in Congress. He became senior counsel at the international law firm Squire, Sanders, and Dempsey, LLP and was named distinguished visiting professor at Case Western University's Mandel School of Applied Social Science.

Stokes was well respected for his unwavering commitment to public service. Among his recognitions and awards for service are the Certificate of Appreciation from the U.S. Commission on Civil Rights, the Congressional Distinguished Service Award, and over twenty-six honorary degrees.

Harold Washington (1922–1987)
Mayor

Washington was born in Chicago on April 15, 1922. After serving with the Army Air Corps in the Pacific theater during World War II, he received a B.A. from Roosevelt University in 1949. Washington then received a J.D. from Northwestern University Law School in 1952.

After graduation Washington worked as an assistant city prosecutor in Chicago, and while establishing a private law practice, he was an arbitrator with the Illinois Industrial Commission from 1960 to 1964.

Running on the Democratic ticket, Washington was elected to the Illinois State House of Representatives (1965–1976) and the Illinois State Senate (1977–1980). While a legislator he helped establish the Illinois Fair Employment Practices Commission and the naming of Martin Luther King Jr.'s birthday as a state holiday. Washington was also concerned with consumer protection legislation and the Illinois Legislative Black Caucus. In 1980 Washington was elected to the U.S. House of Representatives and in 1983, after a tightly contested primary and subsequent election, Washington became Chicago's first African American mayor.

Although Washington's mayoralty was marred by political infighting, he did manage to institute reforms such as increased city hiring of minorities, deficit reduction, the appointment of an African American police commissioner, and reduction of patronage influence. Washington died while in office on November 25, 1987.

Maxine Waters (1938–)
U.S. Congresswoman

Waters was born in St. Louis, Missouri, on August 15, 1938. After graduating from high school she moved to Los Angeles, where she worked at a garment factory and for a telephone company. She eventually attended college and received a B.A. in sociology from California State University. She became interested in politics after teaching in a Head Start program and serving as a delegate to the Democratic National Convention in 1972. She later attended the convention four more times in the same capacity.

 In 1976 Waters was elected to the California State Assembly, and in 1990 she was elected to the U.S. House of Representatives. Waters has served on committees such as the Banking, Finance and Urban Affairs, chaired the Congressional Black Caucus from 1997 to 1998, and served as the chief deputy whip for the Democratic Party. She is a vociferous spokesperson for minorities, the poor, and those often left out of the democratic process. Currently she is seeking debt relief for earthquake-ravaged Haiti and advocating an increase in opportunities for women and minorities in financial service professions.

Andrew Young (1932–)
Mayor, U.N. Ambassador

Andrew Young came into national prominence nearly three decades ago and has become a figure of international prominence and stature. Soft-spoken yet eloquent, Young is widely admired for his incisive thinking and his willingness to express his opinion.

Young was born in New Orleans in 1932, and received a bachelor of science degree from Howard University and a bachelor of divinity degree from Hartford Theological Seminary in 1955. He was ordained a minister in the United Church of Christ and then served in churches in Alabama and Georgia before joining the National Council of Churches in 1957. The turning point of his life came in 1961 when he joined Martin Luther King Jr. and became a trusted aide and close confidante. He became executive vice president of the SCLC in 1967 and remained with King until the latter's murder in 1968.

In 1970 Young, a Democrat, lost a bid for the U.S. House of Representatives to Republican Fletcher Thompson. In the aftermath of the election, Young was appointed chair of the Community Relations Committee. Although the CRC was an advisory group with no enforcement powers, Young took an activist role, pressing the city government on issues from sanitation and open housing to mass transit, consumer affairs, and Atlanta's drug problem. Young's leadership in the CRC led to a higher public profile and answered critics' charges that he was inexperienced in government.

Young launched another bid for the U.S. Congress in 1972. The campaign was difficult for Young since blacks comprised only 44 percent of the voters in Young's congressional district. However, Young captured 23 percent of the white vote and 54 percent of the total vote to win and became the first black representative to be elected from Georgia since Jefferson Long in 1870.

Thereafter, Young was re-elected with ease every two years. He was one of the most vocal supporters of his fellow Georgian Jimmy Carter's campaign for the presidency in 1976. Following President Carter's inauguration, Young left Congress in 1977 to become America's ambassador to the United Nations.

Young's career as a diplomat came to an end in 1979 when he met secretly with a representative of the Palestine Liberation Organization to discuss an upcoming vote in the United Nations. America had a policy that none of its representatives would meet with the PLO as long as it refused to recognize the right of Israel to exist as a state. When the news of Young's meeting leaked out, an uproar ensued. Young had originally told the State Department that the meeting was by chance, but later he admitted that it had been planned. Though the meeting had secured a vote in the United Nations that the United States wanted, the pressure mounted and Young tendered his resignation, which President Carter accepted.

Young became a private citizen, but not for long. When Atlanta mayor Maynard Jackson was limited by law to two terms, Young ran for the office in 1981 and won with 55 percent of the total vote. He took office at a time when Atlanta was going through several economic and social problems. By 1984 the city was in a growth spurt and was attracting new businesses. Young was re-elected decisively in 1985.

At the end of his two terms as mayor, Young ran unsuccessfully for governor of Georgia in 1990. In 1996 Young was the president of Young Ideas, a consulting firm he founded and he also served as chair of the Atlanta Committee for the Olympic Games, an organization responsible for preparing Atlanta to host the 1996 Summer Olympics. Young continues as co-chair of the organization Good Works International and remains an advocate for human rights.

Coleman Young (1918–1997)
Mayor

In 1989, Coleman Young won his fifth term as mayor of Detroit, Michigan. The vote was considered remarkable because even with the heavy unemployment in Detroit, a shortage of cash, and a high crime rate, the voters returned Young to office. In 1993, however, Young decided not to seek re-election for the following term, pledging his support to candidate Sharon McPhail, who ultimately lost the 1993 mayoral race to Dennis Archer.

Part of Young's support stemmed from a sense of revitalization that he breathed into Detroit and the confidence of the voters who believed that though things were rough, the mayor would persevere. A Democrat, and one of the first big-city mayors to support Jimmy Carter's presidential campaign in 1976, Young had a very close relationship with the Carter administration. This relationship proved helpful in securing funds for Detroit.

Young was born in Tuscaloosa, Alabama, in 1918. His family moved to Detroit's east side in 1926 after the Ku Klux Klan ransacked a neighborhood in Huntsville where his father was learning to be a tailor. In Detroit, Young attended Catholic Central and then Eastern High School, graduating from the latter with honors. He had

to reject a scholarship to the University of Michigan when the Eastern High School Alumni Association, in contrast to policies they followed with poor white students, declined to assist him with costs other than tuition.

Young entered an electrician's apprentice school at Ford Motor Company. He finished first in the program but was passed over for the only available electrician job in favor of a white candidate. He went to work on the assembly line, and soon engaged in underground union activities. One day a man Young described as a "company goon" tried to attack him. Young hit him on the head with a steel bar and was fired.

During World War II, he became a navigator in the Army Air Force and was commissioned a second lieutenant. Stationed at Freeman Field, Indiana, he demonstrated against the exclusion of blacks from segregated officers' clubs and was arrested along with one hundred other black airmen, among them the late Thurgood Marshall and Percy Sutton, former president of New York's borough of Manhattan. Young spent three days in jail. Shortly thereafter, the clubs were opened to black officers.

After the war Young returned to his union-organizing activities and in 1947 was named director of organization for the Wayne County AFL-CIO. However, the union fired him in 1948 when he supported Henry Wallace, candidate of the Progressive Party, in the presidential election. The union regarded Wallace as an agent of the Communist Party and supported Harry Truman.

Young managed a dry cleaning plant for a few years and, in 1951, founded and directed the National Negro Labor Council. According to Young, the Council was ahead of its time and successfully prevailed on Sears Roebuck & Co. and the San Francisco Transit System to hire blacks. However, the Council also aroused the interest of the House Un-American Activities Committee, which was then holding hearings around the country at which alleged Communists were required to produce names of people allegedly associated with the Party. Young, who denied he was ever a Communist, refused to name anyone. He emerged from the battle with his self-respect intact, but his Labor Council was placed on the attorney general's subversive list. In 1956 the Labor Council was disbanded. Charges that Young was a Communist were later used against him, unsuccessfully, during his first mayoral campaign.

After working at a variety of jobs, Young won a seat on the Michigan Constitutional Convention in 1961. In 1962 he lost a race for state representative but became director of campaign organization for the Democratic gubernatorial candidate in Wayne County (Detroit). He sold life insurance until 1964 when, with union support, he was elected to the state Senate. In the Senate he was a leader of the civil-rights forces fighting for low-income housing for people dislocated by urban renewal and for an end to discrimination in the hiring practices of the Detroit Police Department.

Young declared his candidacy for mayor of Detroit in 1973 and mounted a vigorous campaign for the office. He won the office after a racially divisive campaign. Among his early successes in office were the integration of the Detroit Police Department and the promotion of black officers into administrative positions. He was able to encourage new businesses to come to Detroit, which was further expanded by his close relationship with President Jimmy Carter's administration. Young was able to negotiate funding for the city.

After the end of Young's fifth term in 1993 he became a professor of urban affairs at Wayne State University. Young had been suffereing from poor health even during his last term in office. On November 29, 1997, Young died of emphysema.

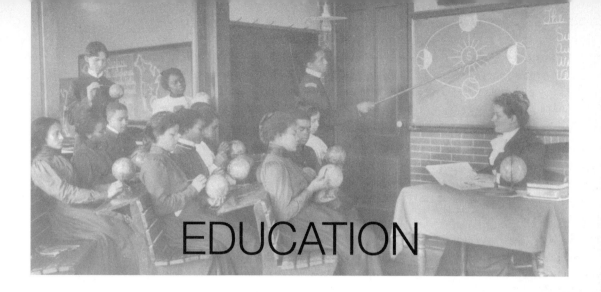

EDUCATION

Since the first arrival of Africans in America, the African American community has worked to sustain a system for educating its youth. In addition to the efforts of individuals, churches and charitable organizations have also played an important role in the creation of educational institutions for blacks in the United States.

Early attempts to educate blacks in America can be traced back to efforts by Christian churches. Although the primary goal of these missionaries was to convert Africans to Christianity, the process often involved general education.

French Catholics in Louisiana were probably the earliest group to begin providing instruction to black laborers in the early 1600s. The French code noir, a system of laws, made it incumbent upon masters to educate slaves.

Pennsylvania Quakers, who opposed the institution of slavery, organized monthly educational meetings for blacks during the early 1700s. One such Quaker, Anthony Benezet, in 1750 established an evening school in his home, which remained successful until 1760. In 1774 Quakers in Philadelphia joined together to open a school for blacks.

The Society for the Propagation of the Gospel in Foreign Parts, organized by the Church of England in 1701 for the purpose of converting African slaves to Christianity, was another organization that provided educational opportunities to blacks. In 1751 the society sent Joseph Ottolenghi to convert and educate blacks in Georgia. Ottolenghi "promised to spare no pains to improve the young children."

Like the church, the anti-slavery movement played an important part in the creation of schools. In 1787 the Manumission Society founded the New York African Free School; by 1820 more than five hundred black children were enrolled. Support increased as other African Free Schools were established in New York, until 1834 when the New York Common Council took over control of the schools.

In 1804 African Episcopalians in Philadelphia organized a school for black children. In 1848 a black industrial training school opened in Philadelphia at the House of Industry. Other Philadelphia schools founded during the nineteenth century included the Corn Street Unclassified School, the Holmesburg Unclassified School, and the Home for Colored Children. By the mid-1860s there were 1,031 pupils in the black public schools of Philadelphia, 748 in the charity schools, 211 in the benevolent schools, and 331 in private schools.

At the close of the Civil War hundreds of thousands of free blacks were left without homes and adequate resources. As a means for providing temporary assistance to the newly freed slaves, numerous organizations were formed.

The New England Freedmen's Aid Society, organized in Boston on February 7, 1862, was founded to promote education among free African Americans. Supporters of the organization included Edward Everett Hale, Samuel Cabot, Charles Bernard, William Lloyd Garrison, and William Cullen Bryant. In New York a similar organization was founded, the National Freedmen's Relief Association, on February 20, 1862. This was followed by the Port Royal Relief Committee, later known as the Pennsylvania Freedmen's Relief Association, founded in Philadelphia on March 3, 1862. In 1863 several of these organizations merged to form the United States Commission for the Relief of the National Freedmen, which in 1865 became the American Freedmen's Aid Union.

During the 1860s Congress passed several Freedmen's Bureau Acts, creating and financing an agency designed to provide temporary assistance to newly freed slaves. Under the acts, the bureau's chief functions were to provide food, clothing, and medical supplies. Working in conjunction with various benevolent organizations, Commissioner General Oliver Otis Howard established and maintained schools, as well as provisions for teachers. By 1870 the bureau operated over 2,600 schools in the South, with 3,300 teachers educating 150,000 students; almost 4,000 schools were in operation prior to the abolition of the agency.

The education of African Americans has been largely a function of independent schools, private institutions founded to meet the educational and employment needs of African Americans.

One of the earliest surviving black independent schools, Tuskegee Normal and Industrial Institute (now Tuskegee Institute), was established in 1881 by an act of the Alabama General Assembly. Booker T. Washington, the school's organizer and first principal, established at the school a cur-

riculum to provide black students with the means to become economically self-supporting.

Similarly, other independent schools developed around the country. In a lecture room at the Christ Presbyterian Church, Lucy Laney in 1883 opened what became the Haines Normal and Industrial Institute in Savannah, Georgia. In 1901 Nannie Helen Burroughs founded the National Training School for Women and Girls in Washington, D.C. By the end of the first year the school had enrolled thirty-one students; twenty-five years later more than two thousand women had trained at the school. In 1901 in Sedalia, North Carolina, Charlotte Hawkins Brown founded the Palmer Memorial Institute.

With only $1.50 and five students, in 1904 Mary McLeod Bethune founded Daytona Normal and Industrial Institute for Girls in Daytona Beach, Florida. Nineteen years later, the institute merged with the Cookman Institute of Jacksonville, Florida, founded in 1872 by D.S.B. Darnell. Some 2,000 students currently study at what is now known as Bethune-Cookman College.

One of the oldest of the historically black institutions of higher education, Wilberforce College (now Wilberforce University), named for the English abolitionist William Wilberforce, was founded in 1856 by the African Methodist Episcopal Church. The school awarded its first degree in 1857. The oldest institution in operation today, Cheyney State in Pennsylvania, was founded in 1837.

Between 1865 and 1871 several predominantly black institutions of higher learning were founded, including Atlanta University (now Clark-Atlanta University), Shaw University, Virginia Union University, Fisk University, Lincoln Institute (now Lincoln University), Talladega College, Augusta Institute (now Morehouse College), Biddle University (now Johnson C. Smith University), Howard University, Scotia Seminary (now Barber-Scotia College), Tougaloo College, Alcorn College (now Alcorn State University), and Benedict College. Religious organizations were instrumental in the founding and support of these early black institutions. Atlanta, Fisk, Tal-

The Tuskegee Institute, established in 1881, is now a national historic site.

ladega, and Tougaloo were founded by the American Missionary Association; Benedict, Shaw, and Virginia Union were founded and supported by the American Baptist Home Mission Society.

Alcorn College, founded in 1871, was the first black land grant college. This was made possible under the Morrill Act of 1862, which provided federal land grant funds for higher education. In 1890 Congress passed the second Morrill Act, also known as the Land Grant Act of 1890. The second act stipulated that no federal aid could be provided for the creation or maintenance of any white agricultural and mechanical school unless that state also provided for a similar school for blacks. As a result, a system of separate black land grant institutions developed, which became the basis of black higher education in the South.

By 1900 there were some thirty-four black institutions in the United States for higher education and more than 2,000 blacks with earned degrees, according to John Hope Franklin in his 1988 publication *From Slavery to Freedom, A History of Negro Americans.*

One of the forerunners in the field of black studies, theologian and educator Reverend Alexander Crummell, along with a group of black intellectuals, founded the American Negro Academy in Washington, D.C., in 1897. The purpose of the organization was to foster scholarship and promote literature, science, and art among African Americans. The organization's members hoped that through the academy, an educated black elite would be born to shape and direct society. Crummell first conceived of the idea of an American Negro Academy while he was a student at Cambridge University in England. The organization's founding members included Paul Laurence Dunbar, William Sanders Scarborough, and W.E.B. DuBois, among other noted educators. Following Crummell's death in 1908, DuBois was elected president of the academy.

In September 1915 Carter G. Woodson, a Harvard Ph.D. graduate, organized the Association for the Study of Negro Life and History (now the Association for the Study of Afro-American Life and History). The association's primary purpose was to promote research, encourage the study of African American history, and publish material on black history. In 1916 the association began publishing the *Journal of Negro History*, for which Woodson served as editor until his death in 1950.

Other early scholars of African American studies include sociologist E. Franklin Frazier (1894–1963); historian George Washington Williams (1849–1991); John Edward Bruce (1856–1924) and Arthur Schomburg, founders of the Negro Society for Historical Research in 1911; and Alain Locke, founder of the Associates in Negro Folk Education in 1934.

In the years that followed the U.S. Supreme Court's 1896 ruling in the *Plessy v. Ferguson* case, segregation in public education became general practice. Prior to the Court's decision in *Brown v. Board of Education of Topeka*, black children were often subjected to inferior educational facilities. By the 1930s, however, a string of school desegregation cases reached the Court.

When Lloyd Lionel Gaines, an African American, was refused admission to the law school of the State University of Missouri, he applied to state courts for an order to compel admission on the grounds that refusal constituted a denial of his rights under the Fourteenth Amendment of the U.S. Constitution. At that time, the state of Missouri maintained a practice of providing funds for blacks to attend graduate and professional schools outside of the state, rather than provide facilities itself. The university defended its action by maintaining that Lincoln University, a predominantly black institution, would eventually establish its own law school, which Gaines could then attend. Until then the state would allow him to exercise the option of pursuing his studies outside the state on a scholarship. Ruling in the case *Missouri ex rel. Gaines v. Canada* in 1938, the Supreme Court ruled that states were required to provide equal educational facilities for blacks within its borders.

Taking an even greater step, in 1950 the U.S. Supreme Court ruled that a separate law school for blacks provided by the state of Texas violated the equal protection clause of the Fourteenth Amendment, when Herman Marion Sweat was refused admission to the law school of the University of Texas on the grounds that substantially equivalent facilities were already available in another Texas school open to blacks only. Ruling in the case *Sweat v. Painter*, the Court ruled that the petitioner be admitted to the University of Texas Law School, since "in terms of number of the faculty, variety of courses and opportunity for specialization, size of the student body, scope of the library, availability of law review and similar activities, the University of Texas Law School is superior."

In 1952 five different cases, all dealing with segregation in public schools but with different facts and from different places, reached the Supreme Court. Four of the cases, *Brown v. Board of Education of Topeka* (out of Kansas), *Briggs v. Elliott* (out of South Carolina), *Davis v. Prince Edward County School Board* (out of Virginia), and *Gebhart v. Belton* (out of Delaware), were considered together; the fifth case, *Bolling v. Sharpe*, coming out of the District of Columbia, was considered separately since the district is not a state.

After hearing initial arguments, the Court found itself unable to reach an agreement. In 1953 the Court heard re-argument. Thurgood Marshall, legal consul for the NAACP Legal Defense and Education Fund, presented arguments on behalf of the black students. On May 17, 1954, the Court unanimously ruled that segregation in all public education deprived minority children of equal protection under the Fourteenth Amendment. (In the Bolling case, the Court determined that segregation violated provisions of the Fifth Amendment, since the Fourteenth Amendment is expressly directed to the states.)

Predominantly black colleges and universities continue to impact the number of graduates and the professional growth of African Americans. Although opportunities are embraced by African Americans to attend majority white institutions, Historic Black Colleges and Universities (HBCUs,) which only make up three percent of institutions of higher learning, continue to produce a significant portion of graduates and professionals. This is especially true in the areas of science, mathematics, and engineering. As the percentage of African American students enrolled in HBCUs continues to decline, the influence of HBCUs remains a strong force in educating African Americans. In 1964 more than 51 percent of all blacks in college were still enrolled in the historically black colleges and universities. By 1970 the proportion was 28 percent, and by fall of 1978, 16.5 percent. As noted in 1977, 38 percent of all blacks receiving baccalaureate degrees earned them at HBCUs. In 1980 there were 190,989 African Americans were enrolled at historically black institutions. In 1988 the total black enrollment reached 217,462, and by 2011 more than 370,000 African Americans or approximately 12 percent of all black college students enrolled at historically black colleagues and universities. In considering degrees HBCUs produce 23 percent of all baccalaureate, 13 percent of all master's degrees, and 20 percent of all first professional degrees earned by African Americans.

The influence of HBCUs remains strong as over half of all professional African Americans are graduates of HBCUs, over 70 percent of African American physicians and dentist, 50 percent of African American public school teachers, 60 percent of engineers, and 40 percent of health professionals all graduated from HBCUs. HBCUs make up nine of the top ten colleges that graduate most of the African American students who go on to earn Ph.Ds. Although the percentage of African American enrollment in HBCUs has declined, the most successful of educated African Americans in many areas are products of these institutions.

For years independent schools have been founded in order to exert greater control, ensure quality in education, and to meet the needs of African American children.

In 1932, in order to promote religious growth in the Muslim community, the Nation of Islam founded the University of Islam, an ele-

mentary and secondary school to educate black Muslim children in Detroit. Clara Muhammad, wife of Elijah Muhammad, served as the school's first instructor. In 1934 a second school was opened in Chicago; by 1965 schools were operating in Atlanta and Washington, D.C. The current system of black Muslim schools, named for Clara Muhammad, is an outgrowth of the earlier University of Islam. As of 1992 there were thirty-eight Sister Clara Muhammad schools in the United States.

Gertrude Wilks and other black community leaders in East Palo Alto, California, in 1966 organized the Nairobi Day School, a Saturday school. In 1969 the school became a full-time school, then closed in 1984.

Also founded as a Saturday school program in 1972, the New Concept Development Center in Chicago set out to create an educational institution that promoted self-respect, cooperation,

While it is now common to see African American students in college, there is still a long way to go before true educational equality exists among all races.

and an awareness of African American history and culture. In 1975 public schoolteacher and nurse Marva Collins founded the Westside Preparatory School in Chicago.

In recent years the educational and social needs of urban youth, particularly African American males, have been given increased attention. Studies show that nearly 40 percent of adult black males are functionally illiterate and that the number of African American males incarcerated far outnumbers the number of black males in college. Addressing these issues, large urban school systems, including Baltimore, Detroit, and Milwaukee, have attempted to create programs that focus on the needs of African American males.

The quality of education for black children remains a function of allocated resources. Efforts at creating alternative schools designed to meet the needs of African American children and to reflect the culture and social experiences of blacks received increased attention. In 1991 the Institute for Independent Education, an organization providing technical assistance to independent neighborhood schools, reported an estimated three hundred such schools serving children of color in the United States.

The African-centered thrust in education has sparked national enthusiasm, debates, and attacks. Whereas many people of African descent see this as a dream come true, others see Afrocentrism as an attack on American fundamentalism.

American fundamentalism can be defined as a Eurocentric world view based on the myth of white supremacy. In other words, the fundamental principles of education in America have been rooted in the theory that whites are superior and that all people of color are inferior. This myth of white supremacy laid the foundation for manifest destiny and eminent domain, thereby giving justification for the annihilation of the Native Americans and the enslavement of Africans.

Afrocentrism is not just historical facts and figures centered around time and space. Afro-

centrism is based on the principles of truth, justice, balance, and order. Afrocentrism presents to black students their own cultural life experiences. The classroom is transformed into a holistic learning environment in which the student is the center. Although Afrocentrism benefits all students, the overall thrust of African-centered education is the re-centering of children of African descent

Many African American children do not graduate, they simply drop out. They become statistics at juvenile centers, group homes, foster care, adoption agencies, prison yards, and graveyards. They are often referred to by such code names as "at risk" and "inner city youth." They are at risk because they often are already within the cycle of failure.

This Eurocentric definition of education, according to many, will continue to change in the twenty-first century. Educating children must be based on the principles of self-determination in which African Americans define, defend, and develop what is in their best interest. African-centered education can instill in youth a sense of self-confidence, pride, and responsibility.

Well into the twenty-first century, blacks continue to be a disproportionate presence in the prison system making up 47 percent of the prison population, and 40 percent of them are black males between the age of seventeen and twenty-seven. Inadequate education along with poverty in urban communities are contributors to high incarceration rates.

In January 8, 2002, the No Child Left Behind Act was signed into law by President George W. Bush. The Act was designed to close the achievement gap between whites and nonwhites. The assessment of the schools, known as the Nation's Report Card, suggested in 2005 that the achievement gap was lessening. Other educators disagreed with the improvement due to lack of funding, distribution of funds, and the lack of the federal government's commitment to imposing mandates in relationship to funding. Others charge that white schools are able to use political clout, not available to minority schools, to obtain waivers from compliance. The central issue continues to reflect the *Brown v Board of Education of Topeka* (1954) controversy of racial isolation. Lacking clout and the ability to practically choose private schools over a failing public school, the African American community may be subjected to the inequities and isolation of a failing school and become "left behind" in this program.

Although some improvement in the achievement of African American students has been realized, the academic gap still remains. More and more community-based schools are offering an independent education that incorporates issues of culture and social experience, as suggested in the African-centered education, as well as meeting the needs of the student. In 1999 the Institute for Independent Education, which offers technical assistance to independent schools, estimated sixty thousand African American children attended community-based schools. The Harlem Children's Zone, a charter school run by Geoffrey Canada, a graduate of Bowdoin College and the Harvard School of Education, is one such school. It is located within a sixty block area in Harlem, New York, and has developed a successful program. The school, which is located in an area of poverty and decay, combines education with social and medical services. Single-gendered schools are also seeing an increasing trend to meet the need of the community. Particularly with the increase in the incarceration and lack of education for African American males, schools like Urban Prep Academy, a charter high school in Chicago, set out to meet the challenge. In 2010 they graduated their first class of 107 young men with 100 percent bound for college.

"Race to the Top" is a program conceived in 2010 by the administration of President Barack Obama in which the Department of Education awards funding to schools and communities that meet a federal criteria for improving education. This government program differs from other programs in that it supports a bottom-up approach through local vouchers, parochial schools, and charter schools verses top-down, or administrative-focused reformation.

BIOGRAPHIES

Molefi Asante (1942–)
University Professor, Author

Asante was born Arthur Lee Smith Jr. on August 14, 1942, in Valdosta, Georgia. His name was legally changed in 1975. He graduated cum laude with a B.A. from Oklahoma Christian College in 1964, received an M.A. from Pepperdine University in 1965, and a Ph.D. from UCLA in 1968.

Asante has taught speech and communications at many universities in the United States. Beginning in 1966 he was an instructor at California State Polytechnic University at Pomona and California State University at Northridge. In 1968 he accepted an assistant professorship at Purdue University in Lafayette, Indiana, where he remained until 1969 when he began teaching at UCLA, advancing from assistant to associate professor of speech. While at UCLA he also served as the director of the Center for Afro-American Studies. In 1973 he accepted the position of professor of communications at the State University of New York. He soon became department chairman, a position he held until 1979 when he became a visiting professor at Howard University in Washington, D.C. In 1981 and 1982 he was a Fulbright Professor at the Zimbabwe Institute of Mass Communications. Since 1980 he has been a professor at Temple University in Philadelphia in the school's Department of Pan African Studies.

Asante is a prolific author with more than twenty-four books dealing with both communication theory and the African American experience. He has published books under both his former and his current name. Some of his recent titles are *Afrocentricity: The Theory of Social Change* (1980), *African Culture: The Rhythms of Unity* (1985), and *The Historical and Cultural Atlas of African Americans* (1991).

Asante is also a founding editor of the *Journal of Black Studies* and has been a member of the advisory board of the *Black Law Journal* and *Race Relations Abstract*.

Lerone Bennett Jr. (1928–)
Historian, Editor

Lerone Bennett Jr. was born in Clarksdale, Mississippi, on October 17, 1928. His family later moved to Jackson, Mississippi. Bennett attended Morehouse College in Atlanta, Georgia, and earned a B.A. degree in 1949. He began his career working for the *Atlanta Daily World* and went on to work for *Jet* magazine and *Ebony* magazine. With *Ebony* Bennett moved up the ranks and was promoted to senior editor in 1958 and executive editor in 1987.

Bennett's historical essays and other writings have made him an influential historian and scholar in the African American community. He explores the issues of race in America and the struggle for equality. Bennett's biography of Martin Luther King Jr., *What Manner of Man* (1964), and the texts *Before the Mayflower: A History of the Negro in America* (1962) and *Forced into Glory: Abraham Lincoln's White Dream* (2000) are among his most outstanding literary contributions. In 2002 Bennett won the American Book Award for lifetime achievement. After more than fifty years, Bennett continues to serve on the editorial staff of *Ebony* magazine.

Mary McLeod Bethune (1875–1955)
Educator, Founder of Bethune-Cookman College

Born on July 10, 1875, in Mayesville, South Carolina, Mary McLeod Bethune received a sporadic education in local schools. She eventually received a scholarship and studied for seven years at the Scotia Seminary in Concord, North Carolina. In 1893 she went on to study at the Moody Bible Institute in Chicago in lieu of a missionary position in Africa. In 1895 she began teaching at the Haines Institute in Augusta, Georgia. Between 1900 and 1904 she taught in Sumter, Georgia, and Palatka, Florida.

In 1904 she founded her own school in Daytona Beach, Florida—the Daytona Educational and Industrial School for Negro Girls. John D. Rockefeller became an early admirer and supporter of the school after hearing a performance by its choir. Bethune went on to found the Tomoka Missions and in 1911 the McLeod Hospital. In 1922 her school merged with the Cookman Institute to become Bethune-Cookman College.

Bethune's work received national attention, and she served on two conferences under President Herbert Hoover. In 1936 President Franklin D. Roosevelt appointed her director of the Division of Negro Affairs of the National Youth Administration. During World War II she served as special assistant to the secretary of war, responsible for selecting Negro WAC officer candidates.

Bethune also served on the executive board of the National Urban League and was a vice president of the NAACP. She received the Spingarn Medal Award in 1935, the Frances A. Drexel Award in 1936, and the Thomas Jefferson Medal in 1942. Bethune was also instrumental in the founding of the National Council of Negro Women. She retired from public life in 1950 on her seventy-fifth birthday and died five years later on May 18, 1955.

Much of Bethune's philosophy involved ennobling labor and empowering African Americans to achieve economic independence. Although a tireless fighter for equality, she eschewed rhetorical militancy in favor of a doctrine of universal love.

Charlotte Hawkins Brown (1883–1961)
Educator, School Founder

Charlotte Hawkins Brown was born Lottie Hawkins on June 11, 1883, in Henderson, North Carolina. When she was seven, her family moved to Cambridge, Massachusetts, to provide a better life for Hawkins and her siblings. She excelled in her schoolwork and by graduation she had changed her name to Charlotte Eugenia to give a more dignified impression. In 1900 Brown enrolled in State Normal School in Salem. After her second year she accepted a job as a teacher at the American Missionary Association Bethany Institute in Sedalia, North Carolina. The school closed a year later.

With the close of the school in Sedalia, Brown was determined, with the help of the community and Northern philanthropists, to open another school. On October 10, 1902, the Alice Freeman Palmer Institute was opened in honor of her friend and mentor. Palmer had provided assistance and guidance to Brown from the time she entered State Normal School. By 1907, when Palmer died, Brown had completed State Normal School, and had taken classes at Harvard University as well as Wellesley and Simmons Colleges. Brown wrote many short stories, essays, and books, but the most famous were "Mammy: An Appeal to the Heart of the South," written in 1919, and a book on social graces, *The Correct Things to Do, to Say, and to Wear*, written in 1941.

Brown continued in her efforts to provide opportunities for African Americans while expanding the school. She was a co-founder of the National Council of Negro Women and served on the board of the YWCA among many other organizations. She was an advocate for civil rights and women's rights. Brown retired from Palmer Institute in 1952 and died in 1961, a decade before the school closed due to financial reasons.

Nannie Helen Burroughs (1879–1961)
Educator

Known as a brilliant orator, Burroughs was a lifelong booster of women's education and a tireless civic organizer. In 1901 the National Training School for Women and Girls opened in Washington, D.C., with Burroughs as president; by the end of the first school year the school had enrolled thirty-one students. In 1934 the name was changed to the National Trades and Professional School for Women. In 1964 the school was again renamed the Nannie Helen Burroughs School, with a new elementary school curriculum.

Burroughs was active in the anti-lynching campaign and a member of the Association for the Study of Negro Life and History. She helped organize the Women's Industrial Club of Louisville and was responsible for organizing Washington, D.C.'s first black self-help program.

Joe Clark (1938–)
Educator, High School Principal

Best known as the feisty, dedicated, baseball bat-wielding school principal portrayed in the film *Lean on Me,* Clark has served as an exemplar of school discipline and boasts a distinguished record of achievements and laurels. A fourteen-year member of the New Jersey Board of Education and an elementary and secondary school principal since 1979, he has been honored by the White House, the NAACP, his alma mater Seton Hall University, and various newspapers and magazines.

Born in Rochelle, Georgia, Clark served in the U.S. Army Reserve from 1958 to 1966. He received a B.A. from New Jersey's William Paterson College in 1960 and his master's degree from Seton Hall in 1974. Between the degrees he served on the Board of Education, and from 1976 to 1979 he was a coordinator of language arts. He then began his career as school principal, and only a few years after he began, the accolades came pouring in. Clark received the NAACP Community Service Award and was named New Jerseyan of the Year by the *Newark Star Ledger* in 1983; the next year *New Jersey Monthly* named him an outstanding educator. In 1985 Clark appeared in Washington, D.C., to receive honors at a presidential conference on academic and disciplinary excellence, and he also took awards from Seton Hall and Farleigh Dickinson University. The National School Safety Center gave Clark the Principal of Leadership Award in 1986 and the National Black Policemen's Association bestowed their Humanitarian Award upon him in 1988.

Clark went on the lecture circuit in 1990, inspiring others. He became director of Essex County Detention House for juveniles in Newark, New Jersey, in August 1995, and in 1996

Clark was chosen as Speaker of the Year by the National Association of Campus Activities.

Kenneth Clark (1914–2005)
Scholar, Social Scientist

Clark was born in the Panama Canal Zone on July 24, 1914, and later moved to Harlem, New York. He received his B.A. in 1935 and his M.S. in 1936 from Howard University. In 1940 Clark was the first African American to earn a Ph.D. from Columbia University. After teaching a brief time at Hampton Institute he moved to City College of New York in 1942, where he remained for the duration of his academic career.

Clark was a key factor in the *Brown v Board of Education of Topeka* of 1954. He had studied the effects of school segregation and served as an expert witness at three of the four cases. His study was a pinnacle document that was read by the justices of the *Brown v Board* case. The doll test, which is the most famous research of Clark and his wife Mamie Phipps Clark, proved that black children had internalized racism by rejecting dolls like themselves and viewing white dolls as good. This was the result of being discriminated against. Clark's contribution made him the premier African American scholar and social scientist of his generation.

Clark worked with programs such as the Harlem Youth Organization Unlimited (HARYOU) that tried to improve integration in public schools. In 1975 he retired from City College and started his own consulting firm to integrate the workforces of the public schools and City College. Clark died on May 1, 2005.

Septima Clark (1898–1987)
Educator, Community Activist

Septima Clark, born on May 3, 1898, in Charleston, South Carolina, was one of eight children born to Peter Poinsette, who was born a slave, and Victoria Warren Anderson Poinsette, who was born free. Clark completed the twelfth grade in 1916 from Avery Institute. She took the

state examination and received a Licentiate of Instruction which allowed her to teach in rural areas. African Americans were not allowed to teach in the public schools of Charleston. Her first position, which was on John's Island, was for a community with poor economic, social, and health conditions. Clark realized it was through education and the rights one has as a citizen that this community could effect a positive change. As a result, Clark dedicated her life to this mission.

In 1937 Clark attended Atlanta University and studied under W.E.B. DuBois and later received her B.A. from Benedict College in 1942. She received her M.A. from Hampton Institute in 1946. After returning to Charleston to teach in the public school system Clark started "citizenship schools" in 1956 at Tennessee's Highland Folk School, a center for civil organizations. When the participation had outgrown the facility, the Southern Christian Leadership Conference (SCLC) offered to take over. Clark became the director of education for the SCLC.

Clark continued her work in educating her community and remained active in the civil rights struggle. She retired from the SCLC in 1974. In 1979 Clark was presented with a Living Legacy Award by President Jimmy Carter. In 1982 she received the Order of the Palmetto, South Carolina's highest award. Clark died on December 15, 1987, in Charleston, South Carolina.

Johnnetta Cole (1936–)
College President

A distinguished scholar, Johnnetta Betsch Cole served on the faculties of Washington State University, University of Massachusetts, Hunter College, and Spelman College, the historically black women's institution in Atlanta, Georgia. Born in Jacksonville, Florida, on October 19, 1936, Cole attended Oberlin College, earning a B.A. in 1957. She went on to earn both her master's degree in 1959 and her doctorate in 1967 from Northwestern University.

Cole held her first teaching post at Washington State University, where she taught anthropology and served as director of black studies. The university dubbed her Outstanding Faculty Member of the Year for 1969 to 1970. As an anthropologist, Cole has done field work in Liberia, Cuba, and in the African American community. A prolific writer, she published in many mainstream periodicals as well as scholarly journals, and contributed and advised the editor of *The Black Scholar*. She headed the Association of Black Anthropologists in 1980, was a fellow of the American Anthropological Association beginning in 1970, and was a board member of the Center for Cuban Studies beginning in 1971.

Cole was a professor of anthropology, at the University of Massachusetts—Amherst from 1970 to 1983, and Hunters College of the City of New York from 1983 to 1987. In 1987 Cole was named president of Spelman College, a women's college and a Historically Black College (HBCU) in Atlanta, Georgia. After retiring from Spelman in 1997 Cole took a professorship at Emory University in Atlanta, Georgia. In 2002 Cole was again chosen as president of an HBCU, Bennett College in Greensboro, North Carolina. After five years of strong leadership and aggressive fundraising, Cole brought Bennett College back from a downward financial spiral. Cole retired in 2007 from Bennett.

Cole has received numerous awards for her scholarship, her service to the community, her leadership and commitment to the African American community and global communities, and her accomplishments. She has also received over forty honorary degrees, the 1990 American Women Award, the Smithsonian's McGovern Behavioral Science Award in 1999, the 2001 Service Award from the United Way of America, and the John W. Gardner Leadership Award in 2006.

Marva Delores Nettles Collins (1936–)
Educator

Schoolteacher Marva Delores Nettles Collins's dedication and ingenuity moved the producers of television's *60 Minutes* to broadcast a feature about her and even inspired a made-for-television film.

The Monroeville, Alabama, native received a bachelor's degree from Clark College in 1957, after which she attended Northwestern University; her teaching career began at the Monroe County Training School in her hometown in 1958. She taught at Delano Elementary School from 1960 to 1975 and has been a fixture at Chicago's Westside Preparatory School ever since.

Collins served as director of the Right to Read Foundation in 1978, and has been a member of the President's Commission on White House Fellowships since 1981. A variety of organizations have honored her, including the NAACP, the Reading Reform Foundation, the Fred Hampton Foundation, and the American Institute for Public Service. Among the institutions that have given her honorary degrees are Washington University, Amherst, Dartmouth, Chicago State University, Howard University, and Central State University.

Anna Julia Cooper (1858–1964)
Civil Rights and Women's Rights Activist, Author

 Cooper was born August 10, 1858, in Raleigh, North Carolina, to Hannah Stanley, a slave, and her master, George Washington Haywood. Cooper attended Saint Augustine's Normal School and Collegiate Institute and became a teacher. She also attended Oberlin College graduating in 1884, but returned to Saint Augustine's to teach. After earning an M.A. also from Oberlin in 1888, Cooper moved to Washington, D.C.

Cooper taught at the Preparatory High School for Colored Youth in Washington, D.C., and became principal of the school from 1902 to 1906. The school was renamed M. Street High School and later the Paul Laurence Dunbar High School. Cooper left the school briefly in 1906 to teach at Lincoln University but returned to the M. Street High School in 1910.

On March 23, 1925, at the age of sixty-six, Cooper earned a Ph.D. from the Sorbonne, making her the fourth African American woman and the first woman in France to earn this degree. Cooper had established herself as an advocate for her race, promoter of women's rights, a lecturer, a writer, and an educator. As a writer she is best known for the text *A Voice from the South* (1892). Cooper died on February 27, 1964, at the age of 105.

Fanny Coppin (1873–1913)
Educator

Fanny Jackson Coppin was born in slavery but rose to prominence in the field of education. After her aunt purchased her freedom, Coppin went on to become the second African American woman to receive a degree from Oberlin College.

Coppin was appointed principal of the women's department of the Institute for Colored Youth, a high school established by Quakers in 1837, and later principal of the entire school. In 1894 Coppin founded the Women's Exchange and Girls' Home. She served as president of the local Women's Mite Missionary Society and the Women's Home and Foreign Missionary Society, and as a vice president of the National Association of Colored Women.

Coppin, an active member of the African Methodist Episcopal Church, served as president of the AME Home Missionary Society and accompanied her husband, Levi J. Coppin, on a missionary venture to South Africa.

Before her death Coppin began writing an autobiography, *Reminiscences of School Life, and Hints on Teaching*.

Howard Dodson Jr. (1939–)
Historian, Author

Born in Chester, Pennsylvania, on June 1, 1939, Howard Dodson Jr. was a top student who earned his B.S. from West Chester State College in 1961, and in 1964 earned an M.A. in history and political science from Villanova University. Dodson was highly interested in the removal of African people to the Western Hemisphere and went on to enter a doctorial program in black history and race relations at the University of California in Berkeley.

Dodson wrote extensively about African American history. He served as editor of *Black World View* magazine in 1977 and published several books, including *Black Photographers Bear Witness: 100 Years of Social Protest* (1989). He was awarded the Association for the Study of Afro-American Life and the History Service Award in 1976 and a Governor's Award for African Americans of distinction in 1982.

In 1984 Dodson took the position as head of the Schomburg Center for Research in Black Culture at the New York Public Library. He was such an effective manager and fundraiser that in 1991 the Center expanded the complex. Dodson has served as consultant to the National Endowment for the Humanities, the African American Museums Association, and the Congressional Black Caucus.

Under Dodson's guidance the Center has a collection of more than ten million items. After more than twenty-seven years of service Dodson retired from the Center in February 2011.

Michael Eric Dyson (1958–)
Scholar, Author, Lecturer

On October 23, 1958, Michael Eric Dyson was born in Detroit, Michigan. Early on in his education he attended Cranbrook Boarding School in Bloomfield Hills, Michigan, for two years. He completed his education at Cass Technical High School in Detroit and later was ordained as a Baptist minister. Dyson attended divinity school at Knoxville College in Tennessee and in 1982 he received his B.A., magna cum laude, from Carson-Newman College. He earned his M.A. in 1991 and his Ph.D. in religion from Princeton University.

Dyson began teaching as an assistant professor at Brown University. His interests were focused toward a larger audience than just the collegiate community. Along with teaching, Dyson wrote film reviews, became a columnist for *Christian Century* and *The Nation*, and wrote his first book, a collection of essays. While seeking to address issues relevant to African American cultural and political concerns he wrote the text *Between God and Gangsta Rap* in 1997. His placement of rap within the cultural context of the African American experience brought him to the attention of the major media. He was considered an authority on this cultural medium and subsequently was asked to speak before a congressional committee, give lecturers on the genre, and to serve as a guest on talk shows.

In 1996 Dyson was appointed as head of the Institute of African American Research at the University of North Carolina at Chapel Hill. He also taught at Columbia University and DePauw University in Chicago before joining the faculty at Penn State in 2002 as the Avalon Foundation Professor in the Humanities and African American Studies.

Dyson continues to bring open, honest, and intellectual discourse to issues of race and other factors which affect the African American community, primarily in the area of pop culture and American influence on African American society. In 2004 Dyson questioned the comments of Bill Cosby regarding Cosby's awareness of all the factors that impact social and economic behavior of lower income African Americans. In 2007 he published *Know What I Mean?: Reflections on Hip Hop* and on April 6, 2009, Dyson started his own radio show with Oprah Winfrey as his first guest. He dedicated to her his seventeenth book, *Can You Hear Me Now?: The Inspiration, Wisdom and Insight of Michael Eric Dyson*.

John Hope Franklin (1915–2009)
Scholar

Franklin's long and distinguished career has included the publication of numerous books of history and biography, numerous awards and honorary degrees, and a position of great stature in the scholarly community.

Franklin was born in Rentiesville, Oklahoma. He received his bachelor's degree from Fisk University in 1935 and then began graduate work at Harvard, which awarded him a master's in 1936 and a Ph.D. in 1941. He taught history at Fisk and St. Augustine's College while working on his doctorate, later moving on to North Carolina College at Durham, Howard University, Brooklyn College (where he chaired the history department), Cambridge University, the University of Chicago, and Duke University. In 1982 Franklin became the James B. Duke professor emeritus of history at Duke.

Among his many publications are such books as *From Slavery to Freedom: A History of Negro Americans* (1947; ninth edition, 2011), *Militant South* (1956), *Reconstruction after the Civil War* (1961), *The Emancipation Proclamation* (1963), *A Southern Odyssey* (1971), and *Race and History: Selected Essays 1938–88* (1990). Franklin continued to write well into his eighties, publishing texts such as the 1998 biography of historian George Washington Williams, co-authoring *Runaway Slaves: Rebels on the Plantation 1790–1860* (1999), and his autobiography, *Mirror to America* (2005).

Twice a Guggenheim Fellow, Franklin received honors from the Fellowship of Southern Writers, Encyclopedia Britannica, and the Publications Prize of the American Studies Association established in his name in 1986. Among numerous other awards, in 1995 he was awarded the Presidential Medal of Freedom by President Bill Clinton and awarded a Harold Washington Literary Award in 2000 for his impressive body of work as an historian. In 2006 Franklin was co-recipient of the Kluge Prize for lifetime achievement in the study of humanity.

In 1997 Franklin was appointed by President Bill Clinton as chair of the White House Initiative on Race and Reconciliation. This initiative allowed various cities and communities across the nation to have a dialogue about the topic of race in America. Many articles, documentaries, and books have been written about John Hope Franklin and his contributions to the study of African American history, his community, and the nation. On March 25, 2009, Franklin died of congestive heart failure.

E. Franklin Frazier (1894–1962)
Sociologist, Activist

Edward Franklin Frazier was born in Baltimore, Maryland, on September 24, 1894. Frazier graduated from Colored High School in 1912 and won a scholarship to Howard University in Washington, D.C. After graduating in 1916, Frazier began teaching at various universities and high schools and spent time in the military. In 1919 he was awarded a scholarship to Clark University in Worcester, Massachusetts, and completed his master's degree in sociology in 1920.

Between 1921 and 1922 Frazier worked as a research fellow at the New York School of Social Work. In the fall of 1922 he moved to Atlanta and accepted a position as a professor of sociology and director of the Atlanta School of Social Work. Frazier combined the teaching of sociology with practical usage. Continuing to research and study primarily the African American family, he began his graduate work for his Ph.D. While pursuing his Ph.D. Frazier found his scholarly focus, which later became known as the "Chicago School of Sociology." He received a fellowship from the University of Chicago and taught at Fisk University while completing his dissertation. In 1932 he received his Ph.D. and published his dissertation, *The Negro Family in Chicago*. In 1934 Frazier was named director of the Department of Sociology at Howard University, and in 1959 he retired and became professor emeritus in sociology and the african studies program. Frazier was also given the American Sociological Association's MacIver Award in 1948 for his contributions in the field of sociology.

Frazier was a prolific writer and wrote numerous books and articles. His works include *Negro Youth at the Crossways: Their Personality Development in the Middle States* (1940), *The Negro in the United States* (1949), and *Black Bour-*

geoisie (1957). Frazier traveled with the United Nations Educational Scientific and Cultural Organization (UNESCO) to Paris, Africa, and Middle Eastern countries. This helped to expand his work to include the struggles of all peoples of African descent. Frazier's last book was *The Negro Church in America,* which was published posthumously in 1964.

Franklin died on May 17, 1962. The Howard University School of Social Work created the E. Franklin Frazier Research Center, inaugurated May 24, 2000, in honor of Frazier's scholarship and his contribution to the university.

Henry Louis Gates Jr. (1950–)
Scholar, Author

 Henry Louis Gates Jr. was born in Keyser, West Virginia, on September 16, 1950. He earned his B.A. in history, summa cum laude, from Yale University in 1973. While attending Clare College in Cambridge, Gates earned a master's degree in 1974 and a Ph.D. in 1979. After graduation he began his academic career as assistant professor of English and director of the Afro-American studies department at Yale University.

In 1981 Gates was selected for a Mac Arthur Foundation Award and went on to republish in 1983 the first novel written by an African American, Harriet E. Wilson's *Our Nig, or, Sketches from the Life of a Free Black in a Two-Story White House, North Showing That Slavery's Shadows Fall Even There*. This publication brought attention to Gates and his scholarship regarding the study of African American literature and culture. From 1983 to 1990 Gates was the recipient of National Endowment of the Arts grants, a PBS television series, a Rockefeller Foundation fellowship, as well as professor of English and African Studies at Cornell University, and the W.E.B. DuBois Professor of Literature at Duke University. In 1990 Gates accepted a position at Harvard University as the W.E.B. DuBois Professor in the Humanities, and in 1991 as chair of the African American studies department.

Gates' writings have been recognized with an American Book Award in 1989 for the book *Signifying Monkey*, and in 1994 he published his memoirs, *Colored People*. He has written numerous books, unearthed lost or ignored periodicals and manuscripts by African Americans, produced a fifty-two-volume series on African American women of the nineteenth century for the Schomburg Center in New York, and developed a multimedia encyclopedia of African American and African culture, *Encarta Africana*.

Gates made national news on July 16, 2009, when he was arrested for breaking into his own Cambridge, Massachusetts, residence. Although he identified himself to the police, he was still arrested. This situation brought cries of racism and further acknowledgment of racial profiling. Although the local police denied allegations of racist conduct, the situation resulted in Gates being invited to the White House after President Barack Obama weighed in on the arrest. On July 30, President Obama, Vice President Joseph Biden, Henry Louis Gates Jr., and the arresting officer, James Crawley, met to discuss the situation.

Gates, currently the Alphonse Fletcher University Professor and director of the W.E.B DuBois Institute of African and African American Research, is the editor and chief of the Oxford African American Studies Center, the first online resource in African American studies and African studies. In 2006 Gates wrote and produced the PBS Documentary *African American Lives*, which utilized genealogy and genetic science to explore African American lives. This production resulted in the book *In Search of Our Roots* (2009). The second part of the series *African American Lives #2* aired in February 2008. The documentary *Looking for Lincoln* aired in February 2009.

mother, was born in Hopkinsville, Kentucky, on September 25, 1952. Hooks's education, which spanned segregated schools and the transition to integrated schools, was a difficult time. Hooks graduated from Hopkinsville High School and earned her B.A. in English from Stanford University in 1973 and her M.A. in English from the University of Wisconsin in 1976. She completed her Ph.D. in 1983 from the University of California, Santa Cruz.

Hooks's academic career began in 1976 as she taught at the University of California and several other institutions. Her first published work was a book of poetry in 1978 and was followed by *Ain't I a Woman: Black Women and Feminism*. This publication placed Hooks in the forefront of black women's issues centering around racism and sexism. Her works continued to focus on the marginalization of women and key issues of race, class, and gender.

Hooks has written over thirty books, including *Talking Back: Thinking Feminist, Thinking Black* (1989), *Happy to Be Nappy* (1999), *Communion: The Female Search for Love* (2002), *Soul Sister: Women, Friendship, and Fulfillment* (2005), *Witness* (2006), and *Teaching Critical Thinking: Practical Wisdom* (2010). Hooks has received numerous awards for her writings and has held a position in African and African American studies and English departments at Yale University, associate professor of women's studies and American literature at Oberlin College, and distinguished lecturer of English literature at the City College of New York.

In 2004 Hooks took the position of distinguished professor in residence at Berea College in Berea, Kentucky.

bell hooks (1952–)
Feminist Scholar, Author

Gloria Jean Watkins, known as "bell hooks," a name taken in honor of her mother and grand-

Ben Jealous (1973–)
President of the NAACP, Community Activist

Ben Jealous became the seventeenth president and chief executive officer of the National Association for the Advancement of Colored People (NAACP) and the youngest person to hold this position in its over one-hundred-year history.

Benjamin Todd Jealous was born on January 18, 1973, in Pacific Grove, California, and grew up in Peninsula, California. As a child his family's involvement with the NAACP and community betterment left a lasting impression on him. He spent summers with his grandparents in Baltimore's Ashburton neighborhood. They were active members in the NAACP. His mother, who is black, was said to be among the first students to desegregate Western High School. His father, who is white, took part in sit-ins to desegregate Baltimore's lunch counters.

Jealous earned his B.A. in 1996 from Columbia University in political science, and in 1998, as a Rhodes Scholar, he earned an M.S. in comparative social research at Oxford University in England. While a student at Columbia, Jealous took an internship with the NAACP Legal Defense Fund. On campus he led successful campaigns for homeless rights and the continuation of full-need financial aid. Protests eventually led to his suspension, along with three other students. While on suspension he became a community organizer in Mississippi and led the campaign for HBCU Initiatives that prevented the closing of two of its three public historically black universities and the conversion of one to a prison. He also served as the managing editor of the *Jackson Advocate*, an historic black newspaper.

From 1999 to 2002 Jealous served as the executive director of the National Newspaper Publishers Association (NNP), an organization of more than 200 black-run newspapers. He launched a Web-based initiative that doubled the number of black newspapers publishing online.

Jealous was director of the U.S. human rights program at Amnesty Internal from 2002 to 2005. He led efforts there against issues such as prison rap, and racial profiling, and from 2005 to 2008 he served as president of the San Francisco-based Rosenberg Foundation, a private nonprofit organization that funds civil and human rights advocacy for California's working families.

Jealous was elected by a sixty-four member board of the NAACP to become the seventeenth president after the resignation of previous president Bruce S. Gordon, who resigned abruptly in March 2007.

He is a board member of the California Council for the Humanities and the Association of Black Foundation Executives, and is a member of the Asia Society.

Charles Spurgeon Johnson (1893–1956)
Scholar, University President

Charles Spurgeon Johnson was born in Bristol, Virginia. He earned a B.A. from Virginia Union University and a Ph.D. from the University of Chicago.

Johnson occupied a number of diverse positions, from editor to administrator. He served as the assistant executive secretary of the Chicago Commission on Race Relations and as research director of the National Urban League, where he founded the organization's journal, *Opportunity*.

In 1928 Johnson was made chairman of Fisk University's Department of Social Sciences, and while there he established the Fisk Institute of Race Relations. In 1933 he was appointed director of Swarthmore College's Institute of Race Relations. In 1946 Johnson was appointed president of Fisk University—the first black to hold the position.

Johnson wrote several books, including *The Negro in American Civilization* (1930), *The Economic Status of the Negro* (1933), *The Negro College Graduate* (1936), and *Educational and Cultural Crisis* (1951).

Mordecai W. Johnson (1890–1976)
University President, Minister

Mordecai Wyatt Johnson was born in Paris, Tennessee, on December 12, 1890. He received a graduate degree from Atlanta Baptist College in

Atlanta, Georgia, and earned a bachelor of divinity degree from Rochester Theological Seminary in Rochester, New York. After being pastor for nine years at the First Baptist Church in Charleston, West Virginia, Johnson decided to continue his graduate studies. In 1912 Johnson attended Harvard Divinity School and graduated in June 1922.

In 1926 Johnson was selected as the eleventh president of Howard University and its first African American president. Although he was criticized by some for not having a terminal degree he was able to create a strong financial foundation for the university and attract some of the most talented persons of the era to the school, including graduate Thurgood Marshall, dean of the law school Charles Hamilton Houston, faculty Alain Locke, historian Rayford Logan, and scientist Charles Drew. Johnson retired from Howard in 1960 after thirty-four years as president and died on September 10, 1976, at the age of eighty-six.

Laurence Clifton Jones (1882–1975)
School Founder, Administrator

Jones was born November 21, 1882, in St. Joseph, Missouri. He was the first African American to graduate from Marshall High School in Marshall, Iowa. Jones attended Central Iowa Business College for a short time and later enrolled in the University of Iowa. He graduated in 1907.

In 1910 Jones started a school in Piney Wood, Mississippi, which was twenty-two miles southeast of Jackson, Mississippi. Through support from the community the Piney Woods School was officially founded on May 17, 1913. Jones and his wife Grace, whom he married in 1912, traveled around fundraising for the school. The Cotton Blossom singers and later the International Sweethearts of Rhythm performed concerts to help support the school financially. In 1954 Jones was selected to be on an episode of the Ralph Edwards television show *This Is Your*

Life. During the show Edwards appealed to his audience to send $1 to support Piney Woods School. As a result the school received $700,000 which was their original endowment fund. The school was damaged by Hurricane Katrina in 2005 but has since been repaired.

Over the years Jones wrote several books, including *Piney Woods and Its Story* (1922). He received several honorary doctorates and an honorary master's degree from Tuskegee University. Jones retired from the presidency in 1974 and died in 1975.

Maulana Karenga (1941–)
Scholar, Activist

Maulana Karenga was born Ronald McKinley on July 14, 1941, in Parsonsburg, Maryland. In the 1950s Karenga's family moved to California. In 1963 he graduated from the University of California in Los Angeles, cum laude, with a degree in political science and in 1964 he earned his M.A. also in political science with a specialization in African studies. Karenga received his first Ph.D. in 1976 from the United States International University in political science and in 1994 a second Ph.D. in social ethics with a focus on the classical African ethics of ancient Egypt from the University of Southern California.

In the 1960s, Karenga founded Us, a cultural and social organization that focuses on black people. He also at this time took the name Maulana Karenga with the title Maulana meaning "master teacher" in Swahili. The philosophy, Kawaida, that guides the organization, seeks "to synthesize the best of African thought and practice in constant exchange with the world." Karenga and the organization Us were important in Black Power conferences, the development of black student movements, Afrocentricity, Egyptian studies, independent school movements, and black theological and ethical discourse, just to cite a few issues that have impacted the black community from the 1960s to the present. Karenga has served as a member of the executive committee that authored the mission statement for the Million Man March/Day of Absence in 1995 and co-edited the book *The Million Man March/Day of Absence: A Commemorative Anthology*. Karenga currently serves as the national chairman of the Us organization and director of the Kawaida Institute of Pan-African Studies. He maintains the organization's motto, "Anywhere we are, Us is," and the three main goals are struggle, service, and institution building.

Karenga is a noted author and has written numerous books with the best-known being *Kwanzaa: A Celebration of Family, Community and Culture* (second edition, 2008). Karenga instituted the tradition of Kwanzaa, which is practiced in the United States and around the world. Also, in 2008 he published *Kawaida and Question of Life and Struggle: African American, Pan-African and Global Issues*. Karenga's commitment to scholarship and intellectual achievement has been acknowledged with many awards such as the Cheikh Anta Diop Award for Excellence in Scholarship 2004 and 2009. Karenga is professor and chair of the Department of Black Studies at the University of California at Long Beach and chair of the University President's Task Force on Multicultural Education and Campus Diversity.

David Levering Lewis (1936–)
Scholar, Author

Lewis was born in Little Rock, Arkansas, on May 25, 1936. He attended Booker T. Washington High School and entered Fisk University on a four-year Ford Foundation Early Entrants Scholarship. Lewis graduated from Fisk in 1956, Phi Beta Kappa in history and earned a master's degree in 1958 from Columbia University. Lewis earned a Ph.D. in modern European and French history from the London School of Economics and Political Science in 1962.

Lewis taught and lectured on French history at universities such as the University of Ghana, Howard University, Cornell University, the Uni-

versity of Notre Dame, and Harvard University. Lewis began to study and research African American history as another aspect of his scholarship. After publishing a biography of Martin Luther King Jr., *Martin Luther King: A Critical Biography* (1971), Lewis became a full professor of history at the University of the District of Columbia in 1974.

After extensive study of the period known as the Harlem Renaissance, Lewis published *When Harlem Was in Vogue: The Politics of the Arts in the Twenties and Thirties* (1981). Returning to biographies, Lewis did research on the prominent scholar W.E.B. DuBois and published *W.E.B. Du Bois: Biography of a Race, 1868–1919*. He was awarded a Pulitzer Prize and a National Book Award for this publication. After winning a MacArthur Foundation "genius grant" Lewis continued his research and published *W.E.B. Du Bois: The Fight for Equality and the American Century, 1919–1963* (2000). He was awarded a second Pulitzer Prize for this publication.

Lewis has received numerous recognitions, including the John Simon Guggenheim Foundation Award, the Bancroft Prize, and the Frances Parkman Prize. He serves as a trustee of the National Humanities Center, a former senator of Phi Beta Kappa, and president of the Society of American Historians from 2002 to 2003. He continues his scholarship and service as the Julius Silver university professor and professor of history at New York University.

Alaine LeRoy Locke (1886–1954)
Scholar

Born on September 3, 1886, in Philadelphia, Locke graduated Phi Beta Kappa with a B.A. from Harvard University in 1907. He was then awarded a Rhodes Scholarship for two years' study at Oxford University in England and did further graduate study at the University of Berlin. Upon returning to the United States, Locke took an assistant professorship in English and philosophy at Howard University in Washington, D.C. He received his Ph.D. from Harvard in 1918, and the same year was made chairman of the philosophy department at Howard, where he stayed until his retirement in 1953.

In 1934 Locke founded the Associates in Negro Folk Education. In 1942 he was named to the Honor Role of Race Relations. A prolific author, Locke's first book was entitled *Race Contacts and Inter-Racial Relations* (1916). His best known works include *The New Negro: An Interpretation* (1925), a book that introduced America to the Harlem Renaissance, and *The Negro in Art: A Pictorial Record of the Negro Artist and of the Negro Theme in Art* (1940). Locke died in New York City on June 9, 1954.

Benjamin E. Mays (1894–1984)
College President

In addition to occupying the president's office at Morehouse, Benjamin Mays wrote, taught mathematics, worked for the Office of Education, served as chairman of the Atlanta Board of Education, preached in a Baptist church, acted as an advisor to the Southern Christian Leadership Council, and was a church historian.

Born in Epworth, South Carolina, Mays attended Bates College and later received his master's degree and Ph.D. from the University of Chicago. He served as a pastor at Georgia's Shiloh Baptist Church from 1921 to 1924, and later taught at Morehouse College and South Carolina's State College at Orangeburg. After a stint at the Tampa Urban League, he worked for the YMCA as national student secretary and then directed a study of black churches for the Institute of Social and Religious Research. From 1934 to 1940 he acted as dean of Howard University's School of Religion, before taking up the presidency of Morehouse from 1940 to 1967. He served in several other distinguished posts, including the Atlanta Board of Education chairmanship and positions at HEW and the Ford Foundation. Mays earned forty-three honorary degrees and the Dorie Miller Medal of Honor, among others.

Arturo A. Schomburg (1874–1938)
Archivist, American Negro Academy President

Born in Puerto Rico, Schomburg, led a richly varied public life. He worked as a law clerk and was a businessman, journalist, editor, lecturer, New York Public Library curator, and Spanish teacher.

In 1911 Schomburg co-founded the Negro Society for Historical Research. He was also a lecturer for the United Negro Improvement Association. Schomburg was a member of the New York Puerto Rico Revolutionary Party and served as secretary of the Cuban Revolutionary Party. In 1922 he headed the American Negro Academy, an organization founded by Alexander Crummell in 1879 to promote black art, literature, and science.

Schomburg collected thousands of works on black culture during his lifetime. In 1926 Schomburg's personal collection was purchased by the Carnegie Corporation and given to the New York Public Library. In 1973 the collection became known as the Schomburg Collection of Negro Literature and History, and the name was later changed to the Schomburg Center for Research in Black Culture.

Shelby Steele (1946–)
Scholar

Steele was born January 1, 1946, in Chicago but grew up in Phoenix, Illinois, a blue-collar suburb of Chicago. He attended high school in Harvey, Illinois, where he was student council president his senior year prior to graduating in 1964. Steel then attended Coe College in Cedar Rapids, Iowa, where he was active in SCOPE—an organization associated with Martin Luther King Jr.'s Southern Christian Leadership Council. He graduated in 1968, and in 1971 received an M.S. in sociology from Southern Illinois University. He went on to receive a Ph.D. in English literature from the University of Utah in 1974. While at

Southern Illinois University he taught African American literature to impoverished children in East St. Louis. Steele is currently a professor of English literature at San Jose State University.

In 1990 Steele published *The Content of Our Character: A New Vision of Race in America,* which won the National Book Critics Circle Award. In this controversial book Steele argued that African American self-doubt and its exploitation by the white and black liberal establishment is as great a cause of problems for African Americans as more traditional forms of racism. Steele has also written articles on this theme for such respected publications as *Harper's, New Republic, American Scholar,* and *Commentary.*

Steele became a senior research fellow at the Hoover Institute at Stanford University in 1994. He was the recipient of the National Humanities Medal and the Bradley Prize in 2006 and published the text *White Guilt: How Blacks & Whites Together Destroyed the Promise of the Civil Rights Era.* In 2007 he wrote *A Bound Man: Why We Are Excited about Obama and Why He Can't Win.* After Obama's successful campaign in 2008, Steele still defended his analysis.

Because of his beliefs Steele has been identified as a black conservative. He continues to write about the issues of race and individual freedoms.

Carter Godwin Woodson (1875–1950)
Scholar

Carter Godwin Woodson was born December 9, 1875, in New Canton, Virginia. He received a B.Litt. degree from Berea College in 1903, a B.A. and an M.A.

in 1907 and 1908 from the University of Chicago, and a Ph.D. from Harvard University in 1912.

 Known as the "Father of Modern Black History," Woodson was a passionate exponent of African American economic self-sufficiency. In 1915 Woodson founded the Association for the Study of Negro Life and History (now the Association for the Study of Afro-American Life and History). One year later, the organization began publishing the *Journal of Negro History.* In 1920 he founded Associated Publishers, Inc., and in 1921 he founded the *Negro History Bulletin.* In 1926 Woodson launched Negro History Week (now Black History Month) to promote the study of African American history.

A historian, author, editor, and teacher, Woodson served as dean of the Howard University School of Liberal Arts and the West Virginia Institute, and he was a Spingarn Medalist. His works include *The Education of the Negro Prior to 1861* (1915), *A Century of Negro Migration* (1918), *The Negro in Our History* (1922), and *The Miseducation of the Negro* (1933).

In an effort to ensure that young people knew their history, Woodson promoted Negro History Week in 1926. It coincided with the birthdays of Booker T. Washington, Abraham Lincoln, and Frederick Douglass. To ensure a resource for information, the Negro History Bulletin was started in 1937. Thanks to his efforts, by 1976 Negro History week had evolved into Black History Month. Woodson died on April 3, 1950.

RELIGION

The first Africans who arrived on North American shores (an event traditionally dated to 1619) brought their own religious world views with them. While a minority had been Muslims or Christians prior to their kidnapping by slave traders, most adhered to their native African religions. There were hundreds of these religions, but, in general, the Africans believed that the world had been created by a high god who removed himself from direct intervention in worldly affairs after the act of creation.

In Africa, worshipers directed their prayers to intermediary spirits, chief among whom were their ancestors, or the "living dead." If proper offering was made to an ancestor, the individual would be blessed with great prosperity, but if the ancestor was slighted, misfortune would result. In addition, the Yorubas worshiped a variety of nature spirits (or orishas). These spirits often possessed their devotees, who then became mediums of their gods. This kind of spirit-possession is a prominent feature of some modern African American religions such as santería, which recently has spread in large urban areas, including Miami and New York. Also a part of the African world view, especially among the Bakongo, was the practice of magic, variously known in the New World as obeah, vaudou (voodoo), or con-

jure. This magic, designed to help friends (myalism) or to hurt enemies (obeah), at one time was widely practiced by Africans throughout the Western Hemisphere.

The type of African spirituality that took root in North America merged elements from many African cultures. Since slave masters intentionally mixed Africans from many tribal backgrounds, no "pure" African religion preserving one tradition emerged. Nevertheless, the longstanding scholarly controversy about the extent to which African traditions have been retained in African-based religions is gradually being resolved in favor of those who see extensive survivals. In addition to singing, church music, and preaching style—aspects where an African influence has generally been conceded—scholars have made persuasive arguments for African survivals in family structure, funeral practices, church organization, and many other areas.

The first sustained effort to convert African Americans to Christianity was made by the Anglican Society for the Propagation of the Gospel in Foreign Parts, which sent missionaries to North America in 1701. These missionaries had little success among the Africans; many blacks mocked those who imitated the whites too closely, and thus resisted the missionaries. In ad-

Martin Luther King III speaks at the Ebenezer Baptist Church in Atlanta, Georgia, on the occasion of his father's eighty-second birthday.

dition, white slave masters often resented losing slaves' time to church services and feared that slaves would lay a claim to freedom through conversion. The numerous colonial laws, starting with Virginia in 1669, that proclaimed that conversion failed to entitle slaves to freedom did not comfort some slave masters, who suspected that Christianity would undermine slave discipline—indeed, some remained unconvinced of the advisability of missionary efforts until emancipation occurred. On the other hand, some slave masters believed the Christianization of Africans to be justification for enslaving them.

Subsequent efforts to convert African Americans to Christianity were more successful. In his seven missionary tours throughout North America between 1742 and 1770, the spellbinding orator George Whitefield effected the conversions of large numbers of both black and white Americans. The ministry of Methodist circuit riders, such as Francis Asbury, was also well received by African Americans at the end of the eighteenth century.

Baptist and Methodist churches were the most successful in attracting black members. Since these churches did not require their ministers be well educated, doors were opened for aspiring African American ministers, many of whom lived in states where teaching African Americans to read and write was forbidden by law. Furthermore, the Baptists and Methodists were not as hostile to the passion of black preachers and congregations as were more staid denominations, such as the Episcopalians. Finally, the anti-slavery stance of notable Methodist and Baptist leaders, such as John Wesley, Francis Asbury, and John Leland, and the greater degree of equality nurtured within many Baptist and Methodist congregations, were attractive to African Americans.

Probably the first organizing effort by African Americans to be successful in an independent black congregation was the Silver Bluff Baptist Church in South Carolina, which came into existence between 1773 and 1775. David George, an African American, and seven other men and women formed its organizing nucleus. George Liele, one of George's associates, often preached at the Silver Bluff Church before immigrating to Jamaica in 1782. Andrew Bryan, one of Liele's converts, founded the First African Baptist Church in Savannah, Georgia, in 1788.

Bryan's life represented the complex predicament faced by African American religious leaders in the antebellum South. In the early years of his ministry, Bryan was whipped and twice imprisoned by whites who feared him. But he bought his freedom, prospered, and eventually came to own much property, including eight black slaves; his death in 1812 was mourned by blacks and whites alike. While many black churches continued to be served by white ministers until 1865, black pastors, licensed ministers, and exhorters ministering to black Baptist and Methodist congregations were not at all unusual at this time, either in the South or the North.

While white preachers urged Black Americans to convert and many predominantly white congregations welcomed them into membership, racial prejudice was never absent from the religious scene. Although the level of discrimination varied from region to region and from congregation to congregation, some factors were relatively constant.

One such factor was the relative scarcity of ordained African American clergy. To take the Methodists as an example, some African American ministers were ordained as deacons within the Methodist Episcopal Church prior to 1820, but none in the four decades thereafter. No African American Methodist minister was ordained by the Methodist Episcopal Church to the higher office of elder or consecrated as a bishop prior to the Civil War, unless he was willing to immigrate to Liberia.

Resistance to discrimination took many forms. In the North, Peter Spencer in Wilmington, Delaware, Richard Allen in Philadelphia, and James Varick in New York, led their black followers out of white Methodist churches and set up independent black congregations. In Allen's case, his departure was preceded by a dramatic confrontation over segregated seating in Philadelphia's white Methodist church. Each of these men then used his congregation as the nucleus of a new black Methodist denomination—Spencer formed the African Union Church in 1807, Allen the African Methodist Episcopal Church (AME) in 1816, and Varick a denomination eventually called the African Methodist Episcopal Zion Church (AME Zion) in 1821.

Meanwhile, in Charleston, South Carolina, a more explosive situation was taking shape. Morris Brown, a black Methodist minister from Charleston who had helped Richard Allen organize the African Methodist Episcopal Church, organized an independent black Methodist church in his home city. The authorities harassed Brown's church and sometimes arrested its leaders. Nevertheless, within a year, more than three-quarters of Charleston's black Methodists had united with him. The oppression of African Americans in Charleston was so severe that many members of Brown's congregation, including prominent lay leaders, joined the insurrection planned by Denmark Vesey to take over the Charleston armory and, eventually, the whole environs of Charleston. The conspirators, apprehended before they could carry out their plans, testified that Brown had not known of their scheme, and the minister was allowed to move to Philadelphia, where Richard Allen made him the second bishop of the African Methodist Episcopal Church.

A few African Americans became acquiescent as a result of Christianity. One such example was Pierre Toussaint, a black Haitian slave who fled in 1787 to New York with his white owners, the Berards, just prior to the Haitian Revolution. In 1811 Mrs. Berard freed Toussaint on her death bed. Over the next forty years, Toussaint became a notable philanthropist, contributing funds to the building of St. Patrick's Cathedral. However, when the cathedral opened, Toussaint did not protest when a white usher refused to seat him for services. Some American Catholics recently revived the controversy over Toussaint by campaigning for his canonization. Many black Catholics have strongly objected, seeing Toussaint as passive and servile and thus a poor candidate for sainthood.

The mid-nineteenth century saw increased anti-slavery activity among many black church leaders and members. Some gave qualified support to the gradual emancipation program sponsored by the American Colonization Society, which sought to encourage free African Americans to emigrate from the United States to Africa to Westernize and Christianize the Africans. Virginia Baptist pastor Lott Cary and Maryland Methodist minister Daniel Coker were the two most prominent African American religious leaders to immigrate to Africa in the 1820s. By the 1850s there were enough black Methodists in Liberia for the Methodist Episcopal Church to consecrate a black bishop, Francis Burns, to serve the Liberian churches. While some Black Americans were migrating to Africa, others migrated to the West Indies—Episcopalian Bishop James T. Holly, for example, settled in Haiti to undertake missionary work.

Because of the extreme repression in the slave states, southern blacks were unable to express openly their views on political issues. They were, however, often able to make their views clear; for example, a white minister who dwelled too long on the Biblical text that servants should obey their masters was apt to find his African American listeners deserting him. In addition, black Christians often held secret meetings in "brush arbors" (rude structures made of pine boughs) or in the middle of the woods. There they could sing spirituals and pray openly for the quick advent of freedom. Slave revolts provided a violent outbreak of dissent much feared by whites. The 1831 revolt of Nat Turner, a Baptist preacher, in Northampton County, Virginia, was suppressed only after tremendous bloodshed had been visited upon both blacks and whites. Frightened whites in the South intensified their surveillance of black churches in the aftermath of the Turner revolt. Even conservative black preachers, such as Presbyterian John Chavis in North Carolina and the Baptist "Uncle Jack" in Virginia, were prohibited from preaching.

Northern African American leaders could afford to be more open and forthright in their political stance. Most rejected outright the views of the American Colonization Society in favor of the immediate abolition of slavery. Presbyterian minister Henry Highland Garnet was a prominent abolitionist urging African American slaves in 1843 to "let your motto be RESISTANCE! RESISTANCE! RESISTANCE!" African Methodist Episcopal bishop Daniel Payne and African Methodist Episcopal Zion bishop Christopher Rush, both emigrants from the Carolinas to the North, were outspoken abolitionists who, after the mid-1840s, became the most prominent leaders in their respective churches. Frederick Douglass was one of the few leading black abolitionists who did not pursue a ministerial career, and even he had briefly served as an African Methodist Episcopal Zion preacher in New Bedford, Massachusetts. Black clergy were extraordinarily active in recruiting black men to join the Union armies during the Civil War, after the Emancipation Proclamation opened up the possibility of military service to them. During the Civil War nearly a dozen black ministers, including the African Methodist Episcopal Church's Henry McNeal Turner, served as chaplains to black army regiments.

The contributions of black women ministers were also vital. Women sometimes served as traveling evangelists, especially within the black denominations. While Sojourner Truth's oratory has become appropriately famous, Maria Stewart, Jarena Lee, Zilpha Elaw, and other early nineteenth-century women also spoke eloquently and, in Lee's and Elaw's cases, traveled widely and labored diligently. None of these women was ordained, but Elizabeth (whose last name is unknown), a former slave from Maryland whose ministry began in 1796, spoke for many female preachers when she was accused of preaching without a license: "If the Lord has ordained me, I need nothing better." Rebecca Cox Jackson left the African Methodist Episcopal Church in the 1830s because she felt that men denied her the chance to exercise her ministry, and she eventually became head eldress of a predominantly black Shaker community in Philadelphia.

During the postbellum years, some black women sought and obtained formal ordination from their denominations. Sarah Ann Hughes, a successful North Carolina evangelist and pastor, was ordained by Bishop Henry McNeal Turner in 1885, but complaints from male pastors caused her ordination to be revoked two years later. Two women were ordained by African Methodist Episcopal Zion bishops not long thereafter— Mary J. Small in 1895 as a deacon and 1898 as an elder, and Julia A.J. Foote in 1894 and 1900. Many women exercised their ministry through para-ecclesiastical structures, such as women's temperance and missionary societies, while others, such as Anna Cooper and the African Methodist Episcopal Church's Frances Jackson Coppin, became renowned educators.

Black church membership grew explosively after the Civil War, especially in the South, where the black clergy played a prominent part in the Reconstruction governments. African Methodist Episcopal minister Hiram Revels became the first African American to serve as a U.S. senator when the Mississippi legislature sent him to Washington, D.C., in 1870. Revels, however, was only the groundbreaker; many black ministers went on to serve in the Congress or in their state governments. African American participation in Reconstruction politics was effective in large part because ministers in the AME and AME Zion Churches, and many black Baptist ministers, carefully and patiently educated their congregation members on every civic and political issue (although one newly established black denomination, the Colored Methodist Episcopal Church, largely stayed away from politics during Reconstruction).

Even though African Americans were largely expelled from southern state governments after the end of political Reconstruction in the 1870s, many black ministers and laity continued to play an active political role on such issues as temperance; often campaigning on behalf of prohibition referenda. The southern white campaign of terror, lynching, and disenfranchisement steadily reduced black political power and participation, however, until the onset of mid-twentieth century civil rights movement.

As the system of racial segregation imposed in the 1880s and 1890s took hold, black minis-ters coordinated a manifold response. First, they challenged new segregation laws, engaging in civil disobedience and boycotts. For example, when the city of Nashville, Tennessee, segregated its streetcars in 1906, influential Baptist minister R.H. Boyd led a black boycott of the streetcars, even operating his own streetcar line for a time. No defeat was ever seen as final.

Second, black ministers helped to nurture a separate set of black institutions to serve African Americans who were excluded from white establishments. The Congregationalists, Baptists, and Northern Methodists established schools in the South for African Americans during Reconstruction, but the African Methodist Episcopal, African Methodist Episcopal Zion, and Christian Methodist Episcopal bishops forged ahead with the establishment of their own network of schools. The black denominations also built up their publishing houses, and the books and periodicals that they published were vital to the black community. Virtually every institution with ties to African American communities received some support from black churches.

Third, some black ministers believed that the civil rights retreats of the late nineteenth century should spur African Americans to leave the United States for a destination where their full civil rights would be respected. A "Back to Africa" movement grew to enable African Americans to find a home where they could run governments, banks, and businesses without interference from whites. Thus, Bishop Turner helped to organize a steamship line to carry Black Americans back to Africa, and two shiploads of black emigrants sailed to Liberia in 1895 and 1896 as a result of his efforts. Some black church leaders, such as Christian Methodist Episcopal bishop Lucius Holsey and AME bishop Richard Cain, held views similar to those advocated by Turner, but many more church leaders opposed Turner's emigrationism vigorously. Simultaneously, African American missionary work continued to occupy the attention of African Americans at the end of the nineteenth century. Under the guidance of Bishops Payne and Turner, for example, the African Methodist Episcopal Church had a strong missionary presence in Sierra Leone, Liberia, and South Africa.

In the past one hundred years, black religious life has become characterized by a far greater degree of diversity and pluralism. At the same time, traditional African American concerns, including the continuing quest for freedom and justice, have been not only maintained but strengthened.

Pentecostalism, which burst on the American scene in 1906, has become a major religious force within the black community. The Church of God in Christ, a Pentecostal denomination, has become the second largest black denomination in the United States. Meanwhile, the charismatic or Neo-Pentecostal movement has revitalized many congregations within mainline black denominations. The Black Nationalism of Bishop Turner helped achieve its full potential in the work of such men as Marcus Garvey (and his chaplain general, George A. McGuire), Elijah Muhammad, and Malcolm X. There has been a spectacular rise of storefront churches, some of which were led by flamboyant showmen such as Father Divine and "Sweet Daddy" Grace. Each of these trends has been significantly aided by the black migrations from the South to the North, which greatly strengthened northern black communities.

Many black ministers became advocates of a "Social Gospel." One of the most famous was the Reverend Ransom of the African Methodist Episcopal Church, who came into prominence between 1901 and 1904 as pastor of an Institutional Church in Chicago. ("Institutional churches" provided a whole panoply of social services to needy members and neighbors, in addition to regular worship.) Social Gospellers highlighted the reality of collective, societal sin, such as the starvation of children and the denial of human rights, and maintained that Christian repentance of these sins must be followed by concrete actions to rectify injustice and to assist the poor. The Reverend Dr. Martin Luther King Jr., was profoundly influenced by this Social Gospel movement.

It is worth recalling that many black religious leaders in the 1960s thought that King's brand of so-cial activism was too radical. One of King's most determined critics during the 1960s was the theologically conservative president of the National Baptist Convention of the U.S.A., Inc., Joseph H. Jackson. The attempt by King's ministerial allies to unseat Jackson as president of the Convention in 1960 and 1961 led to a schism, with King and his supporters forming a new denomination, the Progressive National Baptist Convention. King came under further criticism when, in 1967 and 1968, he made it clear that his advocacy of pacifism extended to opposition to American military involvement in Vietnam.

The Black Theology movement, which grew rapidly after King's assassination, attempted to fashion a critique of the prevalent Christian theology out of the materials that King and Malcolm X provided. One such theologian, Albert Cleage, pastor of the Shrine of the Black Madonna in Detroit, argued that Jesus is a black messiah and that his congregation should follow the teachings of Jehovah, a black god. "Almost everything you have heard about Christianity is essentially a lie," he stated. Cleage was representative of black theologians in arguing that black liberation should be seen as situated at the core of the Christian gospels. In the 1980s black women such as Jacquelyn Grant, Delores Williams, and Katie Cannon formulated "womanist" theologies that sought to combat the triple oppression of race, class, and gender suffered by most black women.

African American churches in the 1990s remained strong, healthy institutions. The largest denomination among the black churches remained the National Baptist Convention of the U.S.A., Inc. While secularization diminished its influence somewhat, the black church continued as the central institution in the black community. Many black churches vigorously confronted such problems as drug abuse and homelessness that were visible symptoms of the increased desperation of the black underclass.

Many churches had strong anti-drug programs. The First AME Church of Los Angeles sponsored a "Lock In" program, which on weekends presented anti-drug messages to youth. Similarly, many congregations had undertaken

An Easter procession outside an AME church in Chicago, 1941.

forceful action against crack houses. Parochial schools, feeding centers, and housing for senior citizens were also part of the black church's outreach to the black community. Many black ministers noted the growing division of the African American community along social-class lines while exhorting middle-class Black Americans to give more generously to programs that aid the poor. James Cone, a leading black theologian, stated that black churches needed to devote less time and attention to institutional survival and more to finding ways to deal with such pressing issues as poverty, gang violence, and AIDS.

Toward this end, black churches participated in a wide variety of ecumenical projects among themselves and with white denominations. The Congress of National Black Churches, a consortium of six black churches, continued to sponsor a variety of projects to improve the economic and social situation of the African American community. Partners in Ecumenism, a project of the National Council of Churches, challenged white denominations to be more responsive to black concerns. At a grassroots level, African American churches successfully joined forces to combat problems that were too large for any congregation to address alone.

This spirit of cooperation inspired individual denominations to explore merging or establishing close working relationships with other denominations with similar backgrounds and traditions.

Black churches also found themselves compelled to address issues related to the multi-ethnic tensions of the 1990s. Leading black pastors in Los Angeles deplored both the violence of police revealed in the Rodney King incident and the violence of inner city rioters, while advocating urgent attention to the problems of inner-city residents. Mainstream Islam, despite raising its own complexities, has also made large gains in the United States. Most African American Muslims do not distinguish between people of different races and worship cordially side-by-side with recent Muslim immigrants from Asia and Africa. Louis Farrakhan's Nation of Islam, however, which retains Elijah Muhammad's black separatist teachings, continues to maintain a devoted following. Because of its very conservative stance on gender issues, Islam has proven to be more popular among black men than among black women.

The cause of gender equality continued to progress slowly in black churches. While two predominantly white denominations, the United Methodist and Protestant Episcopal churches, have elevated black women to the episcopacy in the past decade, none of the largest historically black denominations have done so. Nevertheless, women in some black churches are achieving ever-more-prestigious ministerial assignments. Vashti McKenzie, a former model, disc jockey, and radio program director, was appointed in 1990 as pastor of the Payne Memorial AME Church, a "old-line" church in Baltimore. Her innovative ministry, she says, is designed to "provide a message of hope for a hurting community." There are presently more than six hundred female pastors in the African Methodist Episcopal Church.

Preaching the gospel in a faithful but relevant fashion remained the most important objective of black churches.

Several different groups in the past century have been known as Black Jews. Included among these are the Commandment Keepers, founded in Harlem in 1919 by a Nigerian-born man known as "Rabbi Matthew"; the Church of God and Saints in Christ, founded in 1896 in Lawrence, Kansas, by William Crowdy; and the Church of God founded in Philadelphia by Prophet F. S. Cherry. In terms of doctrine, these groups share little more than a dislike of Christianity and affection for the Old Testament. Some Black Jews claim descent from the Falasha Jews of Ethiopia, who now reside in Israel. However, few Black Jews are recognized as such by orthodox rabbis. The Church of God and Saints of Christ is the largest of these groups.

Members of this religion regard Ethiopian Emperor Haile Selassie, who died in 1975, as God. Marcus Garvey, a Jamaican-born nationalist who advocated a back-to-Africa movement in the United States in the early 1920s, is also a central figure in the faith. Reggae musician Bob Marley, a Rastafarian, helped to increase the religion's popularity in the United States.

Rastas differ on specific dogma, but they basically believe that they are descended from black Hebrews exiled in Babylon and therefore are true Israelites. They also believe that Haile Selassie (whose name before ascending the throne was Lij Ras Tafari Makonnen) is the direct descendent of Solomon and Sheba, and that God is black.

In spite of the movement toward a continued spiritual existence for African Americans, particularly in the South, violence against churches became prevalent. In 1996 the crime of arson against black churches was at its peak. Of the 297 cases of church burnings, 119, or 40 percent, of the burnings were African American churches. By 1998 only 34 percent of the cases were solved. As the investigations continued, those charged with the crimes constituted 68 whites, 37 African Americans, and 1 Hispanic. Arson cases in Alabama gained national attention when three students from the Methodist affiliated University, Birmingham Southern burned nine churches. Five of the churches were white and four were African American.

The last part of the twentieth century and the first part of the twenty-first century continued to see the black church evolve, as middle class enrollment in mega-churches continued to increase. While large African American churches in urban communities like the Ebenezer African Methodist Episcopal Church in Maryland saw memberships increase totaling 23,000, mega-churches in black urban communities were further invigorated by a neo-Pentecostal liturgical style of worship that attracted and evangelized young members. Mega-churches also were a product of reform due to more women in leadership roles and founding the mega-churches. Also groundbreaking was the charismatic and expository preaching style that teaches personal evaluation and transformation, toward successful and economically sound living. Pastors of these new mega-churches also established television ministries, which reach global audiences and address global causes.

A Rastafarian man in Barbados. Rastas believe they are descended from black Hebrews who fled Babylon.

With memberships from 10,000 to 30,000, mega-churches are big business as they provide a wide range of services to the community such as medical clinics, fitness centers, HIV and substance abuse counseling, day-care centers, banks, job training, marriage counseling, and tutoring among other needed services. Some of the largest mega-churches consist of various facilities, large sanctuaries, and multiple worship times to support expanding membership. Some of the larger sanctuaries that provide seating to support growing membership are: Faithful Central Bible Church, pastor Rev. Kenneth Ulmer, in Inglewood California, which is housed in the former home of the Los Angeles Lakers, seats 17,505 and has a membership of 12,000; the Faith Dome of the Crenshaw Christian Center, pastors Rev. Frederick K.C. Price and Rev. Betty Price, in Los Angeles seats 10,146 and has a membership of almost 20,000; Jericho City of Praise Church, Pastor Betty P. Peebles, in Landover, Michigan, seats 10,000 and has more than 15,000 members; The New Birth Missionary Baptist Church, pastor Eddie L. Long, in Lithonia, Georgia, seats 10,000 and has a membership of

25,000; The Potter's House, Bishop T.D. Jakes, in Dallas, Texas, seats 8,200 and has a membership of over 26,000; and the Apostolic Church of God, Rev. Arthur M. Brazier, in Chicago, Illinois, seats 4,500 and has membership over 16,000.

Mega-churches have come under fire regarding the lack of pursuit of civil rights for the poor and disenfranchised and for promoting political agendas and material prosperity which appeared to be a disregard for New Testament warnings against greed. In recognizing that the traditional role of the African American church has been to serve as a central force in stabilizing the community, the mega-church has not only done this, but it has also brought material and political influence into often ignored urban communities. Unlike traditional churches that created a power base for social change, mega-churches generally offer a conservative message rather than challenge the status quo.

BIOGRAPHIES

Noble Drew Ali (1886–1929)
Moorish Science Temple Founder

Noble Drew Ali, whose birth name was Timothy Drew in 1886, was born in North Carolina. He is principally important for his role in establishing the first North American religious movement combining Black Nationalist and Muslim themes with rejection of Christianity as the religion of whites. In 1913 he established the first Moorish Science Temple in Newark, New Jersey. He taught that Black Americans were "Asiatics" who had originally lived in Morocco before enslavement. Every people, including Black Americans, needed land for themselves, he proclaimed, and North America, which he termed an extension of the African continent, was the proper home for Black Americans. The holy book for the Moorish Science Temple was a "Holy Koran" which was "divinely prepared by the Noble Prophet Drew Ali." (This book should not be confused with the Q'uran of Islam.) Every member of the Temple carried a card stating that "we honor all the Divine Prophets, Jesus, Mo-

hammed, Buddha and Confucius" and that "I AM A CITIZEN OF THE U.S.A."

In the 1920s, the Moorish Science Temple expanded to Pittsburgh, Detroit, and Chicago. Drew Ali also started several small businesses, which he and his followers ran. In 1929 Drew Ali was stabbed to death in his Chicago offices in apparent strife over the leadership of the Temple. The Moorish Science Temple survived Drew Ali's death, but the Nation of Islam was able to attract some of its followers.

Richard Allen (1760–1831)
African Methodist Episcopal Church Founder

Born a slave in Philadelphia, Allen converted to Christianity in 1777 and soon thereafter bought his freedom. He traveled widely through the mid-Atlantic states as an exporter. Francis Asbury, the first bishop of the Methodist Episcopal Church, asked Allen to join him as a traveling companion, stipulating that Allen would not be allowed to fraternize with slaves and would sometimes have to sleep in his carriage. Allen refused to accept such an offer, instead settling down in Philadelphia, where he helped to found the Free African Society, an African American society for religious fellowship and mutual aid. One day in the early 1790s, Allen was worshipping in Philadelphia's St. George's Methodist Church when he was pulled off his knees during prayer by white deacons who insisted that Allen was sitting outside the area reserved for African Americans. Allen left, establishing his own church for Philadelphia's African Americans in a converted blacksmith shop in 1794. White Methodists tried to exert their control over his church in various ways, and Allen resisted successfully. In 1816, after the Pennsylvania Supreme Court settled a suit over this church in Allen's favor, Allen called for a conference of black Methodists. The African Methodist Episcopal Church was founded at this conference, and Allen was consecrated as its first bishop. Allen remained both religiously and politically active in his later years, and he was especially active in opposing schemes to colonize free African Americans in Africa.

Carl Bean (c. 1946–)
Clergyman

Carl Bean was born in Baltimore, Maryland, and raised as a member of the Baptist church. From the 1960s to 1982 Bean pursed a singing career by performing at the Apollo Theater and on Broadway and was a recording artist. In 1982 he found a new calling and was ordained as a minister. He began his work in south-central Los Angeles.

Part of Bean's ministry was to help gay and lesbian persons of color, partly due to the experiences he endured from the church as an openly gay man. Since 1985 what began as a study group became the Unity Fellowship Church for African American gays and lesbians. Bean's ministry as pastor of Unity Fellowship also reached out to gangs and anyone who was trying to get their lives together. Bean also founded in 1985 The Minority AIDS Project, which is one of the largest agencies serving African Americans suffering from this disease.

Bishop Carl Bean, D.M., received the NAACP Image Award in 1987 and a Lambda Legal Defense and Education Fund Liberty Award in 1994, among other awards, in recognition of his community service.

Thea Bowman (1938–1990)
Roman Catholic Nun

Born in Canton, Mississippi, in 1938, Thea Bowman, daughter of a medical doctor, joined the Roman Catholic Church at age twelve because of the Catholic education she had received. Three years later, she joined the Franciscan Sisters of Perpetual Adoration. She was extensively educated, earning a Ph.D. in literature and linguistics.

Bowman was a distinguished teacher who taught elementary and high school as well as college. She helped to found the Institute of Black Catholic Studies at Xavier University and was a distinguished scholar known for her writings on Thomas More. But it is probably for the spiritual inspiration that she provided in numerous lectures, workshops, and concerts that she is best remembered. She said that she brought to her church "myself, my black self, all that I am, all that I have, all that I hope to become, my history, my culture, my experience, my African American song and dance and gesture and movement and teaching and preaching and healing."

Calvin O. Butts III (1949–)
Religious Leader

Calvin O. Butts was born in 1949 on the Lower East Side of New York City. The family moved to Queens when Butts was eight; he spent his summers visiting his grandmothers, who both lived in rural Georgia not far from each other. Butts graduated from Flushing High School in 1967, and was then accepted to Morehouse College in Atlanta, Georgia. He later received his master's degree in divinity from Union Theological Seminary and Doctor of Ministry degree in church and public policy from Drew University in New Jersey.

Butts was recruited in 1972 as a junior minister at Abyssinian Baptist Church the oldest Baptist African American church, located in Harlem, New York. Butts assumed the role as pastor of Abyssinian, also considered the first African American mega-church with more than five thousand members, in 1989. Butts's ministry, which is community centered, allowed him to co-found the Abyssinian Development Corporation, which has donated over $300 million to the commercial and housing development of Harlem. He helped to establish the Thurgood Marshall Academy of Learning and Social Change and in 1999 was appointed president of the State University of New York College in Old Westbury, New York. Butts also serves as chairman of the National Affiliate Development Initiative of the National Black Leadership Commission on AIDS. Butts has received numerous award for his service to the community and his commitment toward positive social change.

Katie Cannon (1950–)
Minister, Educator, Feminist

Katie Cannon was born on January 3, 1950, in Kannopolis, North Carolina. She grew up at a time when equality and opportunity for blacks and black women were limited and entrenched with racism. Cannon often worked as a domestic with her aunt. She came to realize that her best chance for a better life was through an education.

Cannon graduated from Barber-Scotia College in Concord, North Carolina, in 1971 with a B.S. degree. She went on to enroll at Johnson C. Smith Seminary of the Interdenominational Theological Center in Atlanta, Georgia. As one of four female students in her class she went on to focus on Old Testament studies and received her master's degree in divinity in 1974. Before resuming her scholarly work she pastored the Ascension Presbyterian Church in New York City and served in an administrative position at the New York Theological Seminary. In 1983, after returning to academia, Cannon received a master's degree and a Ph.D. in philosophy from Union Theological Seminary in Richmond, Virginia. Cannon's scholarship focused not only on philosophy, but on Christian ethics, feminism, and black women.

Cannon is the Annie Scales Roger Professor of Christian Ethics at Union Theological Seminary. She has written numerous books, including *Katie's Canon: Womanism and the Soul of the Black Community* (1997) and *Teaching Preaching* (2002).

Johnnie Coleman (1920–)
Religious Leader, Educator

Johnnie Coleman was born in 1920 in Mississippi. In spite of the fact that she was a girl, she was named after her father. Once graduating from Union Academy and Wiley College, Coleman became a teacher. In 1956 she moved to Kansas City to study at Unity School of Christianity. After suffering racial discrimination Coleman threatened to leave, but her threat won her the opportunity to live on campus like other students.

In 1974 Coleman founded the Universal Foundation for Better Living Inc., which focused on positive thinking. Her focus was derived from the New Thought movement that was prevalent in Chicago in the 1970s. Coleman began a broadcast ministry in the 1980s, and by 1989 twenty-three churches had become part of the Universal Foundation, and her own congregation had grown to membership exceeding twelve thousand.

James Cone (1938–)
Theologian

Born in Fordyce, Arkansas, James Cone received a B.A. from Philander Smith College, a B.D. from Garrett Evangelical Seminary, and an M.A. and Ph.D. from Northwestern University. After teaching at Philander Smith and Adrian Colleges, Cone moved to Union Theological Seminary in 1969. He is currently the Charles A. Briggs Professor of Systematic Theology. Cone is the author of numerous books, including *Black Theology and Black Power* (1969); *The Spirituals and the Blues* (1972); *For My People: Black Theology and the Black Church* (1984); *Martin and Malcolm and America: A Dream or a Nightmare* (1991); and *Risks of Faith* (2001). Perhaps more than any other black theologian, Cone has provided a systematic exposition of the argument that since God, according to the Bible, is on the side of the poor and oppressed, God is siding with the black liberation struggle in the American context. He has made this argument using a diverse set of sources, including the writings of modern European theologians such as Karl Barth, and the writings and speeches of Malcolm X and Martin Luther King Jr. Cone has worked painstakingly in the past two decades to build ties between black, feminist, and third-world liberation theologians.

Suzan Johnson Cook (1957–)
Religious Leader, Author

Suzan Johnson Cook was born in New York City on January 28, 1957. Cook attended Emerson College in Boston, majoring in speech, and graduated cum laude in 1976. Inspired by her role model, Presbyterian minister Katie Cannon, Cook enrolled at the United Theological Seminary in New York and earned an M.Div.; she later enrolled in the United Theological Seminary in Dayton, Ohio, and earned a D.Min. in 1990. Pursuing the path as a minister was a challenge for women, but Cook accomplished her goals. She began preaching at the Mariner's Temple, the oldest Baptist church in Manhattan, in 1983 and remained there for eleven years.

Cook was the first woman to be named as chaplain for the New York City police department in 1990. In 1993 she was chosen by President Bill Clinton to receive a White House fellowship, making her the first to earn such an honor. She also served as domestic policy advisor under President Clinton. In 2010 Cook was nominated for the post of ambassador-at-large for international religious freedom in the State Department by President Barack Obama. Although her nomination was initially placed on hold, she was renominated and confirmed on April 14, 2011, as the first woman and the first African American to hold this position.

Cook's publications include *Too Blessed to Be Stressed* (1998), *Praying for the Men in Your Life* (2003), *Live Like You're Blessed* (2006), and *Moving Up* (2008).

Father Divine (1877–1965)

Mystery shrouds the early identity and real name of Father Divine. There is reason to believe he was born George Baker in 1877 on Hutchinson's Island in Georgia. In 1907 he became a disciple of Sam Morris, a Pennsylvania black man who called himself Father Jehovia. Two years later he switched over to John Hickerson's "Lift Ever, Die Never" group before returning to Georgia, where he began his own campaign to promote himself as a "divine messenger."

Threatened by local authorities (he was once booked as "John Doe, alias God"), Father Divine left Georgia in 1914 and later settled in New York

City, where he worked as an "employment agent" for the few followers still loyal to him. Calling his meeting place Heaven, he soon attracted a larger following and moved to Sayville, Long Island, in 1919. It was at this time that Father Divine began to provide shelter and food to the poor and homeless. Spiritually, Father Divine fostered what amounted to a massive cooperative agency based on the communal spirit of the Last Supper. His movement practiced complete racial equality. Services included songs and impromptu sermons and were conducted without Scripture readings and the use of clergy.

Once he was sentenced to six months in jail as a public nuisance. Four days after his trial, the judge in his case died of a heart attack, whereupon Father Divine was quoted as having said: "I hated to do it." The ensuing publicity enhanced his popularity.

The Divine movement, a non-ritualistic cult whose followers worshipped their leader as God incarnate on Earth, grew rapidly in the 1930s and 1940s, with "Father" speaking out across the country and publicizing his views in the *New Day*, a weekly magazine published by his organization. He set up "Peace Mission Kingdom" throughout the United States and the world. In 1946, he married his "Sweet Angel," a twenty-one-year-old Canadian stenographer known thereafter as Mother Divine.

Father Divine died peacefully in 1965 at Woodmont, an estate he had acquired in the Philadelphia suburbs, and his wife pledged to continue the work of the movement.

Wallace D. Fard (1877–1934)
Religious Leader

The origins of Wallace Fard are reported with conflicting stories. The Nation of Islam contends that Fard was born to mixed parentage with an African American father and a Caucasian mother. He was educated in England and at the University of Southern California as an Arabian diplomat. The Federal Bureau of Investigation alleges that Fard was born in New Zealand or Oregon to

Polynesian or Hawaiian parents. Fard was convicted in 1926 of drug sales and sentenced for six months to six years in the California correctional system. He was released in 1929.

Detroit was where Fard settled after his release from prison. As a door-to-door salesman he taught members of the black community about their health and also about their heritage as black people and the belief in one God, Allah. Fard was influenced by the Moorish Science Temple and the Ahmaddiya Muslim movement. He stated that his true mission was about equality and justice for African Americans. He stared the paramilitary organization, the Fruit of Islam, and established the University of Islam to teach African Americans about their true past and their heritage. In 1931 he designated his follower, Elijah Poole from Georgia, as his supreme minister. Elijah Poole was renamed Elijah Muhammad. The membership reached eight thousand and Fard's influence continued to grow.

In November 1932 the white neighbor of one of Fard's followers was killed as a sacrifice to Allah. Fard was pressured to leave Detroit and in May 1933 after his arrest for disturbing the peace, Fard left Detroit. During the year after Fard left Detroit, he is said to have lived in Chicago while keeping in contact with Muhammad. After that year, little is known of Fard's whereabouts. Muhammad continued to speak of Fard as Allah and that his time in Detroit symbolized his appearance on Earth to African American people. The true origins of Fard are not known, but his influence and teachings are undeniably a key force in the Nation of Islam.

Floyd Flake (1945–)
Religious Leader

Flake was born January 30, 1945, in Los Angeles, California, and grew up in Houston, Texas, one of thirteen children. After high school he became the first in his family to receive a college degree. He earned a B.A. from Wilberforce University in 1970, and earned a M.Div. in 1995 from the United Theological Seminary in Dayton, Ohio.

Flake, who had been ordained as a minister in the A.M.E. Church in the 1960s, accepted the call by his superiors to serve as pastor of the Allen A.M.E. Church in Jamaica, New York, in 1976. He successfully led the revitalization of the church from one thousand to five thousand members and initiated a number of successful programs. In 1987 Flake ran for office and became a member of the U.S. House of Representatives from New York's 6th District. He served until 1997 when he resigned and returned as pastor of Allen A.M.E. Church full time.

Flake's leadership continues to expand the outreach of his church with membership well over twenty-three thousand. His political activities continue and are not only relegated to the Democratic Party but to campaigns that serve the community. Flake is a fellow at the Manhattan Institute for Policy Research and serves as president of Wilberforce University.

"Sweet Daddy" Grace (1881–1960)
United House of Prayer for All People Founder

Sweet Daddy Grace was born Marcelino Manoel da Garcia (and anglicized as Charles Manuel Grace) off the coast of West Africa on Brava, Cape Verde Islands, in 1881. In the early 1900s the Garcia family, consisting of Emanuel and Delomba da Garcia and their nine children, moved to New Bedford, Massachusetts. Grace opened his first church, The House of Prayer, in West Wareham, Massachusetts, in 1921, but his first success occurred five years later when he opened a church in Charlotte. Grace's church, the United House of Prayer for All People, had an ecstatic worship style, where speaking in tongues was encouraged. Grace claimed great powers, including the power of faith healing, and he stated that "Grace has given God a vacation, and since God is on His vacation don't worry Him.... If you sin against God, Grace can save you, but if you sin against Grace, God cannot save you." Even the numerous products that he sold, such as "Daddy Grace" coffee, tea, soaps, and hand creams, were reputed to have healing powers. By the time of his death in 1960, it was estimated that there were hundreds of House of Prayers churches across the country and internationally with over five hundred thousand worshipers.

James Augustine Healy (1830–1890)
Catholic Bishop

James Augustine Healy was the first black Catholic bishop in the United States. For twenty-five years he presided over a diocese covering the states of Maine and New Hampshire.

A native of Macon, Georgia, Healy received his education in the North, first at Franklin Park Quaker School in Burlington, New York, and later at Holy Cross in Worcester, Massachusetts. Healy graduated from the latter with first honors. Healy continued his studies abroad and was ordained in Paris at Notre Dame Cathedral in 1854. He then returned to the United States.

Pastor of a predominantly Irish congregation that was at first reluctant to accept him, Healy performed his priestly duties with devotion and eventually won the respect and admiration of his parishioners—particularly after performing his office during a typhoid epidemic.

Thereafter, he was made an assistant to Bishop John Fitzpatrick of Boston, who appointed him chancellor and entrusted him with a wide variety of additional responsibilities. In 1875 he was named Bishop of Portland, Maine, and in this capacity he founded sixty parishes as well as eighteen schools.

T. D. Jakes (1956–)
Religious Leader

Born Thomas Dexter Jakes in South Charleston, West Virginia, on June 9, 1956, Jakes grew up with a United Pentecostal background. With the death of his father he decided to enter the ministry. In 1979 he founded Greater Emmanuel Temple of Faith in Montgomery, West Virginia.

Jakes continued to hold down a job for the first ten years of his role as pastor until 1982, when the membership was over one thousand, and he turned to full-time ministry.

After moving several times, inclusive of locations in West Virginia and South Carolina, Jakes founded The Potter's House in Dallas, Texas, with fifty families that relocated with him from his location in South Carolina. Jakes's ministry has grown to over thirty thousand members, broadcast to a national and international audience, provides services to the community, and launched initiatives to aid thousands of people in Africa.

Jakes, a charismatic preacher, has published over thirty books and has founded a Christian record label, a movie production company, and numerous other companies. He has received thirteen honorary degrees and received Grammy and Dove Award nominations while winning a Grammy in 2004 for Best Gospel Choir or Chorus Album titled, A Wing and a Prayer.

Absalom Jones (1746–1818)
Religious Leader

Absalom Jones was born a slave in Sussex, Delaware, on November 6, 1746. He was sold away from his mother, five brothers, and one sister in 1762 and taken to Philadelphia. Jones learned to write by begging instruction from anyone he could and buying spelling books with what tips he earned as a house servant. In 1766 he was allowed to attend school at night where he learned the basics of mathematics. Although attempting to purchase his freedom he was freed in 1784 and became a licensed Methodist preacher in 1786. In May 1878 he joined with Richard Allen and others in establishing the Free African Society.

Jones became a leader in the newly established The African Church in St. Thomas in

1794. A year later he was ordained deacon, and in 1804 Jones became the first African American Episcopal priest. Jones was instrumental in the vestry opening a school that continued until 1816 and as a community leader. Jones served as priest of the African Church for twenty-two years. He died on February 13, 1818, at the age of seventy-one.

Leontine T.C. Kelly (1920–)
Methodist Bishop

Leontine T.C. Kelly, the first black woman bishop in any large American denomination, was born in Washington, D.C. She received an M.Div. degree from Union Theological Seminary in Richmond, Virginia, in 1969. She served as a schoolteacher, pastor of Virginia churches, and a staff member of the Virginia Conference of Churches before being elected a bishop in the United Methodist Church in 1984. She presided over the California–Nevada conference until 1989. Kelly was inducted into the National Women's Hall of Fame in Seneca, New York, in 2000.

Isaac Lane (1834–1937)
Colored Methodist Episcopal Church Bishop

A great religious leader and educator whose life spanned more than a century, Isaac Lane was born a slave in Jackson, Tennessee. Self-educated, in 1856 he was granted a license to exhort, a category assigned to blacks who were forbidden to preach, in the Methodist Episcopal Church South.

Lane was ordained a minister in 1865 and in 1873 was made a bishop of the Colored Methodist Episcopal Church (now known as the Christian Methodist Episcopal Church) at a salary so low he had to raise cotton to supplement his income and support his family—which included eleven children. His missionary work was instrumental in establishing the CME Church in Louisiana and Texas. In the 1880s, he established Lane College in Jackson with $9,000 he raised himself.

Jarena Lee (1783–?)
Methodist Church Pioneer

Born in Cape May, New Jersey, Jarena Lee worked as a servant for a family who lived near Philadelphia. She had a conversion experience in 1804 but was unable to find a church with which to unite until she heard Richard Allen, founder of the African Methodist Episcopal Church, preach in Philadelphia. She experienced a call to preach about 1808 and sought permission twice from Richard Allen to exercise her call. On her first attempt in 1809, Allen refused her request, but eight years later he granted it and licensed her as a preacher. Subsequently she traveled widely throughout the North and Midwest, and many of her listeners, especially women, were moved by her eloquent preaching. After Allen's death in 1831, male African Methodist Episcopal preachers in Philadelphia attempted to deny her permission to preach from their pulpits, but she continued her ministry despite such opposition. In 1848 she attempted to form a connection of female African Methodist Episcopal preachers for mutual support, but her organization soon fell apart. Many black women, especially within the African Methodist Episcopal Church, have seen Jarena Lee as a courageous foremother and a model for church activism.

Vashti Murphy McKenzie (1947–)
African Methodist Episcopal Church Bishop

 McKenzie was born May 30, 1947, in Baltimore, Maryland, to a family who had generationally been contributors to the community in publishing, politics, and organization building. McKenzie began her undergraduate work at Morgan State University but left her junior year to marry Stan McKenzie of the Baltimore Bullets basketball franchise. She moved to Phoenix and remained there until her husband's retirement when they returned to Baltimore. McKenzie completed her undergraduate education at the University of Maryland, College

Park earning a B.A in journalism. She began working at her family-owned newspaper, but later felt the calling to the preaching ministry.

To prepare for her role in the ministry, McKenzie attended Howard University in Washington, D.C., and earned a Master of Divinity degree and a doctor of ministry degree from Union Theological Seminary in Dayton, Ohio. In 1985 at the age of thirty-eight she became fully ordained and was appointed the pastor of Oak Street African Methodist Episcopal [AME] Church in Baltimore. In 1990 McKenzie she became the first female pastor of Payne Memorial Church in Baltimore and by 1997 McKenzie was named by *Ebony* magazine as one of the fifteen greatest African American female preachers. After ten years of service Payne Memorial grew from 300 members to 1,700 and McKenzie also contributed to the positive growth of the community through programs and non-profit services. She overcame the challenges of sexism and other obstacles, and on July 11, 2000, she was elected as the first female bishop in the 213-year history of the AME Church.

Bishop McKenzie is bishop of the 18th Episcopal District in Southeast Africa. She has started orphanages and provided support services for children who have lost their parents to the AIDS epidemic. Her publications include *Strength in the Struggle: Leadership Development for Women* (2001) and *Journey to the Well* (2002). She is the recipient of numerous awards while serving as a role model of the achievements that women can accomplish.

William Henry Miles (1828–1892)
Christian Methodist Episcopal Bishop

Born a slave in Kentucky, William Henry Miles was freed by his owner in her will. He joined the Methodist Episcopal Church South and soon felt a call to preach. In 1859 he was ordained a deacon. Uncertain about church affiliation after the war, he investigated the possibility of joining the African Methodist Episcopal Zion Church but soon thought better of it. Thus he remained a preacher in the Methodist Episcopal Church South until its

African American members, those who had decided not to join the African Methodist Episcopal or African Methodist Episcopal Zion Churches, were allowed to form a separate denomination, the Colored Methodist Episcopal Church. At the first general conference of the Colored Methodist Episcopal Church in 1870, Miles was elected one of the denomination's first two bishops. He was an active advocate of black colleges, especially those affiliated with the CME Church, such as Lane College in Jackson, Tennessee, and Paine Seminary in Atlanta, Georgia.

Daniel Alexander Payne (1811–1893)
African Methodist Episcopal Church Bishop, Educator

Payne is a towering figure in the history of African American religion and probably the greatest educator in the history of the African Methodist Episcopal Church. Born to free parents in Charleston, South Carolina, Payne received an excellent education and opened a school for black Charlestonians in 1829. An act of the South Carolina legislature forced him to close the school six years later. Payne traveled north and studied at the Lutheran Theological Seminary in Gettysburg, Pennsylvania. He delivered forceful anti-slavery speeches and, in 1841, switched his affiliation to the African Methodist Episcopal Church. He was ordained one year later and was elected a bishop in 1852.

Payne visited President Abraham Lincoln in the White House in 1862 and was a persistent advocate for emancipation and the freed people. In 1863 Payne bought Wilberforce University from the Methodist Episcopal Church. That university was the flagship school for the African Methodist Episcopal Church, and as its president and chief booster, Payne was the dominant presence there for the next thirty years. After the Civil War, Payne plunged himself deeply into oversight of the missionary work to the southern and western states and eventually to Africa. He was one of the first African

Americans to visit Charleston after its liberation by the Union Army in 1865. He initially was a strong supporter of black ministerial involvement in Reconstruction governments in the South, but Payne (widely known to have an impeccable character) changed his mind after exposure to southerners' corruption and misdeeds soured him on political participation. In 1882 he refused a conductor's order to move to a segregated smoking car, and after the conductor evicted him from the train, protest meetings were held in many American cities. During his last five years of life he published two important books, *Recollections of Seventy Years* (1888) and his well-researched *History of the African Methodist Episcopal Church* (1891).

Adam Clayton Powell Sr. (1865–1953)
Baptist Minister

Adam Clayton Powell Sr., father of the late Harlem congressman named after him, was largely responsible for building the Abyssinian Baptist Church into one of the most celebrated black congregations in the world.

Born in the backwoods of Virginia in 1865, Powell attended school locally and, between sessions, worked in the coal mines of West Virginia. After deciding to enter the ministry, he began his studies at Wayland Academy (now Virginia Union University), working his way through as a janitor and waiter. He later attended the Yale University School of Divinity and served as pastor of the Immanuel Baptist Church in New Haven.

Powell became pastor of Abyssinian in 1908 when it had a membership of only 1,600 and indebtedness of over $100,000. By 1921 the church had not been made solvent but was able to move into a $350,000 Gothic structure at its present location on 138th Street in Harlem.

During the Depression, Powell opened soup kitchens for Harlem residents and served thousands of meals. Later he and his son campaigned vigorously to expand job opportunities and city services in Harlem. Powell retired from Abyssinian in 1937 and died in 1953.

Frederick K.C. Price (1932–)
Religious Leader

Price was born on January 3, 1932, in Santa Monica, California. Price was not reared in the church but while attending a revival with his new wife, Betty Ruth Price, in 1953, Price was "born again" and later received the call to the ministry. He began preaching and pastored in several denominations before establishing his own congregation. In 1973 Price and three hundred parishioners moved to establish the Crenshaw Christian Center in Inglewood, California. His congregation grew as his services included speaking in tongue, healing, and prosperity teachings. By the 1980s Price's radio show *Ever Increasing Faith* was broadcasting to five major cities, and by the 1990s the congregation had outgrown its facility and a new structure was built. The Faith-Dome, dedicated in 1990, has seating for 10,146 persons. By 2002 the Crenshaw Christian Center had over 22,000 members.

Price earned a bachelor's degree in 1978, a Doctor of Ministry in 1988, and a Ph.D. in religious studies in 1992. Price has written numerous books, and in 1998 he received the Horatio Alger Award and Kelly Miller Smith Interfaith Award from the Southern Christian Leadership Conference.

Leon Sullivan (1922–2001)
Baptist Minister

Born in Charleston, South Carolina, Sullivan was ordained to the ministry at age nineteen. He was educated at the Union Theological Seminary in New York, and served as pastor of the Zion Baptist Church in Philadelphia from 1950 to 1988.

Much of his efforts during his ministry were directed toward improving employment prospects of African Americans. During the 1950s, he organized a selective patronage campaign, boycotting Philadelphia-area businesses that had too few black employees. Sullivan's campaign experienced some success, but businesses requested black workers with technical skills that few possessed. Accordingly, Sullivan founded the Opportunities Industrialization Center in 1964 to impart employment skills to inner-city youths. By 1980 the O.I.C. operated programs in 160 cities. He was also a major force in many other economic development initiatives, such as the Philadelphia Community Investment Cooperative. His acceptance within the American business community is well symbolized by his long-time membership on the boards of General Motors and Philadelphia's Girard Bank.

Sullivan is also renowned for his leadership in addressing international issues as they affect the African American community and in particular for his intensive involvement in political and economic reform in South Africa. In the mid-1970s he devised his "Sullivan Principles," which successfully encouraged American-owned companies to hire more black South African workers and to treat them equitably in relation to promotions and working conditions. Sullivan, however, parted company with President Ronald Reagan's "constructive engagement" policy toward South Africa, endorsing instead a policy of South African divestment in 1987.

Sulluvan, who retired in 1988, continued to advocate for assistance and empowerment for the people of Africa. He was honored with the Presidential Medal of Freedom in 1992. In 1999 he published *Global Sullivan Principles of Social Responsibility* and presented the principles to the United Nations, seeking to improve human rights and social justice on a global level. Sullivan died on April 4, 2001 in Scottsdale, Arizona.

Gardner C. Taylor (1918–)
Baptist Minister

Reverend Taylor is widely regarded as the dean of the nation's black preachers. He received a B.A. from Leland College in 1937 and a B.D. from the Oberlin Graduate School of Theology in 1940.

Taylor has long been a community activist. He demonstrated for civil rights, and suffered arrest for civil disobedience with Martin Luther King Jr. in the 1960s, and introduced Nelson

Mandela to a New York audience in 1990. He was a trusted counselor to New York mayor David Dinkins. Taylor served on the New York City Board of Education. He is the past president of the New York Council of Churches and the past vice president of the Urban League in New York City. After forty-two years as pastor of the Concord Baptist Church in Brooklyn, Taylor resigned his post in 1990.

Howard Thurman (1899–1981)
Theologian, Educator

Born in Daytona Beach, Florida, Thurman studied at Morehouse College, Rochester Theological Center, and Haverford College. Thurman, named by *Life* magazine as one of the twelve great preachers of the twentieth century, served as a pastor to a Baptist church in Ohio and, from 1944 to 1953, as pastor to an interracial and interdenominational Fellowship Church he founded in San Francisco. He also served as dean of the chapel at Howard University from 1932 to 1944, and at Boston University from 1953 until his retirement. Thurman was one of the leading theologians of his time, writing *The Negro Spiritual Speaks of Life and Death* and his opposition to segregation and support of the civil rights movement in *This Luminous Darkness*. Altogether, he wrote nineteen books, including an autobiography published in 1979.

Iyanla Vanzant (1954–)
Spiritual Educator, Talk Show Host

Iyanla Vanzant was born Rhonda Harris in Brooklyn, New York, on September 3, 1953. She attended Medgar Evers College and received her B.A., summa cum laude, in 1983 in public administration and later entered the City University of New York Law School at Queens College. In 2001 she earned her M.A. in spiritual psychology from the University of Santa Monica.

Vanzant endured a difficult childhood with various relatives as caregivers and being raped by an uncle at the tender age of nine. By the age of twenty-one she had three children and an abusive husband. Nine years later she escaped this situation only to endure years of public assistance but eventually earning an education and further opportunities. Vanzant went through a period of confusion after leaving her position in the Philadelphia Public Defenders Office. In 1988 she was invited to teach a class for women moving from welfare to work. She produced a workbook to guide their progress, which became her first published work, *Tapping the Power Within: A Path to Self Empowerment for Black Women*. Van-

zant has gone on to publish thirteen works and five best-sellers.

Vanzant has traveled globally sharing her knowledge of self empowerment and hope. She has been on numerous television shows and hosted her own daytime talk show from 2001 to 2002. She is founder of Inner Visions Institute of Spiritual Development and trains life coaches and ministers to teach and motivate others regarding ways to a better life and better communities.

LITERATURE

African American literature in the United States reached an artistic pinnacle in the period between the two world wars with the Harlem Renaissance. Since then the fate of African American writing has reached a level of high visibility; the themes have varied from highly charged and political to private and introspective. The Black Aesthetic Movement of the 1960s and 1970s brought acclaim and prominence to many African American writers and fostered the growth of many black studies departments at universities around the country. In the 1980s and 1990s, African American writers worked in every genre—from scriptwriting to poetry—and the names of African American writers consistently were found on bestseller lists around the country. Black writers no longer were relegated to limited publishing slots because their ingenuity and creativity in getting their work out and developing their audiences created a greater exposure and a greater demand for their work. With the increase in publishing by black writers, well into the twenty-first century, African Americans have earned an increased presence in contemporary fiction reaching out to both black and white readers.

Perhaps the greatest satisfaction for black writers before the 1920s, or the Harlem Renaissance, was to have the freedom to write; in fact, knowing how to read and write was a tremendous accomplishment for many post-Reconstruction African Americans.

For Frederick Douglass, to write stirring diatribes against slavery powerful enough to shake the consciousness of a nation was more a political than an artistic accomplishment. Likewise, when Jupiter Hammon, George Moses Horton, and Frances Harper prosaically wrote about the evils of slavery and racism, their verse seemed somewhat stilted; they followed the molds of Methodism, neoclassicism, and the Bible, traditions ill-suited to their subject matter. However admirable their writing was, they never quite found a vehicle that fit their revolutionary thoughts.

As the bonds of slavery were loosened, black writers clamored to be heard, but the range of their work was limited. Since slavery and plantations were practically the only subjects in their repertoire, early African American works were often locked into these themes. In addition, being a black writer before 1920 was certainly a unique profession, almost an oddity. Many writers were essentially unknown during their lives. Still others, like Phillis Wheatley and Horton, gained a certain amount of acclaim. In fact, a number of blacks, including Paul Laurence Dunbar and Charles W. Chestnutt, became truly appreciated as writers.

White society, however, still controlled much of publishing in America; African American work was often filtered and distorted through this lens. As a result, much of the post-Reconstruction era work by African Americans was an attempt to prove that blacks could fit into middle-American society. In fact, much of the literature of this era was an attempt by blacks to appear happy with their assigned lot. Yet some writers—Dunbar and Chestnutt, for example—tried to break the chains of this imposed expression by presenting a view of black life as it really was, not as society wanted it to be.

Although the accomplishments of writers of this era were remarkable, existing conditions seemed to keep African American letters from truly flourishing. What these authors most notably did was to pave the way for the Harlem Renaissance and to provoke authors to think about and develop a truly African American culture.

The Harlem Renaissance began roughly around World War I and extended into the early 1930s. It began mostly as a movement of African American artists and writers into Harlem from practically every state in the country. The movement also saw that another hub of artistic activity was forming in Washington, D.C. In fact, Harlem artists often journeyed to Washington for a break and a new perspective.

As African American journals such as *Crisis* and *Opportunity* began to appear, it became much easier for black writers to publish in a style that suited their tastes. Also, African American writers were finding that some white patrons in the publishing fields were, in fact, interested in promoting their work. Bohemianism was flourishing, and many of the Harlem Renaissance artists fit this label. Being called "New Negroes," they sought to chisel out a unique, African-centered culture for blacks and to improve race relations while maintaining a distinct cultural identity.

Important writers of this era include Langston Hughes, Countee Cullen, Claude McKay, Nella Larsen, and Zora Neale Hurston. These younger writers were encouraged by the older, established writers, critics, and editors, in-

Langston Hughes was one of the most important authors to come out of the Harlem Renaissance period of literature.

cluding W.E.B. DuBois, with his journal *Crisis*, and Charles S. Johnson, editor of *Opportunity*, a sponsor of many literary contests. In fact, Langston Hughes actually believed that the Renaissance came about directly because of the nurturing of older writers, including Jessie Fauset and Alain Locke.

The Harlem Renaissance was marked by a shift away from the moralizing work, which had been characteristic of much post-Reconstruction writing that decried racism. Even though much of this writing was excellently written and eloquently executed, people like DuBois and Locke realized that it was doing very little to change the consciousness of the country. For this reason, they decided instead to challenge these new writers to produce works that came directly out of personal experience—to communicate the ills of the racist world with art rather than essay. In this way, readers were not struck so bluntly with the grim realities presented by African American writers. These issues could be experienced through the lives of characters and in verse, and the message delivered more subtly and effectively.

As the economic Depression deepened, the Harlem Renaissance slowly faded. Richard Wright's publication in 1940 of *Native Son* marked a new era in African American literature. The years from 1940 to 1955 served as a transition period for black authors; they bridged the wildly creative period of the Renaissance with the more intense creativity and political activity that was to define the work produced during the civil rights movement.

With the publication of his classic novel, Wright maintained that the era of the Harlem Renaissance—with its motto of "art for art's sake"—must die and be replaced instead with works directly intended to end racism. He believed that blacks were an essential part of American society—a belief that was one of the foundations for the ideology of the civil rights movement.

During this time, other black writers, notably poets, were taking a different road in their quest to be heard. Poets such as Gwendolyn Brooks, Melvin B. Tolson, and Robert Hayden were using classical and mythical themes in their works. Indeed, Brooks won a Pulitzer Prize in 1950 for her book *Annie Allen*. These poets used a blend of extreme eclecticism with realistic African American issues. The blend seemed to work, as their writing was met with acceptance in the university community and beyond.

Ralph Ellison's *Invisible Man,* arguably one of the best novels published in America during this century, and James Baldwin's *Go Tell It on the Mountain*, were two other books that brought serious African American issues to mainstream culture. In addition, many African American works were gaining acceptance with the literary establishment and being taught in English classes around the country.

The Black Aesthetic Movement, or the Black Arts Movement, was the first major African American artistic movement since the Harlem Renaissance. Beginning in the early 1960s and lasting through the mid-1970s, this movement was brought on not by white patrons (as the Renaissance had been in part), but by the anger of Richard Wright, Ralph Ellison, and other notable African American writers.

This artistic movement was closely paralleled by the civil rights marches and the call for independence being experienced in the African American community. As phrases like "Black is beautiful" were popularized, African American writers of the Aesthetic Movement consciously set out to define what it meant to be a black writer in white culture. While writers of the Harlem Renaissance seemed to stumble upon their identity within, writers of the Aesthetic Movement were serious about defining themselves and their era before being defined by others.

The Black Aesthetic Movement attempted to produce works of art that would be meaningful to the black masses. Toward this end, popular black music of the day, including John Coltrane's jazz and James Brown's rhythm and blues, as well as street talk, were some of the inspirational forces for their art. In fact, much of the language used in these works was abrasive and shocking—this was often a conscious attempt to show the vitality and power of black activists. These writers tended to be revolutionaries rather than diplomats—Malcolm X was more of an idol than Martin Luther King Jr. In addition, they believed that artists had more of a responsibility than just art: artists also had to be political activists in order to achieve nationalist goals.

Leading writers in this movement include Imamu Amiri Baraka (also known as Leroi Jones), whose poetry was as well known as his political prowess; and Haki R. Madhubuti (Don L. Lee), a poet and essayist who was overwhelmingly popular, selling over 100,000 copies of his books without a national distributor. Ishmael Reed, on the other hand, an early organizer of the Black Aesthetic Movement, later dissented with some of the movement's doctrines; he became inspired more and more by the black magic and

Poet Alice Walker resurrected the work of Zora Neale Hurston as part of the movement to have the voices of African American women heard.

spiritual practices of the West Indies (in what he called the "HooDoo Aesthetic").

Sonia Sanchez was another leading voice of the movement. She managed to combine feminism with her commitment to nurturing children and men in the fight for Black Nationalism. She joined up with the Nation of Islam from 1972 to 1975, and through her association with the Black Aesthetic Movement managed to instill stronger support for that religion.

Many women, however, wrote in response to the Black Aesthetic Movement, protesting the role they felt women were forced to play in the male-oriented Black Nationalist movement. Zora Neale Hurston's work was resurrected by writer and poet Alice Walker and used for inspiration and impetus in their work. These women were also supported by the women's liberation movement, allowing their works to reach a wider audience. In this way, the female-repressive politics of the Black Aesthetic Movement provoked women writers to express their own unique voice. Women-centered

writing in the 1970s also saw authors such as Nikki Giovanni, a vocal and aggressive voice during the Black Aesthetic Movement, take a more direct look at women's roles in the need for social change. Black women were not just feminist as defined by the white women's liberation movement, but they envisioned a movement that was inclusive of a broad cultural and familial need of family and community. Alice Walker coined the word "womanist," which many embraced along with many of the ideologies of feminism. An emerging group also during this time was the lesbian movement which gave voice to writers such as Audre Lorde and feminist and activist June Jordan. Overall during the 1980s, black women writers were at the leading edge of publishing—in quality as well as quantity of work.

Since the Black Aesthetic Movement, African American writing has become more legitimized in America, and black studies departments have emerged in many universities around the country. Variety was the key to African American writing after 1950, and barriers went down in various genres. For example, Octavia Butler and Samuel Delany broke into the world of science fiction. Donald Goines wrote detective fiction that rivaled that of his contemporaries. Novels of both folk history and the urban experience were equally well received, and many artists found that they could straddle more than one genre—Alice Walker and Gayle Jones being good examples—and delve into the worlds of fiction, poetry, essay, and children's books.

Writers after the 1960s seem to have changed the tone by no longer placing as much emphasis on the disparity between black and white in America. In the words of Toni Morrison and John Edgar Wideman, the themes of self-reflection and healing were evident. African Americans were portrayed looking into their own inner worlds for answers, rather than letting themselves be defined by the outer world.

The period from 1975 to the twenty-first century brought more black writers into the mainstream and greater attention to African American literature and black studies programs. Women poets such as Gwendolyn Brooks and Nikki Giovanni, and writers such as Margaret Walker, Paule Marshall, and Nobel Prize winner Toni Morrison were key in literary studies. Writers offered a broad view of the black experience while bringing new perspectives inclusive of post-modern aesthetics and the mixing of genres. Accomplished writers emerged, such as August Wilson, Ntozake Shange, and George Wolf in the theater; Rita Dove and Yusef Komunyakaa in poetry; and Alice Walker, Charles Johnson, and John Edgar Wideman in fiction. Other writers who accentuated their presence in other genres were Walter Mosley with detective novels, Octavia Butler in science fiction, as well as BeBe Moore Campbell, Charles Fuller, Charles Johnson, Gayle Jones, Terry McMillan, and Gloria Naylor who used mixed genres of history revision, magical realism, and popular culture storylines. Unlike past periods these writers shared the stage with other African American writers and were not limited by a publishing world that previously allowed only one or two noted writers at a time.

African American authors have influenced contemporary audiences and earned numerous national and international awards. Pulitzer Prize winners include Rita Dove for poetry (1987), August Wilson a two time winner for playwriting (1987 and 1990), and Alex Haley for his contribution to the literature of slavery (1976). The National Book Award winners since 1975 include, in fiction Alice Walker (1983), Charles Johnson (1990), and in poetry Lucille Clifton (2000).

At the end of the twentieth century and the beginning of the twenty-first century African American writing continues to explore identity but the oppressive legacy of the past has become often only one factor with other issues such as gender, sexual orientation, and individual challenges also being paramount. Writers such as E. Lynn Harris, Omar Tyree, Connie Briso, and Zane have developed a wide following and major booksellers in their area of contemporary black popular fiction. These works are considered largely outside the realm of serious literature and more a function of popular culture and entertainment. Works that have been adapted to films are generally more known by the general public than the literary works themselves, but they continue to create and increase audiences for both popular books and film. The influence of contemporary fiction in expanding reading audiences, both black and white, has continued the interest of mainstream publishers in black writers.

With the success of many programs in African American studies, more writers are coming from academic settings. Afro-Caribbean writers such as Suzan-Lori-Parker, Edwidge Danticat, Colson Whitehead, and Paul Beatty have also reached out to a diverse and growing audience.

BIOGRAPHIES

Maya Angelou (1928–)
Novelist, Poet

Born Marguerite Johnson, Angelou spent her formative years shuttling between St. Louis, Missouri, a tiny, totally segregated town in Arkansas, and San Francisco, where she realized her ambition of becoming that city's first black streetcar conductor.

 During the 1950s she studied dancing with Pearl Primus in New York, later appearing as a nightclub singer in New York and San Francisco. She worked as an editor for *The Arab Observer*, an English-language weekly published in Cairo; lived in Accra, Ghana, where under the Black Nationalist regime of Kwame Nkrumah she taught music and drama; and studied cinematography in Sweden. She became a national celebrity in 1970 with the publication of *I Know Why the Caged Bird Sings*, the first volume of her autobiography, which detailed her encounters with southern racism and a prepubescent rape by her mother's lover.

Angelou pursued her passion in music, performance, poetry, and music, which included writing the first script by an African American woman to be filmed and subsequently nominated for a Pulitzer Prize in 1972. In 1971 she wrote *Just Give Me a Cool Drink of Water 'fore I Die: The Poetry of Maya Angelou*; in 1975, *Oh Pray My Wings Are Gonna Fit Me Well*; in 1979, *And Still I Rise*; and in 1983, *Shaker Why Don't You Sing?* In 1977 she was nominated for an Emmy Award for her portrayal of Nyo Boto in the television adaptation of the bestselling novel *Roots*. In 1993 Angelou appeared in John Singleton's film *Poetic Justice*, then she directed her first feature film, *Down in the Delta* in 1996; and in 2008 she narrated the award-winning documentary *The Black Candle*.

Three more volumes of her autobiography have been published: *Gather Together in My Name* (1974); *Singin' and Swingin' and Gettin' Merry Like Christmas* (1976); and *The Heart of a Woman* (1981). In 1986 *All God's Children Need Traveling Shoes* was published. Angelou's other works include *Mrs. Flowers: A Moment of Friendship*, *Now Sheba Sings the Song*, and *Wouldn't Take Nothing for My Journey Now*.

On January 20, 1993, Angelou read her poem "On the Pulse of Morning" during the inaugura-

tion of President Bill Clinton, which was broadcast all over the world. She was awarded the Spingarn Medal from the NAACP in 1994, the Presidential Medal of Arts in 2000, the Mother Theresa Award in 2006, the Lincoln Medal in 2008, and she also received three Grammy Awards. Angelou has received numerous honorary degrees and continues to be celebrated for her many contributions. She is the Reynolds Professor of American Studies at Wake Forest University.

Houston Baker Jr. (1943–)
Author, Scholar

Baker was born in Louisville, Kentucky, in 1943. He attended Howard University and received his B.A. in English, magna cum laude, and Phi Beta Kappa, and went on to received a master's and doctoral degrees from the University of California at Los Angeles.

As a young scholar Baker moved from a focus in British Victorian literature to the study of African American literature and culture. Beginning with the anthology *Black Literature in America* (1971), Baker published numerous texts that explore black culture. His publications include *No Matter Where You Travel, You Are Still Black* (1979), *Narrative of the Life of Frederick Douglass, An American Slave* (1982), *Black Studies; Rap and the Academy* (1993), *Turning South* (2001), and *Betrayal: How Black Intellectuals Have Abandoned the Ideals of the Civil Rights Era* (2008).

Baker is also a published poet and served as president of the Modern Language Association of America in 1992. He has been honored with awards such as the Guggenheim and Rockefeller Fellowship and received the Hubbell Medal for Lifetime Achievement in American Literary Studies in 2003. Baker is currently the distinguished university professor and professor of English at Vanderbilt University.

James Baldwin (1924–1987)
Novelist, Essayist, Playwright

Born in New York City, Baldwin turned to writing after an early career as a boy preacher in Harlem's storefront churches. He attended Frederick Douglass Junior High School in Harlem and later graduated from DeWitt Clinton High School, where he was editor of the school magazine. Three years later, he won a Eugene Saxton Fellowship, which enabled him to write full time. After leaving the United States, Baldwin resided in France and in Turkey.

 Baldwin's first novel, *Go Tell It on the Mountain*, was published in 1953 to critical acclaim. Two years later, his first collection of essays, *Notes of a Native Son*, again won acclaim. This was followed in 1956 by the publication of his second novel, *Giovanni's Room*. His second collection of essays, *Nobody Knows My Name*, brought him into the literary spotlight and established him as a major voice in American literature. His publications went on to include *Another Country* (1962), which was a critical and commercial success, and *The Fire Next Time* (1963), an immediate bestseller regarded as one of the most brilliant essays written in the history of the black protest. He also published the plays *Blues for Mister Charlie* and *The Amen Corner,* produced on the New York stage; *Tell Me How Long the Train's Been Gone* was published in 1968.

After a silence of several years, he published the 1974 novel *If Beale Street Could Talk*. To many critics, however, the novel lacked the undeniable relevance and fiery power of Baldwin's early polemical essays.

Baldwin's other works include *Going to Meet the Man* (short stories); *No Name in the Street; One Day When I Was Lost,* a scenario based on Alex Haley's *The Autobiography of Malcolm X*; *A Rap on Race with Margaret Mead*; and *A Dialogue with Nikki Giovanni*. He was one of the rare authors who worked well alone or in collaboration. Other books by Baldwin are *Nothing Personal* (1964), with photographs by Richard Avedon; *The Devil Finds Work* (1976), about the movies; his lengthy sixth novel, *Just Above My Head* (1979); and *Little Man, Little Man: A Story of Childhood* (1977), a

book for children. He wrote sixteen books and coauthored three others. Six books have been written about Baldwin's life and writings, including a reference guide and bibliography.

His last three books are *The Evidence of Things Not Seen* (1985), about the killing of twenty-eight black youths in Atlanta, Georgia, in the early 1980s; *The Price of the Ticket: Collected Nonfiction, 1948–1985* (1985); and *Harlem Quartet*.

Baldwin spent most of the remainder of his life in France. In 1986 the French government made him a commander of the Legion of Honor, France's highest civilian award. He died of stomach cancer at his home in France on November 30, 1987, at the age of sixty-three.

Toni Cade Bambara (1939–1995)
Author

Bambara was born in New York City in 1939 as Miltona Mirkin Cade. She shortened her name to Toni while in kindergarten and took the name Bambara when she found among her grandmother's things the name Bambara written on a sketchbook. Bambara received her B.A. from Queens College in New York in 1959 and her M.A. from City College of New York in 1964.

Bambara was active in the nationalist and women's movements and produced work that explored the African American community and focused in particular on African American women. Her works include *Gorilla, My Love* (1972), *The Salt Eaters* (1980), and *If Blessings Come* (1987). Bambara received the American Book Award for *The Salt Eaters*. Her final novel, *Those Bones Are Not My Child,* was published posthumously in 1999.

Bambara died on December 9, 1995, of colon cancer in Philadelphia.

Amiri Baraka (1934–)
Poet, Playwright, Essayist

Baraka was born in Newark in 1934. He attended Rutgers University in Newark, New Jersey, and

Howard University in Washington, D.C. In 1958 he founded *Yugen* magazine and Totem Press. From 1961 to 1964 Baraka worked as an instructor at New York's New School for Social Research. In 1964 he founded the Black Arts Repertory Theater. He has since taught at the State University of New York at Stony Brook, the University of Buffalo, Columbia University, George Washington University, and San Francisco University, and has served as director of the community theater Spirit House in Newark.

In 1961 Baraka published his first book of poetry, *Preface to a Twenty Volume Suicide Note*. His second book, *The Dead Lecturer*, was published in 1964. However, he did not achieve fame until the publication of his play *Dutchman* in 1964, which received the Obie Award for the best Off-Broadway play of the season. The shocking honesty of Baraka's treatment of racial conflict in this and later plays became the hallmark of his work.

In 1966 Baraka's play *The Slave* won second prize in the drama category at the First World Festival of Dramatic Arts in Dakar, Senegal. Baraka's other published plays include *The Toilet* (1964); *The Baptism* (1966); *The System of Dante's Hell* (1965); *Four Black Revolutionary Plays* (1969); *J-E-L-L-O* (1970); and *The Motion of History and Other Plays* (1978).

He edited, with Larry Neal, *Black Fire: An Anthology of AfroAmerican Writing* (1968) and *Afrikan Congress: A Documentary of the First Modern Pan-African Congress* (1972). His works of nonfiction include *Home: Social Essays* (1966), *It's Nation Time; Kawaida Studies: The New Nationalism; A Black Value System, and Strategy and Tactics of a Pan Afrikan Nationalist Party;* and *Funk Love* (1984–1995). More recently, he published *Somebody Blew Up America;* and *Other Poems* (2003) and *Tales of the Out and the Gone* (2006).

In July 2002 Baraka was named Poet Laureate of New Jersey, nine months after the attack on the World Trade Center. A poem he wrote entitled "Somebody Blew Up America" was so controver-

sial it resulted in an effort by state officials to remove Baraka from his post. In 2003, since Baraka could not be removed, the position was abolished.

Baraka has received numerous awards and honors inclusive of the the Obie and the PEN/Faulkner Award as well as prizes from the Guggenheim Foundation, the National Endowment of the Arts, and the Rockefeller Foundation.

Arna Bontemps (1902–1973)
Poet, Novelist

Arna Bontemps was one of the most productive black writers of the twentieth century. Born in Alexandria, Louisiana, and raised in California, Bontemps received his B.A. from Pacific Union College in Angwin in 1923. The next year his poetry first appeared in *Crisis* magazine, the NAACP periodical edited by W.E.B. DuBois. Two years later, *Golgotha Is a Mountain* won the Alexander Pushkin Award, and in 1927, *Nocturne at Bethesda* achieved first honors in the *Crisis* poetry contest. *Personals*, Bontemps's collected poems, was published in 1963.

In the late 1920s Bontemps decided to try his hand at prose, and over the next decade produced such novels as *God Sends Sunday* (1931); *Black Thunder* (1936); and *Drums at Dusk* (1939).

His books for young people include *We Have Tomorrow* (1945) and *Story of the Negro* (1948). Likewise of literary merit are such children's books as *Sad-Faced Boy* (1937) and *Slappy Hooper* (1946). He edited *American Negro Poetry* and two anthologies with Langston Hughes among others.

In 1968 he edited a volume of children's poetry. Other publications were *One Hundred Years of Negro Freedom* (1961); *Anyplace But Here* (published in 1966 in collaboration with Jack Convoy); *Black Thunder* (reprinted 1968); *Great Slave Narratives* (1969); *The Harlem Renaissance Remembered: Essays* (1972, 1984); and *The Old South*.

Bontemps died on June 4, 1973, of a heart attack.

Gwendolyn Brooks (1917–2000)
Poet

Gwendolyn Brooks is one of a select number of blacks to win a Pulitzer Prize. Brooks received this prestigious award in 1950 for *Annie Allen*, a volume of her poetry that had been published a year earlier.

Brooks was born in Topeka, Kansas, moved to Chicago at an early age, and was educated there, graduating from Wilson Junior College in 1936. In 1945 she completed a book of poems, *A Street in Bronzeville*, and was selected by *Mademoiselle* magazine, as one of the year's ten most outstanding American women. She was made a fellow of the American Academy of Arts and Letters in 1946, and received Guggenheim Fellowships for 1946 and 1947.

In 1949 she won the Eunice Tietjen Prize for Poetry in the annual competition sponsored by *Poetry* magazine. She was also poet laureate of the state of Illinois.

Her other books include a collection of children's poems, *Bronzeville Boys and Girls* (1956); a novel, *Maud Martha* (1953); and two books of poetry, *The Bean Eaters* (1960) and *Selected Poems* (1963). She has also written *In the Mecca; Riot; The World of Gwendolyn Brooks; Report from Part One: The Autobiography of Gwendolyn Brooks;* and *To Disembark*. She has edited *A Broadside Treasury* and *Jump Bad: A New Chicago Anthology*.

Brooks received numerous awards and recognition over the years. In 1985 Western Illinois University established the Gwendolyn Brooks Center for African American Literature, and she was inducted into the National Women's Hall of Fame in 1988. She received the Frost Medal from the Poetry Society of America in 1990, and in 1995 received the National Medal of Arts from President Bill Clinton.

Due to complications from cancer, Brooks died on December 3, 2000, at her Chicago home.

William Wells Brown (1815–1884)
Novelist, Playwright

William Wells Brown was the first Black American to publish a novel, the first to publish a drama, and the first to publish a travel book.

Born a slave in Lexington, Kentucky, and taken to St. Louis as a young boy, Brown worked for a time in the offices of the *St. Louis Times*, and then took a job on a riverboat in service on the Mississippi. In 1834 Brown fled to Canada, taking his name from a friendly Quaker whom he met there. While working as a steward on Lake Erie ships, he educated himself and became well known as a public speaker. In 1849 he went to England and Paris to attend the Peace Congress, remaining abroad for five years.

His first published work, *The Narrative of William H. Brown*, went into three editions within eight months. A year later, a collection of his poems was published, *The AntiSlavery Harp*, and in 1852 his travel book *Three Years in Europe* appeared in London.

Brown's *Clotel, or the President's Daughter*, a melodramatic novel about miscegenation, was first published in London in 1853. As the first novel by an African American—which subsequently went through two revisions—its historical importance transcends its aesthetic shortcomings.

Brown's other books include the first black drama *The Escape, or a Leap for Freedom* (1858); *The Black Man: His Antecedents, His Genius, and His Achievements* (1863); *The Negro in the American Rebellion: His Heroism and Fidelity* (1867); and *The Rising Son* (1874).

Octavia Butler (1947–2006)
Novelist

Born in Pasadena, California, Octavia Butler is a graduate of Pasadena City College. She has attended science fiction workshops and is a member of the Science Fiction Writers of America.

Her writing has focused on the impact of race and gender on the future society.

In 1985 Butler won three of science fiction's highest honors for her novella *Bloodchild*: the Nebula Award, the Hugo Award, and the Locus Award. Her other works include *Patternmaster* (1976); *Mind of My Soul* (1977); *Survivor* (1978); *Kindred* (1979); *Wild Seed* (1980); *Clay's Ark* (1984); *Dawn and Xenogenesis* (1987); *Parable of the Sower* (1993); with its sequel, *Parable of the Talents* (1998); and *Fledgling* (2005). Butler also became the first science fiction writer to receive the MacArthur Foundation grant in 1995.

On February 24, 2006, Butler died after hitting her head during a fall at her home in Lake Forest Park, Seattle, Washington.

Charles W. Chesnutt (1858–1932)
Novelist

Born in Cleveland, Ohio, in 1858, Chesnutt moved to North Carolina with his family at the age of eight. Largely self-educated, he was admitted to the Ohio bar in 1887, the same year in which his first story, "The Gophered Grapevine," was published in the *Atlantic Monthly*. This was followed in 1899 by two collections of his stories, *The Conjure Woman* and *The Wife of His Youth*.

His first novel, *The House Behind the Cedars* (1900), dealt with a young girl's attempt to "pass" for white. A year later, *The Marrow of Tradition* examined the violence of the post-Reconstruction period. His final novel, *The Colonel's Dream*, was published in 1905 and typified Chesnutt's basically ingratiating approach to his art, which writers of the Harlem School were later to reject. Chesnutt also wrote a biography, *Frederick Douglass* (1899).

Alice Childress (1920–1994)
Playwright, Novelist

Born in Charleston, South Carolina, Childress studied acting at the American Negro Theatre and attended Radcliffe Institute from 1966 to 1968 through a Harvard University appointment as a scholar-writer. Her plays include *Gold Through the Trees; Just a Little Simple* (based on Langston Hughes's *Simple Speaks His Mind*); and *When the Rattlesnake Sounds: A Play about Harriet Tubman*. Her other books include *A Hero Ain't Nothing but a Sandwich* (novel, 1973); *A Short Walk* (1979); *Rainbow Jordan* (1981); and *Many Closets* (1987). Childress's play *Trouble in Mind* won the Obie Award in 1956 as the best original Off-Broadway production. This made her the first woman to win the award. Many of her plays dealt with issues of miscegenation or race mixing and teen drug issues. She wrote, in the 1980s, a play based on the life of the black woman comedienne Jackie "Moms" Mabley, which was produced in New York City.

Childress died of complications due to cancer on August 14, 1994.

J. California Cooper
Playwright and Short Story Writer

Joan Cooper was born in Berkeley, California. She attended a technical high school and later attended San Francisco State College. Cooper included California in her name when her work was compared to the work of Tennessee Williams and later used the initial of her first name.

Cooper had the skills of a storyteller beginning in her childhood years. Since she chooses not to reveal her birth year the timing of her first endeavor is not known. Cooper began writing plays, producing works such as *Everytime It Rain; System, Suckers, and Success*, and *Ahhh*. By 1978 she had written seventeen plays and was named San Francisco's Best Black Playwright.

After encouragement from poet and author Alice Walker, Cooper began to write short stories. Her first collection *A Piece of Mine* was published in 1984. Subsequent collections include *Home-made Love* (1986), *The Matter Is Life* (1991), *The Future Has a Past* (2000), and *Wild Stars Seeking Midnight Suns* (2006). Cooper also has published novels, including *The Wake of the Wind* (1998), *Some People, Some Other Place* (2004), and *Life Is Short but Wide* (2010), and has been the recipient of the American Book Award in 1986, the James Baldwin Award, and Best Female Writer in Texas.

Cooper's work, which has a strong connection to the "folk," has been described as simple and direct with comparisons made to Langston Hughes and Zora Neale Hurston.

Countee Cullen (1903–1946)
Poet

Born Countee Porter on May 30, 1903, in Baltimore, he was orphaned at an early age and adopted by the Reverend Frederick Cullen, pastor of New York's Salem Methodist Church. At New York University, Cullen won Phi Beta Kappa honors and was awarded the Witter Bynner Poetry Prize. In 1925, while still a student at New York University, Cullen completed *Color*, a volume of poetry that received the Harmon Foundation's first gold medal for literature two years later.

In 1926 he earned his M.A. at Harvard and a year later finished both *The Ballad of the Brown Girl* and *Copper Sun*. This was followed in 1929 by *The Black Christ*, written during a two-year sojourn in France on a Guggenheim Fellowship.

Upon his return to New York City, Cullen began a teaching career in the public school system. During this period, he also produced *One Way to Heaven* (1932); *The Medea and Other Poems* (1935); *The Lost Zoo* (1940); and *My Lives and How I Lost Them* (1942, 1971).

In 1947, a year after his death, Cullen's own selections of his best work were collected in a volume published under the title *On These I Stand*.

Samuel R. Delany (1942–)
Novelist

Born in Harlem, and a published writer at the age of nineteen, Delany has been a prolific writer of science fiction novelettes and novels. His first book was *The Jewels of Aptor* (1962), followed by *Captives of the Flame* (1963). *Babe l17* (1966) and *The Einstein Intersection* (1967) both won Nebula Awards from the Science Fiction Writers of America, as have his short stories "Aye, and Gomorrah" and "Time Considered as a Helix of Semi-Precious Stones," which also won a Hugo Award at the World Science Fiction Convention at Heidelberg. Delany coedited the speculative fiction quarterly, *Quark*, Numbers 1, 2, 3, 4 with his former wife, National Book Award-winning poet Marilyn Hacker. He also wrote *Dahlgren* in 1975, and directed and edited the half-hour film *The Orchid*. He also served as a visiting Butler Chair Professor of English at the State University of New York at Buffalo.

His other books include *Distant Stars* (1981); *Stars in My Pocket Like Grains of Sand* (1984); *Flight from Neveryona* (1985); *Neveryona* (1986); and *The Bridge of Lost Desire* (1988). His nonfiction works include *The Jewel-Hinged Jaw* and *The Motion of Light in Water*, an autobiography.

Delaney's most recent book published in 2008, *Dark Reflections*, explores the experiences of black gay poets. The book was nominated for the Lambda Literary Award. Delaney has received numerous awards for his work and is considered a major African American writer as the genre of science fiction crosses socially constructed lines. He is a professor of English and director of the graduate creative writing program at Temple University in Philadelphia.

Rita Dove (1952–)
Poet, Educator

Dove was born on August 28, 1952, in Akron, Ohio. She received a B.A. from Miami University in Oxford, Ohio, in 1973 and a master of fine arts from the University of Iowa in 1977. Dove also attended the University of Tubingen in Germany in 1974 and 1975.

Dove began her teaching career at Arizona State University in 1981 as an assistant professor. By 1984 she was an associate professor and by 1987 a full professor. In 1989 she joined the University of Virginia's English department, where she continues to teach creative writing.

Dove is a renowned poet, having won the 1987 Pulitzer Prize for poetry for a collection titled *Thomas & Beulah*. Her themes are universal, encompassing much of the human condition and occasionally commenting on racial issues. Among numerous works she has also published *Fifth Sunday* (1985), *Mother Love* (1995), and the play *The Darker Face of the Earth* (1996). In 2009 Dove published *Sonata*, a collection of poems.

Besides the Pulitzer Prize, Dove has received many honors, including a presidential scholarship (1970), two Fulbright scholarships (1974, 1975), two Guggenheim Fellowships (1983, 1984), two Andrew W. Mellon Fellowships (1988, 1989), a fellowship at the Center for Advanced Studies at the University of Virginia (1989–1992), and the Walt Whitman Award (1990).

From 1993 to 1995 Dove was named U.S. Poet Laureate, and from 2004 to 2006 she served as Poet Laureate of the Commonwealth of Virginia. In 2006 she also received the coveted Common Wealth Award of Distinguished Service along with other distinguished recipients.

Paul Laurence Dunbar (1872–1906)
Poet

The first black poet to gain a national reputation in the United States, Paul Laurence Dunbar was also the first to use black dialect within the formal structure of his work.

Born of former slaves in Dayton, Ohio, Dunbar went to work as an elevator operator after graduating from high school. His first book of poetry, *Oak and Ivy*, was privately printed in 1893 and was followed by *Majors and Minors*, which appeared two years later. Neither book was an immediate sensation, but there were enough favorable reviews in such magazines as *Harper's* to encourage Dunbar in the pursuit of a full-fledged literary career. In 1896 Dunbar completed *Lyrics of a Lowly Life*, the single work upon which his subsequent reputation was irrevocably established.

Before his untimely death in 1906, Dunbar had become the dominant presence in the world of American Negro poetry. His later works included *Lyrics of Sunshine and Shadow* (1905), *Li'l Gal* (1904), *Howdy, Honey, Howdy* (1905), *A Plantation Portrait* (1905), *Joggin' Erlong* (1906), and *Complete Poems*, published posthumously in 1913. This last work contains not only the dialect poems that were his trademark, but many poems in conventional English as well. The book has enjoyed such enormous popularity that it has, to this day, never gone out of print. He also published four novels, including *The Sport of Gods, The Love of Landry, The Uncalled,* and four volumes of short stories.

Ralph Ellison (1914–1994)
Novelist, Essayist

Ralph Ellison's critical and artistic reputation rests largely on a single masterpiece, his first and only novel, *Invisible Man*. Acclaimed by virtually all who have read it, the novel was given the National Book Award for fiction in 1952. It had been years in the making, and its success heralded the emergence of a major writing talent.

Ellison was born in Oklahoma City, Oklahoma, and came to New York City in the late 1930s, after having studied music at the Tuskegee Institute for three years. At first interested in sculpture, he turned to writing after coming under the influence of T.S. Eliot's poetry, and as a direct consequence of his friendship with Richard Wright. In 1955 the American Academy of Arts and Letters awarded Ellison the Prix de Rome, which enabled him to live and write in Italy for a time.

Ellison's second published work was *Shadow and Act*, a book of essays that appeared in 1964. Ellison received the Medal of Freedom from President Richard M. Nixon in 1969, and an honorary doctor of letters degree from Wesleyan University in June 1980 "for his insight into the role of the artist in American culture."

Ellison retired as Albert Schweitzer Professor of Humanities at New York University (1970–1980), and in 1974 was awarded an honorary doctor of letters degree by Harvard University. The thirtieth anniversary edition of *Invisible Man,* with a new introduction by Ellison, was published in 1982.

Ellison began his second novel in 1954, and continued to develop it until his death. It was published posthumously in 1999 and titled *Juneteenth.* On April 16, 1994, Ellison died of pancreatic cancer.

Jessie Redmond Fauset (1882–1961)
Author, Editor, Educator

Fauset, the youngest of seven children, was born on April 27, 1882, to Annie Seamon and Reverend Redmond Fauset. Reverend Fauset was pastor of an African Methodist Episcopal church and he championed the cause of racial justice. Fauset's formative years were greatly influenced by her family's commitment to racial uplift. After graduating from high school with honors Fauset attended Cornell on a scholarship set up by Bryn Mawr, a woman's college. Bryn Mawr was not prepared to accept a black woman, so they arranged for the scholarship to Cornell. Fauset graduated in 1905, Phi Beta Kappa, the first black woman to matriculate from Cornell, and in 1919 she received her M.A. from the University of Pennsylvania. Fauset spent several years teaching.

Fauset was a key figure during the Harlem Renaissance and is often referred to as "the Mother of the Harlem Renaissance." She supported the careers of many of the young artists, such as Zora Neale Hurston and Langston Hughes, while serving as editor of *Crisis* magazine from 1919 to 1927. While working for W.E.B. DuBois, the *Crisis* magazine's founder, sales far exceeded other periodicals of the time. Fauset wrote her first novel, *There is Confusion*, in 1924. After leaving *Crisis* in 1927 Fauset establish her own literary career by publishing the novels, *Plum Bun* (1929), *The Chinaberry Tree* (1931), and *Comedy American Style* (1933). Her works focused on the racism and sexism that black women had to confront while educating their audience about the abilities and the deserved opportunities that should be afforded African Americans.

Fauset returned to teaching in her later years. She died on April 30, 1961, of hypertensive heart disease.

Rudolph Fisher (1897–1934)
Physician, Author

Fisher is best known as a leading writer during the Harlem Renaissance and the first to write detective fiction. He was born in Washington, D.C., on May 9, 1897. After experiencing a rigorous primary and secondary education in Rhode Island, he went on to Brown University and earned a B.A. in 1919 with the honors of Phi Beta Kappa and an M.A. in 1920. In that same year Fisher entered the Howard University Medical School. He graduated in 1924, summa cum laude, and began a one-year internship.

While serving as an intern, Fisher published his first short fiction, *The City of Refuge*, in 1925. In 1927 after going into private practice Fisher wrote several short stories and essays that were published in the *Atlantic Monthly* magazine, as well as *McClure's* and *American Mercury*. He wrote his first novel, *The Walls of Jericho,* in 1928. The novel encompasses the social and economic highs and lows of Harlem. In 1932 Fisher wrote *The Conjure-Man Dies,* which was the first black detective novel. Fisher published the children stories *Ezekiel* (1932) and *Ezekiel Learns* (1933), and in 1934 the short stories "Guardians of the Law" and "Miss Cynthie."

Fisher was successful in other areas as well. He was a gifted musician, serving in the 369th Infantry, and he was superintendent of the International Hospital in Manhattan from 1929 to 1930 and a roentgenologist for the New York City Health Department from 1930 to 1934. Fisher died of cancer in New York City on December 16, 1934.

Ernest J. Gaines (1933–)
Novelist, Short Story Writer

Gaines was born on River Lake plantation in Louisiana, which is the same plantation his family lived on since slavery. After emancipation they remained on the land and worked it as sharecroppers. Gaines moved to California in 1949, where he did his undergraduate study at San Francisco State College. In 1959 he received the Wallace Stegner Fellowship in creative writing. The following year he was awarded the Joseph Henry Jackson Literary Award.

His first novel to be published was *Catherine Carmier* (1964). Other novels by Gaines are *Of Love and Dust* (1967); *Barren Summer* (completed in 1963 but never published); *The Autobiography of Miss Jane Pittman* (1971); *A Warm Day in November* (for young people); and *In My Father's House* (1978). The 1974 television production of *The Autobiography of Miss Jane Pittman* with Cicely Tyson boosted his reputation. Another work by Gaines, the novel *A Gathering of Old Men*, published in 1983, has been made into a movie.

In 1993 Gaines published the novel *A Lesson Before Dying* and received, that same year, a MacArthur Foundation "genius grant." Adding a new dimension to the debate over capital punishment, the book received critical acclaim and was awarded the National Book Critics Circle Award for Fiction, and the television adaptation won the Emmy Award as Best Film for Television. In 2005 Gaines published a collection of his work, *Mozart and Leadbelly*.

Nikki Giovanni (1943–)
Poet

Nikki Giovanni, was born Yolande Cornelia Giovanni on June 7, 1943, in Knoxville, Tennessee. She went on to study at Fisk University earning a B.A. in 1967 and spent a year at the University of Pennsylvania School of Social Work. Her first book of poetry, *Black Feeling, Black Talk*, published in the mid-1960s, was followed by *Black Judgment* in 1968. These two were combined as *Black Feeling, Black Talk, Black Judgment* in 1970.

By 1974 her poems were found in many black literature anthologies, and she had also become a media personality through her television appearances, where she read her poetry. Many of her poems were put to soul or gospel music accompaniment. One such recording is *Truth Is on Its Way*.

Giovanni is a prolific author, having written *Recreation; Spin a Soft Black Song; Night Comes Softly: Anthology of Black Female Voices; My House; Gemini: An Extended Autobiographical Statement; Ego Tripping and Other Poems for Young People; A Dialogue* (with James Baldwin); and *A Poetic Equation: Conversations Between Nikki Giovanni and Margaret Walker*. Her other works include *The Women and the Men: Poems* (1975); *Cotton Candy on a Rainy Day* (1978); *Vacation Time* (1980), a collection of poems for children that was dedicated to her son, Tommy; *Those Who Ride the Night Winds* (1984); *Sacred Cows … and Other Edibles* (1988), *Quilting the Black-Eyed Pea; Poems and Not-Quite Poems* (2002), and *Acolytes* (2007). As a lung cancer survivor Giovanni contributed to the anthology *Breaking Silences* (2005).

Giovanni has numerous honorary degrees and awards, which include the Outstanding Women of Tennessee Award in 1985, the Langston Hughes Award for Distinguished Contributions to Arts and Letters in 1996, and the NAACP Image Award for Literature 1998.

Since 1987 Giovanni has been a professor of English at Virginia Tech, in Blacksburg, Virginia.

She is a distinguished university professor and the Gloria D. Smith Professor of Black Studies.

Alex Haley (1921–1992)
Journalist, Novelist

The author of the widely acclaimed novel *Roots* was born in Ithaca, New York, on August 11, 1921, and reared in Henning, Tennessee. The oldest of three sons of a college professor father and a mother who taught grade school, Haley graduated from high school at fifteen and attended college for two years before enlisting in the U.S. Coast Guard as a messboy in 1939.

By 1952 the Coast Guard had created a new rating for Haley, chief journalist, and he began handling U.S. Coast Guard public relations. In 1959, after twenty years of military service, he retired from the Coast Guard and launched a new career as a freelance writer. He eventually became an assignment writer for *Reader's Digest* and moved on to *Playboy*, where he initiated the "Playboy Interviews" feature.

A statue of Alex Haley reading to a group of children in Annapolis, Maryland, near the State House. There is also a statue of the author in Knoxville, Tennessee.

One of the personalities Haley interviewed was Malcolm X—an interview that inspired Haley's first book, *The Autobiography of Malcolm X* (1965). Translated into eight languages, the book has sold over six million copies.

Pursuing the few slender clues of oral family history told to him by his maternal grandmother in Tennessee, Haley spent the next twelve years traveling three continents tracking his maternal family back to a Mandingo youth named Kunta Kinte, who was kidnapped into slavery from the small village of Juffure, in The Gambia, West Africa. During this period he lectured extensively in the United States and in Great Britain on his discoveries about his family in Africa, and he wrote many magazine articles on his research in the 1960s and the 1970s. For his work he received several honorary doctor of letters degrees.

The book *Roots*, was finally published in the fall of 1976 with much publicity and media attention. In January 1977, ABC-TV produced a twelve-hour series based on the book, which set records for the number of viewers. With cover stories, book reviews, and interviews with Haley in scores of magazines and newspapers, the book became the number-one national best-seller, sold in the millions, and was published as a paperback in 1977.

Haley's book stimulated interest in Africa and in black genealogy. The U.S. Senate passed a resolution paying tribute to Haley and comparing *Roots* to *Uncle Tom's Cabin*, written by Harriet Beecher Stowe in the 1850s. Among the book's awards are the National Book Award for 1976 and a special Pulitzer Prize that same year for making an important contribution to the literature of slavery.

Haley received the NAACP's Spingarn Medal in 1977. The ABC-TV network presented another series, *Roots: The Next Generation*, in February 1979 (also written by Haley). *Roots* had sold almost five million copies by December 1978 and had been reprinted in twenty-three languages.

In 1988, Haley conducted a promotional tour for a novella called *A Different Kind of Christmas* about slave escapes in the 1850s. He also promoted a drama, *Roots: The Gift,* a two-hour television program shown in December 1988. Haley died February 10, 1992, of a heart attack.

Jupiter Hammon (c. 1720–c. 1800)
Poet

Hammon was the first black poet to have his work published in America. *An Evening Thought, Salvation by Christ, with Penitential Cries* appeared in 1761, when Hammon was a slave belonging to a Mr. Lloyd of Long Island, New York.

Due to his fondness for preaching, the majority of Hammon's poetry is religious in tone, and is usually dismissed by critics as being of little aesthetic value because of its pious platitudes, faulty syntax, and forced rhymes. Hammon's best-known work is a prose piece, "An Address to the Negroes of the State of New York," delivered before the African Society of New York City on September 24, 1786. This speech was published the following year and went into three editions.

Lorraine Hansberry (1930–1965)
Playwright

Born in Chicago on May 19, 1930, Hansberry studied art at Chicago's Art Institute, the University of Wisconsin, and, finally, in Guadalajara, Mexico.

Hansberry wrote the award-winning play *A Raisin in the Sun* while living in New York's Greenwich Village, having conceived the play after reacting distastefully to what she called "a whole body of material about Negroes. Cardboard characters. Cute dialect bits. Or hip-swinging musicals from exotic scores." The play opened on Broadway on March 11, 1959, at a time when it was generally held that all plays dealing with blacks were "death" at the box office. Produced, directed, and performed by blacks, it was later made into a successful movie starring Sidney Poitier. It was then adapted into *Raisin,* a musical that won a Tony Award in 1974.

Hansberry's second Broadway play, *The Sign in Sidney Brustein's Window,* dealt with "the western intellectual poised in hesitation before the flames of involvement." Shortly after its Broadway opening, Hansberry succumbed to cancer on January 12, 1965, in New York City.

Her books include *To Be Young, Gifted and Black; The Movement: Documentary of a Struggle for Equality;* and *Les Blancs: The Collected Last Plays of Lorraine Hansberry.*

Francis E.W. Harper (1825–1911)
Writer, Poet, Activist

Harper, an activist, poet, writer, and advocate for African American women's rights, was the first African American woman to publish a short story. Her many roles were engaged for the uplift of her people, and in particular for African American women, toward equal rights as persons and citizens.

Harper was born to free parents on September 24, 1825. She attended the most prestigious school, William Watkins Academy for Negro Youth, founded by her uncle in Baltimore, Maryland. Harper became a teacher for Union Seminary in 1850. In 1854 her literary career began with the publication of *Poems on Miscellaneous Subjects* printed in Boston and Philadelphia. The work was reprinted several times and included poems such as "The Slave Mother" and "The Slave Auction" along with other poems that focused on women's issues and other issues of the time. Harper went on to write other dramatic poems, the serialized novel *Minnie's Sacrifice,* and other essays. In 1892 Harper published her best-known novel, *Iola Leroy, or Shadows Uplifted,* which focused on the issues of slavery and Reconstruction and promoted racial pride among African Americans.

Harper is also well known for her fiery speeches on the abolitionist's circuit and her work as an abolitionist poet. Her activism also included work with the YMCA, the Colored Sections of the Women's Christian Suffrage Union in Philadelphia, the American Women's Suffrage Association, and as an organizer for the National Association of Colored Women. Harper died on February 20, 1911, in Philadelphia.

Robert E. Hayden (1913–1980)
Poet

Robert E. Hayden, a graduate of Detroit City College (now Wayne State University), who was chief researcher on African American history and folklore for the Federal Writers Project in 1936, later accomplished advanced work in English, play production, and creative writing at the University of Michigan. While there, he won the Jule and Avery Hopwood Prize for poetry twice. Hayden also completed radio scripts and a finished version of a play about the Underground Railroad, *Go Down Moses*.

His first book of poems, *Heart Shape in the Dust*, was published in 1940 shortly before he assumed the music and drama critic function for the *Michigan Chronicle*. He taught at Fisk University from 1946 to the early 1970s and later at the University of Michigan. His works include *The Lion and the Archer* (with Myron O'Higgins); *A Ballad of Remembrance; Selected Poems; Words in the Mourning Time*; and *The Night-Blooming Cereus*. His other books include *Figure of Time; Angle of Ascent: New and Selected Poems*; and *American Journal* (poems). In 1975 the Academy of American Poets elected him its Fellow of the Year, and in 1976 he was awarded the Grand Prize for Poetry at the First World Festival of Negro Arts in Dakar, Senegal. From 1976 to 1978 he served as consultant in poetry at the Library of Congress. He was a professor of English at the University of Michigan at the time of his death on February 25, 1980.

Chester Himes (1909–1984)
Novelist

Born in Jefferson City, Missouri, on June 29, 1909, Chester Himes was educated at Ohio State University and later lived in France and Spain. In 1945 he completed his first novel, *If He Hollers Let Him Go*, the story of a black working in a defense plant. His second book, *The Lonely Crusade* (1947), was set in similar surroundings. His other books include *The Third Generation* (1954), *Cotton Comes to Harlem* (1965), *Pinktoes* (1962), *The Quality of Hurt: The Autobiography of Chester Himes* (1973), *My Life of Absurdity: The Autobiography of Chester Himes* (1976), and *Black on Black: Baby Sister and Selected Writings* (1973).

Following a stroke, which confined him to a wheelchair, he and his wife lived in Alicante, Spain. In 1977 they returned to New York for the publication of the concluding volume of his autobiography, *My Life of Absurdity*. Himes died in Spain in November 1984, at the age of seventy-five. He was a prolific author of almost twenty books.

Pauline E. Hopkins (1859–1930)
Author, Editor, Playwright, Singer, Actress

Hopkins is best known for bringing light to racial issues through her work. She is remembered as "The Dean of African American women writers," a feminist, and a Pan-Africanist who was focused on the racial history of African American people. Hopkins was born in 1859 in Portland, Maine, and later moved to Boston. She was the great grand-niece of poet James Whitfield. At fifteen Hopkins won a writing contest sponsored by William Wells Brown. Her interest in writing was further realized in the establishment of the Colored Troubadours, a theatrical group. On July 5, 1880, the troupe performed Hopkins' first play, *Slaves' Escape: or the Underground Railroad*. The play was a musical comedy celebrating the bravery of abolitionists and activists such as Frederick Douglass and Harriett Tubman. Hopkins performed with the group for twelve years.

At the turn of the century Hopkins helped establish *The Colored American* magazine. The magazine's first issues in May 1900 included Hopkins's short story "The Mystery Within Us." Her first novel, *Contending Forces*, was published that same year by a Boston firm. Hopkins continued to contribute to the magazine including biographical sketches such as "Famous Women of the Negro Race" and "Famous Men of the Negro Race," serialized versions of three of her novels, *Hagar's Daughter: A Story of Southern Caste Prejudice* (1901–1902), *Winona: A Tale of Negro Life in the South and Southwest* (1902), and *Of One Blood: or The Hidden Self* (1902–1903). Hopkins resigned from the magazine in 1904.

After 1905 Hopkins' career began to decline. She founded her own publishing company, P.E. Hopkins, and in 1916 contributed several articles to local publications. Hopkins suffered severe burns when a bandage saturated with liniment to relieve the neuritis was ignited by an oil stove. As a result, she died on August 13, 1930.

Langston Hughes (1902–1967)
Poet, Novelist, Playwright

Born in Joplin, Missouri, on February 1, 1902, Langston Hughes moved to Cleveland at the age of fourteen, graduated from Central High School, and spent a year in Mexico before studying at Columbia University. After roaming the world as a seaman and writing some poetry as well, Hughes returned to the United States, winning the Witter Bynner Prize for undergraduate poetry while attending Lincoln University. In 1930 he received the Harmon Award, and in 1935, with the help of a Guggenheim Fellowship, he traveled to Russia and Spain.

The long and distinguished list of Hughes's prose works includes *Not Without Laughter* (1930), a novel; *The Big Sea* (1940); and *I Wonder as I Wander* (1956), his autobiography. To this he added such collections of poetry as *The Weary Blues* (1926); *The Dream Keeper* (1932); *Shakespeare in Harlem* (1942); *Fields of Wonder* (1947); *One Way Ticket* (1947); and *Selected Poems* (1959).

Hughes was also an accomplished song lyricist, librettist, and newspaper columnist.

Through his newspaper columns, he created Jesse B. Simple, a Harlem character who saw life on the musical stage in *Simply Heavenly*. There are also several volumes of the *Simple* columns.

Throughout the 1960s, Hughes edited several anthologies in an attempt to popularize black authors and their works. Some of these are *An African Treasury* (1960); *Poems from Black Africa* (1963); *New Negro Poets: U.S.A.* (1964); and *The Best Short Stories by Negro Writers* (1967). Published posthumously were *The Panther and the Lash: Poems of Our Times* (1969) and *Good Morning Revolution: Uncollected Writings of Social Protest.* Hughes wrote many plays, including *Emperor of Haiti and Five Plays by Langston Hughes.* *Mulatto* was produced on Broadway in the 1930s. He also wrote gospelsong plays such as *Tambourines to Glory; Black Nativity;* and *Jericho—Jim Crow.*

Zora Neale Hurston (1891–1960)
Novelist, Folklorist

Zora Neale Hurston, born on January 7, 1891, in Eatonville, Florida, an all-black township, offered perspectives as a black woman, feminist, anthropologist, and a keeper of the culture in her writings. After traveling north as a maid with a Gilbert and Sullivan company, Hurston acquired her education at Morgan State, Howard, and Columbia universities. While at Howard, under Alain Locke's influence, she became a figure in the Harlem Renaissance, publishing short stories in *Opportunity* and serving with Langston Hughes and Wallace Thurman on the editorial board of the magazine *Fire.*

In 1934 *Jonah's Gourd Vine* was published after her return to Florida. An important novel, *Their Eyes Were Watching God,* appeared three years later. *Moses, Man of the Mountain* (1939) was followed in 1948 by *Seraph on the Suwanee.* Her other three works are two books of folklore, *Mules and Men* (1935) and *Tell My Horse* (1938), and *Dust Tracks on a Road* (1942), her autobiography, which was reprinted in 1985 with a new introduction and with several altered or expunged chapters restored.

Toward the end of her life, Hurston was a drama instructor at the North Carolina College for Negroes in Durham. She died in obscurity and poverty on January 28, 1960. With the re-discovery of her work by author Alice Walker in 1973, Hurston's life and her work have earned new audiences.

Charles R. Johnson (1948–)
Novelists, Essayists, Cartoonist

Charles R. Johnson, the second African American man to receive the National Book Award in 1990 for the novel *Middle Passage* is preceded only by author Ralph Ellison the recipient in 1952 for the novel *Invisible Man*.

Johnson was born April 23, 1948, in Evanston, Illinois. He received his B.A. in 1971 from Southern Illinois University in Carbondale, Illinois, and an M.A. in philosophy in 1973. Johnson spent time as a cartoonist but became involved in groups that supported the establishment of African American studies in academia.

Johnson's literary career began in 1974 with the novel *Faith and the Good Thing*. Johnson wrote novels and short stories, which earned him the National Book Award in 1990 for *Middle Passage*, the MacArthur Foundation and the Guggenheim Fellowships. His works include the *Oxherding Tale* (1984); *The Sorcerer's Apprentice* (1986), a series of short stories; *Africans in America* (1998), nonfiction; *Turning the Wheel* (2003), a collection of essays about his experiences as a Buddhist; and *Dreamer: A Novel* (1998). Johnson's innovative and speculative approach to history and philosophy has done much to influence future generations.

Johnson retired after serving as the S. Wilson and Grace M. Pollack Endowed Professor of English at the University of Washington.

Georgia Douglas Johnson (1886–1966)
Poet

As one of the first modern black female poets to gain recognition, Georgia Douglas Johnson, whose collections of verse were published between 1918 and 1930, is an important link in the chain of American black female lyric poets. Johnson's life spanned most of the literary movements of this century, and her Washington, D.C., home was the popular gathering place of early Harlem Renaissance writers.

Johnson was born in Atlanta, Georgia, on September 10, 1886. She was educated in the public schools of the city and at Atlanta University, and she went on to attend Howard University in Washington, D.C., and Oberlin Conservatory of Music in Ohio.

Initially, she was interested in musical composition, but gradually she turned toward lyric poetry. After teaching school in Alabama, she moved to Washington, D.C., with her husband, who had been appointed recorder of deeds by President William Howard Taft. While in the nation's capital, she too engaged in government work and completed such books as *The Heart of a Woman* (1918); *Bronze* (1922); *An Autumn Love Cycle* (1928); and *Share My World*, published in 1962.

Johnson was a prolific writer: more than two hundred of her poems were published in her four literary works, and other poems and several dramas have appeared in journals and books primarily edited by blacks.

James Weldon Johnson (1871–1938)
Poet, Lyricist, Civil Rights Leader

Like W. E. B. DuBois, black intellectual James Weldon Johnson played a vital role in the civil rights movement of the early twentieth century—as poet, teacher, critic, diplomat, and NAACP official. Johnson is perhaps most often remembered as the lyricist for *Lift Every Voice and Sing*, the poem that is often referred to as the black national anthem.

Born in 1871 in Jacksonville, Florida, Johnson was educated at Atlanta and Columbia Universities. His career included service as a school principal, a lawyer, and a diplomat (U.S. consul at Puerto Cabello, Venezuela, and later, in Nicaragua). From 1916 to 1930 he was a key policy maker of the NAACP, eventually serving as the organization's executive secretary.

In his early days, Johnson's fame rested largely on his lyrics for popular songs, but in 1917 he completed his first book of poetry, *Fifty Years and Other Poems*. Five years later he followed this with *The Book of American Negro Poetry*, and in 1927 he established his literary reputation with *God's Trombones*, a collection of seven folk sermons in verse. Over the years, this work has been performed countless times on stage and television.

In 1930 Johnson finished *St. Peter Relates an Incident of the Resurrection*, and three years later, his lengthy autobiography, *Along This Way*.

Johnson died in 1938, following an automobile accident in Maine.

Gayle Jones (1949–)
Novelist, Poet, Short Story Writer

Born in Lexington, Kentucky, in 1949, Gayle Jones received a bachelor's degree in English from Connecticut College in 1971 and a master's degree in creative writing from Brown University in 1973. Jones's work includes two novels, *Corregidora* (1975) and *Eva's Man* (1976), short stories, and several collections of poetry, including *Song for Anninho* (1981), *The Hermit Woman* (1983), and *Xarque and Other Poems* (1985), as well as *Liberating Voices: Oral Tradition in African American Literature* (1991), which focuses on literary criticism.

Much of Jones's work deals with the complexities of the relationships between men and women and the sources of those challenges. Still focusing on women as key subject matter Jones wrote *The Healing* (1998) and *Mosquito* (1999).

After the suicide of her husband in 1998, Jones reverted even more to her reclusive practices.

June Jordan (1936–2002)
Poet, Novelist

Born in Harlem, New York, on July 9, 1936, of parents from Jamaica, in the West Indies, June Jordan attended Barnard College and the University of Chicago. Jordan taught African American literature, English, and writing at several colleges and universities, and was co-founder and co-director of The Voice of the Children, Inc., a creative workshop. Her poems have been published in many magazines, newspapers, and anthologies. She received a Rockefeller grant in creative writing for 1969. Her books for children and young people include *Fannie Lou Hamer* (1972); *His Own Where* (1971), her first novel nominated for the National Book Award; *Who Look at Me* (1969); *Dry Victories* (1972); *New Room, New Life* (1974); and *The Voice of the Children: Writings by Black and Puerto Rican Young People* (1970, 1974), edited by Jordan and Terri Bush. Her books for adults include *Soulscript* (1970), edited by Jordan; *Some Changes* (1971); *New Days: Poems of Exile and Return* (1973); *Things That I Do in the Dark: Selected Poems* (1976); and *Passion: New Poems, 1977–1980* (1980).

Jordon continued to create while diversifying her literary efforts by writing plays and various essays including, *On Call: Political Essays* (1985), *Moving toward Home: Political Essays* (1989), and her memoir, *Soldier: A Poet's Childhood* (2000). In 2001 Jordon was awarded the Barnes & Noble Writers for Writers Award from the Poets & Writers organization. Jordan offered workshops for underserved communities and her unselfish contribution was the basis for the award. Jordan died of breast cancer on June 14, 2002, at her home in Berkeley, California.

John Oliver Killens (1916–1987)
Novelist, Essayist

Killens was born on January 14, 1916, in Macon, Georgia. Killens pursed both an undergraduate and a law degree and was a member of the Army's South Pacific Forces from 1942 to 1945. Killens, influenced by stories he was told as a child, decided to pursue a writing career. Killens's first novel was *Youngblood* (1954), followed by *And Then We Heard the Thunder* (1962), *Sippi* (1967), *The Cotillian, or One Good Bull Is Half the Herd* (1971), and *A Novel on the Life and Times of Alexander Pushkin* (1989). Killens also published essays as well as anthologies.

Killens was honored and presented awards by numerous institutions. In his academic career he taught at Fisk University, Columbia University, and Howard University among others. He died on October 27, 1987, from cancer in Brooklyn, New York.

Jamaica Kincaid (1949–)
Novelist, Short Story Writer

Kincaid was born on May 25, 1949, as Elaine Cynthia Potter Richardson on the island of Antigua. She left at the age of sixteen for the United States. Kincaid became a regular contributor to the *New Yorker* as encouraged by the editor William Shawn. Her first book, *At the Bottom of the River,* was published in 1983 and consisted of seven stories previously printed by the *New Yorker*. This was followed by *Annie John* (1985), *Lucy* (1990), *The Autobiography of My Mother* (1996), *Talk Stories* (2000), *Mr. Potter* (2001), and *Among Flowers: A Walk in the Himalayas* (2005). Kincaid's work focuses on themes of relationships between mother and daughter, family experiences of pain and ambivalence, and identity.

Kincaid teaches at Claremont McKenna College and received an honorary degree from Tufts University in 2011.

Nella Larsen (1891–1964)
Novelist

Nella Larsen was born in 1891 in Chicago, Illinois, of a Danish mother and a West Indian father. She attended Fisk University (High School) in Nashville, Tennessee, from 1909 to 1912, and the University of Copenhagen in Denmark. She also went on to earn a nursing degree from Lincoln School of Nurses in New York City in 1915.

Although working in the field of nursing for over forty years, Larsen was interested in writing also. In the 1920s Larsen was immersed in the literary and political activities of the times. Larsen is best known for her two novels, *Quicksand* (1928), for which she received a bronze medal from the Harmon Foundation, and *Passing* (1929), which earned her the Guggenheim Fellowship in creative writing in 1930. Larsen was the first African American woman to receive this fellowship. Larsen's work focused on black women's sexuality and the social expectations of women of color, particularly those who were of mixed race. She died in New York City on March 20, 1964.

Audre Lorde (1924–1992)
Poet

Audre Lorde was born in New York City on February 18, 1924. She earned a B.A. from Hunter College in 1959 and a master's in library science from Columbia University in 1960; was poet in residence at Tougaloo College; and taught at Lehman College in the Bronx and John Jay College, City College of New York. She received a National Endowment for the Arts grant for poetry and a Cultural Council Foundation grant, also for poetry.

Her books of poetry include *Cables to Rage* (1970); *The First Cities* (1968); *From a Land Where Other People Live* (1973); *Coal* (1968); *The New York Head Shop and Museum* (1974); *Between Ourselves* (1976); *The Black Unicorn* (1978); *Chosen Poems—Old and New* (1982); *Zami: A New Spelling of My Name* (1982); *Sister/Outsider: Essays and Speeches* (1984); *Lesbian Poetry: An Anthology* (1982); and *Woman Poet—The East* (1984). Lorde's poetry has been published in many anthologies, magazines, and lesbian books and periodicals.

In 1980 Lorde published *The Cancer Journal*, a documentation of her experiences once diagnosed with breast cancer in 1978. Lorde continued her battle with cancer for fourteen years and died on November 17, 1992.

Paule Marshall (1929–)
Novelist, Short Story Writer

Paule Marshall was born on April 9, 1929, as Valenza Pauline Burke in Brooklyn, New York. Marshall's parents were from Barbados and she grew up in a neighborhood that supported her West Indian heritage. She grew up with a love for the written word and the world of women telling their stories of life and love.

Marshall's first written work "The Valley Between" was a short story written in 1954 for a class exercise. Her work expanded to include the novels, *Brown Girl, Brownstone* (1959), *The Chosen Place, The Timeless People* (1969), *Praisesong for the Widow* (1983), and *The Fisher King* (2000). Marshall's work focuses on the issues of cultural awareness, the search for identity, and a celebration of the human spirit.

Claude McKay (1889–1948)
Poet, Novelist

Born the son of a farmer in Jamaica (then British West Indies) on September 15, 1889, Claude McKay began writing early in life. Two books of his poems, *Songs of Jamaica* and *Constab Ballads,* were published just after he turned twenty. In both, he made extensive use of Jamaican dialect.

In 1913 McKay came to America to study agriculture at Tuskegee Institute and at Kansas State University, but his interest in poetry prompted him to move to New York City, where he published his work in small literary magazines.

McKay then made a trip abroad, visiting England. While there, he completed a collection of lyrics entitled *Spring in New Hampshire*. In 1922 he completed *Harlem Shadows*, a landmark work of the Harlem Renaissance period.

McKay then turned to the writing of such novels as *Home to Harlem* (1928), *Banjo* (1929), and four other books, including an autobiography and a study of Harlem. *The Passion of Claude McKay: Selected Prose and Poetry 1912–1948,* edited by Wayne Cooper, was published in 1973. During World War II, when Winston Churchill addressed a joint session of the U.S. Congress in an effort to enlist American aid in the battle against Nazism, the climax of his oration was his reading of the famous poem "If We Must Die," originally written by McKay to assail lynchings and mob violence in the South. McKay traveled extensively abroad before returning to the United States, where he died in 1948. His final work, *Selected Poems*, was published posthumously in 1953.

Many of his books or works have been reprinted since his death: *Home to Harlem; Banana Bottom; Banjo; A Long Way from Home* (1970); *Harlem: Negro Metropolis* (1972); and *Selected Poems of Claude McKay* (1971). *Songs of Jamaica* and *Constab Ballads* have been bound together as *The Dialect Poems of Claude McKay*. Also, Wayne F. Cooper's *Claude McKay: Rebel Sojourner in the Harlem Renaissance* (1987) is an important book detailing McKay's life and work.

Terry McMillan (1951–)
Novelist

McMillan was born October 18, 1951, and raised in Port Huron, Michigan. She attended Los Angeles City College, but later transferred to Berkeley and then to Columbia University to study film. She later enrolled in a writing workshop at the Harlem Writers Guild and was accepted at the MacDowell Colony in 1983.

McMillan's early novels include *Mama* (1987), *Disappearing Acts* (1989), and *Waiting to Exhale* (1992). She also edited an anthology of contemporary African American fiction, *Breaking Ice* (1992). McMillan's novel *Waiting to Exhale* remained on the best-seller list for several months, proving that there is a demand for African American literature. After selling three million copies the novel was made into a movie and premiered in 1995. In 1996 McMillan wrote *How Stella Got Her Groove Back,* which was also made into a movie, and her previous novel *Disappearing Acts* became a cable television feature presentation. McMillan received publicity in 2005 when she divorced her husband, twenty-four years her junior, who was fictionalized in her book *How Stella Got Her Groove Back.*

McMillan continued to write about the relationships of African American men and women, and the challenges that women primarily face, with her publication *A Day Late and a Dollar Short* and *The Interruption of Everything* in 2005. In September 2010 McMillan published her long-awaited sequel to *Waiting to Exhale, Getting to Happy.*

James McPherson (1943–)
Short Story Writer

James McPherson, born in Savannah, Georgia, on October 16, 1943, received his B.A. in 1965 from Morris Brown College in Atlanta, a law degree from Harvard University in 1968, and an M.F.A. from the University of Iowa in 1969. He has taught writing at several universities, presently at the University of Iowa, and is a contributing editor of *Atlantic Monthly.*

McPherson's short stories have appeared in several magazines. *Hue and Cry*, a collection of short stories published in 1969, was highly praised by Ralph Ellison. A Guggenheim fellow in 1972–1973, McPherson published a second book of short stories, *Elbow Room,* in 1977 and was given the Pulitzer Prize for fiction in 1978. He taught fiction writing for several years at the University of Virginia in Charlottesville. McPherson was one of the three black writers who in

1981, with Elma Lewis, were awarded five-year grants by the McArthur Foundation of Chicago for exceptional talent. In 1997 McPherson published *Crabcakes,* his memoir, and in 2000 he published a collection of essays, *A Region Not Home: Reflections from Exile.*

Toni Morrison (1931–)
Novelist, Editor

Born Chloe Ardelia Wofford in Lorain, Ohio, on February 18, 1931, Morrison received a B.A. from Howard University in 1953 and an M.A. from Cornell in 1955. After working as an instructor in English and the humanities at Texas Southern University and Howard University, Morrison eventually became a senior editor at Random House in New York City. She has been responsible for the publication of many books by blacks at Random House: Middleton Harris's *The Black Book*, which she edited, and books by Toni Cade Bambara and others. From 1971 to 1972 she was also an associate professor at the State University of New York at Purchase. From 1984 to 1989 Morrison served as Albert Schweitzer Professor of the Humanities at the State University of New York at Albany, after twenty years as a senior editor for Random House. Formerly married, she has two sons.

Morrison's first novel, *The Bluest Eye*, was published in 1969. Her second novel, *Sula*, was published in 1974 and won a 1975 Ohioana Book Award. Morrison's third novel, *Song of Solomon* (1977), was critically acclaimed and received the 1977 National Book Critics Circle Award and the 1978 American Academy and Institute of Arts and Letters Award. Her fourth novel, *Tar Baby* (1981), also received positive reviews. She was elected to the American Institute of Arts and Letters in 1981 and gave the keynote address at the American Writers' Congress in New York City in the fall of that year. She has also written the story for the musical *Storyville*, which is about jazz music originating in the brothels of New Orleans;

the story for the musical *New Orleans*, a New York Public Theater workshop production; and also a screenplay of her novel *Tar Baby*.

Morrison's fifth novel, *Beloved*, was published in 1987. A historical novel, it received rave reviews. In 1988 *Beloved* won both the Pulitzer Prize for fiction and the Robert F. Kennedy Award. *Beloved* was a finalist for the 1988 National Book Critics Circle Award and was one of the three contenders for the Ritz Hemingway prize in Paris, from which no winner emerged, and a finalist for the National Book Award for 1987. In 1993 Morrison's novel *Beloved* was awarded the Nobel Prize for literature. She was the first black woman and the eighth woman to receive this award. Morrison in her writing uses the cultural traditions and experiences that have shaped her life and the life of African American people. She also continues to seek answers about "silences and secrets" that have left much unsaid about those same experiences.

In 1992 Morrison released the novel *Jazz*, followed by *Paradise* (1999), *Love* (2003), and *A Mercy* (2008). At Princeton University Morrison was named the Robert F. Goheen Professor in the Council of Humanities, making her the first black woman writer to hold a named chair at an Ivy League university. Also among her numerous awards are the 1993 Commander of the Arts and Letters, Paris, the National Book Foundation's Medal of Distinguished Contribution to American Letters in 1996, the National Humanities Medal, 2000, and in 2008 she was nominated for a Grammy Award for the Best Spoken Word Album for children, *Who's Got Game?; The Ant or the Grasshopper?, The Lion or the Mouse?, Poppy or the Snake?*

Walter Mosley (1952–)
Novelist

Mosley, born January 12, 1952, is known for his realistic detective novels set in segregated urban black America. Mosley, who was raised in Watts and the Pico-Fairfax district of Los Angeles, had

the unique heritage of an African American father and a white Jewish mother. After having several jobs, including caterer and computer programmer, he settled in New York and began his writing career in 1987. His first published novel was *Devil in a Blue Dress* published in 1990. This novel was well received and followed by *A Red Death* (1991), *White Butterfly* (1992), *Black Betty* (1994), *A Little Yellow Dog* (1996), *Gone Fishin'* (1997), and *Fearless Jones* (2001).

Mosley tried other genres that dealt with different themes and issues in the community he grew up such as *RL's Dream* (1995), *Always Outnumbered, Always Outgunned* (1997), which became a television movie in 1998, *Fear Itself* (2003), and *The Tempest Tales*, which was adapted into his first play *The Fall of Heaven* in 2010.

Mosley's work was recognized during the presidential campaign in 1992 by then candidate Bill Clinton as his favorite mystery writer. Mosley received the O. Henry Award in 1996, "Risktaker Award" from the Sundance Institute in 2005, and the Carl Brandon Society Award for young adult novels in 2006.

Gloria Naylor (1950–)
Novelist

Gloria Naylor was born in New York City, where she currently lives. She received a B.A. in English from Brooklyn College in 1981 and an M.A. in Afro-American studies from Yale University in 1983. She has taught writing and literature at George Washington University, New York University, Brandeis University, Cornell University, and Boston University. In 1983 she won the American Book Award for first fiction for her novel *The Women of Brewster Place*, produced in 1988 for television. Her second novel was *Linden Hills*, published in 1985. Her third novel, *Mama Day* (1988), was written with the aid of a grant from the National Endowment for the Arts. In 1988 Naylor was awarded a Guggenheim Fellowship. In 1993 Naylor published the novel *Bailey's Cafe*, in 1998 *The Men of Brewster Place*, and in 2005 the novel *1996*.

Ann Petry (1908–1997)
Novelist, Short Story Writer

Ann Petry was born October 12, 1908, in Old Saybrook, Connecticut, where her father was a druggist. After graduating from the College of Pharmacy at the University of Connecticut, she went to New York, where she found employment as a social worker and newspaper reporter, studying creative writing at night.

Her early short stories appeared in *Crisis* and *Pylon*. In 1946, after having received a Houghton Mifflin Fellowship, she completed and published her first novel, *The Street*. This was followed by *Country Place* (1947); *The Narrows* (1953); and *Miss Mural and Other Stories* (1971). Her works for children and young people include *The Drugstore Cat; Harriet Tubman; Tituba of Salem Village*; and *Legends of the Saints*. Many of her earlier novels have been reprinted. Petry died on April 28, 1997.

Ishmael Reed (1938–)
Novelist, Poet

Born in Chattanooga, Tennessee, on February 22, 1938, Reed grew up in Buffalo, New York. He attended State University of New York at Buffalo from 1956 to 1960. He later worked as a reporter, taught at different institutions as guest lecturer, and co-founded Reed Cannon & Johnson Communication Company in 1975.

Reed is among the most controversial of African American writers and is often seen as misogynistic and cynical. He seeks to create an alternative black reality through a philosophy and process he calls neohoodooism. Reed's first volume of poetry published in the United States, *Conjure* (1972), which offers a working display of neohoodooism, was nominated for the National Book Award, as was his third novel, *Mumbo Jumbo* (1972). He has also published *Chattanooga* (1973), a second volume of poetry, and novels: *The Freelance Pallbearers* (1967); *Yellow Back Radio Broke Down* (1989); *The Last Days of Louisiana Red* (1974); *Flight to Canada* (1976); *The Terrible Threes* (1989); and *Japanese by Spring* (1992).

Reed published in the 1980s, *The Terrible Twos* (1982), a political satire; and *Reckless Eyeballing* (1986), a farce in which the sinister Flower Phantom punishes feminists for defaming black manhood. Both novels were reissued in paperback in 1988 by Atheneum Publishers. Reed's books of essays include editorials and book reviews such as *Shrovetide in Old New Orleans* (1978), *God Made Alaska for the Indians: Selected Essays* (1983), *Writin' Is Fightin': ThirtySeven Years of Boxing on Paper* (1988), and *Airing Dirty Laundry* (1993), and Reed edited *Multi-America: Essays on Cultural Wars and Cultural Peace* in 1997.

Reed has challenged his talent in many directions, from novelist, poet, and essayist to songwriter, television producer, publisher, and playwright. He has taught at Harvard, Yale, and Dartmouth, and he has lectured at the University of California for over twenty years. He has received numerous prizes such as the Lewis H. Michaux Literary Prize in 1978, fellowships from the Wisconsin Board and Yale University's Calhoun College in 1982, and grants from the National Endowment of the Arts and the MacArthur Foundation.

Sonia Sanchez (1943–)
Poet, Playwright

Sonia Sanchez was born September 9, 1943, in Birmingham, Alabama. She studied at New York University and Hunter College in New York City. She was married to Etheridge Knight, a black writer of poetry and fiction. She taught at San Francisco State College and in the black studies department of Temple University in Philadelphia until her retirement in 1999. She has written both plays, including *Malcolm Man/Don't Live Here No Mo'* (1979) and *Black Cats Back and Uneasy Landings* (1995), and books of poetry including *Homecoming* (1969); *We a BaddDDD People* (1970); *It Is a New Day* (1971); *A Blues Book for Blue Black*

Magical Women (1973); *I've Been a Woman* (1978); *Under a Soprano Sky* (1987); and *Does Your House Have Lions?* (1995). Sanchez has edited two anthologies and a collection of short stories, including *Homegirls and Handgrenades* (1984) and *Shake Loose My Skin* (2000). Sanchez won an American Book Award for *Homegirls and Handgrenades*.

Sanchez has received the Outstanding Arts Award from the Pennsylvania Coalition of 100 Black Women, the National Endowment for the Arts, and a Pew Fellowship in the Arts. She has lectured extensively not only in the United States, but in Africa, Cuba, England, the Caribbean, Australia, Nicaragua, the People's Republic of China, Norway, and Canada.

Ntozake Shange (1948–)
Playwright, Poet, Novelist

Born in Trenton, New Jersey, on October 18, 1948, Paulette Linda Williams, who changed her name to Ntozake Shange in 1971, graduated from Barnard College and received her master's degree from the University of Southern California. She studied African American dance and gave many poetry readings in California. Shange taught at Sonoma Mills College in California from 1972 to 1975. Her play *For Colored Girls Who Have Considered Suicide/When the Rainbow Is Enuf*, a choreopoem, was first produced in California after her dance-drama *Sassafrass* was presented in 1976. *For Colored Girls* was later produced in New York City, where it had a long run before going on to other cities. The production was nominated for an Emmy, a Grammy, and a Tony award. *For Colored Girls* has been published twice as a book, and Shange's book *Three Pieces* (1981) contains *Spell #7, A Photograph: Lovers in Motion* (1979), and *Boogie Woogie Landscapes* (1979). Shange's other books include *Sassafrass, Cypress & Indigo* (1982), *Nappy Edges* (1978), a book of poetry, her novels *Betsey Brown* (1985), *Liliane: Resurrection of the Daughter* (1994), and children's novels *Daddy Says* (2003), *Coretta Scott* (2009)

and the novel, *Some Sing, Some Cry*, co-authored with Ifa Bayeza.

A version of *Betsey Brown* for the stage, with music by the jazz trumpeter and composer Baikida Carroll, opened the American Music Theater Festival in Philadelphia on March 25, 1989. *For Colored Girls Who Have Considered Suicide/When the Rainbow Is Enuf* was revived on Broadway in 1995 and made into a movie in 2010 by African American film director Tyler Perry.

Shange has received awards such as the Obie Award in 1981 for *For Colored Girls*, a Guggenheim Fellowship, and the National Black Theater Festival Award in 1993.

Lucy Terry (1730–1821)
Poet

Lucy Terry is generally considered to be the first black poet in America. In a ballad that she called "Bars Fight," she recreated an Indian massacre that occurred in Deerfield, Massachusetts, in 1746 during King George's War; "Bars Fight" has been hailed by some historians as the most authentic account of the massacre.

Terry was a slave who was sold in Rhode Island to the Terry family in Enfield, Connecticut. She was sold again at the age of five and resided in the household of Ensign Ebenezer Wells of Deerfield, Massachusetts. Terry was taught to read and write and married a free African named Abijah Prince in 1756. She gained her freedom with her husband's assistance and they eventually settled in Guilford, Vermont, in 1764. Terry, the mother of six children, was considered a born storyteller whom many gathered to hear. "Bars Flight" was kept in the town archives and is considered the earliest existing poem by an African American.

Wallace H. Thurman (1902–1934)
Novelist, Playwright, Ghostwriter, Journalist

Thurman, a member of the Harlem Renaissance movement, was born on August 16, 1902. After earning a degree at the University of Utah in 1922 in pre-medicine Thurman moved to New York after a failed attempt to make a west coast version of the Renaissance. He was unsuccessful in promoting and finding publishing support for African American-centered literature based an on African-centered perspective.

In the summer of 1926 Thurman, who was part of a select group of Harlem Renaissance writers, financed *Fire*, a literary magazine that only lasted one issue. The magazine, which was seen as lewd and revolutionary by many of the older generation of scholars, was an attempt at providing another outlet for expression by young writers of the Harlem Renaissance. Thurman spent four years paying back the debt.

Thurman was successful in his writing by having his articles published in prestigious and often white magazines and served as a ghost writer for several magazines and books. He became part of the editorial staff of McFadden Publication. In 1929 Thurman wrote his most well-known work, *The Blacker the Berry the Sweeter the Juice*. In 1932 he published two other novels, *Infants of the Spring* and *The Interne*. Thurman, known to be homosexual and an alcoholic, also suffered from tuberculosis. He died on December 22, 1934, in New York.

Jean Toomer (1894–1967)
Novelist, Poet

Jean Toomer's *Cane*, published in 1923, has been called one of the three best novels ever written by an African American—the others being Richard Wright's *Native Son* and Ralph Ellison's *Invisible Man*. According to Columbia University critic Robert Bone, "*Cane* is by far the most impressive product of the Negro Renaissance."

A mixture of poems and sketches, *Cane* was written during a period in which most black writers were reacting against earlier "polite" forms by creating works marked by literary realism. Toomer even went beyond this realm to the threshold of symbol and myth, using a "mystical" approach that is much more akin to the current mood than it was to the prevailing spirit of his own day. *Cane* sold only five hundred copies on publication, and it was still little known until its recent reprint with new introductions. Much has been written about Toomer and *Cane* in recent years, including a *Cane* casebook.

Born in Washington, D.C., in 1894, Toomer was educated in law at the University of Wisconsin and City College of New York before he turned to writing. The transcendental nature of his writings is said to have stemmed in part from his early study under Gurdjieff, the Russian mystic.

Toomer also published quite a considerable amount of poetry. Much has been written about Toomer, including Robert B. Jones and Margery Toomer Latimer's *The Collected Poems of Jean Toomer* (1988) and Nellie Y. McKay's *Jean Toomer, Artist: A Study of His Literary Life and Work, 1894–1936* (1984, 1987).

Gustavus Vassa (1745–c. 1801)
Narrative Writer

Gustavus Vassa was born in 1745, in Benin, southern Nigeria. At the age of eleven, he was kidnapped and shipped to the New World as a slave. His masters included a Virginia plantation owner, a British officer (who gave him the name Vassa, which he later dropped), and a Philadelphia merchant from whom he eventually purchased his freedom. Vassa then settled in England, where he worked diligently for the elimination of slavery. He even went so far as to present a petition to Parliament calling for its abolition.

His autobiography, *The Interesting Narrative of the Life of Olaudah Equiano, or Gustavus Vassa*, was published in London in 1789 and went through five editions in the next five years. It is regarded as a highly informative account of the evils of slavery as it affected both master and slave. Vassa died around 1801.

Alice Walker (1944–)

Poet, Novelist

Alice Malsenior Walker was born in Eatonton, Georgia, on February 9, 1944, and has lived in Mississippi, New York City, and San Francisco, California. She attended Spelman College in Atlanta, Georgia, from 1961 to 1963, and received her B.A. in 1965 from Sarah Lawrence College in Bronxville, New York.

Walker's first book was a collection of poetry entitled *Once*, published in 1968, followed by her second book, a novel published in 1970, *The Third Life of Grange Copeland*. A second book of poetry, *Revolutionary Petunias and Other Poems*, was published in 1973. She also wrote *In Love and Trouble: Stories of Black Women* (1973); *Langston Hughes, American Poet* (1974), for children; *Meridian* (1976), a novel; *Good Night, Willie Lee, I'll See You in the Morning* (1979), poetry; and *You Can't Keep a Good Woman Down* (1981), short stories.

Walker's book *In Love & Trouble: Stories of Black Women* (1973) won the American Academy and Institute of Arts and Letters' Rosenthal Award. *Revolutionary Petunias and Other Poems* was nominated for the National Book Award and received the Lillian Smith Award. Walker has also received the Merrill Fellowship for Writing, a National Endowment for the Arts grant, a Radcliffe Institute Fellowship, and other honors.

In 1983 Walker's third novel, *The Color Purple* (1982), won the American Book Award in the hardcover category and she became the first African American woman to win the Pulitzer Prize in 1983. Even though the book did receive negative reviews for its depiction of black men, it still became a best-seller in hardcover and paperback. The book was released as a film in 1985, became a box office success, and was later adapted into a play in 2005.

Walker's other books include *In Search of Our Mothers' Gardens: Womanist Prose* (1983); *Zora Neale Hurston Reader*, (1980); *Horses Make the Landscape Look More Beautiful* (1984), a book of poems; *To Hell with Dying* (1988), a book for children; *Living by the Word: Selected Writings, 1973–1987* (1988), a book of essays; *The Temple of My Familiar* (1989), which was both panned and praised by critics; *Possessing the Secret of Joy* (1992); *The Same River Twice: Honoring the Difficult* (1996); *The Way Forward Is with a Broken Heart* (2000); *Now Is the Time to Open Your Heart* (2005); *The Devil's My Enemy* (2008); and *Overcoming Speechlessness* (2010).

In 2001 Walker was inducted into the Georgia Writers Hall of Fame at Emory University in Atlanta and her personal and literary papers were catalogued into their collection beginning in 2007. On December 1, 2005, with Walker's blessing, a theatrical production of *The Color Purple* opened on Broadway with the support of noted producers Quincy Jones and Oprah Winfrey among others. The production, which toured nationally, earned numerous nominations and awards in 2006. The play was on its second national tour in 2010.

Margaret Walker (1915–)

Poet, Novelist

Margaret Abigail Walker was born on July 7, 1915, in Birmingham, Alabama, and received her early education in Alabama, Louisiana, and Mississippi. She earned her B.A. from Northwestern University and her M.A. from the University of Iowa in 1940.

In 1942 Walker published *For My People* and two years later was awarded a Rosenwald Fellowship for creative writing. She has taught English and literature at Livingston College in North Carolina, at West Virginia State College, and at Jackson State College in Mississippi. Her novel *Jubilee* appeared in 1965, and *For My People* was reprinted in 1969. Her other works are *Prophets for a New Day; How I Wrote Jubilee; October Journey*, and *A Poetic Equation: Conversations between Nikki Giovanni and Margaret Walker*. June 17, 1976, was proclaimed Margaret Walker Alexander Day by the mayor of her native Birmingham (Walker married James Alexander in 1943).

Walker's other works include *Richard Wright: Daemonic Genius* (1988). Also, a second edition of *A Poetic Equation: Conversations between Nikki Giovanni and Margaret Walker* was published in 1983. Walker, whose poetry had a profound impact on the African American writers of the Black Arts Movement in the 1960s and the writers of the 1970s, addressed political and cultural issues. Walker died of breast cancer on November 30, 1998.

Dorothy West (1907–1998)
Novelist, Short Story Writer, Journalist

West, born on June 2, 1907, is remembered as one of the writers of the Harlem Renaissance. West was born in Boston, moved to New York, but later returned home and took up residence in their family's summer home on Martha's Vineyard in 1943. West completed her first novel, *The Living Is Easy*, in 1948. West continued to write and submit short stories to the *New York Daily News*.

West's subject matter primarily focused on the life of affluent African Americans. It was not until 1950 that West wrote her second novel, *The Wedding*, which deals with interracial marriage. She was unable to find a publisher, thus leaving the text incomplete until 1992. Jacqueline Onassis, the widow of President John F. Kennedy, took note of the short stories that West had been submitting to the *Daily News*, the local paper at Martha's Vineyard. West had been submitting stories to the *New York Daily News* since the 1970s. Onassis encouraged West to complete her novel and subsequently served as her editor. The novel was published in 1995 and made into a television movie produced by Oprah Winfrey, airing in 1998. West died on August 16, 1998.

Phillis Wheatley (1753–1784)
Poet

Born in Gambia in 1753, Phillis Wheatley was brought to the United States as a slave and received her name from Mrs. Susannah Wheatley, the wife of the Boston tailor who had bought Phillis.

Wheatley received her early education in the household of her master. Her interest in writing stemmed from her reading of the Bible and the classics under the guidance of the Wheatleys' daughter, Mary.

In 1770 her first poem was printed under the title "A Poem by Phillis, A Negro Girl, on the Death of Reverend George Whitefield." Her book *Poems on Various Subjects: Religious and Moral* was published in London in 1773. After a trip to England for health reasons she later returned to the United States and was married. She published the poem "Liberty and Peace" in 1784, shortly before her death. Most of the old books of her poems, letters, and memories about her life were reprinted in the late 1960s and early 1970s. Two books about her are Julian D. Mason Jr.'s *The Poems of Phillis Wheatley* (1966) and William H. Robinson's *Phillis Wheatley, A Biography* (1981). Robinson also compiled and published *Phillis Wheatley: A Bio-Bibliography* (1981).

Although George Washington was among her admirers (she had once sent him a tributary poem, which he graciously acknowledged), her poetry is considered important today largely because of its historical role in the growth of black literature. Wheatley's poetry reflects AngloSaxon models, rather than her African heritage. It is nevertheless a typical example of the verse manufactured in a territory—the British colonies—not yet divorced from its maternal origins. Wheatley died on December 5, 1784.

John Edgar Wideman (1941–)
Novelist

Wideman, born June 14, 1941, in Washington, D.C., moved with his family to Homewood, an African American community in Philadelphia where he grew up. He excelled in his studies and attended the University of Pittsburgh on a Benjamin Franklin scholarship. Wideman, during his undergraduate career, made the Big Five Basketball Hall of Fame, won a creative writing prize, was elected to Phi Beta Kappa, and was selected as a Rhodes Scholar to attend Oxford University in England, making him only the first African American in over fifty years to receive such an honor. Alain Locke, a scholar during the Harlem Renaissance, was the first to receive the honor in 1907. Wideman earned his B.A. in 1963 from the University of Pittsburg and a B.A. from Oxford in philosophy in 1966.

Wideman's first novel, *A Glance Away,* was published in 1967, followed by novels such as *The Lynchers* (1973); *Sent for You* (1983); *Philadelphia Fire* (1990); *The Cattle Killing* (1996); and *Two Cities* (1998). He also published several collections of short stories, including *Brothers and Keepers* (1984) and the collection *Damballah,* reissued in 1998.

Wideman is the only writer to receive the PEN/Faulkner Award twice; 1984 for *Sent for You Yesterday*, and in 1990 for *Philadelphia Fire*. In 1990 Wideman also received the American Book Award for fiction and in 1993 the MacArthur Award. Wideman has received numerous other awards and his work has appeared in periodicals such as *The New Yorker, Vogue, Emerge,* and *The New York Times Magazine*. He is a full professor of creative writing and American studies at the University of Massachusetts in Amherst.

August Wilson (1945–2005)
Playwright

The first of August Wilson's plays was *Ma Rainey's Black Bottom*. First produced at the Yale Repertory Theater and directed by Lloyd Richards, then brought to New York, the play was named the New York Drama Critics Circle's best new play in 1985. Wilson's next play, *Fences*, describing the 1930s, 1940s, and 1950s, was the best new play in 1987 for the New York Drama Critics Circle, after first being produced at the Yale Repertory Theater. Wilson's third play produced in New York, *Joe Turner's Come and Gone*, also started at the Yale Repertory Theater and was

named the best new play in 1988 by the New York Drama Critics Circle. *Joe Turner's Come and Gone* is about 1911 and the earlier period of black migration from the South, sharecropping, and being dispossessed—about a search for cultural roots and identity in a dark and distant past from the psychic burden of years of slavery.

In 1986 Wilson was one of ten writers to win the Whiting Writer's Awards; each writer was given a tax-free check for $25,000. The awards were established in 1985 by the Whiting Foundation to reward "exceptionally promising, emerging talent." In 1988 Yale University gave Wilson an honorary degree.

Wilson's *Joe Turner* opened in Boston before coming to New York. It was produced in 1987 by the Seattle Repertory Theater. *Fences* was also produced in San Francisco in 1987, and it received a Pulitzer Prize and a Tony award. In 1990 Wilson's *The Piano Lesson* was awarded a Pulitzer Prize. He followed this production with *Two Trains Running* (1992) and *Seven Guitars* (1996). Wilson's critique of the lack of support for African American theater by the New York mainstream placed him in the center of this debate. He challenged the notions held by New York critics at the time.

Wilson received numerous awards, including the Washington Literary Award in 2001, and the Laurence Olivier Award in 2002, which made Wilson the first American to receive this prestigious award. Wilson died of liver cancer on October 2, 2005, in Seattle.

Richard Wright (1908–1960)
Novelist

Born on a plantation near Natchez, Mississippi, on September 4, 1908, Wright drew on his personal experience to dramatize racial injustice and its brutalizing effects. In 1938, under the auspices of the WPA Illinois Writers Project, Wright published *Uncle Tom's Children*, a collection of four novellas based on his Mississippi boyhood memories. The book won an award for the best work of fiction by a WPA writer, and Wright received a Guggenheim Fellowship.

Two years later, *Native Son*, a novel of Chicago's Negro ghetto, further enhanced Wright's reputation. A Book-of-the-Month Club choice, it was later a successful Broadway production under Orson Welles's direction and was filmed in South America with Wright himself in the role of Bigger Thomas. He published *Twelve Million Black Voices* in 1941.

In 1945, Wright's largely autobiographical *Black Boy* was selected by the Book-of-the-Month Club and went on to become a second best-seller.

Wright later moved to Paris, where he continued to write fiction and nonfiction, including *The Outsider* (1953); *Black Power* (1954); *Savage Holiday* (1954, 1965); *The Color Curtain* (1956); *White Man Listen* (1957); *The Long Dream* (1958); *Lawd Today* (1963); *Eight Men* (1961); and *American Hunger* (1977), a continuation of Wright's autobiographical work *Black Boy*.

Wright died of a heart attack on November 28, 1960.

BUSINESS ENTREPRENEURS/ MEDIA

African Americans have a long and rich history of entrepreneurship in America; African Americans have been in business since before the Civil War and continue their entrepreneurial tradition today. Segments of the African American population have exhibited the same entrepreneurial spirit as segments of other ethnic groups who have migrated to this country. Very often, however, the history of black entrepreneurship has been either overlooked or misconstrued.

ENTREPRENEURS

Entrepreneurship for African Americans has incorporated ownership as a means to manage and disseminate information for the betterment of the community as well as a means to gain economic opportunities. African American religious publishers were the first entrepreneurs to represent African American interests using print media. This led the way for a variety of businesses and products.

As the United States began to take shape, a number of people of African origin were successful in their attempt to carve out an economic stake for themselves. Anthony Johnson, who accumulated substantial property in Jamestown, Virginia, is believed to be the first person of African descent to have become an entrepreneur in America. Jean Baptist DuSable, a wholesaler and merchant who established the first settlement in Chicago in the early 1770s, was another pre-Civil War era entrepreneur.

Prior to the Civil War, however, slavery defined the existence of most African Americans. Thus, two categories of business persons were able to develop and sustain business enterprises. The first group was composed of free African Americans, numbering approximately sixty thousand, who could accumulate the capital to generate business activity. They developed enterprises in almost every area of the business community, including merchandising, real estate, manufacturing, construction, transportation, and extractive industries.

The second group consisted of slaves who—as a result of thrift, ingenuity, industry, and/or the liberal paternalism of their masters—were able to engage in business activity. Although the constraints of slavery were such that even highly skilled slaves could not become entrepreneurs in the true sense of the word, slaves did, during their limited free time, sell their labor and create products to sell.

The fact that African American entrepreneurship existed at all during the era of slavery is testimony to an entrepreneurial spirit and the determination of a people to achieve economic freedom even under the harshest conditions.

If it was all but impossible for slaves to engage in private enterprise, it was also hazardous for "free" blacks to do so, since they were effectively only half free. Free blacks lived under a constant fear of being labeled as "runaway" slaves and being sold into slavery. In addition, in areas where free blacks lived, laws were passed to restrict their movement and thus their economic freedom. This was one intention, for example, of the laws that Virginia, Maryland, and North Carolina had passed by 1835 forbidding free blacks to carry arms without a license. The right of assembly was also denied blacks throughout the South—leaving it illegal for black civic, business, or benevolent organizations to convene. In addition to reflecting white slave owners' fears of an African American uprising, such legal restriction had the purpose and effect of making it difficult for free blacks to earn a living.

The promise of freedom and political enfranchisement held out by President Abraham Lincoln's Emancipation Proclamation of 1862 was soon undermined by racist judicial rulings. In 1878, in *Hall v. DeCuir*, the U.S. Supreme Court ruled that a state could not prohibit segregation on a common carrier. In 1896, with the *Plessy v. Ferguson* ruling, "separate but equal" became the law of the land. Following these decisions, a pattern of rigid segregation of the races was established that remained the norm until the advent of the civil rights movement in the 1960s.

Nevertheless, even within the context of disenfranchisement and segregation, Booker T. Washington saw the possibility of securing African American economic stability through business development. In 1900 Washington spearheaded the development of the National Negro Business League to encourage black enterprise.

During the early 1900s, although services continued to be the cornerstone of the black business community, blacks found it easier to

The marker on Homer Adolph Plessy's tomb in New Orleans summarizes the case of *Plessy v. Ferguson* that was one of the first legal challenges to the "separate but equal" policies of the Reconstruction South.

raise capital and ventured into more entrepreneurial endeavors.

In 1905, for example, Madame C.J. Walker developed a hair care system that gave dry hair a soft texture; millions of women, both black and white, became customers for Madame Walker's products. Before her death in 1919, Madame Walker had more than two thousand agents marketing her ever-expanding line of products, which made her America's first self-made black female millionaire.

Turn-of-the-century Durham, North Carolina, represented a special case of enterprise and economic resilience. In publications of the time, Durham was referred to as "The Wall Street of Negro America." By the late 1940s, more than 150 businesses owned by African Americans flourished in Durham. Among these businesses were traditional service providers, such as cafes, movie houses, barber shops, boarding houses, pressing shops, grocery stores, and funeral parlors. What distinguished Durham, however, was the presence of large black businesses, including the extremely successful North Carolina Mutual Life Insurance Company.

The civil rights movement prompted the development of legislation and a number of government agencies to ensure the social, political, and economic rights of African Americans. Perhaps the greatest boost to black entrepreneurship came in 1967 with the establishment of the Small Business Administration (SBA) Section 8 (a) program. Under that section of the Small Business Act Amendments, the SBA is authorized to enter into contract with federal agencies on behalf of small and disadvantaged businesses. Entry into the program is contingent upon SBA approval of the business plan prepared by prospective firms. The total dollar value of contracts processed through Section 8 (a) has grown from $8.9 million in 1969 to $2.7 billion in 1985. Through the program, many small and black-owned businesses have been able to stabilize and grow.

Another product of the civil rights movement has been the 1977 Public Works Employment Act. Supplementing the SBA 8 (a) program, the Public Works Employment Act requires that all general contractors bidding for public works projects allocate at least 10 percent of their contracts to minority sub-contractors.

During the early 1980s, the SBA Section 8 (a) program was criticized because less than 5 percent of the firms had achieved open-market competitiveness, which implies that the program is in effect assisting the marginal entrepreneur, as opposed to the promising self-employed minority businessperson.

The fundamental concept of set-aside minority assistance programs was called into question during the height of the Reagan–Bush era. In 1989 the landmark U.S. Supreme Court ruling in *City of Richmond v. Croson* struck down as unconstitutional under the Fourteenth Amendment a city ordinance of Richmond, Virginia, requiring

that 30 percent of each public-construction contract be set aside for minority businesses. The Supreme Court did make a distinction between local/state and federally enacted business development programs, holding that the U.S. Congress has far more authority than the states in formulating remedial legislation.

The *Croson* decision has had a devastating impact on minority businesses. In Richmond, during the month of July 1987 when a lower court first ruled against the city's set-aside program, 40 percent of the city's total construction dollars were allocated for products and services provided by minority-owned construction firms. Immediately following the court's decision, the minority businesses' share of contracts fell to fifteen percent, dropping to less than three percent by the end of 1988. In Tampa, Florida, the number of contracts awarded to black-owned companies decreased 99 percent, and contracts with Latino-owned firms fell 50 percent after *Croson*. Such dramatic decreases in contracts awarded to minority businesses occurred throughout the country. More than thirty-three states and political subdivisions have taken steps to dismantle their racial/ethnic set-aside programs; more than seventy jurisdictions are conducting studies and/or holding hearings to review and evaluate their programs in light of *Croson*.

Although the *Croson* decision limited access for black-owned and other minority firms, the civil rights movement reclaimed some rights for blacks as citizens and entrepreneurs. This supported a trend toward growth. Employment in business firms owned by African Americans grew by 224 percent between 1972 and 1987; the number of firms increased nearly five times, and gross receipts grew by 700 percent. In 1972 there were 187,602 firms listed and by 2002 the number had increased 634.4 percent to 1.2 million. The revenue also grew from $20 billion in 1977 to $88.8 billion in 2002.

Historically, African American businesses have been restricted to the narrow range of service enterprises. They have tended to establish businesses that require relatively limited capital and technical expertise, such as personal services and small-scale retailing. These firms have had to rely heavily on the African American community as their market for goods and services. In 2002 four out of ten black-owned firms provided health care and social assistance, personal services, and repair and maintenance. These services still remain as a key basis for African American businesses. Of the 10,727 African American-owned firms in 2002 with individual revenue of $1 million or more, total revenue for this group has increased to $49 billion versus $40 billion in 1997. Overall African American-owned firms account for five percent of all non-farm businesses in the United States.

The location of corporate headquarters in urban areas has provided increased business opportunity for black business service enterprises. Large cities have become areas where administrative and service functions are the dominant economic activities. The growth in corporate and government administration in central-city business districts has created a need for complementary advertising, accounting, computer, legal, temporary secretarial, and maintenance business services. In 2002, 44 percent of African American-owned firms were located in five key states, with New York having the largest number of firms at 129,324, followed by California 112,873, Florida 102,079, Georgia 90,461, and Texas 88,769. Within those states the key urban areas which have the greatest number of African American firms consists of New York City 98,076, Chicago 39,424, Los Angeles 25,958, Houston 21,226, and Detroit 19,530. These firms generate anywhere from $1.5 million to $5 million in revenue.

With the increase in opportunity for African American-owned firms, the issue of sustainability remains a key concern. African American-owned firms have the lowest survival rates of all ethnic business. In 1997 more than half of African American-owned firms were in the service industry with sixty-three percent of those firms able to survive. Black finance companies and insurance and real estate companies, which are one in every twenty African American-owned firms, have the highest survival rate of seventy-one percent.

Access for qualified African Americans as leaders in a broad range of businesses and corporations has seen an increase. In 1988 there were twenty-five corporate managers but no black executives. By 1993 there were twelve African Americans who were presidents and two CEOs. In 2005 there were eighteen African Americans as CEOs including three women, showing an increase of 300 percent, but still less than one percent of the senior-level positions of America's one thousand largest firms. In 2006 Harpo Inc.'s Oprah Winfrey and RLJ Development's Robert L. Johnson were the first African Americans to be recognized as billionaires, and Reginald F. Lewis became the first CEO of a billion-dollar company.

PUBLISHING
Books

Since black book publishing began in the United States in 1817, three types of publishers have emerged in this sector of the American book publishing industry: religious publishers, institutional publishers, and trade book publishers.

Religious publishing enterprises were established by black religious denominations in order to publish books and other literature to assist clergy and laity in recording denominational history and to provide religious instruction. Some black religious publishers also published books on secular subjects, which were generally related to celebrating some aspect of black culture or documenting black history.

Prior to the Civil War, two black religious publishing enterprises existed. The African Methodist Episcopal Church organized the AME Book Concern in Philadelphia in 1817—the first black-owned book publishing enterprise in the United States. The Colored Methodist Episcopal Church (CME), known as the Christian Methodist Episcopal Church, started the CME Publishing House in 1870, and the AME Sunday School Union and Publishing House was established in Bloomington, Illinois, in 1882, but moved to

Nashville, Tennessee, in 1886. Publishing secular and religious books, the AME Sunday School Union and Publishing House remains today as the oldest publishing unit owned by the AME Church.

One of the most successful black religious publishers to come into existence during the nineteenth century was the National Baptist Publishing Board. Under the leadership of Dr. Richard Henry Boyd and the auspices of the National Baptist Convention, U.S.A., the National Baptist Publishing Board was organized in Nashville in 1896.

During the last decades of the nineteenth century and the early decades of the twentieth century, educational, cultural, social, and political institutions were established to meet the specific needs of Black Americans. Many of these institutions developed publishing programs, which included book publishing.

Hampton Institute became the first black educational institution to publish books when the Hampton Institute Press was established in 1871.

An active publisher until 1940, the Hampton Institute Press published travel books, poetry, textbooks, songbooks, conference proceedings, and the *Southern Workman*, one of the leading national African American periodicals published between 1871 and 1939.

John W. Work's *The Negro and His Song* (1915) was the first book issued under the Fisk University Press imprint. During the 1930s and 1940s, when Charles Spurgeon Johnson chaired the university's Department of Sociology, several important studies were published by Fisk University Press, including E. Franklin Frazier's *The Free Negro Family* (1932); *The Economic Status of the Negro*, by Charles Spurgeon Johnson (1933); and *People versus Property*, by Herman Long and Charles Spurgeon Johnson (1947). The last publication released by the Fisk University Press was *Build a Future: Addresses Marking the Inauguration of Charles Spurgeon Johnson* (1949).

Black cultural and professional organizations and institutions have also developed publishing

A class learns geography at the Hampton Institute, which was the first black educational institution to publish books.

programs that include book publishing. The books published by these organizations have documented areas of black history and depicted various aspects of African American culture.

In 1913, five years after its founding, the National Association for the Advancement of Colored People launched its book publishing program with the publication of three books: *A Child's Story of Dunbar*, by Julia L. Henderson (1919); *Norris Wright Cuney*, by Maude Cuney Hare (1913); and *Hazel*, by Mary White Ovington (1913).

In contrast, the National Urban League first embarked on book publishing in 1927 when it published *Ebony and Topaz*, an anthology of Harlem Renaissance writers, poets, and artists, which was edited by Charles Spurgeon Johnson.

Although the publishing program of the Universal Negro Improvement Association and African Communities League focused on the publication of its newspaper, the *Negro World*, this political organization also published books. Two volumes of *The Philosophy and Opinions of Marcus Garvey*, compiled and edited by Amy Jacques-Garvey, were published under the imprint of the Press of the Universal Negro Improvement Association.

Until the 1960s, most black commercial publishers that engaged in book publishing enterprises were short lived. In 1967, however, Haki Madhubuti founded Third World Press in Chicago. Third World Press is now the oldest continually operating black commercial book publisher in the United States. Other publishers include Just Us Books, which began publishing in 1976; in 1985 Broadside Press was sold, but it continues to operate; in 1993 Genius Press began specializing in romance novels, and other companies were established as interest in diaspora literature increased and a variety of genres that explored the African American experience were more prevalent.

As readership grew from $181 million to $296 million in 1995 and continued to rise, white publishers in response created companies to specifically publish and market African American text. Although many in the black community saw these companies using a formulaic approach to producing books, the overall interest for black books remains high.

Newspapers

The black press in the United States is heir to a great, largely unheralded tradition. It began with the first black newspaper, *Freedom's Journal*, edited and published by Samuel Cornish and John B. Russwurm, on March 16, 1827. The *North Star*, the newspaper of abolitionist Frederick Douglass, was first published on December 3, 1847.

By the 1880s, African Americans' ability to establish a substantial cultural environment in many cities of the North led to the creation of a new wave of publications, including the *Washington Bee*, the *Indianapolis World*, the *Philadelphia Tribune*, the *Cleveland Gazette*, the *Baltimore Afro-American*, and the *New York Age*. By 1900 daily papers appeared in Norfolk, Kansas City, and Washington, D.C.

Founded in 1909 by James H. Anderson, the *Amsterdam News* has become one of the best-known black newspapers in the nation. It was first published on December 4, 1909, in Anderson's home on 132 W. 65th Street in New York City. At that time one of only fifty black "news sheets" in the country, the *Amsterdam News* had a staff of ten, consisted of six printed pages, and sold for two cents a copy. Since then, the paper has been printed at several Harlem addresses.

Among the famous black newspaper editors were William Monroe Trotter, editor of the *Boston Guardian*, a self-styled "radical" paper that showed no sympathy for the conciliatory stance of Booker T. Washington; Robert S. Abbott, whose *Chicago Defender* pioneered the use of headlines; and T. Thomas Fortune of the *New York Age*, who championed free public schools in an age when many opposed the idea.

In 1940 there were over two hundred black newspapers, mostly weeklies with local readerships, and by 1947 circulation of black newspapers had risen to two million readers. The key papers were the *Courier*, the *Afro-American*, the *Defender*, and the *Amsterdam News*. As the 1960s and the civil rights movement swept the country, black newspapers played their part by reporting news and often shedding light on unfair and discriminatory practices. In the 1960s the *Afro-American Press*, in order to provide support for the passing of the Civil Rights Act of 1964, used several of their reporters, disguised as African diplomats, to show discriminatory dinning practices along U.S. Route 1, the main highway between Washington, D.C., and New York. These tactics, along with the filing of lawsuits, challenged Jim Crow laws. Not all papers supported such moves and many that were backed by white supporters were not openly critical of discriminatory systems. This period of media in support of community ideas also opened the door to alternative papers such as *Black Panther* and *Muhammad Speaks*.

During the 1970s and 1980s there was a slow decline in the circulation of black newspapers. The increased role of television, economic issues, and declining influence saw many close their doors. Combining this with the opportunity for young black journalists in white media and the lack of new talent interested in local black papers, many well-established papers such as the *Richmond Afro-American* did not survive. The Internet became another factor that further diminished the readership of not only black newspapers, but the newspaper medium in general.

In spite of the difficulties, many traditional black newspapers continue to operate. With well over three hundred black newspapers still operating, the opportunity to develop technology-based papers has actually expanded the medium with websites as another means of reaching a broader readership.

The National Negro Newspaper Publishers Association was founded in 1940 to represent black newspaper publishers. The organization scheduled workshops and trips abroad to acquaint editors and reporters with important news centers and news sources. One result was a trend to more progressive and interpretive reporting. In 1956 the association changed its name to the National Newspaper Publishers Association [NNPA] and later to the Black Press of America. By 2007 NNPA's readership was over fifteen million readers. In 2001 the organization formed the BlackPressUSA Network, a web resource for the black community, and has provided over twenty-six websites for black newspapers. The black newspaper continues to maintain its focus of serving the black community, which keeps it as an integral part of the information highway.

Magazines

As early as the 1830s, black magazines were being published in the United States. However, it was not until the 1900s that the first truly successful magazines appeared. In 1910 the National Association for the Advancement of Colored People began publishing *Crisis*. In November 1942 John H. Johnson launched the *Negro Digest*, and in 1945 he published the first issue of *Ebony*. The idea for the new magazine came from two *Digest* writers, and the magazine's name was designated by Johnson's wife, Enice Johnson. Its first print run of 25,000 copies sold out immediately. The success of *Ebony* led to the demise of the *Negro Digest*, and in 1951 the magazine ceased publication. However, *Ebony*, which has remained a success, has a circulation rate of almost two million, and in 1951 *Jet* magazine was launched.

Since the founding of *Ebony*, several new and specialized black magazines have appeared. In 1967 *Black American Literature Review*, a journal presenting essays, interviews, poems, and book reviews, was founded. Also in 1967 Project Magazines, Inc. began publishing *Black Careers*. In 1969 the Black World Foundation published the first edition of the *Black Scholar*.

Earl G. Graves, a young businessman, in 1970 embarked on a concept to publish a monthly digest of news, commentary, and informative articles for blacks interested in business enterprise. Within a few short years his magazine, *Black Enterprise*, was accepted as the authority on African Americans in business and as an impor-

A famous fixture at *Ebony* magazine was editor Lerone Bennett, seen here hard at work at his desk. Bennett was promoted from senior to executive editor of the magazine in 1987.

tant advocate for an active, socially responsive black middle class. A second magazine directed at black women founded in 1970, *Essence*, has steadily gained in its circulation since its inception. Featuring health and beauty, fashion, and contemporary living sections, *Essence* is considered one of the top women's magazines. Susan Taylor served as the magazine's editor in chief for nearly twenty years and was a key component of the magazine's success. *Essence*, which in 2002 had a readership of more than seven million, was sold to Time, Inc. in 2005. One factor in the success of many African American publications is the ability to attract advertisers seeking to reach the African American middle class.

The diversity of the magazines available to the African American audience continues to grow with publications such as *O Magazine* launched by media mogul Oprah Winfrey in 2000, and other African American-owned publications such as *Heart & Soul, VIBE, American Legacy,* and *Black Child* just to name a few. Advertisers are able to

reach middle-class black readers through a variety of media, inclusive of *Jet, Ebony,* and *Essence,* which continue to enjoy a healthy readership.

BROADCASTING MEDIA
Radio

African American representation and later ownership in the broadcast industry began in 1929 when black radio pioneer Jack Cooper began hosting a new radio program, *The All-Negro Hour,* on a white-owned Chicago station. A boom period occurred between 1946 and 1955, when the number of black-oriented stations jumped from twenty-four to six hundred.

There were black journalists before there was a broadcast industry, but in the Jim Crow America of the 1920s, there had to be black-oriented radio before there could be black broadcast journalists. That mission fell to a vaudevillian jack-of-all-trades from Cincinnati, Jack L. Cooper (1888–1970).

While early radio shows featured black singing groups, they featured no blacks talking. To Cooper, this "was like taxation without representation," and so on Sunday, November 3, 1929, at 5 P.M., Chicago's white-owned WSBC premiered *The All-Negro Hour,* starring Cooper and friends. Born was the concept of black radio, and Cooper went on to become the nation's first black radio station executive, the first black newscaster, the first black sportscaster, and the first to use radio as a service medium.

The All-Negro Hour was like a vaudeville revue on the air, featuring music, comedy, and serials. Although it ended its run in 1935, Cooper continued with WSBC, pioneering the black-radio format by producing several black-oriented shows. Crucial to that format was local news and public affairs of interest to African Americans.

The first example of public service programming aired December 9, 1938, when Cooper launched the *Search for Missing Persons* show. Aimed at reuniting people who had lost contact with friends and relatives through migration and over time, it reportedly had reunited twenty thousand people by 1950. According to *Ebony* magazine, Cooper also remodeled a van into a mobile unit to relay "on-the-spot news events directly to four radio stations in the Chicago and suburban area," including news flashes from the *Pittsburgh Courier* and interviews with famous personalities who came to town, such as boxer Joe Louis. Cooper also did play-by-play sportscasts of black baseball games from the van.

Listen Chicago, a news discussion show that ran from 1946 to 1952, provided African Americans with their first opportunity to use radio as a public forum. Following Cooper's lead, between 1946 and 1955 the number of black-oriented stations jumped from twenty-four to six hundred. News was a part of the explosion. "We have learned to do newscasts that answer the question, 'How is this news going to affect me as a Negro?,'" Leonard Walk of WHOD Pittsburgh said in 1954. "We have learned that church and

social news deserves a unique place of importance in our daily Negro programming." Yet by and large these broadcasters were not trained journalists. Black stations did not begin to broadcast news as we know it today until the 1960s.

In 1972 the Mutual Black Network was formed for news and sports syndication, under the auspices of the Mutual Broadcasting Network. By the end of the 1970s, the Mutual Black Network had just over one hundred affiliates and 6.2 million listeners. The Sheridan Broadcasting Corporation, a black-owned broadcasting chain based in Pittsburgh, purchased the Mutual Black Network in the late 1970s, renaming it the Sheridan Broadcasting Network. A second African American radio network, the National Black Network, was formed in 1973. Among its regular features was commentary by journalist Roy Wood, which he named "One Black Man's Opinion." In January 1992 the American Urban Radio Network was formed, and the National Black Network has since gone out of business.

The networks were a mixed blessing. They provided their affiliates with broadcast-quality programs produced from an African American perspective. But this relatively inexpensive access to news, sports, and public affairs features discouraged the local stations that subscribed from producing their own shows. News and public affairs staffs at the black-oriented stations remained minimal. There were some notable exceptions. New York's WLIB-AM had a black format that included a highly acclaimed news and public affairs department. A series of shows produced by the station on disadvantaged youth in the city won two Peabody Awards in 1970. After the station was purchased in 1972 by African American civic leader Percy Sutton, the station became "Your Total Black News and Information Station," offering more news and public affairs programming than any other black-formatted radio outlet in the country.

Before 1967 only two black educational outlets existed in the country; by 1990 there were forty black public radio stations. Many of them were community radio stations, owned and operated by nonprofit foundations, controlled by a local board of directors, and relying on listener donations. Others were on college campuses. One of the most successful was WPFW-FM, a 50,000-watt outlet controlled by African Americans, launched in 1977 by the Pacifica Foundation.

Although minority-owned radio stations have increased slightly between 1978 and 1995, the Federal Communications Commission granted tax credit to radio and televisions that sold property to minority owners. The goal of the Commission toward affirmative action was to expand the viewpoints in the industry and broaden ownership beyond primarily white owners. Although the tax credit was eliminated the same year, U.S. Radio, owned by attorney Ragan A. Henry, had become the largest African American radio group in the nation. In 1996 it was reported to have twenty-five stations and was sold for $140 million to Clear Channel Communications of San Antonio, a white organization.

In 1980 Cathy Liggins Hughes, a pioneer in talk and contemporary radio, purchased a radio station in Washington, D.C., making her the first female owner of a station in a dominant market. Hughes who later founded Radio One, Inc., has become the owner of the largest African American broadcasting company in America and the first publicly traded stock on the U.S. stock exchange headed by an African American woman. By 2004 Radio One encompassed sixty-eight stations estimated at three billion dollars.

Television

It took the riots of the 1960s and a stern warning from a federal commission for the broadcast industry to undertake any concentrated hiring of African Americans. When American cities began to burn, blacks held about 3.6 percent of television news jobs. White news directors had to scramble to find black journalists to cover the story. In 1968 the National Advisory Commission on Civil Disorders, known as the Kerner Commission, concluded that "the world that television and newspapers offer to their black audience is almost totally white, in both appearance and attitude." "Within a year," wrote

Noble, "many of us found ourselves working downtown at major radio and TV stations." In 1969 the Federal Communications Commission prohibited discrimination in broadcasting, but by 1973 there were still only seven African American reporters at the three major networks.

In 1980 Howard University launched WHMM-TV, becoming the first licensee of a public television station on a black campus and the only black-owned public television station in the nation. On August 31, 1991, San Francisco's Minority Television Project went on the air with KMTP-TV, which became the nation's second black-owned public television station. One of the principals was Adam Clayton Powell III, son of the late Harlem congressman.

The 1980s saw the explosion of cable television and the decline of the television networks. Black Entertainment Television, founded by former congressional aide Robert L. Johnson, made its debut in 1980 and established a news division by the end of the decade. That division produced a weekly news show, *BET News,* and *Lead Story,* a talk show featuring black pundits. In 2000 BET was sold to Viacom, Inc., an international media giant, which took the control of the station and its programming out of the hand of African Americans. The sale made Robert L. Johnson the first African American billionaire.

Cathy L. Hughes, known for her success as the owner of Radio One, Inc., beginning with the purchase of her first radio station in Washington, D.C., in 1980, partnered with Comcast, one of the nation's largest pay television providers, and launched TV One Inc., a television station catering to the African American lifestyle. By December 2006 the station was seen in over 33 million households. Oprah Winfrey, who successfully orchestrated her career from talk show host of *The Oprah Winfrey Show* in Chicago to media mogul and the first African American female billionaire, launched the Oprah Winfrey Network (OWN) on January 1, 2011. The station's focus is to help all Americans "live their best life."

As technology has opened the door to providing greater access to all aspects of society,

People begin to gather on Michigan Avenue in Chicago in 2009, awaiting the kickoff of the twenty-fourth season of the *Oprah Winfrey Show.*

African Americans have actively been part of this information highway. The World Wide Web offers information on almost any subject that involves the African American experience from newspapers and magazines, organizations and resources, products and businesses, health and wellness, as well as personal sites for social networking.

BIOGRAPHIES: ENTREPRENEURS

Jim Beckwourth (1798–1866)
Trapper, Author

Beckwourth was born on April 26, 1798, to a father from a prominent Virginia family and an African American mother who is said to have been a slave. Beckwourth spent much of his life chasing adventure in the West, and became a well-known mountain man.

By 1842 Beckwourth had been married several times by the informal rules of the frontier, which only required being together as a condition of partnership; he made a living as a trapper and had many exploits in the American West. Once returning to the Rocky Mountains after serving with the U.S. Army during the Seminole wars, Beckwourth decided to open a trading post near what came to be Pueblo, Colorado. In 1850 after joining the California gold rush, he found a mountain pass through to California that bears his name. He opened an inn at the pass and by 1851 was guiding wagon trains through.

Beckwourth became quite famous as his memoirs and stories of his adventures were published in 1856. He later returned to Denver and opened another trading post. Wanting to get back to the adventure in the West, Beckwourth signed up as a scout with the Army to fight the Cheyenne Indians. In 1866 Beckwourth died of food poisoning while riding to a Crow encampment.

Malcolm CasSelle (1970–)
Technology

Malcolm CasSelle was born on March 22, 1970, in Allentown, Pennsylvania. Early in his life CasSelle developed a passion for computers and writing programs. He graduated from Massachusetts Institute of Technology in 1991 and later earned a master's degree from Stanford University. CasSelle was part of the Japan MIT program after his undergraduate work, and while overseas he worked for Shroders Securities and NTT Software Labs. In the States he worked for Apple Computers and Blast Publishing.

In 1995 CasSelle and business partner E. David Ellington co-founded NetNoir Inc., an African American-oriented online website. The site offered a wide scope of news, information, and events within the African American community. CasSelle is currently director of Holo Personal Growth Partners, a marketing and advertising firm.

Kenneth Chenault (1951–)
Corporate Executive

Born June 2, 1951, in Mineola, New York, Kenneth I. Chenault spent his childhood in Hempstead, New York, on Long Island. In 1973 Chenault graduated magna cum laude in history from Bowdoin College and in 1976 he received his J.D. from Harvard Law School.

Chenault joined American Express in 1981 as director of strategic planning for the Travel Related Services. In 1983 he was promoted to vice president of merchandise services and from 1984 to 1986 served as senior vice president and general manager of marketing. Under his direction the division jumped from $150 million to $500 million. In 1991 Chenault was named president of the American Express Card, and in 1993 he was named president of the American Express Travel Related Services U.S.A.

By 1995 Chenault had earned the position of vice chairman of the company and established himself as the highest-ranking African American in corporate America. By 1997 Chenault reached new heights as president and chief operating officer, and in 2001 Chenault was named CEO of American Express, and the second most powerful African American executive. He was an effective and productive leader at the helm of American Express and he inspired others by giving commencement speeches at Howard University in 2008 and Fisk University in 2010.

Comer Cottrell (1931–)
Personal Care Entrepreneur

Comer Cottrell was born on December 7, 1931, in Mobile, Alabama. After graduating from the University of Detroit in 1952 and entering the world of work, Cottrell noticed while working at a post exchange on a military base that there were no hair care products for African Americans. In 1970 Cottrell began his company.

With an empty Los Angeles warehouse, $600, and a typewriter, Cottrell began marketing his first product, hair spray, to barber shops and beauty salons with a moderate degree of success. By 1975 Pro-line opened a distribution center in Birmingham, Alabama, and by 1980 the company had expanded far beyond Los Angeles and moved to Dallas. Pro-line's revenues had increased from $36 million in 1989 to $104 million in 2000. Pro-line continues in its success and the company remains a family affair in its leadership.

Cottrell has been a strong and positive presence in the community. He purchased the property of bankrupt Bishop College in 1986 for $1.5 million. As an advocate for education in the black community he was able to persuade Paul Quinn College, an African Methodist Episcopal church-supported institution to move to the location. Cottrell provided $1.7 million to help with renovations of the site.

Jean Baptiste Point Du Sable (c. 1750–1818)
Chicago Founder

Jean Baptiste Point Du Sable was reportedly born in 1750 in Haiti to a French father and African-born slave mother. It is believed that he was educated in Paris and came to North America through Louisiana or French Canada.

 In the early 1770s Du Sable established the first settlement in an area which was later called Chicago. After a period away from this settlement, serving as a liaison between Native Americans and the British in St. Clair, Du Sable returned to expand the scope of the settlement. He built a poultry house, a bakery, a stable, a horse mill, a dairy, a smokehouse, and a workshop. As a frontiersman he also trapped animals and traded various goods. Because of Du Sable's efforts Chicago became a key center for commerce on the frontier.

In 1788 Du Sable married a Potawatomi woman, Kittihawa, or Catherine, and they had two children. After a failed attempt at becoming chief in 1800 Du Sable sold his holdings and moved to St. Charles, Missouri. He died, it is assumed in poverty, on August 28, 1818.

Ann Marie Fudge (1951–)
Corporate Executive

Ann Marie Fudge was born in Washington, D.C., on April 23, 1951. She attended Simmons College and earned a B.A. with honors in 1973 and an M.B.A. from Harvard Business School in 1977. Fudge began her career in 1973 with General Electric as a manpower specialist but left in 1975 to work for General Mills in Minneapolis. She worked her way up and held various positions in the marketing area until 1986, when Kraft hired her as the associate director of strategic planning. Fudge proved herself a valuable employee and moved through the ranks.

In 1994 Fudge was named executive vice president of the Coffee and Cereals Division of Kraft and in 2000 she became president of the Beverages, Desserts and Post Division. She succeeded in creating double-digit growth and increased market shares. Later in 2000 Fudge decided to retire because of personal experiences and desired goals.

She returned to the world of work in 2003 and became chairperson and CEO of Young and Rubicam Bands, a communications company.

Reginald F. Lewis (1942–1993)
Business Executive

Lewis was born December 7, 1942, in Baltimore, Maryland. He received an A.B. from Virginia State College in 1965 and a law degree from Harvard Law School in 1968. He first worked with the firm of Paul, Weiss, Rifkind, Wharton & Garrison until 1970. He was a partner in Murphy, Thorpe & Lewis, the first African American law firm on Wall Street until 1973. Between 1973 and 1989 Lewis was in private practice as a corporate lawyer. In 1989 he became president and CEO of TLC Beatrice International Holdings Inc. With TLC's leveraged acquisition of the Beatrice International Food Company, Lewis became the head of the largest African American-owned business in the United States. TLC Beatrice had revenues of $1.54 billion in 1992.

Lewis was a member of the American and National Bar Associations and the National Conference of Black Lawyers. He was on the board of directors of the New York City Off-Track Betting Corporation, the Central Park Conservancy, the NAACP Legal Defense Fund, and WNET–Channel 13, the public television station in New York. He was the recipient of the Distinguished Service Award presented by the American Association of MESBIC and the Black Enterprise Achievement Award for the Professions. Lewis died on January 19, 1993, in New York.

Samuel Metters (1934–)
Strategic Planning

Samuel Metters, a native of Austin, Texas, earned his B.S from Prairie View A&M University in architectural engineering and a B.A. from the University of California at Berkeley in architecture and urban planning. He later earned an M.S. in systems management as well as an M.S. and Ph.D. in public administration from the University of Southern California.

Metters began Metters Industries in the basement of his residence in 1981 and in 2010 the company had grown to include six offices nationwide. The firm, which has over 350 employees, works with various agencies to analyze their goals and develop strategic plans to meet those goals. Clients have included the IRS, Northwest Airlines, Howard University, Federal Express, and Fox Studios. In 2002 annual sales were $20 million, down from a high of $34 million.

Rose Meta Morgan (1912–)
Hair Care Entrepreneur

Rosa Meta Morgan was born in Shelby, Mississippi, in 1912. Her father moved the family of thirteen to Chicago when Morgan was six years old. Although Morgan dropped out of school she did attend Chicago's Morris School of Beauty and began earning money styling hair. In 1938 she styled the hair of Ethel Waters, a famous African American actress and entertainer, and was invited to accompany her to New York as her hair dresser.

In 1939 Morgan opened her own salon and was inundated with clients. She leased an old dilapidated mansion and renovated it. Approximately three years later in 1943 she opened the Rose Meta House of Beauty Inc. located in Harlem. Her clientele increased to as many as one thousand customers a week and her staff increased to twenty-nine. Morgan also began making and selling beauty products and fashion designs. Morgan bought and refurbished a new building and in 1955 opened a new location for her House of Beauty. The new location included a dressmaking department, a charm school, a wig salon, and a fitness department. Also in 1955 Morgan married Joe Louis, the boxer, but the marriage was annulled in 1958.

In the early 1960s Morgan co-founded the New Jersey Savings and Loan Association, and in 1965 Morgan founded the Freedom National Bank, the only bank in New York run by an African American and for the African American community. Morgan retired in the 1980s having created some of the most successful and innovative businesses in the African American community. She remained active well into her nineties.

Stanley O'Neal (1951–)
Corporate Executive

Earnest Stanley O'Neal was born in Roanoke, Alabama, on October 7, 1951. His family moved to Atlanta where he worked for General Motors while in high school. O'Neal earned his undergraduate degree in 1974 from the General Motors Institute, later named Kettering University. He was awarded a scholarship from General Motors to attend Harvard Business School where he earned an M.B.A. in 1978. After working for General Motors, first as an analyst and then a director in the treasury division, he left to join Merrill Lynch in 1986. O'Neal served on General Motors's board of directors from 2001 to 2006.

Between 1986 and 2000 O'Neal held key positions at Merrill Lynch as managing director of Investment Banking, head of the Financial Services Group, co-head of the Corporate and Institutional Client Group and CEO of the Private Client Group. O'Neal has been credited with moving the firm from a promoter of stock trading to one that offered wealth management and financial planning.

In 2001 O'Neal was named president and chief operating officer of Merrill Lynch. During the sub-prime crisis in 2007 Merrill Lynch suffered losses of $8 billion, which were assigned to the leadership strategy of O'Neal. He left Merrill that same year in possession of a golden parachute compensation package valued at $161.5 million. On January 18, 2008, O'Neal was named to the board of directors of Alcoa.

Richard Dean Parsons (1948–)
Corporate Executive

Richard Dean Parsons was born on April 4, 1948, in Brooklyn, New York's Bedford-Stuyvesant neighborhood. He graduated high school at the age of sixteen and attended college at the University of Hawaii, where he played varsity basketball. Parsons graduated in 1968 and went on to earn his J.D., at the top of his class, from Union University of Albany Law School in 1971.

Parsons's first position in the work force was as a member of New York governor Nelson Rockefeller's staff. Parsons continued in his position when Rockefeller became vice president under President Gerald Ford in 1974. He stayed in government until 1977 when he left and joined the law firm Patterson, Belknap, Webb & Tyler. He became a partner in the firm in 1979. He had an impressive clientele, including Happy Rockefeller and Estée Lauder.

In 1988 Parsons was named chief operating officer of the Dime Savings Bank of New York and was the first African American male to manage a financial institution. He remained with Dime Savings until 1993. Parsons's leadership was again called upon in 2001 when he was named CEO of the AOL Time Warner Corporation. At Time Warner, Parsons had served, during his tenure, in the positions of chairman and president. As CEO he was able to put the company on the path to sustainable growth, increase their balance sheet, and simplify their corporate structure. Parsons left Time Warner in December 2007. In February 2009 he was named chairman of the board of Citigroup Inc., the eighth largest firm in the United States.

Russell Simmons (1957–)
Music Producer

Simmons was born in the middle-class neighborhood of Hollis in Queens, New York, on October 4, 1957. In 1970 after having some involvement with gangs while a teenager, he decided to take classes in sociology at City College of New York. Although he did not complete college, Simmons saw an opportunity. He recognized the influence that rap music had on young urban African Americans telling their story. The crowds that came to parks and street corners to hear their performances encouraged him to promote local artists and begin Def Jam Recordings in 1984 with partner Rick Rubin. His efforts set the foundation that revolutionized hip-hop.

Simmons's involvement with hip-hop and the fashion that supported this urban music helped to inspire a clothing line Simmons called Phat Farm. It became one aspect of Simmons's multi-faceted business, Rush Communications. The firm encompassed films, television shows, management services, a magazine and advertising company, and clothing. By 1992 Rush Communications was the second largest African American-owned entertainment company in the nation. In 1999 Simmons sold his stake in Def Jam Records to Universal Music Group for $100 million. In 2004 he sold Phat Farm for $140 million.

Naomi R. Sims (1949–2009)
Model, Author, Entrepreneur

Naomi R. Sims was born March 30, 1949, in Oxford, Mississippi. She attended New York University (where she studied psychology) and the Fashion Institute of Technology, both on scholarships.

Sims was a fashion model with the Ford Agency in New York from 1970 to 1973. She was the first African American woman to be a high fashion model and the first to appear in a television commercial. She also appeared on the cover of *Life* magazine.

In 1970 Sims began to lecture and write fashion and beauty articles on a freelance basis. In 1973 she co-developed a new fiber for her line of wigs and founded the Naomi Sims Collection, which by 1977 reported annual revenues of $4 million. Sims has also written a number of books, including *All about Health and Beauty for the Black Woman* (1975), *How to Be a Top Model* (1979), *All about Hair Care for the Black Woman* (1982), and *All about Success for the Black Woman*.

In 1969 and 1970 Sims was voted Model of the Year by International Mannequins and won the Ladies' Home Journal Women of Achieve-ment Award. For her work with underprivileged children in Bedford-Stuyvesant; she also won an award from the New York City Board of Educa-tion. In 1977 Sims was voted into the Modeling Hall of Fame by International Mannequins and made the International Best Dressed List, 1971–73 and 1976–77. Sims has also received recogni-tion for her fund-raising efforts for sickle-cell anemia and cancer research. She belonged to the NAACP and worked closely with drug rehabili-tation programs. Sims died of breast cancer on August 1, 2009, in Newark, New Jersey.

Percy Sutton (1920–2009)
Business Executive, Attorney

Sutton was born on November 24, 1920, in San Antonio, Texas. He graduated from the Phillis Wheatley High School and attended a number of colleges, including Prairie View College, Tuskegee Institute, and the Hampton Institute. His education was interrupted by World War II when he enlisted in the U.S. Army Air Corps. He was promoted to captain and served as a combat intelligence officer in the Italian and Mediter-ranean theaters. He was decorated with Combat Stars for his service.

After his discharge, Sutton attended law school on the G.I. Bill, first at Columbia Univer-sity in New York, and then Brooklyn Law School where he received an LL.B. in 1950. During the Korean conflict Sutton re-enlisted in the USAF and served as an intelligence officer and a trial judge advocate.

Returning to civilian life, he opened a law of-fice in Harlem with his brother and another at-torney. In 1964 he was elected to the New York State Assembly, where he served until 1966. In 1966 he was appointed and later elected to the office of president of the borough of Manhattan, a post he held until 1977. Sutton, with his brother Oliver, and Clarence B. Jones founded the Inner-City Broadcasting Corporation in 1971. They purchased the first black-owned radio sta-tion in New York City, WLIB-AM. In 1987 Sut-ton was awarded the Spingarn Medal by the

NAACP which honors, annually, outstanding achievement by an African American.

Sutton has been a civil rights advocate both as an attorney and a politician. He was a national director of the Urban League and president of the New York branch of the NAACP, and he was voted Assemblyman of the Year by the Intercol-legiate Legislative Assembly in 1966. Sutton has served as a director of the Museum of the City of New York and the American Museum of Natural History.

Sutton died on December 26, 2009, and is buried in his hometown of San Antonio, Texas, in the Gates of Heaven Memorial Cemetery.

John W. Thompson (1949–)
Corporate Executive

John Wendell Thompson was born on April 24, 1949, in Fort Dix, New Jersey. Thompson earned his B.A. in business administration from Florida A&M University in 1971 and earned an M.S. in management sciences from Massachusetts Insti-tute of Technology's Sloan School of Management in 1982.

Thompson joined IBM in 1971 and worked his way through the ranks to the senior level po-sition of general manager of IBM's American unit. In 1999 after twenty-eight years Thompson left IBM and became chief executive officer of Symantec Corporation, a software company. Thompson's leadership strategy focused on cor-porate security solutions and increased the com-pany's revenue from $634 million to $944 million in two years.

Thompson's leadership has broadened the exposure of Symantec and provided services to some of the largest enterprises in the world.

Madam Sarah C. J. Walker
(1867–1919)
Entrepreneur

Walker was born Sarah Breedlove near Delta, Louisiana, in 1867. She was orphaned as a child, raised by a sister in Vicksburg, Mississippi, married at the age of fourteen, and widowed in 1887 at the age of twenty.

Walker moved with her daughter to St. Louis, where she earned a living by taking in laundry and sewing. By 1905 she had become interested in hair care products for African American women and had begun working on a hot comb and her "Wonderful Hair Grower." In 1906 she moved to Denver and, with $1.50 in her pocket, started a hair preparations company. She soon married C.J. Walker, a newspaper journalist who taught her the fundamentals of advertising and mail-order promotion. In 1908 she moved with her daughter to Pittsburgh, where she founded a beauty school that trained cosmetologists in the use of her products. Her husband continued the couple's advertising plan of traveling to different locations to promote her products and train sales agents.

In 1910, with a more central location in mind, she moved to Indianapolis, Indiana, where she established a laboratory and factory and developed a nationwide network of five thousand sales agents, mostly African American women.

Her business prospered and Walker became very wealthy. She had a townhouse in Harlem and a custom-built mansion on the Hudson River near Irvington, New York. She died in New York on May 25, 1919.

Walker was a strong believer in self-reliance and education. She was proud of her accomplishments, especially of providing employment for thousands of African Americans who might otherwise have had less meaningful jobs. Walker was also a genius at marketing, promotion, and mail-order sales. Beneficiaries of her estate included Mary McLeod Bethune's school in Daytona, Florida, and other African American schools, the NAACP, and the Frederick Douglass home restoration project in Florida.

Maggie Lena Walker (1867–1934)
Entrepreneur

Walker was born on or around July 15, 1867, in Richmond, Virginia. She was the daughter of Elizabeth Draper, a former slave, and Eccles Cuthbert, a New York journalist of Irish extraction.

Walker attended Richmond public schools, and after graduating in 1883 she taught in the Richmond schools for three years before marrying building contractor Armstead Walker in 1886.

While she had been in school, Walker joined the Grand United Order of Saint Luke, a mutual aid society that served as an insurance underwriter for African Americans. Walker became active in the organization and held a number of lesser positions before becoming the Right Worthy Grand Secretary in 1899. She soon changed the name of the organization to the Independent Order of Saint Luke and moved its headquarters to Richmond.

In 1903 she became the head of the Saint Luke Penny Bank and the first woman in the United States to hold such a position. Although legally separate, the bank had a close financial association with the Independent Order of Saint Luke. The bank later became the Saint Luke Bank and Trust Company and finally the Consolidated Bank and Trust Company.

By 1924, under Walker's guidance, the Order had a membership of one hundred thousand, a new headquarters building, more than two hundred employees, and its own newspaper, the *Saint Luke Herald*.

Walker was active in many other organizations, including the National Association of Colored Women, the Virginia Federation of Colored Women's Clubs, and the federation's Industrial School for Colored Girls. In 1912 she founded the Richmond Council of Colored Women and was a founding member of the Negro Organization Society, a blanket association for African American clubs and organizations.

She was a board member of the NAACP from 1923 to 1934 and the recipient of an honorary degree from Virginia Union University. In 1927 she received the Harmon Award for Distinguished Achievement.

BIOGRAPHIES: BROADCAST MEDIA

Tyra Banks (1973–)
Model, Talk Show Host

Tyra Banks, a top fashion model who has become a multimedia personality, was born December 4, 1973, in Los Angeles, California. Banks's extraordinary modeling career began in 1991 when her impressive runway performance in Paris, France, earned her a spot in numerous other shows. Banks's career in modeling earned her attention as one of the 50 Most Beautiful People in 1994 and 1996 and Supermodel of the Year in 1997.

In 2005 Banks retired from modeling and began an acting and movie career. With experience as a producer for the television show *America's Next Top Model*, Banks launched *The Tyra Banks Show*, a daytime talk show. The show was very successful and won several daytime Emmy Awards. Banks has started a scholarship at her alma mater for African American girls, founded a camp for teenage girls, and written the book *Tyra's Beauty Inside and Out*. She shares her experiences as a young woman and as an entrepreneur in her role as a motivational speaker. Her talents and burgeoning role as media mogul continues to earn attention.

Ed Bradley (1941–2006)
Journalist, Television News Correspondent

A native of Philadelphia, Pennsylvania, Edward R. Bradley received a B.S. in education from Cheyney State College in Cheyney, Pennsylvania. From 1963 to 1967 Bradley worked as a disc jockey and news reporter for WDAS radio in Philadelphia. From there he moved on to WCBS radio in New York. He joined CBS as a stringer in the Paris bureau in 1971. Within a few months he was transferred to the Saigon bureau, where he remained until he was assigned to the Wash-ington bureau, serving from June 1974 to 1978 as a CBS correspondent.

Until 1981 Bradley served as anchor for the *CBS Sunday Night News* and as principal correspondent for *CBS Reports*. In 1981 he replaced Dan Rather as a correspondent for the weekly news program *60 Minutes*. In 1992 Bradley was made host of the CBS news program *Street Stories*.

Bradley's effective role as correspondent earned eleven Emmy Awards, two Alfred I. DuPont–Columbia University Awards for broadcast journalism, a George Foster Peabody Broadcasting Award, a George Polk Award, and an NCAA Anniversary Award. He also earned in 1992 an Emmy for "Made In China," a segment on *60 Minutes*, in 1993 the Sol Taischoff Award, and in 2000 Bradley was inducted into the Deadline Club Hall of Fame by the New York chapter of the Society of Professional Journalists. Bradley died on November 9, 2006, of complications from leukemia.

James Brown (1951–)
Sports Anchor

Brown, who was born in Washington, D.C., on February 25, 1951, built a career as a sports broadcaster beginning in 1984. After earning a B.A. from Harvard University in 1973, and majoring in government, Brown was drafted by the Atlanta Hawks (but failed to make the team). He began his broadcasting career as an analyst for CBS Sports.

Brown went on to host the 1992 Winter Olympics, the *CBS Sports Saturday/Sunday*, the 1994 Lillehammer Winter Olympics, the Fox Saturday Night Fight programs, and in 2002 he hosted his own show *The James Brown Show*. In 2001 Brown was awarded the prestigious Sportscaster of the Year Award. Brown currently hosts *Inside the NFL* and CBS's *The NFL Today*.

Tony Brown (1933–)
Commentator, Columnist, Producer

Tony [William Anthony] Brown, born in Charleston, West Virginia, is probably best known as the producer and host of one of the longest-running minority affairs programs in history, *Tony Brown's Journal*. Brown received his bachelor of arts degree in 1959 and his master's degree in social work in 1961 from Wayne State University in Detroit. Brown took a job with the *Detroit Courier* as a drama critic. It was during this time that he began to be active in the civil rights movement, helping to organize the 1963 "March to Freedom" with Martin Luther King Jr. in Detroit. After leaving the paper, where he had worked up to the position of city editor, Brown landed a job with the local PBS station, WTVS, where he became involved in television programming and production. At WTVS he produced the station's first series aimed at a black audience, *C.P.T.* (Colored People's Time). He joined the New York staff of the PBS program *Black Journal* in 1970 as the show's executive producer and host—in 1977 the show's name was changed to *Tony Brown's Journal*.

In 1971 Brown founded and became the first dean of Howard University's School of Communications. He continued in that post until 1974. Brown has been an advocate of community and self-help programs. He has written the books *Black Lies, White Lies: The Truth According to Tony Brown* (1995) and *Empower the People: A 7-Step Plan to Overthrow the Conspiracy that Is Stealing Your Money and Freedom* (1998). He has also written, produced, and directed the film *The White Girl*, and has appeared as a commentator for National Public Radio. He is recipient of the NAACP Image Award and serves as president of Tony Brown Productions in New York City.

Xernona Clayton (1930–)
Broadcasting Executive

Clayton was born Xernona Brewster on August 30, 1930, in Muskogee, Oklahoma. She received a B.S. from Tennessee State University in 1952. She also attended the Ru-Jac School of Modeling in Chicago.

Clayton was the first African American woman to have her own television show in the South when she became hostess of the *Xernona Clayton Show* at WAGA-TV in Atlanta. She has

also been a newspaper columnist for the *Atlanta Voice*, taught public school in Chicago and Los Angeles, and has dabbled in photography and fashion modeling.

Clayton has also been active in the civil rights movement. Her first husband, now deceased, was the public relations director for Martin Luther King Jr. Clayton came to the attention of Atlanta officials, who appointed her as community-relations director of the Model Cities Program. She has also raised funds for sickle-cell anemia research and the Martin Luther King Jr. Birthplace Memorial Restoration Committee.

In 1968 Clayton won the Outstanding Leadership Award given by the National Association of Market Developers and a year later the Bronze Woman of the Year in Human Relations award given by Phi Delta Kappa sorority. She is also the recipient of the Georgia Associated Press Award for Superior Television Programming (1969–1971).

Clayton is the founder of the Atlanta chapter of Media Women and a member of the National Academy of Television Arts and Sciences. She has co-starred in a major motion picture, *House on Skull Mountain*. Clayton has remarried and is the executive producer of the Turner Broadcasting Network's Trumpet Awards, honoring the achievements of African Americans.

Don Cornelius (1936–)
Broadcasting Executive

Cornelius, is best known as the announcer and creator of *Soul Train*, one of the most widely watched dance and music shows in the twentieth century, particularly in the African American community. Don Cornelius was born on September 27, 1936, in Chicago, Illinois. After working as a radio announcer and formulating his ideas for a television show, *Soul Train*, it was finally realized on August 17, 1970, and was broadcast in the local Chicago area.

Soul Train had mass appeal particularly for the African American community which had little to no entertainment with community focus. Billed as a dance party, the show's success prompted the spinoff of an award shop specifically for African American artists. By 1992 *Soul Train* had become the longest-running syndicated music program. Although Cornelius retired in 1993 the show continued to run. *Soul Train,* which ran until 2006, holds the record as the longest-running syndicated program in television history. The show, which was sold to Madvision Entertainment in 2008, has been shown as reruns on BET's spinoff station, *Centric,* as of 2009. The Soul Train Awards created in 1986 continues to operate and is regarded with high esteem by the black community and the music community as well.

Cornelius, with his deep voice, is also known for the closing catch phrase of *The Soul Train Show*: "You can bet your last money, it's gonna be a stone gas, honey! I'm Don Cornelius, and as always, we wish you love, peace and soul!"

T. Thomas Fortune (1856–1928)
Journalist, New York Age *Founder*

Timothy Thomas Fortune was one of the most prominent black journalists involved in the flourishing black press of the post–Civil War era.

Born in Florida, on October 3, 1856, the son of a Reconstruction politician, Fortune was particularly productive before his thirtieth year, completing such works as *Black and White: Land, Labor and Politics in the South* (1884) and *The Negro in Politics* (1886), while in his twenties.

Fortune attended Howard University for two years, leaving to marry Carrie Smiley of Jacksonville, Florida. The couple went to New York in 1878, with Fortune taking a job as a printer for the *New York Sun*. In time Fortune caught the attention of *Sun* editor Charles A. Dana, who eventually promoted him to the editorial staff of the paper.

Fortune also edited the *Globe*, a black daily, and was later chief editorial writer for the *Negro World*. In 1900 Fortune joined Booker T. Washington in helping to organize the successful National Negro Business League. His later activity

with Washington gained him more notoriety than his earlier writing, although the writing is clearly more vital in affording him an important niche in the history of black protest.

In 1883 Fortune founded the *New York Age*, the paper with which he sought to "champion the cause" of his race. In time the *Age* became the leading black journal of opinion in the United States. One of Fortune's early crusades was against the practice of separate schools for the races in the New York educational system.

Fortune was later responsible for coining the term "Afro-American" as a substitute for Negro in New York newspapers. He also set up the Afro-American Council, an organization that he regarded as the precursor of the Niagara Movement. In 1907 Fortune sold the *Age*, although he remained active in journalism as an editorial writer for several black newspapers.

Mal Goode (1908–1995)
Television News Correspondent

Malvin Russell Goode had been with the *Pittsburgh Courier* fourteen years when, in 1962, he joined ABC to cover the United Nations. His first test was the Cuban missile crisis that arose just two months later, during which Goode distinguished himself with incisive television and radio reports during the long hours of U.N. debate.

Goode was born in White Plains, Virginia; educated in the public schools of Homestead, Pennsylvania; and graduated from the University of Pittsburgh. He was employed for twelve years as a laborer in the steel mills while in high school and college and for five years after graduation. In 1936 he was appointed to a post in Juvenile Court and became boys work director of the Centre Avenue YMCA, where he led the fight to eliminate discrimination in Pittsburgh branches of the YMCA.

Goode served with the Pittsburgh Housing Authority for six years and in 1948 joined the *Pittsburgh Courier*. The following year he started a career in radio with station KQV, doing a fifteen-minute news show two nights each week. In

1950 he started a five-minute daily news program on WHOD.

Goode was named news director at WHOD in 1952 and he was the first black to hold membership in the National Association of Radio and TV News Directors.

For two months in 1963 he joined with three colleagues to conduct courses in journalism for 104 African students in seminars at Lagos, Nigeria; Addis Ababa, Ethiopia; and Dar es Salaam, Tanzania. Goode died of a stroke on October 12, 1995, in Pittsburgh.

Ed Gordon (1960–)
Television Anchor

Edward L. Gordon III was born in Lansing, Michigan, and attended college at Western University. After graduating with a degree in communications and political science in 1982, Gordon began his broadcasting career in 1983 in Detroit as host of the *Detroit Free Journal*.

Gordon moved to Washington, D.C., in 1988 for an up-and-coming broadcasting company called Black Entertainment Network (BET). Gordon took on the role as newscaster as well as offering several special interest shows such as the 1992 response to the Los Angeles Riots, *Black Men Speak Out*, and the 1996 interview with O.J. Simpson, after Simpson was found not guilty of the murder of his wife. Gordon interviewed presidents and figures of diverse social and political perspectives, which earned him considerable influence in the industry.

In 1996, NBC hired Gordon on a three-year contract for $1.5 million. In 2004 he worked on the CBS news show *60 Minutes* and in 2005 began hosting his own show on NPR, *New & Notes,* focusing on African American issues. Gordon continued to work for BET on specific assignments and later returned to BET in 2010 to host *Weekly with Ed Gordon* among other newsworthy projects.

Earl Graves (1935–)
Publisher, Media Executive

In the 1970s Earl Graves emerged as one of America's leading publishers and exponents of black entrepreneurship. Within a few short years his magazine, *Black Enterprise*, was accepted as the authority on African Americans in business and as an important advocate for an active, socially responsive black middle class.

Born in Brooklyn, Graves graduated from Morgan State College. In 1965 he was hired to a position on the staff of Robert Kennedy, then senator from New York. In 1968 he organized Earl Graves Associates, a firm that serves as a consultant on urban affairs and black economic development, and published *Black Enterprise*. In 1998 Graves started *Black Enterprise Unlimited,* which focused on business and financial concerns of the African American businessperson. Graves was honored for his commitment and outstanding career in the business area with a Spingarn Medal from the NAACP.

Bryant Gumbel (1948–)
Television Anchor

A native of New Orleans, Bryant Gumbel was born on September 29, 1948, and grew up in Chicago. He received a liberal arts degree from Bates College in Lewiston, Maine, in 1970. Before embarking on his career in television, Gumbel was a sportswriter. After submitting his first piece to *Black Sports* magazine in 1971, he was given additional freelance assignments and was soon hired as a staff writer. Within eight months he was elevated to editor in chief.

Gumbel began his broadcasting career in October 1972 when he was named a weekend sportscaster for KNBC, the NBC station in Los Angeles. Within a year, he became weekday sportscaster and was appointed the station's sports director in 1976. He remained in that post until July 1980.

In January 1981 Bryant Gumbel was named co-anchor (with Jane Pauley) of the *Today* show on NBC. Prior to that time, Gumbel had made regular sports reports on *Today*, although his primary responsibilities were with NBC Sports as host of pre-game programming during coverage of the National Football League, Major League Baseball, and other sports broadcasts.

After leaving the *Today* show in 1997, the networks got in a bidding war over Gumbel, which resulted in a five-year $5 million a year contract. He anchored the CBS *This Morning* show in 1999 and returned to television news in 2000. When his contract ended in 2002, he hosted HBO *Real Sports* and served as a NFL announcer in 2005.

Cheryl Willis Hudson (1948–)
Publishing Executive

A native of Portsmouth, Virginia, Cheryl Willis Hudson graduated cum laude from Oberlin College and has studied at Northeastern University and Parsons School of Design. Prior to founding Just Us Books, she worked as an art editor and designer for several publishers, including Houghton Mifflin, Macmillan Publishing, and Arete Publishing.

Hudson as publisher, along with Wade Hudson as president and chief executive officer, founded Just Us Books, Inc. in 1988 to publish children's books and learning material that focus on the African American experience. The company grossed over $1 million in 1995 and has continued to flourish. Just Us Books has been awarded the Parent's Choice Award, the Multicultural Publisher's Exchange Award, and the American Booksellers Association Award "Best Seller of 1994." Hudson is also a published author whose works include *Hold Christmas in Your Heart: African American Songs, Poems and Stories for the Holidays*.

Cathy Hughes (1947–)
Radio and Television Host, Entrepreneur

Catherine (Cathy) Liggins Hughes, born Catherine Elizabeth Woods on April 22, 1947, in Omaha, Nebraska, is the founder of Radio One, Inc., the largest African American-owned broadcasting company in America. Hughes's company also became the first female-owned radio station to dominate in a major market, the first female-owned radio station ranked number one in a major market, and the first publicly traded stock on the U.S. stock exchange headed by an African American woman. Hughes and her son, Alfred C. Liggins II, the president and CEO of the company, dominate in the markets of Atlanta, Baltimore, Washington, D.C., Detroit, and Philadelphia.

Hughes's commitment to the urban market and her success in reaching that market began first with KOWH radio station in Omaha. Hughes began working for Howard University's radio station while serving as lecturer in the School of Communications. She was so successful she became vice president and general manager. Hughes created the popular and copied format, "Quiet Storm," a late night romantic listening, and the twenty-four-hour talk radio from an African American perspective when she purchased her first radio station in Washington, D.C., in 1980. Hughes was strongly invested in the advancement of the black community and consistently addressed topics that were relevant, often controversial, but always geared toward positive community building.

As the result of Hughes's efforts she has been awarded numerous honors such as the Lifetime Achievement Award from the Washington Area Broadcasters Association, the Baltimore NAACP's Parren J. Mitchell Award, and the 2001 National Association of Broadcasters Distinguished Service Award.

On January 19, 2004, Hughes partnered with Comcast, one of the nation's largest pay television providers, and launched TV One Inc., a television station catering to the African American lifestyle. By December 2006 the station was seen in over thirty-three million households. Currently her son, Alfred Liggins III, serves as CEO of Radio One and TV One.

Charlayne Hunter-Gault (1942–)

Journalist

Hunter-Gault was born in Due West, South Carolina, on February 27, 1942. Her involvement in issues concerning her community began in college by breaking the color line, along with another student, at the University of Georgia. She became the first woman to enroll and later graduate receiving her B.A in 1963 in journalism. She went on to work at the *New Yorker*, the *New York Times*, and local television stations. In 1978 Hunter-Gault joined the *MacNeil/Lehrer Report*. She became the program's first woman anchor and she remained there until 1997 when she left to serve as the PBS correspondent in South Africa. She became the bureau chief for PBS in South Africa from 2001 to 2005.

In 2005 Hunter-Gault was inducted into the National Association of Black Journalists Hall of Fame.

John H. Johnson (1918–2005)

Publisher, Media Executive

One of America's foremost business executives, John H. Johnson sat at the head of the most prosperous and powerful black publishing companies in the United States. Beginning with *Negro Digest* in 1942, and following with *Ebony* in 1945, Johnson built a chain of journalistic successes that now also includes *Jet, Ebony Jr., EM: Ebony Man,* and *Ebony South Africa.*

Johnson was born in Arkansas City, Arkansas, on January 19, 1918, and at age six lost his father, a mill worker, and was raised by his mother and stepfather. His segregated schooling was obtained locally until the family moved to Chicago. Johnson attended DuSable High School in Chicago, excelling academically and in extracurricular activities, writing for the yearbook and school paper.

After Johnson graduated, an insurance executive heard a speech he delivered and was so impressed that he offered Johnson a partial scholarship at the University of Chicago. After two years, however, Johnson quit classes. He entered the Northwestern School of Commerce in 1938, studying for an additional two years before joining the Supreme Liberty Life Insurance Company. While running the company's house organ, it occurred to Johnson that a digest of weekly or monthly gathered news items of special interest and importance to the black community might achieve a wide black readership. The idea resulted in the creation of *Negro Digest*, a periodical containing both news reprints and feature articles. Of the latter, perhaps the most beneficial to circulation was Eleanor Roosevelt's contribution, *If I Were a Negro*.

Buoyed by success, Johnson decided to approach the market with yet another offering, a pictorial magazine patterned after *Life*. The first issue of *Ebony* sold out its press run of twenty-five thousand copies and soon became a permanent staple in the world of journalism as large companies began to advertise regularly in it.

In addition to having served as president and publisher of Johnson Publishing Company, Inc., Johnson was chairman and chief executive officer of Supreme Life Insurance Company, chairman of WJPC-AM in Chicago, and president of Fashion Fair Cosmetics. He also developed the Ebony Fashion Fair, a traveling show managed by his wife, Eunice Johnson. He served on the board of directors of the Greyhound Corporation, Verex Corporation, Marina Bank, Supreme Life Insurance Company, and Zenith Radio Corporation. Johnson also served as a trustee for the Art Institute of Chicago and United Negro College Fund; on the advisory council of the Harvard Graduate School of Business; as a director for the Chamber of Commerce of the United States; and on the advertising council of Junior Achievement and Chicago USO. He received honorary doctoral degrees from numerous colleges and universities, and many honors and awards from civil and professional organizations. In 1989 Johnson wrote *Succeeding Against the Odds: The Autobiography of a Great American Business*. Johnson died August 8, 2005, and was succeeded in the company by his daughter, Linda Johnson Rice.

Robert L. Johnson (1946–)
Television Executive

Robert L. Johnson was born April 8, 1946, in Hickory, Mississippi. He earned an undergraduate degree from the University of Illinois in 1968 and a master's degree in public administration from Princeton University in 1972.

Robert Johnson worked for the Washington, D.C., Urban League, the Corporation for Public Broadcasting, and as a press secretary for the Honorable Walter E. Fauntroy, congressional delegate for Washington, D.C., before joining the National Cable Television Association in 1976. While serving as vice president of government relations for the association, Johnson came up with the idea of creating a cable channel aimed at black viewers. In 1989 he took out a $15,000 personal loan to start Black Entertainment Television (BET). Johnson was successful in creating a cable channel that developed programming catering to the interests of the African American community. BET Holding, Inc., also developed channels which offered jazz, films, and other programming.

In addition to running BET, Johnson functions as the publisher of magazines, including *Emerge: A Black America's News Magazine* and *Heart & Soul,* a health and beauty magazine. He also heads Arabesque Books, a line of African American romance novels written by and for African Americans, and MSBET, an interactive website formed in a joint venture with Microsoft Corporation. Johnson has also served on numerous boards.

Johnson has been awarded the *Broadcasting & Cable* magazine's Hall of Fame Award 1997 and Business Leader of the year from *Washingtonian* magazine in 1998, as well as an NAACP Image Award and Distinguished Alumni Award from Princeton University.

In 2001 Johnson sold BET to Viacom for $2.33 million and their assumption of $6 million in company debt.

Tom Joyner (1949–)
Radio Personality

Tom Joyner (also known as "The Fly Jock") is known for reaching more African American listeners than any other radio or electronic medium. Joyner, who simultaneously hosted two radio shows—a morning show in Dallas and an afternoon show in Chicago in the 1980s—has informed and entertained his audience with a variety of programming.

Joyner, born in Tuskegee, Alabama, on November 23, 1949, began in radio after graduating from Tuskegee University. Joyner in his early years in radio learned the need for involvement in the community. Taking this to heart Joyner structured his shows to inform, inspire, and entertain his listeners. In 1994 Joyner became the first African American male to host a nationally syndicated radio show with the debut of the *Tom Joyner Morning Show* on the ABC Radio Network. Joyner's shows have included scholarships to college students in need, done in partnership with the United Negro College Fund and the Tom Joyner Foundation, a nonprofit organization. Also featured are political commentary, comedy bits, and little known black history facts. Joyner was selected to the Radio Hall of Fame in 1998.

In 2003 Joyner founded Reach Media as the parent company of subsidiaries such as Black America Web.com, Tom Joyner Foundation, and also the *Tom Joyner Morning Show*. In 2005 Joyner launched a syndicated television show, but he decided not to continue production due to high costs.

Delano E. Lewis (1938–)
Broadcasting Executive

Delano Eugene Lewis, born in Arkansas City, Kansas, on November 12, 1938, began his career as a lawyer upon earning his degree from the

Washburn University School of Law in 1963. After serving in roles such as the attorney in the U.S. Department of Justice, volunteer for the Peace Corps, and other increasingly more responsible positions, he took a position at the Chesapeake and Potomac Telephone Company. Lewis became the company's president in 1988 and in 1990 their chief executive officer.

 In 1994 Lewis took the position of president and chief executive officer of National Public Radio (NPR). Because of his successes he was asked by Vice President Al Gore to serve as co-chair of the National Information Infrastructure Advisory Committee from 1994 to 1996. The committee's goal was to find new ways to development communication networks. Lewis resigned from NPR in 1998 and became ambassador to South Africa in 1999 to address problems such as the HIV/AIDS epidemic. He served until 2001. In 2006 he was named senior fellow at New Mexico State University, and in 2007 he was named the founding director of New Mexico University's International Relations Institute.

Edward T. Lewis (1940–)

Magazine Publisher

Edward T. Lewis was born in Bronx, New York, on May 15, 1940. Lewis, although well-trained in banking, aspired to branch out on his own. In 1969 after attending an entrepreneur seminar and being inspired to start his own unique black business, the first issues of *Essence* magazine hit the newsstands in May 1970. Although beginning with other partners, within four years only Lewis and Clarence O. Smith continued on with the magazine. The magazine, which was based on reaching the untapped market of black women, took until 1976 before it broke even. By 2002 *Essence* had a readership of 7.6 million and reached African American women ages seventeen to fifty.

In 2000 Essence Communications Partners, the company that publishes *Essence* magazine,

merged with Time, Inc., a subsidiary of AOL Time Warner Inc. Lewis and Smith's partnership ended and each has been acknowledged for their business and entrepreneurial successes. During their partnership Lewis and Smith diversified the company's subsidiaries such as the Essence Awards, Essence Travel, Essence By-Mail, and other ventures, which expanded the scope, exposure, and marketing opportunities for the company. Lewis has received recognition and awards from the American Advertising Federation, the United Negro College Fund, the Democratic Women's Political Caucus, and the Black Women's Forum to name a few. Lewis remains chairman and CEO of Essence Communications Inc.

Haki Madhubuti (1941–)

Poet, Essayist, Publisher

Haki Madhubuti was born Don L. Lee in Little Rock, Arkansas, on February 23, 1942. Madhubuti studied at Wilson Junior College, Roosevelt University, and the University of Illinois, and received a master of fine arts degree from the University of Iowa. Lee was determined to become a writer while preparing himself during his college years. He published his first work, *Think Black*, in 1966; this was followed by *Black Pride; For Black People (and Negroes Too)* (1968); *Don't Cry, Scream; Enemies: The Clash of Races* (1969); *Killing Memory: Seeking Ancestors* (1987); *Black Men: Obsolete, Single, Dangerous?* (1990); *Heart-Love: Wedding and Love Poems* (1998); *Tough Notes: Letters to a Young Black Men* (2001); and *Yellow Black: The First Twenty-one Years of a Poet's Life* (2005). He has taught and served as writer in residence at numerous universities, including Chicago State University, Cornell, Howard, and the University of Illinois.

Lee, who changed his name to Haki Madhubuti in 1973, was one of the founding members of the Organization of Black American Culture Writers Workshop, and has served as vice chairperson of the African Liberation Day Support Committee and on the executive council of the Congress of African People. He has also served as director of the Institute of Positive Education in Chicago, publisher and editor of Third World Press, president of the African American Publishers, and co-director of the National Black Holistic Retreat founded in 1984 by Madhubuti.

Third World Press was founded by Madhubuti in 1967 and has published numerous titles by African American writers, including Frances Cress-Welsing, Gwendolyn Brooks, Chancellor Williams, and Amiri Baraka. Third World Press is currently the longest running continuous African American press in the United States. Madhubuti has received the Distinguished Writers Award from the Middle Atlantic Writers Association and he is the recipient of the Paul Robeson Award from the African American Arts Alliance. He currently serves as director of the Gwendolyn Brooks Center at Chicago State University.

Robert McGruder (1942–2002)
Journalist, Newspaper Editor

Robert McGruder was born on March 31, 1942, in Louisville, Kentucky. He began his newspaper career in 1963 with the *Dayton Journal Herald*. In 1964 he was drafted and served two years in the U.S. Army. McGruder worked at the *Cleveland Plain Dealer* for several years as a reporter, editor, and was selected as managing editor in 1981. McGruder began working at the *Detroit Free Press* in 1986 and became managing editor in 1995. In that year McGruder not only became the first black executive director of the paper, but he also was selected as the first black president of the Associated Press Managing Editors Association.

McGruder was an advocate for diversity in the newspaper industry and supported various campaigns. He utilized opportunities to hire and promote qualified minorities to better serve the entire community. His efforts earned him in 2001 the John S. Knight Gold Medal given as the highest honor bestowed by the parent company Knight Ridder to an employee. After a battle with cancer McGruder died on April 12, 2002. After his death Knight Ridder established the Robert G. McGruder Scholarship to support promising young minority journalists enrolled at Wayne State.

Carl L. Murphy (1889–1967)
Journalist, Publisher

Carl L. Murphy was born in Baltimore, Maryland, on January 17, 1889. He was educated at Howard University in 1911, Harvard University in 1913, and the University of Jena in Berlin in 1913. He served as an educator at Howard University before taking the helm of the newspaper *The Afro-American*. Murphy developed the newspaper into a national voice for African Americans with the largest circulation of a black newspaper.

During the *Brown v. the Board of Education of Topeka*, in 1954, Murphy and his paper were advocates for the community. Once the case was over, Thurgood Marshall publicly acknowledged Murphy's courage and support and in 1955 Murphy was awarded the Spingarn Medal. Murphy died on February 26, 1967.

Norma Quarles (1936–)
Television News Correspondent

Born in New York City, on November 11, 1936, Norma Quarles is an alumna of Hunter College and City College of New York. She first worked as a buyer for a New York specialty shop before moving to Chicago, where she became a licensed real estate broker.

In 1965 she began her broadcast career in Chicago at WSDM-Radio, working as a news reporter and disc jockey. She later returned to New York, where she joined NBC in 1966 for a one-year training program. After three years with KYC-TV in Cleveland, she was transferred to WNBC-TV. In 1978 Quarles moved to NBC News as a correspondent based in Chicago. She had been producing and reporting the *Urban Journal* series for WMAQ-TV for a year at that time. Before joining WMAQ, Quarles was an award-winning reporter for WNBC-TV in New York, where she also anchored the early local news broadcasts during the *Today* show. In 1988 Quarles left NBC, after twenty-one years, to join Cable News Network's New York bureau and was a news anchor from 1988 to 1990.

Quarles is a member of the National Academy of Television Arts and Sciences, Sigma Delta Chi, and a board member of the Governor's National Academy of Television Arts and Sciences. In 1990 she was inducted into the National Association of Black Journalists Hall of Fame and in 1993 received the CINR Golden Circle Award.

Dudley Randall (1914–2000)
Publisher, Poet, Librarian

Dudley Randall was born in Washington, D.C., on January 14, 1914, and was living in Detroit by the time he was nine years old. An early harbinger of Randall's poetic talent was the appearance of one of his poems in the *Detroit Free Press* at the early age of thirteen. After serving in the U.S. Army Signal Corps from 1942 to 1946, Randall worked in the foundry at Ford Motor Company and as a postal carrier and clerk while attending Wayne State University in Detroit. He received his B.A. in 1949 and an M.A. in library science from the University of Michigan in 1951. He also did graduate work at the University of Ghana.

Randall worked in progressively responsible librarian positions at Lincoln University in Jefferson City, Missouri (1951–1954), Morgan State College in Baltimore, Maryland (1954–1956), and the Wayne County Federated Library System in Michigan (1956–1969). From 1969 to 1975 he was a reference librarian and poet in residence at the University of Detroit. In 1969 he also served as a visiting lecturer at the University of Michigan.

Randall's love of poetry led to his founding of the Broadside Press in 1965, and in 1980 he founded the Broadside Poets Theater and the Broadside Poetry Workshop. Randall began Broadside Press to publish his own works, but later expanded it to include other poets. Randall sold Broadside Press in 1985 to Hilda and Donald Vest, who continue to operate the press.

Randall was active in many Detroit cultural organizations and institutions, including the Detroit Council for the Arts and the International Afro-American Museum in Detroit. In 1981 Randall received the Creative Artist Award in Litera-

ture from the Michigan Council for the Arts, and in 1986 he was named the first poet laureate of Detroit. Randall died on August 5, 2000.

Max Robinson (1939–1988)
Television News Correspondent

Born in Richmond, Virginia, on May 1, 1939, Max Robinson attended Oberlin College, Virginia Union University, and Indiana University. He began his career as a news reader at WTOV-TV in Portsmouth, Virginia. In 1965 he worked as a studio floor director at WTOP-TV (now WUSA) in Washington, D.C., before moving on to WRC-TV to work as a news reporter, and to WTOP-TV, where he worked as an anchor.

In 1978 Robinson joined ABC's *World News Tonight,* becoming the first black network anchor. Almost immediately, Robinson took it upon himself to fight racism at whatever cost necessary. ABC management became frustrated with Robinson and moved him to the post of weekend anchor. In 1983 Robinson left ABC for WMAQ-TV in Chicago, where he remained until 1985.

Robinson was the recipient of three Emmy Awards, the Capital Press Club Journalist of the Year Award, the Ohio State Award, and an award from the National Education Association. He taught at Federal City College, in Washington, D.C., and the College of William and Mary, in Williamsburg, Virginia. Robinson died of complications from acquired immune deficiency syndrome (AIDS) on December 20, 1988, in Washington, D.C.

Al Roker (1954–)
Television Broadcaster

Albert Lincoln Roker Jr. was born on August 20, 1954, in New York, to parents with Jamaican and Barbados heritages. Although not initially interested in meteorology, Roker took a class in college which led to a part-time position as a weatherman. After graduating from State University at

Oswego, Roker took several positions at stations in Washington, D.C., and Cleveland, Ohio.

Roker returned to New York in 1983, and in 1995 replaced his retiring long-time supporter and fellow meteorologist, Willard Scott. Roker became the meteorologist on the NBC *Today* show. Roker has since created his own production company and is outspoken on issues both controversial and relevant.

Carl Rowan (1924–2000)
Journalist, Broadcaster

Carl Rowan was born August 11, 1925, in Ravenscroft, Tennessee. He attended Tennessee A&I (now Tennessee State University) in Nashville and Washburn University in Topeka, Kansas. He received his bachelor of arts degree from Oberlin College in 1947; in 1948 he received a master of arts degree from the University of Minnesota.

In 1948 he was hired as a copywriter, later advancing to staff writer, by the *Minneapolis Tribune*, where he worked until 1961. In 1961 he was hired by the U.S. Department of State as deputy assistant secretary for public affairs. After three years with the Department of State, Rowan was appointed U.S. ambassador to Finland by President Lyndon Johnson in 1963, and in 1964 he was appointed director of the United States Information Agency, which operates overseas educational and cultural programs, including the worldwide radio service *Voice of America*. In 1965 Rowan resigned from the USIA.

He authored several books, including *South of Freedom* (1951), *Wait till Next Year: The Life and Story of Jackie Robinson* (1960), *Just between Us Blacks* (1974), and *Breaking Barriers: A Memoir* (1991). He was a syndicated columnist whose work appeared in numerous newspapers across the country.

Rowan served as a political commentator for the Post-Newsweek Broadcasting Company, and

was a frequent panelist on the NBC program *Meet the Press* and the syndicated programs *Agronsky & Co.* and *Inside Washington*. In 1987 he was awarded by Columbia University the Alfred I. DuPont Silver Baton for the television documentary *Thurgood Marshall: The Man*. In 1998 he received the Victory Award for overcoming personal obstacles from the National Rehabilitation Hospital in Washington, D.C. Rowan had learned how to walk again after the amputation of his right leg below the knee. Rowan died on September 13, 2000, of natural causes.

John B. Russwurm (1799–1851)
Newspaper Founder

Born in Port Antonio, Jamaica, on October 1, 1799, Russwurm graduated from Bowdoin College in Brunswick, Maine, in 1826. From Brunswick, Russwurm moved to New York, where on March 16, 1827, he and Samuel E. Cornish published the first edition of *Freedom's Journal*—the nation's first African American newspaper.

In 1829 Russwurm decided to immigrate to Monrovia, Liberia, where he published the *Liberia Herald* from 1830 to 1850. Cornish, who had left the paper in late 1827, resumed his role as editor in 1830, publishing the paper under the name *Rights of All*.

Russwurm went on to serve as superintendent of education in Monrovia, and later as governor of a settlement. Russwurm died on June 9, 1851.

Bernard Shaw (1940–)
Television News Anchor

Bernard Shaw was a Washington anchor for the Cable News Network (CNN) from the time the network went on the air on June 1, 1980, until his departure in February 28, 2001. Shaw often reported first-hand on major international news stories. He was present when the Chinese government's tanks rolled into Tiananmen Square in

May 1989, crushing the student-led pro-democracy movement. In January 1991 Shaw, along with two other colleagues from CNN, was stranded in Baghdad when allied bombing attacks launched Operation Desert Storm. From their hotel room, Shaw and the others provided first-hand accounts of the bombing raid on the city.

Bernard Shaw was born on May 22, 1940, in Chicago. From as early as the age of fourteen he was interested in the things going on in the world. After four years in the Marines Shaw entered college at the University of Illinois in 1963, but left school in 1966 when offered a job in Washington, D.C,. as a White House correspondent. Shaw's first job as a television journalist came in 1971 with CBS News at the network's Washington bureau. He conducted an exclusive interview with Attorney General John Mitchell at the height of the Watergate scandal. Shaw left CBS in 1977 to join ABC News as Miami bureau chief and Latin American correspondent. Shaw was one of the first reporters to file from location on the Jonestown massacre story in Guyana, and he and his team provided the only aerial photos of the mass suicide–murder site. ABC sent Shaw to Iran to report on the 1979 hostage crisis at the American Embassy in Tehran. He then returned to Washington as ABC's senior Capitol Hill correspondent.

Shaw has received numerous awards inclusive of induction into the Society of Professional Journalists in 1995, the Paul White Life Achievement Award from the Radio Television News Director's Association in 1996, induction into the Chicago Journalists Hall of Fame in 1997, and in that same year the Congressional Medal of Honor Society's Tex McCray Award for Journalism. With his final newscast in 2001 he noted it was harder for him to leave than it was to enter since he had invested so much of his life in making his career happen.

Carole Simpson (1940–)
Television News Anchor

Carole Simpson, a native of Chicago, graduated from the University of Michigan with a bachelor of arts degree in journalism and did graduate work in journalism at the University of Iowa. She first entered broadcasting in 1965 as a reporter for a local radio station, WCFL, in Morris, Illinois. In 1968 she moved to radio station WBBM in Chicago, and in 1970 she went to work as a reporter for the Chicago television station WMAQ.

Simpson made her first network appearance as a substitute anchor for NBC *Nightly News* and as anchor on NBC's *Newsbreak* on weekends. In 1982 Simpson joined ABC in Washington as a general assignment correspondent. She is currently an ABC News correspondent and weekend anchor.

Simpson has served as president of the Radio and Television Correspondents Association, as chairperson of the ABC Women's Advisory Board, and as a member of the board of directors of the Washington Chapter of the Society of Professional Journalists, and she is a member of Theta Sigma Phi. She has been awarded the Media Journalism Award, the Milestone Award in Broadcast Journalism from the National Commission of Working Women, and the Silver Bell Award from the Ad Council.

Simpson was awarded Journalist of the Year in 1992 and opened a Leadership Institute for African women journalists in Dakar, Senegal, in 1998. As of 2007 she has served as an educator for Emerson College.

Tavis Smiley (1964–)
Political and Social Commentator

Smiley, who was born on September 13, 1964, in Gulfport, Mississippi, began his involvement in community issues in his college years at Indiana University at Bloomington, Illinois. Also influenced by his involvement with Kappa Alpha Psi Fraternity, service to the community became a key career and life goal. Smiley earned his B.A. in law and public policy in 1986.

Smiley served as an aide to Los Angeles mayor Tom Bradley from 1986 to 1990 and had an unsuccessful run for Los Angeles City Council in 1991. In 1996 Smiley became a social commentator on the *Tom Joyner Morning Show,* a nationally syndicated radio show focusing on urban issues and concerns of the African American community. Through collaboration with Joyner, Smiley hosted *The State of the Black Union,* a series of town-hall meetings about the future of the black community. Smiley continued with *The Tom Joyner Morning Show* until 2008.

Smiley had a successful show on Black Entertainment Television (BET) where he presented news, information, and talk. With the non-renewal of his contract with BET Smiley went on to work for ABC-TV, and CNN. From 2001 to 2004 he hosted *The Tavis Smiley Show* on National Public Radio (NPR). In 2007 Smiley served as the moderator for two presidential campaigns.

In March 2006 The Smiley Group and Third World Press released the book *The Covenant with Black America,* which consisted of essays that offered statistics and a plan of action to move the African American community forward. The book became the number one nonfiction book by a black-owned publisher on the *New York Times* best-seller list.

Smiley has received numerous awards for his contributions to the field of media, including an Image Award from the NAACP and the Mickey Leland Humanitarian Award.

Clarence O. Smith (1933–)
Magazine Publisher

Clarence O. Smith was born on March 31, 1933. Smith, along with Edward T. Lewis, is best known as an investor that helped launch *Essence* magazine, a medium that reached out to African American women's interests as an ignored market share. The magazine launched in May 1970 and by 1976 had broken even. Smith was seen as the salesman in the partnership based on his years in insurance in the 1960s. He was proficient in gaining high profile advertisers. As the company grew other creative venues were developed including the Essence Awards, the Essence-by-Mail, and Essence Art Reproductions.

In 2000 the Essence Communications, Inc., merged with Time, Inc., a subsidiary of Time Warner, the nation's largest publisher. On June 28, 2002, Smith resigned to pursue other interests after a thirty-two-year partnership with Lewis. This brought additional attention since the partnership had just been awarded the *Black Enterprise* Marathon Men Award for the nation's largest black-owned business.

Smith has received many awards for his advocacy for minority representation, and he was a founding member of the African American Anti-Defamation Association. Smith continues his entrepreneurial interest and launched the music production company, You Entertainment, in 2005.

Pierre Sutton (1947–)
Broadcast Executive

Pierre Sutton is president of Inner City Broadcasting Corporation in New York City and president of its radio stations in New York and California. He is the son of Percy E. Sutton, chairman of the board of Inner City Broadcasting and former borough president of Manhattan.

Sutton was born in New York City on February 1, 1947. He received a B.A. from the University of Toledo in 1968 and attended New York University in 1972.

He began his career in 1971 as vice president of Inner City Research and Analysis Corporation, was executive editor of the *New York Courier* newspaper in 1971 and 1972, served as public affairs director for WLIB-Radio from 1972 to 1975, was vice president of Inner City Broadcasting from 1975 to 1977, and became president in 1977. He has served as a board member of the Minority Investment Fund, first vice president of the National Association of Black Owned Broadcasters, chairman of the Harlem Boy Scouts, member of the board and executive committee of the New York City Marathon, trustee of the Alvin Ailey Dance Foundation, board member of the Better Business Bureau of Harlem, and member of the board of the Hayden Planetarium.

Susan L. Taylor (1946–)
Editor, Journalist

Susan L. Taylor was born on January 23, 1946, in New York City. Her parents, who were of Caribbean descent, instilled in her the family legacy of entrepreneurship. After completing high school Taylor decided to create a cosmetic business that by the 1970s was thriving. As a former actress, cosmetologist, and founder of her own cosmetics company, Nequai Cosmetics, Taylor began her relationship with *Essence* magazine as a freelance writer. In 1971 she became the magazine's beauty editor, and from 1971 to 1980 she served as fashion and beauty editor. She moved swiftly through the ranks and in 1981 became the editor in chief. By 1986 Taylor had become senior vice president of Essence Communications, the publisher of the magazine, and by 1991 she had continued her personal growth by earning a degree in sociology from Fordham University.

Taylor has used her talent and influence to support the careers of other artists such as Toni Morrison, Alice Walker, and Terri McMillan. She also brought attention to the rebuilding of New Orleans after Hurricane Katrina, and she has created the Essence Music Festival, which is a yearly event to promote education and information as well as to entertain. Her own writing has also garnered her critical acclaim, and overall Taylor is seen as a model of success and inspiration to black women artists and to the African American publishing community. In 1999 Taylor was the first and only African American woman to be awarded the Henry Johnson Fisher Award, the industry's highest honor given for lifetime achievement. She was also inducted into the Magazine Editor's Hall of Fame. She has numerous other awards as well as honorary doctorates.

Taylor is the founder of the National CARES Mentoring Movement which began in 2006 to support children in achieving their education. She also co-chairs the organization Shared Interest with Danny Glover, which supports the building of houses and business ownership for South Africa.

Ida B. Wells-Barnett (1862–1931)
Editor, Newspaper Owner

Ida Barnett Wells was born in Holly Springs, Mississippi, on July 16, 1862, and educated at Rusk University. She served as editor of the black newspaper, the *Memphis Free Speech*, and in 1892 became part-owner. Through the paper she engaged in a vigorous campaign against the practice of lynching. On May 27, 1882, the paper's offices were destroyed by a mob.

In 1895 she married *Chicago Conservator* editor Ferdinand Lee Barnett. That same year Barnett published her first pamphlet against lynching, *A Red Record*. Over the years Barnett wrote numerous other pamphlets and articles and conducted speaking tours throughout the United States and Europe.

Juan Williams (1954–)
Television and Radio Correspondent

Juan Williams was born in Colon, Panama, on April 10, 1954, and his family moved to Brooklyn, New York, in 1958 when Williams was four years old. Williams went on to graduate from Haverford College in Pennsylvania in 1976 and took a job at the *Washington Post*. In 1987 Williams along with a production crew produced a fourteen-hour PBS series on the civil rights years, 1954 to 1965. This was accompanied by a book *Eyes on the Prize: Civil Rights Years, 1954–1965*. The series won critical acclaim and continues as an important record of ordinary people and their participation during this critical time. While at the *Post* Williams served as editorial writer, columnist, and White House correspondent. He left the newspaper in 1996 to host the television show

America's Black Forum, and then joined FOX News in 1997. In 2000 Williams jointed NPR as the host of the talk show *Talk of the Nation.* His contract was terminated on October 20, 2010, over statements some called "controversial".

Williams, a prolific writer, has published numerous books, essays, and articles. His books include the biography *Thurgood Marshall,* (1998), *This Far by Faith: Stories from the African American Religious Experience* (2003), *Soul Looks Back in Wonder: Voices of the Civil Rights Experience* (2004), *Enough! The Phony Leaders, Dead-end Movements, and Culture of Failure that Are Undermining Black America—And What We Can Do about It* (2006). Williams has received an Emmy Award for his television documentary writing as well as honorary degrees. He was selected by the U.S. Census Bureau to moderate a series of programs in 2010.

Montel Williams (1956–)

Talk Show Host

Montel Williams, a prominent talk show host and motivational speaker, comes from a non-media background. He began his career in the U.S. Marine Corps in 1979 and through a desire to help other, counseled families and servicemen under his command. His ability to reach and motivate others took him to the role of motivational speaker and then to his own talk show, which first aired in 1990. His show handled many controversial topics and sought to find solutions to problems.

In 1999 Williams announced that he has multiple sclerosis but would continue as host while serving as a role model for others. Williams continued the show until November 10, 2010. Williams's show has received many daytime Emmy Awards as well as humanitarian awards for his contributions. These awards include an honorable mention Gracie Award for excellence in the positive portrayal of women, the Nancy Susan Reynolds Award for his episode on teenagers and

AIDS, and in 2002 the Man of Courage Award at the Seventh Annual Race to Erase MS.

Oprah Winfrey (1954–)

Talk Show Host, Media Mogul

Oprah Winfrey's rise to fame is a tale at once moving and inspiring. She was born on January 29, 1954, in Kosciusko, Mississippi. Her name was supposed to have been "Orpah," after a biblical figure in the book of Ruth; accounts vary as to the origin of the misspelling.

Winfrey was a precocious child who asked her kindergarten teacher to advance her to the first grade; Winfrey also skipped the second grade. Her parents, who were not married, separated when she was very young and sent her to live with her grandparents. At the age of six Winfrey moved to Milwaukee to live with her mother. From the time she was nine she was abused sexually by male family members and acquaintances; these events, which she did not discuss publicly until the 1980s, have had a profound effect on her life.

When she was fourteen Winfrey went to live with her father in Nashville, Tennessee, and it was there that her life was put back on track. Her father insisted on hard work and discipline as a means of self-improvement, and Winfrey complied, winning a college scholarship that allowed her to attend Tennessee State University. In 1971 she began working part time as a radio announcer for WVOL in Nashville. Two years later, after receiving a B.A. from Tennessee State, she became a reporter at WTVF-TV in Nashville. From 1976 to 1983 she lived in Baltimore, working for the ABC affiliate WJZ-TV, progressing from news anchor to co-host of the popular show *People Are Talking.* In 1984 she moved to Chicago and took over the ailing morning show *A.M. Chicago.* By September of the next year, the show was so successful that it was expanded to an hour format and renamed *The Oprah Winfrey Show.* The show was placed in syndication and the *The Oprah Winfrey Show* became one of the most popular television programs in history. A talented actress, Winfrey appeared in the motion picture *The Color Purple* (1985) and in the television movie *The Women of Brewster Place* (1989). In 1986 Winfrey founded Harpo, Inc., her own production company ("Harpo" is "Oprah" spelled backwards).

In 2011 after twenty-five successful years hosting *The Oprah Winfrey Show*, Winfrey ended the show after over five thousand broadcasts. She also launched on January 1, 2011, a new television station in collaboration with the Discovery Health Channel called OWN (Oprah Winfrey Network). Winfrey is the richest African American female in America in the twenty-first century, as well as the only African American consistently rated as a billionaire. She is also a philanthropist who donates money to worthy causes, offers scholarships to students for education, and in 2007 she opened The Leadership Academy for Girls in South Africa to promote the education of young girls toward transforming communities and countries. As the most powerful African American woman in America she has used her influence to help and encourage all Americans "to live their best life."

PERFORMING AND VISUAL/APPLIED ARTS

For more than two hundred years African American performers have appeared on the American stage, often in the face of prejudice and bigotry. Showcasing their talents, they have made unique contributions to American performance art. The artistic heritage of today's African American actors, dancers, and comedians can be traced back to the last decades of the eighteenth century.

The first performances by African American actors on the American stage were in plays written by white playwrights, who portrayed blacks as buffoons or intellectually inept characters. In 1769, for example, Lewis Hallam's performance in Charles Dibdin's comedy *The Padlock* was as a West Indian slave character named Mongo, who was a clown to be played by a black. Other white-authored eighteenth-century works that depicted blacks in demoralizing roles were *Robinson Crusoe* (1719) by Daniel Defoe, *Harlequin* (1792), and *The Triumphs of Love* (1795) by John Murdock, which included the native black character named Sambo. Thus, the earliest appearances of blacks on the American stage were as characters devoid of intellectual and moral sensibilities.

New York City's free African American community founded the first African American theater in 1821—the African Grove Theatre, located at Mercer between Bleecker and Prince streets "in the rear of the one-mile stone on Broadway." A group of amateur African American actors organized by Henry Brown presented *Richard III* at the theater on October 1, 1821. The African Grove Theatre subsequently produced *Othello, Hamlet,* and such lighter works as *Tom and Jerry* and *The Poor Soldier, Obi.*

One of the principal actors at the African Grove Theatre was James Hewlett, a West Indian–born black who distinguished himself in roles in *Othello* and *Richard III*. Hewlett later toured England and billed himself as "The New York and London Colored Comedian." Ira Aldridge, who later distinguished himself as one of the great Shakespearean tragic actors, was also a member of the permanent group that performed at the African Grove Theatre. Aldridge was cast in comic and singing roles as well as in Shakespearean tragedies.

It was at the African Grove Theatre that the first play written and produced by an African American was performed on the American stage. The play was William Henry Brown's *The Drama of King Shotaway,* which was presented in 1823.

Because of disturbances created by whites in the audience, the local police raided the African

Grove Theatre on several occasions. The theater evidently was wrecked by police and hoodlums during one of these raids, which forced its closure in late 1823. The theater's black actors, who were determined to preserve their company, continued for several years to present plays at different rented locations throughout New York City.

Talented slaves were among the earliest black entertainers in colonial and antebellum America. On plantations throughout the South slave performers—using clappers, jawbones, and blacksmith rasps—danced, sang, and told jokes for the entertainment of their fellow slaves as well as their masters, who often showcased their talents at local gatherings. Some masters hired out talented slaves to perform in traveling troupes.

During the late 1820s and early 1830s white entertainers, observing the artistry of black performers, began to imitate blacks in their routines.

An actor, circa 1900, in blackface. White performers imitated black routines, including their styles of comedy, song, and dance.

Blackening their faces with cork, these white entertainers performed jigs, songs, and jokes with topical allusions to blacks in their lyrics. Thus, the art of minstrelsy as theatrical material was born.

White minstrel troupes in blackface became very popular on the American stage in the 1830s. Among some of the more famous white minstrel performers were Thomas Dartmouth Rice ("Daddy Rice," the original "Jim Crow"), Edwin Forrest, Daniel Decatur "Dan" Emmett, and the Christy Minstrels with Edwin Pearce Christy.

Some traveling white minstrel troupes used African American performers to enhance the authenticity of their productions. One such troupe was the Ethiopian Minstrels; its star performer was African American dancer William Henry Lane, who used the stage name "Master Juba." Lane was one of the greatest dancers of his generation. Throughout the United States and England "Master Juba" was enthusiastically praised by audiences and critics alike. One anonymous English critic, quoted by dance historian Marian Hannah Winter in Paul Magriel's *Chronicles of the American Dance* (1906), wrote the following critique of one of Lane's performances:

> Juba exceeded anything ever witnessed in Europe. The style as well as the execution is unlike anything seen in this country. The manner in which he beats time with feet, and the extraordinary command he possesses over them, can only be believed by those who have been present at the exhibition.

Black minstrel troupes began to appear in the 1850s, but it was not until after the Civil War that they became established on the American stage. Although black minstrels inherited the negative stereotypes of blacks that white minstrels had established, the African American performer won a permanent place on the American stage, providing a training ground for the many black dancers, comedians, singers, and composers to come. Notable among these stage personalities were: dancer–comedians Billy Kersands, Bert Williams, Bob Height, Dewey "Pigmeat" Martin, and Ernest

Hogan; singers Gertrude "Ma" Rainey and Bessie Smith; and composers James Bland and William Christopher Handy. To a great extent black minstrelsy created a national appreciation for the talent of black stage entertainers, drawing audiences to black shows and other forms of black entertainment for generations to come.

MUSICALS

By the 1890s black producers, writers, and stage performers sought to reform the demeaning images of blacks that were prevalent on the American stage. *The Creole Show,* cast by black producer Sam T. Jack in 1891, was the first all-black musical to depart from minstrelsy. Featuring an all-black chorus line, *The Creole Show* premiered in Boston in 1891 and later played at the Chicago World's Fair for the entire season. In 1895 black producer John W. Isham presented *The Octoroon,* another all-black musical that moved away from the minstrel tradition. *Oriental America,* which Isham also produced in 1896, broke further from minstrel conventions by not closing with the traditional walkaround but with an operatic medley.

Trip to Coontown, written and directed by Bob Cole in 1898, completely broke away from the minstrel tradition. The plot of this all-black musical was presented completely through music and dance. The first musical produced, written, and performed by African Americans on Broadway, it ushered in a new era for blacks on the American stage.

The highly popular *Clorindy: The Origin of the Cakewalk,* with music by composer Will Marion Cook and lyrics by poet Paul Laurence Dunbar, opened in 1898 at the Casino Roof Garden and featured comedian–singer Ernest Hogan. The comic–dance duo of Bert Williams and George Walker premiered their first Broadway musical, *The Policy Player,* in l899. This success was followed by Williams and Walker's *Sons of Ham,* which played on Broadway for two seasons beginning in September 1900. Their *In Dahomey* premiered on Broadway in 1903 and, after a long

run, toured successfully in England. *The Southerners,* with music by Will Marion Cook, opened on Broadway in 1904 with an interracial cast starring Abbie Mitchell. The Williams and Walker team returned to Broadway in 1906 with a new musical, *Abyssinia,* which consistently played to a full house.

In 1902 the versatile Ernest Hogan starred in *The Oyster Man,* which enjoyed a successful run on Broadway; and in 1906 Hogan appeared again on Broadway in *Rufus Rastus.* Bob Cole, J. Rosamond Johnson, and James Weldon Johnson wrote and performed in *The Shoo-Fly Regiment,* another musical that opened on Broadway in 1902. Williams and Walker appeared in their last Broadway production together, *Bandanna Land,* in 1908. George Walker fell into ill health after the show closed and died in 1911. Bert Williams went on to appear in *Mr. Lode of Koal* on Broadway in 1909, and later he was the star comedian performer in the Ziegfeld Follies. The last black musical to open on Broadway before the 1920s was *His Honor: The Barber* in 1911, with S. H. Dudley in the lead.

On May 23, 1921, *Shuffle Along* opened on Broadway, signaling the return of black musicals to "The Great White Way" and the arrival of the Harlem Renaissance on the American stage. Featuring the talented singer–dancer Florence Mills, *Shuffle Along* was written by Flournoy Miller and Aubrey Lyles, with music by Eubie Blake and lyrics by Noble Sissle. Florence Mills quickly became a sought-after performer, appearing in *The Plantation Revue* (which opened on Broadway on July 17, 1922) and touring England. In 1926 Mills returned to Harlem and played the lead in *Black Birds* at the Alhambra Theatre for a six-week run. Subsequently, Mills performed in Paris for six months.

Noble Sissle and Eubie Blake returned to Broadway on September 24, 1924, with their new musical *Chocolate Dandies.* Two years later, Flournoy Miller and Aubrey Lyles opened on Broadway in *Runnin' Wild,* which introduced the Charleston to the country. Bill "Bojangles" Robinson, starring in *Blackbirds of 1928,* dazzled Broadway audiences with his exciting tap-dancing style.

A circa 1935 Theatre Guild production in New York City of *Porgy and Bess.*

Several other black musicals opened on Broadway during the 1920s, including *Rang Tang* (1927), *Keep Shuffling* (1928), and *Hot Chocolates* (1929).

Porgy and Bess opened on Broadway in 1935 and became the major all-black musical production of the 1930s. With music by George Gershwin, this adaptation of the novel by DuBose Heyward (1925) and the play that Dorothy Heyward helped him to adapt (1927), was an immediate success as a folk opera. Todd Duncan was cast as Porgy, with Anne Brown as Bess, and co-median–dancer John W. Bubbles as the character Sportin' Life.

In the 1940s black musicals were scarce on Broadway. *Cabin in the Sky,* starring Ethel Waters, Dooley Wilson, Todd Duncan, Rex Ingram, J. Rosamond Johnson, and Katherine Dunham and her dancers, ran for 165 performances after it opened on October 25, 1940. *Carmen Jones,* perhaps the most successful all-black musical of the decade, opened in 1943 with Luther Saxon, Napoleon Reed, Carlotta Franzel, and Cozy Cole; it had a run of 231 performances and was taken on tour. In 1946 *St. Louis Woman,* which featured Rex Ingram, Pearl Bailey, Juanita Hall, and June Hawkins, played a short run to mixed reviews.

One of the most active periods for African American performers in musical theater occurred between 1961 and the mid-1980s. Many of the black musicals produced during these years, both on and Off-Broadway, enjoyed substantial runs and extended road tours.

Langston Hughes's musical *Black Nativity* opened on Broadway on December 11, 1961, and was directed by Vinette Carroll. The cast was headed by gospel singers Marion Williams and the Stars of Faith, and also featured Alex Bradford, Clive Thompson, Cleo Quitman, and Carl Ford. Although it ran for only fifty-seven performances on Broadway, it toured extensively throughout the United States and abroad.

Black musicals in the late 1960s and 1970s earned considerable success with extended runs and recognition for their productions. *Hallelujah Baby,* which explored five decades of African American history, opened in 1967 and received five Tony Awards including best actor for Robert Hooks, best actress for Leslie Uggams, and best featured actress for Lillian Hayman; *Raisin* opened in 1973, based on Lorraine Hansberry's *A Raisin in the Sun,* and received the Tony Award for the best musical in 1974; *The Wiz,* the longest-running black musical in the history of Broadway with 1,672 performances, opened in 1975 and won seven Tony Awards; *Ain't Misbehavin',* which opened in 1978 and is based on songs by the composer Fats Waller, received a Tony Award for best featured actress, Nell Carter. It played to Broadway audiences for 1,604 performances.

In the 1980s and 1990s productions continued to engage audiences. *Dreamgirls,* which opened at the Imperial Theater on December 20, 1981, captivated Broadway audiences with a cast that included Jennifer Holiday, Cleavant Derricks, Loretta Devine, and Cheryl Alexander. *Dreamgirls* ran for 1,522 performances on Broadway and had an extensive road tour. Jennifer Holiday won a Tony Award for her role as Effie Melody White. *Dreamgirls* was adapted into a feature film in 2006, and new actress Jennifer Hudson won an Oscar for her supporting role as Effie Melody White. *Jelly's Last Jam,* which opened in 1992 as a tribute to Jelly Roll Morton, was a commercial success and earned its playwright George C. Wolfe eleven Tony nominations, with Gregory Hines receiving the best actor award. Wolfe also directed *Bring in 'Da Noise, Bring in 'Da Funk* in 1995. The musical celebrated 300 years of African American history, poetry, music, song, and dance; it received Tony Awards for best choreographer for Savion Glover, best director for Wolfe, and best featured actress for Ann Duquesnay.

More African Americans also took on the role of producer and earned Tony Awards for their work, such as Whoopi Goldberg in 2002 for *Thoroughly Modern Millie,* and Oprah Winfrey in 2006 for *The Color Purple.*

DRAMATICS

Black actors on the dramatic stage, like the performers in all-black musicals, attempted to shed the demeaning image of the African American as projected by most white-produced minstrelsy and drama. The presentation of three plays—*The Rider of Dreams, Granny Maumee,* and *Simon the Cyrenian*—by white playwright Ridgely Torrence at the Garden Theatre in Madison Square Garden on April 5, 1917, was an exceptional and highly successful effort to objectively portray the African American on the dramatic stage.

Dramatic actors during the Harlem Renaissance years remained less active than the black performers in musicals, and the image of the African American projected by white playwrights was generally inadequate. In the 1967 book *Black Drama: The Story of the American Negro in the Theatre,* critic Loften Mitchell recounts, for example, that when Charles Gilpin starred in Eugene O'Neill's *The Emperor Jones* at the Provincetown Theatre in 1920:

> This play, while offering one of the most magnificent roles for a Negro in the American theatre, is the first in a long line to deal with the Negro on this level. O'Neill obviously saw in the Negro rich subject matter, but he was either incapable or unwilling to deal directly with the matter.

Nonetheless, African American actors and actresses had to accept the roles in which they were cast by white playwrights. In 1924 the O'Neill play *All God's Chillun Got Wings* opened at the Provincetown Theatre, with Paul Robeson and Mary Blair, to mixed reviews because of its interracial theme. Rose McClendon starred in Paul Green's Pulitzer Prize–winning *In Abraham's Bosom* in 1926 and was ably supported by Abbie Mitchell and Jules Bledsoe. Marc Connelly's *The Green Pastures* opened on Broadway on February 26, 1930, with Richard B. Harrison playing "De Lawd," and it ran for 557 performances and was taken on an extensive road tour.

Three plays by Langston Hughes that treated African Americans objectively were produced successfully on Broadway in the 1930s. *Mulatto,* which opened in 1935 and starred Rose McClendon and Morris McKenney, had the longest Broadway run of any play written by an African American in the history of the American theater with 373 consecutive performances. It was followed by *Little Ham* (1935) and *Troubled Island* (1936).

Ossie Davis playing the role of Gabriel in the 1930 Broadway play *The Green Pastures*.

In the mid-1930s the Works Progress Administration (WPA) sponsored one of the greatest organized efforts to assist and encourage American actors, especially African American actors. The Federal Theater Project employed a total of 851 black actors to work in sixteen segregated units of the project in Chicago, New York, and other cities from 1935 until 1939, when Congress ended the project. While the project was in operation, black actors appeared in seventy-five plays, including classics, vaudeville contemporary comedy, children's shows, circuses, and "living newspaper" performances. Notable among the black actors who worked in the project, and later became stars on Broadway and in the film, were Butterfly McQueen, Canada Lee, Rex Ingram, Katherine Dunham, Edna Thomas, Thomas Anderson, and Arthur "Dooley" Wilson.

In the wake of the Federal Theater Project the American Negro Theater was established in Harlem by Abram Hill, Austin Briggs-Hall, Frederick O'Neal, and Hattie King-Reeves. Its objective was to authentically portray black life and give black actors and playwrights a forum for their talents. Some of their productions eventually made it to Broadway. In 1944 the theater produced *Anna Lucasta* in the basement of the 135th Street Library in Harlem. It was successful enough to move to Broadway and featured Hilda Simms, Frederick O'Neal, Alice Childress, Alvin Childress, Earle Hyman, and Herbert "Henry" Heard. Abram Hill's *Walk Hard* opened in Harlem in 1946 and became a Broadway production with Maxwell Glanville in the lead. The American Negro Theater provided a training ground for many black actors who later became stars on Broadway and in Hollywood, including Ruby Dee, Ossie Davis, Harry Belafonte, and Sidney Poitier.

One of the most successful all-black plays to appear on Broadway was Lorraine Hansberry's *A Raisin in the Sun* which opened in March 1959. The cast included Sidney Poitier, Ruby Dee, Diana Sands, Claudia McNeil, Louis Gossett Jr., Ivan Dixon, Lonne Elder III, and Douglas Turner Ward. *A Raisin in the Sun,* which won the New York Drama Critics' Circle Award, indicated the future of blacks in the American theater.

As the civil rights movement challenged the national conscience in the 1960s, every facet of African American life changed, including black performing arts. More plays about African Americans by both black and white playwrights were produced, providing increased employment for black actors. On the dance stage more opportunities were opened to blacks as composers, choreographers, and dancers. And many black comedians, by invitation, moved from the "Chitterling Circuit" to posh white-clientele nightclubs and, in some instances, to theaters.

Three events in the 1960s signaled trends that would affect African American dramatic actors for the next thirty years: the production of Jean Genet's play, *The Blacks*; the staging of Leroi Jones's

(Imamu Amiri Baraka) play, *Dutchman*; and the founding of the Negro Ensemble Company.

On May 4, 1961, *The Blacks* by French playwright/author Jean Genet, opened off-Broadway at the St. Mark's Theater. A play about African Americans written for white audiences, *The Blacks* provided employment for a host of black actors, including Roscoe Lee Browne, James Earl Jones, Louis Gossett Jr., Helen Martin, Cicely Tyson, Godfrey Cambridge, Raymond St. Jacques, Maya Angelou, Charles Gordone, and many others who appeared in its road tours. Subsequently, black dramatic actors appeared on and off-Broadway in several major plays by white playwrights. Notable among them were: *In White America* by Judith Rutherford Marechal (1968), with Gloria Foster and Moses Gunn; *The Great White Hope* by Howard Sackler (1968), starring James Earl Jones; and *So Nice, They Named It Twice* by Neil Harris (1975), featuring Bill Jay and Veronica Redd.

On May 23, 1961, when the Leroi Jones play *Dutchman* opened at the Cherry Lane Theatre, the black revolutionary play was introduced to theater audiences. Black actors were provided with the opportunity to perform in roles that not only affirmed blackness but portrayed black political militancy. Several black revolutionary plays subsequently afforded opportunities for black actors, including James Baldwin's *Blues for Mr. Charlie* (1964), with Al Freeman Jr. and Diana Sands; and *The Toilet/The Slave* (1964) by Leroi Jones, starring James Spruill, Walter Jones, Nan Martin, and Al Freeman Jr. In 1991 black revolutionary plays such as *General Hag's Skeezag* continued to provide important roles for black actors.

Perhaps most beneficial to black actors was the founding of the Negro Ensemble Company in New York in 1967. This theatrical production company, initially financed by a three-year grant of $1.2 million from the Ford Foundation, was the brainchild of playwright/actor Douglas Turner Ward. Housed originally at the St. Mark's Theater and currently at Theater Four, the Negro Ensemble is headed by actor Robert Hooks as executive director, Gerald S. Krone as administra-

tive director, and Douglas Turner Ward as artistic director. The Negro Ensemble's objective is to develop African American managers, playwrights, actors, and technicians.

The Negro Ensemble has staged more than one hundred productions, including the work of forty black playwrights, and has provided work for countless aspiring and seasoned black actors. Several plays produced by the Negro Ensemble have eventually gone to Broadway, including Joseph A. Walker's *The River Niger* (1973), which won a Tony and an Obie, and Charles Fuller's Pulitzer Prize–winning *A Soldier's Play* (1981). A plethora of outstanding black actors and actresses have appeared in Ensemble productions, including Marshall Williams, Denise Nicholas, Esther Rolle, Roxie Roker, Adolph Ceasar, Denzel Washington, Moses Gunn, and Barbara Montgomery.

Several black playwrights had plays successfully produced on Broadway independently of the Negro Ensemble Company. Ntozake Shange's widely acclaimed *For Colored Girls Who Have Considered Suicide/When the Rainbow Is Enuf* (1972) had a cast of seven black actresses. August Wilson's *Fences*, which opened on March 26, 1987, and featured James Earl Jones, won the 1987 Pulitzer Prize for drama. Wilson's *Two Trains Running*, which opened April 13, 1992, and starred Roscoe Lee Browne and Laurence Fishburne, received the New York Drama Critic's Circle Award for 1992. Wilson, who is considered the most prolific and celebrated playwright of his time, received numerous awards for his work. Before his death in 2005 he had received New York Drama Critic's Circle Award for seven of his plays, including *Jitney* in 2000.

In 2002 Suzan-Lori Parks won the Pulitzer Prize for her play *Topdog/Underdog,* directed by George C. Wolfe. Other award-winning and up-and-coming playwrights include Cheryl L. West, Kia Corthron, Daniel Beaty, and Marcus Gardley, to name a few.

A merging of dramatic content and gospel music, as created by playwright and media mogul Tyler Perry, has created a theatrical genre that has found a willing audience in the black community.

The performances, which deal with life issues centering in the black community, offer a spiritual and primarily Christian response to problem solving. These plays have been tremendously successful. Perry, who produced his first play *I Know I've Been Changed* in 1992, found his success when he reworked the play and presented it again in 1998. By 2001, with the presence of the character Madea, a sharp tongued and gun packing mature woman (played by Perry in drag), his plays were reported to have entertained as many as 35,000 persons a week. In 2005 Perry expanded his productions to film.

DANCE

Black dance, like other forms of black entertainment, had its beginnings in Africa and on the plantations of early America, where slaves performed to entertain themselves and their masters. White minstrels in blackface incorporated many of these black dance inventions into their shows, while black minstrel dancers, such as "Master Juba" (William Henry Lane), thrilled audiences with their artistry.

Many performers in the early black musicals that appeared on Broadway from 1898 to 1910 were expert show dancers, such as George Walker and Bert Williams. Similarly, in the all-black musicals of the 1920s, performers like Florence Mills and Bill "Bojangles" Robinson captivated audiences with their show dancing. The musical *Runnin' Wild* (1926) was responsible for creating the Charleston dance craze of the "Roaring Twenties."

Hemsley Winfield presented what was billed as "The First Negro Concert in America" in Manhattan's Chanin Building on April 31, 1931. Two suites on African themes were performed, along with solos by Edna Guy and Winfield himself. In 1933 Winfield became the first black to dance for the Metropolitan Opera, performing the role of the Witch Doctor in *The Emperor Jones*.

Austin "Asadata Dafora" Horton, a native of Sierra Leone, electrified audiences in New York with his 1934 production of *Kykunkor.* Dance historian Lynne Fauley Emery concluded in *Black Dance from 1619 to Today* that *Kyunkor* "was the first performance by black dancers on the concert stage which was entirely successful. It revealed the potential of ethnic material to black dancers, and herein lay Dafora's value as a great influence on black concert dance."

Katherine Dunham had her first lead dance role in Ruth Page's West Indian ballet *La Guiablesse* in 1933. In 1936 Dunham received a master's degree in anthropology from the University of Chicago; her thesis, *The Dances of Haiti,* resulted from her on-site study of native dances in the West Indies. For the next thirty years Dunham and her dance company toured the United States and Europe, dazzling audiences with her choreography. During the 1963 to 1964 season Dunham choreographed the Metropolitan Opera's production of *Aida,* becoming the first Black American to do so.

Pearl Primus, like Katherine Dunham, was trained in anthropology. Her research in primitive African dance inspired her first composition performed as a professional dancer, "African Ceremonial," which she presented on February 14, 1943. On October 4, 1944, Primus made her Broadway debut at the Belasco Theater in New York. Her performance included dances of West Indian, African, and African American origin; the concert was widely acclaimed and launched her career as a dancer. Primus traveled to Africa many times to research African dances; in 1959 she was named director of Liberia's Performing Arts Center. She later opened the Primus–Borde School of Primal Dance with her husband, dancer Percival Sebastian Borde, and was involved in the Pearl Primus Dance Language Institute in New Rochelle, New York.

By late 1950s several black dancers and dance companies were distinguishing themselves on the concert stage. Janet Collins was the "première danseuse" of the Metropolitan Opera Ballet from 1951 until 1954. Arthur Mitchell made his debut as a principal dancer with the New York City Ballet in 1955. Alvin Ailey established his company in 1958. And Geoffrey Holder, who made his Broadway debut in 1954 in *House of Flowers,* became a leading choreographer.

Since the early 1960s two of the leading dance companies in the United States, the Alvin Ailey American Dance Theater and the Dance Theater of Harlem, have been headed by black males and composed largely of black dancers. In the 1970s more black women established schools and played a greater role in developing new talent.

The Alvin Ailey American Dance Theater, one of the most renowned troops, was founded in 1958 and has performed before more people throughout the world than any other American dance company. With a touring circuit that has included forty-eight states and seventy-one countries on all continents of the world, the Alvin Ailey American Dance Theater has been seen by more than twenty-three million people. The Alvin Ailey organization consists of three components: the Alvin Ailey American Dance Theater, the Alvin Ailey Repertory Ensemble, and the Alvin Ailey American Dance Center.

Samuel Roberts of the Alvin Ailey American Dance Theater performing "Damn" at the Harbour Festival in Bristol, England on July 31, 2010.

Between 1958 and 1988 the Alvin Ailey Dance Theater performed 150 works by forty-five choreographers, most of whom were black. Notable among these black choreographers have been Talley Beatty, Donald McKayle, Louis Johnson, Eleo Pomare, Billy Wilson, George Faison, Pearl Primus, Judith Jamison, Katherine Dunham, Ulysses Dove, Milton Myers, Kelvin Rotardier, and Gary DeLoatch. More than 250 dancers, again mostly black, have performed with the dance theater. Among its star performers have been Judith Jamison, Clive Thompson, Dudley Williams, Donna Wood, Gary DeLoatch, George Faison, and Sara Yaraborough. A prolific choreographer, Alvin Ailey created numerous works for his dance theater and other dance companies, including *Revelations* (1958); *Reflections in D,* with music by Duke Ellington (1962); *Quintet* (1968); *Cry* (1971); *Memoria* (1974); and *Three Black Kings* (1976). Alvin Ailey choreographed *Carmen* for the Metropolitan Opera in 1973, and *Au Bord du Precipice* for the Paris Opera in 1983.

Alvin Ailey died in 1989, and Judith Jamison was named as director. During her tenure Jamison expanded the groups' goals to include more community programs. In 2002 she was chosen to carry the Olympic torch for the 2002 Winter Games in Salt Lake City, and was awarded the National Medal of the Arts in 2002, to both herself and the Alvin Ailey Dance Foundation. This was the first time a dance organization had been honored with this award. Jamison served as director until July 2011, after twenty-one years of service to the organization. Her successor is choreographer Robert Battle, a former student of the prestigious Juilliard School in New York City, who began choreographing ballets in 1998 and later joined the Ailey dancers.

Other notable contributing companies to dance are: Bill T. Jones/Arnie Zane Dance Company formed in 1982, which is a multiracial company that incorporates within their productions a musical and literary focus; and Forces Of Nature Dance Theater formed in 1981 by Abdel R. Salaam and Olabamidele "Dele" Husbands, which synthesizes American and diaspora cultures and movements. Award-winning choreographers include: George Faison for his work in the 1998 production of *The Lion King*; Donald Byrd, and other choreographers, who earned a Tony Award nomination in 2006 for *The Color Purple*; as well as other successful choreographers such as Geoffrey Holder, Louis Johnson, Bebe Miller, and Donald McKayle.

COMEDIANS

The earliest black comedians in America, like other early black entertainers, were slaves who in their free time entertained themselves and their masters. In the early minstrel shows white comedians in blackface created comic caricatures of blacks, whom they referred to as "coons." When African Americans began appearing in minstrel shows shortly after the Civil War, they found themselves burdened with the "coon" comic caricatures created by white performers. The dance–comedy team of Bert Williams and George Walker were the most famous of the early black comedians, appearing in numerous all-black musicals between 1899 and 1909.

In the all-black musicals of the 1920s a new comic movement emerged: the comedy of style, which emphasized such antics as rolling the eyes or shaking the hips. The venom and bite of black folk humor was replaced by a comedy of style that was more acceptable to the white audiences of these all-black musicals.

Real black folk humor, however, did survive and thrive in black nightclubs and black theaters such as the Apollo in Harlem and the Regal in Chicago in the 1930s, 1940s, and 1950s. In these settings, known as the "Chitterling Circuit," such black comedians as Tim Moore, Dusty Fletcher, Butterbeans and Susie, Stepin Fetchit, Jackie "Moms" Mabley, Redd Foxx, and Slappy White performed without restrictions.

Black comedians enjoyed great exposure during the 1960s. No longer confined to the "Chitterling Circuit," comedians such as Jackie "Moms" Mabley, Redd Foxx, and Slappy White began to perform to audiences in exclusive white clubs as well as to audiences within the black community. They used black folk humor to comment on politics, civil rights, work, sex, and a variety of other subjects. Jackie "Moms" Mabley made two popular recordings: *Moms Mabley at the "UN"* (1961) and *Moms Mabley at the Geneva Conference* (1962). In January 1972, Redd Foxx premiered on television as Fred Sanford in *Sanford and Son,* which remains one of the most popular syndicated shows.

Several younger black comedians came into prominence in the early 1960s. Dick Gregory used black folk humor to make political commentary. Bill Cosby specialized in amusing chronicles about boyhood in America. Godfrey Cambridge, although successful, did not rely on black folk humor. During the late 1960s and the early 1970s, Flip Wilson parodied historical and social experience by creating black characters living in a black world and became extremely popular on television. His cast of characters, which included "Freddy the Playboy," "Sammy the White House Janitor," and "Geraldine," was the epitome of black folk humor as commentary on an array of issues.

Another pivotal black comedian who began his career in the 1960s was Richard Pryor. His well-timed, risqué, sharp folk humor quickly won him a large group of faithful fans. Pryor, who recorded extensively, also starred in several successful films, including *Lady Sings the Blues* (1972), *Car Wash* (1976), and *Stir Crazy* (1980).

During the 1980s and 1990s numerous black comedians have become successful in the various entertainment media. Eddie Murphy made his first appearance on the television show *Saturday Night Live* on November 15, 1980. From television Murphy went on to Hollywood, making his movie debut in the film *48 Hours* in 1982. Starring roles followed in such films as *Beverly Hills Cop* (1984), which was one of the highest grossing comedy films in history, and *Coming to America* (1988). Murphy has established his own company, Eddie Murphy Productions, to create and produce television and film projects. Murphy's career has spanned the roles of actor, producer, director, and voice actor, which have earned him critical acclaim as well as an Oscar nomination and a Golden Globe for best actor for his role in the film *Dreamgirls* (2006).

In the 1990s, as television incorporated more opportunities for stand–up comedians to perform on air, more opportunities came in both the television and film industry. Performers such as Keenen Ivory Wayans and Damon Wayans created a winning comedy show based on situational sketches that launched the careers of Jamie Foxx and David Allen Grier. Other comedians whose careers were launched by television include Martin Lawrence, Will Smith, and Chris Rock. *The Original Kings of Comedy,* a stand-up comedy film directed by Spike Lee, was released on DVD in 2000. It featured Steve Harvey, Bernie Mac, Cedric the Entertainer, and D. L. Hughley as filmed on the last two nights of their *Kings of Comedy* tour. This production brought the comics to the attention of mainstream media. After grossing more than $37 million over the two-year tour, each of the performers subsequently had continued success in their careers with television shows and other stand-up opportunities. *Queens of Comedy,* a spin-off from the *Kings of Comedy,* which was released in 2001, featured Laura Hayes, Adele Givens, Sommore, and Mo'Nique. This production was also successful and brought added attention to black female comics in a predominately male profession.

In 2005 enormously successful comedian Dave Chappelle, who had received critical acclaim for his show *Chappelle's Show* on Comedy Central, walked away from a $50 million contract that required him to continue the show for two more years. Chappelle, who used a comedic sketch format as a vehicle for commentary on race and American culture, no longer saw his vision realized.

Comedians have secured a solid place on television through channels such as Comedy Central and specials that feature selected comedians. Black comedies have also secured a place through television shows such as *Who's Got Jokes* (2006), hosted by comedian Bill Bellamy, and *Last Comic Standing* (2003), which offers a competition for new comedians. These opportunities, along with computer technology that provides an immediate viewing audience for video performances through YouTube and other Internet sites, assures the continued exposure, viability, and success of black comedians.

TELEVISION AND FILM

The rise of television in the 1950s generally had an adverse effect on the American theater. Employment for all actors fell sharply, but especially for black actors. Television had limited access for blacks as segregation was still the law of the land. Actors such as Lena Horne and Sammy Davis Jr. were occasional guests on television, but overall images of blacks were often derogatory. Shows like *The Beulah Show, Amos 'n' Andy,* and *The Little Rascals,* which were on the air between 1950 and 1953, offered no lasting opportunities for blacks.

When the civil rights movement in the 1960s became a continuous part of the airways, blacks broke new ground in lead roles such as Diahann Carroll in the television sitcom *Julia.* By the 1970s situation comedies were the top shows for blacks. Although there were some dramas, comedies thrived. Comedians such as Flip Wilson and Redd Foxx had their own shows, while family comedies included *The Jeffersons* and *Good Times.* Family comedies depicted black life as well as the challenges, successes, and creativity of black urban culture.

The most acclaimed black sitcom of the 1980s was *The Cosby Show,* which ran from 1984 to 1992. This show was popular for all American viewers and its success remains undeniable yet controversial. Many attribute it to the assumed idealized sense of the black upper-middle class family, while others saw it as a colorized version of the stock American family. In spite of these viewpoints the show brought a new perspective of the black family. Television viewers were offered a truthfulness and honesty that kept blacks and whites alike watching. Other shows that continued a view into black culture were *Frank's*

The *Amos 'n' Andy Show* featured two white actors, Charles Correll and Freeman Gosden, playing African Americans in a comedy that was not very flattering and, indeed, derogatory.

Place, from 1987 to 1988, set in New Orleans with a working class focus, and *A Different World* from 1987 to 1993, featuring college students at a historically black college.

Television since the 1990s continues to diversify the images of black cultural experiences. Situation comedies still prevail as the dominant format, and actors such as Will Smith, Martin Lawrence, and Queen Latifah remain popular figures; and the irreverent show *In Living Color* (1990–1994), created by Keenen Ivory Wayans, pushed the envelope of parody. Shows like *Everybody Hates Chris* (2005), and *Tyler Perry's House of Payne* (2007), are shows that continue this tradition in the new millennium. Black actors have also taken major roles on shows such as *Law & Order, CSI:New York,* and *NCIS: Los Angeles.*

The Internet has offered another media opportunity for producers and directors. African Americans on the cutting edge of this new media have created series such as *Buppies,* produced by Tatyana Ali for BET.com and *Diary of a Single*

Mom, produced by award-winning producer and director Robert Townsend. Townsend's series launched in 2009; it offers fourteen-minute episodes and is in its third season. He is looking to produce another series that will be the first to focus on Latino Americans.

African Americans have been a part of the film industry since the 1896 film short *Watermelon Contest,* which catered to the derogatory notions of blacks prevalent at the time. These stereotypical images of African Americans' place in American society continued well into the twentieth century and were bolstered by the film *The Birth of a Nation,* produced in 1915 by D. W. Griffith. African Americans responded to these films by making "race" films, which found themes in every genre of the film industry. Oscar Micheaux was the most successful African American filmmaker at the time, with films such as *Body and Soul* (1925) and *Swing!* (1935).

The post-World War II film industry saw an integration of African American actors such as

Harry Belafonte, Dorothy Dandridge, and Sidney Poitier, who challenged roles that demeaned African Americans in past generations. The 1940s through the 1970s saw African American filmmakers moving toward defining their circumstance and not responding to it. Themes were chosen that were more global, complex, and original.

In the 1970s "blaxploitation" films, as they were called, took a leading role in the African American film industry. The films focused on male-centered power that resisted authority and won. The films were primarily urban and included violence and often the exploitation of women. Films such as Melvin Van Peebles's, *Sweet Sweetback's Baadasssss Song* (1971), *Shaft* (1971), and *Superfly* (1972), were among the most popular.

The end of the twentieth century saw the rise of independent African American filmmakers such as Robert Townsend and one of the most renowned filmmakers, Spike Lee. Townsend produced the satire *Hollywood Shuffle* (1987), among others, and Lee has produced films such as *Do the Right Thing* (1989), *Malcolm X* (1992), and *When the Levees Broke* (2006), among many others. Each used personal and committed resources to create films that reflected and confronted experiences in the African American community. Other filmmakers also brought strong social content and unique aesthetic experiences in their films, including John Singleton's *Boyz n the Hood* (1991), and Julie Dash's film *Daughters of the Dust* (1991). New and innovative filmmakers in the twentieth-first century include: Ava Duvernay operating out of Los Angeles, California; Sam Walton operating out of Harlem, New York; Tanya Elaine Hamilton of Jamaica, West Indies, operating out of Philadelphia, Pennsylvania; John K. Dargan operating out of New York City; Maxwell Addae operating out of Los Angeles, California; and Tim Gordon of Washington, D.C.

African American actors and actresses have contributed greatly to the overall film industry and have been awarded the industry's highest recognition—Oscars presented during the Academy Award shows. Sidney Poitier was the first actor to receive an Oscar for best actor in 1963 for *Lilies of the Field,* only to be followed thirty-eight years later with an Oscar awarded to Denzel Washington in 2001 for *Training Day.* Jamie Foxx received the Oscar for best actor in 2004 for *Ray,* and Forest Whitaker received the Oscar for best actor in 2006 for *The Last King of Scotland.* The Oscar for best supporting actress was first awarded to Hattie McDaniel in 1939 for the film *Gone with the Wind,* followed sixty-two years later with an Oscar awarded to Halle Berry in 2001 for best actress in *Monster's Ball.*

African Americans as filmmakers, producers, actresses, and actors continue to expand and enrich the film industry as a whole. Their films not only increase the awareness of the African American experiences and struggles, but enhance the understanding of human relationships, whether they are presented as comedies or serious storylines. Independent filmmaker Tyler Perry has produced films that cover the dramatic and comedic with such work as *Diary of a Mad Black Woman* (2005), *Madea's Family Reunion* (2006), and *For Colored Girls* (2010), among his many successful films grossing well over $100 million. Oprah Winfrey assisted in the production of independent filmmaker Lee Daniels's film *Precious* (2009), which earned not only critical acclaim but also an Oscar for Mo'Nique as best supporting actress.

African Americans continue to make a tremendous impact on the film industry while addressing issues of social injustice, individual survival, spiritual concerns, self-love, and racial and cultural dynamics that impact all aspects of the African American and American experience.

VISUAL ARTS

The following comment, made over eighty years ago during the height of the Harlem Renaissance, by Alain Locke—one of America's foremost art critics—underscores the promise displayed by African Americans throughout their history in the United States.

The constructive lessons of African art are among the soundest and most needed of art creeds. They offset with equal force the banalities of sterile, imitative classicism and the superficialities of literal realism. They emphasize intellectually significant form, abstractly balanced design, formal simplicity, restrained and unsentimental emotional appeal. Moreover, Africa's art creed is beauty in use, vitally rooted in the crafts, and uncontaminated with the blight of the machine. Surely the liberating example of such art will be as marked an influence in the contemporary work of Negro artists as it has been in that of the leading modernists: Picasso, Modigliani, Matisse, Epstein, Lipchitz, Brancusi and others too numerous to mention.

The substantial contributions of African American artists have been achieved in the face of numerous obstacles. Blacks in the United States and Europe were long cut off from the rich artistic heritage of Africa. As Locke points out, "The liberating example" of African art was used by white Europeans long before it reached African Americans.

From colonial times to the present, black artistic talent has been encouraged and recognized on a very limited basis by reigning establishments and connoisseurs in the United States, though some white institutions, such as the Rosenwald Fund in the early twentieth century, did subsidize promising black artists. More support came later from the Harmon, Rockefeller, Guggenheim, and Whitney Foundations and from government programs, such as the Works Progress Administration (which later became the Works Projects Administration) and the National Endowment for the Arts. State Arts Councils, formed in the 1960s and 1970s, have also provided grants for artists. The need for support, however, has always exceeded the available sponsorships.

Early African American themes and expressions—whether related to slave, sharecropper, or ghetto life—have rarely been regarded as prime moneymakers by leading curators of the art world. Until very recently, few blacks attained the economic security and leisure essential to the patronage of artists. Art history books include the contributions of one or two African American artists and very little about African art, although images of blacks abound: in Egyptian tomb paintings, on Greek vase paintings, in Roman frescoes and mosaics, in medieval illuminated manuscripts, and in Gothic sculpture. If Africans were subjects, might not they also have been artists?

Two black artists in seventeenth-century Europe have been documented. They are Juan de Pareja and Sebastian Gomez. Pareja was a slave, apprentice, and pupil of the great master Velasquez. Many of Pareja's works were of such a quality that they were mistakenly accepted as Velasquez's own and hung in the great museums and mansions of Western Europe. Pareja's paintings, properly credited to him, now hang in the Dulwich Gallery in London, the Prado in Madrid, the Munich Gallery, and the Hermitage in Leningrad. Pareja's talent was recognized in his lifetime, and in 1652 he was manumitted by King Philip IV.

Sebastian Gomez, a servant of Murillo, was discovered painting secretly at night in his master's studio after Murillo's pupils had departed. Murillo made Gomez his student; and eventually Gomez, known as the "Mulatto of Murillo," became famous for paintings and murals in Seville.

Although Pareja and Gomez were black artists, their genius was nurtured in a European setting and tradition. Cut off from their African heritage, they naturally worked in the same style and format as their white contemporaries. Their paintings were devoted to the religious themes and aristocratic portraits desired by the art world of that era.

The only African American artist in colonial America to have left a historical record was Scipio Morehead. Morehead's artistic endeavors appear to have been aided by two prominent women who lived in Boston where he was a slave: the wife of his clergyman master, the Reverend John Morehead, who was a patron of arts, and poet Phillis Wheatley, who was herself a slave. Morehead's style is in keeping with the period—it is classically allegorical, resembling the work of George Romney and Joshua Reynolds, British masters of the era. Although no major work is known to have survived, the small extant portrait of Phillis Wheatley is believed to be Morehead's work.

Certainly there were many black artists and craftspeople in the eighteenth century who did not achieve historical recognition. Fortunately, as scholars have more of a desire to understand the nature and development of the American culture, a more multi-ethnic pattern is beginning to emerge with the basic foundation being Western European, African, and Native American cultures. Records indicate that skilled blacks interested in buying their freedom worked as painters, silversmiths, cabinet and coach makers, ornamentalists, and shipwrights. Eugene Warbourg, for example, a black sculptor from New Orleans, became well known for his ornamental gravestones and eventually went to study in Europe. Bill Day, a celebrated carpenter who owned slaves in his shop, has gained recognition for his interior design as well as his furniture.

Much of the colonial iron work and metal work on eighteenth-century mansions, churches, and public buildings was created and executed by blacks and occasionally reached heights that can be classified as fine art. The artists and artisans, however, are not known.

Emerging African American artists in the eighteenth and nineteenth centuries found that their cultural roots were not recognized. To become professionals they had to simulate European artistic styles. Many were trained by white artists, and they traveled to Europe to study and receive validation. Their works received some degree of popular acceptance, but racism kept them out of the mainstream. Most continued to work in the United States in spite of their status. Some were able to overcome immense obstacles and win recognition for their art, including Edward Mitchell Bannister, Robert Scott Duncanson, Meta Warrick Fuller, Joshua Johnston, Edmonia Lewis, and Henry Ossawa Tanner.

Christ in the Home of Mary and Martha by artist Henry Ossawa Tanner.

Some African American artists attempted to escape the classical tradition into which they were confined and painted themes closer to their heritage and existence. Some fine portraits of black freedmen were painted by talented but obscure black artists in the rural South during the period from 1870 through the early part of the twentieth century. Henry Ossawa Tanner's paintings in the 1880s of poor blacks, for example, belong to this little-known school of African American art.

The turn of the century brought few changes in the approach of most African American artists to their work. They continued to look toward Western Europe for their themes and development of expression, and there was little emphasis given to demonstrating an ethnic consciousness. Two important developments in art helped to push black artists toward cultural and social awareness and a visual aesthetic: the 1913 Armory Show of works by European cubist and modernist painters revealed an interest in, and the influence of, African art forms; and the mainstream American art world developed an interest in genre subjects. These movements toward social realism and abstract formalism in art opened the doors to new interpretations and values in artistic expression.

During the period of transition, from 1900 to the 1920s, many black artists continued to express themselves in imitative styles. They felt that the interest in African American culture was sincere in Europe, and many traveled there to study. New trends emerged, demonstrating expressions of personal dignity and ethnic awareness. The artists of this period—Palmer Hayden, Archibald Motley, Malvin Gray Johnson, William Edouard Scott, Meta Warrick Fuller, and Laura Wheeler Waring—were among the major contributors to this new awareness.

The new respect for negritude and the African idiom that began to manifest itself after World War I is evinced by cultural activities and organizations that developed in major American cities during the 1920s.

From Karamu House, a center for cultural activities founded in 1915 in Cleveland, came such artists as Hughie Lee-Smith, Zell Ingram, Charles Sallee, Elmer William Brown, William E. Smith, and George E. Hulsinger. In 1924 the Spingarn Medals were established. Three years later, the Harmon Foundation was established by philanthropist William E. Harmon to aid African American artists. The foundation offered financial awards and exhibitions and encouraged the growth of art education programs in many black institutions throughout the country. The Harmon Foundation became one of the major organizations involved in the perpetuation and presentation of African American art in the United States and continued to exist until the mid-1960s. Howard University established its first art gallery, under the directorship of James V. Herrings, in 1930.

The 1930s brought the Depression and the Works Progress Administration. Black artists abandoned by the white philanthropists of the 1920s were rescued by the WPA. Aaron Douglas, Augusta Savage, Charles Alston, Hale Woodruff, and Charles White created murals and other works for public buildings under this program. In 1939 the Baltimore Museum Show, the first exhibition of African American artists to be held in a southern region, presented the works of Richmond Barthe, Malvin Gray Johnson, Henry Bannarn, Florence V. Purviance, Hale Woodruff, Dox Thrash, Robert Blackburn, and Archibald Motley. The Harlem Art Center and the Chicago South Side Community Art Center also began with the help of the WPA.

Representation of the African American culture through art became an important goal in the first three decades of the twentieth century. At the urging of Alain Locke, W. E. B. DuBois, and others, creative artists began collaborating in literature, music, theater, and art to increase awareness of their cultural heritage. Aaron Douglas was considered the leading painter of "The Negro Renaissance." Active in New York from 1923 to 1925, Douglas was the first of his generation to depict visual symbols—stylized African figures with overlays of geometric forms—that created a sense of movement and rhythm. The idea spread from Harlem's boundaries, where many black intellectuals and artists from the Caribbean and elsewhere had settled, throughout the United States. This concept, while promoting ethnic awareness and pride, also counteracted the stereotypes and shallow interpretations prevalent in the popular culture.

During this period black artists continued to depict the American social and political landscape in their works. World War II brought a sense of urgency to the search for equality; the integration of the armed services fostered hope for equality in all facets of American life. Seeking greater cultural and professional opportunities, as well as communities of African American intellectuals and artists, many blacks migrated from the South to urban areas in the North. This migration was documented by artists such as Romare Bearden, Beauford Delaney, Jacob Lawrence, and Hughie Lee-Smith.

The influence of the previous decades became evident in the proliferation of muralist art. In her book *Art: African American* (1978),

Samella Lewis notes that exterior murals are an important aspect of African architectural traditions. Charles Alston, John T. Biggers, Jacob Lawrence, and Charles W. White became important muralists during this period. Inspired by Mexican mural artists (who advocated social change through their art), African American artists were especially drawn to the themes, bold forms, and bright colors of such artists as Diego Rivera, David Alfaro Siqueiros, and José Clemente Orozco.

Like their successful white counterparts, African American artists were conscious of the need to study the history, aesthetics, and formal qualities of art. Many continued to go abroad to Paris, Rome, and, before World War II, Germany. Most, however, stayed in the United States and attended classes either at universities such as Columbia, Ohio State, and Pennsylvania State, or at professional art schools such as the Art Institute of Chicago, the New York Art Students' League, and the Philadelphia Academy of Art. Black educational institutions such as Fisk, Hampton, Howard, Morehouse, and Tuskegee emphasized art education as a means of survival, as well as the basis for continuing a future cultural aesthetic in the visual arts.

"Some historians and critics," Lewis notes, "have erroneously assumed that African-American artists are unfamiliar with the formalized techniques of Western aesthetics." Beginning in the 1940s more African Americans were being awarded degrees in art than ever before. Some turned to abstraction, non-objective art (Delilah Pierce), and expressive forms, as seen in many works by Norman Lewis, who for a time was a part of the group known as the Action Painters (Jackson Pollock, a major American artist, was also part of this group). Romare Bearden studied cubism, as did Aaron Douglas. These artists were aware of the African roots of this art form long before American critics began writing about the significant influence of African art on the abstractionist painters of the twentieth century.

The end of World War II saw the beginning of the dismantling of the Jim Crow segregation laws in the South—provocative subjects for artists in the 1940s and 1950s. The period was marked by social unrest as barriers to racial equality slowly broke down, and social and political expressions dominated African American art. Many artists considered it imperative to document, inspire, and champion the "cause." Several artists, however, felt that art should be separate from race and politics. Horace Pippin, William Edmondson, and Clementine Hunter, who were self-taught individuals, and E. Simms Campbell, a cartoonist and successful pictorial journalist for *Esquire* and the *New Yorker,* were among them.

The 1960s saw a great many radical changes in social and cultural aspects of the United States. African Americans throughout the country were demanding political, social, and cultural recognition. No longer satisfied with the limited support of such philanthropic organizations as the Harmon Foundation, these artists looked for alternative forms of exposure. In response, numerous galleries, community art centers, and community art galleries developed.

The search for a black identity and the expression of militancy were the most pervasive themes of black art in the 1960s. Emotions could not always be contained on canvas, channeled into familiar forms, or exhibited in traditional settings. Art literally took to the streets of the ghetto to meet with, appeal to, and celebrate the people, as was richly illustrated in Chicago and Detroit murals. In 1972 African American and Hispanic teenagers in New York City created a colorful art form, "wall graffiti," to express their loyalty and pride. The content of wall graffiti is often merely the name of a street gang, the nickname of the painter, or the name of the street where the painter lives. Some of the paintings, however, depict extravagant scenes with cartoon characters and flamboyant lettering. Toward the end of the 1970s and well into the 1980s this graffiti style became very popular and acquired value in the art market. Several of the young street artists, particularly Jean-Michel Basquiat, were welcomed into the mainstream art world and made into superstars.

In the early 1990s multimedia art forms (initially developed in the 1960s and 1970s and expanded by video and computers in the 1980s) came to the forefront. Artists combining traditional expressive modes (painting, printmaking, sculpture) with dance, drama, and other performance arts were finding alternative exhibition spaces as well, including the natural environment, factories, and school buildings. Traditional materials were often replaced by stones, hair, elephant dung, twigs, bricks, and found objects. Words, symbols, and numbers as images have acquired a new emphasis in much of this experimental art.

By the 1990s mainstream museums across the country, including the Seattle Museum in Washington, the Dallas Museum in Texas, the Brooklyn Museum in New York, the Corcoran Gallery of Art in Washington, D.C., and the Wadsorth Atheneum in Hartford, Connecticut, were sponsoring major exhibits of African American artists' works or displaying collections and artifacts designed to appeal to black audiences.

African American museums include the Studio Museum in Harlem, which began in 1969 initially for artists who needed working space; the Schomburg Center for Research in Black Culture of the New York Public Library, one of the most widely used research facilities in the world devoted to the preservation of materials on black life; the Cinque Gallery in New York, which opened in 1969 and was named after the famous African Joseph Cinqué; the Du Sable Museum in Chicago, established in 1961, which grew out of an art center that was established under the WPA during the Depression; the museum of the National Center of Afro-American Artists in Boston, which began in 1969 and is a multimedia art center featuring dance, theater, visual arts, film, and educational programs; the Museum of African Art in Washington, D.C., established in 1964 to promote and familiarize Americans with the artistic heritage of Africa, was transitioned to the Smithsonian Institution in 1984.

In the 1990s more and more artists used their creativity in media outside traditional forms and textures, and they presented their works not only in established places but orchestrated their own exhibits. Their artistic energy was inspired by the black aesthetic of the black arts movement.

Artists of the twenty-first century confront the issues of race, beauty, and identity pertaining to the individual and within the cultural landscape. Artists such as Kara Walker confront issues of race, exploitation, and violence, while Lorna Simpson uses the gaze of black women in her photography. Charles Bibbs and Synthia Saint James use bright colors and scenes paying tribute to experience at the heart of the community; Barbara Chase-Riboud, William T. Williams, Richard Hunt, Raymond Saunders, and Melvin Edwards, as painters and sculptors, use various materials to create engaging and often critical cultural images. Artists such as Betye Saar and Leah Gilman create computer-generated images to reach a global audience.

BIOGRAPHIES: PERFORMING ARTS

Alvin Ailey (1931–1989)
Dancer, Choreographer

Alvin Ailey Jr. was born on January 5, 1931, in Rogers, Texas. After the Great Depression Ailey followed his mother to Los Angeles, California, where he studied dance at Lester Horton's school in 1949. He joined the Horton Dance Company in 1953, and he assumed the role of artistic director when Horton died that year. Ailey formed his own troupe, the Alvin Ailey American Dance Theater in 1958. In 1965 Ailey took his troupe on one of the most successful European tours ever made by an American dance company. It was held over for six weeks in London to accommodate the demand for tickets, and in Hamburg it received an unprecedented sixty-one curtain calls. A German critic called this performance "a triumph of sweeping, violent beauty, a furious spectacle. The stage vibrates. One has never seen anything like it." In 1970 Ailey's company became the first American modern dance troupe to tour the Soviet Union.

During the mid-1970s Ailey, among his other professional commitments, devoted much time to creating special jazz dance sequences for America's bicentennial celebration. Among numerous honors, including several honorary degrees, Ailey was awarded the NAACP's Spingarn Medal in 1976. Ailey died on December 1, 1989.

Ira Aldridge (1807–1867)
Actor

Ira Aldridge was born July 24, 1807, in New York City. He was one of the leading Shakespearean actors of the nineteenth century. Although he was denied the opportunity to perform before the American public in his prime, the fame that he won abroad established him as one of the prominent figures of international theater.

Aldridge's early dramatic training centered on the African Grove Theatre in New York in 1821. His first role was in *Pizarro*, and he subsequently played a variety of small roles in classical productions before accepting employment as a steward on a ship bound for England.

After studying briefly at the University of Glasgow in Scotland, Aldridge went to London in 1825 and appeared in the melodrama *Surinam, or a Slave's Revenge*. In 1833, he appeared in London's Theatre Royal in the title role of *Othello*, earning wide acclaim. For the next three decades he toured the continent with great success, often appearing before European royalty.

Aldridge died in Lodz, Poland, on August 7, 1867. He was honored by a commemorative tablet in the New Memorial Theatre in StratfordUponAvon, England.

Debbie Allen (1950–)
Actress, Singer, Dancer, Director

Debbie Allen was born in Houston, Texas, on January 16, 1950. A cum laude graduate of Howard University, Allen began her career on the Broadway stage in the chorus line of the hit musical *Purlie* (1972). She then portrayed Beneatha in the Tony and Grammy award–winning musical *Raisin* (1973). Allen was subsequently selected to star in an NBC pilot, *3 Girls 3* (1977), and then appeared on other television hits such as *Good Times* (1976) and *The Love Boat* (1979 and 1983). At this time, with her talent as a choreographer recognized, she worked on such television projects as *Midnight Special* (1977), as well as two films, *The Fish That Saved Pittsburgh* (1979) and *Under Fire* (1981).

The year 1982 was pivotal for Allen. She appeared in the film *Ragtime* and the television series *Fame,* as well as the Joseph Papp television special *Alice at the Palace.* Allen also starred in a dance performance for the Academy Awards ceremonies.

As each season passed on *Fame,* Allen became more involved as choreographer and was soon regularly directing episodes of the series. In 1988 she was selected by the producers to become director of the television sitcom *A Different World.* In another acknowledgment of her stature as a performer and creative talent, she starred in her own television special during the 1988 and 1989 seasons, and began a five-year run doing the choreography for the Academy Awards. She also appeared in other acting opportunities such as *In the House* (1995), *Old Settler* (2001) and *The Painting* (2002). Allen has received two Emmys for choreography, a Golden Globe for best actress in *Fame* (1982–1983), as well as two Emmy nominations in 1998.

Allen co-produced the film *Amistad* (1997) with Steven Spielberg and has been director on other projects such as the television shows *Girlfriends* 2005–2008 and *Everybody Hates Chris* (2006–2009). Among her numerous awards and honors, Allen has received the Career Achievement Award at the Acapulco Black Film Festival (1998), the Lifetime Achievement Award, American Women in Radio and Television (2001), and the Strong, Smart, and Bold Award from Girls Inc.

of Greater Houston (2002). In 2001 Allen opened the Debbie Allen Dance Academy, which offers preparatory programs for youth. She continues to use her talents in directing, producing, acting, and chorography.

Pearl Bailey (1918–1990)
Singer, Actress

Pearl Mae Bailey was born in Newport News, Virginia, on March 29, 1918. After singing at small clubs and touring with the United Service Organizations (USO) she made her stage debut in New York in *St. Louis Woman* (1946), for which she received the Donaldson Award for the best new performer.

In 1950 Bailey appeared in several films including *Carmen Jones, That Certain Feeling,* and *Porgy and Bess*; in 1967 her performance in *Hello, Dolly* earned her a special Tony Award. In 1969 Bailey wrote her autobiography *The Raw Pearl,* in addition to several other books on various issues. In 1975 she was named special advisor to the United Nations and received an award from the Screen Actors Guild for outstanding achievement. In 1980 Bailey gave a one-night concert at Radio City Music Hall in New York. She died on August 17, 1990.

Josephine Baker (1906–1975)
Dancer, Singer

Born in St. Louis, Missouri, on June 3, 1906, Josephine Baker received little formal education; she left school at the age of eight to supplement the family income by working as a kitchen helper and babysitter. While still in elementary school, she took a parttime job as a chorus girl. At seventeen she performed as a chorus girl in Noble Sissle's musical comedy *Shuffle Along,* which played at Radio City Music Hall in 1923. Her next show

was *Chocolate Dandies,* followed by a major dancing part in *La Revue Nègre,* an American production that introduced *Le Jazz Hot* to Paris in 1925.

In Paris, Baker left the show to create her most sensational role, that of the Dark Star of the Folies Bergère. In her act, she appeared topless on a mirror, clad only in a protective waist shield of rubber bananas. The spectacular dance made her an overnight star and a public figure with a loyal following. In true "star" tradition, she catered to her fans by adopting such flamboyant eccentricities as walking pet leopards down the Champs-Élysées.

In 1930, after completing a world tour, Baker made her debut as a singing and dancing comedienne at the Casino de Paris. Critics called her a "complete artist, the perfect master of her tools." In time she ventured into films, starring alongside French idol Jean Gabin in *Zouzou* (1934), and into light opera, performing in *La Créole* (1934), an operetta about a Jamaican girl.

During World War II, Baker served first as a Red Cross volunteer and later did underground intelligence work through an Italian Embassy attaché. After the war the French government decorated her with the Legion of Honor. She returned to the entertainment world, regularly starring at the Folies Bergère, appearing on French television, and going on another extended international tour. In 1951, during the course of a successful American tour, Baker made headlines by speaking out against discrimination and refusing to perform in segregated venues.

Beginning in 1954 Baker earned another reputation—not as a lavish and provocative entertainer, but as a progressive humanitarian. She used her fortune to begin adopting and tutoring a group of orphaned babies of all races, retiring from the stage in 1956 to devote all her time to her "rainbow family." Within three years, however, her "experiment in brotherhood" had taken such a toll on her finances that she was forced to return to the stage, starring in *Paris, Mes Amours,* a musical based in part on her own fabled career.

Baker privately, and without voicing discouragement, survived numerous financial crises. Illness hardly managed to dampen her in-domitable spirit. Through her long life she re-tained her most noteworthy stage attributes—an intimate, subdued voice, coupled with an infec-tiously energetic and vivacious manner.

Baker died in Paris on April 12, 1975, after opening a gala to celebrate her fiftieth year in show business.

Angela Bassett (1958–)
Actress

Angela Basset was born in New York City on August 16, 1958. She grew up in St. Pe-tersburg, Florida. After earn-ing a scholarship from Yale University, Bassett graduated in 1980 with a B.A. in African American studies and went on to earn an M.A. from the Yale School of Drama.

Bassett played several roles on television, in-cluding the 1992 miniseries about the Jackson 5, *The Jacksons: An American Dream*, before landing her breakout role as Tina Turner in the film *What's Love Got to Do with It?* (1993). For her performance she was awarded a Golden Globe and an Oscar nomination for best actress. Bassett also received critical acclaim for her performance as the late Dr. Betty Shabazz in Spike Lee's film *Malcolm X* (1992), as well as an NAACP Image Award for outstanding supporting actress in the film. Bassett also earned an Emmy nomination for her lead role in *The Rosa Parks Story* (2002).

Harry Belafonte (1927–)
Singer, Actor

Born in New York City, on March 1, 1927, Harold George "Harry" Belafonte (originally Belafonete) moved to the West Indies at the age of eight. At thirteen Belafonte returned to New York, where he attended high school. Belafonte joined the Navy in 1944; after his discharge, while working as a janitor in New York, he became interested in drama. He studied acting at Stanley Kubrick's Dramatic Workshop and with Erwin Piscator at the New School for Social Research, where his classmates included Marlon Brando and Walter Matthau. A successful singing engagement at the Royal Roost, a New York jazz club, led to other engagements around the country. But Belafonte, dissatisfied with the music he was performing, returned to New York, opened a restaurant in Greenwich Village, and studied folk singing. His first appearances as a folk singer in the 1950s "helped give folk music a period of mass appeal," according to John S. Wilson in a 1981 *New York Times* article. During his performances at the Palace Theater in New York, Belafonte had audi-ences calypsoing in the aisles.

Belafonte produced the first integrated musical shows on television, which won him two Emmys and resulted in his being fired by the sponsor. Belafonte also appeared on Broadway in *John Murray An-derson's Almanac* (1953); his movies include *Car-men Jones* (1954), *Island in the Sun* (1957), *The World, the Flesh and the Devil* (1958), *Odds Against Tomorrow* (1959), *The Angel Levine* (1970), *Buck and the Preacher* (1972), and *Up-town Saturday Night* (1974).

During the 1980s Belafonte appeared in his first dramatic role on television in the NBC pres-entation of *Grambling's White Tiger,* and in 1981 Columbia Records released his first album in seven years, *Loving You Is Where I Belong*, con-sisting mostly of ballads. He has received nu-merous awards and honors, including the 1982 Martin Luther King Jr. Nonviolent Peace Prize and three honorary doctorates. In 1993 Belafonte received the Thurgood Marshall Award for life-time achievement, and in 1994 the National Medal of Arts. Belafonte continues to be politi-cally and socially active.

Halle Berry (1966–)
Actress, Model

Maria Halle Berry was born on August 14, 1966, in Cleveland, Ohio, to an African American father and a white mother. The couple divorced when Halle was four years old, but she continued to identify herself as an African American. In 1986 she enrolled in Cuyahoga Community College after winning the Miss Teen Ohio beauty pageant. After deciding that majoring in journalism was not for her, Berry moved to Chicago to pursue acting and in 1988 relocated to Manhattan. Her first job in New York was as a catalog model, and her first big acting role was in *Jungle Fever,* a film by Spike Lee in 1991.

 Throughout the 1990s Berry starred in several films, including *Executive Decision* (1996), the comedy *B.A.P.S.* (1997), and *Introducing Dorothy Dandridge* (1998), an HBO film. Berry received for her performance in *Introducing Dorothy Dandridge* the outstanding actress award from the NAACP, a Screen Actors Guild (SAG) Award for best television actress in a miniseries or television movie, and a Golden Globe. Berry followed her performance with a starring role in the film, *Monster's Ball,* which earned her the film industry's highest honor, the Academy Award, in 2002. Berry is the only African American women to receive the award for best actress. She also was honored by the Berlin International Film Festival, the National Board of Review, and the Screen Actors Guild. In April 2007 she was awarded a star on the Walk of Fame.

Berry has been named one of *People* magazine's fifty "Most Beautiful People in the World," and by *Esquire* as the "Sexiest Woman Alive" in 2008, and was featured by *Ebony* as one of the twenty-five African American women "who make everyone stand up and take notice," in 2009.

"Eubie" Blake (c.1883–1983)

Musician, Composer

James Herbert "Eubie" Blake was born in Baltimore, Maryland, on February 7, 1883, or 1887. The son of former slaves, Blake was the last of ten children and the only one to survive beyond two

months. His mother worked as a laundress, his father as a stevedore.

At the age of six Blake started taking piano lessons. He studied under the renowned teacher Margaret Marshall and subsequently was taught musical composition by Llewellyn Wilson, who at one time conducted an all-black symphony orchestra sponsored by the city of Baltimore. At the age of seventeen Blake was playing for a Baltimore nightclub.

In 1915 Blake joined Noble Sissle. That year Blake and Sissle sold their first song, "It's All Your Fault," to Sophie Tucker, and her introduction of the song started them on their way. Blake and Sissle moved to New York and, together with Flournoy Miller and Aubrey Lyles, created one of the pioneer black shows, *Shuffle Along,* in 1921; the show was produced again on Broadway in 1952. *Chocolate Dandies* and *Elsie* followed in 1924.

During the early 1930s Blake collaborated with Andy Razaf and wrote the musical score for Lew Leslie's *Blackbirds.* Out of this association came the hit "Memories of You." During World War II, Blake was appointed musical conductor for the United Service Organizations' (USO) Hospital Unit. In 1946 he announced his retirement and enrolled in New York University.

For many years, Blake's most requested song was "Charleston Rag," which he composed in 1899 and was written down by someone else because Blake could not then read music. Among his most famous songs were "How Ya' Gonna Keep 'Em Down on the Farm," "Love Will Find a Way," and "You're Lucky to Me." Some of his other works include "I'm Just Wild About Harry," "Serenade Blues," "It's All Your Fault," and "Floradora Girls," with lyrics by Sissle.

Though known as the master of ragtime, Blake loved best the music of the classical masters. In the intimacy of his Brooklyn studio, Blake rarely played the music for which the world reveres him. In 1978 Blake's life and career were celebrated in the Broadway musical *Eubie!* Several thousand people attended concerts at the Shubert Theatre and St. Peter's Lutheran Church celebrating Blake's one hundredth birthday on

February 8, 1983. Blake also received honorary doctorates from numerous colleges and universities. He died on February 12, 1983.

John Bubbles (1902–1986)
Dancer, Singer

John Bubbles, inventor of rhythm tap dancing, was born John William Sublett on February 19, 1902, in Louisville, Kentucky. At the age of seven he teamed with a fellow bowling-alley pin boy, Ford "Buck" Washington, to form what became one of the top vaudeville acts in show business. Throughout the 1920s and 1930s Buck and Bubbles played the top theaters in the country at fees of up to $1,750 a week. The two appeared in several films, including *Cabin in the Sky* (1943). Bubbles captured additional fame in the role of Sportin' Life in the 1935 version of *Porgy and Bess*. After Buck's death in 1955, Bubbles virtually disappeared from show business until 1964, when he teamed up with Anna Maria Alberghetti in a successful nightclub act.

In 1979, at the age of seventy-seven and partially crippled from an earlier stroke, Bubbles recreated his characterization of Sportin' Life for a one-night show entitled *Black Broadway* at New York's Lincoln Center. The show was repeated in 1980 for a limited engagement at the Town Hall in New York. In the fall of 1980 Bubbles received a lifetime achievement award from the American Guild of Variety Artists and a certificate of appreciation from the city of New York. Bubbles died on May 19, 1986, at the age of eighty-four.

Anita Bush (1883–1974)
Actress, Singer

Born in Washington, D.C., on August 1, 1883, Anita Bush was involved in the theater from an early age since her father had been the tailor for the Bijou Theater in Brooklyn. In the 1920s Bush was in the Williams and Walker chorus and performed in the productions *Abyssinia* and *Dahomey.*

Bush started her own company in 1915 called the Anita Bush All-Colored Dramatic Stock Company, which launched a new play every two weeks with a great degree of success. The group also launched the careers of Charles Gilpin and Dooley Wilson. The Lafayette Theater, where the group performed, later purchased the rights to the company and changed the name to the Lafayette Players. Although Bush went on to pursue a career in motion pictures, the Lafayette Players provided a venue for many actors and actresses of that time.

Donald Byrd (1949–)
Choreographer

Donaldson Toussaint L'Overture Byrd II was born on July 21, 1949, in New London, North Carolina, but he was raised in Clearwater, Florida. Inspired by a dance lecture-performance when he was sixteen, Byrd earned a scholarship to Yale University, majoring in philosophy. Byrd was eager about being exposed to the theater groups but the racist attitudes of his classmates at Yale were not so welcoming. Byrd transferred in the early 1970s to Tufts University. He began to take dance lessons, and he later moved to New York where he took lessons with the Alvin Ailey dancers. He graduated from Tufts in 1974.

Byrd began to receive acclaim for his choreography in 1977. He had been performing various works and did dance workshops in New York. In 1978 Byrd started his own company, which offered a blend of ballet, classical, modern, and street dance. In 1987 he debuted *Dance at the Gym* for Alvin Ailey and *Prodigal,* performed by his own troupe. In 1992 Byrd won a Bessie Award for the controversial piece *The Minstrel Show.* In 2002 he disbanded his troupe for financial reasons, but continues to create stage productions. In 2006 he choreographed the stage production of *The Color Purple.*

Godfrey Cambridge (1933–1976)
Actor, Comedian

Godfrey MacArthur Cambridge was born in New York on February 26, 1933; his parents had emigrated from British Guiana. He attended grammar school in Nova Scotia while living with his grandparents. After finishing his schooling in New York at Flushing High School and Hofstra College, he went on to study acting.

Cambridge made his Broadway debut in *Nature's Way* (1956), and was featured in *Purlie Victorious,* both on stage in 1961, and later on screen. He also appeared off-Broadway in *Lost in the Stars* (1958), *Take a Giant Step* (1959), and *The Detective Story* (1960). Cambridge won the Obie Award for the 1960–1961 season's most distinguished Off-Broadway performance for his role in *The Blacks.* In 1965 he starred in a stock version of *A Funny Thing Happened on the Way to the Forum.*

As a comedian Cambridge appeared on *The Tonight Show* and many other variety programs. His material, drawn from the contemporary racial situation, was often presented in the style associated with the contemporary wave of black comedians. One of Cambridge's most memorable roles was as the star of a seriocomic Hollywood film, *The Watermelon Man* (1970), in which the comedian played a white man who changes color overnight. Cambridge has also performed dramatic roles on many television series.

During the mid-1970s Cambridge remained in semiretirement, making few public appearances. Cambridge died at the age of forty-three in California on November 29, 1976. His death occurred on a Warner Brothers set, where he was playing the role of Ugandan dictator Idi Amin for the television film *Victory at Entebbe.*

Diahann Carroll (1935–)
Actress, Singer

Diahann Carroll was born Carol Diahann Johnson in the Bronx, New York, on July 17, 1935, the daughter of a subway conductor and a nurse. As a child she was a member of the Abyssinian Baptist Church choir; at the age of ten Carroll won a Metropolitan Opera scholarship. Singing lessons held little ap-

peal for her, however, so she continued her schooling at the High School of Music and Art. As a concession to her parents, Carroll enrolled at New York University, where she was to be a sociology student, but stage fever led her to an appearance on a television talent show that netted her $1,000. A subsequent appearance at the Latin Quarter club launched her professional career.

In 1954 Carroll appeared in *House of Flowers,* winning favorable press notices. In that year she also appeared in a film version of *Carmen Jones,* in the role of Myrt.

Movie and television appearances kept Carroll busy until 1958, the year she was slated to appear as an Asian in Richard Rodgers's *Flower Drum Song.* The part did not materialize. Three years later, Rodgers cast her in *No Strings* as a high-fashion model, a role for which she earned a Tony in 1962.

In the late 1960s Carroll was cast as lead in the television series *Julia,* in which she played a nurse and war widow. She also appeared in the films *Porgy and Bess* (1959); *Goodbye Again* (1961); *Paris Blues* (1961); *Claudine,* with James Earl Jones (1974); *Sister, Sister* (1982); and *The Five Heartbeats* (1991). She has been featured in the television series *Dynasty* and *A Different World* and has written an autobiography. Her many awards include an Oscar nomination in 1974 for the film *Claudine,* and an Emmy nomination for outstanding best actress in a comedy series in 1989 for *A Different World.*

Carroll continued to perform on the small and large screen in the 1990s in films such as *Eve's Bayou* (1998), and *Having Our Say: The Delany Sisters' First 100 Years* (1999), and on the small screen in *Livin' for Love: The Natalie Cole Story* (2002). She has also made appearances on the hit drama *Grey's Anatomy.*

Dave Chappelle (1973–)
Comedian, Actor

David Khari Webber Chappelle was born on August 24, 1973, in Washington, D.C. Chappelle's career was supported by his parents throughout middle and high school as he performed at various comedy clubs beginning at the age of fourteen. Giving himself a year after graduating high school, Chappelle felt confident he could succeed in that year with his comedy. If not, he would enroll in college.

Chappelle is one of the most extraordinary and controversial comedians of the twenty-first century. His aggressive and sometimes irreverent routines were so effective that within a short time he had a budding career. By 1992 he had performed on Russell Simmons's *Def Comedy Jam* which opened the door to late night appearances and movie roles. In his creative ventures he refused to compromise his comedic vision. After a one-man show on HBO called *Dave Chappelle: Killin' Them Softly,* he was offered a chance to do a television show. In 2003 Comedy Central debuted *Chappelle's Show,* a sketch comedy show. The show earned two Emmy nominations and a huge following. With the success of a second season Chappelle was offered a $50 millon contract for a third season. In the midst of taping the season, Chappelle began to evaluate his own personal vision of comedy; he left the show and in 2006 stated his departure was due to creative differences and not rumors of drugs or the need for psychiatric care.

In 2005 Chappelle produced the documentary *Dave Chappelle's Block Party,* where he hosted a neighborhood party and the reunion concert of the group, the Fugees.

Don Cheadle (1964–)

Actor

Donald Frank Cheadle Jr. was born in Kansas City, Missouri, on November 29, 1964, but moved several times throughout his childhood. After high school he attended the California Institute for the Arts in Valencia in 1982. After graduation he found work on well-known television shows such as *Fame, L.A. Law,* and *Hill Street Blues.* It was for his role in the film version of Walter Mosley's novel *Devil in a Blue Dress* (1995) that he received critical acclaim and considerable Hollywood attention. He also received recogni-

tion for his role in Steven Soderbergh's film, *Ocean's Eleven.* Cheadle won the Los Angeles Film Critics Association Award and the National Society of Film Critics Award. He also was awarded a Golden Globe for his portrayal of Sammy Davis Jr. in *The Rat Pack* (1999).

For his performance in *Hotel Rwanda* (2004), Cheadle was nominated for an Oscar. In 2005 he produced and starred in the film *Crash,* which won the Academy Award for best picture, and he won a Screen Actors Guild Award for best supporting actor.

In 2007 Cheadle, along with George Clooney, received the Summit Peace Award for humanitarian work from the Nobel Peace Laureates in Rome for his work to stop genocide and relive the suffering of the people of Darfur.

Hope Clarke (1941–)

Stage Director, Choreographer, Actress

Hope Clarke was born in Washington, D.C., on March 23, 1941. In 1960 she was cast in Leonard Bernstein's touring company of *West Side Story* and later became a dancer with the Katherine Dunham Dance Company and the Alvin Ailey American Dance Theater. She became a principle dancer but later left to pursue acting.

Clarke did acting and choreography and received a Tony nomination for best choreography for her work in the 1992 production of *Jelly's Last Jam,* which was written by George C. Wolfe. In 1995 Clarke did the choreography for *Porgy and Bess,* which was staged by the Houston Grand Opera in celebration of the sixtieth year of George Gershwin's opera.

In 1998 Clarke received a Bessie Award for outstanding achievement as a performance professional. Clarke, in a collaboration with George C. Wolfe, received two Tony nominations for the musical *Caroline; or, Change* (2004).

Bill Cosby (1937–)

Actor, Comedian, Author

William Henry "Bill" Cosby was born in Philadelphia, Pennsylvania, on July 12, 1937. Cosby dropped out of high school to become a medic in the Navy, obtaining his diploma while in the service. Upon becoming a civilian, he entered Temple University, where he played football and worked evenings as a bartender.

 While working as a bartender, Cosby began to entertain the customers with his comedy routines and, encouraged by his success, left Temple in 1962 to pursue a career in show business. He began by playing small clubs around Philadelphia and in New York's Greenwich Village. Within two years he was playing the top nightclubs around the country and making television appearances with Johnny Carson (also acting as guest host), Jack Paar, and Andy Williams. Cosby became the first black to star in a prime-time television series. *I Spy* ran from 1965 to 1968 and won Cosby three Emmy Awards.

In the 1970s Cosby appeared regularly in nightclubs in Las Vegas, Tahoe, and Reno, and did commercials for such sponsors as Jell-O, Del Monte, and Ford Motor Company. From 1969 until 1972 he had his own television series, *The Bill Cosby Show*. During the early 1970s he developed and contributed vocals to the Saturday morning children's show *Fat Albert and the Cosby Kids*. He appeared in such films as *Uptown Saturday Night* (1974), *Let's Do It Again* (1975), *A Piece of the Action* (1977), and the award-winning television movie *To All My Friends on Shore*. During this time he also earned a master's degree and a doctorate in education from the University of Massachusetts.

Cosby was star and creator of the consistently top-rated *The Cosby Show* from 1985 to 1992, author of two best-selling books, *Fatherhood* (1986) and *Time Flies* (1987), and a performer at the top venues in Las Vegas, where he earned $500,000 a week. He also won top fees as a commercial spokesperson for Jell-O, Kodak, and Coca-Cola. He returned to television in 1996 in the series *The Cosby Mysteries* and he joined again with Phylicia Rashad in the comedy sitcom *Cosby*.

While contending with personal issues such as the loss of his son in 1997 and a false paternity suit, Cosby has continued to be active in social and political issues regarding the African American community. The Cosby family made headlines when they donated $20 million to Spelman College in Atlanta. In 2000 Cosby addressed the education system with the book *American Schools: The $100 Billion Challenge*. Cosby has received numerous awards for his contributions, including the Bob Hope Humanitarian Award in 2003 and the Mark Twain Prize for American Humor in 2009.

Dorothy Dandridge (1922–1965)
Actress

Dorothy Dandridge was born on November 9, 1922, in Cleveland, Ohio; her mother was the actress Ruby Dandridge. As children Dorothy and her sister, Vivian, performed as "The Wonder Kids," touring the United States. In 1934 they were joined by a third performer, Etta Jones, and the trio became the Dandridge Sisters. The Dandridge Sisters were a popular act, performing at the Cotton Club in Harlem and in the motion picture *A Day at the Races* (1937). By the 1940s, Dorothy Dandridge had struck out on her own, appearing in the "soundies" (musical shorts) *Easy Street; Yes, Indeed; Cow Cow Boogie; Jungle Jig; Paper Doll;* and *Sing for My Supper*.

Dandridge married Harold Nicholas (of the famed Nicholas Brothers dance team) in 1942, and had a daughter, Harolyn, in 1943. Harolyn was diagnosed as having a severe developmental disability and was sent to an institution; shortly thereafter, Dandridge divorced Nicholas. She carried on a fairly successful career as a nightclub singer during the 1940s and 1950s. Her greatest triumph, however, came as a film actress, particularly in the all-black musical *Carmen Jones* (1954), for which she received an Oscar nomination for best actress, becoming the first African American woman to receive this nomination. Another important role was in *Island in the Sun* (1957), where she was paired romantically with a white man, John Justin—a breakthrough in desegregating the screen. In 1959 Dandridge played

Bess opposite Sidney Poitier's Porgy in the movie version of *Porgy and Bess*. Ultimately, she appeared in over twenty-five films.

Dandridge married the white Las Vegas restaurateur Jack Dennison in 1959, but three years later divorced him and declared personal bankruptcy. She died of an overdose of a prescription antidepressant on September 8, 1965.

Ossie Davis (1917–2005)
Actor

Ossie Davis was born Raiford Chatman Davis on December 18, 1917. He grew up in Waycross, Georgia, and attended Howard University in Washington, D.C., where Dr. Alain Locke suggested he pursue an acting career in New York. After completing service in the Army, Davis landed his first role in 1946 in the play *Jeb,* where he met Ruby Dee, whom he married two years later.

After appearing in the movie *No Way Out* (1950), Davis won Broadway roles in *No Time for Sergeants, A Raisin in the Sun,* and *Jamaica.* In 1961 he and Dee starred in *Purlie Victorious,* which Davis himself had written. Two years later, they repeated their roles in the movie version, *Gone Are the Days.*

Davis's other movie credits from this period include *The Cardinal* (1963), *Shock Treatment* (1964), *The Hill* (1965), *A Man Called Adam* (1966), and *The Scalphunter* (1968).

Davis then directed such films as *Cotton Comes to Harlem* (1970) and *Black Girl* (1972). His play *Escape to Freedom: A Play about Young Frederick Douglass* had its debut at Town Hall in New York and later was published by Viking Junior Books. Davis has also been involved with television scripts and educational programming. *The Ruby Dee/Ossie Davis Story Hour* was produced for television in 1974. The arts education television series *With Ossie and Ruby* appeared in 1981. Davis and Ruby Dee also founded the Institute of New Cinema Artists and the Recording Industry Training Program.

Davis's continued movie appearances include roles in *Let's Do It Again* (1975), *Hot Stuff* (1979), and *Nothing Personal* (1979). Other film credits include *Harry and Son* (1984) and Spike Lee's *School Daze* (1988), *Do the Right Thing* (1989), *Jungle Fever* (1991), and *Get on the Bus* (1996). Davis's last appearances before his death were in the cable television series *The L Word* (2004–2005). David died on February 4, 2005.

Davis and his lifelong partner in life and in the entertainment industry, Rudy Dee, were named to the NAACP Image Awards Hall of Fame in 1989; they also received the American National Medal of the Arts in 1995, the Kennedy Center Honors Award in 2004, and the Lifetime Achievement Freedom Award from the National Civil Rights Museum in 2005. Davis died on February 4, 2005.

Sammy Davis Jr. (1925–1990)
Singer, Dancer, Actor, Comedian

Samuel George "Sammy" Davis Jr. was often called "the world's greatest entertainer," a title that attested to his remarkable versatility as singer, dancer, actor, mimic, and musician.

Davis was born in New York City on December 8, 1925. Four years later, he began appearing in vaudeville shows with his father and uncle in the Will Mastin Trio. In 1931 Davis made his movie debut with Ethel Waters in *Rufus Jones for President*; this was followed by an appearance in *Season's Greetings.*

Throughout the 1930s the Will Mastin Trio continued to play vaudeville, burlesque, and cabarets. In 1943 Davis entered the Army and served for two years by writing, directing, and producing camp shows. After his discharge he rejoined the trio, which in 1946 cracked the major club circuit with a successful Hollywood engagement.

Davis recorded a string of hits ("Hey There," "Mr. Wonderful," "Too Close for Comfort") during his steady rise to the top of show business. In November 1954 he lost an eye in an automobile accident, which fortunately did not interfere with his career. He scored a hit in his first Broadway show, *Mr. Wonderful* (1956), and later repeated this success in *Golden Boy* (1964).

In 1959 Davis played the character Sportin' Life in the movie version of *Porgy and Bess.* Other Davis movies from this period include *Oceans 11* (1960) and *Robin and the Seven Hoods* (1964). His 1966 autobiography *Yes, I Can* became a best seller, and he starred in his own network television series. Davis married three times. His first marriage was in 1959 to singer Loray White. He married his second wife, actress Mai Britt, in 1961; she is the mother of his three children. In 1970 he married dancer Altovise Gore.

In 1968 the NAACP awarded Davis its Spingarn Medal, and in subsequent years Davis continued to appear in films, television, and nightclubs. In 1972 he was involved in a controversy over his support of Richard Nixon, which was publicized by a famous photograph of Nixon hugging Davis at the 1972 Republican Convention. In 1974 Davis renounced his support of Nixon and his programs. In 1980 he marked his fiftieth anniversary as an entertainer, and the Friars Club honored him with its annual life achievement award. In 1989 he appeared in the film *Tap* with Gregory Hines and Harold Nicholas. In 1989 Davis was diagnosed with throat cancer and died on May 16, 1990.

Ruby Dee (1924–)
Actress

Ruby Dee was born Ruby Ann Wallace in Cleveland, Ohio, on October 27, 1924, but grew up in Harlem, New York, and attended Hunter College. In 1942 she appeared in *South Pacific* with Canada Lee. Five years later, she met Ossie Davis while they were both playing in *Jeb.* They were married two years later.

Ruby Dee's movie roles from this period include parts in *No Way Out* (1950), *Edge of the*

City (1957), *A Raisin in the Sun* (1961), Genet's *The Balcony* (1963), and *Purlie Victorious,* written by Davis (1963). Since 1960 she has appeared often on network television.

In 1965 Ruby Dee became the first black actress to appear in major roles at the American Shakespeare Festival in Stratford, Connecticut. She subsequently appeared in movies, including *The Incident* (1967), *Uptight* (1968), *Buck and the Preacher* (1972), *Black Girl,* directed by Davis (1972), and *Countdown at Kusini* (1976). Her musical satire *Take It from the Top,* in which she appeared with her husband in a showcase run at the Henry Street Settlement Theatre in New York, premiered in 1979.

As a team Ruby Dee and Ossie Davis have recorded several talking story albums for Caedmon. In 1974 they produced *The Ruby Dee/Ossie Davis Story Hour,* which was sponsored by Kraft Foods and carried by more than sixty stations of the National Black Network. In 1981 Alcoa funded a television series for the Public Broadcasting System titled *With Ossie and Ruby,* which used guests to provide an anthology of the arts. Other film credits include *Cat People* (1982) and, with Ossie Davis, Spike Lee's *Do the Right Thing* (1989). Dee received an Emmy Award in 1991 for her performance in the miniseries *Decoration,* and in 2008 she received a Screen Actors Guild Award for best supporting actress and an Academy Award nomination for her role in *American Gangster* (2007).

Dee lost her husband and partner, Ossie Davis, in 2005. In 2001 they received the Lifetime Achievement Award from the Screen Actors Guild after the couple had been married and worked together for fifty-two years. The couple also received the Kennedy Center Honors Award in 2004 and the Lifetime Achievement Freedom Award from the National Civil Rights Museum in 2005. Dee continues to appear on television and in film roles.

Suzanne de Passe (1947–)
Producer, Entrepreneur

Suzanne de Passe was born on July 19, 1947, in Harlem, New York. De Passe graduated from

Manhattan High School and briefly attended Syracuse University before landing a job at Motown Records as a creative assistant. De Passe discovered the Jackson 5 and the Commodores, earning the reputation of one who could recognize real talent.

In 1973 de Passe received an Oscar nomination for co-writing the movie *Lady Sings the Blues,* in 1980 her production of *Motown 25* earned an Emmy Award and several Emmy nominations, and in 1989 she earned another Emmy nomination for the TV western miniseries, *Lonesome Dove.* De Passe started her own production company, De Passe Entertainment, in 1992 and produced several shows on the WB television station. In 1995 she was awarded the Charles W. Fries Producer of the Year Award for her contribution to television. She continues to be executive producer on many television shows and productions, including *Zenon, Girl of the 21st Century* (1999), *Cheaters* on HBO in 2000, and the 32nd Annual NAACP Image Awards on Fox Network in 2001. From 2002 to 2008 de Passe was the executive producer of the television variety show, *Showtime at the Apollo.*

De Passe has received numerous awards, including induction into the Black Filmmakers Hall of Fame in 1990, the Time Warner Endowed Chair in Media at Howard University from 2002 to 2005, *Ebony* magazine's Madam C. J. Walker Award in 2004, and in 2006 Producer of the Year Award from the Caucus for Television Producers, Writers and Directors.

André DeShields (1946–)
Actor, Director, Choreographer

André DeShields was born in Baltimore, Maryland, on January 12, 1946, and began his professional career in the production of *Hair* in the 1960s. In the 1970s many opportunities presented themselves, and he co-choreographed two shows for Bette Midler in 1973 and in 1975, he starred in *The Wiz* in 1975, and *Ain't Misbehavin'* in 1978. In 1982 he received an Emmy Award for his performance in *Ain't Misbehavin'*.

In 1997 and 2001 DeShields won both Tony and Drama Desk Award nominations for his performances, and also in 2001 he won an Outer Critics Circle Award for his performance as Noah T. "Horse" Simmons in *The Full Monty*. DeShields served as director of Carnegie Hall's Jazzed, an educational program for public schools. In 2006 he performed in *King Lear* at the Classical Theatre of Harlem.

Bill Duke (1943–)
Actor, Producer, Director

William Henry "Bill" Duke Jr. was born in Poughkeepsie, New York, on February 26, 1943. After earning a B.A. from Boston University in 1964, he went on to earn an M.A. from New York University in 1968. He made his film debut in 1980 in *American Gigolo* and his directorial debut with the film *A Rage in Harlem* in 1991.

Duke has directed the films *Deep Cover* (1992), *Hoodlum* (1997), and *Sister Act 2: Back in the Habit* (1993). His acting roles also include *Menace II Society* (1993), *X-Men: The Last Stand* (2000), and *Get Rich or Die Tryin'* (2005). He continues to take on other acting and directorial ventures, but he currently serves as head of the School of Performing Arts at Howard University in Washington, D.C.

Katherine Dunham (1910–2006)
Dancer, Choreographer

Katherine Dunham was one of the leading exponents of primitive dance in the world of modern choreography.

Born in Joliet, Illinois, on June 22, 1910, Dunham attended Joliet Township Junior College and the University of Chicago, where she majored in anthropology. With funding from a Rosenwald fellowship, she was able to conduct anthropological studies in the Caribbean and Brazil. She later attended Northwestern University, where she earned her Ph.D., MacMurray College, where she received a L.H.D. in 1972, and Atlanta University, where she received a Ph.D.L. in 1977.

In the 1930s she founded the Dunham Dance Company, whose repertoire drew on techniques Dunham learned while studying in the Caribbean. She used her training in anthropology and her study of primitive rituals from tropical cultures to create unique dance forms that blend primitive qualities with sophisticated Broadway stage settings. In 1940 she appeared in the musical *Cabin in the Sky,* which she had choreographed with George Balanchine. She later toured the United States with her dance group; after World War II, she played to enthusiastic audiences in Europe.

Among Dunham's choreographic pieces are *Le Jazz Hot* (1938), *Bhahiana* (1939), *Plantation Dances* (1940), *Haitian Suite (II)* (1941), *Tropical Revue* (1943), *Havana 1910/1919* (1944), *Carib Song* (1945), *Bal Negre* (1946), *Rhumba Trio* (1947), *Macumba* (1948), *Adeus Terras* (1949), *Spirituals* (1951), *Afrique du Nord* (1953), *Jazz Finale* (1955), *Ti 'Cocomaque* (1957), and *Anabacoa* (1963). Under the pseudonym Kaye Dunn, Dunham wrote several articles and books on primitive dance. Referred to as "the mother of Afro-American dance," Dunham founded schools of dance in Chicago, New York, Haiti, Stockholm, and Paris. She also lectured at colleges and universities across the country.

On January 15, 1979, at Carnegie Hall in New York, Dunham received the 1979 Albert Schweitzer Music Award, and selections from her dance repertory from 1938 to 1975 were staged. She also received a Kennedy Center Honors Award in 1983, and induction into the Hall of Fame of the National Museum of Dance in 1987.

In 1990 Dunham's legacy was ensured with contributions to preserve and make available the archives regarding her work. Dunham's technique, which is a key part of renowned dance companies such as Alvin Ailey and the Debbie Allen Dance Company, continues to influence the dances of today. Dunham died at the age of ninety-six on May 21, 2006.

Tracey Edmonds (1967–)
Producer

Tracey Elaine McQuarn Edmonds was born on February 18, 1967, in southern California. Edmonds entered Stanford University at sixteen and designed her own major to fit her interests. She graduated in 1987 with a degree that combined psychology and neurobiology. Edmonds, after earning a real estate license, started her own mortgage company in Newport Beach in the 1980s and later moved her offices to Los Angeles in 1990.

In 1992 after marrying "Babyface" Edmonds, a well-known recording artist, song writer, record producer, and co-founder of LaFace Records, Edmonds started a music publishing company she called Yab Yum publishing. With support from her husband, particularly in the music area, Edmonds became the moving force behind their ventures and the key contributor to the success of the company. The company supported many new artists and eventually expanded into film production with the acclaimed film *Soul Food,* released in 1996. This was followed with the film *Light It Up* in 2000. *Soul Food,* which became an hour-long television series that ran for five seasons, won Edmonds multiple NAACP Image Awards and an Outstanding Drama Series Awards three years in a row. The Edmondses filed for divorce in 2005.

Edmonds has been a major influence in launching the careers of Kimberly Elise, Mekhi Phifer, and Tracee Ellis Ross, to name a few. Edmonds has also been successful in the recent reality-show media with *College Hill* on BET. She has received numerous awards for her achievements, including the Turner Broadcasting Systems Prestigious Tower of Power Award in 2000, The Ebony Magazine Outstanding Women in Marketing and Communications Entrepreneur Award in 2002, and an award from Girls Inc., in 2004, for inspiring young girls to achieve.

Garth Fagan (1940–)
Choreographer

Gawain Garth Fagan was born on May 3, 1940, in Kingston, Jamaica. While still in high school he studied dance and traveled throughout Latin America with the Jamaican National Dance Theatre Company. Fagan graduated with a master's degree from Wayne State University and continued to study with Martha Graham, Alvin Ailey, and others while also becoming a distinguished professor at the State University of New York.

Fagan used the polyrhythm of Afro-Caribbean dance and modern dance to create works for Alvin Ailey and other dance troupes. In 1986 he produced and did the choreography for his work *Queenie Pie* at the Kennedy Center.

Fagan has received numerous awards for his work, including a Guggenheim Fellowship, Choreography Fellowship from the National Endowment for the Arts, and in 1996 he was named among the twenty-five artists for the Fulbright Fiftieth Anniversary Distinguished Fellow. He received a Tony in 1998 for his work in the Broadway production *The Lion King* as well as the Outer Critics Circle Award, the Drama Desk Award, and in 2001, the Samuel H. Scripps American Dance Festival Award.

The Garth Fagan Dance troupe continues to produce works such as *Trips and Trysts* (2000), *****ING* (2004), *Senku* (2006), and *Phone Tag Thanks and Things* (2009). Fagan's work continues to push the limits of dance and to offer innovative interpretations of modern dance and post-modern dance for an evolving world.

Stepin Fetchit (1902–1985)
Actor

Born Lincoln Theodore Monroe Andrew Perry in Key West, Florida, on May 30, 1902, Stepin Fetchit pursued an early career in the Royal American Shows' plantation revues. He and his partner, Ed Lee, took the names "Step 'n' Fetchit: Two Dancing Fools from Dixie." When the duo broke up, Fetchit appropriated "Stepin Fetchit" for himself.

Fetchit appeared in numerous motion pictures in the 1920s and 1930s, including *In Old Kentucky* (1927), *Salute* (1929), *Hearts in Dixie*

(1929), *Show Boat* (1929), *Swing High* (1930), *Stand Up and Cheer* (1934), *David Harum* (1934), *One More Spring* (1936), and *Zenobia* (1939). Fetchit earned a great deal of income from these films and he spent it wildly. His extravagant lifestyle ended when he filed for bankruptcy in the 1930s.

Fetchit made sporadic appearances in films later in his life, among them *Miracle in Harlem* (1949), *Bend of the River* (1952), *Amazing Grace* (1974), and *Won Ton Ton, the Dog Who Saved Hollywood* (1976).

Fetchit's place in movie history is a controversial one. Praised by some critics as an actor who opened doors for other African Americans in Hollywood, he has been berated by others for catering to racist stereotypes and doing little to raise the status of black actors. His characters—lazy, inarticulate, slow-witted, and always in the service of whites—have become so uncomfortable to watch that his scenes are sometimes cut when films in which he appeared are shown on television. Even at the height of his career, civil rights groups protested his roles, which they considered demeaning caricatures. He died on November 19, 1985.

Laurence Fishburne (1961–)
Actor

Laurence John Fishburne III was born in Augusta, Georgia, on July 30, 1961, and made his first stage appearance at the age of ten. By the age of twelve in 1975 he made his film debut in *Cornbread, Earl and Me*. Fishburne continued to do a series of key roles, including co-starring in *Apocalypse Now*, a Francis Ford Coppola war classic.

After a break-out performance in John Singleton's film *Boyz n the Hood* Fishburn was nominated for an Oscar for his 1993 performance of Ike Turner in the film *What's Love Got to Do with It?* In 1995 he played the lead role in the film version of *Othello*. No other film production of this play had featured an African American in the title role. Fishburne's other film credits include the popular film *The Matrix* (1999) as well as the stage production of the play *Two Trains Running* (1992) by renowned playwright August Wilson. He won a Tony for his performance in *Two Trains Running* in 1993 and was awarded an Emmy for his performance in *TriBeCa*.

Fishburne continues to offer outstanding performances in film, theater, and television, including a work that he wrote and starred in, *Once in the Life*, which was produced in 2000. In April 2008 he starred in the production *Thurgood*, a play by George Stevens Jr. That same year he returned to television in the cast of *CSI: Crime Scene Investigation*, a show he left in 2011.

Redd Foxx (1922–1991)

Actor, Comedian

Redd Foxx was born John Elroy Sanford on December 9, 1922, in St. Louis, Missouri, and both his father and his brother were named Fred. As a boy, he concocted a washtub band with two friends and played for tips on street corners, earning as much as $60 a night. At fourteen Foxx and the band moved to Chicago; the group broke up during World War II.

Foxx then moved to New York, where he worked as a rack pusher in the garment district while seeking work in nightclubs and on the black vaudeville circuit. While in New York he played pool with a hustler named Malcolm Little, who later changed his name to Malcolm X.

In the early 1950s Foxx tried to find work in Hollywood. He had a brief stint with *The Dinah Washington Show* but mostly survived by performing a vaudeville act and working as a sign painter. His comedy act was adult entertainment, which limited his bookings.

Foxx's first real success came in 1955, when he began to record party records. He ultimately made more than fifty records, which sold over twenty million copies. His television career was launched in the 1960s with guest appearances on *The Today Show, The Tonight Show,* and other variety programs. He also began to appear in Las Vegas nightclubs.

Foxx's most famous role was that of Fred Sanford, the junkman on the popular NBC series *Sanford and Son,* which began in 1972. It was the second most popular role on television (after Archie Bunker in *All in the Family*). As a result, Foxx became one of the highest paid actors in show business. In 1976 it was reported that he was earning $25,000 per half-hour episode, plus twenty-five percent of the producer's net profit. Throughout the long run of *Sanford and Son,* Foxx disputed with his producers over money. Originally, he was not receiving a percentage of the show's profits, which led him to sit out several episodes; a breach of contract suit filed by the producers resulted. There were racial undertones to these disputes, with Foxx referring to himself as a "tuxedo slave" and pointing to white stars who owned a percentage of their shows. Eventually, Foxx broke with the show and with NBC.

Foxx then signed a multimillion-dollar, multiyear contract with ABC, which resulted in a disastrous comedy variety hour that he quit on the air in October 1977. The ABC situation comedy *My Buddy,* which he wrote, starred in, and produced, followed. In 1978, however, ABC filed a breach of contract suit. In 1979 Foxx was back at NBC planning a sequel to *Sanford and Son.* He also made a deal with ABC, which in 1981 was suing him for a second time, allegedly to recover advances not paid back.

In 1976 Foxx performed in the MGM movie *Norman, Is That You?* He continued his appearances in nightclubs in Las Vegas and New York. In 1979 the book *Redd Foxx, B.S.* was published, composed of chapters written by his friends.

In 1973 Foxx received the Entertainer of the Year award from the NAACP. In 1974 he was named police chief of Taft, Oklahoma, an all-black village of 600 people. He also ran a Los Angeles nightclub to showcase aspiring young comedians, both black and white. In addition, Foxx did numerous prison shows, probably more than any other famous entertainer, which he paid for himself. Redd Foxx died on October 11, 1991.

Al Freeman Jr. (1934–)

Actor

Albert Cornelius Freeman Jr. was born in San Antonio, Texas, on March 21, 1934, and made numerous and varied contributions to the fields of theater, television, and motion pictures. His first Broadway play was *The Long Dream* (1960), which opened the door to performances both on and off-Broadway, including *Blues for Mr. Charlie* (1964), and *Medea* (1973), as well as films such as *Black Like Me* (1964), *Dutchman* (1967), and *Once upon a Time … When We Were Colored* (1995).

Freeman's credits also include television series such as *Law and Order, The Cosby Show,* and the daytime series *One Life to Live* from 1972 to 1985, for which he received an Emmy.

Morgan Freeman (1937–)

Actor

Born in Memphis, Tennessee, on June 1, 1937, Morgan Freeman grew up in Greenwood, Mississippi. He joined the U.S. Air Force in 1955 but left a few years later to pursue an acting career in Hollywood, taking classes at Los Angeles City College. He moved to New York City in the 1960s. Freeman's first important role was in the shortrunning off Broadway play *The Nigger Lovers* in 1967. Soon thereafter, he appeared in the all-black version of the musical *Hello, Dolly!*

Americans who grew up in the 1970s remember Freeman fondly as a regular on the public television program *The Electric Company* in which he appeared from 1971 to 1976; his most notable character was the hip Easy Reader. More theater roles followed in productions of *The Mighty Gents* (1978), *Othello* (1982), *The Gospel at Colonus* (1983), and *The Taming of the Shrew* (1990).

In 1987 Freeman was cast in the Broadway play *Driving Miss Daisy.* He won an Obie Award for his portrayal of Hoke, the chauffeur for a wealthy white woman in the American South. Freeman recreated his Broadway role for the 1989 movie version of the play and received an Academy Award nomination for best actor. In the same year, Freeman appeared in the highly successful movie *Glory* (1989) about an all-black Union regiment in the Civil War. Morgan has added to his credits *The Shawshank Redemption* (1994), *Million Dollar Baby,* which earned him a Screen Actors Guild Award, and *Invictus* (2009), which earned Freeman an NAACP Image Award for Outstanding Actor.

In 2006 Freeman was honored with the Lifetime Achievement Award by the Mississippi Institute of Arts and Letters; in 2008 he received Kennedy Center Honors; and in 2011 he was awarded a Lifetime Achievement Award by the American Film Institute.

Antoine Fuqua (1966–)

Director

Antoine Fuqua was born on January 19, 1966, in Pittsburgh, Pennsylvania. After spending the earlier part of his career directing music videos for stars such as Prince, Stevie Wonder, Usher, and Toni Braxton, he began a career in film making. In 2000 he directed Jamie Foxx in *Bait* and added other films such as *Training Day* (2001) and *Shooter* (2007). Denzel Washington's performance in *Training Day* earned him an Academy Award for best actor.

Charles Gilpin (1878–1930)

Actor

Charles Gilpin was born on November 20, 1878, in Richmond, Virginia. In 1890 he traveled with various vaudeville companies. He toured with the Pan-American Octette company from 1911 to 1914 before starting his own company, the Lafayette Theatre company, in 1916.

In 1920 Gilpin was chosen by Eugene O'Neill to play the lead in his play *The Emperor Jones*. He played this role until 1924 with critical acclaim for his performance. In 1921 Gilpin was awarded the NAACP Spingarn Medal for his accomplishments. Gilpin's career ended when he lost his voice in 1926. He died on May 6, 1930.

Danny Glover (1947–)
Actor

A native of San Francisco, California, Danny Lebern Glover was born July 22, 1947. He attended San Francisco State University and trained at the Black Actors Workshop of the American Conservatory Theatre.

Glover went on to appear in many stage productions, including *The Island, Macbeth, Sizwe Banzi Is Dead,* and New York productions of *Suicide in B Flat, The Blood Knot,* and *Master Harold … and the Boys,* which won him a Theatre World Award.

Glover's film credits include *Escape from Alcatraz* (1979), *Chu Chu and the Philly Flash* (1984), *Iceman* (1984), *Witness* (1985), *Places in the Heart* (1985), *The Color Purple* (1985), *Lethal Weapon* (1987), *Bat*21* (1988), *Lethal Weapon 2* (1989), *Predator 2* (1990), *A Rage in Harlem* (1991), *Lethal Weapon 3* (1992), *Lethal Weapon 4* (1998), *Beloved* (1998), *Dreamgirls* (2006), and *2012* (2009).

On television Glover appeared in the hit series *Hill Street Blues* (1981), the miniseries *Chiefs* (1983), *Lonesome Dove* (1989), and other projects, including *The Face of Rage* (1983), *Mandela* (1987), *A Place at the Table* (1988), *A Raisin in the Sun* (1989), *Many Mansions* (1989), *Freedom Song* (2000), and *Brothers & Sisters* (2007–2008).

Glover's awards are numerous and include the Theatre World Award in 1982, MTV Movie Award in 1993, and induction into the Black Filmmakers Hall of Fame in 1998, five NAACP

Image Awards from 1989 to 2001, and a Lifetime Achievement Award from the Los Angeles Pan African Film Festival in 2003.

Savion Glover (1973–)
Choreographer

Savion Glover was born November 19, 1973, in Newark, New Jersey. By the age of seven Glover had taken drumming and tap lessons and had proved his natural talent for dance. He became the youngest person to enroll at the Newark Community School for the Arts. Glover's rhythm tap dancing, which is a form of tap that uses every aspect of the foot, earned him a role in the Broadway musical *The Tap Dance Kid*, first as an understudy and then as the lead in 1984. In 1989 he performed again on Broadway in the musical *Black and Blue* and was nominated for a Tony Award. Also in 1989 he had a role in the film *Tap,* which cast many of the tap masters.

In 1992 Glover became the youngest recipient of the National Endowment for the Arts grant. He continues to bring his unique style of tap, which he calls "free-form and hard core," to the stage and screen in productions such as *Bring in 'Da Noise, Bring in 'Da Funk,* which in 1996 won Glover four Tony Awards, including best choreographer. In 2007 he created stop-motion choreography for the main character in *Happy Feet,* an animated film.

Whoopi Goldberg (1949–)
Actress, Comedienne

Born Caryn E. Johnson in Manhattan's Chelsea District in New York, on November 13, 1949, Whoopi Goldberg began performing at the age of eight at the children's program at Hudson Guild and Helen Rubinstein Children's Theatre. After trying her hand at theater, improvisation, and chorus parts on Broadway, she moved to San Diego in

1974 and appeared in repertory productions of *Mother Courage* and *Getting Out.*

Goldberg joined the Black Street Hawkeyes Theatre in Berkeley as a partner with David Schein, then went solo to create *The Spook Show,* performing in San Francisco and later touring the United States and Europe.

In 1983 Goldberg's work caught the attention of Mike Nichols, who created and directed her Broadway show a year later. She made her film debut in *The Color Purple* (1985), winning an NAACP Image Award as well as a Golden Globe Award.

Goldberg has had roles in numerous films, including *Jumpin' Jack Flash* (1986), *Clara's Heart* (1988), *Ghost* (1990), for which she won an Academy Award as best supporting actress, *Sister Act* (1992), *Sarafina* (1992), and *Homie Spumoni* (2007). On television she received an Emmy nomination in 1985 for her guest appearance on *Moonlighting,* had a recurring role on *Star Trek: The Next Generation,* and was a founding member of the *Comic Relief* benefit shows.

Goldberg's career is one of a trailblazer. She was the first African American woman to host the Academy Awards four times—1994, 1996, 1999, and 2002. She is one of only a few actors who have the major awards of an Oscar (*Ghost*), a Tony (*Thoroughly Modern Millie*), an Emmy (*Beyond Tara: the Extraordinary Life of Hattie Mc-Daniel*), and a Grammy (*Whoopi: Direct from Broadway*). In 2001 she was honored with a star on the Walk of Fame and awarded the Mark Twain Prize for American Humor.

From August 2006 to March 2008 Goldberg hosted a national syndicated talk radio show *Wake up with Whoopi,* and on September 4, 2007, she became the moderator and co-host of the television talk show *The View.*

Louis Gossett Jr. (1936–)
Actor

Born in Brooklyn, New York, on May 27, 1936, Louis Gossett Jr. began acting at the age of sev-

enteen when a leg injury prevented him from pursuing his first love—basketball. In 1953 he surpassed over 445 contenders for the role of a black youngster in *Take a Giant Step,* for which he received a Donaldson Award as best newcomer of the year.

While performing in *The Desk Set* in 1958, Gossett was drafted by the professional basketball team the New York Knicks, but decided to remain in the theater. Ultimately, he appeared in more than sixty stage productions, including such plays as *Lost in the Stars* (1958), *A Raisin in the Sun* (1959), *The Blacks* (1961), and *Murderous Angels* (1969).

On television Gossett played character roles in such series as *The Nurses, The Defenders,* and *East Side, West Side.* In 1977 he won an Emmy for his performance in the acclaimed miniseries *Roots.* He also starred in such films as *Skin Game* (1971), *The Deep* (1977), *An Officer and a Gentleman* (1983), *Iron Eagle* (1986), *Iron Eagle II* (1988), *Daddy's Little Girl* (2007), *The Least Among You* (2009), and *Why Did I Get Married Too?* (2010).

In 1989 Gossett starred in his own television series, *Gideon Oliver,* followed by television shows such as *Ray Alexander: A Taste for Justice* (1994), *The Inspectors* (1998), *For Love of Olivia* (2001), *Stargate SG-1* (2005–2006), and *ER* (2009).

Gossett includes among his awards an Academy Award, two Golden Globes, and an Emmy Award.

Dick Gregory (1932–)
Comedian, Activist

Richard Claxton Gregory was born on October 12, 1932, in St Louis, Missouri. Since his father was often absent from the home the family endured poverty and were on welfare. In defending himself against the taunts of other children, Gregory learned that laughter was liberating and resulted in less bullying. Gregory practiced his comedy from that point on and into his years in the U.S. military.

Discharged from the military in 1956, Gregory pursued a career in stand-up comedy. After a failed venture with a club he opened, Gregory got the opportunity in 1961 to perform at the Playboy Club and ended up with a three-year contract. Gregory's performances lead to national network exposure on shows like the *The Jack Paar Show*.

With the civil rights movement of the 1960s Gregory used his visibility to bring attention to the racism and inequities going on in the country. Eventually Gregory withdrew from entertainment and fully committed himself to the movement. In the 1970s Gregory was involved in health and nutrition issues and founded Health Enterprises, which focused on marketing a diet drink.

Gregory returned to the stage in 1990 to a new generation, and in 2000 he published *Callus on My Soul: A Memoir*. Gregory remains a highly sought speaker. He has received numerous honorary degrees and awards including The Ebony-Topaz Heritage and Freedom Award, and the Wellness of You 2001 Tree of Life Award. Gregory is a social activist who speaks out against injustice while infusing the experience with humor.

Pam Grier (1949–)

Actress

Pam Grier was born on May 26, 1949, in Winston-Salem, North Carolina. Grier's father had a military career, which kept her family moving often until she was fourteen. The family settled in Denver, Colorado, and after high school she enrolled in Metropolitan State College. In 1967 she entered the Miss Colorado Universe contest in hopes of winning prize money to assist with her tuition. Although she won second place she caught the eye of an agent.

Grier's first film role was in 1969, but throughout the 1970s she was a box office draw.

Her films were categorized as part of the blaxploitation film movement, but the characters had confidence and strength. Her films include *Coffy* (1973) and *Foxy Brown* (1974). By the 1980s and 1990s Grier had moved into television with a regular role on *Miami Vice* and had appeared in movies such as *Jackie Brown* (1997), *Jawbreakers* (1999), and *Bones* (2001).

Grier's roles as a strong confident African American woman had a powerful influence on the African American community by showing a view beyond the stereotypes and negative images that permeated the American social perspective. Grier received the NAACP Image Award in 1986, an award from the National Black Theater Festival, and the African American Film Society, and was named by *Ebony* as one of the "100 Most Fascinating Black Women" of the twentieth century.

Juanita Hall (1901–1968)

Singer, Actress

Born on November 6, 1901, in Keyport, New Jersey, Juanita Hall studied at the Juilliard School of Music after singing in Catholic church choirs as a child. Hall devoted her life to music as a singer in choirs and in stage and movie productions.

Her first major stage appearance was in Ziegfeld's *Show Boat* in 1928. Her lengthy stage career culminated in her role as Bloody Mary in Richard Rodgers and Oscar Hammerstein's *South Pacific* in 1949. Hall went on to appear in *Flower Drum Song* and the movie versions of both shows. She served as a soloist and assistant director of the Hall Johnson Choir (1931–1936), conducted the Works Progress Administration Chorus in New York City (1936–1941), and organized the Juanita Hall Choir in 1942.

Hall performed at the London Palladium and was a guest on *The Ed Sullivan Show* and *The Perry Como Show*. She was the recipient of a Donaldson, a Tony, and the Bill Bojangles Awards. Hall died February 28, 1968, in Bay Shore, New York.

Henry Hampton (1940–1998)
Filmmaker

Henry Eugene Hampton Jr. was born on January 8, 1940, in St. Louis, Missouri, and went on to earn his B.A. from Washington University in 1961. In 1968 he started a production company called Blackside Inc., which focused on documentaries and films about the black experience.

Hampton's company produced over sixty films with the goal of effecting social change. From 1968 to 1998 his projects at Blackside were numerous and include *America's War on Poverty*, a five part series, *Code Blue*, and *An American Experience*. Hampton is best known for his 1987, fourteen-hour documentary *Eyes on the Prize: American's Civil Rights Years (1954-1965)* which captured over 20 million viewers when the series was aired on primetime PBS stations. In 1990 he produced *Eyes on the Prize II: America at the Racial Crosssroads* (1966 – mid-1980s). His work earned him numerous awards and honors, including six Emmys, an Academy Award nomination, and the Dupont-Columbia Award for excellence in journalism. Hampton's documentary *I'll Make Me a World*, a six-hour series on African American creative artists, was presented in 1999 in memoriam after his death in 1998.

Hill Harper (1966–)
Actor, Author

Francis Harper, better known as Hill Harper, was born on May 17, 1966, in Iowa City, Iowa. Harper graduated magna cum laude from Brown University, he earned a J.D. cum laude from Harvard Law School, and a Master of Public Administration from the John F. Kennedy School of Government at Harvard University.

Harper began in film and television in 1993 on the series *Married with Children*. He went on to a featured role in Spike Lee's *Get on the Bus* (1996) and *He Got Game* (1998). Hill is best known for his role on the popular television show *CSI: NY*.

Harper is the author of three books, including *The Conversation: How Black Men and Women Can Build Loving, Trusting Relationships*, published in 2010. He has been awarded the NAACP Image Award for outstanding actor in a drama series for three consecutive years, 2008, 2009, and 2010.

Leonard Harper (1899–1943)
Dancer, Choreographer

Leonard Harper was born into a show-business family in Birmingham, Alabama, in 1899. When his father died he took care of the family by working in vaudeville. Harper later traveled to Chicago and met a new partner who became his wife. The couple, Harper and Blake, broke the color barrier and performed on the Shubert's Select white theatre circuit in 1921 and performed in formal attire unlike other black acts.

In 1922 after touring the United States and later London, Harper pioneered a form of musical production involving an intimate nightclub scene. Hired as floor manager for clubs during the Harlem Renaissance, such as Connie's Inn, the Plantation Club, the Cotton Club, Smalls Paradise, and the Apollo Theatre, Harper broke new ground for nightclub entertainment. He took his musical experiences and produced the stage show *Hollywood Follies*. He performed in various other stage productions and produced *Keep Shufflin'* (1928) and *Hot Chocolate* (1929) with music composed by Fats Waller. The production featured Louis Armstrong and Cab Calloway. Leonard Harper died in 1943 while rehearsing a nightclub show.

Robin Harris (1953–1990)
Comedian, Actor

Robin Harris was born on August 30, 1953, in Chicago, Illinois. Harris attended Ottawa University in Kansas and upon graduation began to pursue comedy. Inspired by comedians such as Redd Foxx, Harris began to make a name for himself as master of ceremony at the Comedy Act Theater in Los Angeles, California, in 1985.

Spike Lee recognized Harris's talent and cast him in *Do the Right Thing* in 1989, followed by film roles in *I'm Gonna Get You Sucka* and *Harlem Nights*. In 1990 Harris also had a role in *House Party*. Harris's career became hectic as he landed an HBO comedy special, a voice-over for the animated film *Bebe's Kids,* and the release of a comedy album. Harris was unable to handle the heavy schedule and died on March 18, 1990, of heart failure. Both his HBO special and the animated movie *Bebe's Kids* were released posthumously.

Richard B. Harrison (1864–1935)
Actor

Richard B. Harrison was born in Canada in 1864 and moved to Detroit, Michigan, as a young boy. There he worked as a waiter, porter, and handyman, saving whatever money he could to attend the theatrical offerings playing in town. After studying drama in Detroit, he made his professional debut in Canada in a program of readings and recitations.

For three decades, Harrison entertained black audiences with one-man performances of recitations from *Macbeth, Julius Caesar,* and *Damon and Pythias,* as well as poems by Shakespeare, Poe, Kipling, and Paul Laurence Dunbar. In 1929, while serving on the faculty of North Carolina A&T State University as drama instructor, he was chosen for the part in *The Green Pastures.*

Harrison was one of the few actors to gain national prominence on the basis of one role, his characterization of "De Lawd" in *The Green Pastures.* When he died in 1935, Harrison had performed as "De Lawd" 1,656 times. His work earned him the 1930 Spingarn Medal and numerous honorary degrees.

Gregory Hines (1946–2003)
Dancer, Actor

Born in New York City on Valentine's Day in 1946, Gregory Hines began dancing with his brother Maurice under the instruction of tap dancer Henry LeTang. When Gregory was five, the brothers began performing professionally as the Hines Kids. Appearing in nightclubs and theaters around the country, they were able to benefit from contact with dance legends such as Charles "Honi" Coles, Howard "Sandman" Sims, the Nicholas Brothers, and Teddy Hale.

As teenagers the two brothers performed as the Hines Brothers. When Gregory reached the age of eighteen, the two were joined by their father, Maurice Sr., on drums, and the trio became known as Hines, Hines and Dad. They performed internationally and appeared on *The Tonight Show*. Eventually, Gregory tired of touring and settled in California, where he formed the jazz-rock band Severance.

After a distinguished career as a tap dancer, Hines made an unusual transition to dramatic actor. He subsequently moved back to New York and landed a role in *The Last Minstrel Show* (1978). He later appeared in such Broadway musicals as *Eubie!* (1978), *Sophisticated Ladies* (1981), and *Comin' Uptown* (1990), as well as feature films, including *The Cotton Club* (1985), *White Nights* (1985), *Running Scared* (1985), and *Off Limits* (1988). Hines starred in the 1989 TriStar film *Tap* with Sammy Davis, Jr., not only acting and dancing, but singing as well.

On television Hines appeared in the series *Amazing Stories* and the special *Motown Returns to the Apollo,* which earned him an Emmy nomination. When not appearing in films or television, he toured internationally with a solo club act. *Gregory Hines,* his first solo album, was released by CBS/Epic in 1988. The album was produced by Luther Vandross, who teamed with Gregory for a single, "There's Nothing Better Than Love," which reached number one on the R&B charts in 1987.

Hines received numerous awards, including the Dance Educators of America Award and the Theater World Award. The recipient of numerous Tony nominations, Hines received the award in 1992 for best actor in a musical for his role in *Jelly's Last Jam*. Hines died of liver cancer on August 9, 2003.

Geoffrey Holder (1930–)

Actor, Dancer, Choreographer, Costume Designer, Director, Author

 Geoffrey Holder was born on August 1, 1930, in Port-of-Spain, Trinidad. At an early age he left school to become the costume designer for his brother's dance troupe, which he took over in 1948. Holder led the dancers, singers, and steel band musicians through a series of successful small revues to the Caribbean Festival in Puerto Rico, where they represented Trinidad and Tobago. His appearances with his troupe in the mid-1950s were so popular that he is credited with launching the calypso vogue.

Early in his career, Holder appeared in New York as a featured dancer in *House of Flowers* (1954). He later performed with the Metropolitan Opera and as a guest star on many television shows. Film credits include the James Bond adventure *Live and Let Die* (1973) and *Dr. Doolittle* (1967), the children's classic starring Rex Harrison.

A successful artist in many areas, Holder received two Tony Awards in 1976, as director and costume designer for the Broadway show *The Wiz*, the all-black adaptation of *The Wizard of Oz*. In 1978 he directed and choreographed the successful Broadway musical *Timbuktu*. In 1982 Holder appeared in the film *Annie* based on the hit Broadway musical, playing Punjab—a character from the original comic strip; and in 1992 he appeared in the film *Boomerang,* starring Eddie Murphy.

Holder received a Guggenheim Fellowship to pursue painting; his impressionist paintings have been shown in galleries such as the Corcoran in Washington, D.C. Holder also has written two books. *Black Gods, Green Islands,* published in 1969, is a retelling of West Indian legends; his *Caribbean Cookbook,* which Holder also illustrated, is a collection of recipes.

Holder is married to the ballet dancer Carmen de Lavallade.

Lena Horne (1917–2010)

Singer, Actress

Lena Mary Calhoun Horne was born on June 30, 1917, in Brooklyn, New York. She joined the chorus line at the Cotton Club in 1933, and then left to tour as a dancer with Noble Sissle's orchestra. She was given a leading role in *Blackbirds of 1939,* but the show folded quickly, whereupon she left to join Charlie Barnett's band as a singer. She made her first records (including the popular "Haunted Town") with Barnett. In the early 1940s she also worked at New York's famous Cafe Society Downtown.

Horne was called the most beautiful woman in the world, and her beauty was no small factor in the success of her stage, screen, and nightclub career. She went to Hollywood, where she became the first black woman to sign a term contract with a film studio. Her films included *Panama Hattie* (1942), *Cabin in the Sky* (1943), *Stormy Weather* (1943), and *Meet Me in Las Vegas* (1956). In 1957 she took a break from her film and nightclub schedule to star in her first Broadway musical, *Jamaica.* Her popular recordings included "Stormy Weather," "Blues in the Night," "The Lady Is a Tramp," and "Mad about the Boy."

Throughout the 1960s and 1970s, Horne appeared in nightclubs and concerts. On May 12, 1981, she opened a one-woman show called *Lena Horne: The Lady and Her Music* to critical and box-office acclaim. Although it opened too late to qualify for a Tony Award nomination, the show was awarded a special Tony at the June ceremonies. In December of that year she received New York City's highest cultural award, the Handel Medallion, for her contribution to the city's intellectual and cultural life.

Horne was married for twenty-three years to Lennie Hayton, a white composer, arranger, and conductor, who died April 24, 1971. She had been married previously to Louis Jordan Jones. A generous and gracious woman, Horne quietly devoted much time to humanitarian causes.

Between 1994 and 1998 Horne released four new recordings: *We'll Be Together Again, An*

Evening with Lena Horne, Lena Horne at Metro-Goldwyn-Mayer: Ain't It the Truth, and *Being Myself.* Lena Horne died on May 9, 2010.

Djimon Hounsou (1964–)
Actor

Djimon Hounsou was born in West Africa on April 24, 1964. He moved to Paris, France, with his parents at age thirteen, and he became a high fashion model. He caught the attention of the film industry as star of the film *Amistad* (1998), which recounts the historical experience of Joseph Cinqué, an African who lead a slave revolt in the 1800s. In 2004 Hounsou received an Oscar nomination for his performance in the film *America,* and a second Oscar nomination in 2006 for the film *Blood Diamond.*

Samuel L. Jackson (1948–)
Actor

 Samuel L. Jackson was born in Chattanooga, Tennessee, on December 21, 1948, and grew up with an interest in theater. While at Morehouse College he earned a dramatic arts degree and moved to New York City to pursue his career.

Jackson began to make progress after Spike Lee noticed him in a 1981 stage production of *A Soldier's Story.* He later collaborated with Lee and had roles in his films *School Daze* (1988) and *Do the Right Thing* (1989), among other films. Jackson received critical acclaim for his role as a crack addict in the film *Jungle Fever* (1991). He won several awards for his performance, including a Cannes Film Festival award for best supporting actor. He also garnered attention for his roles in *Patriot Games* (1992), *Jurassic Park* (1993), and *Menace II Society* (1993). His career continued on a high note with the film *Pulp Fiction* (1994).

Jackson continues to have roles in key films and many blockbusters that showcase his talents. In 2000 he had the starring role in *Shaft,* followed by 2002 roles in *Changing Lanes* and *Star Wars: Episode II—Attack of the Clones*. In 2009, Jackson signed a nine-picture deal with Marvel Comics to play the character Nick Fury.

Judith Jamison (1943–)
Choreographer

Born in Philadelphia, Pennsylvania, on May 10, 1943, Judith Jamison started to study dance at the age of six. She was discovered in her early twenties by the choreographer Agnes de Mille, who admired her spontaneous style.

From 1965 to 1980 Jamison was a principal dancer for Alvin Ailey's American Dance Theater, performing a wide gamut of black roles that Ailey choreographed for her. She has made guest appearances with many other dance companies, including the American Ballet Theatre, and with such opera companies as the Vienna State Opera and the Munich State Opera. In the 1980s Jamison scored a great success on Broadway in *Sophisticated Ladies,* a musical featuring the music of Duke Ellington. In 1988 she formed her own modern dance company, the Jamison Project.

In 1989, with the death of Alvin Ailey, Jamison was named the artistic director of Alvin Ailey American Dance Theater. The company continued to travel worldwide and performed at the 1996 and the 2002 Olympic Games. Jameson also developed the Women's Choreography Initiative to encourage young women performers.

Jamison's work as a choreographer includes *Hymn* (1993), *Riverside* (1995), *Sweet Release* (1996), *Echo: Far from Home* (1998), and *Double Exposure* (2002). Her awards include the Dance USA Award in 1998, with Jamison being the youngest recipient; in 2000 she received Kennedy Center Honors; in 2002 she was the recipient of the National Medal of Arts; and in 2003, she received the Making a Difference Award from the NAACP.

Jamison announced her retirement as artistic director of the Alvin Ailey American Dance Theater in June 2011, passing the mantle to a long time member of the group, Robert Battle.

Bill T. Jones (1952–)
Dancer, Choreographer

Bill T. Jones was born in Bunnell, Florida, on February 15, 1952, and his family later moved to New York. In high school Jones was very athletic and when he enrolled in State University of New York at Binghamton in the 1970s he chose the dance department. Jones and college friend Arnie Zane became lovers and colleagues and formed a dance company to pursue their common interest of dance.

After returning to New York from Amsterdam, Jones and Zane formed another dance company that gained critical acclaim. With the death of Zane in 1988 due to AIDS, Jones channeled his grief into the creative work *Absence,* which was performed in 1989; after the loss of another member of the company, he wrote *D-Man in the Waters,* also performed in 1989. His works include *Mother of Three Sons* (1991); he has directed *Lost in the Stars, Dream on Monkey Mountain,* and *Still/Here,* a PBS documentary. Jones has done collaborative work with Toni Morrison, Max Roach, and Jessye Norman. Jones has continued to write socially conscious works that address sexuality, cultural experiences, and individuial differences.

Jones has received numerous awards including the MacArthur Foundation Fellowship in 1994, the Isadora Duncan Dance Award in 2001, the Dorothy and Lillian Gish Prize in 2003, the Wexner, and the Lifetime Achievement Award in 2005, and a Tony Award in 2010 for best choreography for his work in the play *Fela!* Jones was also honored at the Kennedy Center in 2010.

James Earl Jones (1931–)
Actor

James Earl Jones (whose father, Robert Earl Jones, was featured in the movie *One Potato, Two Potato*) was born on January 17, 1931, in Tate County, Mississippi, and raised by his grandparents on a farm near Jackson, Michigan. He turned to acting after a brief period as a pre-medical student at the University of Michigan (from which he graduated cum laude in 1953) and upon completion of military service with the Army's Cold Weather Mountain Training Command in Colorado.

After moving to New York, Jones studied at the American Theatre Wing, making his off-Broadway debut in 1957 in *Wedding in Japan.* Since then, he has appeared in numerous plays, on and off-Broadway, including *Sunrise at Campobello* (1958), *The Cool World* (1960), *The Blacks* (1961), *The Blood Knot* (1964), and *Anyone, Anyone* (1965).

Jones's career as an actor progressed slowly until he portrayed Jack Jefferson in the Broadway smash hit *The Great White Hope.* The play was based on the life of Jack Johnson, the first black heavyweight champion. For this performance Jones received the 1969 Tony Award for the best dramatic actor in a Broadway play, and a Drama Desk Award for one of the best performances of the 1968–1969 New York season.

By the 1970s Jones was appearing in roles traditionally performed by white actors, including the title role in *King Lear* and an award-winning performance as Lenny in John Steinbeck's *Of Mice and Men.*

In 1978 Jones appeared in the highly controversial *Paul Robeson,* a one-man show on Broadway. Many leading blacks advocated a boycott of the show because they felt it did not measure up to the man himself. Many critics, however, gave the show high praise.

In 1980 Jones starred in Athol Fugard's *A Lesson from Aloes,* a top contender for a Tony Award that year. He also appeared in the Yale Repertory Theater Production of *Hedda Gabler.* In the spring of 1982 he costarred with Christopher Plummer on Broadway in *Othello,* a production that was acclaimed as among the best ever done. In 1987 Jones received a Tony Award for his performance in August Wilson's Pulitzer Prize–winning play *Fences.*

Jones's film credits include *Dr. Strangelove* (1964) and *Field of Dreams* (1989). He was the screen voice of Darth Vader in *Star Wars* (1977), *The Empire Strikes Back* (1980), *and Return of the*

Jedi (1983). His credits also include *The Sandlot* (1993), *The Lion King* (1994), *Cry, the Beloved Country* (1995), *A Family Thing* (1996), and *Finder's Fee* (2001). Among numerous television appearances, Jones portrayed author Alex Haley in *Roots: The Next Generations* (1979), *Under One Roof* (1995), *The Feast of All Saints* (2001), and *Welcome Home, Roscoe Jenkins* (2008).

In 1976 Jones was elected to the board of governors of the Academy of Motion Picture Arts and Sciences. In 1979 New York City presented him with the Mayor's Award of Honor for Arts and Culture. He received an honorary doctorate of humane letters from the University of Michigan in 1971 and the New York Man of the Year Award in 1976. In 1985 he was inducted into the Theater Hall of Fame. Among Jones's many awards, including Emmys and Golden Globes, is a 2009 Lifetime Achievement Award from the Screen Actors Guild.

Woodie King Jr. (1937–)
Producer, Director, Writer

Woodie King Jr. was born in Mobile, Alabama, on July 27, 1937, but grew up in Detroit, Michigan. Initially King wanted to be an actor and study his craft with other actors such as Vincent Price and Helen Hayes only to be frustrated by the lack of opportunities for black actors.

While attending Wayne State University, King met other students who had similar interests and formed a group. With the production of a play that allowed them to perform in New York, King decided to remain in New York in 1964 and eventually started his own company.

King's company, named The New Federal Theatre (NFT) after the government-sponsored theater of the 1930s, found a great degree of success. Many writers, including J. E. Franklin, Ron Milner, Ed Bullins, Damien Leake, Alexis DeVeaux, and Dr. Endesha Hollard, brought national attention. Such notable actors as Jackee Harry, Morgan Freeman, Denzel Washington, Phylicia Rashad, Laurence Fishburne, Robert

Downey Jr., Debbie Morgan, and Lynn Whitfield also launched their careers there.

King also co-produced productions such as *For Colored Girls Who Have Considered Suicide When the Rainbow Is Enuf* (1976), and has co-authored anthologies and collections of essays.

In 1977 King was awarded the Obie Award for sustained achievement, and the Actors' Equity Association's Paul Robeson Award in 2004. King continues to produce and co-produce works at NFT, which serves as a place where writers from different backgrounds can showcase their work.

Martin Lawrence (1965–)
Comedian, Actor

Martin Lawrence was born in Frankfurt, West Germany, on April 16, 1965, and grew up in Landover, Maryland. Lawrence knew early on that he wanted to be in entertainment. His opportunity came in the 1990s when he got roles in the sitcom *What's Happening Now!* as well as in the films *Do the Right Thing* (1989), *House Party* (1990), *House Party 2* (1991), *Boomerang* (1992), and *House Party 3* (1994). More recently, Lawrence has appeared in films such as *Big Momma's House* (2000), *Black Knight* (2001), *Big Momma's House 2* (2007), and Disney's *College Road Trip* (2008), co-starring Raven Symone.

In 1992 his comedic style earned him his own show, *Martin*, which lasted until 1997. In 1996 Lawrence received an Image Award from the NAACP.

Canada Lee (1907–1952)
Actor

Canada Lee was born Leonard Lionel Cornelius Canegata in Manhattan, New York, on May 3, 1907. After studying violin as a young boy, he ran off to Saratoga to become a jockey. Failing in this, he returned to New York City and began a boxing career. In 1926, after winning ninety out of one hundred fights, including the national amateur lightweight title, he turned professional. Over the next few years he won 175 out of some 200 fights against such top opponents as Jack Britton and Vince Dundee. In 1933 a detached retina brought an end to his ring career. He had acquired the name Canada Lee when a ring announcer could not pronounce his real name.

In 1934 Lee successfully auditioned at the Harlem YMCA for his first acting role, which was in a Works Progress Administration production of *Brother Moses.* In 1941 Orson Welles, who had met Lee in the Federal Theater Project's all-black production of *Macbeth,* chose him to play Bigger Thomas in the stage version of Richard Wright's famed novel, *Native Son.*

In 1944 Lee served as narrator of a radio series called *New World Comin',* the first such series devoted to racial issues. That same year, he also appeared in Alfred Hitchcock's film *Lifeboat,* and in the Broadway play *Anna Lucasta.* Lee's activism against racism and discrimination resulted in his name being placed on a blacklist in Hollywood and he also was suspected of being a communist.

In 1950 Lee starred in a British production of *Cry, the Beloved Country.* Lee, stressed by the blacklisting, had a heart attack and died on May 8, 1952.

Spike Lee (1957–)
Filmmaker

Shelton "Spike" Lee was born March 20, 1957, in Atlanta, Georgia. His family moved briefly to Chicago, Illinois, before settling in New York in 1959. Lee received a B.A. in mass communication in 1979 from Morehouse College. After a summer internship at Columbia Pictures in Burbank, California, Lee enrolled in New York University's prestigious Institute of Film and Television. He

received an M.A. in filmmaking in 1983. While at New York University he wrote and directed *Joe's Bed-Stuy Barbershop: We Cut Heads,* for which he won the 1982 Student Academy Award given by the Academy of Motion Picture Arts and Sciences. The movie was later shown on public television's *Independent Focus* series.

Notable films by Lee include *She's Gotta Have It* (1986), *School Daze* (1988), *Do the Right Thing* (1989), *Mo' Better Blues* (1990), *Jungle Fever* (1991), *Malcolm X* (1992), *Crooklyn* (1994), *Girl 6* (1996), *Bamboozled* (2000), and *Miracle at St. Anna* (2008). *She's Gotta Have It* won the L.A. Film Critics New Generation Award and the Prix de Jeunesse at the Cannes Film Festival.

Lee produced the documentary *4 Little Girls* (1997) about the four little girls who died in the Birmingham church bombing in 1963, which won an Academy Award, and *When the Levees Broke* (2006) about the Hurricane Katrina disaster.

Lee has also written two books: *Spike Lee's Gotta Have It: Inside Guerrilla Filmmaking* (1987) and *Uplift the Race* (1988). He has established a fellowship for minority filmmakers at New York University and is a trustee of Morehouse College. Lee's production company, Forty Acres and a Mule Filmworks, is located in Brooklyn, New York.

Jackie "Moms" Mabley (1894–1975)
Comedienne

Jackie "Moms" Mabley was born Loretta Mary Aiken in Brevard, North Carolina, on March 19, 1894, and entered show business as a teenager when the team of Buck and Bubbles gave her a bit part in a vaudeville skit called "Rich Aunt from Utah."

With the help of comedienne Bonnie Bell Drew, Mabley developed a monologue and was soon being booked on the black vaudeville circuit. Influenced by such acts as Butterbeans and Susie, she developed her own comic character, a world-weary old woman in a funny hat and droopy stockings, delivering her gags with a mixture of sassy folk wisdom and sly insights.

Her first big success came in 1923 at Connie's Inn in New York. Engagements at the Cotton Club in Harlem and at Club Harlem in Atlantic City followed.

Moms Mabley was noticed by white audiences in the early 1960s. Her record album *Moms Mabley at the U.N.* became a commercial success and was followed by *Moms Mabley at the Geneva Conference*. In 1962 she made her Carnegie Hall debut on a program with Cannonball Adderley and Nancy Wilson. Her subsequent Broadway, film, television, and record successes made her the favorite of a new generation.

Moms Mabley died on May 23, 1975, at the age of seventy-eight in a White Plains, New York, hospital.

Bernie Mac (1957–2008)
Comedian, Actor

Bernard "Bernie Mac" McCullough was born October 5, 1957, in Chicago, Illinois. After realizing the power of comedy, Bernie Mac decided that was what he wanted to do. His career began to take off in 1990 when he won the Miller Lite Comedy Search. He received a spot on the HBO *Def Comedy Jam*, which led to a role in the film *Mo' Money* (1992). Mac later wrote his own show on HBO, *Midnight Mac,* which earned him a nomination for a CableACE Award in 1995.

In 1997 Mac joined three other comics on the *Original Kings of Comedy Tour,* featuring D. L. Hughley, Cedric the Entertainer, and Steve Harvey. The tour became the highest grossing comedy tour in history. The tour was filmed by Spike Lee and became a highly successful DVD. Following this success Mac went on to do a series of films including *Ocean's 11* (2001) and launched *The Bernie Mac Show* in 2001, which ran for five years. He was featured in films such as *Charlie's Angels 2: Full Throttle* (2003), *Mr. 3000* (2004), *Guess Who* (2005), *Transformers* (2007), *Ocean's 13* (2007), and posthumously, *Soul Men* (2008) and *Old Dogs* (2009).

Due to complications associated with a diagnosis of sarcoidosis, Bernie Mac died on August 8, 2008, from pneumonia.

Hattie McDaniel (1898–1952)
Actress

Hattie McDaniel was born on June 10, 1898, in Wichita, Kansas, and moved to Denver, Colorado, as a child. After a period of singing for Denver radio as an amateur, she entered vaudeville professionally and by 1924 was a headliner on the Pantages Circuit.

By 1931 McDaniel had made her way to Hollywood. After a slow start, during which she supported herself as a maid and washer woman, she gradually began to acquire more movie roles. Her early film credits include *Judge Priest* (1934), *The Little Colonel* (1935), *Show Boat* (1936), *Saratoga* (1937), and *Nothing Sacred*. Her portrayal of a "mammy" figure in *Gone with the Wind*, a role for which she received an Oscar in 1940 as best supporting actress, is still regarded as a definitive interpretation. She was the first African American to receive an Oscar.

McDaniel subsequently appeared in films such as *The Great Lie* (1941), *In This Our Life* (1942), *Johnny Come Lately* (1943), *Since You Went Away* (1944), *Margie* (1946), *Never Say Goodbye* (1946), *Song of the South* (1946), *Mr. Blandings Builds His Dream House* (1948), *Family Honeymoon* (1948), and *The Big Wheel* (1949).

In addition to her movie roles, McDaniel enjoyed success in radio during the 1930s as HiHat Hattie, and during the 1940s in the title role of the very successful *Beulah* series. McDaniel died on October 26, 1952.

Butterfly McQueen (1911–1995)
Actress

Born Thelma McQueen on January 8, 1911, in Tampa, Florida, Buttterfly McQueen began her career in the 1930s performing as a radio actress in *The Goldbergs, The Danny Kaye Show, The Jack Benny Show,* and *The Beulah Show.* She also appeared on stage in *Brown Sugar* (1937), *Brother Rat* (1937), and *What a Life* (1938).

McQueen's portrayal of Prissy in *Gone with the Wind* (1939) rivals Hattie McDaniel's Oscar-winning role as the "mammy," and is certainly as popular with audiences as Vivien Leigh's Scarlett O'Hara or Clark Gable's Rhett Butler. After her role in *Gone with the Wind,* McQueen was cast in other motion pictures such as *I Dood It* (1943), *Cabin in the Sky* (1943), *Mildred Pierce* (1945), and *Duel in the Sun* (1946). She appeared as Oriole on the television series *Beulah* from 1950 to 1952.

Given her outspokenness against racism and discrimination and her refusal to play stereotypical servant roles, McQueen's appearances after this period were sporadic. In 1968 she won accolades for her performance in the Off-Broadway play *Curley McDimple.* She was cast in the television program *The Seven Wishes of Joanna Peabody* in 1978, and the film *The Mosquito Coast* in 1986. McQueen received a B.A. in Spanish from New York City College in 1975. She died on December 22, 1995, from severe burns due to a fire in her home.

Oscar Micheaux (1884–1951)
Filmmaker, Author

Oscar Devereaux Micheaux was born January 2, 1884, in Metropolis, Illinois. Little is known about his early years other than his leaving home at age seventeen and his brief work as a Pullman porter. In 1904 he began homesteading in Gregory County, South Dakota.

Micheaux was a farmer who loved to read and had a flair for writing. In 1913 he wrote, published, and promoted *The Conquest: Story of a Negro Pioneer.* This novel was followed by *Forged Note: Romance of the Darker Races* in 1915 and *The Homesteader* in 1917. Much of his writing was melodramatic and probably autobiographical.

In 1918 the Lincoln Picture Company, an independent African American film producer, tried to buy the film rights to *The Homesteader.* When Micheaux insisted that he direct the planned movie, the deal fell through. Micheaux went to New York, where he formed the Oscar Micheaux Corporation. Between 1919 and 1937 Micheaux made about thirty films, including *Body and Soul,* a 1924 movie in which Paul Robeson made his first cinematic appearance.

Although Micheaux was an excellent self-promoter of his books and films, his company went into bankruptcy in 1928. By 1931, however, Micheaux was back in the film business, producing and directing *The Exile* (1931) and *Veiled Aristocrats* (1932). Between 1941 and 1943 he wrote four more books, *Wind from Nowhere, The Case of Mrs. Wingate, Masquerade,* and *The Story of Dorothy Stansfield.* In 1948 he made his last film, *The Betrayal.*

None of Micheaux's films achieved critical acclaim but they were quite popular with African American audiences and attracted a limited white following. Although his characters broke with the black stereotypes of the day, the themes of his movies ignored racial injustice and the day-to-day problems of African Americans.

Micheaux was known as a hard worker and a natty dresser who consumed neither alcohol nor tobacco. Although he made a great deal of money, he squandered it all and died penniless in Charlotte, North Carolina. Conflicting dates are given for his death: March 26, 1951, and April 1, 1951.

Florence Mills (1895–1927)
Dancer

Florence Mills was born in Washington, D.C., on January 25, 1895. She made her debut at the age of five in *Sons of Ham.* In 1903 the family moved to Harlem and she joined her sisters in an act called the Mills Trio in 1910. She later appeared with a group called the Panama Four, which included Ada "Bricktop" Smith.

In 1921 Mills appeared in *Shuffle Along,* a prototype for African American musicals, and her success led to a long engagement at the Plantation, a New York night spot. After a successful appearance in London, she returned to the United States in 1924 to star in *From Dixie to*

Broadway, in which she performed her trademark song, "I'm a Little Blackbird Looking for a Bluebird." Later, her own Blackbirds revue was a great success in London and Paris.

Mills returned to the United States in 1927. Exhausted by her work abroad, she entered the hospital on October 25 for a routine appendectomy, and died suddenly a few days later.

Arthur Mitchell (1934–)
Dancer, Choreographer

Arthur Mitchell was born in Harlem, New York, on March 27, 1934, and attended New York's famed High School of Performing Arts. Mitchell was the first African American male to receive the high school's dance award in 1951.

Upon graduation in 1952 Mitchell enrolled on a scholarship in the School of American Ballet, run by the eminent choreographer George Balanchine, who also directed the New York City Ballet. In 1955 Mitchell was invited by Balanchine to join the New York City Ballet. Before long he was a principal dancer in the company, performing in such works as *Agon* and *A Midsummer Night's Dream*.

Mitchell left the New York City Ballet in 1969 to establish the Dance Theatre of Harlem (DTH), which he founded to give young African Americans an opportunity to get out of the ghetto through the arts. Mitchell and DTH have received numerous awards and citations, including the Changers Award given by *Mademoiselle* magazine in 1970, and the Capezio Dance Award in 1971. DTH and Mitchell were honored at the White House by President George W. Bush in 2006.

Mitchell himself has received numerous awards including Kennedy Center Honors and the National Medal of Arts in 1993, a Lifetime Achievement Award from the School of American Ballet in 1995, induction into the Dance Hall of Fame in 1999, a Gold Medal at the Sixth New York

International Ballet Competition in 2001, and a Fletcher Foundation Fellowship in 2005 for his contributions to the African American community.

Mo'Nique (1967–)
Actress

Mo'Nique Imes was born December 11, 1967, in Woodland, Maryland. Mo'Nique graduated from Milford Mill High School in Baltimore County and attended Morgan State University. In 1991, after an open-mic competition, she was hired to do comedy acts. After moving to Atlanta, more opportunities came her way. Determined to advance her career, Mo'Nique appeared on the television shows *Showtime at the Apollo*, *Def Comedy Jam*, and *Comic View*.

In 1999 Mo'Nique debuted her own television series *The Parkers*. This was followed by a spot on the *Queens of Comedy Tour*, which showcased four African American female comics. Later came movie roles in films such as *3 Strikes* (2000), *Baby Boy* (2001), and *Two Can Play at That Game* (2001). Mo'Nique was subsequently offered her own talk show, *The Mo'Nique Show*, by BET.

Many of the ventures pursued by Mo'Nique have been successful, from her full-figured clothing line, to her book *Skinny Women Are Evil: Notes of a Big Girl in a Small-minded World* in 2003, to her show called *F.A.T. Chance* (2005–2007), a beauty pageant for full-figured women, which was shown on the Oxygen network.

The range of Mo'Nique's talent was evident when she won the Academy Award for best performance by an actress in a supporting role for the film *Precious* (2010). Her performance also earned her a Screen Actors Guild Award for best supporting actress, and a Golden Globe.

Eddie Murphy (1961–)
Actor, Comedian, Producer

Edward Regan "Eddie" Murphy was born on April 3, 1961, in the Bushwick section of Brooklyn, New York, the son of a New York City policeman and an amateur comedian. As a youngster he performed imitations of cartoon characters; as he grew older he began preparing comic routines with impressions of Elvis Presley, Jackie Wilson, Al Green, and the Beatles.

Murphy attended Roosevelt Junior-Senior High School on Long Island and hosted a talent show at the Roosevelt Youth Center before beginning to call local talent agents to secure bookings at Long Island nightclubs. He was a little known stand-up comedian when he made his first appearance on the late night television show *Saturday Night Live* in 1980. He made a memorable impression and within three years was hailed as a major new star based on his work in the hit films *48 Hours* (1982) and *Trading Places* (1983).

After his success with the first two Paramount films, Murphy starred in *Beverly Hills Cop* (1985) and its sequel *Beverly Hills Cop II* (1987), which were two of the major box office hits of the decade. Murphy appeared in *The Golden Child* (1986), an effort at light-hearted fantasy, and followed it with the concert film *Eddie Murphy: Raw* (1987). Other film appearances include *Coming to America* (1988), *Harlem Nights* (1989), *Boomerang* (1992), *The Distinguished Gentleman* (1992), *Doctor Dolittle* (1998), *Life* (1999), *Nutty Professor II: The Klumps* (2000), *Shrek* (2001), *I Spy* (2002), *Daddy Daycare* (2003), *Shrek 2,* (2004), *Norbert* (2007), *Imagine That* (2009), *Nutty Professor* (2010), *Shrek Forever After* (2010), and *Tower Heist* (2011).

Murphy has earned recognition for his films, including Golden Globe Awards for *Beverly Hills Cop III* (1994), *The Nutty Professor* (1996), and *Dreamgirls* (2006).

Murphy's work as a comedian and actor, both on telelvision and film, as well as his singing career, have created a body of work that rivals the most successful of Hollywood entertainers.

Clarence Muse (1889–1979)
Actor, Director

Clarence Muse was born in Baltimore, Maryland, on October 14, 1889, though his parents came from Virginia and North Carolina, and his grandfather from Martinique. After studying law at Dickinson University in Pennsylvania, Muse sang as part of a hotel quartet in Palm Beach, Florida. A subsequent job with a stock company took him on tour through the South with his wife and son. Coming to New York, he barely scraped together a living, mostly performing as a vaudevillian.

Muse established himself as an actor and singer after several plays with the now famous Lincoln Theatre group and in 1922 after joining the Lafayette Players in Harlem he performed the dual role of *Dr. Jekyll and Mr. Hyde*. Having white roles played by blacks in whiteface created quite a controversy and set Muse apart from other black actors.

Muse's first movie role was in *Hearts in Dixie* (1929), produced at the William Fox Studio, in which Muse played a ninety-year-old man. Later, he returned to the stage for the role of a butler in the show that was to be called *Under the Virgin Moon*. After Muse wrote the theme song, the title was changed to *When It's Sleepy Time Down South*. Both the song and the show were hits.

Perhaps best known for his film acting, Muse was also successful as a director, playwright, and actor on the stage. When the Federal Theatre Project in Los Angeles presented Hall Johnson's *Run, Little Chillun*, Muse directed the show. After its successful two-year run, Muse made the screen adaption *Way Down South* (1939).

During Muse's career, he appeared in 219 films, and was at one time one of the highest paid black actors, often portraying faithful servant "Uncle Tom" characters. His movie credits include *Huckleberry Finn* (1931), *Cabin in the Cotton* (1932), *The Count of Monte Cristo* (1934), *So Red the Rose* (1935), *Show Boat* (1936), *The Toy Wife* (1938), *The Flame of New Orleans* (1941), *Tales of Manhattan* (1942), *Heaven Can Wait* (1943), *Night and Day* (1946), *An Act of Murder*

(1948), *Porgy and Bess* (1959), *Buck and the Preacher* (1972), and *Car Wash* (1976). His last film was *Black Stallion* in 1979. He also appeared over the years in concerts and on radio.

Muse died October 13, 1979, the day before his ninetieth birthday. He had lived in Perris, California, on his Muse-a-While Ranch.

Fayard Nicholas (1917–2006) and Harold Nicholas (1924–2000)
Dancers

The Nicholas Brothers were one of the great tap dance teams of the first half of the twentieth century. Their acrobatics and precision were admired by the likes of Fred Astaire and George Balanchine, and their appearances in motion pictures provide a record of their astounding abilities.

Their professional debut came on the radio program *The Horn and Hardart Kiddie Hour* in 1931. The following year they became a featured act at Harlem's Cotton Club. They made their first Broadway appearance in the Ziegfeld Follies of 1936; this was followed by *Babes in Arms* in 1937.

The Nicholas Brothers' film debut was in *Pie Pie Blackbird* in 1932, and they appeared in several other movies in the 1930s and 1940s, including *Sun Valley Serenade* (1941) and *Stormy Weather* (1943). The latter is particularly memorable for the sequence in which they are featured.

Harold Nicholas married actress Dorothy Dandridge in 1942, but the couple later divorced. Harold costarred with Gregory Hines in the movie *Tap* in 1989, and Fayard won a Tony Award for best choreographer for the Broadway musical *Black and Blue* in the same year. In 1992 the Nicholas Brothers were honored by the Kennedy Center. In 1998 a gala was given at Carnegie Hall in their honor: *From Harlem to Hollywood: A Tribute to the Nicholas Brothers' Tap Legends*. In 2003 they were inducted into the Hall of Fame of the National Museum of Dance. Harold Nicholas died in 2000, and Fayard Nicholas died in 2006.

Frederick O'Neal (1905–1992)
Actor

Frederick O'Neal was born August 27, 1905, in Brookville, Mississippi. After his father's death in 1919, he moved with his family to St. Louis, Missouri, finishing high school there and appearing in several Urban League dramatic productions.

In 1927, with the help of some friends in St. Louis, O'Neal founded the Aldridge Players, the second African American acting troupe in America. For the next ten years, he played in thirty of its productions. In 1937 he came to New York, and three years later he helped found the American Negro Theatre. Today its alumni include such established stars as Sidney Poitier, Earle Hyman, Harry Belafonte, Ruby Dee, Ossie Davis, and Hilda Simms.

O'Neal himself starred in *Anna Lucasta* (1944), for which he won the Clarence Derwent Award and the New York Drama Critics' Circle Award for the best supporting performance by an actor on Broadway. He was later featured in *Take a Giant Step* (1953), *The Winner* (1956), and several other stage productions. His films include *Pinky* (1949) and *The Man with the Golden Arm* (1956). He has also appeared on several television dramatic and comedy shows.

In 1964 O'Neal became the first black president of Actors' Equity, a fitting tribute to his long years of service to the American theater as both actor and teacher. In 1970, after devoting himself full time to Actors' Equity, O'Neal was elected international president of the Associated Actors and Artistes of America, the parent union of all show-business performers' unions. He became president and chairman of the board of the Schomburg Center for Research in Black Culture to raise money to conserve and preserve materials in the center, to solicit material, and toward construction of a new building. He has been a member of the New York State Council on the Arts, president of the Catholic Interracial Council, chairman of the AFL-CIO Civil Rights Committee, and vice president of the A. Philip Randolph Institute. In 1980 he received the Distinguished Trade Unionist Award from the National Urban Coalition and a special tribute from the Black Filmmakers Hall of Fame. O'Neal died on April 27, 1992.

Tyler Perry (1969–)
Actor, Playwright

Tyler Perry was born Emmitt R. Perry Jr. on September 14, 1969, in New Orleans, Louisiana. As a young adult Perry began journaling, which led to his first play in 1992. He moved to Atlanta but not until 1998 was his play well received by his audience. *I Know I've Been Changed* was produced and later followed by a series of plays such as *Diary of a Mad Black Woman* (2001), *Madea's Family Reunion* (2002), *Why Did I Get Married?* (2004), *Meet the Browns* (2004), and *Madea Goes to Jail* (2005).

In 2005 Perry launched his film career and brought many of his characters from the stage to the screen. The character of Madea, which is Perry dressed as a woman who behaves as a gun packing, tough talking matriarch, added a comic side to many of his films just as the character did for his plays. Perry has produced several films, including *Diary of a Mad Black Woman* (2005), *Madea's Family Reunion* (2006), *Daddy's Little Girls* (2007), *Why Did I Get Married?* (2007), and *For Colored Girls* (2010).

Perry has also produced two television comedy series, *House of Payne* and *Meet the Browns*.

Sidney Poitier (1927–)
Actor

Sidney Poitier was born on February 20, 1927, in Miami, Florida, but moved to the Bahamas with his family at a very early age. At age fifteen he returned to Miami; he later rode freight trains to New York City, where he found employment as a dishwasher. After Pearl Harbor, he enlisted in the Army and served on active duty for four years.

Back in New York, Poitier auditioned for the American Negro Theater but was turned down by director Frederick O'Neal. After working diligently to improve his diction, Poitier was accepted in the theater group and received acting lessons in exchange for doing backstage chores.

Poitier made his Hollywood debut in *No Way Out* (1950), followed by successful appearances in *Cry, the Beloved Country* (1952), *Red Ball Express* (1952), *Go, Man, Go!* (1954), *Blackboard Jungle* (1956), *Good-bye, My Lady* (1956), *Edge of the City* (1957), *Band of Angels* (1957), *Something of Value* (1957), *The Defiant Ones* (1958), *Porgy and Bess* (1959), and *Lilies of the Field* (1963), among others. Poitier starred on Broadway in 1959 in Lorraine Hansberry's award-winning *A Raisin in the Sun*, and repeated this success in the movie version of the play in 1961.

In 1964 Poitier became the first black to win an Oscar for a starring role, receiving this award for his performance in *Lilies of the Field*. Seven years earlier Poitier had been the first black actor nominated for the award for his portrayal of an escaped convict in *The Defiant Ones*.

Subsequent notable film appearances include performances in *To Sir with Love* (1967), *Heat of the Night* (1967), *Guess Who's Coming to Dinner* (1968; with Spencer Tracy and Katharine Hepburn), *Buck and the Preacher* and *A Warm December* (1972 and 1973; both of which he also directed), *Uptown Saturday Night* (1974), and *A Piece of the Action* (1977). After years of inactivity Poitier performed in two additional films, *Little Nikita* and *Shoot to Kill* (both released in 1988). His directing ventures include *Stir Crazy* (1980; with Richard Pryor and Gene Wilder), *Hanky Panky* (1982; with Gene Wilder and Gilda Radner), and the musical *Fast Forward* (1985).

Poitier spent two years writing his memoirs, *This Life*, published by Knopf in 1980. In 1981 Citadel Press published *The Films of Sidney Poitier*, by Alvin H. Marill. Among the numerous awards that Poitier has received, he was selected in 1999 by the American Film Institute as one of the greatest male stars of all time, and he was granted an Honorary Academy Award in 2001 for his outstanding contributions to American cinema.

Pearl Primus (1919–1994)
Dancer, Choreographer

Pearl Primus was born in Port of Spain, Trinidad and Tobago, on November 29, 1919. Originally intending to pursue a career in medicine, she received a B.A. in pre-medical sciences and biology from Hunter College, with graduate work in medical education and psychology. But in the 1940s America did not welcome blacks or women in medicine, and after seeking employment in vain, Primus sought assistance from the government's National Youth Administration. She was put into a youth administration dance group, and by 1941 was accepted into New York City's New Dance Group. Her professional debut was at the Young Men's Hebrew Association in New York City on February 14, 1943. In April of that year, she began appearing at Café Society Downtown, the famed New York City nightclub, but left after ten months for an appearance on Broadway at the Belasco Theatre. By this time she had her own dance company, Pearl Primus, Percival Borde and Company. She toured Africa and the southern United States, and incorporated what she learned into her choreography.

Primus's anthropological approach to dance made her one of the most purposeful figures in that medium; for her, dance was education, not merely entertainment. Her aim was to show audiences and dancers alike the African roots of dance. Primus was best known for the dances *African Ceremonial* and *Strange Fruit,* which were incorporated into her *Solos for Performance at the Café Society* (c. 1944), and *Hard Times Blues* (1945). Primus died on October 29, 1994.

Richard Pryor (1940–2005)
Comedian, Actor

Richard Franklin Lennox Thomas Pryor III was born on December 1, 1940, he was raised by his grandmother in the Peoria, Illinois, brothel she ran. His mother worked there as a prostitute. His parents married when he was three years old but the union did not last. His grandmother was a strict disciplinarian and young Richard was often beaten.

In school Pryor was often in trouble with the authorities; he was expelled from high school for striking a teacher. In 1958 he joined the Army and spent two years in Germany. He returned to Peoria after his military service and during the early 1960s began his work as a stand-up comic on a local circuit. He moved to New York City's Greenwich Village in 1963, where he honed his stand-up routine. A 1964 appearance on *The Ed Sullivan Show* led to his first movie role in *The Busy Body* (1966), followed by bit parts in *The Green Berets* and *Wild in the Streets* (both 1968). During this time Pryor continued to play to live audiences.

In 1972 Pryor played Piano Man in *Lady Sings the Blues* and earned an Academy Award nomination for his performance. Throughout the 1970s Pryor continued his work as a stand-up comic and contributed his writing talents to television's *The Flip Wilson Show* and *Sanford and Son,* as well as Mel Brooks's film *Blazing Saddles* and Lily Tomlin's television special, *Lily,* for which he won an Emmy. He won two of his five Grammy Awards for his comedy albums *That Nigger's Crazy* (1974) and *Bicentennial Nigger* (1976).

Pryor wrote and starred in *The Bingo Long Traveling All-Stars and Motor Kings* in 1976 and received raves for his work in *Silver Streak,* also in 1976. In 1979 the comedian's film *Richard Pryor: Live in Concert* brought his stand-up act to millions.

In 1978 Pryor suffered a major heart attack and in 1980, while freebasing cocaine, he set himself ablaze and suffered severe injuries. He addressed these incidents in his second concert movie, *Richard Pryor: Live on the Sunset Strip* (1982). In 1985 Pryor co-wrote, directed, and starred in *Jo Jo Dancer, Your Life Is Calling,* a semi-autobiographical tale of a comedian who relives his life immediately following a near fatal accident. Pryor's other popular films include *Stir Crazy* (1980), *Bustin' Loose* (1981), *The Toy* (1982), *Some Kind of Hero* (1982), *Brewster's Millions* (1985), *Critical Condition* (1987), *Moving* (1988), and *See No Evil, Hear No Evil* (1989). Pryor co-starred with Eddie Murphy in *Harlem Nights* (1989), and he performed with Gene Wilder in *Another You* (1991).

With great success as a stand-up comedian, writer, actor, and recording star, Pryor received a star on the Walk of Fame in 1993, and he was awarded the first Mark Twain Prize for American Humor in 1998. He won the MTV Lifetime Achievement Award in 2000, and was voted the Best Stand-up Comedian of All Time by Comedy Central in 2004. Although Pryor had been diagnosed with multiple sclerosis in 1986, he died on December 10, 2005, of cardiac arrest. He was awarded posthumously a Grammy Lifetime Achievement Award in 2006.

Phylicia Rashad (1948–)
Actress

Phylicia Rashad was born on June 19, 1948, in Houston, Texas, and until 1985 was known as Phylicia Ayers-Allen. Her sister is the famous Debbie Allen; both sisters received early instruction in music, acting, and dance. Phylicia graduated magna cum laude from Howard University in 1970 with a B.F.A. in theater.

Early in her career, Rashad played the character Courtney Wright in the soap opera *One Life to Live.* Her big break came with *The Cosby Show,* in which she and Bill Cosby presided over the Huxtable family for seven years, from 1985 to

1992. Known to millions as Claire Huxtable, "America's Favorite Mom" Rashad has led a distinguished acting career on television and the stage. Rashad has also appeared in Broadway and Off-Broadway productions of *The Cherry Orchard* (1973), *The Wiz* (1975), *Zora* (1981), *Dreamgirls* (1981), *A Raisin in the Sun* (1984), and *Into the Woods* (1988). In 2008 Rashad starred in the Tyler Perry film *For Colored Girls,* which is a film remake of the 1970s play by Ntozake Shonga, *For Colored Girls Who Have Considered Suicide When the Rainbow Is Enuf.*

In 1999 she was honored by the National Council of Negro Women with the Dorothy L. Height Dreammaker Award. Rashad earned a Tony Award in 2004 for her stage performance in *A Raisin in the Sun,* making her the first African American lead actress to receive the award; and in 2009, she received an Image Award from the NAACP for her performance in the television version of the play. Rashad has also received two honorary doctorates—one from Providence College in Rhode Island and one from Barber-Scotia College in North Carolina.

Lloyd Richards (1919–2006)
Theatrical Director, Educator

Lloyd Richards was born in Toronto, Ontario, Canada, on June 29, 1919. In 1944 he earned a degree from Wayne State University in theater after first considering law. After serving in World War II, he moved to New York to purse his career in the theater.

In 1959, at the urging of Sidney Poitier, Richards directed Lorraine Hansberry's *A Raisin in the Sun,* a play that received critical acclaim and maintains a classic status among plays. The play ran for 530 performances. Richards began teaching at Hunters College and New York University while continuing to work with artists such as August Wilson, Charles Fuller, and Henry Hwang.

In 1979 Richards became dean of the Yale School of Drama and artistic director of the Yale Repertory Theatre. He remained there until 1991.

Under his direction at Yale many famous plays were produced at the theater such as the Pulitzer Prize-winning plays *Fences* and *The Piano Lesson* by August Wilson. There were also prominent actors who came to the theater, including Angela Bassett, Glenn Close, Colleen Dewhurst, and James Earl Jones. After his departure from Yale, Richards continued to guide, direct, encourage, and produce new playwrights, plays, and stage production.

Richards's awards included induction into the Theater Hall of Fame in 1990, Directors Award from the National Black Theatre Festival, a National Medal of Arts in 1993, and the Huntington Award for lifetime achievement in 1995. Lloyd Richards died of heart failure on June 29, 2006.

Bill "Bojangles" Robinson (1878–1949)
Dancer

Bill Robinson was born on May 25, 1878, in Richmond, Virginia. Having been orphaned early, he was raised by his grandmother, a former slave. By the time he was eight, he was earning his own way by dancing in the street for pennies and working as a stable boy.

In 1887 Robinson toured the South in a show called *The South Before the War.* The following year, he moved to Washington, D.C., where he again worked as a stable boy. By 1896 he had teamed up with George W. Cooper. This act was successful on the Keith circuit until the slump of 1907 caused it to fold. Robinson returned to Richmond and worked as a waiter until a year later when he was taken up by a theatrical manager and became a cabaret and vaudeville headliner.

In 1927 Robinson starred on Broadway in *Blackbirds,* and in 1932 he had top billing in Harlem's *Heaven,* the first all-black motion picture with sound. Later, he scored a Hollywood success by teaching his famous stair dance to Shirley Temple in *The Little Colonel* (1935). Robinson made fourteen movies, including *The Littlest Rebel* (1935), *In Old Kentucky* (1935), *Rebecca of Sunnybrook Farm* (1938), *Stormy Weather* (1943), and *One Mile from Heaven* (1937).

Throughout his long career on stage and in movies, Robinson was known as the "King of Tap Dancers." Robinson died on November 25, 1949.

Chris Rock (1965–)
Comedian, Actor

Christopher Julius Rock III was born in Andrews, South Carolina, on February 7, 1965. After leaving school at the age of seventeen, Rock was determined to do stand-up comedy. In 1986 he met Eddie Murphy who mentored him and provided a role in *Beverly Hills Cop II*; he also landed a role in *New Jack City* in 1991, which earned him critical claim for his performance. In 1993 Rock joined *In Living Color* for one season.

Rock's stand-up comedy and film career saw progress. He wrote and directed several shows, and in 1996 he earned two Emmy Awards for his comedy special *Chris Rock: Bring the Pain.* He went on to have a series on HBO, *The Chris Rock Show,* which won him an Emmy for best writing in 1999. Rock landed film roles in *Nurse Betty* (2000), *Down to Earth* (2001), *Osmosis Jones* (2001), and *Bad Company* (2002). With some controversy Rock also hosted the 2005 Academy Awards show.

Rock continues to bring a new perspective as shown in the success of his show *Everybody Hates Chris,* which Rock wrote and produced, based on his own life experiences. He also has co-written/directed or produced films that include *Head of State* (2003), *I Think I Love My Wife* (2007), and *Death at a Funeral* (2010). Rock made his Broadway debut in *The Motherfucker with the Hat* (2010).

Richard Roundtree (1942–)
Actor

Richard Roundtree was born in New Rochelle, New York, on July 9, 1942. He graduated from New Rochelle High School and attended Southern Illinois University on a football scholarship. After brief stints as a suit salesman and a model, he began a stage career with the Negro Ensemble Company. Roundtree is best known as John Shaft, the tough, renegade detective from the *Shaft* films. With *Shaft* (1971) and its sequels, *Shaft's Big Score* (1972) and *Shaft in Africa* (1973), Roundtree reached the peak of his career and became a pop icon.

Roundtree appeared in the television miniseries *Roots* (1977) and has subsequently appeared in the films *Embassy* (1972), *Charlie One Eye* (1973), *Earthquake* (1974), *Diamonds* (1975), *Man Friday* (1976), *Se7ven* (1995), *When We Were Colored* (1996), *Shaft* (2000), *Heroes* (2007), *Lincoln Heights* (2008), and *Knight Rider* (2009). He continues to be cast in various television programs and motion pictures.

Roundtree is a survivor of breast cancer and is an active member of the American Cancer Society.

John Singleton (1968–)
Filmmaker

John Daniel Singleton was born on January 6, 1968, in South Los Angeles, California. After graduating from high school in 1986 he enrolled in the University of Southern California's prestigious Film Writing Program, which is part of their School of Cinema–Television. While there he formed an African American Film Association and did a six-month director's internship for *The Arsenio Hall Show*. He twice won the school's Jack Nicholson Award for best feature-length screenplays. Before graduating in 1990 he signed with the well-known Creative Artists Agency.

Singleton was soon approached by Columbia Pictures to sell the film rights to *Boyz n the Hood,* his original screenplay and college thesis. Singleton agreed, but only if he could be the movie's director. The movie was released in July of 1991 to mixed critical reviews. Although its first showings were marred by movie-house violence, the film garnered Singleton an Academy Award nomination for best director. He became the youngest director and the first African American to be so honored.

Since *Boyz n the Hood* Singleton has done a short cable television film for Michael Jackson entitled *Remember the Time* (1992), followed by *Poetic Justice* (1993), *Higher Learning* (1995), *Rosewood* (1997), *Shaft* (2000), *Baby Boy* (2001), *2 Fast 2 Furious* (2003), *Four Brothers* (2005), and *Abduction* (2011).

Noble Sissle (1889–1975)
Lyricist, Singer

Noble Sissle was born on July 10, 1889, in Indianapolis, Indiana. He reaped his early successes teamed with the great musician/composer Eubie Blake. Sissle wrote the lyrics and sang them in performance; Blake composed and played the music. Together the two created such songs as "I'm Just Wild about Harry," "It's All Your Fault," "Serenade Blues," and "Love Will Find a Way."

The 1921 show *Shuffle Along,* the first black musical with a love theme, made Sissle and Blake famous. Joining forces with the writing and comedy team of Flournoy Miller and Aubrey Lyles, Sissle and Blake wrote the words and music to more than a dozen songs for the show. *Shuffle Along* became a huge success in the United States and Europe, where it had a prolonged tour. As with most black performers in the early 1900s, Sissle and his troupe had to travel as far as twenty or thirty miles out of their way to find a place to eat and sleep, since blacks were not welcomed in the white hotels of the towns where they played.

Other Sissle and Blake shows included *Chocolate Dandies* (1924) and *Keep Shufflin'* (1928). Noble Sissle died December 17, 1975, at his home in Tampa, Florida.

Will Smith (1968–)
Actor, Singer

Born Willard Christopher Smith on September 25, 1968, in Wynnefield, Pennsylvania, Will Smith grew up in a middle-class black neighborhood but attended predominantly white Catholic schools. At the age of eighteen Smith and friend Jeff Townes formed the rap group DJ Jazzy Jeff and the Fresh Prince. In 1987 the duo released their second album, which was widely successful. The single on the album "Parents Just Don't Understand" won a Grammy Award for the best rap performance. The duo went on to release three more albums.

In 1996 Smith landed a role in a sitcom based on the life experience of Benny Medina, *The Fresh Prince of Bel-Air*. The sitcom, which ran from 1991 to 1996, found its success in the goofy, carefree attitude of Smith. He appeared in *Bad Boys* (1995), and he established himself as a box-office draw in the film *Independence Day* (1996), followed by *Men in Black* (1997), *Enemy of the State* (1998), *Wild Wild West* (1999), and an Oscar-nominated portrayal of Muhammad Ali in *Ali* (2001). Smith's almost yearly releases continue to have a box office draw, including *Men In Black II* (2002), *I, Robot* (2004), *Hitch* (2005), *The Pursuit of Happyness* (2006), *I Am Legend* (2007), and *Seven Pounds* (2008).

Smith has continued to put out rap albums, which include major singles such a "Getting Jiggy With It" and "Just the Two of Us," as well as solo and collaborative albums, including *Willenium* (1999), *Born to Reign* (2002), and *Lost and Found* (2005).

Smith and his wife, actress Jada Pinkett Smith, continue to support philanthropic causes for disaster relief, children's health, and many other organizations.

Wesley Snipes (1962–)
Actor

Born in Orlando, Florida, on July 31, 1962, Wesley Trent Snipes spent his childhood in the Bronx, New York. At the age of twelve he appeared in his first off-Broadway production, a minor role in the play *The Me Nobody Knows*. His interest in dance led him to enroll in New York's High School for the Performing Arts. Before he completed the curriculum, however, his mother sent him back to Orlando to finish school, where he continued to study drama.

Upon high school graduation, Snipes was awarded a scholarship to study theater at the State University of New York at Purchase. Snipes subsequently appeared in Broadway and Off-Broadway productions, including Wole Soyinka's *Death and the King's Horsemen* (1986), Emily Mann's *Execution of Justice* (1986), and John Pielmeier's *The Boys of Winter* (1985). He has also appeared in Michael Jackson's video *Bad* and in the HBO production *Vietnam War Story*, for which he received cable television's best actor award.

Snipes's film appearances include roles in *Wildcats* (1986), *Streets of Gold* (1986), *Major League* (1989), and *King of New York* (1990). In 1990 Snipes appeared in Spike Lee's *Mo' Better Blues*, with Denzel Washington. This was followed by a role in Mario Van Peebles's *New Jack City* (1991), Spike Lee's *Jungle Fever* (1991), *White Men Can't Jump* (1992), *Passenger 57* (1992), *Rising Sun*, (1993), *Blade* (1998), *Disappearing Acts* (2000), *Blade II* (2002), and between 2004 and 2010 at least nine films that have gone directly to DVD distribution.

Snipes has been awarded numerous honors, including Image Awards from the NAACP, Blockbuster Entertainment Awards, and a best actor award at the Venice Film Festival. In 2010 Snipes was convicted on charges of failing to file a U.S. Federal Income Tax return and entered prison on December 9, 2010, to serve a term of approximately three years.

Wanda Sykes (1964–)
Comedienne, Actress, Writer

Wanda Sykes was born on March 7, 1964, in Portsmouth, Virginia. Her comic abilities were evident in high school, and she enrolled in theater classes to support her comedic interests. She graduated from Hampton University in 1986 with a B.S. degree and went to work for a high-tech communications company, temporarily putting aside her comedic interests. In 1987 Sykes entered a comedy competition and received encouraging reviews. In 1992, after performing in many comedy clubs, she began to pursue a career in stand-up comedy full time.

Sykes became friends with Chris Rock who had Sykes open for his show, and eventually she became a writer for his television show *The Chris Rock Show* from 1997 to 2000. Sykes secured writing opportunities while pursuing her own stand-up comedy, which dealt with issues of the African American community, gay marriage, politics, and sports. Her quick wit and insults earned her Emmys in 2002, 2004, and 2005 for work on HBO's *Inside the NFL*. Sykes went on to appear in numerous television shows and series such as *Curb Your Enthusiasm* and *The Drew Carey Show.* Her HBO comedy special *Wanda Sykes: Sick and Tired* debuted in October 2006.

Sykes has appeared in numerous films, including *Monster-in-Law* (2005), *My Super Ex-Girlfriend* (2006), *Evan Almighty* (2007), and the television series *The New Adventures of Old Christine* (2006–2010). Sykes continues to do comedy, and published her first book in 2004, *Yeah, I Said It,* which contains humorous essays.

Robert Townsend (1957–)
Actor, Director,

Robert Townsend was born on February 6, 1957, in Chicago, Illinois, and joined an acting group at age sixteen to pursue his desire to be an actor.

Townsend secured a role in *Cooley High* in 1975. He later moved to New York and found steady work. He landed a recurring role on a public television series, and at one point he tried out for *Saturday Night Live* but lost the spot to fellow artist Eddie Murphy.

Townsend continued to do films until 1982, when he moved to Los Angeles and learned the filmmaking process. In 1986, backed with savings and credit cards, Townsend released his first movie *Hollywood Shuffle.* Townsend, produced, directed, and starred in the highly successful film. Townsend has continued to use his writing and directing abilities to direct the concert film *Eddie Murphy: Raw* (1987), and the film *The Five Heartbeats* (1991). Other films include *The Meteor Man* (1993), *Up, Up, and Away* (2000), and *Phantom Punch* (2009).

Townsend has been honored with two CableACE Awards and several NAACP Image Awards for his accomplishments. He has continued to perform in sitcoms such as *Parenthood* (1995–1999), host variety shows such as *Motown Live* (1998), to direct the Lifetime cable network's dramatic trilogy *Love Songs* (1999) and produce the television films *Carmen: A Hip Hopera* and *10,000 Black Men Named George* in 2001. Towsend briefly served as director of programming for the Black Family Channel in 2007, but has since put his efforts in The Robert Townsend Foundation toward created content in films.

Billie "Buckwheat" Thomas (1931–1980)
Actor

Billie "Buckwheat" Thomas was born on March 12, 1931, and became one of the principal characters in the *Our Gang* cast in 1934. He appeared in ninety-three episodes, the last in 1944. Film historian David Bogle described the character of Buckwheat as "a quiet, oddball type, the perfect little dumdum tagalong." Buckwheat succeeded the character Farina, and like Farina, his gender was ambiguous: he was in most respects a boy, but wore dresslike gingham smocks, and in some episodes sported pigtails. Comedian Eddie Murphy's parodies of Buckwheat in the 1980s were enormously popular; Buckwheat's generally unintelligible speech, blank expression, and untidy hair provided a wealth of material for Murphy's routine.

Billie Thomas pursued little acting after the *Our Gang* series ended. He died on October 10, 1980, at the age of 49.

Cicely Tyson (1933–)
Actress

Cicely Tyson was born in Harlem, New York, on December 19, 1933, and was raised by a religious and strict mother who associated movies with sin and forbade Cicely to go to movie theaters. Blessed with poise and natural grace, Tyson became a model and appeared on the cover of America's two foremost fashion magazines, *Vogue* and *Harper's Bazaar,* in 1956. Interested in acting, she began to study drama. In 1959 she appeared on a CBS culture series, *Camera Three,* with what is believed to be the first natural African hair style worn on television.

Tyson won a role in an Off-Broadway production of Jean Genet's *The Blacks* (1961), for which she received the 1962 Vernon Rice Award. She then played a lead part in the CBS series *East Side, West Side.* Tyson subsequently moved into film parts, appearing in *The Comedians* (1967) and *The Heart Is a Lonely Hunter* (1968).

During the early 1970s Tyson emerged as America's leading black dramatic star. She achieved this through two sterling performances—as Rebecca, the wife of a southern sharecropper in the film *Sounder* (1972), and as the lead in a television special, *The Autobiography of Miss Jane Pittman* (1974), the story of an ex-slave who, past her hundredth year, challenges racist authority by deliberately drinking from a "white only" water fountain as a white deputy sheriff looks on. Tyson was nominated for an Academy Award for *Sounder* and was named best actress by the National Society of Film Crit-

ics. She won an Emmy for *The Autobiography of Miss Jane Pittman.*

In 1978 Tyson portrayed Harriet Tubman in *A Woman Called Moses,* and Chicago schoolteacher Marva Collins in a made-for-television movie in 1981. On television, she has appeared in *Roots* (1977), *Wilma* (1977), *King* (1978), the miniseries *The Women of Brewster Place* (1989), *Oldest Living Confederate Widow Tells All* (1994), *Mama Flora's Family* (1998), and *A Lesson before Dying* (1999). Tyson's other film appearances include *The Blue Bird* (1976), *Bustin' Loose* (1981), *Fried Green Tomatoes* (1991), *Diary of a Mad Black Woman* (2005), *Idlewild* (2006), and *Why Did I Get Married Too?* (2010).

Tyson was presented with a honorary degree from Marymount College in 1979 and from Morehouse College in 2009.

Leslie Uggams (1943–)
Singer, Actress

Born in the Washington Heights section of New York City on May 25, 1943, Leslie Uggams enjoyed a comfortable childhood. She made her singing debut at the age of six, performing with the choir of St. James Presbyterian Church in New York, and followed shortly thereafter with her acting debut in the television series *Beulah.* Uggams developed her poise and stage presence early in life, attending the Professional Children's School, where she was chosen student body president in her senior year.

Uggams subsequently won $25,000 on the popular television quiz show *Name That Tune,* which renewed her interest in a singing career. In 1961 Uggams became a regular on *The Mitch Miller Show,* a variety show featuring old favorites. She was at the time the only black performer appearing regularly on network television.

Throughout the 1960s Uggams appeared in numerous nightclubs and had several supper club and television engagements. Her big break came when she was signed as a replacement for Lena Horne in *Hallelujah Baby,* a 1967 show that presented a musical chronicle of the civil rights movement. Uggams won instant stardom and received a Tony Award for her performance.

In 1977 Uggams appeared as Kizzy in the television adaption of Alex Haley's novel *Roots*. In May 1982 she performed in a new Broadway show, *Blues in the Night,* at the Rialto Theater in New York City. She has also appeared on television in *Backstairs at the White House*, a 1979 miniseries, and *The Book of Lists* in 1982; in the film *Skyjacked* (1972); and in the musicals *Jerry's Girls* (1986), *The Great Gershwin* (1987), and *Anything Goes* (1989).

Uggams returned to the stage in 1998 in the title role of *The Old Settler.* In 2001 her performance in *King Hedley II* won Uggams a Tony nomination for best actress. Uggams join the cast of *Thoroughly Modern Millie* in 2003, and she received two Tony nominations for *On Golden Pond* in 2005.

Mario Van Peebles (1957–)
Director, Actor, Producer, Writer

Mario Cain Van Peebles was born on January 15, 1957, in Mexico City, Mexico, but traveled the world. His father Melvin Van Peebles (a filmmaker, actor, and director) and his mother Maria Marx (a German actress) presented a world of nonconformity through their racial mix and adventurous spirits that embraceed the world as they saw it. After settling in San Francisco, Mario made his acting debut at age eight and his screen debut on his controversial film *Sweet Sweetback's Baadasssss Song* at age fourteen.

After studying both the acting and business side of the film business Van Peebles debuted as a film director in 1991 with the film *New Jack City.* Controversy followed the film regarding its violence, which resulted in widespread media attention. The film was produced for $8.5 million and grossed over $100 million.

Van Peebles has appeared in films such as *Stompin' at the Savoy* (1992) and *Mama Flora's Family* (1998), and has both acted and directed in films such as *Possee* (1993), *BAADASSSSS!* (2003), and *Kerosene Cowboys* (2010). Mario Van Peebles continues to direct, write, and act in films. In *No Identity Crisis,* a book co-written with his father in 1990, he embraces the gifts and the differences that have supported the Van Peebles's contributions to the film industry.

Melvin Van Peebles (1932–)
Filmmaker, Actor, Writer

Melvin Van Peebles was born on August 21, 1932, in Chicago, Illinois, but grew up in Phoenix, Illinois. In 1953 he graduated from Ohio Wesleyan University with a B.A. in English literature. After spending time in the Netherlands and the breakup of his family, Van Peebles moved to France, where he had his first success writing a novel using his self-taught French.

While in France in 1967 Van Peebles received good reviews on his play *The Story of a Three Day Pass* and decided to return to the United States. In 1971 he produced the film *Sweet Sweetback's Baadasssss Song* on a budget of $500,000 in only nineteen days. The film, which awakened Hollywood to black audiences, grossed over $13 million. Although the film is said to have introduced blaxploitation films and is controversial for its violence (thus earning an "X" rating), the film used mostly a black crew and broke into an industry that had ignored a key part of the American viewing audience.

Van Peebles's success allowed him to produce works on Broadway such as *Don't Play Us Cheap: Know Your Business* in 1972, the 1981 television miniseries *The Sophisticated Gents,* and ultimately to direct his son Mario in the film *Identity Crisis* in 1990. Van Peebles has continued to collaborate with his son as well as write and direct.

Van Peebles has received many awards, including first prize at the Belgian Film Festival in 1971, an Emmy Award in 1987, "Honorary President" for the French Black Roots Film Festival, and in 2000 the Acapulco Black Film Festival's International Films Competition, and the Byron E. Lewis Trailblazer Award.

Ben Vereen (1946–)

Dancer, Actor

Ben Vereen was born October 10, 1946, in the Bedford Stuyvesant section of Brooklyn, New York, and attended the High School for the Performing Arts in Manhattan. His dancing ability was discovered almost accidentally after he had been sent to dance school by his mother. Vereen has since been called America's premier song-and-dance man.

Ben Vereen made his stage debut in 1965 in *The Prodigal Son*. He went on to appear in *Sweet Charity* (1966), *Golden Boy* (1968), *Hair* (1968), and *No Place to Be Somebody* (1970). Vereen is best known for his Broadway role in *Pippin* (1972), for which he won a Tony Award. He was also nominated for a Tony for his costarring role in *Jesus Christ Superstar* (1971). His film appearances include roles in *Funny Lady* (1975), *All That Jazz* (1979), and *The Zoo Gang* (1985).

Vereen has starred in the ABC comedy series *Tenspeed and Brown Shoe* in the 1980s and is known for his television specials, including the highly acclaimed *Ben Vereen: His Roots* (1978), which won seven Emmy Awards. He also portrayed Louis "Satchmo" Armstrong and received wide acclaim for his role of Chicken George in television's adaption of Alex Haley's *Roots* (1977) and for his performance in *Jubilee*.

Vereen has continued to work in film performing in *Why Do Fools Fall in Love* (1998), *Feast of All Saints* (2001), and *Idlewild* (2006); and on Broadway performing in *I'm Not Rappaport* (2002) and *Wicked* (2005). Because of his concert tours in the 1990s Vereen became the first entertainer to earn three awards from the American Guild of Variety Artists—Entertainer of the Year, Rising Star, and Song and Dance Star.

Denzel Washington (1954–)

Actor

Denzel Hayes Washington was born on December 28, 1954, in Mt. Vernon, New York. He attended an upstate private high school, the Oakland Academy, and then entered Fordham University as a pre-med major. Washington did not originally intend to become an actor, but when he auditioned for the lead role in a student production of Eugene O'Neill's *The Emperor Jones,* he won the part over theater majors. His performance in that play, and later in a production of *Othello,* led his drama instructor to encourage Washington to pursue an acting career.

Washington's first major role was in the Off-Broadway drama *A Soldier's Story*; Washington recreated his role when the play was adapted into a motion picture in 1984. He played Dr. Phillip Chandler on the television series *St. Elsewhere* and appeared in a string of films, including *Carbon Copy* (1981), *Cry Freedom* (in which he portrayed South African activist Steven Biko; 1987), *The Mighty Quinn* (1989), *Glory* (1989), *Mo' Better Blues* (1990), *Mississippi Masala* (1992), *Malcolm X* (1992), *Devil in a Blue Dress* (1995), *He Got Game* (1998), *The Hurricane* (1999), *Training Day* (2001), and *American Gangster* (2007).

Washington has expanded his role to that of director in the films *Antwone Fisher* (2002), and *The Great Debaters* (2007), which he co-produced with Oprah Winfrey. His latest films include *The Book of Eli* and *Unstoppable,* both released in 2010.

Washington's numerous awards include an Oscar for best supporting actor in *Glory* in 1990; two Golden Globes as well as the Silver Beard Award from the Berlin International Film Festival in 1993, the Image Award from the NAACP in 1999 for outstanding actor in the film *The Hurricane* (based on a true story about the life of incarcerated boxer Rubin Carter), and for his performance in *The Great Debaters* in 2007, and an Oscar for best actor in 2002 for his performance in the film *Training Day,* which also earned best actor awards from the Los Angeles Film Critics Association and the American Film Institute. Washington returned to the stage in 2010 and won a Tony Award for his performance in the play *Fences*.

Ethel Waters (1896–1977)
Actress, Singer

The distinguished career of Ethel Waters spanned half a century and made its mark in virtually all entertainment media—stage, screen, television, and recordings.

Ethel Waters was born on October 31, 1896, and spent most of her childhood in Chester, Pennsylvania. By the age of seventeen she was singing professionally at the Lincoln Theatre in Baltimore. During this early phase of her career, she became the first woman to perform W.C. Handy's "St. Louis Blues" on stage.

After several years in nightclubs and vaudeville, Waters made her Broadway debut in the 1927 review *Africana*. In 1930 she appeared in *Blackbirds*; and in 1931 and 1932 she starred in *Rhapsody in Black*. The following year she was featured with Clifton Webb and Marilyn Miller in Irving Berlin's *As Thousands Cheer*. In 1935 she costarred with Beatrice Lillie in *At Home Abroad,* and three years later she played the lead in *Mamba's Daughters*.

In 1940 Waters appeared in the stage version of *Cabin in the Sky,* a triumph that she repeated in the 1943 movie version. Her other film appearances include *Rufus Jones for President* (1931), *Tales of Manhattan* (1941), *Cairo* (1942), *Stage Door Canteen* (1943), and *Pinky* (1949).

Her autobiography, *His Eye Is on the Sparrow,* was a 1951 Book-of-the-Month Club selection. The title is taken from a song that she sang in her 1950 stage success, *Member of the Wedding*.

The Wayans Brothers
Entertainers, Filmmakers

Brothers Keenen Ivory (born June 8, 1958), Damon Kyle (born September 4, 1960), Shawn

Mathis born January 19,1971, and Marlon (born July 23, 1972), grew up in a family of ten siblings in New York City in one of Manhattan's housing complexes.

Keenen and Damon both struck out to make a career in stand-up comedy, with each taking his own route. Damon was doing films and stand-up and at one point landed a spot on *Saturday Night Live*. Keenen was also doing stand-up as well as several television series. The two came together in the film *Hollywood Shuffle* in 1987. After Keenen's success with the film *I'm Gonna Git You, Sucka* in 1988 (a hilarious send-up of 1970s "blaxploitation" films), he wrote and produced the television comedy series *In Living Color*. In 1990 Damon joined the cast as the show offered outrageous parody and was often irreverent.

Damon left *In Living Color* after four seasons and continued to appear in films such as *Blankman* (1994), *Celtic Pride* (1996), and also continued to write. Keenen's most successful television series as a writer to date has been *My Wife*

Keenen Ivory Wayans

and Kids, which ran from 2001 to 2005. Damon Waynons was awarded the People's Choice Award in 2002 and he continues to offer insight and humor in his writing and acting. He released the novel *Red Hats* in 2010.

Keenen Wayans has continued to write and direct and has been most successful with the directing and writing of the film series: *Scary Movie* (2000), *Scary Movie 2* (2001), and *Scary Movie 3* (2003).

Shawn and Marlon Wayans first appeared on the entertainment scene in Keenen Wayans's film, *I'm Gonna Git You, Sucka* in 1988, and later joined the cast of *In Living Color,* from 1990 to 1994. In 1994 Shawn and Marlon wrote the film *Scary Movie,* which premiered in 2000 and was directed by Keenen Wayans. It was highly successful as it satirized horror movies of the day.

In 2004 Shawn and Marlon starred in the film *White Chicks,* which was directed by Keenen Wayans. Although the film was criticized for its

Marlon Wayans

questionable content, the Wayans brothers continue to act, write, and produce while offering a comedic perspective.

Forest Whitaker (1961–)
Actor, Director

Forest Whitaker was born on July 15, 1961, in Longview, Texas. He made his first appearance in movies in the 1982 film *Fast Times at Ridgemont High.* It was Whitaker's breakout performance in *Bird* (1988), in which he portrays the jazz icon Charlie Parker, that brought him critical acclaim. Films that followed this success include *The Crying Game* (1992) and *Panic Room* (2002).

In 2006 Whitaker again showed his talent in the film *The Last King of Scotland.* His performance earned him an Academy Award as best actor in 2007, and in that same year he received an Emmy for his performance in the television series *ER.* Whitaker has added directing to his credits, including *A Rage in Harlem* (1991), *Waiting to Exhale* (1995), and *First Daughter* (2004).

Bert Williams (1874–1922)
Comedian, Dancer

Born on November 12, 1874, in Nassau, Bahamas, Egbert Austin "Bert" Williams moved to New York with his family and then on to California, where he graduated from high school. After studying civil engineering for a time, he decided to try his hand at show business.

In 1895 Williams teamed with George Walker to form a successful vaudeville team. Five years later, they opened in New York in *Sons of Ham* and were acclaimed for the characterizations that became their stock-in-trade—Walker as a dandy and Williams in blackface, complete with outlandish costumes and black dialect. The show ran for two years.

In 1902 their show *In Dahomey* was so popular that they took it to England, where it met with equal success. The partners continued to produce such shows as *The Policy Players* (1899), *Bandanna Land* (1908), and *Abyssinia* (1906) until Walker's death in 1909.

Thereafter, Williams worked as a featured single in the Ziegfeld Follies, touring America for ten years in several versions of the show. His most famous songs were "Woodman, Spare That Tree," "O, Death, Where Is Thy Sting," and "Nobody," his own composition and trademark.

Considered by many to be the greatest black vaudeville performer in the history of the American stage, Williams died of pneumonia on March 4, 1922.

Billy Dee Williams (1937–)
Actor

A screen, television, and stage actor with impressive credits, Billy Dee Williams was born William December Williams in Harlem, New York, on April 6, 1937. Williams was a withdrawn, overweight youngster who initially planned to become a fashion illustrator. While he was studying on scholarship at the School of Fine Arts in the National Academy of Design, a CBS casting director helped him secure bit parts in several television shows, including *Lamp Unto My Feet* and *Look Up and Live*.

Williams then began to study acting under Sidney Poitier and Paul Mann at the Harlem Actors Workshop. He made his film debut in *The Last Angry Man* (1959), then appeared on stage in *The Cool World* (1960), *A Taste of Honey* (1961), and *The Blacks* (1962). He later appeared briefly on Broadway in *Hallelujah Baby!* (1967) and in several Off-Broadway shows, including *Ceremonies in Dark Old Men* (1970).

Williams's next major role was in the acclaimed television movie *Brian's Song* (1970), a performance for which he received an Emmy nomination. Motown's Berry Gordy then signed Williams to a seven-year contract, after which he starred in *Lady Sings the Blues* (1972) and *Mahogany* (1976) with Diana Ross. His last movie

for Gordy was *The Bingo Long Traveling All-Stars & Motor King* (1976).

Williams appeared in two of George Lucas's *Star Wars* adventures, *The Empire Strikes Back* (1980) and *Return of the Jedi* (1983). He has appeared in numerous television movies, including *Scott Joplin* (1977), *Christmas Lilies of the Field* (1979), and the miniseries *Chiefs* (1983). When he was cast opposite Diahann Carroll in the prime time drama *Dynasty,* his reputation as a romantic lead was secured. At the end of the decade, he starred in action films such as *Oceans of Fire* (1986) and *Number One with a Bullet* (1987).

Williams has remained impressive and influential in film and on television acting in films such as such a *Code Name: Eternity* (1999), *The Ladies Man* (2000), *Good Neighbor* (2001), *Undercover Brother* (2002), *Hood of Horror* (2006), and *This Bitter Earth* (2009). He has also appeared in television episodes of *Lost* (2007) and *The Boondocks* (animated; 2010).

Vanessa Williams (1963–)
Model, Singer, Actress

Vanessa Lynn Williams was born on March 18, 1963, in Tarrytown, New York. Williams made history in 1983 when she became the first African American to win the title of Miss America. By 1984 she had to relinquish her title due to compromising photos published by *Penthouse.*

Williams went on to pursue her singing career and she signed a record deal in 1988. Beginning with her first album *The Right Stuff,* which made it to *Billboard's* Top-10 list, she has had success. Her second album contained the hit single "Save the Best for Last" and her third album, which went triple platinum, earned Williams three Grammy nominations. She has continued to put out albums/CDs with commercial success.

Williams's film debut began with *Under the Gun* (1988). Other notable roles include the films

Eraser (1996) and *Soul Food* (1997), and television movies *Stompin' at the Savoy* (1992), *The Odyssey* (1997), and *Don Quixote* (2000). She has starred on the television series *Ugly Betty,* which ended in 2010, and she joined the cast of the series *Desperate Housewives* in 2011.

Flip Wilson (1933–1998)
Comedian, Actor

Born Clerow Wilson on December 8, 1933, in Jersey City, New Jersey, Flip Wilson was the tenth in a family of twenty-four children, eighteen of whom survived. The family was destitute and Wilson was a troublesome child during his youth in Jersey City; he ran away from reform school several times and was ultimately raised in foster homes.

Wilson's comic talents first surfaced while he was serving in the Air Force. Sent overseas to the Pacific, Wilson entertained his buddies with preposterous routines. Back in civilian life, he worked as a bellhop and part-time showman. Opportunity struck in 1959 when a Miami businessman sponsored him for one year at $50 a week, thus enabling Wilson to concentrate on the evolution of his routine. For the next five years or so, Wilson appeared regularly at the Apollo Theatre in Harlem. In 1965 he began a series of nationwide appearances on *The Tonight Show.* Long-term contracts and several hit records followed in quick sequence, and Wilson became firmly established as one of the truly innovative talents in the comedy profession. He reached the pinnacle of the entertainment world with a series of original routines and ethnic characters rivaled only by those of Bill Cosby. His hilarious monologues, seen on a number of network television shows, made him the most visible black comedian of the early 1970s.

With *The Flip Wilson Show* in the early 1970s, Wilson became the first black to have a weekly prime-time television show under his own name. He became famous for his original character creations, such as "Geraldine." On January 31, 1972, he appeared on the cover of *Time*

magazine. In 1976 he made his dramatic debut on television in the ABC series *The Six Million Dollar Man.*

During the early 1980s, Wilson appeared in numerous nightclubs and television specials. He also made comedy albums, including *The Devil Made Me Buy This Dress,* for which he received a Grammy Award. Wilson died on November 25, 1998, of liver cancer.

George C. Wolfe (1954–)
Playwright

George Costello Wolfe was born on September 23, 1954, in Frankfort, Kentucky. Inspired early on to have a career in the theater, Wolfe earned a B.A. in theater from Pomona College in 1976. In 1979 he also earned an M.F.A. in dramatic writing and musical theater from New York University.

Wolfe wrote his first play in 1985 but received limited reviews from the critics. With the production of the play *The Colored Museum* in 1986, Wolfe received critical acclaim and was awarded an Obie. The play was also broadcast on PBS. In 1992 Wolfe debuted his play *Jelly's Last Jam,* which was well received by the New York community. The play was produced on Broadway and it received eleven Tony nominations and won the Drama Desk Award. Wolfe continues to write and direct and support other playwrights in their work.

Wolfe has received numerous awards for his work, including a Tony Award in 1993 for producing Part One of *Angels in America: Millennium Approaches,* and in that same year Wolfe was named artistic director and producer of the Joseph Papp Public Theater/New York Shakespeare Festival. He has also been awarded the Drama Desk, Outer Critics Circle, Dramalogue, and Obie Awards, and was named person of the year by the National Theater Conference.

Although Wolfe stepped down from the Public Theater in 2004, and has since immersed himself in other endeavors, he still actively supports the work of the Public Theater. Wolfe directed the film *Lackawanna Blues* in 2004, as well as the Pulitzer Prize-winning play *Topdog/Underdog* by playwright Suzan-Lori Parks. His latest film venture, *Nights in Rodanthe,* opened in 2008.

BIOGRAPHIES: VISUAL AND APPLIED ARTS

Charles Alston (1907–1972)

Painter, Sculptor, Muralist

Charles Alston was born on November 28, 1907, in Charlotte, North Carolina. He earned his B.A. and M.A. from Columbia University and studied at the National Academy of Art in New York. Alston was a key figure in the Harlem Renaissance as he helped to create a community of artists. He recognized the talents of artists such as Jacob Lawrence and was acquainted with artists such as Langston Hughes. Alston combined modern styles with non-Western influences to create an African American perspective. As a result of his talent, he was awarded several scholarships and grants that helped to launch his career.

In the 1960s Alston produced close-up portraits of great black figures such as Frederick Douglass and Martin Luther King Jr. Alston's painting and sculptures are a part of the art collections of IBM and the Detroit Institute of Art, and his murals grace the walls of Harlem Hospital in New York. Alston's most recognized works include *Exploration and Colonization* (1949), *Blues Songs* (1958), *Nobody Knows* (1966), and *Frederick Douglass* (1968). Alston died on April 27, 1972.

Benny Andrews (1930–2006)

Painter

Andrews was born in Plainview, Georgia, on November 13, 1930. He earned a B.F.A. from the Art Institute of Chicago in 1958. He is considered a figural painter as he addresses images and issues of suffering and injustice. His work has represented the Holocaust, black migration, and Hurricane Katrina. His work has appeared at the Boston Museum of Fine Arts, the Martha Jackson Gallery in New York, and other galleries around the country. His most notable works include *The Family, The Boxer, The Invisible Man,* and *Womanhood.*

Andrews taught at the New York School of Social Research and Queens College in New York. He also served at the National Endowment of the Arts from 1982 to 1984 as visual arts program director. He received numerous awards, including a Rockefeller Foundation Award in 1987 and a National Endowment for the Arts Painting Fellowship in 1986. Andrews died on November 10, 2006.

Ernie Barnes (1938–2009)

Painter

Ernest Eugene "Ernie" Barnes Jr. was born on July 15, 1938, in Durham, North Carolina. He began his career in sports playing football for the Washington Redskins. Even though he attended North Carolina Central University from 1957 to 1960 majoring in art and playing football, he left when he was drafted. Barnes played for several teams in the National Football League before retiring due to an injury in 1966.

Barnes continued to paint during his football career and became known among his teammates as "Big Rembrandt." After he retired he landed a contract to paint for the American Football League and New York Jets owner Sonny Werblin. His art, which was referred as sports art, is figurative in that it emphasizes and even exaggerates to enhance physical characteristics, humor, or mood. Barnes was selected as the official artist for the 1994 Olympics. He received further exposure for his work when his paintings appeared on the popular television series, *Good Times.*

Barnes's work has appeared on album covers and in many prized personal collections. He work has also been exhibited at the California Museum of Science and Industry. Barnes died on April 27, 2009, in Los Angeles, California, from a rare blood disorder.

Richmond Barthé (1901–1989)
Sculptor

James Richmond Barthé was born in Bay St. Louis, Mississippi, on January 28, 1901. He studied at the Art Institute in Chicago. Although initially having a passion for painting, Barthé first received attention for a sculpture he created in 1927. He was subsequently commissioned to do busts of Henry Ossawa Tanner and Toussaint L'Ouverture. His work most often depicted African Americans in everyday life and in the South. His notable works include *Mother and Son, The Boxer, Singing Slave,* and *Henry Ossawa Tanner.*

Barthé's work has been exhibited in many galleries including the Metropolitan Museum of Art in New York City. He was awarded a Rosenwald Fellowship, presented a one-man show of his work in Chicago, and was one of fifteen artists chosen to modernize the sculptures in the Catholic churches in America. In 1943 he was awarded a Guggenheim Fellowship and in 1943, *The Boxer* was purchased by the Metropolitan Museum of Art in New York. In 1953 he created a forty-foot statue of Jean Jacques Dessalines, leader of the 1804 revolution for the city of Port-au-Prince. Barthé's last known sculpture was of actor James Garner in appreciation for his assistance in difficult times. Barthé died on March 6, 1989, in Pasadena, California.

Jean-Michel Basquiat (1960–1988)
Painter

Jean-Michel Basquiat was born in Brooklyn, New York, on December 22, 1960. He attracted the New York art world with his trendy personal appearance and his flair as a musician and artist at the age of eighteen. In February 1985, he was featured on the cover of the *New York Times Magazine,* shoeless but wearing a suit, shirt, and tie. He began spray-painting on buildings in the 1970s using the signature "SAMO" (meaning "same old shit"). In 1980 "The Time Square Show" brought him to the immediate attention of the art world in the United States and Europe. In a brief, tragic career, Basquiat gained attention from wealthy collectors as a young artist discovered by Andy Warhol and promoted by other art consultants. His works are autobiographical and deliberately "primitive" in style.

Basquiat began his career illegally spray-painting images on buildings throughout the city, and he has said that his subject matter was "royalty, heroism and the streets." Basquiat died of a drug overdose on August 12, 1988. His notable works include: *Self Portrait as a Heel #3; Untitled* (History of Black People); *Hollywood Africans;* and *CPRKR* (in honor of Charlie Parker).

The Whitney Museum of American Art in New York City owns many of the 600 works Basquiat produced, reportedly valued in the tens of millions of dollars. The Whitney Museum mounted a retrospective exhibit of his work from October 23, 1992, to February 14, 1993.

Romare Bearden (1911–1988)
Painter, Collagist

Romare Bearden was born in Charlotte, North Carolina, on September 2, 1911. His family moved to Pittsburgh and later to Harlem. Bearden studied with George Grosz at the Art Students League and later, on the G.I. Bill, went to Paris where he met Henri Matisse, Joan Miró, and Carl Holty. Bearden was a product of the new generation of African Americans who had migrated from the rural areas of the South to the urban areas of the North. His work reflected the era of industrialization and would become the visual images that depicted city life, the music (jazz), and the people. Bearden's earlier works belonged to the school of social realism, but after his return from Europe his images became more abstract.

In the 1960s Bearden changed his approach to picture-making and began to make collages, soon becoming one of the best known collagists in the world. His images are haunting montages of his memories of past experiences, and of stories told to him by other people. They are for Bearden "an attempt to redefine the image of man in terms of the black experience." His notable works include *Street Corner, He Is Arisen, The Burial, Sheba,* and *The Prevalence of Ritual.*

Bearden's work can be seen at the Museum of Modern Art, Pennsylvania Academy of the Fine Arts, and the Library of Congress. Bearden died on March 2, 1988, due to complications from bone cancer. In 2002 the scholar Molefi Kete Asante listed Bearden on his list of the 100 greatest African Americans.

John Biggers (1924–2001)
Painter

Born in Gastonia, North Carolina, on April 13, 1924, John Biggers derived much of his subject matter from the contributions made by blacks to the development of the United States. While teaching at Texas Southern University, Biggers significantly influenced several young black painters. Biggers became a leading figure in social realism as a painter, sculptor, printmaker, and teacher, as well as an outstanding surrealistic muralist.

Some of his most powerful pieces were created as a result of his study trips to Africa: *The Time of Ede, Nigeria,* a series of works done in the 1960s, are prime examples. His notable works include *Cradle, Mother and Child, The Contributions of Negro Women to American Life and Education,* and *Shotgun, Third Ward, #1.* His work is displayed at the Houston Museum of Fine Arts, the Dallas Museum of Fine Arts, Howard University, and Pennsylvania State University. Biggers died in 2001.

Camille Billops (1933–)
Sculptor, Photographer, Filmmaker

A sculptor of note in the art and retailing world, Camille Billops was born in Los Angeles, California, on August 12, 1933, and graduated from California State College in 1960. She then studied sculpture on the West Coast under a grant from the Huntington Hartford Foundation. In 1960 she had her first exhibition at the African Art Exhibition in Los Angeles, followed by an exhibit at the Valley Cities Jewish Community Center in Los Angeles in 1963. In 1966 she participated in a group exhibition in Moscow. Her multifaceted artistic talents, which include poetry, book illustration, and jewelry making, have earned the praise of critics throughout the world, particularly in Sri Lanka and Egypt, where she has lived and worked.

Billops has also taught extensively. In 1975 she was active on the faculties of the City University of New York and Rutgers at Newark, New Jersey. In addition, she conducted special art courses in the New York City jail (the Tombs), and in 1972 she lectured in India for the U.S. Information Service on Black American artists. She participated in an exhibit at the New York Cultural Center in 1973.

She has received grants for films from such institutions as: the New York State Council on the Arts in 1987, 1988, and 1989; the New York Foundation for the Arts in 1989; Rockefeller Foundation in 1991; and the National Endowment for the Arts in 1994.

In 1992 Billops won the prestigious Grand Jury Prize for best documentary at the Sundance Film Festival with *Finding Christa,* an edited combination of interviews, home movies, still images, and dramatic acting. Her most notable films include *Older Women and Love* (1987), *The K.K.K. Boutique Ain't Just Rednecks* (1994), and *A String of Pearls* (2002). Her other notable works include *Tenure, Black American,* and *Portrait of an American Indian* (ceramic sculptures), and *Year after Year* (painting).

Robert Blackburn (1920–2003)
Printmaker

Robert Hamilton Blackburn was born December 10, 1920, in Summit, New Jersey, and his family later moved to Harlem, New York City. He studied at the Harlem Workshop, at the Art Students League under Augusta Savage, and at the Wallace Harrison School of Art. His exhibits include *Art of the American Negro* (1940), *Contemporary Art of the American Negro* (1966), exhibits in New York's Downtown Gallery and the Albany Museum, and numerous print shows in the United States and Europe. His work is represented in the Library of Congress, the Brooklyn and Baltimore museums, and the Atlanta University Collections. He was a member of the art faculty of Cooper Union.

Along with his other accomplishments, he founded the Printmaking Workshop as an artist-run cooperative in 1949. In 1971 it was incorporated as a nonprofit printmaking studio for work in lithography, etching, relief, and photo processes. The workshop, which is a magnet for third-world and minority artists and reflects Blackburn's warmth and encouraging personality, remains a haven for artists "to turn out prints for the love of it" and to do anything from experimental hodgepodge to polished pieces. In 1988 Bob Blackburn and the Printmaking Workshop were given the Governor's Art Award for making "a significant contribution to the cultural life of New York State." His notable works include *Boy with Green Head, Blue Thing, Space Shapes,* and *Negro Mother.* In 1992 Blackburn was awarded the prestigious John D. and Catherine T. MacArthur Foundation Awards worth $375,000. The award went to support his workshop. Blackburn died in New York City on April 21, 2003.

Selma Burke (1900–1995)
Sculptor, Educator

Selma Hortense Burke was born December 31, 1900, in Mooresville, North Carolina, and received her training as a sculptor at Columbia University in New York. She also studied with Aristide Maillol in Paris and with Povolney in Vienna. World War II interrupted her work in Europe and she returned to the United States to continue her artistic and humanitarian pursuits. Burke is best known for her relief sculpture rendering of Franklin Delano Roosevelt that was later minted on the American dime. She also produced a statue of Martin Luther King Jr. that stands in Marshall Park in Charlotte, North Carolina.

The Pearl S. Buck Foundation Woman's Award was given to Burke in 1987 for her professional distinction and devotion to family and humanity. Her notable works include *Falling Angel, Peace,* and *Jim.* Burke, who enjoyed an artistic career that spanned more than sixty years, died of cancer on August 29, 1995.

Stephen Burrows (1943–)
Fashion Designer

Stephen Burrows was born September 15, 1943, in Newark, New Jersey. He studied at his grandmother's knee as a boy and started making clothes at a young age. He later studied at the Philadelphia Museum College of Art from 1961 to 1962, and at the Fashion Institute of Technology in New York City from 1964 to 1966.

With a partner Burrows opened a boutique in 1968. He worked for Henri Bendel from 1969 to 1973 and returned to Bendel's in 1977. From 1974 to 1977 he and a partner ran a Seventh Avenue firm. Known for his unique color combinations, he used patches of cloth for decorative motifs in the 1960s. His top-stitching of seams in contrasting threads and top-stitched hems, known as "lettuce hems" because of their fluted effect, were widely copied. His designs show an inclination toward asymmetry and a preference for soft, clinging, easy-moving fabrics such as chiffon and matte jersey. His clothes were adopted readily by disco dancers, for whom he designed clothing in natural fabrics with non-constricting, light, and airy qualities. He won a Coty American Fashion

Critics' Award in 1974, and a special Coty Award in 1977. After staying out of the public eye in the 1980s, Burrows returned to Henri Bendel to design evening wear in 1993.

Elizabeth Catlett (1915–)
Sculptor, Painter

The granddaughter of North Carolina slaves, Elizabeth Catlett was born on April 15, 1915, and raised in northwest Washington, D.C. As a young woman she attempted to gain admission to a then all-white art school, Carnegie Institute of Technology in Pittsburgh, Pennsylvania. She was refused entry and instead went to Howard University and graduated as an honor student in 1937. In 1940 she went on to study at the University of Iowa, where she became the first of their students to receive an M.F.A.

Her exhibition history dates back to 1937 and includes group and solo presentations at all the major American art museums as well as institutions in Mexico City, Moscow, Paris, Prague, Tokyo, Beijing, Berlin, and Havana. Catlett's public sculpture can be found in Mexico City, Mexico; Jackson, Mississippi; New Orleans, Louisiana; Washington, D.C.; and New York City. Her work is represented in the permanent collections of over twenty museums throughout the world.

Catlett accepted teaching positions at various black colleges to earn a living, but by 1946 she had moved to Mexico, where she eventually settled. Always a champion of the oppressed—concerned with the documentation of economic, social, and political themes—Catlett became deeply involved with the civil rights movement, and it greatly affected her philosophy of life and art. Between 1941 and 1969 Catlett won eight prizes and honors, four in Mexico and four in America. Her notable works include *Black Unity* (1968), *Target Practice* (1970), *Mother and Child* (1972), and *Woman Resting* (1981). In 1995 Catlett created a lithograph called *Children with Flowers* to benefit the Smithsonian Associates Art Collectors Program's educational and cultural programs; and in 2003 she designed a memorial to the author Ralph Ellison, which is in West Harlem, New York.

Catlett was awarded an honorary degree from Morgan State University in 1993, and from the New York School for Social Research in 1995. In 2003 she was awarded the Lifetime Achievement Award from the International Sculpture Center.

Barbara Chase-Riboud (1939–)
Sculptor, Writer

Barbara Chase-Riboud was born in Philadelphia, Pennsylvania, on June 26, 1939. Encouraged by her parents she studied piano, ballet, and dance. She attended Temple University and received a B.F.A. in art in 1956, and an M.F.A. from Yale University in 1960. After earning a fellowship from the John Hay Whitney Foundation, Chase-Riboud

A bronze statue by artist Barbara Chase-Riboud.

was able to travel to Rome during her college years and returned after completing her studies at Yale. She has resided in Europe since 1961.

As a sculptor Chase-Riboud uses mixed-media to explore issues of race and society. Her most notable works are *Exploration in the City of Light: African American Artists in Paris, 1945–1965* and *Three Generations of African-American Women Sculptors.* Chase-Riboud has established herself as a writer, publishing such works as *The President's Daughter* (1994), *Portrait of a Nude Woman as Cleopatra* (poetry; 1987), and *Hottentot Venus: A Novel* (2004).

Robert Colescott (1925–2009)

Painter

Robert Colescott was born August 25, 1925, in Oakland, California. He earned his B.A. from the University of California in 1949 and his M.A. in 1952. His works are best known for their satirical content while exploring race and other stereotypes and taboos. They are in the Metropolitan Museum of Art, the Portland Art Museum, the Delaware Museum of Art, and the University of Massachusetts's fine art collection. His most notable pieces include *Eat Dem Taters, Shirley Temple Black, Bill Robinson White,* and *The Desire for Power.*

Colescott died on June 4, 2009, at his home in Tucson, Arizona.

Beauford Delaney (1910–1979)

Painter

Born in Knoxville, Tennessee, on December 30, 1910, Beauford Delaney was described by his elder brother Samuel as a "remarkably dutiful child." His father, the Reverend Samuel Delaney, and his mother, Delia Johnson Delaney, understood and recognized Beauford's artistic talent, as well as that of his brother Joseph, and they encouraged them to develop their skills. For Beauford Delaney, recognition came by way of an elderly

white artist of Knoxville, Lloyd Branson. Branson gave him lessons and after a time urged him to go to a city where he might study and come into contact with the art world.

In 1924 Beauford Delaney went to Boston to study at the Massachusetts Normal School, and he later studied at the Copley Society, where he took evening courses while working full-time at the South Boston School of Art. From Boston, Delaney moved on to New York.

Delaney assumed the life of a bohemian in New York, living in the Village in coldwater flats. Much of his time was spent painting the portraits of the personalities of the day, such as Louis Armstrong, Ethel Waters, and Duke Ellington. In 1938 Delaney gained national attention when *Life* magazine, in an article on "negroes," featured a photograph of him surrounded by a group of his paintings at the annual outdoor exhibition in Washington Square in New York. In 1945 Henry Miller wrote the essay "The Amazing and Invariable Beauford Delaney," which was later reprinted in *Remember to Remember.* The essay describes Delaney's bohemian life-style in New York during the 1940s and 1950s.

In the 1950s Delaney left New York with the intention of studying in Rome. Taking the *Ile de France,* he sailed to Paris, next visiting Greece, Turkey, and Northern Italy—but he never got to Rome. Returning to Paris for one more visit, Delaney began to paint, make new friends, and create a social life filled with the famous and the soon-to-be-famous, like James Baldwin, who at that time had not yet become a renowned novelist. Paris was to become Delaney's permanent home.

By 1961 Delaney was producing paintings at such an intense rate that the pressure began to wear upon his strength, and he suffered his first mental collapse. He was confined to a clinic in Vincennes, and his dealer and close friends began to organize his life, hoping to relieve some of the pressure, but it was of little use. For the rest of his life, Delaney was to suffer sporadic breakdowns, and by 1971 he was back in a sanitarium, where he remained until his death in 1979.

Delaney's numerous exhibitions included the Artists Gallery in New York (1948); the Roko Gallery in New York (1950–1953); the Musée d'Art Moderne in Paris (1963); the American Negro Exposition in Chicago (1940); and Newark Museum (1971). His work can be found in the collections of the Whitney Museum of American Art, New York; the Newark Museum, New Jersey; and Morgan State College, Baltimore, Maryland. Notable works include *Greene Street, Yaddo, Head of a Poet,* and *Snow Scene.*

Aaron Douglas (1899–1979)
Painter

Born in Topeka, Kansas, on May 26, 1899, Aaron Douglas achieved considerable eminence as a muralist, illustrator, and academician. As a young man Douglas studied at the University of Nebraska, Columbia University Teachers College, and L'Académie Scandinave in Paris. He had one-person exhibits at the University of Kansas and the University of Nebraska and also exhibited in New York at the Gallery of Modern Art. In 1939 Douglas was named to the faculty of Fisk University and later became head of its department of art.

In 1992 Fisk opened a new gallery in his memory. Douglas is considered the most important painter and illustrator of the "Negro Renaissance," now known as the Harlem Renaissance. His notable works include murals at Fisk and in the Countee Cullen Branch of the New York City Public Library, and illustrations in books by Countee Cullen, James Weldon Johnson, Alain Locke, and Langston Hughes. Marian Anderson and Mary McLeod Bethune are among the many African Americans he painted or rendered in charcoal. Douglas died on February 3, 1979.

David C. Driskell (1931–)
Painter, Historian

Born in Eatonton, Georgia, on June 7, 1931, David Clyde Driskell studied at Howard Univer-

sity and Catholic University of America, where he received an M.A. in 1962. He also studied at the Skowhegan School of Painting and Sculpture and the Netherlands Institute for History of Art. He has taught at Talladega College, Fisk University, the Institute for African Studies of the University of Ife in Nigeria, and the University of Maryland at College Park.

Immediately after the death of Alonzo Aden, Driskell was asked to direct the gallery that housed the important Barnett–Aden collection of African American art. He has curated and mounted important exhibitions, including the impressive *200 Years of African American Art,* shown at major museums across the country.

A recipient of many awards, including the John Hope Award, prizes from the Danforth Foundation, American Federation of Arts, and Harmon Foundation, Driskell has exhibited at the Corcoran Gallery of Art, National Museum, and Rhodes National Gallery in Salisbury, Rhodesia. Notable works include *Movement, the Mountain, Still Life with Gateleg Table, Shango Goen, Rainmaker, Foreign Post,* and *Hands Up.*

Robert Duncanson (1821–1872)
Painter

Robert Duncanson was the son of an African American woman and a Scottish-Canadian man. Born in Seneca County, New York, in 1821, he would spend much of his childhood in Canada. At some point in his youth, he and his mother moved to Mt. Healthy, Ohio, where in 1840 the Western Freedmen's Aid Society, an anti-slavery group, raised funds to send him to Glasgow, Scotland, to study art. Returning to Cincinnati three years later, Duncanson advertised in the local newspaper as the proprietor of a daguerreotype studio. Even though he had begun gaining a reputation as a painter, he continued to work at daguerreotype until 1855, when he started to devote all of his time to his painting. Like many landscape artists of this time, Duncanson traveled around the United States drawing compositions from the images of nature before him. In

Landscape painting by Robert Duncanson, c. 1870.

1853 he made his second trip to Europe—this time to visit Italy, France, and England.

Duncanson was painting during and after the Civil War era; though with the exception of his painting *Uncle Tom and Eva,* he made no attempts to present the turmoil that was taking place in America or the social pressures that he experienced. In September 1872 Duncanson, while at the height of his success, suffered a severe mental breakdown and ended his life on December 21 in the Michigan State Retreat in Detroit. His notable works include murals in the Taft Museum and *Bishop Payne.*

William Edmonson (1882–1951)

Sculptor

William Edmonson, a stonecutter and self-taught sculptor, was born in Nashville, Tennessee, in 1882. He supported himself working as a hospital orderly at Baptist Hospital and through other menial jobs. His work was discovered by Mrs. Meyer Dahl-Wolfe, who had an extensive private collec-

tion and brought him to the attention of the Museum of Modern Art. In an exhibition of self-taught artists, his work was received extremely well. In 1937 he was the first African American to have a one-person exhibit at the museum. Private collectors and museums have purchased his few sculptures, which are vigorously executed and original.

Inspired by biblical passages, Edmonson engraved tombstones and worked on his sculpture, which he did in limestone, at the home he shared with his mother and sister. He continued to live alone and work there after their deaths, until he died in 1951. Notable works include *Choir Girls, Lion,* and *Crucifixion.*

Tom Feelings (1933–2003)

Illustrator

Tom Feelings was born in Brooklyn, New York, on May 19, 1933. After he completed high school he studied at the Cartoonists and Illustrators' School in New York City. While in school he created the comic strip *Tommy Traveler in the World of Negro*

History, published in the Harlem paper *New York Age.* After graduating in 1964 he traveled to Ghana to help support the new independent nation. He left in 1966 and later traveled to Guyana to administer a project for children's books.

Feelings began illustrating African American books and in particular children's books in the late 1960s. His work included illustrations in *Moja Means One: A Swahili Counting Book* (illustrated with his wife), which won a Caldecott Honor Award in 1972, and two collaborations with Maya Angelou titled *Now Sheba Sings the Song* in 1987, and *Soul Looks Back in Wonder* in 1993. In 1995 Feelings published *The Middle Passage,* which was twenty years in the making and is considered his masterpiece.

Feelings's awards are numerous, including the Distinguished Service to Children through Art Award from the University of South Carolina, a National Endowment for the Arts grant, two outstanding achievement awards from the New York School of Visual Arts, and three Coretta Scott King Awards. He died on August 25, 2003.

Meta Fuller (1877–1968)

Sculptor

Meta Vaux Warrick Fuller was born on June 9, 1877, in Philadelphia, Pennsylvania, and educated at the School of Industrial Art and the Pennsylvania Academy, Fuller pursued her interest in sculpture by studying with Charles Grafly and with Auguste Rodin at the Académie Colarossi in Paris. After studying in Europe she returned to Philadelphia and immersed herself in black life. She drew her themes from black life and in 1907 was commissioned to sculpt scenes for the Negro Pavilion at the Jamestown Tercentennial Exposition. She was the first black woman to receive a federal commission. Although her work was not always popular she continued to create. As the first African American woman to become a professional artist, Fuller was part of the transitional period between the artists who chose to simulate Euro-American subjects and styles and the later periods to follow. Her African American figures in *The Wretched,* exhibited at the Paris Salon in 1903 and 1904, did not suit popular tastes, but they were sincere expressions of the talented artist.

Fuller married and settled in the Boston area where, in 1910 most of her works were destroyed by fire. In spite of this she went on to produce *Ethiopia Awakening,* a sculpture that anticipated the voices of the Harlem Renaissance. In 1956 she sculptured the head and hands of ten notable black women for a set of dolls for the National Council of Negro Women, and she dedicated the piece *The Good Shepard* to the clergy who walked with Martin Luther King Jr. on March 9, 1955. The Boston Art Club, the Harmon Foundation, and many other galleries have exhibited her works, and representative pieces of her sculpture can be found in the Cleveland Museum. Fuller continued to create works for the Framingham Center Library well into her eighties. She died on March 18, 1968.

Sam Gilliam (1933–)

Painter

Born in Tupelo, Mississippi, on November 30, 1933, Sam Gilliam produces hanging canvases that are laced with pure color pigments rather than shades or tones. The artist bunches these pigments in weird configurations on drooping, drape-like canvases, giving the effect, in the words of a *Time* magazine critic, of "clothes drying on a line." His canvases are said to be "like nobody else's, black or white."

Gilliam received his M.A. from the University of Louisville, and was awarded National Endowment of Humanities and Arts grants. He has had one-man and group shows at the Washington Gallery of Modern Art, Jefferson Place Gallery, Adams-Morgan Gallery in Washington, D.C., the Art Gallery of Washington University in St. Louis, Missouri, the Speed Museum in Louisville, the Philadelphia Museum of Art, the Museum of Modern Art, the Phillips Collection and Corcoran Gallery of Art, both in Washington, D.C., the San Francisco Museum of Art, the

The sculpture *Color of Metals*, by Sam Gilliam, is mounted on a wall inside the Philadelphia Veterans Administration building.

Walker Art Center in Minneapolis, and the Whitney Museum of American Art. He is represented in the permanent collection of over forty-five American museums.

Gilliam's work has been included in several group exhibitions, including the *First World Festival of Negro Arts* in Dakar, Senegal (1966), *The Negro in American Art* at UCLA (1967), and the Whitney Museum's *American Art Annual* (1969).

In 1980 Sam Gilliam was commissioned, with thirteen other artists, to design an art piece for installation in the Hartsfield-Jackston Atlanta International Airport terminal in Georgia—one of the largest terminals in the world and the first to install contemporary artwork on its walls for public viewing. In 1983 the first retrospective of his work was exhibited. His notable works include *Herald* (1965), *Watercolor 4* (1969), *Carousel Change* (1970), *Mazda* (1970), *Plantagenets Golden* (1984), and *Golden Element Inside Gold* (1994).

Tyree Guyton (1955–)
Multimedia Artist

Tyree Guyton was born on August 24, 1955, in Detroit, Michigan. Guyton, who spent his life in the same area of urban Detroit, began an ongoing project of transforming his neighborhood. In 1984, after taking art classes and infusing the influence of his mother toward color and decor, he used dots, stripes, bright colors, and any and all discarded objects from junk piles to transform his home. Guyton not only transformed his home but many other homes on Heidelberg Street where he lived. His use of mixed media had a social impact of deterring negative elements from the street while gaining the praise of the neighborhood, art critics, and art lovers.

Guyton's work, called the *Heidelberg Project* after the street where he lived, was considered an artistic success and was placed on the city's art tour. He was named the Michiganian of the Year and received the Governor's Art Award. Although there was some criticism of the project by those who preferred traditional neighborhoods, his community and the art world saw it as innovate and inspiring. Guyton received the David A. Hammond Memorial Scholarship and the Spirit of Detroit Award, among others.

Although Guyton's neighborhood was a part of the city's tour, several of the houses were bulldozed in 1991 and Guyton sued the city. Eventually the suit was dropped, but by 1999 the project had been partly dismantled. Gyton has been an artist in residence at Marygrove College, Syracuse University School of fine arts, and Harvard University, and his work can be viewed at the Studio Museum of Harlem, the University of Michigan Museum of Art, and the Kresge Art Museum.

Sargent Johnson (1888–1967)
Sculptor

Sargent Johnson was born in Boston, Massachusetts, in 1888. His father was Swedish and his mother was Cherokee and Negro. Johnson studied at the Worchester Art School and, in 1915 moved to San Francisco. His work was presented at the San Francisco Artists Annual festival from 1925 to 1931, the Harmon Foundation from 1928 to 1931, and again in 1933, and the American Negro Exposition in Chicago in 1940.

Johnson worked with various media, but his style is considered as figurative. Johnson received many other awards for his work, notably among which are *Sammy, Esther,* and *Forever Free.* Johnson died in 1967.

William H. Johnson (1901–1970)
Painter

Born in Florence, South Carolina, on March 18, 1901, William H. Johnson studied at the National Academy of Design; the Cape Cod School of Art, under Charles Hawthorne; in southern France from 1926 to 1929; and in Denmark and Norway from 1930 to 1938. Johnson was a pioneering black modernist whose ever-developing work went from abstract expressionist landscape and flower studies influenced by Vincent Van Gogh, to studies of black life in America, and finally to abstract figure studies in the manner of Georges Rouault. His exhibits include the Harmon Foundation, which awarded him a gold medal in 1929; Aarlins, Denmark, 1935; the Baltimore Museum, 1939; and the American Negro Exposition in Chicago, 1940. He produced one-person shows in Copenhagen in 1935, and at New York's Artists Gallery in 1938. His notable works include *Booker T. Washington, Young Man in Vest, Descent from the Cross,* and *On a John Brown Flight.* Johnson died on April 13, 1970.

Joshua Johnston (c.1763–c.1824)
Painter

Born about 1763, Joshua Johnston is the first known black portrait painter from the Baltimore area. At least two dozen paintings have been attributed to this artist, who was listed as a "free house-holder of colour, portrait painter." He was listed in the Baltimore directories in various studio locations.

Johnston was the son of George Johnston and a slave woman. Johnston was freed in 1782, after completing an apprenticeship with a Baltimore blacksmith or upon turning twenty-one, whichever came first as stated by the manumission papers. In either case, Johnston was most likely self-taught as a painter. A portraitist in the true style of the period, his work now seems quaint and sensitive. Only one black subject has been attributed to him, *Portrait of a Cleric.* Notable works include *Portrait of Adelia Ellender, Portrait of Mrs. Barbara Baker Murphy,* and *Portrait of Sea Captain John Murphy.*

Jacob Lawrence (1917–2000)
Painter

Born on September 7, 1917, in Atlantic City, New Jersey, Jacob Lawrence received his early training at the Harlem Art School and the American Artist School. His rise to prominence was ushered in by his series of biographical panels commemorating important episodes in African American history. Capturing the essential meaning behind a historical moment or personality, Lawrence created several series, each consisting of dozens of small paintings that depict a particular event in American history, such as *The Migration Series* ("... and the Migrants keep coming"), which traces the migration of the African American from the South to the North, or the events of a person's life (e.g., Toussaint L'Ouverture and John Brown). A narrative painter, Lawrence related the "philosophy of Impressionism" in his work.

Lawrence was a visual American historian. His paintings record the African American in trade, theater, mental hospitals, neighborhoods, or running in the Olympic races. Lawrence's works are found in such collections as the Metropolitan Museum of Art, the Museum of Modern Art, the Whitney Museum of American Art, the National Museum of American Art, and the Wadsworth Atheneum in Hartford, Connecticut.

Lawrence's notable works include *The Life of Toussaint L'Ouverture* (forty-one panels; 1937); *The Life of Harriet Tubman* (forty panels; 1939); and *The Negro Migration Northward in World War* (sixty panels; 1942). His commissioned work in later years include a print for the 1976 U.S. Bicentennial, an invitation to paint the presidential inauguration of Jimmy Carter, illustrations for John Hersey's special edition book *Hiroshima* in 1983, and a poster for the National Urban League in 1984.

Lawrence was awarded the National Medal of Arts in 1990. He died on June 9, 2000.

Edmonia Lewis (1845–1907)
Sculptor

Edmonia Lewis was America's first black woman artist and also the first of her race and gender to be recognized as a sculptor. Born on July 4, 1845, in Albany, New York, she was the daughter of a Chippewa woman and a free black man. From 1859 to 1863, under the patronage of a number of abolitionists, she was educated at Oberlin College, the first American college to admit women into an integrated environment.

After completing her schooling, Lewis moved to Boston, where she studied with Edmund Brackett and did a bust of Colonel Robert Gould Shaw, the commander of the first black regiment organized in the state of Massachusetts during the Civil War. In 1865 she moved to Rome, where she soon became a prominent artist. Returning to the United States in 1874, she fulfilled many commissions, including a bust of Henry Wadsworth Longfellow that was executed for the Harvard College Library.

Her works are fine examples of the neo-classical sculpture that was fashionable during her lifetime. Notable works include *Hagar in the Wilderness, Forever Free, Hiawatha,* and *Old Arrow-Maker and His Daughter*. Lewis died September 17, 1907.

Geraldine McCullough (1917–2008)
Sculptor

Geraldine Hamilton McCullough was born in Kingston, Arkansas, on December 1, 1917. She attended the Art Institute of Chicago and earned a B.A. in 1948, and an M.A. in 1955. After receiving first prize in an art competition at Atlanta University in 1961, McCullough decided to try her hand at sculpting. She made her debut in 1963 and won the George D. Widener Gold Medal in 1965, for her steel and copper structure *Phoenix*. McCullough's work was inspired by African ritual art.

McCullough was a guest artist of the Russian government, and her work has been exhibited at the Smithsonian Institution and the Women's Museum. Following her retirement from Dominican University (previously Rosary College) after twenty-two years, she was awarded an honorary doctorate. McCullough died on December 15, 2008.

Archibald Motley (1891–1981)
Painter

Born in New Orleans, Louisiana, on October 7, 1891, Archibald Motley evinced his artistic talent by the time he attended high school. His father wanted him to become a doctor, but Archibald insisted on art and began formal education at the Art Institute of Chicago, earning his living by working as a day laborer. During this time Motley came in contact with the drifters, scavengers, and hustlers of society, who are now immortalized in his street scenes. Motley touched on many topics and themes in his work, but none was more gratifying to him than his candid depictions of Black Americans.

Black Belt by artist Archibald Motley.

His genre scenes are highly stylized and colorful and are often associated with the Ash-Can school of art, which was popular in the 1920s. His scenes are influenced by jazz culture and black migration from the South as in his sculpture *Bronzville at Night.*

In 1928 Motley had a one-person show at the new galleries in downtown New York and became the first artist, black or white, to make the front page of the *New York Times.* He was awarded a Guggenheim Fellowship in 1929 and studied in France. He was the recipient of a Harmon Foundation Award for an early portrait. His notable works include *The Jockey Club, The Plotters, Parisian Scene, Black Belt,* and *Old Snuff Dipper.* Motley died on January 16, 1981.

John Outterbridge (1933–)
Sculptor

John Wilfred Outterbridge was born in Greenville, North Carolina, on March 12, 1933. He studied at A&T University in Greensboro, North Carolina. He also studied at the Chicago Academy for the Arts, the American Academy of Art, both in Chicago, and at the Art Center School of Design in Pasadena, California.

Outterbridge's works are either tributes to ancestors or they create or contribute to "street art," which incorporates structures and symbols or words to address and explore community concerns. His notable works are *Shoeshine Box, Mood Ghetto,* and *Ethnic Heritage Group.* Outterbridge was awarded the Malcolm X Freedom Award by the New Afrikan People's Organization in 1990, the National Endowment for the Arts Visual Arts Fellowship, and the J. Paul Getty Visual Arts Fellowship in 1994. He has also received an honorary degree from the Otis College of Arts and Design.

Gordon Parks (1912–2006)
Photographer, Composer, Writer, Director

 Gordon Parks was born on November 30, 1912, in Fort Scott, Kansas. After the death of his mother, Parks went to St. Paul, Minnesota, to live with relatives. While there he attended Central High School and Mechanical Arts High School. Despite having fond childhood memories of his father on the family farm, Parks had a dysfunctional upbringing that lasted into young adulthood. Parks worked at a large variety of jobs including janitor, busboy, and semi-pro basketball player. Always interested in the arts, Parks also tried sculpting, writing, and touring with a band, but these artistic endeavors were largely without focus.

In 1933 Parks joined the Civilian Conservation Corps, and in the late 1930s, while working as a railroad porter, he became interested in photography as a medium in which he could finally focus his considerable artistic talents. After purchasing a used camera, Parks worked as a freelance photographer and as a photo-journalist. In 1942 he became a correspondent for the Farm Security Administration, and from 1943 to 1945 he was a correspondent for the Office of War Information. After the war he worked for Standard Oil Company of New Jersey, and in 1948 he became a staff photographer for *Life* magazine. He soon achieved national acclaim for his photographs, and in the mid-1950s he began doing consulting work on Hollywood productions. In the 1960s Parks began doing television documentaries, and in 1966 he published his biography, *A Choice of Weapons*.

Parks is also the author of *The Learning Tree* (1963), *Born Black* (1971), *Gordon Parks: Whis-*

pers of Intimate Things (1971), *Moments without Proper Names* (1975), *To Smile in Autumn* (1979), and *Voices in the Mirror* (1991). In 1968 Parks produced, directed, and wrote the script and music for the movie production of *The Learning Tree*. Parks also directed and scored the movies *Shaft* (1971), *Shaft's Big Score* (1972), *The Super Cops* (1974), and *Leadbelly* (1976).

Parks was the recipient of the NAACP's Spingarn Medal (1972), the Rhode Island School of Design's Presidents Fellow Award (1984), and Kansan of the Year (1986); and in 1988 President Ronald Reagan presented him with the National Medal of Arts. In 1989 Parks received from the Library of Congress the National Film Registry's classic film honor for *The Learning Tree*; that same year he received the New York Mayor's Award. The Library of Congress acquired Parks's personal papers and archives on July 7, 1995. Parks died in 2006 of cancer.

Howardena Pindell (1943–)
Painter

Born April 14, 1943, in Philadelphia, Pennsylvania, Howardena Pindell received her education at Boston University, where she earned a B.F.A. in 1965, and Yale University, where she obtained her M.F.A. in 1967. She first gained national recognition for her artistic skills with the exhibition *American Drawing Biennial XXIII* at the Norfolk Museum of Arts and Sciences in Virginia in 1969. By the mid-1970s Pindell's work began appearing in such exhibitions as *Eleven Americans in Paris* at the Gerald Piltzer Gallery, Macherin, France, 1975; *Recent Acquisitions; Drawings* at the Museum of Modern Art, New York, 1976; and *Pindell: Video Drawings* at the Henie-Onstad Art Centre, Oslofjord, Norway, 1976.

Around this same time, Pindell began to travel throughout the world as a guest speaker. Some of her lectures included "Current American and Black American Art: A Historical Survey" at Madras College of Arts and Crafts, Madras, India, 1975; and "Black Artists, U.S.A.," Academy of Art, Oslo, Norway, 1976. She is currently a professor of art at the State University of New York at Stony Brook.

Pindell's work is part of the permanent collections of over thirty museums, including the Brooklyn Museum, High Museum in Atlanta, Newark Museum, Fogg Museum in Cambridge, Massachusetts, Whitney Museum of American Art, Museum of Modern Art, and the Metropolitan Museum of Art. Pindell has received two National Endowment for the Arts Fellowships and a Guggenheim Fellowship.

Pindell's awards include the Studio Museum in Harlem Award, and the Distinguished Contribution to the Profession Award from the Women's Caucus for Art in 1996.

Jerry Pinkney (1939–)
Illustrator

Jerry Pinkney was born on December 22, 1939, in Philadelphia, Pennsylvania. His primary focus for illustrations has been children's books, but he has contributed to the U.S. Postal Service's Black Heritage Stamp Collection with images of Benjamin Banneker, Martin Luther King Jr., Scott Joplin, Jackie Robinson, Sojourner Truth, Carter G. Woodson, Whitney Moore Young, Mary McLeod Bethune, and Harriet Tubman. Pinkney also taught at various universities and shared his skill with diverse audiences.

Books notable for Pinkney's illustrations are *The Tale of Uncle Remus, Call It Courage, Self Portrait,* and *Back Home* (written by his wife, Gloria Pinkney). His work often focuses on folktales, myths, and legends. He has supported many artists in their work including that of Julius Lester's *John Henry* (1994), and Robert D. San Souci's *The Hired Hand: An African American Folktale* (1997).

He has received numerous honors for his work, which include the Coretta Scott King Awards for *The Patchwork Quilt* (1986), *Half a Moon and One Whole Star* (1987), *Mirandy and Brother Wind* (1988), and a Caldecott Honor Book for *Mirandy and Brother Wind* (1989) and *The Talking Eggs* (1990).

Horace Pippin (1888–1946)
Painter

Horace Pippin was born on February 22, 1888, in West Chester, Pennsylvania, and painted steadily from 1920 until his death in 1946. Among his most vivid portrayals on canvas are the battle scenes that he remembered from his own experience in World War I, during which he was wounded and partially paralyzed.

Pippin's earliest works are designs burned into wood with a hot poker; to accomplish this he had to guide his right arm with his left hand. He did not complete his first oil painting until 1930—after working on it for three years. He painted scenes of family reunions, biblical stories, and historical events. His notable works include *John Brown Goes to a Hanging, Flowers with Red Chair, The Den, The Milk Man of Goshen,* and *Dog Fight over the Trenches.* Pippin, whose work has been ranked in the company of Henri Rousseau because of his accomplishments as a self-taught artist, died July 6, 1946.

James A. Porter (1905–1970)
Painter, Art Historian

James Amos Porter was born in Baltimore, Maryland, on December 22, 1905. He studied at Howard University, where he earned a B.S. in 1927; the Art Students League in New York; the Sorbonne in Paris; and New York University, where he received his M.A. He was awarded numerous travel grants that enabled him to study African and European art firsthand.

Among his ten one-person shows are exhibits at Port-au-Prince, Haiti, 1946; DuPont Gallery, Washington, D.C., 1949; and Howard University, 1965. His works are in the collections of Howard University, Lincoln University, Missouri, the Harmon Foundation, IBM, and others. He was the author of the classic *Modern Negro Art* (1943) and numerous articles, making him the first African American art historian.

In 1953 Porter became chair of the department of art and director of the Gallery of Art at

Howard University, a position he held until his death. He was a delegate to the UNESCO Conference on Africa, held in Boston in 1961, and to the International Congress of African Art and Culture in Salisbury, Southern Rhodesia, in 1962. In 1965, at the twenty-fifth anniversary of the founding of the National Gallery of Art, he was named "one of America's Most Outstanding Men of the Arts." His notable works include *On a Cuban Bus, Portrait of F. A. as Harlequin, Dorothy Porter,* and *Nude.* Porter, who was a painter of considerable scholarship who also earned acclaim as a writer and educator, died on February 28, 1970.

Faith Ringgold (1930–)
Painter, Fiber Artist

Born in Harlem, New York, on October 8, 1930, Faith Ringgold was raised by parents who made sure she would enjoy the benefits of a good education. She attended the City College of New York, receiving her B.S. in 1955, and her M.F.A. in 1959. She is a professor emeritus of art at the University of California at San Diego.

Committed to a revolutionary perspective both in her political subject matter and her unconventional aesthetic, Ringgold is a symbolic expressionist whose stark paintings are acts of social reform directed toward educating her audience. Her most intense focus has been upon the problems of being black in America. Her works highlight the violent tensions that tear at American society, including discrimination suffered by women.

Her boldly political work has been well received and widely shown. She has had several one-person shows, the first in 1968; and her paintings are included in the collections of the Chase Manhattan Bank, the Museum of Modern Art, the Bank Street College of Education, and the Solomon R. Guggenheim Museum.

In 1972 Ringgold became one of the founders of the Women Students and Artists for Black Liberation, an organization whose principal goal is to make sure that all exhibitions of black artists give equal space to paintings by men and women. She donated a large mural depicting the roles of women in American society to the Women's House of Detention in Manhattan.

Aesthetically, Ringgold believes that "black art must use its own color, black, to create its light, since that color is the most immediate black truth." Her most recent paintings have been an attempt to give pictorial realization to this vision.

Her first quilt *Echoes of Harlem* was completed in 1980, and was followed by *The Sunflower Quilting Bee at Arles,* and *Who's Afraid of Aunt Jemima?* In 1991 she illustrated and wrote the children's book *Tar Beach.* Notable works include *The Flag Is Bleeding, Flag for the Moon, Die Nigger, Mommy & Daddy,* and *Soul Sister, Woman on a Bridge.*

Ringgold has received many awards and accolades inclusive of the 1992 Caldecott Honor Book for her book *Tar Beach,* and a 1996 award from the National Museum of Women in the Arts for her accomplishments.

Betye Saar (1926–)
Painter, Sculptor

Betye Saar was born in Los Angeles, California, on July 30, 1926. She went to college, got married, and raised her children—all while creating artwork made of discarded pieces of old dreams: postcards, photographs, flowers, buttons, fans, and ticket stubs. Her motifs range from the fetish to the everyday object. In 1978 Saar became one of a select group of American female artists to be discussed in a documentary film entitled *Spirit Catcher: The Art of Betye Saar.* It appeared on WNET-13 in New York as part of the series *The Originals: Women in Art.* Her exhibitions include an installation piece especially designed for the Studio Museum in Harlem in 1980, and several one-person exhibitions at the Monique Knowlton Gallery in New York in 1981.

Saar studied at Pasadena City College, the University of California (where she received her B.F.A.), Long Beach State College, the University of Southern California, San Fernando State College, and Valley State College, California. She was a teacher at Hayward State College in California, and she has exhibited throughout the United States. Her notable works include *The Vision of El Cremo, Africa, The View from the Sorcerer's Window,* and *House of Gris Gris* (a mixed-media installation with daughter Alison Saar), and *The Liberation of Aunt Jemima.*

Synthia Saint James (1949–)
Illustrator, Writer

Synthia Saint James was born on February 11, 1949, in Los Angeles, California. Her skill as an illustrator is self-taught. Her work, which uses bright colors and celebrates everyday life, has been exhibited internationally and has graced the covers of countless books and on canvas. Authors such as Terry McMillan and Alice Walker have used her art as covers. Many companies and corporations have commissioned her work for their products, posters, and events; Saint James was also commissioned to create the first Kwanzaa stamp for the U.S. Postal Service that debuted on October 2, 1997.

Saint James combined her skill as an illustrator and her interest in children's books to produce books such as *The Gift of Kwanzaa* (1994) and *Sunday* (1996), among others. She has also done illustrations for the books *No Mirror* (1998) and *Girls Together* (1999). Saint James's work has been exhibited in the National Museum of Women in the Arts, Musee des Duncans in Paris, France, and the Art Institute of Chicago.

Augusta Savage (1892–1962)
Sculptor

Augusta Savage was born on February 29, 1892, in Green Cove Springs, Florida, and studied at Tallahassee State Normal School, at Cooper Union in New York City, and in France as the recipient of Carnegie and Rosenwald Fellowships. She was the first black to win acceptance to the National Association of Women Painters and Sculptors.

In the 1930s she taught in her own School of Arts and Crafts in Harlem and helped many of her students take advantage of WPA projects for artists during the Depression. Most of her sculptures are clay or plaster since she could not afford bronze. Her style is expressive and inspirational. A leading sculptor who emerged during the Negro Renaissance, Savage was one of the artists represented in the first all-black exhibition in America, sponsored by the Harmon Foundation at International House in New York City. In 1939 her symbolic group piece *Lift Every Voice and Sing* was shown at the New York World's Fair Community Arts Building. Other notable works include *The Chase, Black Women, Lenore, Gamin, Marcus Garvey,* and *W. E. B. DuBois.*

Charles Searles (1937–2004)
Painter, Educator

Charles R. Searles was born in Philadelphia, Pennsylvania, in 1937. He studied at Fleicher Art Memorial and completed four years at Penn Academy of Fine Arts. His work is noted for its rhythmic quality, the human form, and the use of colors. Notable works are *Cultural Mix, Rhythmic Forms, Play Time,* and *Celebration.*

Searles's works are in the collections of the Smithsonian Institution, Dallas Museum of Art, Montclair Art Museum, and Howard University. As an educator, he taught at several institutions including the Philadelphia College of Art, Brooklyn Museum Art School, Jersey State College, and Bloomfield College. Searles died in 2004.

Norma Sklarek (1928–)
Architect

Norma Merrick Sklarek was born in New York City, on April 15, 1928. She earned her B.A. from Barnard College in 1950. In 1954 Sklarek became the first African American woman to be named a fellow of the American Institute of Architects.

Sklarek worked as an architect for five years before taking a position in 1960 with Gruen and Associates in Los Angeles, California. She remained there for the next twenty years. During this time she also served on the faculty of New York City College from 1957 to 1960, and UCLA from 1972 to 1978. In 1980 she became vice president of Welton Becket Associates before accepting a partnership in 1985, which formed Siegel, Sklarek and Diamond—a female-owned architectural firm and the largest of its kind. Sklarek retired in 1992.

Sklarek's most notable structures are the U.S. Embassy in Tokyo; Courthouse Center, Columbus, Indiana; City Hall, San Bernardino, California; and Terminal One, Los Angeles International Airport.

Moneta Sleet Jr. (1926–1996)
Photographer

Moneta Sleet Jr. was born February 14, 1926, in Owensboro, Kentucky. He studied at Kentucky State College under Dr. John Williams, a family friend who was dean of the college and an accomplished photographer. Sleet earned his B.A. in 1947; after serving in World War II, Williams offered him the opportunity to set up a photography department at Maryland State College in 1948. By 1950 Sleet had moved to New York, where he obtained a master's degree in journalism from New York University. In 1955 Sleet moved to Chicago and began working for Johnson Publishing as staff photographer for *Ebony* and *Jet* magazines.

In 1969 Sleet became the first African American to win a Pulitzer Prize in photography. Although employed by *Ebony,* he was eligible for the award because his photograph of Coretta Scott King at her husband's funeral was picked up by a wire service and published in daily newspapers throughout the country.

Sleet has won awards from the Overseas Press Club of America, National Urban League, and the National Association of Black Journalists. His work has appeared in several group exhibitions at museums, including the Studio Museum in Harlem and the Metropolitan Museum of Art. In 1970 solo exhibitions were held at the City Art Museum of St. Louis and at the Detroit Public Library. In 1986 Sleet was featured in two retrospective exhibits—one at the New York Public Library and one sponsored by the Philip Morris Companies.

Sleet was a member of the NAACP and the Black Academy of Arts and Letters. In 1989 he was inducted into the University of Kentucky's Journalism Hall of Fame.

Willi Smith (1948–1987)
Fashion Designer

Born on February 29, 1948, in Philadelphia, Pennsylvania, Willi Smith studied at the Parsons School of Design on a scholarship, and his work became popular during the 1960s. He was known for his designer wear for men and women, made from natural fibers that were fun, cross-seasonal, and affordable. His line of clothes, known as Willi-Wear, consisted of sportswear pieces that mixed readily with his own designs as well as those of others. Smith was known for an innovative mixing and matching of plaids, stripes, and vivid colors. Smith had his clothes manufactured in India, traveling there several times a year to supervise the making of his functional and practical collections.

In 1983 Willi Smith received the Coty American Fashion Critics' Award for women's fashion. He died in 1987.

Henry Ossawa Tanner (1859–1937)
Painter

 Henry Ossawa Tanner was born on June 21, 1859, in Pittsburgh, Pennsylvania. Tanner chose painting rather than the ministry as a career, overcoming the strong objections of his father, an African Methodist Episcopal bishop. After attending the Pennsylvania Academy of Fine Arts, he taught at Clark University in Atlanta, supplementing his

salary by working as a photographer. Some of Tanner's most compelling work—such as *The Banjo Lesson* (1890)—was produced during this period, with Tanner emerging as the most promising black artist of his day. Alain Locke called Tanner the leading talent of the "journeyman period" of Black American art.

In 1891, however, Tanner abandoned black subject matter and left the United States for Paris, where he concentrated on religious themes. In 1896 his *Daniel in the Lion's Den*, a mixture of realism and mystical symbolism, won honorable mention at the Paris Salon. The following year the French government purchased his *Resurrection of Lazarus*. In 1900 Tanner received the Medal of Honor at the Paris Exposition and the Lippincott Prize.

Tanner died on May 25, 1937. His notable works include *Flight into Egypt, The Annunciation, Thankful Poor,* and *The Sabot Makers*.

Alma Thomas (1891–1978)
Painter

Alma W. Thomas was born in Columbus, Georgia, on September 22, 1891, but her family later moved to Washington, D.C. Thomas enrolled in Howard University and became its first graduate in art in 1924. She earned an M.A. from Columbia University. Only after Thomas retired from teaching was she able to devote herself full time to painting.

In her later years Thomas received many awards and honors with her work in the collections of the National Museum of American Art at the Smithsonian Institution, Howard University, and the Metropolitan Museum. Her notable works are *The Eclipse, Arboretum Presents White Dogwood, Elysian Fields, Red Sunset,* and *Old Pond Concerto*. Thomas died on February 24, 1978, at Howard University Hospital.

James Van Der Zee (1886–1983)
Photographer

James Van Der Zee was born on June 29, 1886, in Lenox, Massachusetts. His parents had moved there from New York in the early 1880s after serving as maid and butler to Ulysses S. Grant, who then resided on 34th Street in New York City. The second of six children, James grew up in a family of creative people. Everybody painted, drew, or played an instrument; so it was not considered out of the ordinary when, upon receiving a camera in 1900, Van Der Zee became interested in photography.

By 1906 Van Der Zee had moved to New York, married, and was taking odd jobs to support his growing family. In 1907 he moved to Phoetus, Virginia, where he worked in the dining room of the Hotel Chamberlin in Old Point Comfort, Virginia. During this time he also worked as a photographer on a part-time basis. In 1909 he returned to New York.

By 1915 Van Der Zee had a photography job as assistant in a small concession in the Gertz Department Store in Newark, New Jersey. With the money he saved from this job he was able to open his own studio on 135th Street in 1916. World War I had begun and many young soldiers came to the studio to have their pictures taken. Over the course of a half-century, James Van Der Zee recorded the visual history of Harlem. His subjects included Marcus Garvey, Daddy Grace, Father Divine, Joe Louis, Madame Walker, and many other famous African Americans.

In 1969 the exhibition *Harlem On My Mind,* produced by Thomas Hoving, then director of the Metropolitan Museum of Art, brought Van Der Zee international recognition. Van Der Zee died in 1983.

Carrie Mae Weems (1953–)
Photographer, Conceptual Artist

Carrie Mae Weems was born on April 20, 1953, in Portland, Oregon, and earned her B.F.A. from the California Institute of the Arts in 1981, and her M.F.A. from the University of California at San Diego in 1984. She also received an M.A. in African American folklore from the University of California at Berkeley.

An artist who explores stereotypes, especially of black women, Weems has exhibited widely in the last few years. Formerly a photo-documentarian, Weems also teaches filmmaking and photography at Hampshire College in Amherst, Massachusetts. Her new works are "about race, gender, class and kinship."

She has exhibited at the Rhode Island School of Design and Wadsworth Atheneum in Hartford, Connecticut. Weems has won numerous awards for her work, including Photographer of the Year by the Friends of Photography, and Distinguished Photographer's Award in 2005. Her notable works include *Mirror, Mirror, Black Woman with Chicken, High Yella Girl, Colored People, Family Pictures and Stories,* and the *Ain't Jokin'* and *American Icon* series.

Edward T. Welburn (1950–)
Automobile Designer

Edward T. Welburn was born in 1950, in Philadelphia, Pennsylvania. His father owned a body shop and instilled in Welburn an appreciation for automobile design. After graduation from Howard University, having studied fine arts and sculpture, he was hired by General Motors (GM) in 1972. In 1975 he moved to the Oldsmobile Studio and stayed there for twenty years. He worked his way up to chief designer in 1989, and to the head of a winning design team in 1992. Welburn's design of the GM Olds Achieva was awarded the Outstanding Design of the model year. He was also awarded the Society of America Award for Design Excellence for his part in the design of the Oldsmobile Aerotech 1992.

Welburn is a member of the Founders Society of the Detroit Institute of Arts, and was named Alumnus of the Year in 1989 by Howard University's Student Association.

James Lesesne Wells (1902–1993)
Artist, Printmaker

James Lesesne Wells was born in Atlanta, Georgia, on November 2, 1902. Early on he was interested in becoming an artist. Wells won the Harmon Foundation Award in 1916 with first prize in painting and second prize in woodworking. Determined to go to college and complete his education, Wells worked for two years to earn the money. He spent one year at Lincoln University and then completed his B.S. degree from Teacher's College at Columbia University in 1927, and earned an M.S. from Columbia in 1938.

Following undergraduate studies Wells continued to purse his interests in painting and printmaking. He was invited to join the faculty of Howard University in 1929, after his work was seen in the International Modernists exhibition. Wells remained at the university for thirty-nine years and mentored artists such as Charles Alston and Jacob Lawrence.

As Wells continued his craft of printmaking and painting over the years, he won the George E. Haynes prize in 1933; won first prize in a religious art exhibition by the Smithsonian in 1958; was awarded a Presidential Citation by President Jimmy Carter for Lifetime Contributions in 1980; "James L. Wells Day" was declared in Washington, D.C., in 1984; and the National Black Arts Festival named Wells a "living legend" in 1991. Wells died of congestive heart failure in 1993.

Charles White (1918–1979)
Painter

Charles White was born on April 2, 1918, in Chicago, Illinois. White won a celebrated Rosenwald Fellowship, which allowed him to travel in the South for two years. As a result of his experiences and his skill, he was commissioned in 1940 to paint a mural showing black people's contributions to American democracy. By 1947 White had his first one-man show, which brought him worldwide attention. White's work focused on the human experience and the respect for the human being, but he only painted black people.

White continued to create, using black and white as a symbolic color motif. White was awarded the Gold Medal at the International Show in Germany, the Adolph and Clara Obrig

Prize in 1971 and 1975, and received an honorary doctorate from Columbia University. White's notable works include *Let's Walk Together, Frederick Douglass Lives Again, Women,* and *Gospel Singer.* He died in Los Angeles in 1979.

Paul Revere Williams (1894–1980)
Architect

Paul Revere Williams was born in Los Angeles, California, on February 18, 1894, and graduated from the University of California at Los Angeles. He later attended the Beaux Arts Institute of Design in Paris; he received honorary degrees from Howard University, Lincoln University, and Atlanta University as well as Hampton Institute.

Williams became a certified architect in 1917, and after working for Reginald Johnson and John Austin, distinguished designers and architects, he opened his own firm in 1923. Williams was known as America's "architect to the stars." Williams designed a total of 3,000 buildings, including some 400 homes for such celebrities as Cary Grant, Barbara Stanwyk, William Holden, Frank Sinatra, Betty Grable, Bill "Bojangles" Robinson, and Bert Lahr. He also co-designed the first federally funded public housing project.

In 1926 he was the first black to become a member of the American Institute of Architects. He served on the National Monument Commission, an appointee of President Calvin Coolidge, and was awarded the Spingarn Medal from the NAACP. His notable works include Los Angeles County Airport, Palm Springs Tennis Club, and Saks Fifth Avenue at Beverly Hills. Williams died on January 23, 1980.

William T. Williams (1942–)
Painter

Born in Cross Creek, North Carolina, on July 17, 1942, William T. Williams studied at a community college and later at Pratt Institute in Brooklyn, New York. He received his M.F.A. from Yale University in 1968. Williams had his first show at the Reese Paley Gallery in 1971. His work is considered that of an abstract expressionist painter.

Williams avoids labels and association with any particular movement or school. Critics have viewed Williams's work in comparison to that of Joseph Albers and the Bauhaus traditions from Europe. Williams's own statements about his work point to such subjects as the city, architecture, tension, things in flux, order from disorder, Africa, and the United States.

Williams's work has been exhibited at the Studio Museum in Harlem, Wadsworth Atheneum, the Art Institute of Chicago, and the Whitney Museum of American Art. He has received awards such as the Guggenheim Fellowship, two awards from the National Endowment for the Arts, and a Joan Mitchell Foundation Award. His notable works include *Elbert Jackson L.A.M.F. Port II, Big Red for N.C.,* and *Buttermilk.*

John Wilson (1922–)
Painter, Printmaker, Sculptor

John Wilson was born on April 14, 1922, in Boston, Massachusetts. Wilson studied at the Boston Museum of Fine Arts; the Fernand Leger School in Paris; and at El Instituto Politecnico and the Escuela de las Artes Del Libro in Mexico City. In 1947 he earned his B.A. from Tufts University.

Wilson's notable works include *Roxbury Landscape* (1944), *Trabajador* (1951), and *Child with Father* (1969), covering the spectrum of oil, print, and graphics. Wilson also created the Martin Luther King Jr. commemorative statue at the U.S. Capitol in Washington, D.C., in 1983, and the *Eternal Presence* monument at the National Center of Afro-American Artists in Boston in 1987.

Wilson's work is in the collections of the Museum of Modern Art, Schomburg Collection, and Atlanta University.

Hale Woodruff (1900–1980)
Painter, Muralist

Hale Woodruff was born in Cairo, Illinois, in 1900, but he later moved to Nashville, Tennessee. He graduated from the John Herron Art Institute in Indianapolis, Indiana, and after winning a Harmon Foundation competition, went to Paris to study his craft; he also studied with Henry Ossawa Tanner and attended L'Académie Scandinave and the Academie Moderne. Once back in the United States, Woodruff became an art instructor for Atlanta University in 1931. Woodruff's work was abstract while expressing heritage and reality.

As a muralist Woodruff was commissioned by Talladega College for *The Amistad Murals* about slave revolts. In 1948 he teamed with Charles Alston for a mural about African Americans' contribution to California history for the Golden State Mutual Life Insurance Company. In 1950 he developed a series of mural panels titled, *The Art of the Negro*. Other notable works by Woodruff include *Ancestral Remedies* and *The Little Boy*. Woodruff died in 1980.

The painting *Savoy* by Richard Yarde is located in the Joseph P. Addabbo Federal Building in Queens, New York.

Richard Yarde (1939–)

Painter

Richard Yarde was born in Boston, Massachusetts, in 1939. He studied at the School of the Museum of Fine Arts and at Boston University, where he earned his B.F.A. in 1962, and his M.F.A. in 1964. He has taught at Boston University and has received numerous awards for his art, including Yaddo Fellowships, 1964, 1966, and 1970; McDowell Colony awards, 1968 and 1970; and the Blanche E. Colman Award, 1970.

The Boston Museum of Fine Arts, Wadsworth Atheneum, Rose Art Museum, Museum of the National Center of Afro-American

Artists, and Studio Museum in Harlem have all exhibited his works. He has held one-person shows at numerous galleries and universities. His works are in many collections, such as the Wadsworth Atheneum in Hartford, Connecticut. He has received an Arts and Letters Award from the American Academy of Arts and Letters in 1995, and the Commonwealth Award for Fine Arts in 2002. His notable works include *The Stoop, Passage Edgar and I, The Corner, Paul Robeson as Emperor Jones, Head and Hands I, Josephine's Baffle Triptych,* and *Richard's Cards.*

MUSIC

CLASSICAL

When the first Africans arrived in 1619 on the eastern coast of what is now the United States, they brought with them a rich musical heritage. In the culture from which these slaves were taken, music and dance accompanied almost every public activity. Each community had professional musicians, and everyone, from the youngest to the oldest, played, sang, and danced. Because theirs was an oral tradition, they did not need sheet music to bring their songs and dances with them—they carried it all in their heads. They brought to the new world not only their songs and dances, but their love of and need for music as an integral part of daily life, and they participated in the music of their new world from the very beginning.

As slaves, the Africans assumed the lives and culture of their owners; they learned the Europeans' language, religion, and music. They sang English psalms and hymns in church as they converted to Christianity. They heard folk and popular tunes in the taverns and homes. Some slaves in the South studied with itinerant music teachers. The most talented musicians gained professional-level skills that were quickly put to use by the whites. Bonded servants and slave musicians, playing instruments such as the violin, flute, and piano, provided much of the recreational music for their masters, playing at dance balls and dancing schools. On self-sufficient plantations in the South, the most musical of the domestic slaves provided evening "entertainments." Once public concerts became possible and popular in the New World, a few talented slaves gave public concerts. The pianist Thomas "Blind Tom" Green Bethune began public concertizing while still a slave, and he continued to perform after emancipation.

As a free black middle class arose in the nineteenth century and the popularity of public concerts increased, black musicians began to provide "art music" for both black and white audiences. As in white middle- and upper-class communities, genteel songs and piano pieces could be heard in the parlors of the comfortable and well-off members of the black communities; music also accompanied most public celebrations and ceremonies. As the black middle class grew, it could support more professional musicians and music educators. Singing schools and private lessons in instruments were available to anyone interested. During much of the nineteenth century, the best black artists toured throughout the United States and Europe, performing for black and white audiences alike.

In the nineteenth century a typical "art music" concert showcased a variety of musical pieces. Songs, arias, and ensemble vocal pieces were performed in the same show as chamber, band, and orchestral numbers. The most popular singers tended to be women, including Elizabeth Taylor Greenfield, called the "Black Swan," and Matilda Sissieretta Jones, known as the "Black Patti" after the contemporary reigning white diva, Adelina Patti.

Men dominated the realm of instrumental music. Pianists included John William Boone and Samuel Jamieson in addition to Blind Tom. John Thomas Douglas, Walter F. Craig, and Edmond Dede played the violin. Morris Brown Jr., Robert Jones, Jacob Stans, William Appo, James Hermenway, Francis Johnson, and Aaron J. R. Connor conducted all-black orchestras, bands, and choruses; most composed music as well. The original Colored American Opera Company of Washington, D.C., and the Theodore Drury Colored Opera Company, both established in the second half of the nineteenth century, were the earliest long-lasting black opera companies.

During most of the nineteenth century African American musicians performed for both black and white audiences. Toward the end of the century, however, white audiences began to favor European over American performers, and white musicians over black. Despite their obvious success in classical music, by the beginning of the twentieth century African Americans were not considered suitable as classical musicians, and white audiences accepted them only on the vaudeville and minstrel stage. Whites considered blacks unable to contribute to art music as either performers or composers. In response to composer Scott Joplin's attempt to produce his opera *Treemonisha* in New York, for example, the *New York Age* stated on March 5, 1908, "Since ragtime has been in vogue, many Negro writers have gained considerable fame as composers of that style of music. From the white man's standpoint of view … after writing ragtime, the Negro does not figure." This was the prevailing attitude for some time.

Flutist Dorothy Antoinette Handy wrote in the preface of her *Black Women in American Bands and Orchestras* (1981) that her book "originated in the mind of a fourteen-year-old Black American female who decided that she wanted to be a symphonic orchestral flutist…. She went to a New Orleans Philharmonic concert, and shortly before the end proceeded backstage from the reserved for colored section to the orchestra's first flutist. Question: 'Are you accepting any pupils?' Answer: 'Do you mean that you, a Negro, want to study flute?'" Unfortunately, this attitude has continued to reign in the second half of the century as well. In 1975 San Francisco Symphony Orchestra timpanist Elayne Jones, the only black first-chair player in a major American orchestra, filed a suit claiming contract violation on grounds of racism and sexism because she was denied tenure. She lost her case.

Despite this opposition African Americans have never been absent from the world of classical music. While the merits of compositions by African American composers have been undeniable, they have often been ignored. For much of the twentieth century they have been denied entrance to this country's major metropolitan (white) symphonies, though they have constantly worked toward inclusion. William Grant Still's *Afro-American Symphony* became the first symphonic work written by a black composer to be performed by a major symphony orchestra when it was performed in 1931 by the Rochester Philharmonic Symphony. In 1933 Florence Price became the first black female to have a symphony played by a major orchestra when the Chicago Symphony Orchestra performed her *Symphony in E Minor* at the Chicago World's Fair. In 1934 Price conducted her *Concerto in F Minor* in Chicago. In 1955 William Grant Still became the first African American to conduct a major orchestra in the deep South when he led the New Orleans Symphony Orchestra.

On March 18, 1974, the first four records of the *Black Composers Series* were formally released by Columbia Records. These LPs featured works by Chevalier de Saint-Georges, Samuel Coleridge-Taylor, William Grant Still, George Walker, Ulysses Kay, and Roque Cordero, under the artistic direction of Paul Freeman. This *Black Composers Series* grew out of an agreement between

CBS and the Afro-American Music Opportunities Association (AAMOA) for at least twelve recordings of approximately twenty black composers.

The Center for Black Music Research, established in 1982 at Chicago's Columbia College, has actively contributed to the research publications and performances of contemporary and historic compositions. They have an ever-growing library and computer database of resources used by scholars all over the country. African American classical and popular music has received more and more attention in the mainstream academic world as musicologists and ethnomusicologists have begun to focus their attention in that direction.

In the 1970s two national black opera companies were formed. Opera/South was founded in 1970 by Sister Elise of the Catholic order of the Sisters of the Blessed Sacrament, and by members of the Mississippi Inter-Collegiate Opera Guild (Jackson State University, Utica Junior College, and Tougaloo College). In addition to staging

grand opera, the company performed operas by black composers, including *Highway No. 1 USA* and *A Bayou Legend,* both by William Grant Still, and *Jubilee* and *The Juggler of Our Lady,* both by Ulysses Kay. In 1973 Sister Elise, along with Margaret Harris, Benjamin Matthews, and Wayne Sanders, organized Opera Ebony. Performers with these two companies have included conductors Leonard de Paur, Margaret Harris, and Everett Lee; pianist Way Sanders; and singers Donnie Ray Albert, William Brown, Alpha Floyd, Ester Hinds, Robert Mosely, Wilma Shakesnider, and Walter Turnbull. These companies—as well as the Houston Opera Company, which, in 1975 produced Scott Joplin's *Treemonisha*—have served as a showcase for black talent, and have launched the careers of a number of performers.

As in other areas of American life, the civil rights struggle continues in the realm of classical music. Programs to support young black artists, begun as a response to the civil rights movement

New York City's Metropolitan Opera House at Lincoln Center. There were no black artists at the Met until after World War II. As of 2011, there are eleven principal singers, two conductors, and a stage director who are African Americans.

in the 1960s, died as a result of the economic recession of the 1970s. A 1981 survey by the National Urban League indicated that of the nearly 5,000 musicians playing regularly in fifty-six leading orchestras, only seventy were black. Only a half dozen of the 538 members of the "Big Five" orchestras—in New York, Boston, Chicago, Cleveland, and Philadelphia—were black. Few employ black conductors. The American Symphony Orchestra League published a report in 1992 with similar findings. The 146 orchestras that participated in the survey reported that of a total 8,326 positions, only 133 were filled by black musicians.

In the early 1980s the Metropolitan Opera had fifteen black artists on its roster, and the New York City Opera had eleven singers in principal roles, with two conductors and one stage director. Prior to World War II, there were no black singers in any opera house in the United States. As the twenty-first century progresses, the limited presence of African Americans in major symphonies remains few to none. In 2010 the New York Philharmonic had only one African American musician, the Chicago Symphony had no African American musicians, and the Detroit Symphony had three members. There are various reasons given for the limited progress of African American artists in the orchestras, including equal access, racism, career isolation, and the overall lack of musicians in the pipeline. To impact the lack of future participants, the Chicago Youth Center was started to train minorities, the St. Louis Symphony opened a music school, and the Detroit Symphony began working with the public schools like many other symphonies have begun to do. In spite of challenges, conductor Kazem Abdullah made his debut at the Metropolitan Opera House in January 2009, and singers Martina Arroyo, Florence Ouivar, and Barbara Hendrick share their talent with the world.

BLUES—JAZZ

The period after Reconstruction (1867–1877), for blacks who still primarily lived in the agrarian South, was entrenched in injustice, brutality, and a disregard for the laws that were passed to protect and promote their role as citizen. The blues was a musical response to the pain and suffering that was experienced. The blues, which was clearly defined by 1880, was not only sad and sorrowful in a worldly sense, but it still offered hope in such a cruel world. The most influential blues artists were Robert Johnson from the Mississippi Delta who used stylized vocals accompanied by his guitar; "Father of the Blues" William Christopher (W. C.) Handy, who wrote blues ballads and recorded them and wrote them down for sheet music; and the first professional blues singer Gertrude "Ma" Rainey, known as the "Mother of the Blues," who with a powerful voice made her first recording in 1923.

The blues genre, which is the essence of the individual story told primarily by a singer and an instrument, has inspired and been incorporated into every facet of African American and American music. Blues, which is often referred to by regions, encompasses the Country Blues, the St. Louis Blues, the Chicago Blues, the Memphis Blues, the Delta Blues, and the Mississippi Blues. With the singer-instrument as a key component in the blues experience, new trends include acoustic blues and electric blues.

With the introduction of recording, blues was transformed in the urban communities of the 1920s through improvisation and refined into a new form that is jazz. Blues is the precursor to ragtime, rhythm and blues, gospel, rock and roll, and soul music. The 1960s saw a renewed interest in the blues and many artists and groups have gained new attention. Currently, both past audiences and new enthusiasts continue to celebrate this music. As white blues singers become a greater presence in the blues community, the historical birth and cultural roots of this African American genre has caused many to see these new voices as misrepresenting this important original art form. With racism, segregation, and white supremacy creating real and spiritual lines between the races in embracing change, celebration offers a means of healing.

This home in Florence, Alabama, was where W. C. Handy was born in 1873.

Born of the encounter between African music—including work songs, gospel, spirituals, blues, and songs for dancing—and European musical traditions, jazz has become a musical form that is loved, admired, and played all over the world.

By the late nineteenth century a dance music called ragtime had become very popular, particularly the compositions of Scott Joplin. The heavily syncopated rhythms and sprightly melodies of ragtime had a distinctly African American flavor. About the same time, a form of Black American folk music called the blues coalesced into a twelve-bar pattern that made it adaptable to popular song writing. The blues has a unique harmonic quality derived from a "flattening" of the third and seventh notes of the tempered scale (creating what are called blue notes) and, while seemingly simple, lends itself to infinite variation. The blues had an impact not only on jazz but also on rock and soul, both of which would be unthinkable without the blues element.

Jazz was born when ragtime (primarily an instrumental music) and blues (at first primarily a vocal style) came together, and though this process was taking place in many parts of America, it was in New Orleans that the basic language of jazz was first spoken. This was due not only to the rich musical tradition of this port city (with its international atmosphere), but also because social conditions in New Orleans, while certainly not free from racist elements, were less restrictive than in other large American cities at the time. Thus, there was much contact among musicians of varied ethnic backgrounds. Many historical accounts of jazz mistakenly overemphasize the importance of the New Orleans red light district (called Storyville). While early jazz certainly was performed there, many other outlets for musicmaking existed, including dances, parades, carnivals, and traditional New Orleans funerals at which a band would accompany the casket from church to cemetery with mournful strains, and then lead the march back to town with livelier music such as ragtime or jazz.

Musicians from New Orleans began to tour the United States in about 1907. Although their music made a significant impression wherever they went, their intricate style of collective improvisation, in which each instrument in the band had its own specific role, was not easily absorbed. It is another myth of jazz history that most of these early jazz players were a special breed of self-taught "naturals"; in fact, almost all of them had good basic musical training that included learning how to read music.

Jazz developed almost simultaneously with the phonograph; without the dissemination of jazz recordings, it is unlikely that jazz would have spread as quickly as it did. By studying recorded performances, musicians anywhere could learn at least the rudiments of jazz, a spontaneous music in which improvisation played a considerable role. Jazz improvisation does not mean, as is often believed, inventing music on the spot, without guidelines. It does mean adding one's own ideas to a common musical text and taking liberties as long as they fit within a shared framework. In addition, a jazz musician's personal style is based on tonal qualities, a distinctive approach to rhythm and phrasing, and a vocabulary of melodic and thematic characteristics. Taken together, these ingredients make it possible for a seasoned listener to identify who is playing in a jazz performance.

Ironically, the first New Orleans jazz to be recorded was performed by a white group, the Original Dixieland Jazz Band, in 1917. By then, black musicians had already made records, but they were not in a jazz idiom. It would take several more years for the best black New Orleans players to make records. In the meantime, however, some of them had already visited Europe, notably Sidney Bechet, the great clarinetist and soprano saxophonist who has been called the first great jazz soloist. But it was a somewhat younger musician from New Orleans, Louis Armstrong, who made the biggest impact on the future of jazz.

In 1922 Armstrong was brought to Chicago (by then the center of jazz activity) by his mentor and fellow trumpeter Joe "King" Oliver. He made his first records there, and came to New York two years later to join the band of Fletcher Henderson.

Henderson's band was the first musically significant big band in jazz. While most New Orleans jazz bands used an instrumentation of trumpet, trombone, clarinet, piano, guitar (or banjo), bass (string or brass), and drums, the early big bands used three trumpets, one or two trombones, three reeds (saxophonists doubling clarinet), and rhythm section instruments. They employed written scores (called arrangements), but gave the soloists freedom to improvise their contributions.

Armstrong's arrival was a revelation to the Henderson band. His first solos on the band's records stand out like diamonds in a tin setting. What Louis brought to jazz was, first of all, his superior sense of rhythm, which made other players sound stiff and clumsy in comparison. He discovered the rhythmic element called "swing" that sets jazz apart from other music—a kind of rhythmic thrust that seems to float and soar. In addition, his sound on the trumpet was the

Jazz musicians on the streets of New Orleans are still a common sight, even after Hurricane Katrina decimated the city in 2005.

biggest and most musically appealing yet heard, and he had exceptional range and powers of execution. Further, his gifts of melodic invention were so great that he can be said to have laid the foundation for jazz as a medium for personal expression by an instrumental soloist.

One of the first Henderson colleagues to get Armstrong's message was tenor saxophonist Coleman Hawkins, who soon created the first influential jazz style on his instrument. Also greatly affected was the band's chief arranger, Don Redman, who was the first to translate Armstrong's innovations to big-band arranging. Many others followed suit, especially after Armstrong, now back in Chicago, began to make records with his own studio groups, the Hot Fives and Hot Sevens.

By the late 1920s jazz had become a mainstay of American popular dance music and had spread to Europe as well. Black American musicians were touring worldwide, including such places as China and India, and wherever they went, their music made an impression. Yet there was still quite a gap between jazz at its best and the more commercially acceptable versions of it. Not until the advent of the so-called "Swing Era" in the 1930s did unadulterated jazz reach a level of popular acceptance that, thus far, remains unmatched.

This level of acceptance was primarily due to the big bands, which had reached a new height of artistic maturity. Duke Ellington, aptly called the greatest American composer, led big-band music to this level of sophistication. He gradually created a perfect balance between written and improvised elements for his unique band, which included such great soloists as Johnny Hodges (alto sax), Harry Carney (baritone sax), Barney Bigard (clarinet), Cootie Williams, and Rex Stewart (trumpets). In late 1927, Ellington's band began an important engagement at Harlem's famous Cotton Club. Through appearances there, regular network radio broadcasts, and many recordings, Ellington's music was widely disseminated. His band visited Europe for the first time in 1933.

Important work was also done at this time by Redman and by Benny Carter, a brilliant multi-instrumentalist and arranger–composer. Fletcher Henderson had not previously arranged music for his band, but he began to do so in the early 1930s and soon became one of the best. Such efforts laid the foundation for the success of Benny Goodman, a white clarinetist and bandleader, who commissioned the best black arrangers and was the first white bandleader to hire black musicians.

By 1936 the Swing Era was under way. Black dance styles that developed at such places as Harlem's Savoy Ballroom swept the nation, and young people jitterbugged to the sounds of an astonishing number of excellent bands; those led by Jimmie Lunceford and Count Basie stood out among the many. The big bands spawned a host of gifted young players and brought into the limelight many giants with established reputations in the jazz community, such as Armstrong, who led his own big bands from 1929 to 1947.

World War II brought economic and social changes that affected the big bands. During the war, gasoline rationing impeded the constant touring that was a source of livelihood for the bands. After the war, the advent of television wrought fundamental changes in the ways people sought entertainment. Among the chief victims of the new stay-at-home trend was ballroom dancing. The big bands went into rapid decline, and only a handful were able to survive, among them the bands of Ellington and Basie.

Meanwhile, the music itself had also undergone fundamental changes. The singers whose popularity was first established through their work with the bands became stars in their own right. The new generation of players who had come to maturity by way of big-band experiences were eager to express themselves at greater length than most big-band work permitted, and they were coming up with new and potentially radical musical ideas.

The most advanced soloists of the Swing Era, such as Roy Eldridge (trumpet), Lester Young (tenor sax), Art Tatum (piano), and Sid Catlett (drums) had been extending the rhythmic, harmonic, and technical resources of their instruments. Two young geniuses, guitarist Charlie Christian (featured with Benny Goodman) and bassist Jimmy Blanton (featured with Duke Ellington), revolutionized the language of their respective instruments.

Christian was among the many notable players who, in the early 1940s, participated in jam sessions (informal musical get-togethers) at Minton's Playhouse, a nightclub in Harlem where pianist Thelonious Monk and drummer Kenny Clarke were in the regular house band. At Minton's, experimentation took place that fed into the new jazz mainstream and led to the advent of modern jazz around 1944 and 1945.

The chief creators of this new jazz language were trumpeter (and bandleader–composer) Dizzy Gillespie and alto saxophonist–composer Charlie Parker, both of whom had put in time with leading big bands. While working together in the band of pianist Earl Hines (the father of modern jazz piano style) in 1943, they began to solidify their mutually compatible ideas. When they joined forces in a small group in 1945, on records and in live performances, bebop (as the new jazz style soon was called) came into being.

Though bebop was solidly grounded in earlier jazz styles, it seemed different to the public; the average listener often was unable to follow the intricate rhythmic and harmonic elaborations of the boppers. Furthermore, the bop musicians, unlike most of the jazz players who preceded them, were less concerned with pleasing the public than with creating music that fulfilled their artistic ambitions (Gillespie, however, was an exception, perhaps because his irrepressible sense of humor made him a natural entertainer).

In any case, the advent of bop went hand in hand with a change in the audience for jazz. By the mid-1930s, small clubs catering to jazz connoisseurs had begun to spring up in most large urban areas. The biggest and most famous concentration was in New York City, in two blocks of West 52nd Street, which soon became known as "Swing Street." In such clubs, musicians could perform for knowledgeable listeners without making musical compromises; most of the clubs were too small for dancing, so people came strictly to listen. By this time, people all over the world had become seriously interested in jazz. Some studied and documented its origins and history; others collected, researched, and classified jazz records. Publications like *Downbeat* and *Metronome* arose, catering to musicians and serious fans. These magazines, as well as the prestigious *Esquire,* conducted polls and conferred awards; in the mid-1940s, *Esquire* presented these awards at a huge all-star jazz concert on the stage of the Metropolitan Opera House in New York.

Jazz concerts had been a rarity in the 1920s. Then in 1938 Goodman staged one at Carnegie Hall, and beginning in 1943, Duke Ellington gave an annual concert there. By the late 1940s jazz concerts were regular events, among them the famous "Jazz at the Philharmonic" all-star tours. Thus, the stage was set for the acceptance of jazz not simply as music for entertainment and dancing, but as a form worthy of serious artistic consideration.

Bebop was soon succeeded by radical new forms of jazz. In 1959 a young Texas-born alto saxophonist, Ornette Coleman, brought his adventurous quartet to New York, setting off a controversy with music that seemed to have abandoned most of the harmonic and structural principles of jazz. In fact, Coleman's music was deeply rooted in the blues and in well-established improvisational jazz procedures, and in time his music was accepted as part of the jazz tradition.

By the 1960s so-called avant-garde jazz was very much in evidence. In 1956 trumpeter Miles Davis, who had worked with Charlie Parker and had led his own very influential groups (one of which gave birth to a style known as "cool jazz"), hired a little known tenor saxophonist, John Coltrane. With Coltrane, Davis introduced in 1958 a modal approach to jazz improvisation that was based on scales rather than harmonies. Coltrane soon formed his own group, which took modality much farther and extended improvisation both in length and intensity. Cecil Taylor, a virtuoso of the keyboard, further stretched the boundaries of jazz. Davis experimented with electronics and the rhythms of rock and soul. The bassist and composer Charles Mingus, deeply influenced by Ellington and Parker, found new and imaginative ways of combining written and improvised jazz. Tenor saxophonist Sonny Rollins, while remaining rooted in traditional harmonic music, expanded solo improvisation dramatically. And by the end of the 1960s Albert Ayler, a tenor saxophonist with roots in rhythm-and-blues music, brought another new and intensely personal voice to jazz.

The many gifted players who emerged from Chicago's Association for the Advancement of Creative Music in the 1960s pursued their various approaches with stirring results in such groups as the Art Ensemble of Chicago, the World Saxophone Quartet, and Lester Bowie's Brass Fantasy.

When Coltrane died suddenly in 1967 jazz was at the height of its experimental, expansionist stage, much of it inspired by the social and political upheaval of the time. By then, the term "free jazz" had begun to replace "avant-garde" and many young musicians were following in the footsteps of Coltrane and other innovators. But within a few years of Coltrane's death, the storm quieted. Experimentation did continue through the late 1980s, but by the early 1970s it had become clear that the period of rapid and sometimes overpowering changes in jazz had come to an end.

In its place came a period of what might be called "peaceful coexistence" of many kinds of jazz. A number of young musicians turned to the rich tradition of jazz, among them the gifted trumpeter Wynton Marsalis (also an expert classical player) and several other remarkable musicians from New Orleans, including Wynton's brother Branford (tenor and soprano saxophones), trumpeter Terence Blanchard, and alto saxophonist Donald Harrison. These young players have rejected "fusion" with electronics and rock as well as the practices of "free jazz" instead looking to the bebop tradition and Armstrong and Ellington for inspiration.

In the late 1980s jazz musicians paid tribute to traditional jazz forms with the development of "repertory jazz," which refers to the perform-

ances of big-band compositions and arrangements. The most notable of these ensembles are the Lincoln Center Jazz Orchestra—with Wynton Marsalis as artistic director—specializing in the music of Ellington, and the Smithsonian Jazz Masterpiece Ensemble, jointly directed by David Baker and Gunther Schuller, two master musicians with classical as well as jazz training. Female jazz vocalists continue to offer their agile and improvisational skills to the form through the works of Cassandra Wilson, Nnenna Freelon, and Shirley Horn, and jazz instrumentalists Regina Carter, JoAnn Brackeen, and Geri Allen.

It is difficult to predict where jazz will go next but one thing is certain, the story of jazz is one of the most remarkable chapters in the history of twentieth-century artistic creativity. Jazz continues to permeate almost every aspect of musical forms in the country. It has been celebrated through jazz festivals in almost every major city in America and many other major cities across the globe. The popularity has supported the interest in performers and the production of the music. Jazz as well as blues scholars have incorporated these musical forms into degree programs promoting a continuing generation of performers and those who appreciate the music. There are more than 500 colleges and universities that offer these opportunities.

POPULAR, FUNK, AND GOSPEL

Since the turn of the twentieth century, black music—whether gospel, rhythm and blues, soul, funk, or rap—has shaped American popular music. More recently, its impact can be heard in the emergence of world music coming out of Africa, South America, and the Caribbean Islands. From the church to the concert stage, thousands of gifted African American singers and musicians have bestowed upon America and the world a gift of unbounded spirit.

The foundation of twentieth-century black popular music is rooted in the sounds of several folk styles, including black minstrel and vaudeville tunes, blues, and ragtime. The music of the African American church, however, has played one of the most significant roles in the evolution of black popular music.

Inextricably bound to the spirituals sung by slaves, the gospel style came to dominate the black religious experience in America. By the turn of the century, gospel music had reached popularity as black religious songwriters began to publish their own compositions. One of the earliest and most influential of these writers was Charles Albert Tindley, a Maryland-born Methodist preacher, who was responsible for writing several gospel music classics. His song "I'll Overcome Someday" resurfaced more than a half decade later as "We Shall Overcome," the anthem of the civil rights movement in the 1960s. Tindley's 1905 composition "Stand by Me" became a major hit for singer Ben E. King and the Drifters during the 1960s.

Tindley's music subsequently influenced Thomas A. Dorsey, whose talents as a religious songwriter, accompanist, and choir director earned him the title "the father of gospel music." Before dedicating his life to the Baptist church, Dorsey spent his youth as an itinerant blues pianist, performing under the name Georgia Tom. Like other bluesmen/preachers such as the Reverend Gary Davis, Blind Willie McTell, and Gatemouth Moore, Dorsey performed both secular and religious music. In 1928, for example, he not only co-wrote the blues hit "Tight Like That" with guitarist Hudson "Tampa Red" Whitaker, but also composed his first gospel song, "If You See My Savior Tell Him You Saw Me."

Four years later, Dorsey abandoned his career as a blues and jazz pianist to devote himself to a form of religious music that historian Michael W. Harris describes as a gospel–blues style melding black religious and popular music into a unique and passionate form of gospel. During the Great Depression Dorsey's new style of gospel served as an uplifting spiritual release from the pervasive poverty experienced in the black community. The performance of two of Dorsey's songs at the 1930 National Baptist Convention created a wave of enthusiasm for gospel across the nation. In the fol-

lowing year, Dorsey organized the world's first gospel choir. In 1932 he began a forty-year career as choir director at Chicago's Pilgrim Baptist Church. During his stay at Pilgrim Baptist, he launched the golden age of gospel music (c.1945–1960), training and accompanying singers from Sallie Martin to Mahalia Jackson.

The advent of the phonograph around the turn of the century helped to heighten the popularity of gospel music. The distribution of records helped break down the musical isolation imposed upon blacks since slavery, allowing them to reach audiences outside their own communities. Recorded by the Victor label in 1902, the Jubilee singing and camp meeting shouts of the Dinwiddie Colored Quartet appeared as one of the first black recordings. In the 1920s black religious music became popular with the race record (a title designating the segregated sale of African American recordings). By 1924 Paramount Records sponsored its own Jubilee singers, and within three years Columbia Records began to send engineers into the field to record the richly complex harmonies of gospel quartets. Also popular were recorded sermons backed by occasional musical instruments, and evangelistic guitars, known commonly as "jack legs," which brought street-singing gospel blues to a wider audience.

After a decline in recordings by evangelists during the 1930s and early 1940s, gospel music experienced an immense rise in popularity as hundreds of independent recording labels appeared after World War II. During the 1940s numerous gospel quartets went on the road as full-time professionals, while thousands more sought work on weekends. Dressed in flowing robes and fashionably designed dress suits, quartets incorporated dance routines and expressive shouts into their performances. Throughout the postwar period male gospel groups like the Five Blind Boys from Mississippi, the Mighty Clouds of Joy from Los Angeles, and the Sensational Nightingales from Memphis sang *a cappella* (without instruments) on numerous recordings.

As black veterans returned home from World War II, they found not only a new gospel sound, but an exciting blues style being played by small combos—jump blues. With its roots in boogie woogie and the blues–swing arrangements of artists like Count Basie, Cab Calloway, Louis Jordan, and Lucky Millinder, this new blues style acquired an enormous following in black urban communities across the country. Unlike the swing-era big bands, jump blues groups featured fewer horns and a heavy rhythmic approach marked by a walking boogie bass line, honking saxophone solos, and a two–four drum pattern. Among the greatest exponents of postwar jump blues were guitarist T–Bone Walker, saxophonist Eddie "Cleanhead" Vincent, and blues shouter Big Joe Turner.

Soon, many jump blues ensembles began to feature singers versed in a smooth gospel-influenced vocal style. In 1949 the popularity of this style led *Billboard* magazine to change its black pop chart title to rhythm and blues, thus coining the name of this new music. Just as gospel emerged from blues and religious spirituals and hymns, rhythm and blues drew upon gospel, electric urban blues, and swing jazz to create a vibrantly modern sound appealing to the younger generation of postwar blacks. Some of the early recordings exemplifying the gospel influence on rhythm and blues were Cecil Grant's 1945 hit "I Wonder," Roy Brown's 1947 classic "Good Rocking Tonight," and Wynonie Harris's 1949 disc "All She Wants to Do Is Rock."

It was not long before this kind of raw-edged rhythm and blues emerged from hundreds of independent recording labels that appeared across the country in the postwar era. With the increased availability of rhythm and blues recordings, a handful of black radio disc jockeys became locally famous as the first promoters and salesmen of this music. Bringing their colorful street language to the airwaves, pioneer black DJs such as Al Benson and Vernon Winslow not only helped to popularize rhythm and blues, but set the trend for modern pop radio.

In the early 1950s numerous gospel quartets and street corner singing groups set out to establish careers in the black popular music scene. Influenced by gospel music and the secular singing of groups like the Inkspots, vocal groups performed complex harmonies in a cappella style. As they would for rap artists in decades to come, street corners in urban neighborhoods became training grounds for thousands of young aspiring African American artists. This music, known as doo-wop, first arrived on the scene with the formation of the Ravens in 1945. Not long afterward, there followed a great succession of doo-wop groups. One of these, the Orioles, scored a nationwide hit in 1953 with "Crying in the Chapel"—a song that, for the first time in black popular music, walked an almost indistinguishable line between gospel and mainstream pop music. In the same year, Billy Ward formed the Dominoes, featuring lead singer Clyde McPhatter, the son of a Baptist minister.

In the wake of the success of these vocal groups, numerous gospel singers left the church to become pop music stars. In 1952, for example, the Royal Sons became the Five Royales, the Gospel Starlighters (with James Brown), and finally the Blue Flames. Five years later, a young gospel singer named Sam Cooke landed a number-one pop hit with "You Send Me," a song that achieved popularity among both black and white audiences.

The strong relationship between gospel and rhythm and blues was evident in the music of more hard-edged R&B groups like Hank Ballard and the Midnighters. Maintaining a driving blues-based sound, Ballard's music, while featuring gospel-based harmonies, retained secular themes, as evinced in his 1954 hit "Work With Me Annie." However, the capstone of gospel R&B appeared in the talents of Georgia-born pianist and singer Ray Charles, who hit the charts in 1954 with "I Got a Woman," which was based upon the gospel song "My Jesus Is All the World to Me." Charles's 1958 recording "What I'd Say" is famed for its call-and-response pattern, which directly resembled the music in Holiness churches.

The rise of white rock and roll around 1955 served to open the floodgates for thousands of black R&B artists longing for a nationwide audience. A term applied to black R&B and its white equivalents during the mid-1950s, rock and roll represented a label given to a music form by the white media and marketplace in order to attract a mass multi-racial audience. As black music writer Nelson George explained, naming this music rock and roll "dulled down the racial identification and made young white consumers of Cold War America feel more comfortable." Taken from a term common among the Delta and electric blues cultures, rock and roll was actually rhythm and blues rechristened with a more "socially acceptable" title.

Thus, the majority of R&B performers never made the distinction between rhythm and blues and rock and roll. One R&B artist who established a prosperous career in rock and roll was New Orleans–born pianist Antoine "Fats" Domino. Although he had produced a great amount of strong R&B material before his career in rock and roll, Domino did not hit the charts until 1955 with "Ain't That a Shame," followed by the classics "Blueberry Hill," "I'm Walkin," and "Whole Lotta Loving." Another R&B pianist/singer to enter the rock and roll field was Little Richard Penniman, a former Pentecostal gospel singer whose career in pop music began in 1956 with the hit "Tutti Frutti." Before entering a Seventh Day Adventist seminary in 1959, Little Richard produced a string of hits: "Long Tall Sally," "Rip It Up," "The Girl Can't Help It," and "Good Golly Miss Molly."

In 1955 as Fats Domino's New Orleans style R&B tunes climbed the charts, a young guitarist from St. Louis named Chuck Berry achieved nationwide fame with the country-influenced song "Maybelleine," which reached number five on the charts. Backed by bluesman Muddy Waters's rhythm section, "Maybelleine" offered a unique form of R&B, combining white hillbilly, or rockabilly, with jump blues; Berry revolutionized R&B by featuring the guitar as a lead, rather than a rhythm, instrument. Modeled after his blues–guitar mentor T–Bone Walker, Berry's double-string guitar bends and syncopated up-stroke rhythm created a driving backdrop for his colorfully poetic tales of teenage life. A very eclectic and creative musician, Berry incorporated the

sounds of urban blues, country, calypso, Latin, and even Hawaiian music into his unique brand of R&B. His classic "Johnny B. Good," recorded in 1958, became a standard in almost every rock and roll band's repertoire, including 1960s rock guitar hero Jimi Hendrix.

Berry was not the only African American to take an interest in country music. Ray Charles's crossover into country music in the early 1960s caused controversy in many circles. In 1959 Charles recorded "I'm Moving On," a country tune by Hank Snow. Despite opposition, Charles went on to record a fine collection of songs in 1962 entitled *Modern Sounds in Country Music.* Filled with soulful ballads and backed by colorful string sections, the session produced two classic numbers: "You Don't Know Me" and "I Can't Stop Loving You." Its popularity spawned the 1963 sequel *Modern Sounds in Country Music: Volume 2,* which produced several more hits, including Hank Williams's "Your Cheating Heart" and "Take These Chains From My Heart."

Unlike those of other mainstream black country artists, Charles's renditions remained immersed in his unique gospel–blues sound. Before Charles's entrance into the country music field there had been many African American country artists, but it was not until 1965, when Charley Pride arrived on the country music scene with his RCA recordings "Snakes Crawl at Night" and "Atlantic Coastal Line," that a black artist emerged as a superstar in the country tradition. Pride's songs were so steeped in the country tradition that many radio listeners were astounded when they found out his racial identity. With the arrival of Pride, there appeared other black country artists like Linda Martell from South Carolina, O. B. McClinton from Mississippi, and Oklahoma-born Big Al Downing and Stoney Edwards. The most noted of these artists, Edwards recorded two nationwide hits in 1968 with Jesse Winchester's "You're on My Mind" and Leonard Cohen's "Bird on a Wire."

The most dominant form of black popular music of the 1960s emerged under the powerful gospel-influenced rhythm and blues style known as soul. As music historian Peter Guralnick wrote, soul music was a "brief flowering" of a distinctly southern-inspired black music that "came to its own no earlier than 1960," crossed over by 1965 or 1966, and, despite lingering traces of its influence throughout the culture, was spent as a controlling force by the early 1970s. Since it paralleled the civil rights and black power movements of the 1960s, soul embodied a sense of racial pride and independence. Such themes are evident in the soul music of Curtis Mayfield, an artist whom Nelson George describes as "black music's most unflagging Civil Rights activist." Mayfield's "People Get Ready" (1965), "We're a Winner" (1965), and "Choice of Color" (1969) represented messages of racial advancement and social change.

Although racial pride played an important role in the rise of soul, one of its main attributes was its relationship to the music of the black church—for there existed during the 1960s a distinct pattern among the careers of soul artists. Many African American artists, for instance, after establishing a career in gospel music became R&B and then soul artists. Among the artists who followed this pattern were soul singers Solomon Burke, Wilson Pickett, and Otis Redding.

One could say soul was the intensification of the gospel influence in popular black music. Soul artists from Joe Tex to "Lady of Soul" Aretha Franklin cultivated and refined a burningly passionate form of singing filled with gospel-influenced shouts and screams. With the incorporation of the electric bass, which replaced the acoustic bass featured on most of the R&B music of the 1940s and 1950s, these singers were provided with a modern pulsing rhythm that inspired them and the entire band to reshape the sound of black music.

In 1965, when Otis Redding hit the charts with the ballad "I've Been Loving You Too Long" and Wilson Pickett released the recording "Midnight Hour," a dynamic veteran of the gospel and rhythm and blues circuit named James Brown climbed the charts with the powerful soul number "Out of Sight." A self-created legend, Brown was

soul music's uncompromising individualist. As "Soul Brother No. 1," he achieved commercial success with his legendary 1963 LP *Live at the Apollo,* a record many critics believe best captures his explosive onstage energy. Throughout the 1960s Brown astounded audiences with his ability to lead a full horn and rhythm section through spontaneous changes in the musical form by a sudden gesture or a quick vocal command. Later in the decade, Brown and his powerful rhythm section, the Famous Flames, produced a number of classic soul numbers such as the 1967 recordings "Papa's Got a Brand New Bag" and "Cold Sweat," and the 1968 racial–political statement "I'm Black and I'm Proud." The "James Brown Sound" not only had a profound impact on the development of funk and jazz fusion, but it also helped shape the sound of African popular music.

During the 1960s, as soul music gained a mass following in the black community, a black-owned and family-run Detroit record company emerged as one of the largest and most successful African American business enterprises in America. In 1959 Berry Gordy, a Detroit entrepreneur, songwriter, and modern jazz enthusiast, established the Motown Record Corporation.

With its headquarters located in a modest two-story home, the company proudly displayed a sign on its exterior reading "Hitsville USA." Taking advantage of the diversity of local talent, Gordy employed Detroit-based contract teams, writers, producers, and engineers. Motown's studio became a great laboratory for technological innovations, advancing the use of echo, multi-tracking, and over-dubbing. In the studio, Gordy employed the city's finest jazz and classical musicians to accompany the young singing talent signed to the company.

Unlike the soul music emerging in studios like Stax Records in Memphis and Muscle Shoals Sounds in Alabama, Motown's music was also marketed at the white middle class; Gordy called his music "The Sound of Young America," and he sought to produce glamorous and well-groomed acts. "Blues and R&B always had a funky look to it back in those days," explained Motown pro-

The birth of Motown occurred in Detroit, where the Motown Museum (Hitsville, U.S.A.) remains a popular attraction to music lovers everywhere. In this 2009 photo, people gather to remember Michael Jackson, who got his start there with the Jackson 5.

ducer Mickey Stevenson. "We felt that we should have a look that the mothers and fathers would want their children to follow."

Thus, Motown set out to produce a sound that it considered more refined and less "off-key" than the music played by mainstream soul and blues artists. In its early years of operation, Motown retained an R&B influence as evinced in songs like the Marvelettes's "Please Mister Postman" (1961), Mary Wells's "You Beat Me to the Punch" (1962), and Marvin Gaye's "Pride and Joy" (1963).

One of the main forces responsible for the emergence of a unique "Motown sound" appeared in the production team of Brian and Eddie Holland, and Lamont Dozier, or H–D–H, as they came to be known. Utilizing the recording techniques of Phil Spector's "wall of sound," the H–D–H team brought fame to many of Motown's "girl groups" such as Martha and the Vandellas and the Supremes, featuring Diana Ross.

From 1966 to 1967 H–D–H began to use more complex string arrangements based upon minor-chord structures. This gave rise to what has been referred to as their "classical period." As a result, many Motown songs reflected the darker side of lost love and the conditions of ghetto life. This mood was captured in such songs by the Four Tops as "Reach Out, I'll Be There," "Burnadette," and "Seven Rooms of Gloom."

After the Holland–Dozier–Holland team left Motown in 1968, the company faced numerous artistic and economic problems and fell into a state of decline. A year later, Gordy signed the Jackson Five, the last major act to join the label before its demise. The Jacksons landed thirteen consecutive hit singles, including "ABC" and "I'll Be There." In 1971 Gordy moved the Motown Record Corporation to Los Angeles, where the company directed its efforts toward making films. Through the late 1970s and early 1980s Motown continued to sign such acts as the Commodores, Lionel Richie, and DeBarge. But in 1984 Gordy entered into a distribution agreement with MCA records and eventually sold Motown to an entertainment conglomerate.

Upon the waning of Motown in the 1970s, a new African American music style appeared that met the demands for a harder-edged dance music. The origins of what became funk can be traced to several sources: the music of James Brown, the rhythm patterns invented by New Orleans drummer Ziggy Modeliste, and the slapping electric bass style of Sly and the Family Stone member Larry Graham. Funk capitalized on the modern guitar styles of Jimi Hendrix and Johnny "Guitar" Watson. It also brought the synthesizer to the forefront of pop music, which gave funk a textual and rhythmic quality unlike the music played by the soul bands of the 1960s.

By the 1970s a number of groups played in the funk idiom, including soul veterans Curtis Mayfield and the Isley Brothers, and Maurice White's Earth, Wind, and Fire. Under George "Funkenstein" Clinton, there appeared a series of aggregate bands bearing the titles Parliment, Funkadelic, Bootsy's Rubber Band, the Horny Horns, and the Brides of Funkenstein, to name a few. Blending psychedelic guitar lines, complex chord work, and vocal distortion, Parliment–Funkadelic created a gritty funk style that sought to counter the sounds of the disco craze of the 1970s.

Other bands to join the funk scene were Kool and the Gang, the Ohio Players, and the Commodores. Although less abrasive in style than Parliment–Funkadelic, these groups retained a soul-influenced sound in an era when the commercial sounds of disco dominated the popular music scene.

While funk sold millions of records and received extensive radio airplay in the mid-1970s, rap music emerged within a small circle of New York artists and entertainers. In neighborhoods in Upper Manhattan and the South Bronx, disc jockeys at private parties discovered how to use "little raps" between songs to keep dancers on their feet. From behind the microphone DJs created a call-and-response pattern with the audience. Taking advantage of their status as master of ceremonies, they often boasted of their intellectual or sexual prowess. "Soon a division of labor emerged," explains musical historian Jefferson Morley. "DJs concentrated on perfecting the techniques of manipulating the turntables, while masters of ceremonies (MCs or rappers) concentrated on rapping in rhymes." Through the use of a special stylus, rappers moved records back and forth on the turntable to create a unique rhythmic sound, known within the rap culture as needle rocking.

Long before the modern rap, or hip-hop, culture appeared, however, there were African American artists who performed in a rap-style idiom. In 1929, for instance, New York singer–comedian Pigmeat Markham gave performances representative of an early rap style.

Rap music is also rooted in the talking jazz style of a group of ex-convicts called the Last Poets. During the 1960s this ensemble of black street poets rapped in complex rhythms over music played by jazz accompanists. Last Poets member Jalal Uridin, recording under the name Lightning Rod, released an album entitled *Hustler's Convention*. Backed by the funk band Kool and the Gang, Uridin's recording became very influential to the early New York rappers.

One of the first New York rap artists of the early 1970s was Jamaican-born Clive Campbell, also known as Kool Herc. A street DJ, Herc developed the art of sampling, the method of playing a section of a recording over and over in order to create a unique dance mix. Others to join the New York scene were Black Nationalist DJ Afrika Bambaataa from the southeast Bronx and Joseph Saddler, known as Grandmaster Flash, from the central Bronx. Flash formed the group Grandmaster Flash and the Three MCs (Cowboy, Kid Creole, and Melle Mel). Later he added Kurtis Blow and Duke Bootee, who founded the Furious Five.

Rap music did not reach a broad audience, however, until 1980, when the Sugar Hill Gang's song "Rapper's Delight" received widespread radio airplay. As rap groups assembled during the decade, they began to use their art to describe the

Rap music has gained in popularity worldwide. Here, British rapper Tinie Tempah performs in Helsinki, Finland.

harsh realities of inner-city life. Unlike early rap music, which was generally upbeat and exuberant in tone, the rap style of the 1980s exhibited a strong sense of racial and political consciousness. Toward the end of the decade, rap came to express an increasing sense of racial militancy. Inspired by the Nation of Islam and the teachings of martyred race leader Malcolm X, rap groups like Public Enemy turned their music into a voice supporting black power. Public Enemy's second LP, *It Takes a Nation of Millions to Hold Us Back,* sold over one million copies. Their song "Fight the Power" appeared in director Spike Lee's film *Do the Right Thing.* The group's third album, *Fear of a Black Planet,* was released in 1990. While it is a statement against "western cultural supremacy," explained group member Chuck D., it is also "about the coming together of all races" in a "racial rebirth."

Women have also played a role in the shaping of rap music. Rap artists such as Queen Lat-

ifah and the group Salt-N-Pepa represent a growing number of female rappers who speak for the advancement of black women in American society. Queen Latifah has emerged a critic of the male dominance in the music industry and the sexist image of women presented by some male rap artists.

Aside from the issues of racial protest, rap has generally been associated, especially in the mass popular culture, with themes regarding misogyny, sexual exploits, and youth culture. In other instances, rap seeks to educate young listeners about the dangers of inner-city life. But regardless of its style or message, rap is the voice of young African Americans. Like the music of its predecessors, rap is filled with artistic energy and descriptions of the human experience. "Rap is no fad," contends renowned producer Quincy Jones, "and it's not just a new kind of music. It's a whole new subculture that's been invented by the disenfranchised."

Rap music transitioned from the 1980s hardcore approach to the "gangsta" rap of the 1990s, which focused on violence and a lack of optimism, to issues of technique and rhymes in the late 1990s. Rappers such as Lil' Wayne, 50 Cent, and Kanye West lead the way in the twenty-first century along with veteran Jay-Z, as perspectives have become quite diverse, from party to gangsta. Regional styles, social messages, freestyle and other approaches also have created a category of rappers that not only rap, but also are producers, such as "Babyface" Edmonds, R. Kelly and Sean "Puffy" Combs.

With the death of music icon, Michael Jackson in 2009, popular music suffered a great lost. Jackson, who was rehearsing for his final tour, *This Is It,* died unexpectedly of cardiac arrest in his Los Angeles home on June 25. He was fifty years old. The entire nation and the world mourned his death. Jackson's influence as an artist is unparalleled as his contributions to the music scene spanned well over forty years beginning with the success of his family group The Jackson Five in 1970. The rehearsal tapes of Jackson's preparation for his final tour were released as a documentary film featuring interviews, rehearsals, and backstage footage of Jackson. The film opened at theaters in October 2009 and earned $23 million in its opening week. The film went on to earn $260.8 million and became the number-one grossing film of all time. Although legal issues are still unresolved regarding Jackson's death, presumably due to illegal and irresponsible prescription and use of medication, the final tribute *This Is It* did a great deal to provide closure for the family and Jackson's millions of fans.

Popular music has seen many extraordinary artists such as Beyoncé, Mary J. Blige, Ne-Yo, Usher, Chris Brown, and Keyshia Cole, who bring fresh sounds to rhythm and blues (R&B) and other genres. Reminiscent of Donny Hathaway and Marvin Gaye, neo-soul artists such as Musiq Soulchild, have added an even more direct connection to past styles of R&B.

Gospel, a melding of blues, jazz, folk, and rap music has continued to skyrocket in popularity as it reaches audiences not only with an interest in sacred music, but to audiences seeking a more contemporary sound that expresses a variety of emotions. Artists such as Kirk Franklin, Yolanda Adams, and BeBe and CeCe Winans have had crossover successes with secular audiences. These successes have also come through collaborations with other secular artists, which in combination have helped to make some of the biggest selling gospels albums that the genre has experienced. Over the past thirty years gospel has grown to be a multimillion-dollar industry reaching a diverse audience. Many of the artists are more transparent in their personal experiences and many more have ministries such as artist Donnie McClurkin. Many new artists such as "Toney," a preacher's son, use technology, rap, and religion to create gospel music for the new generation.

Popular music overall is an artistic collection of expressions that cover the scope of poetry, cultural critique, romance, celebration, spirituality, and funk. As a voice of "the people," the direction is carried forward by the will, desire, and aspiration of the people.

BIOGRAPHIES: CLASSICAL MUSIC

Michael Abels (1962–)

Composer

Michael Abels was born in Phoenix, Arizona, in 1962. He studied at the University of Southern California in Los Angeles and was esteemed for his composition *Queries*. After focusing his studies on African American music and the black church he collaborated with the Reverend James Cleveland regarding an arrangement for his recording. This opened the door to a commission from the Phoenix Symphony and other opportunities.

Abels's best known works are *Global Warming*, written in 1991, and *Fredericks Fables*, in 1994. His other works include *Dance for Martin*, which premiered in 1997, and *Tribute*, which premiered in 2001, inspired by the heroes of the 9/11 attacks. Abels has received two Meet the Composer Residencies (MTC), with one at the Watts Tower Arts Center and the other with the Richmond Symphony for 2001 to 2002. He continues to earn critical acclaim for his compositions.

Adele Addison (1925–)

Singer

Born on July 24, 1925, in New York, Adele Addison studied voice and attended Westminster Choir College. She did graduate studies at Princeton University and summer sessions at Berkshire Music School. While still attending Princeton she debuted in Boston in 1948.

In 1955 Addison made her professional debut at the New York Opera as Mimi in Puccini's *La Bohème*. Although she did perform in more operatic roles she preferred recitals. In 1959 Addison performed as Bess in the film version of *Porgy and Bess*. In 1963 Addison toured the Soviet Union as a member of a U.S. cultural exchange, and later in the 1960s she decided to teach on a collegiate level. In 2001 Addison received an honorary degree from Manhattan School of Music where she taught for many years.

Marian Anderson (1902–1993)
Singer

Marian Anderson was born on February 27, 1902, in Philadelphia, Pennsylvania. As a young choir girl she demonstrated her vocal talents by singing parts from soprano, alto, tenor, and bass. At the age of nineteen she began studying with Giuseppe Boghetti, and four years later she appeared as soloist with the New York Philharmonic. After a short engagement with the Philadelphia Symphony Orchestra, she traveled to Europe on a scholarship granted by the National Association of Negro Musicians.

At the peak of her career, Anderson was regarded as the world's greatest contralto. When she made her Town Hall debut in New York on December 31, 1935, her performance was described by Howard Taubman, the *New York Times* reviewer, as "musicmaking that probed too deep for words."

On Easter Sunday in 1939 Anderson gave what is perhaps her most memorable concert— singing on the steps of the Lincoln Memorial after having been barred, because of her race, from making an appearance at Constitution Hall by the Daughters of the American Revolution (an action that prompted Eleanor Roosevelt to resign in anger from the DAR). Her concert drew a crowd of more than 75,000.

In 1955 after years of successful concert work, she made her Metropolitan Opera debut in Verdi's *Un ballo in maschera.* Two years later, a U.S. Department of State tour took her around the world. In September of 1958 she was named to the U.S. delegation to the United Nations.

In 1982, when Anderson celebrated her eightieth birthday, Grace Bumbry and Shirley Verrett sang a tribute to her at New York City's Carnegie Hall. Anderson established scholarships to support and encourage other singers who had to endure and eventually break the racist barriers that permeated America.

T. J. Anderson (1928–)
Composer, Educator

T. J. Anderson was born on August 17, 1928, in Coatesville, Pennsylvania. His love of music was realized early on when he played with a jazz group while still in junior high school. Anderson earned a bachelor's degree in music from West Virginia State College in 1950, a master's degree in music education from Pennsylvania State University in 1951, and a Ph.D. from the University of Iowa. In his studies he was guided by Darius Milhaud, Philip Bezanson, and Richard Hervig. After several teaching opportunities he joined the faculty of Tufts University and remained there throughout his career.

Anderson began to receive numerous commissions for his compositions in 1961. Anderson's skills include the techniques of jazz, blues, spirituals, big band, chamber music, ensembles, and full orchestra. His commissions drew on his many skills and included works such as *Transitions, A Fantasy for Ten Instruments, Thomas Jefferson's Orbiting Minstrels, Contraband,* and *Variations on a Theme.* Notable artists requesting his skills include Derek Walcott, Nobel Prize winner, and Yo-Yo Ma, master cellist. Anderson's abilities were also shown as he conducted the Black Music Repertory Ensemble in 1988.

David N. Baker (1931–)
Composer, Educator

David Nathaniel Baker was born on December 21, 1931, in Indianapolis, Indiana. He received a bachelor's degree in 1953, and a master's degree in music education from Indiana University in 1954. He also studied at Berklee School of Music and the Lenox School of Jazz earning a diploma in 1959. He played for various bands in the 1950s and 1960s, including the bands of Quincy Jones, Wes Montgomery, and Lionel Hampton.

Baker continued to perform with various groups as well as compose after joining the faculty of the University of Indiana in 1966. Baker, who has a catalog of well over 2,000 commissioned works, including jazz, symphonic works, chamber music, ballet, and film scores, is also conductor and artistic director of the Smithsonian Jazz Masterworks Orchestra.

Baker has received numerous awards, including induction into the National Association of Jazz Educators' Hall of Fame in 1981, the American Jazz Masters Award from the National Endowment for the Arts in 2000, an Emmy Award in 2003, and the Kennedy Center's Living Jazz Legend Award in 2007.

Kathleen Battle (1948–)
Singer

Soprano Kathleen Battle was born in Portsmouth, Ohio, on August 13, 1948, and is a graduate of the University of Cincinnati's College-Conservatory of Music, having received both bachelor's and master's degrees in music.

Battle made her Metropolitan Opera debut in 1977 as the Shepherd in *Tannhäuser* and has also been heard there as Sophie in *Werther,* and Blondchen in *The Abduction from the Seraglio.* The 1980–1981 season included performances in *The Italian Girl in Algiers,* as well as debuts with the Zurich Opera and the Lyric Opera of Chicago. In 1982 she received critical praise for her depiction of Rosina in the Met's production of *The Barber of Seville.*

In the 1987–1988 season Battle returned to the Metropolitan Opera to sing the role of Zerbinetta in Strauss's *Ariadne auf Naxos.* She has sung in major music festivals and with major orchestras, including the New York Philharmonic, Cleveland Orchestra, and Los Angeles Philharmonic, and she has recorded such works as *Ari-* *adne auf Naxos* and Mahler's *Symphony No. 4.* In 1993 she sang with Jessye Norman in a program of spirituals at Carnegie Hall with James Levine conducting. Her recordings include collaborations with trumpeter Wynton Marsalis in a recording of baroque arias, Gershwin with Herbie Hancock, and Janet Jackson with her album *janet.*

In 1994 Battle was removed from her performance at the Metropolitan Opera due to claims of unprofessional behavior. Since that time Battle has focused on studio recordings and further collaborations with various artists. In 2008 she performed "Superwoman" on the American Music Awards telecast, and in February of the same year she performed at Carnegie Hall in a piano-accompanied recital of works by Schubert, Liszt, and Rachmaninoff.

Battle has received numerous awards and honorary doctorates, including five Grammy Awards, one Emmy, and an Image Award from the NAACP in 1999.

"Blind Tom" Bethune (1849–1908)
Pianist

Thomas Greene "Blind Tom" Bethune was born into slavery on May 25, 1849, in Columbus, Georgia. Blind from birth, he was a musical prodigy. His owner, James Bethune, allowed him access to the family's piano, and realizing at once the financial possibilities, arranged for informal musical training. It soon became apparent that Tom needed only to hear a piece to be able to play it.

"Blind Tom" began performing for the profit of his owner while still a slave and a child, and he continued to tour the North and South during the Civil War. After the war the Bethune family retained financial control over his performances through contracts. Tom performed in the United States and in Europe. His repertoire consisted of the usual concert fare, including serious classics by composers like Bach, Beethoven, and Chopin; fancy virtuosic pieces by composers such as Gottschalk and Liszt; improvised variations on contemporary popular ballads and arias; and his own light compositions, few of which survive today. He was said to have been able to play any one of seven thousand pieces on command. Tom retired in 1898 and died June 4, 1908.

Harolyn Blackwell (1955–)
Singer

Harolyn Blackwell was born November 23, 1955, in Washington, D.C. Her musical talents were nurtured by her teacher of piano and voice who encouraged her to perform throughout her high school years. Blackwell attended Catholic University majoring in classical music and theater, and subsequently moved to New York after graduation to perform in the twenty-fifth anniversary revival of *West Side Story*.

Blackwell returned to Chicago for an apprenticeship in opera and became a finalist in a regional audition for the Metropolitan Opera (Met). Her vocal success resulted in her 1989 debut at the Met as Poussette in *Manon*. She continued at the Met until 1997, performing in various roles such as Susanna in *The Marriage of Figaro* and Gilda in *Rigoletto*. Blackwell returned to Broadway in 1997 for a revival of *Candide* by Leonard Bernstein.

Blackwell continues to perform at opera houses across the country, including the Lyric Opera of Chicago, the San Francisco Opera, the Seattle Opera, and the Met. She has also sung with the Pittsburgh Symphony, the Cincinnati Symphony, and London Symphony Orchestra among others. In 2006 Blackwell sang at the White House in honor of the Dance Theater of Harlem.

"Blind" Boone (1864–1927)
Pianist

John William Boone, called "Blind Boone", was born on May 17, 1864, near Miami, Missouri. His music career began with the support of his home town community in Warrensburg, Missouri. Funds were raised so that he could attend the In-

stitute for the Education of the Blind in St. Louis, Missouri. Boone struck out on his own with three years of training on the piano. After meeting and partnering with John Lange, the Blind Boone Concert Company was formed to support Boone and provide a stipend for his mother. This successful partnership lasted until Lange's death in 1916.

A concert of Boone's would consist of classical, popular, dance, and piano improvisation. Boone often wrote pieces to include in his concerts. He was able to continue his company after 1916 in spite of the prevailing racist challenges and he was able to give back to the African American community. Boone's last concert was in 1927, shortly before his death.

Grace Bumbry (1937–)
Singer

Born in St. Louis, Missouri, on January 4, 1937, Grace Bumbry, like many black singers, had her first exposure to music in a church choir singing with her brothers and her parents at the Union Memorial Methodist Church in St. Louis. After studying voice locally, she won a nationwide talent contest in 1954 and went on, with scholarship aid, to study successively at Boston University and Northwestern University. At the latter school, she attended master classes in opera and lieder taught by the famed singer and teacher Lotte Lehmann.

In 1959 Bumbry traveled to various European countries, performing in the operatic capitals of the world. On July 23, 1961, Wieland Wagner, grandson of Richard Wagner, shocked many traditionalists by selecting Bumbry to sing the role of Venus in *Tannhäuser*, a role that conventionally calls for a figure of so-called Nordic beauty—usually a tall and voluptuous blond. Bumbry gave a performance that won acclaim from even the harshest of critics, who praised her physical radiance and brilliant singing.

Bumbry, a mezzo-soprano, is the first black performer to have sung at the Wagner Festival in

Bayreuth, Germany, and one of the few singers who can boast of having been called to play a command performance at the White House. Bumbry was a guest of the Kennedys, singing at a formal state dinner opening Washington's official social season in 1962.

In 1974 Bumbry performed with the Met in *Cavalleria rusticana.* On December 6, 1981, Bumbry participated in a benefit concert at Carnegie Hall put on by Artists to End Hunger. On January 31, 1982, she appeared at Carnegie Hall again, sharing the stage with Shirley Verrett to pay tribute to Marian Anderson.

In the 1987–1988 season Grace Bumbry performed with the San Francisco Opera as Abigaille in *Nabucco,* and starred as Lady Macbeth in a new production of *Macbeth* in Los Angeles. She celebrated her twenty-fifth anniversary at the Convent Garden's Royal Opera with a series of performances of *Tosca* and appeared at the Vienna State Opera in the same role. In 1990 she toured with her own troupe, the Grace Bumbry Musical Heritage Ensemble, which she established to focus on the preservation and performance of Negro spirituals. Bumbry continues to teach and encourage others. Her primary residence is in Salzburg, Austria.

Bumbry's awards include induction into the St. Louis Walk of Fame, Italy's Premio Giuseppe Verdi Award, France's Commandeur de L'Ordre des Arts et Lettres, and in 2009 she was honored at the Kennedy Center for her contributions to the arts.

"Harry" Burleigh (1866–1949)
Composer, Arranger, Singer

Born into a poverty-stricken family on December 2, 1866, in Erie, Pennsylvania, Henry Thacker "Harry" Burleigh was unable to receive any formal musical training until he was an adult. In 1892 at the age of twenty-six he moved from his home in Erie to New York City, where he won a scholarship to the National Conservatory of Music (1892–1896). After graduation he pursued a very successful singing career that included concerts throughout the United States and Europe.

He was soloist at St. George's Protestant Episcopal Church in New York for fifty-three years, and at Temple Emanu-El for twenty-five. Burleigh toured as a recitalist performing in Europe and England. He also worked on Broadway and served as a private voice and composition instructor.

As a composer and arranger, Burleigh was the first to arrange spirituals in the style of art songs and was the first African American composer to receive critical acclaim for his art songs. As a performer, he established the tradition of concluding recitals with a group of spirituals. His art-song compositions included settings of poetry by Robert Burns and Langston Hughes, and he composed several pieces for violin and piano. He was a member of the American Society of Composers, Authors, and Publishers (ASCAP), and sat on its board of directors. He received an honorary master's degree from Atlanta University in 1918, and an honorary doctorate from Howard University in 1920. He died on December 12, 1949.

Will Marion Cook (1869–1944), Violinist, Conductor, Composer

Born on January 27, 1869, in Washington, D.C., Will Marion Cook wrote and directed in both popular and classical venues. He was well educated in the classical genres—he entered Oberlin Conservatory when he was fifteen to study violin, studied further in Berlin between 1887 and 1889, and attended the National Conservatory of Music in New York.

In 1890 he shifted his energies from performing to conducting. He directed an orchestra in Washington, D.C., in 1890, and performed at the Chicago World's Fair in 1893. In 1898 he became active in writing and directing black musical comedies in New York, producing the first such show to play in a major theater for a wide audience. He organized choral societies and promoted all-black concerts. He directed the New York Syncopated Orchestra, which traveled Europe, and taught and sponsored many young and talented black musicians. In addition to his musicals, he wrote art songs, choral works, instrumental pieces, and operas. Cook died in New York in 1944.

Roque Cordero (1917–2008)
Composer, Educator

 Roque Cordero was born on August 16, 1917, in Panama. He studied clarinet and string instruments and began to write songs and study compositions when he was seventeen. In 1943 he came to the United States to study at Hamline University in St. Paul, Minnesota, and to study conducting with Dimitri Mitropoulos at the University of Minnesota, where he earned a B.A. in art.

Cordero's work has been presented in the United States as well as in Latin American and Europe. His works include *Rapsodia Campesina, Violin Concerto,* and *Third String Quartet,* which earned him several awards. His other awards include a Guggenheim Fellowship, an honorary professorship at the University of Chile, and a Koussevitzky International Recording Award. He also served as professor of music at Illinois State University for over fifteen years. Cordero died on December 27, 2008.

Anthony Davis (1951–)
Composer, Pianist

Anthony Davis was born in Paterson, New Jersey, on February 20, 1951. He earned a bachelor's degree in music from Yale in 1975. As a Lustman Fellow at Yale, Davis taught composition and Afro-American studies. He returned to Yale after graduation in 1990 as a visiting professor of music. After moving to New York he formed his own group, *Episteme.* He wrote compositions for jazz, opera, instrumentals, and voice, and by 1990 Davis had established a reputation through over twenty commissions for his compositions.

Davis's most well-known operas are *Tania* (1992), *Amistad* (1977), and *X: The Life and Times of Malcolm X* (1986). In addition to operas he has composed music for the Pulitzer Prize-winning Broadway production of *Angels in America Part I: Millennium Approaches,* which premiered in 1993.

Davis served as artistic advisor of the American Composers Orchestra's Imrpovisel festival and conference, 2003–2004. The conference featured a solo piano performance by Davis of his composition *Wayang V.* In 2009 the La Jolla Symphony premiered Davis symphonic composition *Amistad.*

Mary Cardwell Dawson (1894–1962)
Opera Director

Mary Cardwell Dawson was born in Meridian, North Carolina, on February 14, 1894. Her family later moved to Pittsburgh, Pennsylvania. Dawson graduated from the New England Conservatory of Music and the Chicago Musical College. In 1927 she founded the Cardwell School of Music and the renowned Cardwell Choir. The group was so successful they made an appearance at the New York World's Fair. Dawson was president of the National Association of Negro Music from 1939 to 1941.

After a successful performance of Verdi's *Aida* in 1941 Dawson was so frustrated by the discrimination that prevented not only her and other professionals and students from getting into the world of opera that she started the Nation Negro Opera Company (NNOC) in 1941. Washington, D.C., became the central location for NNOC, but there were chapters in major cities such as Baltimore, Chicago, Cleveland, Pittsburgh, and Red Bank, New Jersey. The company produced major operas such as *Faust, Aida,* and *La Traviata.* Their most performed opera was *The Ordering of Moses.* Dawson died in 1962.

William Levi Dawson (1899–1990)
Composer

William Levi Dawson was born on September 26, 1899, in Anniston, Alabama. He studied composition and trombone at Tuskegee at the age of fifteen. After moving to Kansas City he went on to earn a bachelor's degree in music in 1925. He earned a master's degree in 1927 from the Conservatory of Music. Dawson established himself as a composer and published numerous arrangements of spirituals. Dawson became the head of Tuskegee Music Institute in 1931.

Dawson's most famous work, *Negro Folk Symphony,* was performed in 1934 at the Philadelphia Orchestra. It was the first African American composition to be premiered by a major U.S. orchestra. After Dawson took a trip to Africa, where he studied African rhythms and techniques and their influence on African American spirituals, he added a new dimension to his spiritual arrangements. His arrangements, which have an authentic feel, remain staples for many choral groups. His compositions combine European form with a nationalistic focus based on folk culture and African influences. He died in 1990.

James DePreist (1936–)
Conductor

Born in Philadelphia, Pennsylvania, on November 21, 1936, James DePreist studied piano and percussion from the age of ten, but he did not decide on a musical career until he reached his early twenties. After graduating from high school, he entered the Wharton School of the University of Pennsylvania as a pre-law student, receiving a B.S. in 1958, and an M.A. in 1961. DePreist also studied music history, the theory of harmony, and orchestration at the Philadelphia Conservatory of Music, and he studied composition with the distinguished American composer Vincent Persichetti.

In 1962 the U.S. State Department sponsored a cultural exchange tour of the Near and Far East, engaging DePreist as an American specialist in music. During this tour DePreist was stricken with polio, which paralyzed both of his legs, and was flown home for intensive therapy. Within six months he had fought his way back to the point where he could walk with the aid of crutches and braces. Courage, determination, and talent carried him to the semi-finals of the 1963 Dimitri Mitropoulos International Music Competition for Conductors.

In 1964 DePreist captured first prize in the Mitropoulos International Competition and on June 28, 1965, he conducted Marian Anderson's farewell concert at Robin Hood Dell in Philadelphia (DePriest is a nephew of Marian Anderson). DePriest made his European debut with the Rotterdam Philharmonic in 1969; in 1971 he was selected to become associate conductor with the National Symphony in Washington, D.C. He made his London debut in 2005 and served as permanent conductor of the Tokyo Metropolitan Symphony Orchestra from 2005 to 2008.

DePriest has been awarded numerous doctorates and honors, including awards from the American Academy of Arts and Sciences, the Royal Swedish Academy of Music, and the National Medal of Arts for artistic excellence in 2005.

Robert Nathaniel Dett (1882–1943)
Composer, Arranger, Conductor

Robert Nathaniel Dett was born in Drummondville, Ontario, Canada, on October 11, 1882. His family later moved to Niagara Falls, New York. Dett's musical training began in 1901 when he studied at Halstead Conservatory in Brockport, New York. In 1903 he enrolled at the Oberlin Conservatory graduating in 1908 with a degree in music. Between 1913 and 1932 Dett held several teaching jobs, which included Lane College, Lincoln Institute, and Hampton Institute. In 1932 he moved to Rochester, New York, and earned a master's degree from the Eastman School of Music.

From 1932 to 1943 Dett spent time as a choir director and continued to compose. His choral compositions include *Chariot Jubilee, The Ordering of Moses: Biblical Folk Scenes, Enchantment, In the Bottoms,* and *Magnolia.* Dett was a founding member of the National Association of Negro Musicians in 1919.

Dett joined the faculty at Bennett College, in Greensboro, North Carolina, and was the director of the Women's Army Corps chorus in 1943. That same year he died of a heart attack.

Dean Dixon (1915–1976)
Conductor

Dean Dixon was born in Manhattan, New York, on January 10, 1915, and graduated from DeWitt Clinton High School in 1932. Exposed to classical music by his parents (as a small boy he was regularly taken to Carnegie Hall), Dixon formed his own amateur orchestra at the Harlem YMCA while still in high school. On the basis of a successful violin audition he was admitted to the Juilliard School, where he received his bachelor's degree in 1936; three years later, he acquired his master's degree from Columbia.

The Dean Dixon Symphony Society, which he formed in 1932, began to receive financial support from the Harlem community in 1937. In 1941, at the request of Eleanor Roosevelt, Dixon gave a concert at the Heckscher Theater in New York. He was later signed by the musical director of NBC Radio to conduct the network's summer symphony in two concerts. Two months after the NBC concerts he made his debut with the New York Philharmonic. Dixon was the first black and, at twenty-six, the youngest musician ever to conduct the New York Philharmonic Orchestra.

Unable to find a position in the United States, Dixon went abroad and worked with orchestras in Germany, Australia, and Sweden. He was conductor for the Israel Philharmonic from 1950 to 1951, and the principal conductor of the Sydney Symphony Orchestra from 1964 to 1967. He returned to the United States in 1970 and served as guest conductors for several orchestras. He died in 1976.

Mattiwilda Dobbs (1925–)
Singer

Mattiwilda Dobbs was born in Atlanta, Georgia, on July 11, 1925. She attended Spelman College and graduated with a major in voice in 1946. She also studied at Columbia University Teacher College and earned a master's degree. Dobbs traveled throughout Europe and gained additional training in voice from Pierre Berman in Paris. In 1951 Dobbs became the first African American to sing a principal role at La Scala in Milan, Italy.

A pioneer, Dobbs debuted in San Francisco in 1955 as the first African American to play a major role in the San Francisco Opera company. She debuted at the Metropolitan Opera as the first African American to sing a romantic lead, and she became the first African American singer to perform at the Bolshoi Theatre in the Soviet Union.

Dobbs has served as artist-in-residence at Spelman College and taught classes at Howard University through the 1970s. She was elected to the board of directors of the Metropolitan Opera in 1989.

Robert Todd Duncan (1903–1998)
Singer, Actor, Educator

Robert Todd Duncan was born February 12, 1903, in Indianapolis, Indiana. He graduated from Butler University with a B.A. in music and received an M.A. in music from Columbia University Teachers College. Duncan was very successful as a concert singer and premiered in the opera Porgy and Bess with an all-black cast in 1934. Duncan sang the lead role of Porgy. He became the first African American member of the New York City Opera from 1945 to 1946.

Duncan did several movie roles such as Cabin in the Sky (1943) and Show Boat (1944). For his role in Lost in the Stars Duncan received the New York Drama Critics' Circle Award and the Tony Award in 1950. He continued to teach following his retirement in 1967. Duncan died in 1998.

Leslie B. Dunner (1956–)
Conductor, Clarinetist, Composer

Leslie B. Dunner was born in New York City, on January 5, 1956. He earned a B.A. from the Eastman School of Music in clarinet performance in 1976, and an M.A. in music history from Queen's College. He received his doctorate from the College-Conservatory of Music of the University of Cincinnati in 1982.

Dunner has had various roles including conductor at the Detroit Symphony, the Annapolis Symphony, principle director of the Joffre Ballet in Chicago, and guest conductor for the Warsaw Philharmonic and the New York City Ballet. He also worked with the Dance Theatre of Harlem. His honors include the 1991 James Weldon Johns Award and the American Symphony Orchestra League Award in 1994.

Aaron Paul Dworkin (1970–)
Violinist, Educator

Aaron Paul Dworkin was born in Monticello, New York, on September 11, 1970. A bi-racial child who was adopted when he was two weeks old by a white couple, Dworkin has said that his diverse experiences allowed him to see art as a way to bridge differences. He received his B.A in music in 1997, and his M.A. in music in both acoustic and electric violin performance from the University of Michigan School of Music. He also studied at Interlochen Art Academy in Michigan and the Peabody Institute.

In pursuing his career and often finding himself as the sole African American, Dworkin founded the Sphinx Organization to help young African American and Latino artists in meeting challenges of racism, isolation, and access into the world of classical music. It has become a national non-profit organization.

Dworkin, an accomplished electric and acoustic violinist, received a MacArthur Fellowship in 2005 for his work in classical music. The Sphinx Organization was awarded one of eight 2005 National Governor's Awards in the area of artistic production for distinguished service to state government. Dworkin serves as a member of the Obama National Arts Policy Committee. He has produced two CDs, *Ebony Rhythm* and *Bar-talk*.

Simon Lamont Estes (1938–)
Singer

A native of Centerville, Iowa, Simon Lamont Estes was born on March 2, 1938. He attended the University of Iowa and received a full scholarship to Juilliard, studying under Sergius Kagan and Christopher West. He won the Munich International Vocal Competition in 1965, and was the silver medalist in the Tchaikovsky Competition in 1966.

Estes, a bass-bariton, made his operatic debut as Ramfis in *Aida* at the Deutsche Opera Berlin and since then has appeared in most of the world's major opera houses, including La Scala, the Hamburg State Opera, the Bavarian State Opera of Munich, the Vienna State Opera, the Lyric Opera of Chicago, the San Francisco Opera, and the Zurich Opera. After having been spurned by many of the major U.S. opera houses it was not until 1982 that he made his debut at the Metropolitan Opera (foregoing the honor of singing the national anthem on baseball's opening day because it coincided with his Met debut). He went on to perform at the Met for six consecutive season in operas such as *Parsifal, Elektra, Porgy and Bess,* and *Aida.*

Estes has appeared as soloist with most of the world's leading symphony orchestras. Estes was the first black man to sing at the Bayreuth Festival, appearing in the title role of a new production of *Der Fliegende Holländer,* a portrayal he repeated there in three subsequent seasons. He has also performed recitals and orchestral engagements in numerous European cities, including Paris, Zurich, Brussels, Munich, Bonn, Madrid, and Bordeaux. His North American highlights include appearances with the Chicago Symphony Orchestra conducted by Sir Georg Solti, and the Montreal Symphony conducted by Charles Dutoit. In addition to having recorded *Der Fliegende Holländer,* Estes has recorded Handel's *Messiah,* Fauré's *Requiem,* Beethoven's *Symphony No. 9,* numerous spirituals, and highlights from *Porgy and Bess.* In July 2010 he performed at the World Cup during the opening gala's "Tribute to South Africa" in Johannesburg, South Africa.

Emma Hackley (1867–1922)
Singer, Choral Director, Educator

Emma Azalia Hackley did as much to promote African American musicians as she did to promote traditional African music. She was born in 1867, in Tennessee. She received her musical training while growing up in Detroit, Michigan, where she studied voice and piano and began giving local recitals at an early age. She attended the University of Denver, where she received her bachelor's degree in music in 1900. In 1905 she traveled to Paris, where she continued her studies.

Hackley performed concerts extensively during the early years of the twentieth century, but gradually turned to developing and supporting the careers of other talented young black artists. Through recitals, concerts, lectures, and demonstrations, she raised funds for scholarships; in 1908 she established an ongoing scholarship to promote and fund study abroad. She sponsored debut recitals for young performers and helped many find good college-level teaching positions. Many of the artists she supported and promoted went on to become successful musical leaders in their own right.

Hackley founded and directed the Vocal Normal Institute in Chicago between 1915 and 1917. In the last years of her life she organized large community concerts promoting the importance of black folk music, raising the level of public interest and pride in African American musical heritage. So significant was her contribution that twenty years after her death, the National Association of Negro Musicians established the Hackley Collection at the Detroit Public Library for the preservation of materials relating to black musicians.

Dorothy Antoinette Handy (1930–2002)
Flautist, Educator, Writer

Dorothy Antoinette Handy was born on October 29, 1930, in New Orleans, Louisiana. She decided early in life that the flute was her instrument of choice. She studied at Spelman College in Atlanta and the New England Conservatory of Music in Boston, where she earned her B.A.

in music in 1952; she received an M.A. in music from Northwestern University, in Evanston, in 1953, and an arts diploma from the National Conservatory in Paris in 1955. After becoming first chair with the Orchestre International in 1954, Handy was able to secure opportunities in the United States.

Handy played with orchestras such as the Chicago Civic Symphony, the Richmond Symphony, and the Symphony of the New World. She continued to perform in a career that lasted twenty-five years. Handy spent time as an instructor at various institutions and has published research about African American music. As a result of receiving a Ford Foundation Humanities Fellowship, Handy published *Black Women in American Bands and Orchestras* (1981), *The International Sweethearts of Rhythm* (1983), *Black Conductors* (1995), and *Jazz Man's Journey* (1999). In 1990 Handy was selected as director of the music program for the National Endowment of the Arts; she retired in 1993 and died October 21, 2002.

Roland Hayes (1987–1977)
Singer

 Roland Hayes was born to former slave parents in Curryville, Georgia, on June 3, 1887. His father, a tenant farmer, died when Hayes was twelve. Determined that her seven children would receive an education, Hayes's mother sent them to Chattanooga, Tennessee, where they set up a rotating system whereby one brother worked while the others attended school. Hayes was employed in a machine shop, but when his turn came to go to school he passed it up, continuing to supply the family income while he studied at night.

In 1917 Hayes became the first black to give a recital in Boston's Symphony Hall. Three years later, he traveled to London and gave a royal command performance, followed by other successes throughout Europe. His tenor voice was used to good advantage in programs blended from Negro spirituals, folk songs, operatic arias, and German lieder.

Hayes gave a well-received farewell concert at Carnegie Hall in New York on his seventy-fifth birthday in 1962. During his career he received many awards and citations, including eight honorary degrees and the NAACP's Spingarn Medal for the most outstanding achievement among blacks. Hayes died in Boston on January 1, 1977, at the age of eighty-nine. His success in the concert field played a great part in broadening the opportunities later afforded to such singers as Paul Robeson and Marian Anderson.

Amadi Hummings (1969–)
Violist, Educator

Hummings was born in New York City in 1969, and attended North Carolina School of the Arts to begin his formal training. He also studied at the New England Conservatory and earned his master's degree from Indiana University in 1994.

As a concerto soloist Hummings has performed with symphonies all over the world, including the Virginia Symphony, the Salisbury Symphony, the National Symphony of Ecuador, and at the Costa Rica International Music Festival as well as the San Juan Island Festival. His performances are numerous despite serving as a faculty member at James Madison University and the Atlanta University Center, as well as currently serving as the music director of the Harlem Symphony Orchestra.

Isaiah Jackson (1945–)
Conductor

Isaiah Jackson was born in Richmond, Virginia, on January 22, 1945; he earned a B.A. from Harvard University in 1966, cum laude in Russian history and literature. After determining that he wanted to become a musician, Jackson earned a master's degree from Stanford University in music in 1969. He studied with Nadia Boulanger in France before going to Juilliard School of Music

to earn another master's degree and a doctorate in musical arts in 1973.

Jackson has served as a guest conductor at New York Philharmonic in 1978, Boston Pops in 1983, the Berlin Symphony Orchestra from 1989 to 1991, and many other guest roles in numerous countries. Jackson was also the first conductor of color at the Cape Town Philharmonic Orchestra, guest conductor at the Royal Ballet of London, and conductor at the Vienna Symphony.

Jackson's awards include the Governor's Award for the Arts from the Commonwealth of Virginia, 1979 and 1991, and he has most recently concluded a seven-year term achieving the status of conductor emeritus for the Pro Arte Chamber Orchestra of Boston. He also serves as instructor at the Harvard Extension School and the Berklee College of Music.

J. Rosamond Johnson (1873–1954)
Composer

John Rosamond Johnson, brother of writer and lyricist James Weldon Johnson, was born in Jacksonville, Florida, in 1873. He received his musical training at the New England Conservatory and briefly studied under composer Samuel Coleridge-Taylor.

Eager to pursue a career in show business, Johnson teamed up with lyricist and vaudeville entertainer Bob Cole in 1899. With lyrics supplied by his brother James, Johnson and Cole wrote numerous songs, including "Under the Bamboo Tree," "Congo Love Songs," "My Castle on the Nile," and "Lift Every Voice and Sing," which premiered in 1900.

Johnson and Cole also wrote, directed, and produced several musicals, including *The Shoo-Fly Regiment* in 1907, and *The Red Moon* in 1910. In addition to songwriting, Johnson and his brother edited several collections of Negro spirituals for solo or piano in 1925 and 1926. Johnson published on his own two more collections in 1936 and 1937.

Scott Joplin (c.1867–1917)
Pianist, Composer

Scott Joplin was born about 1867 in eastern Texas, and he came from a musical family who encouraged him to study music. His father bought him a piano, and Joplin studied classical piano with a local German music teacher. When he left home, however, he could only find musical work in such venues as bars and brothels. In 1894 he settled in Sedalia, Missouri, to teach piano and study theory and composition at George R. Smith College for Negroes. In 1899 he published "The Maple Leaf Rag," which was enormously successful; his piano rags appealed greatly to the public and within a few years he had achieved financial success with his ragtime compositions. He was able to create works that provided royalties for life, but he also sought to expand his compositions.

Joplin composed larger works in the same style. He completed a ballet in 1899, and his first opera in 1908 (the score of which is now lost); he also wrote a second opera, *Treemonisha*. He was determined to produce this opera and see it performed, but had no luck. He personally financed the publication of the vocal score and produced a non-staged version of the opera for critics, but New York audiences were not ready for an opera about blacks by a black composer, and no one would give financial backing to a full production.

After the "Ragtime Renaissance" of the early 1970s Joplin's opera was given a world premiere at the Atlanta Memorial Arts Center in Georgia in 1972, and has been performed elsewhere many times, including a masterful performance by the Houston Grand Opera Company. In 1976 Joplin's work was also awarded a Pulitzer Prize for contributions to American music.

Ulysses Simpson Kay (1917–1995)
Composer, Educator

Ulysses Simpson Kay was born on January 7, 1917, in Tucson, Arizona. He came from a musical family and was the nephew of jazz cornetist King Oliver. Kay studied voice, piano, and several different instruments. He graduated from the University of Arizona with a degree in music in 1938, and a master's degree from the Eastman School of Music in Rochester in 1940.

Kay received critical acclaim with the performance of his composition *Of New Horizons* in 1944, and it was followed by *Suite for Orchestra* in 1945, which won Kay a prize from Broadcast Music Incorporated. Kay won many awards such as the Prix de Rome (1949), a Fulbright Foundation grant (1950), and the Guggenheim Fellowship (1964), which allowed him to continue writing compositions and scores. Some of his works include film scores such as *Southern Harmony: Four Aspects for Orchestra* (1975), and *Frederick Douglass* (1991). Kay taught at several universities beginning in 1965, and retired from Lehman College, City University of New York, in 1988. Kay died in Teaneck, New Jersey, on May 20, 1995.

Tania León (1943–)
Composer, Conductor, Pianist

Tania León was born on May 14, 1943, in Havana, Cuba. She studied at Carlos Alfredo Peyrellado Conservatory earning a B.A. in 1963, and from New York University earning a B.S. in 1971, and an M.S. in 1975. Her first position was as an accompanist and music director of what became the Arthur Mitchell Dance Theatre of Harlem. León premiered her compositions in Spoleto, Italy, with the dance company at the Festival of Two Worlds in 1970. She later served as music director and conductor for the Broadway production of *The Wiz* in 1978. She left the Dance Theatre of Harlem in 1980 and served as music director for the Alvin Ailey Dance Company for the 1983–1984 season.

León was on the faculty of Brooklyn College and was the Revson Composer for the New York Philharmonic from 1993 to 1996. Her works include *Bata* (1985), *Heart of Ours* (1988), *Crabeli* (1992), *Scourge of Hyacinths* (1994), *Para Viola y Orquesta* (1995), and *Hechizos* (1995).

León's awards include the Celebrate Brooklyn Achievement Award (1990), Academy Institute Award in Music from the American Academy and Institute of Arts and Letters (1991), and the Latin Women of Hope, Bread and Roses Cultural Project (1995).

Henry Jay Lewis (1932–1996)
Conductor, Double Bassist

Henry Jay Lewis was born on October 16, 1932, in Los Angeles, California. He joined the Los Angeles Philharmonic as a double bassist at the age of sixteen in 1948. This position made Lewis the first African American to play with a major American orchestra. Once drafted into the U.S. Army in 1954, Lewis used his musical talents to conduct the Seventh Army Symphony orchestra and returned to the Los Angeles Philharmonic as an assistant conductor once he was discharged. He remained at the Philharmonic from 1961 to 1965.

Lewis was a pioneer, as he founded the String Society of Los Angeles in 1959, was the music director for the Los Angeles Opera Company, was the first African American to serve as music director and conductor of the New Jersey Symphony (a major American orchestra in 1968), and the first African American to conduct the Metropolitan Opera orchestra in 1972. He was also founder of the Black Academy of Arts and Letters. Lewis had other major positions as conductor and continued to tour until his death in 1996.

Dorothy Maynor (1910–1996)
Soprano

Dorothy Maynor was born on September 3, 1910, in Norfolk, Virginia. Maynor began singing in her father's church. She earned a B.S from Hampton Institute in 1933, and she attended the Westminster Choir College in Princeton, New Jersey, in 1939. Maynor debuted at the Berkshire Musical Festival in Tanglewood, Massachusetts, in 1939 to rave reviews.

Maynor began touring after her debut, singing arias and spirituals; she also made numerous recordings. In 1952 she became the first African American to perform at Constitution Hall in Washington, D.C. She continued to be active until the death of her husband in 1963. In 1975 she became the first African American on the board of directors of the Metropolitan Opera, a site where she had not been allowed to perform. Maynor, who was director of the Harlem School of the Arts (originally located in the St. James Presbyterian Church), fully retired after she raised $3.5 million to build the school its own building in 1979.

Bobby McFerrin (1950–)
Singer, Songwriter, Conductor

Robert "Bobby" McFerrin Jr. was born on March 11, 1950, in New York City, to parents Robert McFerrin Sr. and Sara McFerrin, who were well-known opera singers. After his family moved to Los Angeles in 1958, McFerrin later attended Sacramento State University and Cerritos College for a while. In 1977 he decided to focus on a singing career and earned himself the opportunity to sing with artists such as George Benson and Herbie Hancock. His first album was *Bobby McFerrin* and his most popular song is "Don't Worry, Be Happy," which was released in 1988 and topped the music charts.

McFerrin turned to conducting and made his debut in 1990 with the San Francisco Symphony. He later released the recording *Medicine Music* in 1992, and *Hush* with Yo-Yo Ma, which went gold in 1996 on the classical charts. McFerrin's concert-length version of *Porgy and Bess* is on the *Billboard* charts of classical bestsellers.

McFerrin is known as one of the world's best innovators and improvisers and has used his talents in all genres of music from the concert hall to television to the classroom. McFerrin is an active part of the Saint Paul Chamber Orchestra and he became the creative chair in 1994. He has also developed a program to encourage youth to be involved in classical music. McFerrin has received numerous awards, which include ten Grammys, and is considered one of the greatest jazz artists of all time by his peers.

Robert McFerrin (1921–2006)
Singer, Educator

Born in Marianna, Arkansas, on March 19, 1921, baritone Robert McFerrin began his studies at Fisk University but later transferred when he won a scholarship to the Chicago Musical College, obtaining a bachelor's degree there. He sang the title role in *Rigoletto* with the New England Opera Company in 1950, and was a baritone soloist in the Lewisohn Stadium Summer Concert Series in 1954. McFerrin made his Metropolitan Opera debut in 1955, singing the role of Amonasro in *Aida* and became the first African American male to sing at the Met. He performed at the Metropolitan Opera until 1958.

In 1959 McFerrin sang the role of Porgy for the film *Porgy and Bess* by George Gershwin. The film version starred Sidney Poitier as Porgy. After the film McFerrin stayed in Los Angeles and taught voice. McFerrin has served as a guest professor of voice at Sibelius Academy in Finland and Roosevelt University in Chicago. He has also served as a member of the voice faculty at Nelson School of Fine Arts in Nelson, British Columbia, Canada. Despite having suffered a stroke, McFerrin sang with his son (renowned vocalist Bobby McFerrin) at the St. Louis Symphony in 1993. McFerrin has received numerous awards, including a Lifetime Achievement Award from the International Professional Opera Companies and Opera Volunteers International, and a brass star and bronze plaque embedded in the St. Louis Walk of Fame.

Leona Mitchell (1949–)
Singer

Leona Mitchell was born on October 13, 1949, in Enid, Oklahoma, the daughter of a minister and a piano teacher. She received her education from Oklahoma City University in 1971. Mitchell made her European debut as a soprano in Barcelona, Spain, in 1974, and her U.S. debut at the Metropolitan Opera (Met) as Michaela in Bizet's *Carmen* in 1975. In 1988 she played the role of a Nubian princess in *Aida,* which became her signature role. She played this role in Switzerland, Chile, Madrid, and Cairo from 1997 through 2001.

Mitchell was a leading spinto soprano at the Met for eighteen years and performed in major symphony houses all over the world. She was inducted into the Oklahoma Music Hall of Fame, the Oklahoma Women's Hall of Fame in 1983, and is a Grammy Award-winning soprano. Although a teacher and performer she still finds time to return to Enid, Oklahoma, to perform benefits to help children.

Dorothy Rudd Moore (1940–)
Composer, Singer

Dorothy Rudd Moore was born on June 4, 1940, in New Castle, Delaware. She earned a B.Mus. from Howard University in 1963, attended the American Conservatory of Fontainebleau in France in 1963, followed by private lessons with Chou Wen-chung in 1965, and Lola Hayes in 1972. Between 1965 and 1971 Moore taught at the Harlem School of the Arts, New York University, and the Bronx Community College. After that time she taught private voice, piano, and sight-singing lessons.

Moore's work includes orchestral music, opera, and chamber pieces. Her compositions include *Dirge and Deliverance, Flowers of Darkness* (commissioned by her husband, Kermit Moore), and *Reflections.* Her opera, *Frederick Douglass,* which took eight years to complete, was commissioned by Opera Ebony. Moore wrote the libretto as well as the music and it premiered in New York City.

Moore's awards include the Lucy E. Moten Fellowship (1963), the American Music Center grant (1972), the New York State Council of the Arts grant (1985), and other distinguished recognitions for her contributions. She is considered one of the most prolific women composers in the United States.

Kermit Moore (1929–)
Cellist, Composer, Conductor

Kermit Moore was born in Akron, Ohio, in 1929. He studied at the Cleveland Institute of Music and earned a B.A. in 1951, and an M.A. at New York University in 1952. In 1956 he was awarded an artist's diploma from the Paris National Conservatory. His debut was in 1949 at New York's Town Hall. Moore has performed with major European orchestras such as the Orchestre de la Suisse Romande as well as recitals at the New York's Lincoln Center, Carnegie Recital Hall, and universities throughout the United States and the world.

In 1964 Moore co-founded the Symphony of the New World in New York and is a co-founder of the Society of Black Composers. He has conducted for Arthur Mitchell's Dance Theatre of Harlem and at the ANTA Theatre on Broadway in New York. Moore's honors include the Edgar Stillman Kelley Award, the Lili Boulanger Award in Paris, and a medal presented by the Société des Artistes Professionals Belgique.

Undine Smith Moore (1904–1989)
Composer, Educator

Undine Smith Moore, a native of Jarret, Virginia, was born on August 25, 1904. She was one of the most important and influential music educators of the twentieth century, as is evident by her numerous awards and honors. She received honorary doctorates from Virginia State University in 1972, and from Indiana University in 1976. The mayor of New York City presented her with a certificate of appreciation, she received the seventh annual Humanitarian Award from Fisk University in 1973, she won the National Association of Negro Musicians Award in 1975,

and in that same year Mayor Remmis Arnold of Petersburg, Virginia, proclaimed April 13 as Undine Moore Day.

Moore received her B.A. and B.M. degrees from Fisk University in Nashville, and an M.A. and professional diploma from Columbia University's Teachers College in New York. She also studied at the Juilliard School of Music, Manhattan School of Music, and Eastman School of Music in Rochester, New York. She taught at Virginia State College in Petersburg from 1927 to 1972, where she co-founded and directed the Black Music Center in 1969, and was co-director until 1972. She also served as visiting professor at numerous other schools, including Carleton College in Northfield, Minnesota; St. Benedict College in St. Joseph, Minnesota; St. Johns University in Collegeville, Minnesota; and Virginia Union University in Richmond.

As a composer, Moore wrote for a variety of ensembles. Many of her works are for chorus, and she has also written for solo voice, piano, organ, flute, and clarinet. Her works have received much recognition, and her *Afro-American Suite*, commissioned by D. Antoinette Handy's Trio Pro Viva, has been performed widely. Her cantata "Scenes" in 1982 from *The Life of a Martyr: To the Memory of Martin Luther King* received a Pulitzer Prize nomination. Other compositions include *Afro-American Suite* for flute, violoncello, and piano, *Lord We Give Thanks to Thee* for chorus, and *Daniel, Daniel, Servant of the Lord* for chorus. Moore died in Petersburg, Virginia, on February 6, 1989.

Jessye Norman (1945–)
Singer

Soprano Jessye Norman was born in Augusta, Georgia, on September 15, 1945, to a musical family. Her mother, a school teacher and amateur pianist, provided the family with piano lessons. At the age of sixteen Norman went to Philadelphia to compete for the Marian Anderson Scholarship. She did not win this competition, but once the director of the music department at

Howard University heard her sing, she was granted a full four-year scholarship.

Norman graduated with honors from Howard in 1967, and went on to study at the Peabody Conservatory in Baltimore, Maryland, and at the University of Michigan, where she received a master's degree in 1968.

In 1968 Norman entered the Bavarian Radio Corporation's International Music Competition, receiving first prize. In 1969 she made her debut with the Deutsch Opera in Berlin as Elisabeth in Wagner's *Tannhäuser,* and in 1970 she made her Italian opera debut. Norman has performed at La Scala in Milan, Wolf Trap in Virginia, the Tanglewood Music Festival, and the Royal Opera House in Covent Garden, England. She has appeared with some of the world's leading orchestras.

Following a temporary leave from opera in the mid-1970s Norman returned to the stage. In the 1980s and 1990s Norman performed in Strauss's *Ariadne auf Naxos.* She has since made numerous concert appearances and several recordings, including Berg's *Lulu Suite,* Berlioz's *Les nuits d'été* and *Romeo and Juliette,* Bizet's *Carmen,* Mahler's *Kindertotenlieder,* and a recent album entitled *Lucky to Be Me.* Norman made her U.S. operatic debut in 1982 as Jocasta in Stravinsky's *Oedipus Rex* with the Opera Company of Philadelphia. During this time Norman also performed and recorded many award winning operas that were televised.

Norman's career flourishes as she continues to receive numerous awards for her work such as Kennedy Center Honors (1997), several Grammy awards as well as the Grammy Lifetime Achievement Award (2006), numerous honorary degrees from American universities, and the National Medal of Arts presented by President Barack Obama (2009).

Julia Perry (1924–1979)
Composer, Conductor

Julia Amanda Perry was born in Lexington, Kentucky, in 1924, and grew up in Akron, Ohio. She

went on to earn bachelor's and master's degrees from Westminster Choir College, and in 1948 studied at the Juilliard School and the Berkshire Music Center in Massachusetts. She was awarded two Guggenheim Fellowships, one in 1954 and one in 1956, which allowed her to spend the decade of the 1950s studying in Europe.

Upon her return to the United States in 1959, Perry taught at several universities and continued to compose. She specialized in vocal music and produced twelve symphonies. Her works include *Stabat Mater* (for contralto; 1951), *Homage to Vivaldi* (for orchestra; 1954), and *Homunculus C.F.* (for piano, harp and percussion; 1960). Perry suffered a debilitating stroke in 1971, which deterred her work but she taught herself to write and continue with her work. She died on April 29, 1979.

Awadagin Pratt (1966–)
Pianist, Violinist, Conductor

Awadagin Pratt was born on March 6, 1966, in Pittsburgh, Pennsylvania. After his family moved to Illinois, Pratt attended the University of Illinois, majoring in music, at the age of sixteen. He also attended the Peabody Conservatory of Music in Baltimore and earned performance certificates in piano and violin in 1986, and conducting in 1992. His career gained momentum after Pratt won the Hamburg International piano composition in 1992, and the Avery Fisher Career Grant in 1994.

Pratt made his debut in 1994 at the Lincoln Center with the New York Philharmonic. He performs as many as thirty concerts a year in the United States and Europe, and serves as assistant professor and artist in residence at the University of Cincinnati's Conservatory of Music. Pratt is considered a virtuoso not only because of his unconventional attire when performing, but he gravitates to technically demanding pieces that require retrospection. He also chooses pieces that build an enthusiasm for classical music and brings his diverse audiences together.

Pratt's recordings include *A Long Way from Normal* (1994), *Beethoven Piano Sonatas* (1995), *Live from South Africa* (1997), *Transformations* (1999), and *Play Beach* (2002).

Florence Price (1887–1953)
Composer, Pianist

Florence Price was born in 1887, in Little Rock, Arkansas, and grew up in Chicago. She studied music with her mother, a talented soprano and concert pianist. In 1902 she enrolled in the New England Conservatory of Music in Boston, majoring in piano and organ. After graduating in 1907, she returned to Little Rock as a music educator, performer, and composer. In 1927, due to racial tensions, she moved to Chicago and pursued further musical education. In the early 1920s Price's compositions began to receive notice. She won the Rodman Wanamaker Foundation Award for a piano sonata and her *Symphony in E Minor*; the Chicago Symphony Orchestra premiered this work at the Chicago World's Fair in 1933. She also presented a program of her pieces at the fair, and the Women's Symphony Orchestra of Chicago performed some of her works. In 1934 she appeared as soloist in her *Concerto in D Minor* at the Chicago Musical College and in Pittsburgh. That same year she conducted a performance of her *Concerto in F Minor* with pianist/composer Margaret Bonds as the soloist.

Her fame grew steadily. In 1940 she performed her *Concerto in One Movement* with the WPA Symphony Orchestra in Detroit, which played her *Symphony No. 3 in C Minor* in the same program. The Forum String Quartet of Chicago and faculty members of the Music School of the University of Illinois performed some of her chamber music. The British conductor Sir John Barbirolli commissioned her to write a suite for strings, which he presented in Manchester, England. Marian Anderson sang Price's *Songs to the Dark Virgin* in her second

American concert tour, receiving rave reviews. In addition to her larger orchestral and chamber works, she wrote many art songs, spiritual arrangements, and choral pieces, as well as piano, organ, and violin works. Price died from a stroke on June 3, 1953.

Leontyne Price (1927–)
Singer

Mary Violet Leontyne Price was born on February 10, 1927, in Laurel, Mississippi. Price was encouraged by her parents, who were amateur musicians, to sing and play the piano at an early age. In 1949 she received her bachelor's degree from the College of Education and Industrial Arts (now Central State College) in Wilberforce, Ohio, where she had studied music education in hopes of becoming a music teacher.

Price received a scholarship to study at the Juilliard School of Music in New York City. While appearing in a student production of Verdi's *Falstaff*, she was noticed by composer and music critic Virgil Thomson, who later cast her in her first professional role in a revival of his opera *Four Saints in Three Acts*.

Between 1952 and 1954 Price performed the role of Bess in a revival of Gershwin's *Porgy and Bess*. In 1954 Price made her debut at New York's Town Hall. From there she went on to appear in Puccini's *Tosca* in 1955, Mozart's *The Magic Flute* in 1956, and Poulenc's *Dialogues of the Carmelites*. Between 1958 and 1960 she appeared at Verona, Vienna, Covent Garden, and La Scala. Price had become one of the world's leading sopranos.

On January 27, 1961, Price made her Metropolitan Opera debut in Verdi's *Il Trovatore,* a performance for which she received a standing ovation that lasted forty-two minutes. She has since appeared in numerous Met productions, including Puccini's *The Girl of the Golden West* and the world premiere of Samuel Barber's *Antony and Cleopatra* in 1966. Price continued to do opera appearances until the 1970s when she focused more on recitals and solo performances. In 1977 Price was awarded the San Francisco Opera

Medal in honor of the twentieth anniversary of her debut with the company. On April 20, 1982, Price opened the convention of the Daughters of the American Revolution in Constitution Hall with a concert honoring Marian Anderson. In 1985 she retired and gave her final performance at New York's Lincoln Center in the title role of Verdi's *Aida*.

Price came out of retirement in 2001 to sing her rendition of "America the Beautiful" at Carnegie Hall. The concert was dedicated to the victims of the 9/11 attacks on the World Trade Center. Her honors include the Presidential Medal of Freedom in 1964, Kennedy Center Honors in 1980, National Medal of the Arts in 1985, the Mississippi Governor's Lifetime Achievement Award in 2000, and she was honored as one of the first recipients of the National Endowments of the Arts Award in 2008.

Kay George Roberts (1950–)
Conductor, Violinist

Kay George Roberts was born in Nashville, Tennessee, on September 16, 1950. She began her music career playing the violin with the Nashville Symphony in her senior year in high school and played through her senior year in college. Roberts graduated from Fisk University in 1972. She attended Yale University focusing on conducting and earned an M.A. in music in 1975, an M.A. in musical arts in 1976, and a doctorate in musical arts in 1986. Roberts was the first African American woman to earn a doctor of musical arts degree in conducting from Yale University. While earning her degree she was under the guidance of master conductor Otto-Werner Mueller, who arranged for her to lead rehearsal performances of the Nashville and the Atlanta Symphony Orchestras.

Roberts was music director of the New Hampshire Philharmonic in 1982 and has been guest conductor for major orchestras, including the Orchestra della Svizzera Italiana, the Cleveland, Detroit, Dallas, and Nashville Symphonies, and the Bangkok Symphony, Thailand. Beginning in 1978 she has served as a music faculty member for the University of Massachusetts, Lowell, while balancing the demands of conducting and teaching.

Roberts is the founder and music director of the Lowell-based New England Orchestra, principle conductor for Opera North, Inc. in Philadelphia, cover conductor for the Boston Symphony Orchestra, the Cleveland Orchestra, and the Detroit Symphony Orchestra. Her many awards and honors include "The Certificate of Special Congressional Recognition" from the U.S. House of Representatives for community service, University of Massachusetts Presidents' Public Service Award, and Woman of the Year by Girls Incorporated of Greater Lowell.

Paul Robeson (1898–1976)
Singer, Actor

 Born in Princeton, New Jersey, on April 9, 1898, Paul Robeson was the son of a runaway slave who put himself through Lincoln University and later became a Presbyterian minister. Robeson entered Rutgers College (now Rutgers University) on a scholarship, and he won a total of twelve letters in track, football, baseball, and basketball. In addition to his athletic exploits, his academic ability gained him Phi Beta Kappa honors in his junior year.

In 1923 Robeson received a law degree from Columbia University, financing his schooling by playing professional football. While at Columbia, Robeson was seen by Eugene O'Neill in an amateur play. After making his professional debut in *Taboo* (1922), Robeson appeared in O'Neill's *All God's Chillun Got Wings* and *The Emperor Jones*. Called upon to whistle in the latter play, Robeson sang instead, and his voice met with instant acclaim. In 1925 he made his concert debut with a highly successful program of all African American music. He went on to such stage successes as *Show Boat, Porgy and Bess,* and *Othello*.

A world traveler in the Soviet Union, Asia, and Europe, Robeson spoke several languages, including Chinese, Russian, Gaelic, and Spanish. Robeson's political affiliations at times tended to attract even more publicity than his artistic career. In 1950 for instance, his passport was revoked after he refused to sign an affidavit as to whether or not he had ever belonged to the Communist Party. Eight years later, the U.S. Supreme Court ruled that the refusal to sign such an affidavit was not valid grounds for denial of a passport. Robeson subsequently settled in London, making a number of trips to the continent (and to the Soviet Union as well) before returning to the United States in 1963.

Robeson played an active role in civil and human rights issues. He was a co-founder of the Council on African Affairs, and a member of the Joint Anti-Fascist Refugee Committee, and the Committee to Aid China. Robeson died January 23, 1976, in Philadelphia, Pennsylvania.

Chevalier de Saint-George (1745–1799)
Violinist, Composer

Joseph Boulogne, Chevalier de Saint-George, was born on the Caribbean island of Guadeloupe on December 25, 1745, to an African slave mother and a French Father. He displayed his talent on the violin early in life. He studied with François Gossec, whom he succeeded as concertmaster of the celebrated Concert des Amateurs in 1769. Saint-George made his debut as an opera composer at the Comédie-Italienne in 1777. His musical output was enormous, including several operas, symphonies concertantes, a dozen string quartets, violin concertos, and other instrumental and vocal works. His music left an impact on the world of opera because of his virtuosity and ability to use one melodic line after another in a single work. He is remembered mainly for his quartets and violin concerti. Saint-George, considered the first man of African ancestry to have made a major impression on European music, died on June 22, 1799.

Philippa "Duke" Schuyler (1931–1967)
Pianist, Composer

Philippa "Duke" Schuyler was born on August 2, 1931, in New York. The daughter of the African American journalist George Schuyler and satirical novelist Josephine Cogdell from a wealthy white Texas family, her birth was a way to prove the theory that mixed race produced a hybrid that manifested the best of both races. This theory was a form of eugenics or racial purity, but it was based on race mixing.

Schuyler was a child prodigy and her talents as a pianist were nurtured by her parents. By five years old, with an IQ of 185 attested to by New York University, she was playing Mozart. Schuyler had no formal training and what instruction she had ended at fifteen. Her childhood was one of isolation but she was not free from racism when she traveled in the United States.

In her late teens Schuyler began performing with various orchestras including the Detroit, Chicago, and New York symphonies. She went to Europe first in 1952 and subsequently visited over eighty countries while touring. Schuyler received numerous awards for her achievement, including a Distinguished Achievement Award from the National Negro Opera Company, and a gold and silver medal from the Emperor of Ethiopia. Her popularity waned as she became an adult and Schuyler began searching for her identity. When she died in 1967 in a helicopter crash, she was helping to rescue children from Vietnam.

George Shirley (1934–)
Singer

George Irving Shirley was born April 18, 1934, in Indianapolis, Indiana, and moved to Detroit in 1940. There he began giving vocal recitals in churches and decided on a musical career after playing baritone horn in a community band. In

1955 he graduated from Wayne State University in Detroit with a bachelor's degree in musical education.

After his discharge from the Army in 1959, he began serious vocal studies with Themy S. Gerogi. In June of that year he made his operatic debut as Eisenstein in Strauss's *Die Fledermaus,* performing with the Turnau Players at Woodstock. A year later, he won the American Opera auditions, whereupon he journeyed to Milan, Italy, making his opera debut there in Puccini's *La Bohème.* In 1961 his career was given tremendous impetus by his victory in the Metropolitan Opera auditions. Two years later, he made his debut at Carnegie Hall with the Friends of French Opera, singing opposite Rita Gorr in Massenet's *La Navarraise,* and in 1968 he won a Grammy for singing the role of Ferrand in the RCA recording of Mozart's *Cosi fan tutte.*

Shirley has sung with several of the Met's leading divas, including Renata Tebaldi in *Simon Boccanegra* and Birgit Nilsson in *Salome.* In 1974 he sang the title role in Mozart's *Idomeneo* at the Glyndebourne Festival, and he remained a favorite at the Met over the years. He became the first black performer to be placed on contract, and subsequently remained a regular performer for eleven years. In 1990 Shirley was featured with the Deutsche Opera of Berlin and performed as a soloist in the premiere of Richard Strauss's *Friedenstag* at Carnegie Hall

Shirley has also been an educator serving from 1980 to 1987 as voice professor at the University of Maryland; and in 1987 Shirley became a voice professor for the University of Michigan Musical Society.

William Grant Still (1895–1978)

Composer, Conductor

William Grant Still was born on May 11, 1895, in Woodville, Mississippi. Since both of his parents were musicians and his father was the town's bandmaster, he received his early musical training at home.

Intending to study medicine, Still enrolled at Wilberforce College but left before graduating. He began to seriously consider a career in music, and after working with various jazz musicians, including W. C. Handy and Paul Whiteman, Still enrolled at Oberlin College Conservatory of Music.

Still became the first African American composer to have a large-scale work performed by a major American orchestra when the Rochester Philharmonic Orchestra performed his *Afro-American Symphony* in 1931. In 1936 Still became the first African American to conduct a major American orchestra when he conducted the Los Angeles Philharmonic in a program of his work. He was also the first African American composer to have an opera performed by a major opera company when the New York City Opera performed his *Troubled Island* in 1949.

Still considered that folk music was the best source for presenting American music separate from the European models that permeated most music of the time. He was highly influenced by blues and jazz and used their structures in the music that he created. Still's 1930 symphony, *Afro-American Symphony,* was the first of five symphonies that he wrote.

Still was awarded the Harmon Award in 1928 for his contribution to black culture. He was the winner of two Guggenheim Fellowships—one in 1944 and the other in 1961. In 1961 the National Federation of Music Clubs awarded him $1,500 for his composition *The Peaceful Land.* His major works include his composition *Song of a New Race,* the symphonic poem *Darker America,* the suites *Pages from Negro History* and *The American Scene,* and numerous songs and arrangements of spirituals.

Still's health began to fail in 1970, and he died in Los Angeles on December 3, 1978.

Shirley Verrett (1931–2010)
Singer

Born to a musical family on May 31, 1931, in New Orleans, Louisiana, Shirley Verrett moved to California at the age of five, but had no formal voice training during her childhood—largely because her father felt that singing would involve his daughter in too precarious a career. Still, he offered his daughter the opportunity to sing in church choirs under his direction. She attended Ventura College, where she majored in business administration. By 1954 she was a prosperous real estate agent, but her longing for an artistic career had become so acute that she decided to take voice lessons in Los Angeles and train her sights on the concert stage anyway.

After winning a television talent show in 1955, she enrolled at the Juilliard School on a scholarship, earning her diploma in voice some six years later. Her debut at New York's Town Hall in 1958 was not a sensational one. However, by 1962 at Spoleto, Italy, she delivered an excellent performance in *Carmen,* and a year later she performed at Lincoln Center in New York, where her recital was said to be "simply without flaws, simply a great event in the annals of American musicmaking."

By 1964 her Carmen had improved so dramatically that the *New York Herald Tribune* critic was able to claim it as "the finest" performance "seen or heard in New York" for the past generation. Other performances in such roles as Orfeo in Gluck's *Orfeo ed Eurydice,* Ulrica in Verdi's *Un Ballo de maschera,* and Leonora in Beethoven's *Fidelio* have been met with comparable acclaim.

In 1982 Verrett appeared with Grace Bumbry in a concert honoring Marian Anderson on her eightieth birthday. Her yearly recital tours took her to the major music centers throughout the country. During the 1986–1987 season the successes for Verrett included a series of operas staged especially for her by the Paris Opera: Rossini's *Mose,* Cherubini's *Medee,* and Gluck's *Iphigenia en Tauride* and *Alceste.* She made a triumphant return to the Metropolitan Opera in 1986 as Eboli in *Don Carlo* and also starred that year in a new production of *Macbeth* with the San Francisco Opera. In the 1987–1988 season Verrett made her long-awaited Chicago Lyric Opera debut as Lucena in *Il Trovatore.*

Verrett continued to perform both in the United States and Europe. In 1994 Verrett made her Broadway debut as Nettie Fowler in the Tony Award-winning revival of *Carousel* at the Lincoln Center's Beaumont Theater. She joined the faculty of the University of Michigan School of Music in 1996 and also served as professor of voice and the James Earl Jones University Professor of Music. Verrett died on November 5, 2010, of heart failure after a long illness.

George Walker (1922–)
Pianist, Composer

George Theophilus Walker was born on June 27, 1922, in Washington, D.C. He earned his B.A. in music from Oberlin College in 1941, and earned an artist diploma from Curtis Institute in Philadelphia. He also earned an artist diploma from the American Academy at Fontainebleau, France, in piano in 1947, but found it difficult to survive as a black concert pianist. Although he was the first African American to perform in New York's Town Hall in 1945, he continued to struggle. Hitting a low point in 1953 with ailing parents, he enrolled in the Ph.D. program at the Eastman School of Music. He earned his Ph.D. in 1956 as the first black student to earn a doctorate.

After several positions at universities he joined the faculty of Rutgers University in 1969. Walker was able to write and compose for piano as well as full orchestra. He wrote four sonatas, as well as for solo voice and chorus. His works include *Lyric for Strings* (1941), *Address for Orchestra* (1959), *Variations for Orchestra* (1972), *Sinfonia No. 2* (1984), *Four Spirituals for Orchestra* (1990), *Lilacs* (1995), and *Tangents for Chamber Orchestra* (1999). Walker has been awarded two Guggenheim Fellowships, the American Academy and Institute of Arts and Letters Award in 1992, and a Pulitzer Prize for Music in 1996 for his *Lilacs for Soprano or Tenor and Orchestra.* He was also inducted into the American Classical Music Hall of Fame in 2000.

William Warfield (1920–2002)

Singer

William Warfield was born on January 22, 1920, in West Helena, Arkansas. His family moved to Rochester, New York, where he later attended the Eastman School of Music earning a bachelor's degree in music in 1942. Warfield made his debut at New York's Town Hall in 1950, which resulted in a tour of Australia under the guidance of the Australian Broadcasting Commission. He also toured Africa, the Middle East, and Europe. Warfield appeared in several television roles and his most recognized role was Porgy from *Porgy and Bess*.

Warfield's baritone voice was said to electrify the stage and earned him a great following. He appeared with great orchestras and conductors. In 1974 he accepted a position as professor of music at the University of Illinois School of Music; and in 1984 he was elected president of the National Association of Negro Musicians, which he held until 1990. Warfield joined the Schiller Institute in 1996 and remained active until his death in 2002.

André Watts (1946–)

Pianist

André Watts was born June 20, 1946, in Germany. His father was an African American soldier and his mother was Hungarian. Watts made his debut at nine years old at a Philadelphia Orchestra's children concert and again at sixteen when he performed on television as conducted by Leonard Bernstein. When he completed his performance on television of Liszt's *E-flat Major Piano Concerto,* Watts received a standing ovation by the audience. Watts appeared on other television programs that were produced by PBS, BBC, and the Arts and Entertainment Network.

Watts continued to perform at summer festivals, but he also performed at the Los Angeles Philharmonic, Minnesota Orchestra, Lincoln Center, St. Louis, Atlanta, Cincinnati, and Seattle Symphonies, and the Dallas Symphony. In 1976 he performed a concert that was the first solo recital televised in history. Watts has received awards that include the National Society of Arts and Letters Gold Medal (1982), Avery Fisher Prize (1988), Distinguished Alumni Award from the Peabody Conservatory of Johns Hopkins University (May 1997), and the Jack I. and Dora B Hamlin Endowed Chair in Music from Indiana University (2004).

Camilla Williams (1919–)

Singer

Camilla Williams was born in Danville, Virginia, on October 18, 1919, and studied at Virginia State College. She earned her B.S. in 1941, and won several competitions as well as being awarded the Marian Anderson Fellowship in 1943 and 1944. Also in 1944 Williams performed on RCA Radio. Williams made her debut in 1946 with the New York City Opera in the title role in Puccini's *Madame Butterfly.* She spent the next six years with the Opera performing in various leading roles.

In 1954 Williams performed her signature role Cio-Cio San with the Vienna State Opera making her the first African American to sing the part. Williams toured throughout the United States and Europe and was a soloist at the Berlin Philharmonic, the Vienna Symphony, the New York Philharmonic, and the BBC Symphony. In 1977 Williams was appointed to the voice faculty of Indiana University, and in 1984 she was instructor for the Central Conservatory of Music in Beijing, China.

Williams' awards include Harvard University's Outstanding African American Singer/Pioneer (1996), being named as one of eight women to be honored during the Library of Virginia's Women's History Month (2007), and she was bestowed with a "Tribute to Camilla Williams" program at New York's Schomburg Center for Research in Black Culture (2009).

BIOGRAPHIES: BLUES AND JAZZ

Henry "Red" Allen (1908–1967)
Trumpeter

Henry "Red" Allen was born on January 7, 1908, in New Orleans, Louisiana. Allen began his career by playing trumpet with his father's band and later played with other bands such as John Handy's band in 1925, and the riverboat band of Fate Marble in 1926. Allen became a member of King Oliver's Creole Jazz Band in St. Louis and traveled with the band before returning to New Orleans in 1928. Allen got his first recording deal when Victor Records was looking for a performer to compete with Louis Armstrong.

Over the next few years Allen played with the Luis Russell Band, the Fletcher Henderson Band, and the Mills Blue Rhythm Band between 1929 and 1937. His solo career paralleled that of Louis Armstrong and set the standard for the swing era. In 1937 Allen returned to New Orleans and played with Russell's Band, which featured Louis Armstrong. Allen continued to record his solo records with musicians such as Billie Holiday, Lena Horne, and Art Tatum, and much later with Jelly Roll Morton and Sidney Bechet.

His recordings include *Truckin, Down South Camp Meeting, Hocus Pocus,* and *Wrappin' It Up.* Allen transformed his style over the years from fluid and light, to a move away from tradition, to finally a modern sound that played to jazz influences. Allen remains a key influence in the swing era.

Louis Armstrong (1901–1971)
Trumpeter

Born in New Orleans, Louisiana, on August 4, 1901, Louis Armstrong was one of the most influential and durable of all jazz artists, and quite simply one of the most famous of the twentieth century.

Armstrong was raised by his mother in the Third Ward section of New Orleans. On New Year's Eve in 1914 Armstrong was arrested in New Orleans for firing a pistol and sent to the Colored Waif's Home. It was there that he first learned to play the cornet. His skill increased with the experience he gained from playing in the Home's band. When he was finally released from the institution, he was already proficient enough with the instrument to begin playing for money.

Befriended by his idol King Oliver, Armstrong quickly began to develop the jazz skills that, until then, he had only been able to admire from a distance. When Oliver left for Chicago in 1919, a place opened up for Armstrong as a member of the Kid Ory and His Creole Jazz Band in New Orleans. In 1922 Oliver asked Armstrong to join him in Chicago as second cornet with his Creole Jazz Band. The duets between "Dippermouth" (as Armstrong was called) and "Papa Joe" (Oliver's nickname) soon became the talk of the Chicago music world.

Two years later Armstrong joined the Fletcher Henderson Band at the Roseland Ballroom in New York City. In 1925 he returned to Chicago to play with Erskine Tate, switching from cornet to trumpet, the instrument he played from then on. During the next four years he made a series of recordings that profoundly influenced the course of jazz. Armstrong recorded *Hot Fives and Hot Sevens,* which showcased his skill and technique in swing and in the art of improvisation.

In 1929 Armstrong returned to New York in the revue *Hot Chocolates,* where he scored his first triumph with the performance of a popular song (Fats Waller's "Ain't Misbehavin'"). This success was a turning point in his career. He now began to front big bands, playing and singing popular songs rather than blues or original instrumentals.

In 1932 Armstrong headlined a show at the London Palladium, where he acquired the nickname "Satchmo." From 1933 to 1935 he toured Europe, returning to the United States to film *Pennies from Heaven* with Bing Crosby. He continued to evolve from the status of musician to that of entertainer, and his singing soon became as important as his playing. In 1947 he formed a small group that was an immediate success. He continued to work in this context and toured throughout the world.

Armstrong experienced a tremendous success in 1964 with his recording of "Hello Dolly," which knocked the Beatles off the number one spot on the Top 40 list—a great feat in the age of rock. Though his health began to decline, he maintained a heavy schedule of international touring. When he died in his sleep at home in Corona, Queens, two days after his seventieth birthday, he had been preparing to resume work despite a serious heart attack suffered some three months before. "The music—it's my living and my life" was his motto.

Louis Armstrong's fame as an entertainer in the later stages of his extraordinary career sometimes made people forget that he remained a great musician to the end. More than any other artist, Armstrong symbolized the magic of jazz, a music unimaginable without his contribution. "You can't play a note on the horn that Louis hasn't already played," said Miles Davis, and contemporary musicians like Wynton Marsalis echo that opinion.

In 1988 after its use in the motion picture *Good Morning, Vietnam,* Armstrong's recording of "What a Wonderful World" became a surprise hit, climbing to number eleven on the *Billboard* chart. In 1992 a Louis Armstrong Archive was established at Queens College in New York. It includes his personal papers, private recordings, memorabilia, and instruments.

"Count" Basie (1904–1984)
Pianist, Bandleader

William "Count" Basie was born on August 24, 1904, in Red Bank, New Jersey. His musical career ranges from a boyhood spent watching the pit band at the local movie theater (he later learned the organ techniques of Fats Waller by crouching beside him in the Lincoln Theater in Harlem) to his dual triumphs in 1957 when his group became the first American band to play a royal command performance for the Queen of England, and the first black jazz band ever to play at the Waldorf Astoria Hotel in New York City.

During the early 1920s Basie toured in vaudeville. Stranded in Kansas City, he joined Walter Page's Blue Devils, which featured Jimmy Rushing as the singer. After this band broke up, Basie joined Bennie Moten and in 1935 formed his own band at the Reno Club in Kansas City, where a local radio announcer soon dubbed him "Count."

At the urging of critic John Hammond, Basie brought his group to New York City in 1936. Within a year he had cut his first record and was well on his way to becoming an established presence in the jazz world.

The Basie trademark was his rhythm section, which featured Basie's clean, spare piano style and outstanding soloists like Lester Young and Sweets Edison in the early years, and Lucky Thompson, J. J. Johnson, Clark Terry, and Benny Powell in the later period.

Except for the years 1950 and 1951 when he had a small group, Basie led a big band for almost forty years. Immune to changing fashion, the Basie band completed numerous global tours and successful recording engagements without ever suffering an appreciable decline in popularity.

In 1974 on his seventieth birthday, the Count was honored at a "Royal Salute" party by virtually every big name in jazz. Count Basie was honored again at Radio City Music Hall in New York City in 1982. Among those in attendance were Dionne Warwick and Lena Horne. Count Basie is generally regarded as the leader of the best jazz band in the United States and, consequently, one of the major influences on jazz. Basie died on April 26, 1984.

Sidney Bechet (1897–1959)
Saxophonist, Clarinetist

Sidney Bechet was born on May 14, 1897, in New Orleans, and began playing the clarinet at six years old. He played in various bands and later joined Will Marion Cook's Southern Syncopated Orchestra in 1919 and toured Europe. While in Europe he purchased a soprano saxophone and from then on it became his primary instrument. Bechet came back to the United States briefly and made his debut in recordings playing with Clarence Williams and other blues singers in 1923. He was very popular and had distinguished himself both in Europe and the United States with his talent and technique with the saxophone.

Bechet lived in Europe from 1925 to 1929 and returned to the United States in 1931 to join the Noble Sissle Orchestra. He also worked with Duke Ellington, Mamie Smith, and others. Bechet had a hit record in 1938 titled "Summertime." He saw his band beginning to decline with the success of the Ellington, Armstrong, and Basie bands. Bechet returned to France in 1949 and remained there until his death from cancer in 1959.

Art Blakely (1919–1990)
Drummer, Bandleader

Art Blakely was born on October 11, 1919, in Pittsburgh, Pennsylvania. Blakely's career began with playing the piano but was quickly changed to the drums, based on a club owner's demand that was backed by a pistol. Blakely was guided by the drummer and bandleader Chick Webb while serving as his valet. Blakely teamed up with pianist Mary Lou Williams in 1937.

Blakely formed his own band in 1948. He spent time with jazz greats such as Fletcher Henderson, Billy Eckstine, Charlie Parker, Dizzie Gillespie, and Sarah Vaughan, and later he traveled to Africa and learned poly-rhythmic techniques on the drum. Blakely also embraced Islam and took the name Abdullah Ibn Buhaina. Blakely's first group was the Jazz Messengers, a seventeen-piece band. There was an array of talented sidemen who passed through the band such as Clifford Brown, Benny Golson, Wayne Shorter, Lee Morgan, Bobby Timmons, and Jymie Merritt. The band's trademark releases included Timmons's "Moan," Golson's "Along Came Betty" and "Blues March", and Shorter's "Ping Pong."

In 1960 the Jazz Messengers was the first American jazz band to play in Japan. Blakely continued to encourage and support the artists that came through the band. Blakely died at the age of seventy-one in 1990.

Jimmy Blanton (1918–1942)
Bassist

Born in St. Louis, Missouri, on October 15, 1918, Jimmy Blanton played with the Jeter-Pillars Orchestra and the Fate Marable Band before joining Duke Ellington in 1939. Until this time the string bass rarely played anything but quarter notes in ensembles or solos; but Blanton began sliding into eighth and sixteenth-note runs, introducing melodic and harmonic ideas that were totally new to the instrument. During his brief life Blanton changed the course of jazz history by originating a new way of playing the string bass. Playing the instrument as if it were a horn, he shifted it from rhythmic backup to melodic focal point. His skill put him in a different class from his predecessors; it made him the first true master of the bass and demonstrated the instrument's potential as a solo vehicle. Blanton died in 1942 of tuberculosis.

William Lee Conley Broonzy
(1893–1958)
Guitarist, Singer

Born June 26, 1893, in Scott, Mississippi, William Lee Conley Broonzy (often called "Big Bill") learned how to play initially on a homemade fiddle. After a stint in the Army he switched to the guitar and joined the Papa Charlie Jackson Band. In 1927 Broonzy began recording and touring with Black Bob and Memphis Minnie, and in 1938 he performed at Carnegie Hall. His appearances at Carnegie Hall were based on John Hammond's *Spirituals to Swing* series in which Broonzy performed with Benny Goodman and Louis Armstrong.

In the 1940s and 1950s Broonzy continued to tour through the South and in Europe. He wrote hundreds of songs, including "All by Myself" and "Key to the Highway." Broonzy died on August 15, 1958, of cancer.

Raymond Matthews Brown (1926–2002)
Bassist

Raymond Matthews Brown was born on October 13, 1926, in Pittsburgh, Pennsylvania. He studied piano and bass under Jimmy Hinsley and Snookum Russell. In 1945 after moving to New York he played with Charlie Parker, Bud Powell, and Dizzy Gillespie. After marrying Ella Fitzgerald in 1948 he led a trio for her until their divorce in 1952. His time with the Oscar Peterson Band began in 1951 and was the most successful as they were very popular and in demand for concerts.

In the 1970s Brown continued to perform as well as manage other groups. From 1976 to 1977 Brown was the musical director of the Concord Summer Festival; he received a National Endowment of the Arts American Jazz Master Fellowship in 1995. Brown died while on tour on July 2, 2002.

Ruth Brown (1928–2006)
Singer

Ruth Brown was born on January 12, 1928, in Portsmouth, Virginia. Brown's singing style was highly influenced by Dinah Washington and Sarah Vaughan. In 1950 her big break came when Blanche Calloway, the sister of Cab Calloway, became her manager.

Brown had a strong association with Atlantic Records during the 1950s, which was beneficial for both. Brown had a string of hits that included "Mama, He Treats Your Daughter Mean" (1953), "Oh, What Dream" (1954), and "Don't Deceive Me" (1960). Brown left the industry for a while primarily to raise her family and resurfaced in the 1970s. Brown died in October 2006 from complications from a stroke.

"Cab" Calloway (1907–1994)
Singer, Dancer, Bandleader, Writer

Cabell "Cab" Calloway III was born on December 25, 1907, in Rochester, New York, but his family later moved to Baltimore, Maryland. His older sister, Blanche, found work in Chicago and sent for her younger brother. Calloway briefly attended Crane College in Chicago before getting involved in the theater and as a bandleader. In 1928 he became the bandleader for Marion Handy's Alabamians, which disbanded after their performance in New York. Choosing to stay in New York, Calloway spent time in the theater and later formed another band called Cab Calloway and his Orchestra. Because of his animated and enthusiastic performance as bandleader he was hired at the Cotton Club to play alternate engagements with Duke Ellington in 1929. It was at the Cotton Club that Calloway's most famous song "Minnie the Moocher" was performed during a radio broadcast. When he forgot the words he used a call response technique with the audience and replaced the words with scatting sounds like *Hi-de-he-de-ho*. The song was considered a hit and Calloway remained at the Cotton Club for nine years. He began to write songs that used scat words as part of the lyrics.

Calloway continued to lead his band after the Cotton Club run and went on to perform in the 1943 film *Stormy Weather* with Lena Horne and Bill "Bojangles" Robinson. He was also in the Broadway revival of *Porgy and Bess* in 1952, the production of *Hello, Dolly* with Pearl Bailey in the 1960s, and other films. Calloway died in November 1994.

Benny Carter (1907–2003)
Saxophonist, Trumpeter, Composer, Bandleader

Bennett "Benny" Lester Carter was born August 8, 1907, in New York City, and was primarily a self-taught musician. He enrolled in Wilberforce College in 1925 but left to join the Horace Henderson Orchestra. Carter started his own big band in 1933 and later moved to Paris and London. He wrote several tunes for Benny Goodman before leaving the United States.

Carter returned in 1938 and worked with both great musicians and composers. Admired and respected by generations of musicians, many of whom "went to school" in his bands (including Sid Catlett, Miles Davis, J. J. Johnson, Max Roach, and Teddy Wilson), Carter helped shape the language of big-band jazz. His scoring for saxophone sections was especially influential. On the alto saxophone, he and Johnny Hodges were the pacesetters before Charlie Parker and bebop. He had few peers as a trumpeter and composed many standards.

Carter was the first black composer to break the color barrier in the Hollywood film studios. He scored many major films and television shows, including *M Squad*. Carter received an honorary doctorate in music from Princeton University, where he taught, in 1974. He was the subject of what is considered to be one of the best biographies of a jazz artist ever published—*Benny Carter: A Life in American Music*, in 1982. In 1988 he toured Europe, visited Japan with his own band, performed in Brazil for the first time in his career, and recorded three albums. He continued at the same pace in 1993. Carter was

awarded the Kennedy Center Honors for Lifetime Achievement in 1996. He died in 2003.

Betty Carter (1930–1998)
Singer

 Lillie Mae Jones, also known as Betty Carter, was born in Flint, Michigan, on May 16, 1930. Early on, Carter studied at the Detroit Conservatory of Music. By the time she was sixteen she was working with Lionel Hampton and had been performing under the name of Lorene. Carter also made a good showing at the Apollo Theater in Harlem. She was given the nickname "Betty BeBop" by Lionel Hampton and she became known as Betty Carter. In the 1950s Carter worked with artists such as Max Roach, Dizzy Gillespie, and Miles Davis. Carter made her first recording in 1955, followed by a second, which was not released for almost thirty years.

Carter earned critical acclaim when she did a series of duets with Ray Charles in 1961. When the industry was suffering in the 1960s, Carter started her own label, Bet-Car, and re-established herself. She performed at the Newport Jazz Festival in 1977 and 1978. In 1980 a documentary film was produced about her entitled *But Then, She's Betty Carter*. Carter signed with Verve Records and recorded "Now It's My Turn" (1976), "Look What I Got" (1988), "It's Not About the Melody" (1992), and "I'm Yours, You're Mine" (1996). In 1988 she won a Grammy for the album *Look What I Got*. Carter remained active and continued to promote up-and-coming artists. She died on September 26, 1998. Carter's signature style of wild scat–singing and heavy hitting interpretations of classical songs has left an indelible impression on the jazz world.

Ray Charles (1932–2004)
Singer, Pianist, Bandleader

Ray Charles was born Ray Charles Robinson on September 27, 1930, in Albany, Georgia. Blinded at the age of six by glaucoma, Charles received his first musical training at a school for the blind in St. Augustine, Florida. He left school at the age of fifteen to play local engagements. Within two years after the death of his parents he formed a trio that had some success in the Northwest. Influenced by smooth pop and rock styles Charles got his first rhythm and blues chart topper with "Baby Let Me Hold Your Hand," followed by "I Got a Woman," released in 1955. Charles's songs at this time began to include the groans and shouts reflective of his gospel musical arrangements.

 In 1957 his first album was released, consisting of a potpourri of instrumentals drawn from pop, gospel, and modern jazz sources. His singing and piano playing found favor particularly with a number of jazz artists who opposed what they felt was a growing tendency for jazz to become over-scored and under-felt. In Charles they saw an artist who had restored both a sense of "soul" and instrumental "funkiness" to the jazz idiom.

Charles had a string of hits through the 1960s such as "Hit the Road" and "I Can't Stop Loving You". He was so influential that he was inducted into the Rock and Roll Hall of Fame in 1986, received the National Medal of the Arts in 1993, was awarded more than ten Grammys, and received numerous degrees and other honors. Actively involved with a film about his life starring Jamie Foxx, Charles took time to train, encourage, and challenge Foxx musically. Charles, who had been battling cancer, died on June 10, 2004, after giving Foxx his blessings for the film. The film opened on June 10, 2004, and Foxx won an Academy Award as best actor for his performance in 2005.

Clifton Chenier (1925–1987)
Accordion Player

Clifton Chenier was born on June 25, 1925, a Creole French speaker from Opelousas, Louisiana. He was taught the basics of the accor-

dion by his father. Regional success came for Chenier when he signed with Elko Records in 1954, and had his first recording session in Lake Charles, Louisiana. It included "Cliston's Blues" and "Louisiana Stomp." His hit record "Ay 'Tite Fille" ("Hey Little Girl") was released in May 1955 which earned him national attention. In 1976 he performed on the premiere PBS music show Austin City Limits to reignite interest in his music with one of his best known albums *Bogalusa Boogie*.

Chenier's work was recognized with a Grammy Award for his album *I'm Here* in 1983. He and his group traveled throughout the world and he is often referred to as the "King of Zydeco." Chenier suffered from diabetes and died of related kidney issues on December 12, 1987. In 1989 he was posthumously inducted into the Blues Hall of Fame.

Charlie Christian (1916–1942)
Electric Guitarist

Charlie Christian, born on July 29, 1916, and raised in Oklahoma City, Oklahoma, did for the electric guitar what Jimmy Blanton did for the bass. Christian joined Benny Goodman in 1939, and after only two years with the Goodman Sextet he achieved great fame as the first electric guitarist to play single-string solos. In his afterhour activities at such Harlem clubs as Minton's, he was an early contributor to the jazz revolution that would one day come to be called bop.

In 1941 Christian was hospitalized with tuberculosis; he died the following year. His recordings are still an inspiration to young guitarists.

Ornette Coleman (1930–)
Saxophonist, Composer, Bandleader

Ornette Coleman, born March 9, 1930, was a student of jazz and in particular improvisation. His approach was not centered on harmonic patterns but on the melodic and expressive elements. He began his career with carnivals and rhythm and blues bands but found it difficult to continue be-

Clifton Chenier (far right) plays accordion in Cankton, Louisiana, during the 1975 Mardi Gras celebrations. His brother Cleveland accompanies him on the washboard.

cause of his unconventional style. In the 1950s Coleman formed a group and released his first album, *Something Else* (1958). He moved to New York and his recordings *Free Jazz* (1960), which used free meters and tempos, caused controversy among jazz musicians.

Coleman continued to perform his "free jazz" and joined with the London Symphony for the recording *The Skies of America* (1972). In 1994 Coleman was awarded a MacArthur Fellowship, and in 2007 he was awarded a Pulitzer Prize for his 2005 performance that included a quartet consisting of Coleman playing the trumpet, violin, and alto saxophone, along with two acoustic double bass players and drummer. Coleman continues to perform and compose.

John Coltrane (1926–1967)
Saxophonist, Bandleader

John Coltrane (or just "Trane," as he was known to many) was the last great innovator to profoundly influence the course of jazz. John William Coltrane was born September 23, 1926, in Hamlet, North Carolina. He first played the clarinet taught to him by his father, then alto saxophone in high school. Upon graduation he moved to Philadelphia and continued to study music, winning several scholarships. After playing in a Navy band in Hawaii, he started his professional career with rhythm and blues bands, joining Dizzy Gillespie's big band (on alto) in 1949. When Gillespie scaled the band down to a sextet in 1951, he had Coltrane switch to tenor saxophone. After stints with two great but very different alto saxophonists, Earl Bostic and Johnny Hodges, Coltrane was hired by Miles Davis in 1955. At first some musicians and listeners didn't care for what they felt was Coltrane's harsh sound, but as the Davis Quintet became the most popular jazz group of its day, Coltrane was not only accepted but began to influence younger players. He briefly left Davis in 1957 to work with Thelonious Monk and further develop what was already a highly original style. Back with Davis, he participated in the great *Kind of Blue* record dates.

In 1959, while still with Davis, Coltrane composed and recorded "Giant Steps," a piece so harmonically intricate that it staggered most of his fellow saxophonists. Coltrane later formed his own quartet with pianist McCoy Tyner, bassist Jimmy Garrison, and drummer Elvin Jones. In 1960 they recorded the song "My Favorite Things" from the musical and film *The Sound of Music* in a performance that featured Coltrane's soprano saxophone and lasted more than fifteen minutes. This performance became such a hit with the jazz audience that it sustained Coltrane's popularity even when he began to experiment with unusual and demanding music. The quartet became one of the most tightly knit groups in jazz history; the empathy between Coltrane and Elvin Jones was astonishing, and in their live performances, the four musicians would sometimes play for more than an hour, creating music so intense that some listeners likened it to a religious experience.

Coltrane was a deeply spiritual man. One of his masterpieces, the suite "A Love Supreme" and an accompanying poem, was his offering to God. The quartet's live recordings at the Village Vanguard and Birdland became instant classics, and Coltrane was regarded as the leading figure of the avant-garde jazz of the 1960s. The quartet broke up in 1966, and Coltrane searched for new modes of expression, never complacent about his work at any time in his career. His death at forty-one of liver cancer came as a shock to the jazz world. He died on July 17, 1967. Coltrane has become a legend whose influence continues, though few have attempted to emulate the unconventional style of his later years when he stretched the limits of his instrument.

Turiya Alice Coltrane (1937–2007)
Pianist, Harpist, Composer, Bandleader

Turiya Alice Coltrane was born on August 27, 1937, in Detroit, Michigan. Although she had earned a scholarship to the Detroit Institute of Technology, her skills with the piano, organ, and harp, and playing for choirs, churches, and R&B groups encouraged her to join a local group and travel. In 1959 she traveled to Paris, and in 1962 she met and married jazz artist John Coltrane.

After her husband's death in 1965, Alice Coltrane took over the role as pianist in her husband's group, and she pursued her interest in composition and created works that combined classical and jazz with Eastern instrumentations. In 2002 she released *Eternity,* and in 2004 she returned to performing. Turiya Alice Coltrane died on January 12, 2007, of respiratory failure.

Miles Davis (1926–1991)
Trumpeter, Bandleader

Miles Dewey Davis Jr. was born in Alton, Illinois, on May 26, 1926. His family later moved to St. Louis, Missouri, in 1927. His father gave him a trumpet for his thirteenth birthday. As a teenage musician in St. Louis in the early 1940s, Davis sat in with his idols Charlie Parker and Dizzy Gillespie when they passed through town, and with the Billy Eckstine Band.

In 1945 Davis's well-to-do dentist father sent him to the Juilliard School of Music in New York. Within a short time, Davis was working the 52nd Street clubs with Parker and Coleman Hawkins, and touring with the bands of Billy Eckstine and Benny Carter. Davis recorded with Parker for the first time in 1945.

In 1949 Davis formed a nine-piece band with Lee Konitz, Gerry Mulligan, John Lewis, and Max Roach. The group was short lived, but its recordings had a great impact on musicians and defined "cool" jazz. In 1955 Davis formed a quintet with John Coltrane featured on tenor saxophone. Success came in the following year, when Davis made his first record with arranger Gil Evans, *Miles Ahead.* This was followed by two other collaborations with Evans, *Porgy and Bess* and *Sketches of Spain,* both landmarks in jazz. In 1958 came *Kind of Blue,* an album by a new sextet with Coltrane and the additions of Cannonball Adderley on alto saxophone and Bill Evans on piano. This album established modal improvisation in jazz and set the stage for Coltrane's explorations on his own.

Davis continued to introduce new ideas in his music and give exposure to new talent. He played a major role in the transition from the hard, aggressive stance of bop to the softer, more subtle side of jazz. By 1964 he had Wayne Shorter on saxophones, Herbie Hancock on piano, Ron Carter on bass, and the sensational eighteen-year-old Tony Williams on drums. This group explored unconventional musical territory, mostly in the realm of rhythmic and harmonic freedom. In 1968, however, Davis got restless again and was attracted by the possibilities of electronic instruments. Hancock, Chick Corea, Joe Zawinul, and Keith Jarrett were among the keyboard players who worked with Davis during this period, starting with the album *Bitches Brew,* which ushered in the concept of jazz fusion.

Some of his many fans, and quite a few musicians, did not care for the music Davis was producing at this point, but he remained unaffected by his critics. He gradually moved farther away from traditional jazz into an unclassifiable and ever-changing music that appealed to a young audience not generally interested in jazz. In the late 1970s Davis became a cult figure and his famous reserve (he had long been known for not acknowledging applause, walking off the stand when he wasn't playing, and being a difficult interview subject) was replaced by an open manner; he began smiling more often, waving to the audience, shaking hands with those nearest the stage, and giving frequent and amiable interviews.

After some time away from performing due to poor health, Davis returned to performing in the 1980s and experimented with hip hop and rap. Davis died on September 28, 1991.

Willie Dixon (1915–1992)
Guitarist, Singer, Songwriter

Willie Dixon was born on July 1, 1915, in Vicksburg, Mississippi. In his early years Dixon spent time as a boxer, was jailed as a conscientious objector regarding the Army, and sang with several recording groups. Dixon found his niche when he was hired as a session bass player for Chess Records in 1948. He later took on roles as in-house writer, recording artist, and session player.

It was Dixon's songwriting skills that helped support the careers of numerous artists with releases such as "Hoochie Coochie Man" for Muddy Waters, "I Ain't Superstitious" for Howlin' Wolf, and "Wang Dang Doodle" for KoKo Taylor. By the 1960s Dixon was in full swing and wrote songs for himself as well for others. Dixon released the album *I Am the Blues* under his own name as artist.

Dixon is credited with writing over 500 songs as well as leaving his mark on recordings as session player. In the 1970s he sued A&R Music (Chess Publishing Company) and secured the rights to songs and royalties and helped other artists do the same. Dixon died on January 29, 1992.

"Duke" Ellington (1899–1974)
Pianist, Composer, Bandleader

 Edward Kennedy Ellington, nicknamed "Duke" in his teens for his dapper dress style and courtly manners, was born into a middle-class family in Washington, D.C., on April 29, 1899. After graduating from high school, he was offered an art scholarship at Pratt Institute in New York, but he'd already had a taste of bandleading and preferred to stay with music. He had some success in his hometown, mainly because he had the biggest band advertisement in the telephone book, but

in 1923 he felt the urge to go to New York, where careers were made. He didn't succeed immediately (he later said that he and his friends were so broke they had to split a hot dog three ways), but by 1924 he was leading his Washingtonians at a Broadway nightclub and making his first records. That early band was only five pieces, but it had grown to ten by the time the young pianist–composer opened at the Cotton Club, the most famous Harlem night spot.

Ellington's unique style evolved during a five-year stay at the Cotton Club. Unlike most other bands, he played primarily his own music with a few pop tunes occasionally thrown in. This included "Tiger Rag," "Black and Tan Fantasy," and "The Mooch." Also, unlike other bands, Ellington kept the same players with him once he'd decided that he liked their style. He had a great sense of their potential and some of his bandsmen stayed with him for decades—none longer than baritone saxophonist Harry Carney, who was in the band from 1927 until the end. Many became stars in their own right (Johnny Hodges, alto saxophone; Cootie Williams, trumpet; Barney Bigard, clarinet), but somehow they always sounded better with Ellington, who knew just how to write for what he called their "tonal personalities." Ellington's scoring for the band was also strictly his own, and other arrangers found it hard to copy him.

By 1933 Ellington was ready for his first European tour; performing in London and Paris, the band, whose many recordings had prepared the way, was enthusiastically received. Back home, the band had already appeared in films (and would soon make more), and they had received valuable exposure on radio and on records (Ellington was among the first musicians to truly understand the importance of records, and to realize that making good ones required something different from playing in public). In 1935, deeply touched by the death of his mother, Ellington composed "Reminiscing in Tempo," his longest work to that date; most of his songs were tailored to the time limit of a little over three minutes imposed by the 78-rpm technology.

The band reached a first peak in 1940, when almost all of the musicians had been aboard for many years. Two exceptions were of key importance to the music—tenor Ben Webster and bassist Jimmy Blanton, who both joined in 1939. Billy Strayhorn, also a newcomer, didn't play in the band but quickly became essential to Ellington as an associate composer–arranger. Strayhorn spent the rest of his life with Duke and his men. A second peak was reached in 1956 when the band gave a tremendous performance at the Newport Jazz Festival, which fortunately was recorded; the album, highlighted by "Crescendo and Diminuendo in Blue," featuring twenty-seven choruses by tenor man Paul Gonsalves, became the best-selling Ellington record of all—and Duke made more records than any other jazz artist. It was Duke's success as a composer of popular songs that allowed him to keep the big band going through five decades; included among his hits are "Solitude," "Mood Indigo," "Sophisticated Lady," "Satin Doll," and "Don't Get Around Much Any More." All began as instrumentals. Ellington's major longer works include "Black, Brown and Beige," "Harlem," "Such Sweet Thunder," and "Far East Suite," the last two in collaboration with Strayhorn.

Ellington and his astonishing creations have been an inspiration to generations of musicians, most recently to Wynton Marsalis, who has done much to keep the Ellington legacy in the forefront of American music both in his own composing and in his efforts to get Ellington's music performed live (with the Lincoln Center Jazz Ensemble, for example). There can be no doubt that Duke Ellington (who was also a brilliant pianist) will stand as one of the greatest composers of the twentieth century. Ellington died on May 24, 1974, of cancer.

James Reese Europe (1881–1919)
Bandleader

James Reese Europe was born in Mobile, Alabama, on February 22, 1881. His family moved to Washington, D.C., when he was ten, and he studied violin with the U.S. Marine Band. As an adult he later moved to New York. In 1906 he organized the New Amsterdam Musical Association and in 1910 formed the Clef Club Orchestra.

During World War I, Europe directed the 369th Infantry Regimental Band, which performed throughout France and was a major force in the development of jazz in that country. Following his return to the United States, Europe toured the country with his band. In 1919 he was fatally stabbed by a member of his band while on tour.

Ella Fitzgerald (1918–1996)
Singer

Ella Fitzgerald was born on April 25, 1918, in Newport News, Virginia. She looked to music for solace when her mother died in 1932. Discovered in 1934 by drummer–bandleader Chick Webb at an amateur contest at Harlem's Apollo Theater, she cut her first side with Webb a year later, and he became her legal guardian. In 1938 she recorded "A Tisket, A Tasket," a novelty number that brought her commercial success and made her name widely known among the general public. Among musicians, Fitzgerald's reputation rests on her singular ability to use her voice like an instrument, improvising effortlessly in a style filled with rhythmic subtleties.

By the mid-1950s Fitzgerald had become the top jazz singer. Her series of recordings for Verve Records from 1955 to 1959 in multi-volume song books are among her greatest contributions to American music. Fitzgerald has emerged as the top female vocalist in virtually every poll conducted among jazz musicians and singers. No other vocalist has been so unanimously acclaimed. She is fondly known as "The First Lady of Song." During her career she was awarded over twelve Grammys, a Grammy Lifetime Achievement Award in 1967, a National Medal of the Arts, and the Kennedy Center for the Performing Arts Medal, among others. Fitzgerald suffered

from diabetes, which resulted in the amputation of both her legs. Fitzgerald's last performance was at Carnegie Hall in 1991. She died on June 15, 1996, in Beverly Hills.

Erroll Garner (1921–1977)
Pianist, Composer

Erroll Garner was born on June 15, 1921, in Pittsburgh, Pennsylvania. He taught himself to play piano and played primarily by ear. After dropping out of school, he arrived in New York in 1944, and he played most of the clubs on 52nd Street. His fame began to grow as he played on local radio, and in 1949 he released "Laura," which was massively successful. He formed his own group, and in 1958 he released Concert by the Sea, considered as one of the best selling jazz albums.

Garner was best known for his composition "Misty," which was a hit in 1959, but it was a hit for five other artists. The last re-release was in 1975 for Clint Eastwood's film Play Misty for Me. Garner played with orchestras, traveled throughout Europe, and wrote scores for films. Garner died of lung cancer on January 2, 1977.

Dizzy Gillespie (1917–1993)
Trumpeter, Bandleader

Born on October 21, 1917, John Birks "Dizzy" Gillespie received his early musical training in his native Cheraw, South Carolina. After moving to Philadelphia in 1935 and gaining more professional experience there, he joined the Teddy Hill Band, replacing his early idol Roy "Little Jazz" Eldridge.

Gillespie toured Europe with Teddy Hill in 1939, and when he returned to New York to play with Cab Calloway, his bop experimentation was already beginning to develop and his career as arranger began. Gillespie recorded his first "bop" solo with Les Hite in 1942. After working with Ella Fitzgerald, Benny Carter, Charlie Barnett, Earl Hines, and others, he joined Billy Eckstine's band in 1944. Gillespie and Charlie Parker were the cofounders of the revolutionary movement in jazz during the 1940s—the phenomenon known as bop or bebop. Eckstine, whose band at one time included both Gillespie and Parker, defined Parker's role more as instrumentalist, while Gillespie acted more as writer and arranger. Whatever their particular contributions were, however, it cannot be disputed that the sum total of their ideas brought about a change in jazz that continues to be felt today. Gillespie and Parker released bebop recordings *Shaw Nuff, Salt Peanuts,* and *Hot House,* and in 1946 Gillespie split from Parker and started his own band.

Gillespie's signature look of horn-rimmed glasses, beret, goatee, and the trumpet with the bell angled upward at a 45-degree angle was established by 1948. This was complimented by his puffed-out checks and rhythmic flair. Gillespie toured Europe, the Middle East, and Latin America with big bands and quintets subsidized by the U.S. State Department. He ultimately became a revered elder statesman of jazz. His dizzying speed and ingenuity along with his use of African clave in swing compositions have made him a true jazz great and many of his compositions jazz standards. Gillespie died on January 6, 1993, in Englewood, New Jersey.

Dexter Gordon (1923–1990)
Saxophonist, Bandleader

Dexter Gordon was born in Los Angeles, California, on February 27, 1923, to a prominent physician whose patients included famous jazz musicians. Gordon joined Lionel Hampton's newly formed big band in 1940. He was with Louis Armstrong in 1944, and later that year he joined the Billy Eckstine Band. After freelancing in New York, he returned home and in 1946 recorded "The Chase," a "tenor battle" with Wardell Gray, which became one of the biggest modern jazz hits. He teamed up with Gray on and off until 1952, when he was jailed for two years for heroin possession.

Gordon made a major comeback in the early 1960s with a series of much acclaimed recordings. In 1962 he settled in Copenhagen, and the Danish capital became his headquarters for the next fourteen years, though he made brief playing visits to the United States. In 1977 he came home for good, forming his own group and winning many new fans. In 1986 he starred in the French feature film *Round Midnight,* in which his portrayal of a character (based on Lester Young and Bud Powell) won him an Oscar nomination for best actor.

Gordon was the premier tenor saxophone stylist of bebop, but his strong, swinging music transcends categorization. He greatly influenced the young John Coltrane. Gordon died on April 26, 1990, in Philadelphia, Pennsylvania.

Buddy Guy (1936–)
Guitarist

Born on July 30, 1936, in Lettsworth, Louisiana, Buddy Guy began playing acoustic guitar as a teenager emulating Guitar Slim and Lightnin' Slim, Southern blues artists. Guy went to Chicago in 1957 and made his mark on the club scene. Unlike other guitarists he changed his presentation from sitting to standing, wandering off stage with a long cord as support, or even throwing chairs. His antics brought him as much attention as his abilities as a guitarist. Guy cut two singles for Cobra Records, "This is the End" and "Try to Quit You Baby," and when Cobra closed, Guy went to Chess Records.

Guy was at Chess Records from 1960 to 1967 and created a noteworthy body of work, including "Let Me Love You Baby," "Ten Years Ago," "My Time after Awhile," and "No Lie." He also played as session guitarist for Muddy Waters, Howlin' Wolf, Little Walter, and Koko Taylor. His albums after this point were not so well received, but his live performances were considered legendary. In 1991 he released his first album in over ten years and earned a Grammy. Buddy Guy was inducted into the Louisiana Music Hall of fame in 2008.

Lionel Hampton (1908–2002)
Vibraphonist, Pianist, Bandleader

Lionel Hampton was born on April 20, 1908, in Louisville, Kentucky. He was raised in Chicago, Illinois, and moved to California in 1928. Hampton was the first jazz musician to feature the vibraphone, or vibes—an instrument that has since come to play a vital role in jazz. His first recorded effort with the instrument was in 1930 on "Memories of You" with the Les Hite band in California, which included Louis Armstrong.

Hampton later left Hite's band to form his own Los Angeles group. When Benny Goodman heard him in 1936, he hired him to play on a record date with Teddy Wilson and Gene Krupa, and he then persuaded him to join the quartet on a permanent basis.

Hampton played with the Goodman Quartet until 1940, the year he formed his own big orchestra. The following year his band scored its first big hit, "Flyin' Home." Other famous songs include "On the Sunny Side of the Street," "Hot Mallets," and "He! Ba-Ba-Re-Bop."

Hampton enjoyed great success and continued to tour the world even after celebrating his eightieth birthday in 1989. Hampton helped to launch the careers of many well-known musicians, including Dinah Washington, Betty Carter, Dexter Gordon, Clark Terry, Clifford Brown, and Johnny Griffin. In 1981 he became a professor at Howard University and was honored at the Kennedy Center in 1995. Hampton died on August 31, 2002.

Herbie Hancock (1940–)
Pianist, Composer, Bandleader

Herbert "Herbie" Jeffrey Hancock was born April 12, 1940, in Chicago, Illinois. His music career began when he played Mozart with the Chicago Symphony at the age of eleven. After graduating from Grinnell College in Iowa in 1960, he joined trumpeter Donald Byrd and moved to New York in 1961. Although initially known as a pianist, Hancock has also turned to electronic music as a vehicle of communication, experimenting with the electric guitar, electric bass, electric piano, echoplex, phase shifter, and synthesizer.

From 1963 to 1968 Hancock traveled and played with Miles Davis and established himself as a composer and instrumentalist of the first rank. While with Davis, Hancock recorded with numerous other groups and became firmly established as a major jazz figure. Between 1969 and 1972 Hancock released two albums with Davis, and he released three fusion albums before his 1974 release of *Headhunters,* which is a blend of pop, funk, and jazz. His other projects include *On Future 2 Future* (2001), *Possibilities* (2005), and *Rivers: The Joni Letters* (tribute to Joni Mitchell; 2007).

Hancock has won many awards, including Downbeat Jazzman of the Year (1974), MTV Video Awards for his hit single "Rockit" (1984), and an Academy Award for the best score for the film *Round Midnight* (1986). Hancock has won numerous reader-poll music awards from *Keyboard* and *Playboy* magazines, plus fourteen Grammy Awards. Hancock is considered one of the all-time best jazz pianists.

W. C. Handy (1873–1958)
Trumpeter, Composer, Bandleader

William Christopher "W. C." Handy was born on November 16, 1873, in Florence, Alabama. After studying at Kentucky Musical College, Handy toured with an assortment of musical groups and became the bandmaster of the W. A. Mahara Minstrels in 1896.

In 1909, during a political campaign in Memphis, Handy wrote "Mr. Crump," a campaign song for E. H. "Boss" Crump. Three years later, the song was published as the "Memphis Blues," which made blues a legitimate category of music. Other works that have become perennial favorites are "Yellow Dog Blues" (1914), "Joe Turner Blues" (1915), "Beale Street Blues" (1916), "Careless Love" (1921), and "Aunt Hagar's Blues" (1922).

In the 1920s Handy became a music publisher in New York. Despite his failing sight, he remained active until his death on March 29, 1958. Although Handy began as a cornetist and bandleader in the 1890s, he achieved fame through his work as a composer, and became known as the "Father of the Blues." The film of his life story, *Father of the Blues,* based on his autobiography published in 1941, hit the silver screen months after Handy's death, and it starred Nat King Cole. Handy's songs extended beyond the world of jazz and into the field of popular music. Their popularity continues unabated today.

Lil Hardin-Armstrong (1898–1971)
Pianist, Singer

Lil Hardin-Armstrong was born Lillian Beatrice Hardin in Memphis, Tennessee, on February 3, 1898, but her family later moved to Chicago. Hardin-Armstrong was classically trained on the piano at Fisk University in Nashville, Tennessee. After playing with several other bands and leading her own band at the Dreamland Café, she joined King Oliver's Creole Jazz Band in 1921. It was then that Hardin-Armstrong met Louis Armstrong as he was the featured trumpeter. Lil and Louis were both married to other people at the time, but Lil arranged for their divorces and they were married in 1924. Lil led her own bands while with Louis and wrote music for his "Hot Five and Hot Seven" concerts. They divorced in 1938 but remained friends.

Hardin-Armstrong continued to work as an accompanist and cut twenty-six vocal slides for Decca Records from 1937 to 1940. She traveled in Europe and returned to the United States in the 1950s. Her songs include "Bad Boy" and "Just for a Thrill." Hardin-Armstrong died of a heart attack at a memorial for Louis Armstrong. She died on August 27, 1971, two months after Armstrong died.

Coleman Hawkins (1904–1969)
Saxophonist

Born on November 21, 1904, in St. Joseph, Missouri, Coleman Hawkins had already begun musical training by nine years old. He studied four years on the piano and cello and decided to take up the tenor saxophone. Hawkins studied at Washburn College in Topeka, Kansas, in 1922. He played with Fletcher Henderson's band from 1923 to 1934, during which time he was influenced by Lester Young and Stan Getz and developed his own signature style. In 1939, after spending five years touring Europe, he recorded his biggest hit "Body and Soul." Hawkins went back on tour through Europe.

In 1944 Hawkins formed an all star group for a recording session that included Thelonious Monk and Max Roach. Hawkins was an innovator who understood the intricacies of chord progressions and influenced many great saxophonists of the modern jazz era. He earned many accolades and awards. Hawkins died on May 19, 1969.

Roy Haynes (1925–)
Drummer, Bandleader

 Roy Owen Haynes was born on March 13, 1925, in the Roxbury section of Boston, Massachusetts. Haynes turned professional in his late teens. He went on the road with Luis Russell's big band before joining Lester Young's sextet and established his reputation. Settling in New York, he worked

with Charlie Parker and Dizzy Gillespie, then he toured in Sarah Vaughan's trio from 1953 to 1958.

Other important associates include Stan Getz, Gary Burton, Thelonious Monk, and John Coltrane. Haynes recorded prolifically with these and many others and also did recordings as leader of his own groups, including the "Hip Ensemble" (1960). Haynes is one of the originators and greatest exponents of modern jazz drumming. He is both a fantastic soloist and a creative ensemble drummer. His foot is undoubtedly the fastest ever, and his playing has an elegance that is reflected in his stylish appearance—he was once chosen by *Esquire* magazine as one of America's ten best-dressed men. Never out of date, Haynes in his sixties teamed up with such modernists as Pat Metheny and Chick Corea, and he consistently picks young players for his group.

Haynes's career as a drummer continued through the 1990s as he played for the Newport and Monterey jazz festivals in 1979, he joined Chick Corea's band trio in 1981, and he released the records *Homecoming* and *When It's Haynes It Roars* in 1996. Chick Corea toured with Haynes to celebrate Bud Powell's career, and Haynes released *The Roy Haynes Trio* on Universal in 2000. Haynes was awarded the Mid-Atlantic Art Foundation Living Legacy Award in 2010, and he received a Grammy Lifetime Achievement Award on February 12, 2011.

Fletcher Henderson (1897–1952)
Bandleader, Arranger, Pianist

Born in Cuthbert, Georgia, on December 18, 1897, James Fletcher Hamilton Henderson Jr. came to New York in 1920 to study chemistry. To earn spending money, he took a job as house pianist and musical director for Black Swan, the first record company owned and operated by blacks. Chemistry soon took a back seat, and in 1924 he was persuaded by some of his recording studio colleagues to audition with a band for a new club. The band got the job and soon gradu-

ated to the Roseland Ballroom on Broadway, where they played for eight years, toured, and made hundreds of records.

Henderson's band was the first big band to earn a reputation playing jazz, and it was the starting point for some of the greatest stars of the day, among them Louis Armstrong, Coleman Hawkins, and Benny Carter. It was the arranger and saxophonist Don Redman who shaped the band's early style. When he left in 1928 Carter and others, including Fletcher's younger brother Horace (also a pianist and arranger) took over. It was not until 1933 that Fletcher himself began to write full time for his band; he had such a talent for arranging that he soon became one of the architects of swing. Ironically, just as he hit his stride as a writer, his band fell on hard times in 1939, and for a brief while he gave it up and became a freelance arranger, contributing significantly to the library of the newly formed Benny Goodman Band.

Henderson led another big band in the 1940s but not with the same degree of success. Henderson's unique style of arranging voice along with the music and brass with reed instruments had a direct influence on swing and popular music in general. Henderson died on December 29, 1952.

Earl "Fatha" Hines (1903–1983)
Pianist, Bandleader

Born in Pittsburgh, Pennsylvania, on December 28, 1903, Earl Kenneth Hines (known worldwide as Earl "Fatha" Hines) grew up in a musical home: his father played the trumpet and his mother played the organ. Hines originally planned a concert career, but he was soon caught up in the world of jazz. Forming his own trio while still in high school, he began to play in local clubs before moving on to Chicago in 1925.

While there, he made a brilliant series of records with Louis Armstrong's Hot Five, and he soon became known as "the trumpet-style pianist." The intricacy of his style was well beyond that of his contemporaries, but served as a touchstone for a succeeding generation of pianists.

Hines formed his own band at the Grand Terrace in Chicago in 1928. For the next twenty years this band served as a proving ground for many great instrumentalists and innovators of the period (from Budd Johnson and Trummy Young in the early era to Dizzy Gillespie and Charlie Parker in the later years).

From 1948 to 1951 Hines worked with Armstrong again, and played a long engagement in San Francisco. In 1963 a New York recital revitalized his career, and he enjoyed great success in Europe, Japan, and the United States. He recorded prolifically with many jazz greats and was the recipient of numerous awards and honors, including two solo performances at the White House. Except for increased technical proficiency, the piano style of Earl "Fatha" Hines barely changed from what it was in the late 1920s. He died on July 22, 1983. "Piano Man" is inscribed on his tombstone.

Billie Holiday (1915–1959)
Singer

Billie Holiday, dubbed "Lady Day" by Lester Young, was one of the greatest jazz singers of all time. She was born Eleanor Fagan on April 7, 1915, in Baltimore, Maryland. While still a young girl, she moved from Baltimore to New York City, and in 1931 she began her singing career in an assortment of Harlem night spots. In 1933 she cut her first sides with Benny Goodman. From 1935 to 1939 she established her reputation with a series of records made with Teddy Wilson. Holiday also sang with the bands of Count Basie, Artie Shaw, and Lester Young.

In such classic records as "Strange Fruit" and her own "God Bless the Child," she departed from popular material to score her greatest artistic triumphs, depicting the harsh reality of Southern lynching and the personal alienation she had experienced. The 1939 release of "Strange Fruit" was rejected by her own label Columbia, which refused to record it. By 1944, with the release of "Lover Man," Holiday's sound reflected more of a pop sound.

At one time addicted to drugs and alcohol, Holiday wrote in her 1956 autobiography *Lady Sings the Blues* that "all dope can do for you is kill you—and kill you the long, slow, hard way." The subject of a feature film starring Diana Ross, several books, and videos, Billie Holiday is still a powerful force in music decades after her untimely death on July 17, 1959.

John Lee Hooker (1917–2001)
Singer, Guitarist

John Lee Hooker was born in Clarksdale, Mississippi, on August 22, 1917. He had a great interest in gospel music and was taught by his stepfather to play the guitar. His big break came in 1948 when he went to Memphis and cut a demo for Bernie Besman, a record label owner. "Boogie Chillun" and "Sally Mae" were big hits, and Hooker followed the success with "Crawling King Snake" in 1949 and "In the Mood for Love" in 1951, which also topped the charts. He continued to put out successful records throughout the 1950s and the 1960s.

In the 1970s and 1980s Hooker traveled throughout the United States and Europe and collaborated with many artists, including Canned Heat, Bonnie Raitt, and Van Morrison. He also appeared in films such as *The Blues Brothers* in 1980. Hooker recorded over a hundred songs, received a Grammy Award, and was inducted into the Rock 'n' Roll Hall of Fame in 1991. Hooker died on June 21, 2001.

Lightnin' Hopkins (1912–1982)
Singer, Guitarist

Sam John Hopkins (known as "Lightnin'") was born on March 15, 1912, in Houston, Texas. He became interested in blues when he met Blind Lemon Jefferson. In 1920 Hopkins traveled with Jefferson and served as one of his guides while learning his techniques. Hopkins played the Houston bar circuit after his time with Jefferson and teamed up with his cousin, blues singer Texas Alexander.

It was not until 1946, when Aladdin Records teamed Hopkins and pianist Wilson "Thunder" Smith together, that some degree of success occurred. The regional hits "Katie May" and "Shotgun Blues" were successful for the duo. Hopkins made the charts again in the 1950s, reinvented himself as a "folk blues legend," and traveled in the United States, Canada, and Europe. He died of throat cancer on January 30, 1982.

Howlin' Wolf (1910–1976)
Singer, Harmonica Player

Blues singer and harmonica player Howlin' Wolf was born Chester Arthur Burnett on June 20, 1910, in West Point, Mississippi. He learned to play the harmonica from blues musician Sonny Boy Williamson and made his first recording in 1950, when his baying style of singing won him the name Howlin' Wolf.

Wolf was picked up by Chess Records in Chicago in 1953. He was paired with guitarist Hubert Sumlin and they were paired with Willie Dixon, a staff writer. In 1956 they released songs such as "The Red Rooster, Back Door Man," and "Wang Dang Doodle". This duo lasted until 1964, when Wolf recorded his solo work "Killing Floor."

Wolf's best-known recordings include "Moanin' at Midnight, Poor Boy", and "My Country Sugar Mama." By the 1970s rock and roll groups such as the Doors and Jeff Beck were recording Wolf's work. Wolf had become increasingly ill and died on January 10, 1976.

Alberta Hunter (1895–1984)
Singer

Alberta Hunter was born on April 1, 1895, in Memphis, Tennessee. After her father left, her

mother remarried and Hunter, unhappy with her new family, ran away to Chicago, Illinois, at the age of eleven. She found work and later began singing in south side nightclubs. By 1919 Hunter had established her reputation, and she wrote the song "Down Hearted Blues" in 1921, which became Bessie Smith's first hit. In 1924 Hunter moved to New York and began recording under pseudonyms. Hoping to escape racism and experience more success, she went to Europe from 1927 to 1937. She found that success in Europe did not mean success in the United States.

Hunter performed in several plays, including *Mamba's Daughter* in 1939, and she began working with the United Service Organizations (USO). She traveled with them to both theaters of World War II and during the Korean War and performed blues and popular songs. She returned to Chicago and continued to perform until her mother died in 1954. Hunter decided to give up performing and become a nurse. After being a nurse for twenty years, Hunter was forced to retire only to have her employers discover she was eighty-two and not the expected seventy. In 1977 Hunter began singing again and continued to perform at the Cookery in New York until her death in 1984.

Illinois Jacquet (1922–2004)
Saxophonist, Bandleader

Jean-Baptiste Illinois Jacquet was born on October 25, 1922, in Broussard, Louisiana, and was raised in Texas. The man who contributed to making the tenor sax the most popular jazz horn began as an altoist; it was Lionel Hampton who made him switch to tenor when he joined Hampton's new big band in 1942. Soon thereafter, Jacquet recorded his famous solo on "Flyin' Home" and made both his own and the Hampton band's name.

After stints with Cab Calloway and Count Basie, Jacquet joined the Jazz at the Philharmonic touring group, in which he starred in tenor "battles" with Flip Phillips and others. He soon formed his own swinging little band and became a mainstay in the international jazz circuit, a position he still occupied in the 1990s. He formed a successful big band in the 1980s that toured Europe and recorded; the European tour and other incidents in Jacquet's life as a musician are part of the documentary film *Texas Tenor*, which premiered at the 1992 JVC Jazz Festival.

Jacquet was one of the first to "overblow" the tenor saxophone, reaching high harmonics that were dismissed by some as a circus stunt but appealed to audiences; eventually, of course, such overblowing became part of the instrument's vocabulary, as in the later work of John Coltrane and the style of David Murray. He died of a heart attack in 2004.

Elmore James (1918–1963)
Singer, Guitarist

Elmore James was born on January 27, 1918, near Richland, Mississippi. James learned in his teens how to play music on a homemade instrument. As he got older, James played at local nightclubs and admired the styles of Robert Johnson. James eventually developed his own distinctive style of playing the slide guitar. He began to play whenever possible with Robert Johnson, Howlin' Wolf, and Sonny Boy Williams, a harmonica player. This led to radio shows and recording sessions for James. James formed his own band in the 1930s but was drafted into the armed service for three years.

James's first recording was in 1951 with the famous release "Dust My Broom." This song became a top hit and the signature song for him. He moved to Chicago, formed the band Broomdusters, and recorded numerous songs that made the charts, some of which are considered blues classics. One of his last recordings before legal and other problems took precedence was "The Sky Is Crying." James suffered a heart attack in Chicago and died on May 24, 1963.

Etta James (1938–)
Singer

Born Jamesetta Hawkins on January 25, 1938, in Los Angeles, California, Etta James was a singer in church as early as five years old. By twelve she had moved to San Francisco, formed a trio, and had begun working for bandleader Johnny Otis. In 1954 she inverted her first name to Etta James and took that as her stage name. She also recorded the song "The Wallflower" with her group Peaches, which was her nickname. In 1955 James began her solo career with the song "Good Rockin Daddy."

James signed with Chess Records in 1960 and recorded her debut album *At Last*, followed by hits "Something's Got a Hold on Me" (1962), "Stop the Wedding" (1962), and "In the Basement" (1966), among others. In performance she used her skills with gospel to rock the house. Her success continued through the 1960s with Chess Records in spite of problems with a heroin addiction.

After a lull in her career, a resurgence in James's music occurred in the 1990s. She was inducted into the Rock and Roll Hall of Fame in 1993; she released *Blues to the Bone* in 2004, and *All the Way* in 2006. With the release of the film *Cadillac Records* in 2009, her music (and in particular her song "At Last") gained renewed attention. James continues to perform blues, soul, jazz, and gospel. She was diagnosed with leukemia in 2011 and is undergoing treatment.

"Blind" Lemon Jefferson (1893–1929)
Guitarist, Singer

Lemon Jefferson was born in September 1893, in Couchman, Texas. Blind from birth he would walk to the nearest town of Worthham, Texas, and play in front of a shop or store for money. Jefferson became very popular, subsequently moving to Dallas when he was twenty and playing at brothels, saloons, and parties. He hired young musicians such as T-Bone Walker and Lightin' Hopkins to be his guides while traveling in Texas, Louisiana, Mississippi, Alabama, and Virginia.

Jefferson's high, booming, two-octave voice, shouting style, driving guitar technique, and brilliant improvisations brought him much success. In 1925 he moved to Chicago and made an estimated eighty recordings with Paramount Records between 1926 and 1929. Jefferson is thought to be the first country blues singer to become a recording star. On December 29, 1929, after a night of heavy-drinking, Jefferson got lost coming home from a party and froze to death.

J. J. Johnson (1924–2001)
Trombonist

James Louis Johnson was born in Indianapolis, Indiana, on January 22, 1924. He began playing the saxophone, but by the age of fourteen he had moved to the trombone. Johnson left home at eighteen and over the next few years played for Snookum Russell, Benny Carter, Count Basie, and Illinois Jacquet. In 1944 he played at the first jazz at the Philharmonic concert and later recorded with Miles Davis.

Johnson's skill as a trombonist was already legendary as he performed at high speed and was able to adapt the instrument to the demands of "bop." By 1959 Johnson had reorganized his sextet but disbanded them almost immediately. He turned to composing and took on several commissions. He began writing for films such as *Cleopatra Jones* and *Shaft,* and for television shows such as *The Mod Squad.* Johnson returned briefly to performing in 1977. He died on February 4, 2001.

Robert Johnson (1911–1938)
Singer, Guitarist

Robert Leroy Johnson was born on May 8, 1911, in Hazelhurst, Mississippi. He first tried his hand with the harmonica as a teenager, but he had no real talent at it. Years later, after getting married and losing his wife during childbirth, Johnson committed himself to playing music. He spent a year studying guitar with Ike Zimmerman, a blues musician. His skill on the guitar matured so quickly that many believed he sold his soul to the devil to get such power in his playing. It is said

that Johnson may have promoted this myth himself but not necessarily with the same meaning.

After Johnson released his first recording "Terraplane Blues," he toured Chicago, the Delta, and St. Louis, and he went on to record twenty-nine songs between 1936 and 1937 for the American Record Corporation. The songs include "Cross Road Blues," "Love in Vain," "Hellhound on My Trail," "I Believe I'll Dust My Broom," "Walking Blues," and "Sweet Home Chicago." The story regarding his death is that Johnson was poisoned by a jealous husband in Three Forks, Mississippi, in 1938. After being warned not to drink from an offered bottle, Johnson did so anyway and died a few days later, convulsing with symptoms akin to that of strychnine poisoning. He died at the age of twenty-seven. It was not until after 1960 that a renewed interest in his music allowed it to reach a broader audience. His contribution to the blues genre lies in his ability to play a bass line on the bottom strings and a melody on the top along with rundowns and turnbacks, which were new in his day.

B. B. King (1925–)
Singer, Guitarist, Bandleader

Riley B. King was born on September 16, 1925, in Indianola, Mississippi. His career started when, as a boy of fourteen, he met a preacher who played the guitar. King soon owned his own guitar; he bought it for $8, paid out of meager wages from working in the cotton fields. From that time on, King spent his spare time singing and playing the guitar with other budding musicians in the town and listening to blues guitarists who came to Indianola clubs. In the early 1940s he traveled to a nearby town to play on street corners. Sometimes he'd come home with as much as $25.

After World War II, King hitchhiked to Memphis where a musician-relative got him a performing job at the 16th Street Grill. He was paid $12 a night, plus room and board, five nights a week. King then found a spot on a newly opened radio station in Memphis called WDIA. He played ten minutes each afternoon and then became a disc jockey. The station named him "The Boy from Beale Street," and thereafter Riley B. King was known as "B. B."

King's first record was made in 1949 for RPM, and in 1951 he released "Three O'Clock Blues," which was a number-one record on the rhythm and blues charts. While promoting his record in Twist, Arkansas, King was inspired to name his guitar after a woman who caused a fight between two men and a fire that almost cost him his life. The guitar came to be known as Lucille. King continued his successes and released "The Thrill Is Gone" in 1969, which earned him a Grammy in 1971. A series of personal appearances on major television shows increased his popularity. King toured Europe for the first time in 1969, starting at the Royal Albert Hall in London and continuing through England, France, Germany, Switzerland, Denmark, and Sweden. Returning to the United States, he joined a fourteen-city tour with the Rolling Stones. Twenty years later, he toured with the Stones again.

By the 1980s King had reached legend status as he continued to perform. He won a Grammy for his blues recording *Blues 'n' Jazz* in 1984, he was awarded a Grammy for lifetime achievement in 1988, was inducted into the Rock and Roll Hall of Fame in 1987, awarded the Presidential Medal of Arts in 1990, and honored at the Kennedy Center in 1995. B. B. King is one of the most successful artists in the history of the blues. He continues to tour, performing on average 250 concerts per year.

Abbey Lincoln (1930–2010)
Singer

Anna Marie Wooldridge, known as Abbey Lincoln, was born on August 6, 1930, in Chicago, Illinois. Lincoln's professional career began after winning a singing contest in the 1950s. She sang in nightclubs such as the famous Blue Note in New York City. She was actively involved in the civil rights

movement, and in the 1960s she began recording such jazz releases as *We Insist! And Freedom Now,* with jazz musician Max Roach. Lincoln traveled throughout Africa, Asia, and Europe.

Lincoln's acting career earned her roles in films such as *The Girl Can't Help It* (1956), and films with accomplished co-stars such as Ivan Dixon in *Nothing but a Man* (1964), and Sidney Poitier and Beau Bridges in the film *For Love of Ivy* (1968). Lincoln also appeared in Spike Lee's film *Mo' Better Blues* (1990).

Lincoln was inducted into the Black Filmmakers Hall of Fame in 1975, and she received the National Endowment of the Arts NEA Jazz Masters Award in 2003. Lincoln died on August 14, 2010.

Branford Marsalis (1960–)
Saxophonist, Bandleader

Fourteen months older than his brother Wynton, Branford Marsalis was born on August 26, 1960, in New Orleans, Louisiana. His career began professionally in 1980 playing baritone saxophone for Art Blakely and subsequently touring Europe. Between 1983 and 1987 Marsalis played on his brother Wynton's debut record as well as his own debut record, and he later joined the rock group Sting for his solo debut album. Marsalis also recorded a classical record while in London. In 1987 he was awarded a Grammy for best jazz instrumental performance solo.

Marsalis has gained equal fame with his brother due in part to his wide exposure as bandleader for the *Tonight* show from 1992 to 1995. He has received many awards, including several Grammy nominations for his jazz recordings, and recognition for movie soundtracks such as Spike Lee's *Mo' Better Blues*. He received a Grammy in 2001 for his album *Contemporary Jazz*. Marsalis's interests also extend to movie roles. Marsalis is a gifted player whose many recordings, including some as sideman with brother Wynton, show him to be a warm and consistently inventive soloist and an imaginative leader–organizer.

Wynton Marsalis (1961–)
Trumpeter, Bandleader

 Born October 18, 1961, into a musical family in New Orleans, Louisiana, (his father, Ellis Marsalis, is a prominent pianist and teacher), Wynton Marsalis was well schooled in both the jazz and classical traditions. At seventeen he won an award at the prestigious Berkshire Music Center for his classical prowess; a year later, he left the Juilliard School of Music to join Art Blakely's Jazz Messengers.

After touring and recording in Japan and the United States with Herbie Hancock, Marsalis made his first album (in 1981), formed his own group, and toured extensively on his own. Soon after, he made a classical album and in 1984 became the first instrumentalist to win simultaneous Grammy Awards as best jazz and best classical soloist. In 1997 he won the first non-classical Pulitzer Prize for his oratorio *Blood on the Fields*. Marsalis collaborated with the New York City Ballet director and created the works *Jazz/Six Syncopated Movements* and *Jump Start*. He also received a great deal of media coverage—more than any other serious young musician in recent history.

A brilliant virtuoso of the trumpet, with total command of any musical situation, Marsalis has made himself a potent spokesperson for the highest musical standards in jazz, to which he is firmly and proudly committed. He has urged young musicians to acquaint themselves with the rich tradition of jazz and to avoid the pitfalls of "crossing over" to pop, fusion, and rock. Adherence to these principles and his stature as a player has made his words effective. He has composed music for films and ballet and is a co-founder of the Lincoln Center Jazz Ensemble. He also teaches in outreach programs for institutions such as the New England Conservatory of Music.

Carmen McRae (1920–1994)
Singer, Pianist

Carmen Mercedes McRae was born in Harlem, New York, on April 8, 1920. Her natural talent on the keyboards won her numerous music scholarships. During her teen years, she carefully studied the vocal style of Billie Holiday and incorporated it into her own style. A highlight of her career came when Holiday recorded one of McRae's compositions, "Dream of Life." After finishing her education, McRae moved to Washington, D.C., and worked as a government clerk by day and a nightclub pianist–singer by night. In the early 1940s she moved to Chicago to work with Benny Carter, Mercer Ellington, and Count Basie. By 1954 she had gained enough attention through her jazz and pop recordings to be dubbed a "new star" by *Downbeat* magazine. She continued to travel and perform in nightclubs and jazz clubs in the United States and all over the world and produce projects showing her range and abilities with artist such as Sammy Davis Jr., Louis Armstrong, and Betty Carter, to name only a few.

In 1983 McRae recorded an album in honor of her inspiration Billy Holiday entitled *For Lady Day*. McRae appeared in film roles beginning in 1967 with *Hotel*. In 1993 she was awarded the NAACP Image Award, and in 1994 she was honored with a National Endowment for the Arts American Jazz Masters Award. She died from a stroke on November 10, 1994.

Charles Mingus (1922–1979)
Bassist, Composer, Bandleader

Charles Mingus, born on April 22, 1922, in Nogles, Arizona, grew up in the Watts area of Los Angeles. Starting on trombone and cello, he eventually settled on the bass and studied with Red Callender, a noted jazz player, and Herman Reinshagen, a classical musician. He also studied composition with

Lloyd Reese. Early in his professional career he worked with Barney Bigard in a band that included the veteran New Orleans trombonist Kid Ory, and he toured briefly in Louis Armstrong's big band; he also led his own groups and recorded with them locally. After a stint in Lionel Hampton's band, which recorded his interesting composition "Mingus Fingus," he joined Red Norvo's trio, with which he came to New York in 1951.

 Settling there, he worked with many leading players, including Dizzy Gillespie and Charlie Parker, and he founded his own record label Debut. He also formed his first of many so-called jazz workshops, in which new music (mostly his own compositions) was rehearsed and performed. Mingus believed in spontaneity as well as discipline, and he often interrupted his band's public performances if the playing didn't measure up. Some musicians refused to work with him after such public humiliations, but there were some who thought so well of what he was trying to do that they stayed with him for years. Drummer Dannie Richmond was with Mingus from 1956 to 1970 and again from 1974 until the end. Other longtime "Mingusians" include trombonist Jimmy Knepper, pianist Jaki Byard, saxophonists Eric Dolphy, Booker Ervin, John Handy, and Bobby Jones, and trumpeter Jack Walrath.

Mingus's music was as volatile as his temper, filled with ever-changing melodic ideas and textures, and shifting, often accelerating, rhythmic patterns. He was influenced by Duke Ellington, Art Tatum, and Charlie Parker, and his music often reflected psychological states and his views on social issues. Mingus was a staunch fighter for civil rights and wrote such protest pieces as "Fables of Faubus," "Meditations on Integration," and "Eat That Chicken." He was also steeped in the music of the Holiness Church ("Better Git It in Your Soul," "Wednesday Night Prayer Meeting") and in the whole range of the jazz tradition ("My Jelly Roll Soul," "Theme for Lester Young," "Gunslinging Bird," "Open Letter to Duke"). Himself a

virtuoso bassist, he drove his sidemen to their utmost, often with vocal exhortations that became part of a Mingus performance. He composed for films and ballet and experimented with other forms; his most ambitious work, an orchestral suite called *Epitaph,* lasts more than two hours and was not performed in full until years after his death. He died January 5, 1979, in Cuernavaca, Mexico, of amyotrophic lateral sclerosis, a disease with which he struggled valiantly, composing and directing (from a wheelchair) until just before his death. Mingus was often in financial trouble and once was evicted from his home, but he also received a Guggenheim Fellowship in composition and was honored by President Jimmy Carter at a White House jazz event in 1978.

At its best, Mingus's music—angry, humorous, always passionate—ranks with the greatest in jazz. He also wrote a strange but interesting autobiography, *Beneath the Underdog* (1971). A group called Mingus Dynasty continued to perform his music into the 1990s.

Memphis Minnie (1897–1973)
Guitarist, Singer

Lizzie Douglas, known as Memphis Minnie, was born on June 3, 1987, in Algiers, Alabama. Douglas learned to play the guitar and the banjo and at age thirteen ran away to Memphis. She played on the street, medicine shows, and jug bands until 1929, when she married "Kansas" Joe McCoy who also played the guitar. A Columbia Records producer heard Douglas and her husband playing, and she was signed for her first recording "Bumble Bee," which was a hit. She also recorded "Hoodoo Lady," which showed her style moving from country to a more urban style. By 1939 she had split from McCoy and married Little Son Joe Lawlers. Douglas formed a touring company and in the 1940s recorded songs such as "Digging My Potatoes," "Me and My Chauffeur," and "I'm So Glad."

Douglas continued producing records and touring. She married for a third time and returned to Chicago in the early 1950s. Douglas retired in 1957 and died on August 6, 1973. Douglas is one of the few prolific female blues artists who earned the respect of her peers with her musicianship.

Thelonius Monk (1917–1982)
Pianist, Composer

Thelonious Sphere Monk was born on October 10, 1917, in Rocky Mount, North Carolina. His family later moved to New York. Beginning with his teen years he toured with an evangelist group, later studied at Juilliard, and worked with several bands. He made his debut as a leader starting in 1947. After losing his right to work in New York because of a heroin arrest he struggled until 1957, when he landed a six month run at the Five Spot Cafe in New York, where John Coltrane was also performing.

In 1964 Monk signed with Columbia Records and he produced the album *Monk's Dream*, which is his bestselling album. He also produced studio albums such as *Criss Cross* (1963) and *Underground* (1968). His music performances became more and more in demand and he continued to tour. Because of health issues his last tour was from 1971 to 1972.

Along with Charlie Parker and Dizzy Gillespie, Thelonious Monk was a vital member of the jazz revolution that took place in the early 1940s. Some musicians (among them Art Blakely) have said that Monk actually predated his more renowned contemporaries. Monk's unique piano style and his talent as a composer made him a leader in the development of modern jazz. Aside from brief work with the Lucky Millinder Band, Coleman Hawkins, and Dizzy Gillespie, Monk generally was the leader of his own small groups. He has been called the most important jazz composer since Duke Ellington. Many of his compositions ("Round Midnight," "Ruby My Dear," "Epistrophy," "Blue Monk," "Straight No Chaser," and "Well, You Needn't") have become jazz standards.

Monk was unique as both an instrumentalist and a composer, maintaining his musical integrity and his melodic originality. He died in Englewood, New Jersey, on February 17, 1982.

"Jelly Roll" Morton (1890–1941)
Composer, Pianist, Bandleader

Ferdinand Joseph LeMenthe Morton, known professionally as Jelly Roll Morton, was born on October 20, 1890, in New Orleans, Louisiana. Morton, who had been abandoned by his father, was cared for by primarily his grandmother after the death of his mother. When Morton's grandmother discovered his wild lifestyle, she put him out. The 1920s were the peak decade in Morton's up-and-down career. He was a much-in-demand pianist in his hometown while still in his teens, working in the Storyville "houses." Restless and ambitious, he hit the road, working in vaudeville, hustling pool, running gambling halls, occasionally playing piano, and traveling as far as Alaska and Mexico. He finally settled in Chicago in 1923, made his first records, worked for a music publisher, and with characteristic arrogance, let everybody know that he was the greatest.

In the mid-1920s Morton made some wonderful recordings for Victor Records, the leading label of that day, under the name Jelly Roll Morton and with his group the Red Hot Peppers. Most were his own compositions, all were his arrangements, and they showed that he was a major talent—quite possibly the first real composer in jazz, if not the inventor that he so often professed to be. In 1927 he moved to New York, still with a Victor contract but no longer doing as well, and when big-band swing came to the forefront, Morton's career took a dive. He had made his last commercial records in 1930.

Alan Lomax, a folklorist for the Library of Congress, was intrigued by Morton's Storyville days and some of the songs he sang. He urged Morton to make a recording of his life story, interspersed with fine piano playing, for Lomax's archives. Morton was then living in Washington, D.C., managing an obscure nightclub. After the Library of Congress sessions, Victor Records was persuaded to record Morton again, and he was briefly back in the spotlight. Failing health and restlessness led him to drive to California to be with a female companion. But the trip made him ill, and he died in his fiftieth year, on July 10, 1941, just before a revival of interest in traditional jazz that would have given him the break he needed.

In 1992 the musical *Jelly's Last Jam* opened with great success on Broadway. It was loosely based on Morton's life as a force behind the introduction of jazz in the early twentieth century and featured new arrangements of his music.

Joe "King" Oliver (1885–1938)
Cornetist

Joseph Oliver was born on May 11, 1885, in Abend, Louisiana. Oliver started his career playing the trombone but switched to the cornet. He began playing with the Melrose Brass Band in 1907 and played with several other brass bands as he perfected his skills. Oliver first earned the sobriquet "King" in 1917 after establishing himself as the best cornetist against the likes of Freddie Keppard, Manuel Perez, and a host of other early New Orleans jazz musicians. Oliver soon teamed up with Kid Ory and organized what would become the leading jazz band in New Orleans.

During the Storyville era, Oliver met and befriended Louis Armstrong. Lacking a son of his own, Oliver became Armstrong's "unofficial father," sharing with him the musical knowledge that he had acquired over the years. In return, Armstrong treated him with great respect, referring to him as "Papa Joe."

With the end of the Storyville era, Oliver left and Armstrong replaced him in Ory's band. In 1922 Oliver summoned Armstrong to Chicago to play in his Creole Jazz Band as second cornetist; a year later the band made the first important recordings by a black jazz group.

The work of Oliver and Armstrong put Chicago on the jazz map of the United States. However, changing tastes caused Oliver's music to decline in popularity, and by the time he moved to New York in 1928, his best years were behind him.

Beginning in 1932, Oliver toured mainly in the South before ill health forced him to give up music. He died in Savannah, Georgia, where he worked in a poolroom from 1936 until his death in 1938.

Charlie "Bird" Parker (1920–1955)
Saxophonist

Charles Christopher Parker Jr., known as "Bird," "Yard," or "Yardbird," was born August 29, 1920, in Kansas City, Missouri. He left school at sixteen to become a professional musician in his hometown, where he joined pianist Jay McShann from 1940 to 1942, with whom he recorded his first sides. At this time Parker met Dizzy Gillespie. The two men had independently formulated similar ideas about the direction of jazz, and they cofounded the bop movement some four years later.

In the early 1940s Parker played with the bands of Earl Hines, Cootie Williams, and Andy Kirk, as well as the original Billy Eckstine band— the first big band formed expressly to feature the new jazz style in its solos and arrangements.

In 1945 Parker cut a series of remarkable sides with Gillespie that put bebop on the map. Although Parker was revered by a host of younger musicians, his innovations were at first met with a great deal of opposition from traditionalist jazz musicians and critics.

In 1946 Parker, addicted to heroin, suffered a breakdown and was confined to a state hospital in California. Six months later he was back recording with Erroll Garner. The records Parker made between 1945 and 1948 are considered his greatest work, which include the Koko session, "Relaxin at Camarillo," "Night in Tunsia," "Embraceable You," "Donna Lee," "Omithology," and "Parker's Mood." From this point until his death from a heart attack in 1955, he confined most of his activity to working with a quintet, but he also recorded and toured with a string section and visited Europe in 1949 and 1950. He made his final public appearance in 1955 at Birdland, the club that had been named in his honor. He died a week later on March 12, 1955.

The influence of Charlie Parker on the development of jazz has been felt not just in the realm of the alto saxophone, but in the whole spectrum of jazz ideas. The astounding melodic, harmonic, tonal, and rhythmic innovations he introduced have made it impossible for any jazz musician from the mid-1940s to the present to develop a musical style without reflecting some of Parker's influence, whether it is acknowledged or not.

Charley Patton (c.1887–1934)
Singer, Guitarist

Charlie (better known as Charley) Patton was born between 1887 and 1891, in Edwards, Mississippi. He is among the earliest of blues singer-guitar players. Spending most of his life in the Delta region of Mississippi, he moved to the Will Dockery Plantation in Sunflower County in 1897. It was there that he began to compose in the twelve-bar patterns that came to be known as the standard blues form. Patton was popular in live performances that showcased his hoarse voice, flashy style, and repertoire of ragtime, spirituals, ballads, and blues. They caused quite a commotion as workers would leave their work in the fields to get a look at this music great.

Patton did not record his music until 1929, when he recorded sixty songs for Paramount Records in less than five years, including his famous hit "Pony Blues." Many of the techniques he perfected in live performances became standard in the region's blues style, such as using the guitar like a drum to reinforce beats, and popping the bass strings. Patton died on April 28, 1934.

Oscar Pettiford (1922–1960)
Bassist

Oscar Pettiford was born on September 30, 1922, on an American Indian reservation in Oklahoma and raised in Minneapolis, Minnesota. Until he was nineteen, he toured with the family band (consisting of his father and eleven children) and was well known in the Midwest. In 1943 Charlie Barnet heard him in Minneapolis and hired him to team up with bassist Chubby Jackson. Pettiford left Barnet later that year to lead his own group on 52nd Street, and he also played with Coleman Hawkins, Duke Ellington, and Woody Herman.

Pettiford was the leading bassist in the modern era of jazz. Building his own style on the foundation established by Jimmy Blanton, Pettiford achieved renown as the most technically capable and melodically inventive bassist in the jazz world of the late 1940s.

Pettiford's fame grew during the 1950s through his recordings and his tours of Europe and the Orient. His best known compositions are "Tricrotism," "LaVerne Walk," "Bohemia after Dark," and "Swingin' till the Girls Come Home." In 1958 he settled permanently in Europe, where he continued to work until his death in Copenhagen in 1960.

Bud Powell (1924–1966)
Pianist

Earl Rudolph "Bud" Powell was born on September 27, 1924, in New York City. He was a child prodigy who began his career in 1943 with the Cootie Williams orchestra and played in Harlem on 52nd Street as bebop came into existence. In 1945, in a racial incident, Powell was severely beaten about the head by a Philadelphia policeman. As a result of this he suffered from headaches and mental breakdowns throughout the remainder of his life.

Between 1947 and 1951 Powell was able to produce some of his best work, which included "Dance of the Infidels," "Hallucinations," "Bouncing with Bud," and "Tempus Fugit." Although Powell continued to have some erratic times while performing, he also had notable times such as the 1953 Massey Hall Concert. Powell spent time in Paris from 1954 to 1964 with success even though he spent some time in the hospital. He returned to New York in 1964 and, after a few concerts, died on July 31, 1966. Powell changed the use of the left hand striding that had been a standard of the jazz piano.

Sun Ra (1914–1993)
Pianist, Composer, Bandleader

Considered the most controversial of jazz musicians, Sun Ra was born Herman Poole Blount on May 22, 1914, in Birmingham, Alabama. Although professing at times to be from the planet Saturn, Blount played rhythm and blues in Chicago and spent time playing with Fletcher Henderson's band beginning in 1947.

In 1950 Blount legally changed his name to Le Sony'r Ra but was known professionally as Sun Ra. He assembled a band to play his mystical and unusual music. By 1953 his band Arkestra began with advanced pop and expanded to playing avant-garde. His concerts challenged the seriousness of his work as he often had anything from primitive electric keyboards to fire-eaters and plate twirlers as in the later years of his performances. Sun Ra continued to perform in the United States and spent some time doing concerts in France, Germany, Egypt, and the United Kingdom. Despite his eccentricity, he was an innovative performer. Sun Ra died on May 30, 1993, following a series of strokes.

"Ma" Rainey (1886–1939)
Singer

Ma Rainey was born Gertrude Pridgett on April 26, 1886, in Columbus, Georgia. She gave her first public performance as a twelve year old at the local Springer Opera House. At age eighteen she married singer–dancer William "Pa" Rainey, and the duo embarked on a long entertainment career. Around 1912 Rainey introduced a teenaged Bessie Smith into her act, a move that was later seen as having a major impact on blues–jazz singing styles.

Rainey produced her first record in 1923 and later did recordings with Fletcher Henderson, Louis Armstrong, and Coleman Hawkins, racking up the biggest record sales of that era for Paramount Records. By 1928 she had recorded one hundred songs, including "See See Rider" and "Bo Weavil Blues," which became blues classics. Rainey stopped recording in 1928 but continued to tour the South for a few more years. She retired from singing in 1935 and managed the two theaters she owned in Georgia. She died on December 22, 1939. Ma Rainey, the "Mother of the Blues," enveloped the 1920s with her powerful, message-oriented blues songs, and she is remembered as a genuine jazz pioneer. Her strong and communicative voice lives on in the more than one hundred recordings she made in her lifetime, singing of the many facets of black experience.

Don Redman (1900–1964)
Saxophonist, Composer

The first composer–arranger of consequence in the history of jazz, Donald Matthew Redman was born in Piedmont, West Virginia, on July 29, 1900. He was a child prodigy who played trumpet at the age of three, joined a band at six, and later studied harmony, theory, and composition at the Boston and Detroit conservatories. In 1924 he joined Fletcher Henderson's band as lead saxophonist and staff arranger, and in 1928 became leader of McKinney's Cotton Pickers. He remained leader of the band for four years working with jazz legends such as Fats Waller, Louis Armstrong, Benny Carter, and Coleman Hawkins. Redman was known throughout the

1920s as a brilliant instrumentalist on several kinds of saxophones. He also made many records with Bessie Smith, Louis Armstrong, and other top-ranking jazz artists.

During most of the 1930s Redman led his own band, which was regarded as one of the leading black orchestras of the day and the first to play a sponsored radio series. He also wrote for many other prominent bands, black and white, and was considered the first to write jazz for big band.

In 1951 Redman became musical director for Pearl Bailey. From 1954 to 1955 he appeared in a small acting role in *House of Flowers* on Broadway. He continued to arrange and record until his death in 1964.

Jimmy Reed (1925–1976)
Singer, Guitarist

Jimmy Reed was born Mathis James Reed on September 6, 1925, in Dunleith, Mississippi. He and his childhood friend Eddie Taylor taught themselves how to play the guitar and the harmonica. After spending time in the Navy, Reed returned to Chicago and decided to pursue a career playing the guitar. In 1953, after being rejected by Leonard Chess of Chess Records, Reed was able to interest the newly formed record label Vee Jay in his music, and he and Eddie Taylor began their career in earnest. Between 1955 and 1961 Reed placed eighteen singles on the *Billboard* rhythm and blues chart.

Reed was known for his simple and straightforward style and the ease of a listener in understanding the words. Some say he distilled the essence of the blues. Some of his best known recordings are "Baby, What You Want Me to Do," "Bright Lights," "Big City," "Honest I Do," "You Don't Have to Go," "Going to New York," "Ain't That Lovin You Baby", and "Big Boss Man." Reed worked sporadically in the 1970s and died on August 29, 1976.

Max Roach (1924–2007)
Percussionist, Composer

Maxwell Lemuel Roach was born on January 10, 1924, in Newland, North Carolina. As one of the key figures in the development of modern jazz, Roach was in the first group to play bebop on 52nd Street in New York, led by Dizzy Gillespie from 1943 to 1944, and he later worked with Charlie Parker's finest group from 1947 to 1948. In 1954 he joined the brilliant young trumpeter Clifford Brown as coleader of the Clifford Brown–Max Roach Quintet. After Brown's untimely death in a car crash, Roach began to lead his own groups of various sizes and instrumentation (including interesting work with solo and choral voices, an all-percussion band, and a jazz quartet combined with a string quartet). His many compositions include *We Insist! Freedom Now*. This suite, written with singer Abbey Lincoln (who was his wife at the time), was one of the first jazz works with a strong and direct political and social thrust.

A phenomenally gifted musician with a matchless percussion technique, Roach developed the drum solo to new heights of structural refinement; he has been an influence on every drummer to come along since the 1940s. Beginning in 1972 Roach was a professor of music at the University of Massachusetts; in 1988 he became the first jazz artist to receive a MacArthur Fellowship—the most prestigious (and lucrative) award in the world of arts and letters. Roach continued as a professor until the mid-1990s while taking on various musical projects. One such project was *To the Max*, which contained a variety of his techniques, concertos for drum solos, and other works. He traveled with his quartet into the twenty-first century. Roach died on August 16, 2007.

"Sonny" Rollins (1930–)
Saxophonist, Bandleader

Theodore Walter "Sonny" Rollins was born on September 7, 1930, in New York City. He did not find his passion in music until he learned to play the saxophone in 1944. Rollins made his recording debut at nineteen with the song "Audubon," in such fast company as J. J. Johnson and Bud Powell. Distinctively personal from the start, his style developed through work with Thelonious Monk, Powell, Art Blakely, and Miles Davis. In 1955 he joined the Clifford Brown–Max Roach Quintet. Later that year he recorded *Saxophone Colossus,* which featured thematic improvisations. With a piano-less trio he recorded *Way Out West,* focusing on show tunes (1957), and *Freedom Suite,* regarding the lack of integration in America (1958).

In 1959 Rollins took two years off from active playing to study and practice. When he reappeared at the helm of his own quartet in 1961, he surprised even those who knew the quality of his work with the power and conviction of his playing. In 1972 he was named a Guggenheim fellow, in 2002 he won a Grammy for his album *This Is What I Do,* and in 2006 he received another Grammy for his performance of the song "Without a Song."

Though briefly overshadowed by John Coltrane, Rollins has been the unchallenged master of modern jazz tenor saxophone, with a sound and style completely his own. He often draws on his West Indian heritage for melodic and rhythmic inspiration. He is one of the undisputed masters of extended improvisation, often playing all by himself as his group "lays out" in amazement—a feeling shared by his listeners. Among many other honors he was awarded the Medal of Arts from President Barack Obama on March 2, 2011. His album *Road Show, Volume 2* was released in the fall of 2011.

Jimmy Rushing (c. 1901–1972)
Singer

James Andrew Rushing was born on August 26, 1901 (some sources indicate 1902 or 1903), in Oklahoma City, Oklahoma. He played piano and violin as a boy, but he entered music professionally as a singer in the after-hours world of California in 1925. After that, Rushing was linked with several leading bands and musicians: Walter Page from 1927 to 1928; Benny Moten in 1929; and from 1936 to 1949 he was a mainstay of the famed Count Basie Band.

Rushing formed his own small group when he left Basie and in the ensuing years worked most often as a "single." Following the revival of the blues in the mid-1950s, Rushing regained widespread popularity.

His nightclub and festival engagements were always successful, and his world tours, on his own and also with Benny Goodman, earned him critical acclaim and commercial success. His style has endured across four decades of jazz largely due to its great warmth, a sure, firm melodic line, and a swinging use of rhythm. Rushing died of leukemia on June 8, 1972. The song "Mister Five by Five," written in tribute to Rushing, is an apt physical description of this singer, who was one of the greatest male jazz and blues singers.

Bessie Smith (1894–1937)
Singer

Bessie Elizabeth Smith was born on April 5, 1894, in Chattanooga, Tennessee. They called her "The Empress of the Blues," and she had no peers. Her magnificent voice, dramatic sense, clarity of diction, and incomparable timing and phrasing set her apart from the competition and made her appeal to lovers of both jazz and blues. Her first record, "Down Hearted Blues," sold more than a million copies in 1923, when only Enrico Caruso and Paul Whiteman were racking up those kind of figures.

By then, Bessie Smith had been singing professionally for fifteen years, but records by black singers had only been made since 1920, and usually by less earthy singers. She already had a large following and had appeared in big shows, so the timing was right—not least for Columbia Records, which she pulled out of the red. Before long she was backed by the best jazz players, including Louis Armstrong; and by 1925 she starred in her own touring show, which traveled in a private Pullman car. By 1927 she was the highest paid black artist in the world, and in 1929 she made a short film, *St. Louis Blues,* that captures for posterity some of her magnetism as a stage performer. But tastes in music were changing rapidly, and though Smith added more popular songs to her repertoire and moved with the times, the Depression nearly killed the jazz and blues record business. In 1931 Columbia dropped her, and she was soon touring as a "single."

John Hammond brought her back to the studios in 1933. Her records were wonderful, her singing as powerful and swinging as ever, but these recordings didn't sell and turned out to be her last. She still found plenty of work on the traveling circuit, but the money was not what it had been in the 1920s. On the road early one morning on September 26, 1937, in Mississippi, Smith was fatally injured in a collision. In 1968 Columbia reissued all of her records, then did so again on compact disc in the 1990s, with very positive results.

Esperanza Spalding (1984–)
Bassist, Singer, Composer

Esperanza Spalding was born on October 18, 1984, in Portland, Oregon. She was homeschooled much of her early years and upon leaving high school earned a GED. At fifteen she encountered the acoustic bass and chose it as her instrument. She studied at Portland State University and earned her B.A. degree in three years and was hired as an instructor in the Berklee College of Music in Boston in 2005.

Spalding tours extensively with artists such as Regina Carter, Dave Samuels, and Patti Austin. She also heads her own trio. Her first release was on a Barcelona–based imprint in 2006 entitled *Juno,* which was followed by her first album release in 2008 entitled *Esperanza.* It remained on contemporary jazz charts for seventy weeks. That album was followed by *Chamber Music Society,* released in 2010. Esperanza gained world attention when President Barack Obama asked her in 2009 to play at the Peace Prize Ceremony and the Nobel Peace Prize Concert. Spalding, who has a Brazilian and Afro-Cuban style, plays the gamut of genres from blues, funk, hip-hop, and pop fusion. She won a Grammy for best new artist at the 53rd Grammy Awards in 2011 and is the first jazz artist to win this award.

Billy Strayhorn (1915–1967)
Composer, Arranger, Pianist

William Thomas Strayhorn was born in Dayton, Ohio, on November 29, 1915, and was raised in Pittsburgh, Pennsylvania. Early on he showed an unusually sophisticated gift for writing both music and lyrics. While still in his teens he wrote "Lushlife," which was one of several songs he showed to Duke Ellington in 1938. Ellington recorded Strayhorn's song "Something to Live For"; soon after, Strayhorn, who was also a gifted pianist, joined the Ellington entourage in New York. Ellington first thought of him as a lyricist (something he was always looking for) but soon found out that Strayhorn also had a knack for arranging.

Before long the two had established a working relationship that remains unique in the history of music—a collaboration so close that they were often unsure of who had written which part of a given composition. Each man continued to work on his own; however, among the Strayhorn-signed contributions to Ellington's repertoire in the 1940s, there were standouts such as "Take the A Train," "Passion Flower," "Chelsea Bridge," and "Rain Check."

Self-effacing and modest to a fault, Strayhorn stayed out of the limelight. But musicians and serious Ellington fans knew just how much he contributed to the band's work during his lifetime. Strayhorn's death on May 31, 1967, inspired Ellington's album *And His Mother Called Him Bill.*

Art Tatum (1909–1956)

Pianist

Considered a wizard on the keyboard, Arthur Tatum Jr. was born on October 13, 1909, in Toledo, Ohio. Nearly blind from birth, he was noted for the musical imagination he brought to life by his exceptional facility. Harmonically, he matched the boppers in sophistication—young Charlie Parker took a job as dishwasher in a club where Tatum worked so he could hear him every night. Rhythmically, he anticipated modern jazz developments and could play rings around anyone, regardless of their instrument.

Blind in one eye and partially sighted in the other, Tatum began his professional career in 1932 as accompanist to singer Adelaide Hall. One year later he made his first recording, which included "Tiger Rag." By 1943 his reputation was on a high note and he formed a quartet, which became very popular, that included Slam Stewart, Tiny Grimes, and Everett Barksdale. Tatum did a series of solo performance beginning in 1953 that were recognized and considered examples of his best work.

Though Tatum enjoyed a full career, recording prolifically—mostly as a soloist but also as leader of a trio (with electric guitar and bass, patterned on Nat King Cole's)—his career came a bit too soon to benefit from the acceptance that later came to jazz as a concert hall music. The concert hall, in which he rarely had the chance to perform, was Tatum's ideal medium. As it was, he often played "after hours" for the edification of fellow musicians, as a challenger to newer players, and to better his own skills, setting seemingly impossible tempos or picking tunes with the toughest "changes." Tatum died of uremia on November 4, 1956.

Billy Taylor (1921–2010)

Pianist, Composer, Educator

Few musicians have done more to promote jazz than William "Billy" Taylor Jr., who was born in Greenville, North Carolina, on July 24, 1921. Taylor was instrumental in attaining proper respect and recognition for African American music. In the 1950s he began contributing articles to major magazines like *Esquire,* and he appeared on what was then known as "educational" television. He was at that time already well established as a pianist on the New York scene, having arrived in the Big Apple shortly after graduating from Virginia State College in 1942. Taylor became a regular on Swing Street (52nd Street in Manhattan), and later he was the house pianist at Birdland. He started leading his own trios in 1951.

Taylor earned a doctorate in music education from the University of Massachusetts in 1975; his dissertation was later published as *Jazz Piano: History and Development,* and became the text for a course offered on National Public Radio (NPR). Taylor led an eleven-piece band for television's *David Frost Show* from 1969 to 1972, was founder and director of the program *Jazz Alive* on NPR, and was a regular on CBS-TV's *Sunday Morning.* He has served on several boards and panels, notably the prestigious National Council on the Arts.

Taylor received numerous awards including the National Medal of Arts in 1992; in 2001 he was honored with the Jazz Living Legend Award from the American Society of Composers, Authors and Publishers, and he was elected to the Hall of Fame for the International Association for Jazz Education. Taylor died on December 28, 2010.

Koko Taylor (1928–2009)

Singer, Songwriter

Born Cora Walton on September 28, 1928, in Bartlett, Tennessee, Koko Taylor became one of the few blues women who reached star status in a field dominated by men. Taylor lost her mother at four years old and was raised by her father along with five siblings in a poor environment. She was nicknamed Koko because of her love of chocolate. During her youth, Taylor was exposed to gospel music and the blues she heard on the radio, such as Bessie Smith, Memphis Minnie, and Muddy Waters. Known as the "Queen of the Chicago Blues," Taylor moved to Chicago in her twenties with her fiancé, and worked as a maid during the day, while they both visited blues clubs at night.

In 1963 Taylor was approached by Willie Dixon, who recorded several singles for her and secured her a contract with Chess Records. Among the recordings was Taylor's famous hit "Wang Dang Doodle," which secured her place as a blues singer. In 1975 Taylor performed at the Ann Arbor Jazz Festival, which was released as an album and brought Taylor an even larger audience and following. She received the W. C. Handy Award for best contemporary female artist in 1980. Taylor earned a Grammy nomination for the album *I Got What It Takes* and won her first Grammy in 1984.

Taylor continued to perform after the loss of her husband in 1989. Her comeback at the Chicago Blues Festival began performances of up to one hundred dates a year. In 1993 she recorded *A Force of Nature* and in 2000 *Royal Blue*. Taylor died on May 19, 2009, due to complications from surgery.

McCoy Tyner (1938–)
Pianist, Composer, Bandleader

Alfred McCoy Tyner was born on December 11, 1938, in Philadelphia, Pennsylvania. He attended the Granoff School of Music and later joined the Art Farmer and Benny Golson Jazztet. In 1955 Tyner, just seventeen years old, joined the John Coltrane quartet. He became an intricate part of the quartet and played on classic recordings such as *Live at the Village Vanguard* and *A Love Supreme*. On his own, Tyner pursued the roles of composer and bandleader with his piano trio, which included Avery Sharpe and Aaron Scott.

He won a Grammy nomination in 1972 for his album *Sahara*. Tyner and his trio continued to be in demand well into the 1990s; he joined with artists such as Burt Bacharach in 1996 and Stanley Clarke in 1998. In 2005 he began a project with the Blue Note in New York City.

Tyner continues to compose and perform and has received numerous awards, including Grammy Awards in 1994, 1995 and 2004, a Jazz Master Award from the National Endowment of the Arts in 2002, and a Presidential Merit Award from the Grammy Foundation in 2008.

Sarah Vaughan (1924–1990)
Singer

Sarah Lois Vaughan was born on March 27, 1924, in Newark, New Jersey. Vaughan was a contralto with a range of three octaves; she had a voice of such beauty, range, and power, her ear so sure, her musicality so rare that she could have become an opera star. Fortunately for jazz lovers, she went the way of jazz and brought joy to her listeners from the time she started singing professionally in 1943.

Vaughan had begun singing and accompanying the choir on piano in church in her native Newark, and she had sung pop songs at high school parties when, on a dare, she entered the Wednesday night amateur contest at Harlem's famed Apollo Theater. Billy Eckstine happened to be backstage, and he ran out front as soon as he heard her voice and later recommended Vaughan to his boss, bandleader Earl Hines. Hines came, heard her sing, and hired her—and she did win the amateur contest, which meant a week's work at the Apollo. Charlie "Bird" Parker and Dizzy Gillespie were both in the Hines band at the time, although they and Vaughan left Hines when Eckstine decided to start his own band. By 1945 Vaughan had made her first records under her own name, which included the classic "Lover Man," and she was the only singer to record with Bird and Dizzy together.

A year later she started her solo career. Though she had some big pop hits during her long and rich career, she never strayed from jazz for long. Her records with jazz artist greats Count Basie, Roy Haynes, Benny Carter, Clifford Brown, and Gerald Wilson in the late 1950s remain classics as well as her recording with Miles Davis. Incredibly, as she got older, she got better, losing none of her amazing top range and adding to the bottom range, while her mastery of interpretation continued to improve. Her fans called her "The Divine One." Her best known songs include "It's Magic," "Broken-hearted Melody," "Misty," and "Send in the Clowns." Vaughan died on April 3, 1990, in Los Angeles, California.

T-Bone Walker (1910–1975)
Singer, Guitarist

Aaron Thibeaux "T-Bone" Walker was born on May 28, 1910, in Linden, Texas. Walker's mother moved the family to Dallas when his father left to avoid working in the fields and the strict Christian rules of her family. Walker worked for a time as Blind Lemon Jefferson's guide but later joined Dr. Breeding's medicine show in 1925 and performed as a dancer and banjo player. Under the name Oak Cliff T-Bone (T-Bone a corruption of his middle name) he made his first two recordings in 1929 and later played with Fats Waller and Louis Armstrong. In 1939 Walker recorded his first song on the electric guitar. When he recorded the "T-Bone Blues," his reputation as an excellent singer and guitarist was secure. He went solo in 1940 and recorded "Mean Old World" and "I Got a Break, Baby." His performances included playing the guitar behind his head while doing the splits and playing the guitar with his teeth (which was copied by the artists Chuck Berry and Jimi Hendrix).

Walker was considered one of the key originators of the Texas and California blues. He continued to perform for large crowds and recorded classics such as "Call It Stormy Monday," "T-Bone Shuffle," "Bobby Sox Blues", and "Long Skirt Baby Blues." In the 1950s Walker had health issues as the result of a car accident but continued to record for Atlantic Records. In 1970 he was awarded a Grammy for his album *Good Feeling,* which he recorded in France. He died on March 16, 1975.

Thomas "Fats" Waller (1904–1943)
Composer, Pianist, Singer, Bandleader

Weighing in at over three hundred pounds and standing more than six feet tall, Thomas Wright Waller, a preacher's son, was born in Greenwich Village, New York, on May 21, 1904, and came by his nickname naturally. He was, as one of his many good friends said, "all music." His father wanted him to follow in his footsteps, but Fats liked the good times that came with playing the piano well, which he could do almost from the start. At fifteen he turned professional, backing singers in Harlem clubs and playing piano for silent movies at the Lincoln Theater. He played accompanist for Alberta Hunter and Bessie Smith. Wherever he went, people loved him, and he loved to spread joy. Few pianists have been able to match his terrific beat. He was also a master of the stride piano style. He loved to play Bach, especially on the organ, and he was the first to play the organ as a jazz instrument. In 1932 world-famous Marcel Dupré invited Fats to play the organ at the Notre Dame Cathedral in Paris.

Waller's talent for writing songs soon became evident. His first and biggest hit was "Ain't Misbehavin'" in 1929; others include "Honeysuckle Rose," "Blue Turning Gray Over You," and "The Jitterbug Waltz." He also wrote "London Suite" for solo piano, and the score for the Broadway hit *Hot Chocolate.*

Waller was a great performer on the new medium of the 1920s—the radio. He had a constant line of patter to go along with his great piano and carefree singing. He also made it to Hollywood. His finest medium, however, was recorded music. His big break came in 1934 while playing at a party given by George Gershwin. With his contagious rhythms and his ability to delight the crowd, he was offered a contract by an executive from Victor Records who was at the party. With his small group and the occasional big band, he cut more than five hundred sides between 1934 and his untimely death at thirty-nine in 1943. His personality came across on records, and no matter how trite the tune, he turned it into a jazz gem. Unfortunately, Waller suffered from ill health in the midst of a successful and productive career, partly due to his huge appetite and excessive drinking. He had just finished filming *Stormy Weather,* and his first complete Broadway musical was becoming a hit, when he died of pneumonia on December 15, 1943.

Dinah Washington (1924–1963)
Singer

Dinah Washington, born Ruth Lee Jones on August 29, 1924, in Tuscaloosa, Alabama, had a style that defied categorization, but it is seen as laying the groundwork for numerous rhythm and blues and jazz artists. Like many black singers, Washington got her start singing gospel—in her case, at St. Luke's Baptist Church on Chicago's South Side. She toured churches with her mother, playing the piano and singing solos, until opportunity beckoned in the form of an amateur talent contest at Chicago's Regal Theater. Her triumphant performance there led to shows at local nightclubs, and in 1943 the nineteen-year-old singer successfully auditioned for a slot in Lionel Hampton's band. She was soon discovered by composer and critic Leonard Feather, and together Washington and Feather created several chart toppers, including "Baby Get Lost," "Salty Papa Blues," "Evil Gal Blues," and "Homeward Bound." She gained legendary status with "What a Difference a Day Makes" and "Unforgettable."

Washington proved to be such a versatile artist that she was acclaimed by blues, jazz, gospel, pop, and rhythm and blues audiences alike. Aretha Franklin dedicated one of her early albums to Washington, labeling it simply "Unforgettable." Washington died of an overdose of alcohol and pills on December 14, 1963, in Detroit.

Muddy Waters (1915–1983)
Guitarist, Harmonica Player, Singer

Muddy Waters, who was born McKinley Morganfield on April 4, 1915, in Fork, Mississippi, grew up in Clarksdale on Stovall's Plantation. Waters was raised by his grandmothers after his mother died in 1918. He taught himself how to play the harmonica and later took up the guitar by the age of seventeen. He began running a juke joint and performing concerts. In 1941 Alan Lomax from the Library of Congress went to Stovall to record country and blues musicians and recorded Waters. As a result, the sessions were released in 1942 as *Down On Stovall's Plantation.* Waters moved to Chicago in 1943 to pursue a professional career. After working as a side man for Chess Records, Waters recorded "I Feel Like Going Home" in 1948, which became his first national hit on the rhythm and blues charts.

In the 1950s Waters was recording with blues artists Little Walter Jacobs, Jimmy Rogers, Elgin Evans, Otis Spann, and Big Crawford making them the hottest group at the time. Waters and his band released "I'm Your Hoochie Coochie Man," "Got My Mojo Working," "Tiger in Your Tank," and "Mannish Boy." As the members of the band branched out on their own, Waters and his country blues on the electric guitar continued to gain attention, including young white British groups such as Eric Clapton and Mike Bloomfield.

Waters played at Carnegie Hall and the New Port Jazz Festival in 1960, and in the 1970s established the Muddy Waters Production Company. Waters won six Grammy Awards between 1971 and 1979, and he was inducted into the Rock and Roll Hall of Fame in 1987 and the Blues Foundation Hall of Fame in 1980. Muddy Waters died in his sleep from heart failure on April 30, 1983.

Ben Webster (1909–1973)
Saxophonist

Born in Kansas City, Missouri, on March 27, 1909, Benjamin Francis Love Webster as a teenager decided on the saxophone as his instrument of choice after having played the piano. He was a member of the family band led by Lester Young's father. Webster moved to New York in 1931 and made a name for himself as a disciple of Coleman Hawkins. He played for various bands, including Fletcher Henderson, Cab Calloway, and Benny Carter, and he joined Duke Ellington's Band from 1940 to 1943.

In the 1950s Webster moved to the West Coast and recorded with artists such as Billie Holiday and Coleman Hawkins. Webster left for his first European trip in 1965 and decided to stay due to the lack of opportunities in the United States. He settled in Copenhagen, continuing to play and perfect his music until his death on September 20, 1973.

Mary Lou Williams (1910–1981)
Pianist, Composer, Arranger

Most women who have achieved fame in jazz have been singers, including Bessie Smith and Betty Carter. A singular exception to this rule was Mary Lou Williams, dubbed the "First Lady of Jazz." Born in Atlanta, Georgia, on May 8, 1910, and raised in Pittsburgh, Pennsylvania, Mary Elfrieda Scruggs had already performed in public at the age of six and was a professional by thirteen. Three years later she married saxophonist John Williams, with whom she made her record debut. When he joined Andy Kirk's band she took over the group. Soon she was writing arrangements for Kirk, and in 1931 she became the band's pianist and musical director.

Though she also wrote for Benny Goodman, Tommy Dorsey, and Earl Hines, among other bands, she stayed with Kirk until 1942 helping to make the band one of the swing era's best. She also served as staff arranger for Duke Ellington's band and contributed some fifteen works to the group. Settling in New York, she led her own groups (sometimes all female) and began to compose longer works, including the *Zodiac Suite,* performed at Town Hall in 1946. A champion of modern jazz, she gave advice and counsel to such rising stars as Dizzy Gillespie and Thelonious Monk.

Williams lived in England and France from 1952 to 1954. When she returned home she retired from music for three years, but was coaxed out by Gillespie. Resuming her career, she toured widely, wrote several religious works (including a jazz mass performed at St. Patrick's Cathedral), ran her own record label from 1955 to 1963, and in 1977 she became artist in residence and teacher of jazz history and performance at Duke University, a position she held until her death on May 28, 1981. As pianist, composer, and arranger, Mary Lou Williams ranks with the very best as she adapted her style to the many styles of the jazz era.

"Sonny Boy" Williamson (1899–1965)
Singer, Harmonica Player

"Sonny Boy" Williamson, who stands as the ultimate blues legend, was born Aleck Ford "Rice" Miller on December 5, 1899, in Glendora, Mississippi. In the 1930s Miller was traveling and performing throughout the Delta under the name of Little Boy Blue, and by 1940 he was appearing on *King Biscuit Time*—the first live blues radio show. The sponsor of the show had Little Boy Blue pose as the Chicago Blues star John Lee "Sonny Boy" Williamson. The plan worked for the show, but after the real Chicago-born "Sonny Boy" Williamson was murdered in 1948, Miller took the name as the new, and only "Sonny Boy" Williamson. Aleck Ford Miller thus came to be known as Sonny Boy Williamson, aka Sonny Boy Williamson II, and aka Sonny Boy Williams, songwriter, blues harmonica player, and singer.

It was not until the period between 1951 and 1954 that Williamson was able to record his first single "Eyesight to the Blind," which was a hit; and it was not until 1955 that he recorded his first session for *Chess Records*, "Don't Start Me Talkin." Williamson had his first European tour in 1963 and had great success playing concert tours with British blues-rock groups such as the Yardbirds and the Animals, which were released as live albums. After two years he returned to the United States and later died of a heart attack in Helena, Arkansas, on May 25, 1965. Williamson was inducted into the Blues Hall of Fame in 1980.

Nancy Wilson (1937–)
Singer

Nancy Wilson was born in Chillicothe, Ohio, on February 20, 1937. Her interest in singing was showcased in performances for family and at church, and her influences were Billy Eckstine, Nat "King" Cole, Ruth Brown, and LaVerne Baker. After a short time in college she began to pursue her music career by spending three years touring with the Rusty Byrant's Carolyn Club Band. Wilson moved to New York in 1959. Within weeks she had secured the manager of her choice, John Levy, and the record label of her choice, Capital Records; and she had recorded four songs, including "Guess Who I Saw Today?" and "Sometimes I'm Happy." Wilson's recordings were so successful that between 1960 and 1962 Capital Records released five more of her albums.

Wilson's career has contained variety as she has appeared on numerous variety shows and popular television programs; she also hosted her own show, *The Nancy Wilson Show,* which won her an Emmy in 1975. As the industry changed she continued to record and in 1995 became the host for the National Public Radio Jazz Profiles series. Wilson completed a Christmas album in the 1990s and channeled the proceeds to MCG Jazz, which helps to support youth education programs for minorities.

Wilson has been honored with the 2005 NAACP Image Award, three Grammy Awards, a Star on the Hollywood Walk of Fame, the 2005 Trumpet Award for African American Achievement, the Oprah Winfrey's Legends Award, and honorary doctorates. Wilson has retired from touring but continues to perform for selected gatherings or causes. Although Wilson is clearly a jazz singer, her career includes pop, ballads, show tunes, and cabaret, done in her own unique and engaging style.

Lester "Prez" Young (1909–1959)
Saxophonist

Born August 27, 1909, in Woodville, Mississippi, Lester Willis Young is the one who dubbed Billie Holiday "Lady Day" when both were with Count Basie, and it was Lady Day in turn who christened Lester Young "President" (later shortened to "Prez").

As a youth, Young was instructed by his father on the trumpet, violin, saxophone, and drums. His family moved to New Orleans and at thirteen he traveled on the carnival circuit in the Midwest with his musical family, choosing to concentrate on the tenor saxophone. In the 1930s Young toured with King Oliver and Walter Page and spent a short time with Count Basie.

When Young took over Coleman Hawkins's chair in Fletcher Henderson's orchestra, he was criticized for not having the same style as his predecessor. As a result of this, he returned to Kansas City to play first with Andy Kirk, and then with Count Basie from 1936 to 1940. During the Basie years Young surpassed Hawkins as the vital influence on the tenor saxophone. Hardly a tenor man from the mid-1940s through the 1950s achieved prominence without building on the foundations laid by Lester Young.

Young entered the Army in 1944 and suffered racial indignities that left a traumatic mark on his life. Once returning to civilian life he continued to work in small bands and toured with the Jazz at the Philharmonic units. Young suffered a complete breakdown in 1955 but made a comeback the next year. He died within hours of returning from a long engagement in Paris. Young's death on March 15, 1959, was the result of mental problems and alcoholism.

BIOGRAPHIES: POPULAR, FUNK, AND GOSPEL MUSIC

Yolanda Adams (1961–)
Gospel Singer

 Yolanda Adams was born October 27, 1961, in Houston, Texas, and had many musical influences, including gospel music. Her commitment to music resulted in teaching elementary school during the week and singing on the weekends. As a result of her solo as a part of a Southeast Inspiration Choir's performance, Thomas Whitfield collaborated with Adams and produced the gospel album *Just as I Am* in 1988. Between 1990 and 1997 Adams released four successful albums and recorded with such gospel greats as Albertina Walker. Adams later signed with the label Elecktra, which resulted in the album *Mountain High Valley Law* in 1999, which reached double platinum and included the crossover hit "Open My Heart." This song reached number one on the gospel charts and number ten on the R&B charts, which resulted in some backlash regarding whether the inference in the lyrics was sacred or secular.

After a brief hiatus Adams released a new album in 2005 with Atlantic Records. Adams's combination of traditional gospel with jazz and blues has created a body of work that has earned her numerous awards, including four Grammy Awards, seven NAACP Image Awards, three BET Awards, and the Stellar Awards Hall of Fame in 2003. She has performed with numerous other artists and has appeared on various television shows. In 2007 she became the host of her own morning show with TV One and she continues to inspire and inform others about faith and hope through her music.

Vanessa Bell Armstrong (1953–)
Gospel Singer

Vanessa Bell Armstrong was born October 2, 1953, in Detroit, Michigan. While still a youth Armstrong was mentored by her church choir director, Mattie Moss Clark, in 1966. Armstrong began performing with gospel greats such as the Mighty Clouds of Joy and the Winans Family and was often compared with Aretha Franklin, also of Detroit.

Armstrong's debut album was released in 1984, *Peace Be Still,* which took her to the top of gospel charts and earned her a recording contract with R&B label Jive Records. Armstrong has been successful in not only music, but she also has done television and film. Her records continue to succeed as she combines gospel with contemporary urban music. Her releases include the single "You Bring Out the Best In Me" (1987), and albums *Chosen* (1991), *Something on the Inside* (1993), *The Secret Is Out* (1995), and the acclaimed live record *Desire of My Heart* (1998), which she co-produced.

Armstrong has received some criticism for not staying with traditional gospel themes. In 2001 she released the album *Brand New Day,* which focuses on more traditional themes, while in 2007 she returned to her unique offering of gospel and contemporary urban music with the release of *Walking Miracle.* Armstrong was presented with a lifetime achievement award from Gospel Superfest in 2004.

Nicholas Ashford (1943–2011) and Valerie Simpson (1948–)
Singers, Songwriters

One of the most enduring songwriting teams to emerge from Motown has been Nicholas Ashford and Valerie Simpson who have created numerous hits and have written chart toppers for artists from Ray Charles to Diana Ross.

Nicky Ashford was born in Fairfield, South Carolina, on May 14, 1943, and Valerie Simpson was born in the Bronx section of New York City on August 26, 1948. The two met in the early 1960s while singing in the same choir at Harlem's White Rock Baptist Church. With Ashford's gift for lyrics and Simpson's exceptional gospel piano and compositional skills, the two began to write for the staff of Scepter Records in 1964. Two years later, their song "Let's Go Get Stoned" became a hit for Ray Charles.

In 1962 Ashford and Simpson joined Motown's Jobete Music where they wrote and produced hit songs for Marvin Gaye and Tammi Terrell, including "Ain't Nothing Like the Real Thing," "Good Loving Ain't Easy to Come By," and "Onion Song." Next they worked with Diana Ross, who had just set out to establish a solo career, producing such hits as "Remember Me," "Reach Out (and Touch Somebody's Hand)," and an updated version of "Ain't No Mountain High Enough."

Ashford and Simpson's success as songwriters led them to release their own solo recording *Exposed* in 1971. After signing with Warner Brothers in 1973, they recorded a number of hit albums: *Is It Still Good to Ya* (1978), *Stay Free* (1979), *A Musical Affair* (1980), and their biggest seller, *Solid* (1985), which hit number twelve on pop charts.

After retiring from recording in the late 1980s, Ashford and Simpson finally returned to performing and launched their own label, Hopsack & Silk, in 1996. They subsequently released the album *Been Found,* in collaboration with Maya Angelou. Ashford and Simpson's music continues to be a part of the airways reaching fans from generations new and old school.

Anita Baker (1958–)

Singer

Anita Baker was born on January 26, 1958, in Toledo, Ohio, and was raised in Detroit, Michi-

gan in a single-parent, middle-class family. She first sang in storefront churches, where it was common for the congregation to improvise on various gospel themes. After graduating from Central High School, Baker sang in the Detroit soul/funk group Chapter 8. Although Chapter 8 recorded the album *I Just Want to Be Your Girl* for the Ariola label, the group's lack of commercial success caused it to disband, and for the next three years Baker worked as a receptionist in a law firm.

In 1982, after signing a contract with Beverly Glen, Baker moved to Los Angeles and recorded the critically acclaimed solo album *Songstress.* Following a legal battle with Glen, Baker signed with Elecktra and recorded her hit album *Rapture* in 1986. As the album's executive producer, Baker sought "a minimalist approach" featuring simple recording techniques that captured the natural sounds of her voice. The album's single "Sweet Love" brought Baker immediate crossover success. Baker's follow-up effort, the multi-platinum-selling *Giving You the Best I Got,* is considered one of the finest pop music albums of the 1990s. Her third effort, *Compositions,* recorded in 1990, features a number of notable back-up musicians, including Detroit jazz guitarist Earl Klugh. Albums that followed were *Rhythm of Love* in 1994 with the hit single "I Apologize," and *My Everything,* released in 2004.

One of the most sophisticated soul divas to emerge in the 1980s, Baker considers herself "a balladeer" dedicated to singing music rooted in the tradition of gospel and jazz. Inspired by her idols Mahalia Jackson, Sarah Vaughan, and Nancy Wilson, Baker brings audiences a sincere vocal style that defies commercial trends and electronic overproduction.

The winner of eight Grammys, two NAACP Image Awards, and two American Music Awards, Baker brings audiences music of eloquence and integrity that draws acclaim even from many of her contemporaries.

Chuck Berry (1926–)
Singer, Songwriter, Guitarist

Charles Anderson Edwards "Chuck" Berry, considered "the Father of Rock and Roll," was born on October 18, 1926, in St. Louis, Missouri, to a middle-class family. He and his family were active in church and he sang in the choir. As a teenager he was taught to play the acoustic guitar by jazz guitarist Ira Harris. After years of various jobs, a stint in prison for robbery, and getting married, Berry purchased his first electric guitar in 1950. He began performing and using his trademark move, the duck walk. Berry attributes the move to a desire to hide wrinkles on his only suit during a performance.

In 1955 Berry, while performing in Chicago, recorded "Maybellene" in hopes of getting a record contract. Berry later performed for Chess Records and, based on his song "Ida Red," they signed him. Berry reworked "Maybellene" before re-recording it and it reached number one on the R&B charts and crossed over to the pop charts reaching number five. "Maybellene" combined Chicago blues, country guitar, and storytelling and is considered the first true rock and roll song. Berry followed this hit with "Roll Over, Beethoven" (1956), "School Days" (1957), "Rock and Roll Music" (1957), "Sweet Little Sixteen" (1958), and "Johnny B. Goode" (1958). His hits continued in the 1960s with "Nadine" and "Dear Daddy" and in the 1970s with "Rock It."

Berry was the first guitar hero of rock and roll, and his 1950s jukebox hits remain some of the most imaginative poetic tales in the history of popular music. Berry was influenced by blues artists like T–Bone Walker and the picking styles of rockabilly and country musicians, and his solo guitar work brought the guitar to the forefront of R&B. His driving ensemble sound paved the way for the emergence of bands from the Beach Boys to the Rolling Stones. Berry was awarded the Grammy Lifetime Achievement Award in 1984, inducted into the Rock and Roll Hall of Fame in 1986, and received Kennedy Center Honors in 2000.

Mary J. Blige (1971–)
Singer, Songwriter, Actress

Mary Jane Blige, known as the "Queen of Hip-Hop Soul," was born on January 11, 1971, in Bronx, New York. She had a difficult childhood as her mother, who suffered with depression and alcoholism, struggled to care for Blige and her three siblings. Blige began to use drugs in response to her circumstances, quit school, and went to work. Her initial break as a singer came in 1989 when a tape she made was passed from her mother, to a friend, to R&B record executives Jeff Redd and Andre Harell of Uptown Records. As a result Blige began singing backup for artists at Uptown Records. In 1991, with the help of Sean "Puffy" Combs, Bilge cut her first solo album *What's the 411*, which went multiplatinum and it was followed in 1995 with *My Life*.

Blige moved to MCA Records after 1997 and continued to write many of her songs, which are based on her life experiences. Blige produced albums including *Mary* (1997), *No More Drama* (2001), *Reflections* (2006), and *Growing Pains* (2008). Blige has also made appearances on television series and in movies. In respect for the difficult journey that resulted in her sobriety, she started the first phase of her foundation to help other women, by opening the Mary J. Bilge Center for Women in 2003. Blige's awards include six Grammy Awards and seven multi-platinum records. She continues to write and produce her award-winning music, which is a combination of soul and hip-hop.

James Brown (1933–2006)
Singer, Bandleader

Born in Barnell, South Carolina, on May 3, 1933, James Brown moved to Augusta, Georgia, at the age of four. Although he was raised by various relatives in conditions of economic deprivation, Brown possessed an undaunted determination to succeed at an early age. When not picking cotton, washing cars, or shining shoes, he earned extra money by dancing on the streets and at amateur contests. In the evening, Brown watched shows by such bandleaders as Louis Jordan and Lucky Millinder.

 At fifteen Brown quit school to take the R&B group the Flames. During the same period he also sang and played drums with R&B bands. Brown toured extensively with the Flames, performing a wide range of popular material, including the Five Royales's "Baby Don't Do It," the Clovers's "One Mint Julep," and Hank Ballard and the Midnighters's hit "Annie Had a Baby."

In 1956 Brown's talents caught the attention of Syd Nathan, founder of King Records. In the same year, after signing with the Federal label, a subsidiary of King, Brown recorded "Please Please Please." After the Flames disbanded in 1957, Brown formed a new Flames ensemble, featuring former members of Little Richard's band. Back in the studio the following year, Brown recorded "Try Me," which became a Top-50 pop hit. On the road, Brown polished his stage act and singing ability, producing what became known as the "James Brown Sound."

After the release of *Out of Sight*, Brown's music exhibited a more polyrhythmic sound as evidenced in staccato horn bursts and contrapuntal bass lines. Each successive release explored increasingly new avenues of popular music. Brown's 1967 hit "Cold Sweat" and the 1968 release "I Got the Feeling" not only sent shock waves through the music industry, they served as textbooks of rhythm for thousands of aspiring musicians. In 1970 Brown disbanded the Flames and formed the JBs, featuring Bootsy Collins. The group produced a string of hits like "Super Bad" and "Sex Machine." Among Brown's other commercially successful efforts was the

1988 hit "Living in America," which appeared on the soundtrack of the film *Rocky IV.*

Brown produced *Star Time,* a boxed set of his hits, released in 1991. He continued to do selected appearances and received accolades for his enormous contribution to music all over the world. Brown's impact on American popular music has been of seismic proportion. His explosive onstage energy and intense gospel and R&B-based sound earned him numerous titles such as "The Godfather of Soul," "Mr. Dynamite," and "The Hardest Working Man in Show Business." During the 1960s and early 1970s, Brown's backup group emerged as one of the greatest soul bands in the history of modern music, one that served as a major force in the development of funk and fusion jazz. James Brown died on December 25, 2006, in Atlanta, Georgia, due to complications from pneumonia.

Shirley Caesar (1938–)
Gospel Singer

The leading gospel singer of her generation, Shirley Caesar was born in Durham, North Carolina, on October 13, 1938. One of twelve children born to gospel great "Big Jim" Caesar, Shirley sang in church choirs as a child. By age fourteen, Caesar was on the road as a professional gospel singer, touring the church circuit on weekends and during school vacations. Known as "Baby Shirley," Caesar joined the Caravans in 1958. Featured as an opening act in the show, Caesar worked the audience to a near fever pitch. When Inez Andrews left the Caravans in 1961, Caesar became the featured artist and provided crowds with powerful performances of such songs as "Comfort Me," "Running for Jesus," and "Sweeping Through the City."

After leaving the Caravans in 1966, Caesar formed her own group, the Shirley Caesar Singers. Her sheer energy and pugnacious spirit made her one of the reigning queens of modern gospel. Her first album, *I'll Go,* remains one of her most critically acclaimed. In 1969 she released a ten-minute sermonette with the St. Louis

Choir, which earned her a gold record. In 1971 Caesar earned her first Grammy for best soul gospel performance for the song "Put Your Hand in the Hand of the Man from Galilee." After winning the first Grammy as a black woman since Mahalia Jackson, Caesar went on to earn six more Grammys, eight Dove Awards, and induction into the Gospel Hall of Fame in 1982.

Caesar has performed on Broadway in several successful plays, including *Mama I Want to Sing and Sing!* She was elected to the city council of Durham, North Carolina, with the goal of providing housing and caring for the poor and elderly. She continues to perform up to 150 concerts a year and records with T. D. Jakes, a popular and charismatic minister.

Mariah Carey (1970–)
Singer, Songwriter, Producer, Actress

 Carey was born on March 27, 1970, in Long Island, New York. Her father was an engineer and her mother was a vocal coach who had been a soloist with the New York City Opera. In 1987 Carey moved to New York to pursue her singing career. She was introduced to Columbia/Sony's music president and CEO Tommy Mottola, who heard her recordings and offered her a contract. Carey was married to Mottola from 1993 to 1998.

Carey's 1990 debut album *Mariah Carey*, which produced four number-one singles, began her long run of number-one records. Between 1991 and 2008 Carey earned fourteen more number-one hits, including "Vision of Love," "Love Takes Time," "Somebody," "I Don't Wanna Cry," "Emotions," "I'll Be There," "Dream Lover," "Hero," "Fantasy," "One Sweet Day," "Always Be My Baby," "Honey," "My All," "Heartbreaker," "Thank God I Found You," "We Belong Together," "Don't Forget about Us," and "Touch My Body." Carey, who wrote and produced most of her songs, had some of the biggest opening weeks with her albums and surpassed Elvis Presley with number-one hits.

Projects in the film industry were also apart of Carey's production, but she did not earn the type of success that her records did. She appeared in *Glitter* (2001), *Tennessee* (2008), *Don't Mess with the Zohan* (2008), and *Precious* (2009).

Carey, with her five octave range voice, holds the title as the third best-selling female artist in the music industry. She also has the title for the most number-one records ever recorded by any artist with the exception of the Beatles. Carey has received numerous awards for her music, including Grammy Awards for best vocal performances, best R&B song, best female R&B vocal performance, and the World Music Award's best selling female artist of the millennium.

James Cleveland (1932–1991)
Gospel Singer, Pianist, Composer

Born on December 5, 1932, in Chicago, Illinois, James Cleveland first sang gospel under the direction of Thomas Dorsey at the Pilgrim Baptist Church. Inspired by the keyboard talents of gospel singer Roberta Martin, Cleveland later began to study piano. In 1951 Cleveland joined the Gospelaires, a trio that cut several sides for the Apollo label. With the Caravans, Cleveland arranged and performed on two hits: "The Solid Rock" and an up-tempo reworking of the song "Old Time Religion."

By the mid-1950s Cleveland's original compositions had found their way into the repertoires of numerous gospel groups, and he was performing with such artists as the Thorn Gospel Singers, Roberta Martin Singers, Mahalia Jackson, the Gospel Allstars, and the Meditation Singers. In 1960 Cleveland formed the Cleveland Singers, featuring organist and accompanist Billy Preston. The smash hit "Love of God," recorded with the Detroit-based Voices of Tabernacle, won Cleveland nationwide fame within the gospel community. Signing with the Savoy label, Cleveland and keyboardist Billy Preston released a long list of classic albums, including *Christ Is the Answer* and *Peace Be Still*. As a founder of the Gospel Workshop of America in 1968, Cleveland organized annual conventions that brought together thousands of gospel singers and songwriters. A year later he helped found the Southern California Community Choir.

In 1972 he was reunited with former piano understudy Aretha Franklin, who featured Cleveland as a guest artist on the album *Amazing Grace.* A recipient of the NAACP Image Award, Cleveland also acquired an honorary degree from Temple Baptist College. Although the commercial gospel trends of the 1980s caused a downturn in Cleveland's career, he continued to perform the gutsy blues-based sound that brought him recognition from listeners throughout the world.

Known by such titles as "King James" and the "Crown Prince," the Reverend James Cleveland emerged as a giant of the postwar gospel music scene. Likened to the vocal style of Louis Armstrong, Cleveland's raw bluesy growls and shouts appeared on more recordings than those of any other gospel singer of his generation. Cleveland died February 9, 1991, in Los Angeles, California.

George Clinton (1941–)
Singer, Songwriter, Bandleader

George Clinton was born on July 22, 1941, in Kannapolis, North Carolina. His family later moved to New Jersey where he began working at a barber shop. During this time he started a doo-wop quintet he called the Parliaments. After landing a deal with Reviolet Records the group released their first hit in 1967, "I Just Wanna Testify." When the record company went out of business the group's name remained in litigation so the group was renamed the Funkadelics in 1968. *Maggot Brain,* one of Funkadelics early albums, was a compliment to the psychedelic rock that had come on the scene. It was not until 1972 that the name Parliaments could be reclaimed. Clinton kept both names and used them for different record labels.

By the 1970s the Parliaments offered fantasy-oriented works such as "Flash Light," "Mothership Connection," and "Aqua Boogie." The Funkadelics catered to a more commercial theme with albums such as *One Nation under a Grove* and *Uncle Jam Wants You.* Out of this group Clinton helped bass player Bootsy Collins to become a funk master in his own right.

Clinton's Parliaments and Funkadelics released over forty singles on the R&B charts and had three platinum albums during the 1970s. With legal issues again surrounding the label, Clinton went solo in 1982 and called his group the P. Funk All Stars and released the album *Computer Games,* which had the hits "Atomic Dog" and "Loopzilla." The 1990s saw a renewed interest in Clinton and his music as rappers such as Tupac, Snoop Dog, and other artists sampled his music.

Clinton, the Father of P. Funk, which equates to "pure" funk, turned the concept of funk created by James Brown into an institution and an art form that has influenced the direction of musical styles from rap to rhythm and blues. Clinton has appeared on numerous albums with artists such as Missy Elliott, Dr. Dre, and Outkast. Clinton tried to gain rights to his songs from the 1960s and 1970s but lost because of an agreement he had signed in 1983. In 1997 Clinton was inducted into the Rock and Roll Hall of Fame along with fifteen other group members from the Parliaments and Funkadelics, and received an Image Award for lifetime achievement by the NAACP. Clinton continues to write and tour and has plans to release a new album.

Natalie Cole (1950–)
Singer

Natalie Cole was born on February 6, 1950, in Los Angeles, California, the second daughter of jazz pianist and pop music legend Nat "King" Cole. During the early 1970s Cole performed in nightclubs while pursuing a degree in child psychology at the University of Massachusetts. In 1975 she recorded her first album, *Inseparable,* at Curtis Mayfield's Curtom Studios. Her other albums include *Thankful* (1978), *I'm Ready* (1983), *Dangerous* (1985), *Everlasting* (1987), and *Good to Be Back* (1989). In 1991 Cole released a twenty-two-song collection of her father's hits. The album, which contains a re-mixed version of the original title track "Unforgettable," features a duet between Cole and her father and earned her a Grammy Award for record of the year and album of the year.

In 1966 Cole released the album *Stardust,* which features a duet with her father, "When I Fall in Love," and earned her another Grammy. Cole's style over the years, which has encompassed jazz, pop, and R&B, were represented well in her album *The Sahara,* released in 1999. She has produced an array of songs that reflect the classic and smooth jazz styles of Ella Fitzgerald and the soul searching sounds of R&B done by Aretha Franklin while still creating her own unique vocal quality reflective of the legacy of her father's vocal style.

Cole has won numerous awards, including Grammys, NAACP Image Awards, and other accolades for her singing as well as praises for continuing to win her battle with drugs. In 2000 she published her autobiography *Angel on My Shoulder* about her life, and in 2001 she starred in a television movie also about her life entitled *Living For Love: The Natalie Cole Story.* She signed with Verve Records in 2002 and released the album *Leavin'* in 2006, which debuted at number one on the jazz charts and also appeared on the *Billboard* chart.

Sean Combs (1969–)
Music Executive, Entrepreneur

Sean John Combs (also known as "Puffy," "Puff Daddy," "P. Diddy," and "Diddy") was born on November 4, 1969, in Harlem, New York. He attended Howard University majoring in business but dropped out to take an internship at Uptown Records. After moving through the ranks he left and started his own company Bad Boy Entertainment in 1993. By 1996 Combs's company had sold over a $100 million worth of recordings. In a memorial to his friend and artist Notorious B.I.G., who was murdered in 1997, Combs produced the single "I'll Be Missing You," which launched the record *No Way Out* in 1997. This was Combs's first album and it made platinum status in sales. His second album in 1999 was *Forever,* which coincided that year with his Sean John clothing line.

Combs continues to produce albums, including his 2008 release *Press Play.* He has become involved in the film industry with the movie *Made,* and has performed on Broadway. He has appeared in the television film version of the Lorraine Hansberry's play *A Raisin in the Sun* (2004), has become involved in reality television with his show *Making the Band* (2002), and has produced *Notorious,* a film about the life of Christopher Wallace, also known as Notorious B.I.G. Combs continues to explore new ventures with great success; he has become an international mogul with influence in the areas of music and fashion.

Sam Cooke (1931–1964)
Singer, Songwriter

Born in Clarksdale, Mississippi, on January 2, 1931, Sam Cooke grew up the son of a Baptist minister in Chicago, Illinois. At the age of nine Cooke, along with two sisters and a brother, formed a gospel group called the Singing Children. As a teenager he joined the gospel group the Highway QCs, which performed on the same bill with nationally famous gospel acts.

By 1950 Cooke replaced tenor Rupert H. Harris as lead singer for the renowned gospel group the Soul Stirrers. Cooke's first recording with the Soul Stirrers, "Jesus Gave Me Water," was recorded for Art Rupe's Specialty label. Although the song revealed the inexperience of the twenty-year-old Cooke, it exhibited a quality of immense passion and heightened feeling. Under the pseudonym Dale Cooke, Sam recorded the pop song "Loveable" in 1957. That same year, in a session for producer Bumps Blackwell on the Keen label, Cooke recorded "You Send Me," which climbed to number one on the rhythm and blues charts. On the Keen label, Cooke recorded eight more consecutive hits, including "Everyone Likes to Cha Cha Cha," "Only Sixteen," and "Wonderful World," all of which were written or co-written by Cooke.

When his contract with the Keen label expired in 1960, Cooke signed with RCA and was assigned to staff producers Hugo Peretti and Luigi Creatore. In August Cooke's recording "Chain Gang" reached the number-two spot on the pop charts. Under the lavish production of Hugo and Luigi, Cooke produced a string of hits such as "Cupid" (1961), "Twistin' the Night Away" (1962), and "Another Saturday Night" (1963). Early in 1964 Cooke appeared on *The Tonight Show* and debuted two songs from his new album, which included the gospel-influenced composition "A Change Is Gonna Come."

Cooke's sophisticated vocal style and refined image made him one of the greatest pop music idols of the early 1960s. One of the first gospel artists to cross over into popular music, Cooke produced songs of timeless quality, filled with human emotion and spiritual optimism.

On December 11, 1964, Cooke checked into a $3-a-night motel, and managed to get in a scuffle with a woman hotel guest and the night manager. After a brief physical struggle, the manager fired three pistol shots, which mortally wounded Cooke. The singer left behind a catalogue of classic recordings and more than one hundred original compositions, including the hit "Shake," which was posthumously released in 1965.

singing in his father's Holiness Church. Along with his brother and sister, Crouch formed the Crouch Trio, which performed at their father's services as well as on live Sunday-night radio broadcasts. In the mid-1960s Crouch was discovered by white Pentecostal evangelists and subsequently signed a contract with Light, a white religious record label.

During the late 1960s Crouch, inspired by the modern charismatic revival movement, began adopting street-smart language and informal wardrobe. After forming the Disciples in 1968, Crouch recorded extensively and toured throughout the United States and Europe. His California style of gospel music combines rock, country music, and soul with traditional gospel forms. During the 1970s Crouch's back-up groups incorporated both electronic and acoustic instruments, including synthesizers. Many of his songs have become standards in the repertoire of modern gospel groups. Among his most famous songs are "I Don't Know Why Jesus Loved Me," "Through It All," and "The Blood Will Never Lose Its Power."

Crouch continued his songwriting and released *No Time to Lose* in 1984. With the loss of his father, mother, and brother in a short time, he re-evaluated his decision about going into the ministry and taking over his father's church. In 1994 he released *Mercy* while committing to the leadership of his father's church. In 1996 Crouch released the album *Tribute: The Songs of Andraé Crouch,* which showcased many of the persons influenced by Crouch's gospel music. His awards include Grammys, numerous Dove Awards, an Oscar nomination for the score of *The Color Purple* (1986), among many others honors and recognition for his songwriting and music.

Andraé Crouch (1942–)
Gospel Singer, Pianist

An exponent of a modern pop-based gospel style, Andraé Crouch became one of the leading gospel singers of the 1960s and 1970s. Born on July 1, 1942, in Los Angeles, California, Crouch grew up

Antoine "Fats" Domino (1928–)
Singer

Born in New Orleans on February 26, 1928, Antoine Domino began playing in nightclubs. In 1949, while playing with bassist Billy Diamond's group, he was discovered by a talent scout from

Imperial Records. Along the way he had acquired the nickname Fats and titled his first release *Fat Man*. Domino released other records, but it was not until 1955 that he began to reap real success.

Domino released "Ain't that a Shame" followed by "Blueberry Hill" (1956), "Blue Monday" (1957), and "I'm Walkin'" (1959). Over a six-year period Domino released thirty-five top hits. When his contract with Imperial ran out in 1963 Domino signed with ABC and several other labels during the 1970s and 1980s. He continues to tour in the United States and Europe and was awarded the National Medal of Arts in 1998.

Thomas A. Dorsey (1899–1993)
Gospel Composer, Arranger

Thomas A. Dorsey, known as the "Father of Gospel Music," was born on July 1, 1899, in Villa Rica, Georgia. Dorsey was raised in a church environment and occasionally traveled with his father. He moved to Chicago in 1916 to pursue his music interests. Dorsey attended the Chicago School of Composition and Arranging between 1919 and 1921. In the 1920s he was known for his skills as a blues arranger and composer. After he had a religious conversion at the National Baptist Convention, his focus became religious music. His first song after that experience was "If I Don't Get There." Dorsey's conversion was not readily accepted by traditionalists, and his songs were not initially well received.

In 1927 when Dorsey's song "If You See My Savior" was performed at the National Baptist Convention his opportunities and commitment to religious composition and arrangement were secure. Dorsey, in 1931, had organized a choir at Chicago's Ebenezer Baptist Church and started his own publishing company. He also co-founded the National Convention of Gospel Choirs and Choruses. Dorsey created a network of training, celebrating, and selling gospel music, which had a tremendous impact on its national

exposure. In spite of the success, Dorsey suffered the loss of his wife in childbirth and wrote the most celebrated of his songs, "Precious Lord Take My Hand."

Dorsey helped the career of many singers including Mahalia Jackson, Clara Ward, and Dolores Barrett. He traveled extensively in the United States and in Europe. By the 1980s Dorsey was suffering with Alzheimer's. He died in January 1993 in Chicago.

Dr. Dre (1965–)
Rapper, Producer

André Romelle Young, known as Dr. Dre, was born on February 18, 1965 in Los Angeles, California. As a disc jockey for parties he took on the name Dr. Dre. In homage to his favorite basketball player, Julius Erving, he took on the name "Dr. J." Dre went on to become a member of the group World Class Wreckin' Cru in 1982 and later the controversial group N.W.A. (Niggaz Wit Attitudes). That year Dre also produced the first album of rapper Easy E titled *Easy-Duz-It,* which went platinum. In 1989 N.W.A. put out a record release on Dre and Easy E's Ruthless Records label. N.W.A. continued to have releases on their record label, but in 1991 Dre left Ruthless Records to co-found Death Row Records with Suge Knight.

Dre had not given up on his own music and produced the solo album *The Chronic* in 1993. He received a Grammy Award for this album and his performance. He left Death Row Records and started his own label, Aftermath Entertainment, in 1996 to pursue his own vision for the label. That same year he discovered rapper Eminem, who has dominated the rap charts followed by 50 Cent a few years later. Dre has received numerous awards for his innovation and his risk taking and received a Lifetime Achievement Award in 2000. Dre released his album *Detox* in 2009 and continues to bring new and innovative voices to the rap genre.

Jermaine Dupri (1972–)
Producer

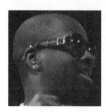

Jermain Dupri Mauldin was born on September 23, 1972, in Asheville, North Carolina. He had an early interest in performing and was a dancer on a national tour with rappers and other performers between 1984 and 1987. Dupri envisioned his career moving in the area of production and produced his first musical group in 1987, the Silk Tymes Leather. Dupri went on to produce other major groups in the 1990s such as Kriss Kross. In 1992 he launched his own record company and became a major factor in the success of many artists.

Dupri has kept abreast of trends and has the ability to recognize and prepare artists for their audiences. He has worked with major artists such as TLC, Usher, Alicia Keys, Mariah Carey, Bow Wow, and Janet Jackson, with whom Dupri developed a relationship. His contributions have earned him several Grammys and other prestigious awards, including the best R&B song in 2006, "We Belong Together."

Kenneth "Babyface" Edmonds (1958–)
Songwriter, Producer

Kenneth Brian Edmonds was born on April 10, 1958, in Indianapolis, Indiana. One of his early ventures into music was becoming a member of the group the Deele in which he played the guitar, keyboard, and synthesizer. In 1983 he successfully co-wrote a song for Midnight Star, "Slow Jam."

Edmonds incorporated his childhood nickname "Babyface" into his name and went solo in 1983 using both his voice and his abilities as a songwriter. As a singer his career focused on black audiences and media such as BET. As a songwriter he secured opportunities for soundtracks such as *Ghostbusters* (1989) and the *House Party* films (1990–2001). In 1989 Edmonds started LeFace Records and successfully managed the careers of Toni Braxton and TLC. Edmonds's reputation as a music producer and songwriter resulted in songs for Michael Jackson, Whitney Houston, Madonna, Eric Clapton, Boys II Men, and many other artists whose careers reached both black and white audiences. Edmonds was awarded three consecutive Grammy Awards for producer of the year between 1995 and 1997.

Edmonds has ventured further into filmmaking and television; he produced the successful film *Soul Food* (1997), *Josie and the Pussycats* (2001), and the BET reality series *College Hill* (2004—). He has established himself as a music producer and songwriter who has found success in areas previously dominated by whites. He also continues to produce his own music with the release of the album *Playlist* in 2007 featuring the original songs "The Soldier Song" and "Not Going Nowhere."

Missy Elliott (1971–)
Rapper, Singer, Songwriter

Melissa Arnette Elliott was born in Portsmouth, Virginia, in 1971. In high school Elliott was part of a singing group with three other girls called Sista. When Elliott graduated from high school in 1990, the group was signed by a subsidiary of Elektra Records after they were seen performing at a concert. When the record release fell through Elliott joined with a friend, Timbaland, and they became a team with Elliott writing and Timbaland producing. Together they made connections in the industry and contributed to the albums of Aaliyah and other artists. In 1966 Elliott contributed to a video by Gina Thompson, "The Things that You Do," which made record executives take her role as rap artist and songwriter seriously. Elektra signed Elliott to a contract for her own album and to run her own record label called Gold Mind in 1997. Her first album release was *Supa Dupa Fly*.

Elliott's songwriting, which is powerful, creative, humorous, sexually charged, and innovative, continued with the albums *Da Real World* (with the hits "She's a Bitch" and "Hot Boyz"; 1999), *Miss E...So Addictive* (with two major hits, capturing a Grammy for best rap solo performance; 2001), *Under Construction* (which went double platinum; 2002), *This is a Test* (with hit single "Work It" (which won a Grammy for best female solo performance in 2003), and *Respect M.E.* (non-U.S., which earned more awards and accolades; 2006). Elliot has ventured into film, advertising, a clothing line, and has created and supported organizations that support the community. In 2010 Elliott released the album *Block Party*.

50 Cent (1976–)
Rapper, Actor, Entrepreneur

Curtis James Jackson III (known professionally as 50 Cent) was born on July 6, 1976, in Queens, New York. He has gone from rapper to entrepreneur worth over $400 million and earned a place of global influence in the music industry.

50 Cent grew up in South Jamaica, New York, and was raised by his grandmother after the death of his mother, which was assumed to be drug related. He sold drugs as a means to support himself knowing the limits of his grandmother's income. By fifteen he was the neighborhood drug king bringing in $150,000 per week. Guided by Jam Master Jay, a successful rapper from his neighborhood, 50 Cent perfected his writing craft and signed a deal with Jam Master Jay in 1997. 50 Cent moved to Columbia Records in 1999 but was later dropped after he was shot nine times by an assailant. His true "thug" life was more than Columbia could handle.

50 Cent had been doing mix-tapes on the underground music scene for several years and returned to that after he recovered from his gunshot wounds. 50 Cent had his first single in 2002, "Wanksta," which appeared on the soundtrack of the movie *8 Mile*, a movie about 50 Cent's hero Eminem. 50 Cent's debut album, *Get Rich or Die Trying*, was released in 2003. Many of his songs target other rappers or engage in feuds. Others songs are autobiographical. Also in 2003, 50 Cent was granted his own label, G-Unit Records, by Interscope records. He released his third album, *Curtis*, in 2007 and has the album *Black Magic* scheduled for release in 2012.

Other ventures for 50 Cent include a film company, Cheetah Vision, as well as collaborating and promoting various products. One of his projects, a Vitamin Water Drink through the company Glaceau, was purchased by Coca-Cola for $4.1 billion.

Roberta Flack (1939–)
Singer, Pianist

Born in Asheville, North Carolina, on February 10, 1939, Roberta Flack moved to Washington, D.C., with her parents at the age of nine. Three years later she studied classical piano with prominent African American concert musician Hazel Harrison. After winning several talent contests, Flack won a scholarship to Howard University where she graduated with a bachelor's degree in music education. During the early 1960s Flack taught music in the Washington, D.C., public school system.

While playing a club date in 1968, Flack was discovered by Les McCann, whose connections resulted in a contract with Atlantic Records. Flack's first album, *First Take*, appeared in 1970 and included the hit song "The First Time Ever I Saw Your Face." Throughout the 1970s Flack landed several hits, such as "Killing Me Softly with His Song" and "The Closer I Get to You," a duet with Donny Hathaway. In the early 1980s Flack collaborated with Peabo Bryson to record the hit "Tonight I Celebrate My Love for You." Flack toured in the 1980s and in 1991 hit the top-ten chart with "Set the Night to Music," a duet with Maxi Priest. She released *The Very Best of Roberta Flack* in 2006.

Roberta Flack has received numerous Grammys and was honored with a star on Hollywood's legendary Walk of Fame in 1999. She has performed with acclaimed orchestras all over the world and founded the Roberta Flack School of Music at the Hyde Leadership Charter School in Bronx, New York.

Aretha Franklin (1942–)
Singer, Pianist, Songwriter

Daughter of the famous Reverend Charles L. Franklin, Aretha Franklin was born on March 25, 1942, in Memphis, Tennessee. Raised on the east side of Detroit, Michigan, Franklin sang at her father's New Bethel Baptist Church. Although she began to study piano at age eight, Franklin refused to learn what she considered juvenile and simple tunes. Thus, she learned piano by ear, occasionally receiving instruction from individuals like the Reverend James Cleveland. Franklin's singing skills were modeled after gospel singers and family friends, including Clara Ward, and R&B artists like Ruth Brown and Sam Cooke.

At fourteen, Franklin quit school to go on the road with her father's Franklin Gospel Caravan, a seemingly endless tour in which the family traveled thousands of miles by car. After four years on the road, Aretha traveled to New York to establish her own career as a pop artist. In 1960 she signed with Columbia Records's talent scout John Hammond, who described her as an "untutored genius, the best singer … since Billie Holiday." Her six-year stay at Columbia, however, produced only a few hits and little material that suited Franklin's unique talents.

In 1966 Franklin signed with Atlantic Records and, in the following year, she recorded a session for producer Jerry Wexler that resulted in the hit "I Never Loved a Man (The Way That I Loved You)." That same year, Franklin's career received another boost when her reworking of Otis Redding's song "Respect" hit the charts. Franklin's first album, *I Never Loved a Man,* was followed by a succession of artistically and commercially successful albums: *Aretha Arrives* (1967), *Lady Soul* (1968), *Aretha Now!* (1968), and *This Girl's in Love with You* (1970). Her prominence grew so great that Franklin appeared on the cover of *Time* magazine in 1968.

During the 1970s Franklin continued to tour and record. In 1971 she released the live album *Aretha Live at the Filmore West,* backed by the horn and rhythm section of Tower of Power. Her next release was in 1972, *Amazing Grace,* which featured the Reverend James Cleveland and the Southern California Community Choir. In 1980 she appeared in the film *The Blues Brothers.* Five years later in 1985 Franklin scored her first big commercial success in over a decade with the album *Who's Zooming Who?* featuring the single "Freeway of Love." In 1988 she released a double live album *One Lord, One Faith*—an effort dedicated to her father who had passed away the previous year. The 1990s saw Franklin recording a track on the soundtrack for the film *Waiting to Exhale* (1995), performing at the VH-1 concert "Divas Live," and receiving the National Medal of the Arts (1999).

In 2003 Franklin released her studio album *So Damn Happy* and in 2008 she collaborated with Mary J. Blige on *Never Gonna Break My Faith,* which earned Franklin her eighteenth Grammy Award. She received her nineteenth Grammy for "A House Is Not a Home," a track from a tribute record for Luther Vandross (2005). Also in 2005 she was awarded the Presidential Medal of Honor. Franklin sang at the inauguration of President Barack Obama in January 2009, and at the twenty-five-year celebration to mark the end of Oprah Winfrey's show in Chicago in May 2011. Franklin started her own record label, Aretha Records, in 2004 and released the album *A Woman Falling Out of Love* (2010).

Writing at the beginning of the 1990s, Atlantic Records producer Jerry Wexler observed that "it's easy to forget that a quarter century ago there was no one singing like Aretha Franklin." He added, "Today, pop music is rich with glorious voices, females in Aretha's mold." As Queen of Soul, Franklin has reigned supreme for the last four decades. Her music incorporates gospel, jazz, blues, and pop; and her voice brings spiritual inspiration to her gender, race, and the world.

Kirk Franklin (1970–)
Gospel Singer

Kirk Franklin was born on January 26, 1970, in Fort Worth, Texas. In the absence of both parents, he was raised by an aunt who saw his musical talents as early as four years old. His aunt supported his musical training by selling aluminum cans and keeping him solidly in the church, and by the time Franklin was eleven years old he was leading the church adult choir. After some years of rebellion and the shooting death of a close friend Franklin devoted himself to writing and producing music. Even though fully immersed in traditional gospel music, Franklin was fully aware of R&B, rock, and pop music. At nineteen he made his first recording, and in 1992 he formed a seventeen-member group called The Family.

Franklin's break came in 1992 when GospoCentric Records heard one of Franklin's tapes and signed him to a recording contract. His debut album *Kirk Franklin and The Family* sold more than one million copies and broadened the audience for gospel music. Almost all of Franklin's records have been gold or platinum regarding sales. He has worked with some of the most important and influential names in gospel music today, including Shirley Caesar, Donnie McClurkin, Richard Smallwood, and Mary Mary. His albums include *Whatcha Lookin' 4* (1996) and *Nu Nation* (1997).

Franklin's music, which blends gospel, hip hop, and R&B, includes songs such as "Caught Up," "The Blood Song," "Imagine Me," "911," "Brighter Day," "He Reigns," and "Awesome God

Lookin Out". He has earned numerous Grammy Awards and other accolades for his ability to reach across boundaries and bring gospel music to more diverse, and more generations of, audiences.

Marvin Gaye (1939–1984)
Singer, Songwriter

Marvin Pentz Gay Jr. (the final "e" on his surname was not added until the early 1960s) was born on April 29, 1939, in Washington, D.C. The son of a Pentecostal minister, he was raised in a segregated slum-ridden section of Washington, D.C., and experienced a strict religious upbringing. As Gaye later recalled, "Living with my father was like living with a king, a very peculiar, changeable, cruel, and all-powerful king." Thus Gaye looked to music for release. Around the age of three, he began singing in church. While attending Cardoza High School, Gaye studied drums, piano, and guitar. Uninspired by his formal studies, Gaye often cut classes to watch James Brown and Jackie Wilson perform at the Howard Theatre.

Soon afterward, Gaye served a short time in the Air Force and received an honorable discharge in 1957. Returning to Washington, D.C., Gaye joined the doo-wop group, the Marquees. After recording for Columbia's subsidiary label, Okeh, the Marquees moved to the Chess/Checker label where they recorded with Bo Diddley. Although the Marquees performed their own compositions and toured regularly, they failed to gain popularity. It was not until they were introduced to Harvey Fuqua, who was in the process of reforming the Moonglows, that the Marquees attracted notice in the pop music world. Impressed by their sound, Fuqua hired the Marquees to form a group under the new name Harvey and the Moonglows. Still under contract at Chess, Fuqua brought the Moonglows to the company's studio in Chicago to record the 1959 hit the "Ten Commandments of Love."

In 1960 Fuqua and Gaye traveled to Detroit, where Fuqua set up his own label and signed with Motown's subsidiary, Anna. After a stint as a back-up singer, studio musician, and drummer in Smokey Robinson's touring band, Gaye signed a contract with Motown as a solo artist. Released in 1962, Gaye's first album was a jazz-oriented effort entitled *The Soulful Moods of Marvin Gaye.* With his sights on a career modeled after the ballad singer Frank Sinatra, Gaye was not enthusiastic when Motown suggested he record a dance record of rhythm and blues material. Nevertheless, Gaye recorded the song "Stubborn Kind of Fellow" in 1962, which entered the top-ten R&B charts. This was followed by a long succession of Motown hits, such as "Hitch Hike" (1963), "Pride and Joy" (1963), "Can I Get a Witness?" (1963), and "Wonderful One" (1964).

Motown's next projects for Gaye included a number of vocal duets, the first of which was with singer Mary Wells on the 1964 album *Together.* In collaboration with singer Kim Weston, Gaye recorded the 1967 hit album *It Takes Two.* His most successful partnership, however, was with Tammi Terrell. During their two-year association Gaye and Terrell recorded, under the writing and production team of Ashford and Simpson, such hits as "Ain't No Mountain High Enough" (1967), "Your Precious Love" (1967), and "Ain't Nothing Like the Real Thing" (1968).

Back in the studio as a solo act Gaye recorded the hit "Heard It Through the Grapevine" (1968). With his growing success Gaye achieved greater creative independence at Motown, which led him to co-produce the 1971 hit album *What's Going On,* a session that produced the best-selling singles "What's Going On," "Mercy Mercy (The Ecology)," and "Inner City Blues (Make Me Wanna Holler)."

After his last album for Motown, *In Our Lifetime,* Gaye signed with CBS Records in April 1981, and within the next year he released the Album *Midnight Lover,* featuring the Grammy Award–winning hit "Sexual Healing." On Sunday, April 1, 1984, Gaye was shot dead by his father in Los Angeles, California. Despite his public image, Gaye had suffered from years of inner conflict and drug abuse. "This tragic ending can only be softened by the memory of a beautiful human being," described long-time friend Smokey Robinson. "He could be full of joy sometimes, but at others, full of woe, but in the end how compassionate, how wonderful, how exciting [were] Marvin Gaye and his music."

Berry Gordy Jr. (1929–)
Songwriter, Producer, Entrepreneur

From assembly line worker to impresario of the Motown Record Corporation, Berry Gordy Jr. emerged as the owner of one of the largest black-owned businesses in American history. A professional boxer, songwriter, producer, and businessman, Gordy is a living legend, a self-made man who, through his determination and passion for music, helped to create one of the most celebrated sounds of modern music.

The seventh of eight children, Gordy was born on November 28, 1929, in Detroit, Michigan. Berry Gordy Sr., the owner of a grocery store, a plastering company, and a printing shop, taught his children the value of hard work and family unity. Despite his dislike for manual labor, Berry possessed a strong desire to become commercially successful. After quitting high school to become a professional boxer, Berry won several contests before leaving the profession in 1950. A year later Gordy was drafted into the Army, where he earned a high school equivalency diploma.

Upon returning from a military tour of Korea in 1953, Gordy opened the 3–D Record Mart, a jazz-oriented retail store. Forced into bankruptcy Gordy closed the store in 1955 and subsequently took a job as an assembly line worker at Ford Motor Company. His nightly visits to Detroit's thriving jazz and R&B scene inspired Gordy to take up songwriting. In 1957 one of Gordy's former boxing colleagues, Jackie Wilson, recorded the hit "Reet Petite," a song written by Gordy, his sister Gwen, and Billy Davis. Over the next four years the Gordy (Berry)–Gwen–Davis writing team provided Wilson with four more hits, "To Be Loved," "Lonely Teardrops," "That's Why (I Love You So)," and "I'll Be Satisfied."

By 1959 Billy Davis and Gwen Gordy founded the Anna label, which distributed material through Chess Records in Chicago. Barrett Strong's recording of "Money (That's What I Want)," written by Gordy and Janie Bradford, became the label's biggest-selling single. With his background as a writer and producer with the Anna label, Gordy decided to start his own company. In 1959 he formed Jobete Music Publishing, Berry Gordy Jr. Enterprises, Hitsville USA, and the Motown Record Corporation. Employing a staff of local studio musicians, writers, and producers, Berry's label scored its first hit in 1961 with Smokey Robinson's "Shop Around." By the mid-1960s Gordy had assembled a wealth of talent, including the Supremes, the Four Tops, the Marvelettes, Marvin Gaye, and Stevie Wonder.

In 1971 Gordy relocated the Motown Recording Corporation to Los Angeles. Although most of the original acts and staff members did not join the company's migration to the West Coast, Gordy's company became one of the country's top black-owned businesses. Throughout the 1970s and 1980s Motown continued to produce motion pictures and artists like the Jackson Five, the Commodores, Lionel Richie, Rick James, and DeBarge. In 1982 Gordy, faced with financial problems, signed a distribution agreement with MCA, and in 1988 he sold the recording company to MCA for $61 million. Gordy's induction into the Rock and Roll Hall of Fame in 1988 brought recognition to a giant of the recording industry who helped transform the sound of popular music. Gordy's contributions as a songwriter were recognized in 2001 when he was inducted into the Independent Music Hall of Fame.

Al Green (1946–)

Singer, Songwriter, Preacher

Albert Green was born on April 13, 1946, in Forrest City, Arkansas. Green was interested in both religious and popular music and formed a quar-

tet with his brothers, Walter, William, and Robert, known as The Green Brothers. In 1967 the family moved to Grand Rapids, Michigan, where Green formed a group with his friends called Al Green and the Soulmates. They recorded the song "Back Up Train," which made number four on the charts but the group later disbanded. It was not until 1968 that Green was signed to Hi Records in Memphis.

After some success with the Temptations's remake, "I Can't Get Next to You," Green got his first smash hit, "Tired of Being Alone." In 1972 this hit was followed by "Let's Stay Together" and his biggest selling album *I'm Still in Love with You*. He had the successful singles from the album, including "Light My Fire," "For the Good Times," and "Love and Happiness." Green's vocal style, along with the influences of church and R&B, established these as music classics. After a religious awakening, and later suffering second degree burns inflicted by his girlfriend who later committed suicide, Green made one more record for Hi Records before leaving in 1977.

Green left secular music in 1980 to devote himself to the role of pastor of the Full Gospel Tabernacle in Memphis, Tennessee, as well as to maintain his music with a gospel focus. In 1985 he signed with A&M Records and recorded *Soul Survivor* in 1987. Green's concerts showed him exhibiting the control of a polished artist by holding his audience with his vocal acuity while surrendering to the spiritual and emotional humility of abandonment as a believer. Green made a comeback to popular music alongside gospel music in 2003 with the album *I Can't Stop,* followed by *Everything's Okay* in 2005. In 2008 he captured a new generation of listeners with the album *Lay It Down* with neo-soul artists John Legend, Anthony Hamilton, and Corrin Bailey Rae, which earned them two Grammy Awards. Green was inducted into Rock and Roll Hall of Fame in 1995, the Gospel Hall of Fame in 2004, and the Songwriters Hall of Fame in 2004.

Tramaine Hawkins (1951–)
Singer

Born on October 11, 1951, in San Francisco, California, Tramaine Aunzola Davis Hawkins began singing at the age of four and sang with the girl group Heavenly Tones while still a child. When the group got offers to sing more secular music Hawkins left because she knew that gospel music was her calling. In 1960 she was a part of the Northern California State Choir that recorded the hit "Oh Happy Day." The choir's name was changed to the Edwin Hawkins Singers, and it toured Europe through 1970. Hawkins left soon after when the group began doing club dates.

Hawkins continued her focus on gospel music releasing *Tramaine* (1980), *Determined* (1983), *Spirit of Love* (1985), *Tramaine: Treasury* (1986), *Freedom* (1987), and *The Joy that Floods My Soul* (1988). In 1990 Hawkins brought together singers outside the gospel world to participate in a live-recording project. Artists such as Carlos Santana, a rock guitarist, Jimmy McGriff, a jazz organist and Stanley Turrentine, a jazz tenor saxophonist, combined with traditional gospel and other styles to create what is called contemporary gospel. She released *All My Best to You* and *Higher Place* in 1994; and in 1996 the broad appeal of gospel music resulted in a Lincoln Center festival that focused on gospel music with Hawkins as one of the artists performing.

Hawkins has released numerous albums and has won several awards, including two Grammys, two Dove Awards, an Image Award from the NAACP, a Stellar Award, and a Gospel Music Excellence Award.

Isaac Hayes (1942–2008)
Singer, Pianist, Producer

Born on August 20, 1942, in Covington, Tennessee, Isaac Lee Hayes Jr. moved to Memphis at age seven, where he heard the sounds of blues and country-western, and the music of idol Sam Cooke. Through the connections of saxophonist Floyd Newman, Hayes began a career as a studio musician for Stax Records in 1964. After playing piano on a session for Otis Redding, Hayes formed a partnership with songwriter Dave Porter that was responsible for supplying a number of hits for Carla Thomas, William Bell, and Eddie Floyd.

The first real break for the Hayes–Porter team came when they were recruited to produce the Miami-based soul duo Sam Moore and Dave Prater. In the span of four years, Hayes and Porter succeeded in making Sam and Dave the hottest-selling act for Stax, producing such hits as "Hold On I'm Coming," "Soul Man," and "I Thank You!" It was the "raw rural southern" sound, recalled Hayes, that made these recordings some of the finest pop hits of the 1960s.

During this period Hayes and Porter continued to perform in a group that established them as an underground legend in the Memphis music scene. In the late 1960s Hayes's solo career emerged in an impromptu fashion when a late-night session with drummer Al Jackson and bassist Duck Dunn prompted Stax to release his next effort. *Hot Buttered Soul* went double platinum in 1969. Its extended rap–soul version of the country song "By the Time I Get to Phoenix" set a trend for the disco/soul sound of the 1970s. Following the 1970 release of the albums *To Be Continued* and *The Isaac Hayes Movement*, Hayes recorded the soundtrack for the film *Shaft* and the album *Black Moses* in 1971.

Hayes left the Stax label to join ABC in 1974. To promote his career Hayes recorded the disco albums *Chocolate Chip* (1975), *Disco Connection* (1975), and *Groove-A-Thon* (1976). In 1979 he earned a gold record for "Don't Let Go," which was released on the Polydor label, and in 1986 he signed with Columbia Records and released the album *U-Turn*.

Hayes took on numerous acting roles, including *Escape from New York* (1996), Comedy Central's animated series *South Park* (1997–2006), *I'm Gonna Git You Sucka* (1998), and *Hustle and Flow* (2005). He was inducted into the Rock and Roll Hall of Fame in 2002. Hayes died of a stroke August 10, 2008.

Jimi Hendrix (1942–1970)
Guitarist, Songwriter

On November 25, 1942, in Seattle, Washington, Johnny Allen Hendrix was born to an enlisted Army soldier and a teenage mother. Four years later, Johnny Allen was renamed James Marshall Hendrix. Because of his mother's fondness for nightclub life and his father's frequent absences, Hendrix was a lonely yet creative child. At school he won several contests for his science fiction–based poetry and visual art. At the age of eight Hendrix, unable to afford a guitar, strummed out rhythms on a broom. Eventually he graduated to a fabricated substitute made from a cigar box, followed by a ukulele, and finally an acoustic guitar that his father had purchased.

By the late 1950s Hendrix began to play in local bands in Seattle. While a teenager he played along with recordings by blues artists like Elmore James and John Lee Hooker. After a twenty-six-month stint (1961–1962) in the 101st Airborne Division, Hendrix played in the Nashville rhythm and blues scene with bassist Billy Cox. For the next three years, Hendrix performed under the name Jimmy James, backing up acts such as Little Richard, Jackie Wilson, Ike and Tina Turner, and the Isley Brothers.

In 1964 Hendrix moved to New York City where he performed in various Greenwich Village clubs. While in New York he formed the group Jimmy James and the Blue Flames. After being discovered by producer and manager Chas Chandler, former bassist with the Animals, Hendrix was urged to leave for England. Arriving there in 1966 Hendrix, along with bassist Noel Redding and drummer Mitch Mitchell, formed the Jimi Hendrix Experience. In 1967, after touring Europe, the trio hit the charts with a cover version of the Leaves's song "Hey Joe." In the same year, the group released the ground-breaking album *Are You Experienced.*

In 1968 the Experience recorded *Axis: Bold as Love,* which led to extensive touring in the United States and Europe. On the Experience's next album, *Electric Ladyland,* Hendrix sought to expand the group's trio-based sound. A double-record effort *Electric Ladyland* featured numerous guest artists such as keyboardists Steve Winwood and Al Kooper, saxophonist Freddie Smith, and conga player Larry Faucette. The record also contained "All Along the Watchtower," a song written by Hendrix's musical and poetic idol Bob Dylan.

After the Experience broke up in 1969, Hendrix played the Woodstock Music and Arts Festival with the Gypsy Sons and Rainbows, featuring bassist Billy Cox. Along with drummer Buddy Miles, Hendrix and Cox formed the Band of Gypsys, and in 1970 the group released an album under the same title. Months later, Mitchell replaced Miles on drums. In August the Mitchell–Cox line-up played behind Hendrix at his last major performance, which was held at England's Isle of Wight Festival. On September 18, 1970, Hendrix died in a hotel room in England.

When Hendrix arrived on the international rock music scene in 1967 he almost single-handedly redefined the sound of the electric guitar. His extraordinary approach has shaped the course of music from jazz fusion to heavy metal.

Whitney Houston (1963–)
Singer, Actress, Model

Born on August 9, 1963, Whitney Elizabeth Houston grew up in East Orange, New Jersey. She made her singing debut as a member of the New Hope Baptist Choir at age eleven. Later, Houston appeared as a back-up singer on numerous recordings, featuring her mother Cissy Houston and her cousin Dionne Warwick. Despite her success as a fashion model who has graced the covers of magazines from *Glamour* to *Cosmopolitan,* Houston found the profession "degrading" and subsequently quit in order to seek a career in music.

By age nineteen Houston had received several recording contract offers. In 1985 she released her debut album on the Arista label entitled *Whitney Houston,* which produced four hits: "Saving All My Love for You," "You Give Good Love," "How Will I Know," and "The Greatest Love of All."

Houston's second album, *Whitney,* appeared in 1987. As with her first effort it produced a number of hits, including "I Wanna Dance with Somebody," "Didn't We Almost Have It All," "So Emotional," "Where Do Broken Hearts Go?," and "Love Will Save the Day." Following the success of her second record, Houston released *One Moment in Time* in 1988 and the slickly produced *I'm Your Baby Tonight* in 1990. In 1992 Houston married singer Bobby Brown, whom she divorced in 2007, and she made her acting debut in the film *The Bodyguard,* co-starring Kevin Costner. The film's soundtrack that Huston released stayed on the charts for fourteen weeks and she won a Grammy Award for album of the year.

Houston appeared in the films *Waiting to Exhale* (1995) and *The Preacher's Wife* (1996); she also released songs on the soundtracks, which resulted in more number-one hits for Houston. She earned another Grammy for her 1998 release *My Love Is Your Love.* Houston's personal issues of finance, family, and health kept her in the tabloids and created detractors from her music and her career. In 2009 Houston began a comeback tour that saw challenges both at home and abroad; her performance generated a lack-luster and sometimes disappointing response from her fans.

Jennifer Hudson (1981–)
Singer, Actress

Jennifer Kate Hudson was born on September 12, 1981, in Chicago, Illinois. She grew up singing in the church choir, and after graduating from Dunbar Vocational Career Academy in 1999 she embraced singing opportunities such as singing for a year on a Disney cruise ship.

In 2004 Hudson auditioned and became a finalist on the reality/talent search show *American Idol.* Hudson earned the role of Effie White in the film *Dreamgirls* (2006), a remake of the play by the same name from the 1970s. Her performance earned her the prestigious Academy Award for best supporting actress, a Golden Globe, and an NAACP Image Award, among other recognitions. Hudson has also been in the films *The Secret Life of Bees* (2008), *Sex and the City* (2008), and *Winnie* (a biopic based on the life of Winnie Mandela; 2010).

In October 2008 Hudson suffered personal tragedy with the violent deaths of her mother, brother, and nephew. She continues to consider film roles while pursuing her music and performing at venues such as Super Bowl XLIII in 2009. Hudson released her debut album *Jennifer Hudson* (2008) and *I Remember Me* (2011).

Phyllis Hyman (1949–1995)
Singer

Phyllis Hyman was born on July 6, 1949, in Philadelphia, Pennsylvania, one of seven brothers and sisters. Hyman pursued a career in entertainment by moving to New York in the early 1970s. She formed her own band by 1974, Phyllis Hyman and the PH Factor, and performed on a regular basis on New York's Upper West Side. Her career took off in 1976 when Norman Connors had Hyman perform the ballad "Betcha By Golly Wow," a remake of a Stylistic's hit on his album. As a result Hyman was signed to the Arista label in 1977 and released her first solo album *Phyllis Hyman.*

Hyman later released the album *Somewhere in My Lifetime* (1978) followed by *You Know How to Love Me* (1979). Her first top-ten single "Can't We Fall in Love Again" was released in 1981 while performing on Broadway. Hyman performed in the Duke Ellington revue *Sophisticated Ladies,* which earned her a nomination for a Tony Award. She was a part of the cast for three years.

Hyman signed with the Philadelphia International label in 1986 and became a part of the Philly sound with writers and producers Gamble and Huff. She released the album *Living All Alone* (1984), and she appeared in the films *School Daze* (1988) and *The Kill Reflex* (1989). Her album *Prime of My Life* (1991) brought her much critical acclaim with the Top 100 hit "Don't Wanna Change the World" and two top-ten R&B singles "Living in Confusion" and "When You Get Right Down to It." The album went gold in 1992.

Hyman, who suffered from addiction and depression, committed suicide on June 30, 1995. She was found in her room just before a scheduled performance at the Apollo Theater. Hyman is remembered in equal stature to Sarah Vaughan and other such artists with extraordinary instruments and emotional commitment to the music. Her rich and soulful sound mingled with her own personal struggles and created a connection to the music by both Hyman and all who heard her.

Ice Cube (1969–)

Singer, Actor

Born O'Shea Jackson on June 15, 1969, in Los Angeles, California, Ice Cube grew up in the west side of the city's south-central area. While in the ninth grade Jackson wrote his first rhyme in typing class. Prompted by his parents to pursue an education after high school, he attended a one-year drafting course at Phoenix Institute in 1988. In the following year Ice Cube achieved great commercial success as a member of N.W.A. (Niggaz Wit Attitudes). Ice Cube was one of the group's founding members and wrote or co-wrote most of the material for N.W.A.'s first two albums. Ice Cube's authoritative baritone won him a legion of fans for his N.W.A. rap anthem "Gangsta Gangsta."

After leaving N.W.A., Ice Cube released his solo album *AmeriKKKa's Most Wanted* (1990), which went gold within three months. He went on to produce *Kill at Will* (1991), *The Predator* (1992), which debuted at numbers one and two on the Pop and R&B charts, *War and Peace* (1998), a best seller, volume two of *War and Peace* (2000), and *Laugh Now, Cry Later* (2006), which features Lil Jon and Scott Storch who produced the lead single "Why We Thugs." Ice Cube was awarded a Lifetime Achievement Award at the Hip-Hop Music Awards in 2000.

In 1991 Ice Cube made his acting debut in director John Singleton's film *Boyz n the Hood,* in which he gave a powerful performance in the role of Doughboy. He has gone on to have a very active career in films such as *Higher Learning* (1995), *Friday* series (1995, 1999, 2002, and 2011), *Anaconda* (1997), *Three Kings* (1999), *Barbershop* (2002), and *Barbershop 2* (2004). In 2011 he turned to television and produced the series *Are We There Yet?,* based on the box-office hit of the same name staring Ice Cube in 2005. Ice Cube has been a successful director, writer, and producer, and one of the most successful hip-hop artists to make the transition to acting.

Behind his gangster image, rapper Ice Cube is a serious artist dedicated to racial advancement and black pride. A staunch spokesperson for Black Nationalism, Ice Cube looks upon his music as a means of launching a "mental revolution" to awaken African American youths to the value of education and the creation of private black economic enterprises.

Janet Jackson (1966–)

Singer

The youngest child of a family of talented children, Janet Damita Jo Jackson was born on May 16, 1966, in Gary, Indiana. Jackson began performing with her brothers at age six, doing impressions of famous stars like Mae West and Cher. She made her professional singing debut at one of the Jackson Five's shows in the Grand Hotel in Las Vegas. Before she was ten years old Jackson was spotted by television producer Norman Lear, which resulted in her guest appearances on such television shows as *Fame, Good Times,* and *Diff'rent Strokes.*

In 1982 Jackson's debut album for the A&M label, *Janet,* contained only a few minor hits. Teamed with producers Jimmy Jam and Terry Lewis, Jackson released her more commercially successful album *Dream Street.* Her 1986 release *Control* scored six hit singles, including "What Have You Done for Me Lately?," "Nasty," "When I Think of You," "Control," "Let's Wait Awhile," and "Pleasure Principle." Under the direction of Jam and Lewis, Jackson released the dance-oriented album *Janet Jackson's Rhythm Nation 1814* in 1989, which went quadruple platinum. Among the record's numerous singles were "Miss You Much," "Come Back to Me," and "Black Cat." Jackson became the first artist to have five hits from a single album, which also earned her three American Music Awards.

After an extensive world tour in 1990, Jackson left the A&M label to sign a contract with Virgin Records in 1991, which guaranteed her an advance of over $30 million. In 1993 Jackson released her fifth album, *Janet,* and received an Oscar nomination for her song "Again," which was part of the soundtrack for *Poetic Justice,* in which Jackson had a starring role. She earned her fourteenth gold single for "Any Time, Any Place." The song "That's the Way Love Goes" earned her a Grammy nomination.

Jackson continued to find success in the recording industry with her next album, *The Velvet Rope* (1997), which had impressive responses, and several albums that followed. Jackson won an American Music Award in January 2002 as the favorite female pop/rock artist. Her career faltered in 2004 when her appearance at the Super Bowl with Justin Timberlake resulted in a "wardrobe malfunction" that revealed her right breast. Her fans and the Federal Trade Commission were upset as this was during the family hour and some thought the stunt had been intentional. Jackson

apologized for the incident. She did not appear at the Grammy Awards that year and dropped out of a television role to play Lena Horne. Jackson has become more involved in the film industry over the years taking roles in the films *The Nutty Professor* (1996), *The Nutty Professor II: The Klumps* (2000), *Why Did I Get Married?* (2007), and *Why Did I Get Married Too?* (2010).

Mahalia Jackson (1912–1972)
Gospel Singer

Born Mahalia Jackson on October 26, 1912, in New Orleans, Louisiana, she was nicknamed "Halie." The third of six children, Jackson grew up in New Orleans and absorbed the sounds of parade music and brass bands. She later discovered the blues, a music labeled the "devil's music" by regular church-goers, and listened secretly to recordings of singers like Mamie Smith and Bessie Smith.

In 1927 at the age of thirteen Jackson moved to Chicago where she joined the Greater Salem Baptist Church. Two years later, Jackson met the gospel musician and songwriter Thomas A. Dorsey who invited her to sing at the Pilgrim Baptist Church. In 1937 Jackson recorded four sides for the Decca label, including the song "God's Gonna Separate the Wheat from the Tares."

Jackson's big break came in 1947 when she released gospel music's first million-selling record "Move on Up a Little." In 1949 her song "Let the Holy Ghost Fall on Me" won the French Academy's Grand Prix du Disque. Soon afterward, she toured Europe and recorded the gospel hit "In the Upper Room." During the 1960s Jackson became a musical ambassador. Not only did she perform at the White House and at London's Albert Hall, but she sang at the 1963 March on Washington, as well as at Martin Luther King Jr.'s funeral ceremony in 1968.

On January 27, 1972, Jackson died in Chicago of a heart condition. At her funeral at Great Salem Baptist, some forty-five thousand mourners gathered to pay their respects. She was hailed as the world's greatest gospel singer, and her rich contralto voice became a national institution. Through live performances, recordings, and television appearances, Jackson elevated gospel music to a level of popularity unprecedented in the history of African American religious music.

Michael Jackson (1958–2009)
Singer, Songwriter, Dancer, Choreographer

The fifth of nine children, Michael Joseph Jackson was born on August 29, 1958, in Gary, Indiana. As a child, Michael, along with his brothers Tito, Jermaine, Jackie, and Marlon, formed the Jackson Five. Under the tutelage of their father, Joe, the five boys learned to sing and dance. On weekends the family singing group traveled hundreds of miles to perform at amateur contests and benefit concerts.

After two years on the road, the group landed an audition with Motown Records. Upon signing with the label in 1969, the Jackson Five hit the charts with the number-one hit "I Want You Back," a song arranged and produced by Berry Gordy Jr. On recordings and television shows, Michael's wholesome image and lead vocal style attracted fans from every racial and age group. During the group's stay at Motown from 1969 to 1975, the Jackson Five scored thirteen consecutive top-twenty singles such as "ABC," "The Love You Save," and "I'll Be There."

During his years as lead vocalist for the Jackson Five, Michael had signed a separate contract with Motown in 1971 and pursued a solo career that produced the hits "Got to Be There" (1971), "Ben" (1972), and "Just a Little Bit of You" (1975). While cast in the role of the scarecrow in the 1978 Motown film *The Wiz,* Jackson met producer Quincy Jones, who later collaborated with him to record the hit album *Off the Wall* (1979) on the Epic label. Two years later, guided by the production skills of Jones, Jackson recorded the biggest-selling album of all time, *Thriller.* "All the brilliance that had been building inside Michael Jackson for twenty-five years just erupted," commented Jones. "I was electrified, and so was everybody on the project." Jackson co-wrote the song "We Are the World" (1985) for the African famine relief fund. After Jackson joined Jones to produce the album *Bad* (1987), he led the most commercially successful tour in history.

The 1990s saw the release of Jackson's album *Dangerous* (1991) with hits such as "Black or White" and "Remember the Time," and the release of *HIStory: Past, Present, and Future, Book I* (1995). During this time Jackson dealt with accusations of child abuse and sexual molestation and stood trial in 2005. He was acquitted of all charges. In 2009 Jackson signed a contract with Anschutz Entertainment Group I for $50 million to do ten shows at London's arena. On June 25, 2009, Jackson collapsed at his home in Los Angeles and was pronounced dead at the UCLA Medical Center from cardiac arrest following acute propofol intoxication. His funeral was televised on July 7, 2009, from the Staples Center in Los Angeles; more than 3.1 million people watched the service. Jackson has amassed the largest audience following of any African American singer in the history of popular music. There were tributes by artists such as Mariah Carey, Stevie Wonder, John Mayer, and Jermaine Jackson. Jackson's death was ruled a homicide due to acute intoxication of a powerful anesthetic with other sedatives as factors. Jackson's personal physician pled not guilty but remains under investigation. As of January 8, 2011, no charges have been filed.

Jay-Z (1969–)
Rap/Hip-Hop Artist, Entrepreneur

Born Shawn Corey Carter on December 4, 1969, in Brooklyn, New York, Jay-Z grew up in the Marcy Projects. Nicknamed "Jazzy" he began free-styling in his neighborhood as early as the 1990s. Jay-Z released his first single in 1994 called "I Can't Get Wit That." He decided to create his own opportunities by forming the Roc-A Fella Record label and released his debut album *Reasonable Doubt* in 1996. His next album *In My Lifetime, Volume 1* was released in 1997 by Def Jam Records while working with executive producer Sean "Puffy" Combs. His biggest hit came in 1998 when he released *Volume 2 ... Hard Knock Life,* which went multiplatinum. This album was followed by *Volume 3 ... Life and Times of S. Carter,* released in 1999, which was also successful.

Jay-Z partnered with Damon Dash and began developing other artists. In 2001 he released the album *The Blueprint,* which featured new artists and debuted at number one. Jay-Z's albums continued to produce top selling singles such as "Excuse Me, Miss" and "Bonny and Clyde" from his 2003 re-release of *The Blueprint 2.1.* After releasing *The Black Album* in 2003, Jay-Z retired and became the first African American executive of a major record label. As an executive and entrepreneur, he discovered artists such as Rihanna and started the clothing line Rocawear. Jay-Z came out of retirement in 2005 and released his comeback album *Kingdom Come* in 2006.

In 2009 after marrying long-time girlfriend and mega star Beyoncé Knowles, Jay-Z released the record *The Blueprint 3,* with the single "Empire State of Mind," featuring Alicia Keys, reaching number one on *Billboard* charts. Jay-Z was CEO of his original label, Rock-A-Fella, and held the same position at Def Jam Records; he has become co-owner of The 40/40 Club, and is part owner of the NBA's New Jersey Nets as well as having investments in real estate, cosmetics, and fine art.

Bobby Jones (1939–)
Television Host, Gospel Singer

Bobby Jones was born on September 18, 1939, in Henry County, Tennessee. He graduated from high school at fifteen and became a schoolteacher in Nashville, Tennessee, after earning his master's degree from Tennessee State University (TSU) at

nineteen. In 1970, while teaching reading skills at Tennessee State, he began singing on the gospel circuit. He did this while being an active church member and an activist in the civil rights movement and for the community. In 1976 he helped present the first Black Expo featuring workshops on community and cultural issues as well as gospel. When asked by BET's owner Robert L. Johnson to bring gospel music to his network, Jones left in 1980 to host *The Bobby Jones Gospel Hour.*

Jones continued to perform internationally and throughout the United States and later started his own record label, GospoCentric. He was invited to the White House to perform for President Ronald Regan and to the Kennedy Center for the Performing Arts. Jones has received a Grammy, Dove Awards, and three Stellar Awards. He maintained his position at TSU and earned a Ph.D. at Vanderbilt University in Nashville. In 1989 he produced a new show *Video Gospel.* He continues to perform and feature other artists in his work. He released the albums *Faith Unscripted* (2007), *The Ambassador* (2007), and *Comin' Back Hard* (2009). Jones continues to be known for his efforts to spread gospel music to audiences all over the world.

Quincy Jones (1933–)
Trumpeter, Arranger, Producer

Quincy Delightt Jones Jr. was born on March 14, 1933, in Chicago, Illinois. At age ten Jones moved to Bremerton, Washington. As a member of Bumps Blackwell's Junior Orchestra, Jones performed at local Seattle social functions. In 1949 Jones played third trumpet in Lionel Hampton's band in the local Seattle club scene. After befriending jazz bassist Oscar Pettiford, Jones established himself as an able musician and arranger.

From 1950 to 1953 Jones performed as a regular member of Hampton's band, and he subsequently toured the United States and Europe.

During the mid-1950s Jones began to record jazz records under his own name. In 1956 he toured the Middle East and South America with the U.S. State Department Band headed by Dizzy Gillespie. Aside from performing trumpet with the likes of jazzmen Lionel Hampton and Dizzy Gillespie, Jones is popular music's quintessential music producer, producing numerous artists from Frank Sinatra to Michael Jackson.

In 1961 Jones was appointed musical director at Mercury Records. In search of new musical horizons, Jones began to produce popular music, including Leslie Gore's 1963 hit "It's My Party." Jones's growing prestige at Mercury led to his promotion to vice president of the company, marking the first time an African American had been placed in an executive position at a major label. During this time Jones also began to write and record more than fifty film scores. In 1967 he produced the music score for the movie *In the Heat of the Night*. He also produced the music score for Alex Haley's television miniseries *Roots* (1977) and co-produced the film *The Color Purple* with Steven Spielberg (1985). After his production of the 1978 Motown-backed film *The Wiz,* Jones went on to produce the film's star Michael Jackson on such recordings as *Off the Wall* (1979) and the record-breaking hit "Thriller" (1985). Jones's *Back on the Block* (1990) has been praised by critics.

Jones released *Miles & Quincy Live at Montreux* (1991), the album *Q's Juke Joint* a collection of African American post-slavery songs (1993 and 1995). The Quincy Jones Entertainment Company was formed in 1994 and collaborated with Time/Warner to produce motion pictures, television, cable, and magazines. His company produced with network support *The Fresh Prince of Bel-Air* (1990–1996), *In the House* (1995–1999), *Mad TV* (1995–2009), and *VIBE* magazine (1993). Jones published his autobiography *Q: The Autobiography of Quincy Jones* (2001). Jones has earned numerous awards and accolades, including seventy-nine Grammy nominations, twenty-seven Grammy Awards, Oscar nominations, a Grammy Legend Award in 1991, and the Humanitarian Award at the BET Awards in 2008.

Alicia Keys (1981–)
Singer

Alicia Keys was born Alicia Augello Cook on January 25, 1981, in New York City. She began taking piano lessons at the age of seven and later attended and graduated from Manhattan's Professional Performance Arts School at the age of sixteen. Her talent was recognized while she was in high school, which resulted in Keys signing a contract with Arista Records in 1998. Although Keys earned a full scholarship to Columbia University she decided to focus on her music career.

Keys released her debut album in 1999, *Songs in A Minor* with J Records, a new label created by Clive Davis. Her album, which she both wrote and produced, went platinum five times. Keys received Grammy Awards for best new artist, and best female R&B vocal performance in 2002. After releasing the album *Diary* in 2005, Keys became the first female R&B singer to have three consecutive number-one debut singles, and she received four Grammy Awards for the album.

Keys made her acting debut in the film *Smokin' Aces* (2007), followed by *The Secret Life of Bees* (2009). Successful as a multitalented artist, Keys has been active as a philanthropist and organizer for humanitarian causes as well. She co-founded Keep a Child Alive, a nonprofit to help kids with HIV or AIDS, and she is a board member of Frum Tha Ground Up, which seeks to inspire youths to excel. Keys received the BET Humanitarian Award in 2009.

Chaka Khan (1953–)
Singer

Chaka Khan was born Yvette Marie Stevens on March 23, 1953, at Great Lakes Naval Training Station, Illinois. She grew up in Chicago and decided to change her name to Chaka Khan after attending the Yoruba Tribe African Arts Center. Her career took off while singing with the group Rufus, which was signed to a contract by ABC Records. Their first album *Rufus* was released in 1973 to a moderate response. With Rufus's second album the group recorded the song "Tell Me Something Good" written by Stevie Wonder, which featured Khan and became a big hit. With subsequent albums and songs featuring Khan, came a string of successes, including *Rufusized* (1974), *Rufus Featuring Chaka Khan* (1975), and *Ask Rufus* (1977). Khan began her solo career in 1978.

In the 1980s and 1990s Khan collaborated with various artists and made an indelible mark on the industry with her sultry voice and vocal stylings. She released several albums, including *Chaka Khan* (1979), *What Cha' Gonna Do for Me?* (1981), *I Feel for You* (1985), *Destiny* (1986), and *The Woman I Am* (1992). Khan has collaborated with Quincy Jones, Joni Mitchell, George Benson, Prince, Freddie Hubbard, and Chick Corea, to name just a few. Khan received an ASCAP Rhythm and Soul Heritage Award (1998) and the Granville White Lifetime Achievement Award (2000). Khan released an album on her own label, Earth Song Records, and later signed with Sony BMG's label Burgendy Records in 2006; she released *I-Khan Divas and Funk This* in 2007.

Gladys Knight (1944–)

Singer

Born May 28, 1944, in Atlanta, Georgia, Gladys Maria Knight was raised in a family that valued education and the sounds of gospel music. At age four Knight began singing gospel music at the Mount Moriah Baptist Church. When she was eight Knight won first prize on the television program *Ted Mack's Amateur Hour* for a rendition of the song "Too Young." Between the years 1950 and 1953 Knight toured with the Morris Brown Choir of Atlanta, Georgia, in 1973. Around this same time, Knight

joined her sister Brenda, brother Merald, and her cousins William and Eleanor Guest to form a local church singing group. In 1957 the group took the name the Pips upon the suggestion of cousin and manager James "Pips" Woods.

Two years later Langston George and Edward Patten replaced Brenda Knight and Eleanor Guest. Though Gladys periodically left the group, she rejoined in 1964. After recording for several record labels, the Pips finally signed with Motown's subsidiary, Soul. Despite the lack of commercial success, the group released a number of fine recordings under the supervision of Motown's talented production staff, including Norman Whitfield and Ashford and Simpson. In 1967 the group released the single "I Heard It Through the Grapevine," which reached number two on the *Billboard* charts. Following a long string of hits on Motown, the Pips signed with the Buddah label in 1973, releasing the album *Imagination*, which provided the group with two gold singles, "Midnight Train to Georgia" and "I've Got to Use My Imagination."

By the late 1970s the group, faced with legal battles and contract disputes, began to fall out of popular vogue. For three years the group was barred from recording or performing together. As a result of an out-of-court settlement in 1980, the Pips signed a new contract with CBS, where they remained until 1985. Joined by Dionne Warwick and Elton John, Knight recorded the Grammy Award–winning gold single "That's What Friends Are For" in 1986. Released in 1988, the title cut of the Pips' *Love Overboard* album became their biggest-selling single in decades. That same year, Knight recorded the theme for the James Bond film *License to Kill*. Released on the MCA label, Knight's 1991 album *Good Women* features guest stars Patti LaBelle and Dionne Warwick. In 1994 Knight released *Just for You*, took a recurring role in the television series *New York Undercover*, and dealt with family and personal issues.

In 2001 Knight released the album *At Last*, which earned her a Grammy for best traditional R&B vocal album. She has received numerous awards, including induction into the Rock and

Roll Hall of Fame (1995), a Grammy for best gospel performance for the song "Heaven Help Us All," a duet with Ray Charles (2005), a Lifetime Achievement Award from BET (2005), and her seventh Grammy for the best choral group for "One Voice," which she performed with the Saints Unified Voices (2007).

Beyoncé Knowles (1981–)

Singer, Actress

Beyoncé Gisele Knowles was born in Houston, Texas, on September 4, 1981. She was interested in music as a child and sang in the church choir; she also participated in pageants, which allowed her to showcase her singing. In 1990 Beyoncé and LaTavia Roberson formed a group they called Girls' Tyme. The group added Kelendria Rowland as a member in 1992, and LeToya Luckett in 1993. After several name changes the group chose Destiny's Child. Although the group signed with Elektra Records in 1995, it was dropped and signed with Columbia Records in 1996. Their debut album *Destiny's Child* (1998), which went platinum, was followed by *The Writing's on the Wall* (1999), which earned them two Grammys. The group made changes in the members but they continued to release records well into 2004 with phenomenal success.

Beyoncé released her first solo album, *Dangerously in Love* (2003). The album was so successful that it went multiplatinum, and it was selected by the Rock and Roll Hall of Fame as one of the 200 definitive albums in music history. She released *B'Day* (2006) and *I Am ... Sasha Fierce* (2008). Beyoncé's musical talents have also earned her four MTV Music Awards, fourteen Grammy Awards, and nine Billboard Music Awards. She is the first African American woman to win the American Society of Composers, Authors and Publishers Songwriter of the Year Award (2001), and she is only the second women to receive such an award.

Beyoncé has performed with numerous artists and has contributed to soundtracks on films such as *Men in Black* (1997), *Charlie's Angels* (2000), and *Dreamgirls* (2006). She has also acted in the films *Austin Powers in Goldmember* (2002), *The Fighting Temptations* (2003), *Cadillac Records* (2008), and *Obsessed* (2009), and will star in the anticipated film *A Star Is Born*. Beyoncé continues to explore different entertainment opportunities and interests, including collaborating with her mother in a clothing line, while actively being involved in philanthropic endeavors.

Patti LaBelle (1944–)

Singer

Patti LaBelle, born Patricia Louise Holt Edwards, on May 24, 1944, in Philadelphia, Pennsylvania, was still a teenager when she started the group known as LaBelle and the Bluebelles. The group, which had several name changes, was called LaBelle when they had their biggest hit with the song "Lady Marmalade." The group disbanded in 1976 and LaBelle began her solo career.

In the 1980s and 1990s LaBelle found much success with singles such as "New Attitude" (1985), "On My Own" in a duet with Michael McDonald (1986), and albums such as *Burnin'* (1991), *Gems* (1994), and *Flame* (1997). She released a studio album *When a Woman Loves* (2000), and *The Gospel According to Patti LaBelle* (2006). LaBelle joined with former LaBelle members to release the album *Back to Now* (2008).

LaBelle has received numerous awards including Emmy and Grammy nominations, a Grammy for best R&B vocal performance (1992), the Soul Train's Lady of Soul Award (2001), and induction into the Apollo Legends Hall of Fame (2009). LaBelle has taken roles in film and television and has performed on Broadway in the gospel musical *Your Arm's Too Short to Box with God* (1982). LaBelle continues to perform at selected gatherings and wows her audience with her range, power, and the presentation of the music.

Little Richard (1932–)
Singer, Pianist

 One of twelve children, Richard Wayne Penniman was born on December 5, 1932, in Macon, Georgia. As a child in Macon, Richard heard the sounds of gospel groups, street musicians, and spiritual-based songs emanating from homes throughout his neighborhood. Nicknamed the "War Hawk" for his unrestrained hollers and shouts, Richard was once asked to stop singing in church because his voice projected with such intensity. Richard's first song before an audience was with the Tiny Tots, a gospel group featuring his brothers Marquette and Walter. Later Richard sang with his family in a group called the Penniman Singers and appeared at churches, camp meetings, and talent contests.

In high school Richard played alto saxophone in the marching band. After school he took a part-time job at the Macon City Auditorium where he watched the bands of Cab Calloway, Hot Lips Page, Lucky Millinder, and Sister Rosetta Thorpe. At age fourteen Richard left home to become a performer in Doctor Hudson's Medicine Show. While on the road he joined B. Brown's Orchestra as a ballad singer, performing such compositions as "Good Night Irene" and "Mona Lisa." Not long afterward, he became a member of the traveling minstrel show of Sugarfoot Sam from Alabama.

Richard's first break came in 1951 when the RCA label recorded him live on the radio, producing the local hit "Every Hour." Richard and his band, the Tempo Toppers, traveled to New Orleans and eventually played the Houston rhythm and blues scene where he attracted the attention of Don Robey, president of Peacock Records. After cutting some sides for the Peacock label, Richard sent a demo tape to Art Rupe's Los Angeles–based Specialty label. Under the direction of Specialty's producer Bumps Blackwell, Richard recorded the 1956 hit "Tutti Frutti" at J&M Studios in New Orleans. Richard's subsequent sessions for Specialty yielded a long list of classic hits such as "Long Tall Sally" (1956), "Lucille" (1957), "Jenny, Jenny" (1957), and "Keep a Knockin'" (1957). In 1957 Richard appeared in the films *The Girl Can't Help It* starring Jane Mansfield (1956) and *Don't Knock Rock* with Billy Haley (1957).

From 1957 to 1959 Richard released several gospel recordings and toured with artists like Mahalia Jackson. In 1962 Richard embarked on a rock and roll tour of Europe with Sam Cooke. A year later, Richard hired an unknown guitarist, Jimi Hendrix, who went under the pseudonym of Maurice James. In Europe Richard played on the same bills as the Beatles and the Rolling Stones.

In 1958 Richard quit his rock and roll career to enter the Oakland Theological College in Huntsville, Alabama. By the 1970s, Richard pursued a career as a full-fledged evangelist and performer. In 1979 he set out on a nationwide evangelist tour. In the following decade, he appeared in the film *Down and Out in Beverly Hills* (1986) and recorded "Rock Island Line" on the tribute album to Leadbelly and Woody Guthrie entitled *Folkways: A Vision Shared* (1988).

Flamboyantly dressed, with his hair piled high in a pompadour, Little Richard is a musical phenomenon, an entertainer hailed by pop superstar Paul McCartney as "one of the greatest kings of rock 'n' roll." Richard's image, mannerisms, and musical talent set the trend for the emergence of modern popular music performers from Jimi Hendrix to Prince. Richard's continuing activity in show business represents the inexhaustible energy of a singer who had a profound impact on the careers of artists like Otis Redding, Eddie Cochran, Richie Valens, and Mitch Ryder.

Richard has been honored with numerous awards, including special Grammy Awards for his contributions (1993), a Lifetime Achievement

Award from the Rhythm and Blues Foundation (1994), induction into the NAACP Hall of Fame (2002), and induction into the Songwriters Hall of Fame (2003). A television movie about his life was released entitled *Little Richard* (2000). Richard toured throughout the 1990s and performs at selected venues. In 2007 the Mojo Topp 100 named his original hit "Tutti Frutti" as a record that helped give birth to rock and roll.

LL Cool J (1968–)

Rapper, Actor

LL Cool J was born James Todd Smith on January 14, 1968, in Bay Shore, Long Island, New York. His grandparents raised him in Queens, New York, after his parents divorced. He had a special bond with his grandfather through their shared love of music. In his pre-teens LLCool J (Ladies Love Cool James) dreamed of being the greatest rapper ever.

As part of the Def Jam family, headed by Russell Simmons and Rick Rubin, LL Cool J released his first record, "I Need a Beat," when he was sixteen years old. With the success of the record, his debut album *Radio* was released in 1985. A song from the album, "I Can't Live without My Radio," was a platinum selling record that opened the door to a performance of that single on the film *Krush Grove* (1985).

LL Cool J's career continued to be successful with major hits such as "I Need Love" (1985) and "Going Back to Cali" (1989), and albums *Mama Said Knock You Out* (1990), *Mr. Smith* (1995), *Featuring James T. Smith* (2001), *Todd Smith* (2006), and *Exit 13* (2008). He also took acting roles in a wide variety of films, including *The Hard Way* (1995), *Deep Blue Sea* (1999), *Kingdom Come* (2001), and *Rollerball* (2002). While continuing to further his career in film and music LL Cool J has devoted time to philanthropic organizations such as the Camp Cool J Foundation and Youth Enterprises, which work toward positive child welfare initiatives.

Ludacris (1977–)

Rapper, Actor

Ludacris, born Christopher Brian Bridges on September 11, 1977, in Champaign, Illinois, grew up listening to his parents' old school music. By the age of twelve he had moved on to rap and joined a Chicago hip-hop group called Loudmouth Hooligans. His family later moved to Atlanta, Georgia, where he actively polished his rap skills in talent shows and clubs, and later as a disc jockey doing rap voice-overs on station promos on Atlanta radio.

In 1999 Ludacris (meaning, "off the chain crazy") debuted with the album *Incognegro,* which he released independently through his company, Disturbing the Peace Entertainment. The success of the album attracted media attention. Ludacris decided to sign with the newly established Def Jam South and released *Back for the First Time* (2000), which contained a majority of the songs from his first independent album. This became the first album of Def Jam South. It was followed with *Word of Mouf* (2001), *Chicken and Beer* (2003), and *The Red Light District* (2004). Ludacris has been described often as a gansta rapper because many of his lyrics are controversial in their frequent use of profanity, violence, and overtly sexual lyrics. However, his albums still have gone platinum two to three times over.

In 2006 Ludacris promoted himself as having grown up and began offering a more mature persona, releasing the album *Release Therapy* with the single "Money Maker."

Master P (1967–)

Rapper, Actor, Music and Film Executive

Master P was born Percy Robert Miller on April 27, 1967, in New Orleans, Louisiana. He spent his early years playing basketball, but after a sports injury changed his focus, he went to junior college and took business courses. Master P later moved to Richmond, Virginia, and opened a record store, No Limits, and began to produce gangsta rap albums.

Master P released his debut album, *The Ghetto's Tryin' to Kill Me* (1994), selling the recordings from the trunk of his car. In 1997 he produced two collections of rap artists: *Down South Hustlers, Vol. 1* and *West Coast Bad Boys, Vol. 1*, which were also successful. Master P turned his attention to the film industry in 1998 and was successful with the films *I Got the Hook Up* and *MP Da Last Don*. He then moved to Baton Rouge, Louisiana; and by 1998 his No Limits Record Company had incorporated over twelve businesses, including music, films, sports management, and a clothing line. In 1998 he tried unsuccessfully to re-capture a basketball career by trying out for the Fort Wayne Furies and later the Charlotte Hornets, but his success as a musician and businessman continued to grow by leaps and bounds.

In 1999 Master P continued with his own music releasing the albums *Only God Can Judge Me* (2004), *Good Side Bad Side* (2004), and *America's Most Luved Bad Guy* (2006). Master P has used his business savvy to increase his influence and he supports the community with the Master P Foundation. He has incorporated his son Percy Romeo Miller Jr. into his business and has supported him in music and other investment opportunities.

Curtis Mayfield (1942–1999)

Singer, Songwriter, Producer

Born on June 3, 1942, in Chicago, Illinois, Curtis Lee Mayfield learned to sing harmony as a member of the Northern Jubilee Singers and the Traveling Souls Spiritualist Church. In 1957 Mayfield joined the Roosters, a five-man doo-wop singing group led by his close friend Jerry Butler. Renamed the Impressions, the group released the

1958 hit "Your Precious Love," featuring Butler's resonant baritone and Mayfield's wispy tenor. But in the following year Butler left the group to pursue a solo career. In search of material, Butler collaborated with Mayfield to write the hit songs "He Will Break Your Heart" (1960) and "I'm a-Telling You" (1961).

In 1960 Mayfield recruited Fred Cash to take Butler's place in the newly reformed group, the Impressions. In the next year the Impressions hit the charts with the sensual soul tune "Gypsy Women." In collaboration with Butler, Mayfield also established the Curtom Publishing Company. With the loss of original members Richard and Arthur Brooks, the three remaining members of the Impressions, Mayfield, Cash, and Sam Gooden, continued to perform as a trio. Under the direction of jazz musician/arranger Johnny Pate, the Impressions recorded "Sad, Sad Girl and Boy" and the rhythmic gospel-based song "It's Alright," released in 1963.

Also during this time Mayfield wrote a number of songs for his Chicago contemporaries, including "The Monkey Time" for Major Lance (1963), "Just Be True," for Gene Chandler (1964), and "It's All Over Now," for Walter Jackson (1964). Writing for the Impressions, however, Mayfield turned to more socially conscious themes reflecting the current of the civil rights era. Mayfield's finest message or "sermon" songs were "People Get Ready" (1965), "We're a Winner" (1968), and "Choice of Colors" (1969).

After leaving the Impressions in 1970, Mayfield released his debut album *Curtis*. On his 1971 album *Curtis Live!*, Mayfield was accompanied by a tight four-piece back-up group that included guitar, bass, drums, and percussion. Mayfield composed the score for the 1972 hit film *Superfly*. The soundtrack became Mayfield's biggest commercial success, providing him two hits with the junkie epitaph "Freddie's Dead," and the wah-wah guitar funk classic "Superfly." Despite his commercial success, Mayfield spent the remainder of the decade in collaboration with other artists, working on such projects as the soundtrack for the film *Claudine,* featuring Gladys Knight and the Pips (1974), and the production of Aretha Franklin's album *Sparkle* (1978).

Throughout the next decade, Mayfield continued to record such albums as *Love Is the Place* (1981) and *Honesty* (1982). Joined by Jerry Butler and newcomers Nate Evans and Vandy Hampton, the Impressions reunited in 1983 for a thirty-city anniversary tour. In 1983 Mayfield released the album *Come in Peace With a Message of Love*. But in August of 1990, while performing at an outdoor concert in Brooklyn, New York, Mayfield received an injury that left him paralyzed from the neck down. In the following year, Mayfield's contributions to popular music were recognized when the Impressions were inducted into the Rock and Roll Hall of Fame. Mayfield's health declined due to his paralysis, and he died on December 26, 1999.

Notorious B.I.G. (1972–1997)

Rapper

Notorious B.I.G. was born Christopher George Latore Wallace on May 24, 1972, in Brooklyn, New York. He is also known as Biggie Smalls and Big Poppa. While being involved in the drug trade in his neighborhood of Bedford-Stuyvesant he would battle rap artists and make amateur tapes with the group Old Gold Brothers. With his lyrical presentation and superior freestyle, he caught the attention of A&R records and was signed by the subsidiary, Uptown Records. He began working with A&R's director Sean "Puffy" Combs. B.I.G. released his first solo track in 1993, "Party and Bullshit," which was on the soundtrack of the film *Who's the Man*. In 1994 he released the album *Ready to Die*. The album was successful based on the singles "Juicy," "One More Chance," and "Big Poppa." He was named rap artist of the year by the Billboard Awards in 1995.

In 1995 B.I.G. was arrested in connection with a robbery and assault, and in 1996 he was arrested in New York regarding marijuana possession. When Tupac Shakur was robbed and shot several times he publicly accused B.I.G of being involved. B.I.G. was also caught up in the heated East Coast-West Coast rivalry and there were other rumors of misconduct and disrespect that were publicly aired by Shakur in his album *Hit Em Up*. When Shakur was murdered in 1996, B.I.G.'s possible role in the death was a part of the rumor mill. B.I.G. focused his attention ironically on his second album, *Life after Death* (1997).

On March 9, 1997, Notorious B.I.G. was gunned down in Los Angeles, California, after a Soul Train Awards ceremony after-party. His second album was released posthumously and went platinum ten times over. Notorious B.I.G., a six-foot-three-inch 300-pound presence, left an indelible mark on the rap world. Some of his unreleased material was presented in the album *Born Again* (1999), and his words, music, and style continue to be sampled and appreciated by other artists.

Teddy Pendergrass (1950–2009)

Singer

Theodore DeReese "Teddy" Pendergrass was born on March 26, 1950, in Philadelphia, Pennsylvania. He began his professional career as a drummer. Pendergrass began singing with Harold Melvin and the Blue Notes, a doo-wop group, and they signed with Gamble and Huff's Philadelphia International label. With his powerful and soulful voice Pendergrass earned the lead spot with the Blue Notes and in 1972 the group produced singles such as "I Miss You," and "If I Don't Know You by Now."

In 1976 Pendergrass left the group to pursue a solo career. With his Teddy Bear Orchestra he released singles such as "I Don't Love You Anymore" (1976), and "Close the Door" (1978), and other singles that made female fans more and more receptive to Pendergrass and his sexy style. In 1982 as a result of a car crash, Pendergrass was paralyzed from the neck down.

Pendergrass returned to singing and signed with Elektra/Asylum Records in 1983. Although his voice lacked some of the luster that existed before the accident, his power to engage and please the audience with his expression and sexy sultry baritone sounds still earned him a huge following of both women and men. He released *Love Language* (1984), which went gold, *Workin' It Back* (1985), *Joy* (1988), and *Little More Magic* (1993). Pendergrass also released *You and I* (1997), and *Teddy with Love* (2002). He officially retired in 2006 and remained an advocate for the disabled. Pendergrass died on January 13, 2009, while trying to recover from colon cancer surgery.

Charley Pride (1939–)
Singer

Born on March 18, 1939, in Sledge, Mississippi, Charley Frank Pride grew up listening to late-night radio broadcasts of the Grand Ole Opry. Although he taught himself guitar at age fourteen, Pride soon turned his attention to a professional baseball career. At age sixteen he left the cotton fields of Sledge for a stint in the Negro American League. During his baseball career, Pride sang on public address systems and in taverns. In 1963 country singer Red Sovine heard Pride's supple baritone voice and arranged for him to attend an audition in Nashville a year later. This led to a recording contract with the RCA label, which produced the 1964 hit "Snakes Crawl at Night."

Throughout the 1960s Pride toured incessantly, appearing at concert dates and state fairs, as well as on radio and television. In 1967 Pride made his debut at the Grand Ole Opry and within the same year hit the charts with singles "Does My Ring Hurt Your Finger?" and "I Know One." By the time he received the Country Music Award for Entertainer of the Year in 1971, Pride had already achieved tremendous success as a major figure in the American popular cultural scene.

During the 1980s, Pride not only continued to find success as a music star, but he also became a successful entrepreneur. Making his home on a 240–acre estate in north Dallas, Texas, Pride emerged as a majority stockholder in the First Texas Bank and part owner of Cecca Productions.

He owns real estate, radio stations, and the Charley Pride Theater in Branson, Missouri. He also has a publishing company, the Pride Group. Pride, the first African American superstar of country music, was inducted into the Grand Ole Opry (1993). He has received several American Music and Country Music Association awards and was awarded the Academy of Country Music's Pioneer Award (1994). Pride, an internationally acclaimed three-time Grammy winner, was inducted into the Country Music Hall of Fame (2000).

Prince (1958–)
Singer, Songwriter, Producer

The son of a jazz pianist, Prince Rogers Nelson was born on June 7, 1958, in Minneapolis, Minnesota. Named after the jazz trio Prince Rogers Trio in which his father was the pianist, Prince by the age of fourteen taught himself to play piano, guitar, and drums. Drawn to many forms of rock and soul, Prince explained that he never grew up in one particular culture. "I'm not a punk, but I'm not an R&B artist either—because I'm a middle-class kid from Minnesota."

It was his eclectic taste that led to Prince's creation of the Minneapolis sound. After forming the band Grand Central in high school in 1973, Prince renamed the group Champagne and eventually recruited the talents of composer Morris Day. In 1978 Prince signed with Warner Brothers and recorded his debut album, *For You*. His follow-up album, *Prince* (1979), featured the hit "I Wanna Be Your Lover." Rooted in the music of Sly and the Family Stone and Jimi Hendrix, Prince released his third album, *Dirty Mind* (1980).

Two years later, Prince achieved superstardom with his album *1999,* an effort that was followed by a spectacular tour composed of Prince and the Revolution, the Time, and the bawdy girl trio Vanity 6. Prince's film soundtrack *Purple Rain* (1984), which received rave reviews for his portrayal of a struggling young musician, grossed

$60 million at the box office in the first two months of its release. Near the end of 1985 Prince established his own record label, Paisley Park, the warehouse/studio located in the wooded terrain of Chanhassen, Minnesota. The same year, Prince released the album *Around the World in a Day,* featuring the hit singles "Raspberry Beret," "Paisley Park," and "Pop Life."

Prince's next film project, *Under the Cherry Moon* (1986), filmed in France, was completed under his direction. The soundtrack *Parade: Music from Under the Cherry Moon,* produced a number of hit singles, including "Kiss" and "Mountains." After reforming the Revolution, Prince released *Sign of the Times* (1987), which included a duet with Sheena Easton, "I Could Never Take the Place of Your Man." Following the album *Lovesexy* (1988), Prince recorded several songs that appeared on the soundtrack for the film *Batman* (1989). This was followed by another film soundtrack, *Graffiti Bridge* (1990).

In September 1992, Prince signed a six-album contract with Warner Brothers. Backed by his new first-rate ensemble, the New Power Generation, Prince embarked on a nationwide tour in April 1993, which proved the most impressive since his commercial breakthrough in the early 1980s. Prince has not only become an owner of his own nightclub, the Grand Slam, he has contributed a set of original music to the Joffre Ballet's production of *Billboards,* which opened in January 1993 to rave reviews.

As a result of a dispute with Warner Brothers Prince denounced his stage name and created a symbol to represent him. He was often referred to as "the artist, formerly known as Prince" which was referenced from 1993 through 2000. He released *Musicology* (2004), which won two Grammys, and *3121* (2006). Prince continues to push convention and produce innovative work.

Queen Latifah (1970–)
Singer, Actress

Queen Latifah, born Dana Elaine Owens on March 18, 1970, in East Orange, New Jersey, re-

ceived her name "Latifah," which means "delicate" and "kind" in Arabic, from a cousin when she was eight years old. She began performing in high school as the human beat box for the rap group Ladies Fresh. In 1989 she launched her solo recording career with the album *All Hail the Queen.* Her other recordings include *Nature of a Sista'* (1991), featuring the single "Latifah Had It Up 2 Here," and *Black Reign* (1993). In 1993 she also released "U.N.I.T.Y.," which is considered a feminist anthem and earned her a Grammy Award in 1994. She later released *She's the Queen: A Collection of Hits* (2002), and *The Dana Owens Album* (2004).

In 1991 Latifah began managing the careers of other rap artists through her New Jersey–based Flavor Unit Records and Management Company, for which she serves as the CEO. In addition, Latifah also appeared in the television show, "Living Single, with co-stars Kim Fields, Erika Alexander, and Kim Coles, on the Fox Television Network (1993–1998). She has also made appearances on *Fresh Prince of Bel-Air,* and in such films as *House Party 2* (1991), *Jungle Fever* (1992), *Set It Off* (1996), *Living Out Loud* (1998), *The Bone Collector* (1999), and *Chicago* (2001), which earned her an Oscar nomination. Her film roles have continued to expand as seen in the movies *Bringing Down the House* (2003), *Beauty Shop* (2005), *Last Holiday* (2007), and *The Secret Life of Bees* (2008).

Otis Redding (1941–1967)
Singer, Songwriter

Born on September 9, 1941, in Dawson, Georgia, Otis Ray Redding Jr. moved with his parents at age three to the Tindall Heights housing project in Macon. In grade school Redding played drums and sang in a church gospel group, and a few years later he learned the vocals and piano style of his idol, Little Richard. Quitting school in the tenth grade, Redding went on the road with Little Richard's former band, the Upsetters. But Redding's first professional break came when he joined Johnny Jenkins and the Pinetoppers. Redding's debut single was a Little Richard imitation tune, "Shout Bamalama" (1960). Accompanying Jenkins to a Stax studio session in Memphis, Redding was afforded some remaining recording time. Backed by Jenkins on guitar, Steve Cropper on piano, Lewis Steinberg on bass, and Al Jackson on drums, Redding cut "Hey Hey Baby" and the hit "These Arms of Mine" (1962).

Signed to the Stax label, Redding released the album *Pain in My Heart* (1963). Backed by members of Booker T. and the MGs, Redding's follow-up album *Otis Blue: Otis Redding Sings Soul* featured the hit "Respect" (1965). In the next year, Redding broke attendance records at shows in Harlem and Watts. After releasing a cover version of the Rolling Stones' song "Satisfaction" (1966), Redding embarked on a European tour that included an appearance on the British television show *Ready Steady Go!*

In August 1966 Redding established his own record company, Jotis, which was distributed through the Stax label. Following a few commercially unsuccessful ventures, Redding recorded singer Arthur Conley, who provided the label with the million-selling single "Sweet Soul Music." Redding's recordings "Try a Little Tenderness" and the vocal duet "Tramp," featuring Carla Thomas, hit the charts in 1967. Redding, backed by the MGs, performed a stunning high-paced set at the Monterey Pop Festival on June 16, 1967. On December 10, Redding's career came to an tragic end when the twin-engine plane carrying him to a concert date in Wisconsin crashed in Lake Monona, just outside Madison. As if in tribute, Redding's song "Sitting on the Dock of the Bay," released a few weeks after his death, became his first gold record.

Lionel Richie (1949–)
Singer, Songwriter, Pianist

Lionel Brockman Richie Jr. was born on June 20, 1949, in Tuskegee, Alabama. He grew up on the campus of Tuskegee Institute with his his Army systems analyst father and school principal mother. Richie's grandmother Adelaide Foster, a classical pianist, became his music instructor and introduced him to the works of Bach and Beethoven. While a freshman at the Tuskegee Institute, Richie formed the Mighty Mystics who, along with members of the Jays, became the Commodores. Combining gospel, classical, and country-western music, the Commodores emerged as a formidable live act throughout the 1960s and 1970s. After signing with the Motown label, the group landed its first hit in 1974 with the song "Machine Gun." In 1981 Richie recorded the hit theme song for Franco Zefferelli's film *Endless Love.*

A year later Richie released his first solo album, *Lionel Richie* (1982), which featured the hits "Truly," "You Are," and "My Love." His follow-up release *Can't Slow Down* (1983) produced five more hits: "All Night Long (All Night)," "Running with the Night," "Hello," "Stuck on You," and "Penny Lover." In collaboration with Michael Jackson, Richie co-wrote "We Are the World" (1985) for USA for Africa, the famine relief project organized and produced by Quincy Jones. In 1985 Richie received an Oscar nomination for best original song for his composition "Say You, Say Me." A year later Richie's third album, *Dancing on the Ceiling* (1986), provided him with the hits "Dancing on the Ceiling," "Love Will Conquer All," "Ballerina Girl," and "Se La."

Richie was inducted into the Songwriters Hall of Fame in 1994. After personal and health concerns in the 1990s, Richie moved to Mercury Records and released *Louder than Words* (1996), followed by *Time* (1998), *Renaissance* (2001), *Encore* (2002), *Just For You* (2004), and *Coming Home* (2006). Richie's music has reached across generations and allowed new listeners to enjoy the smooth sound of this five-time Grammy winner, Oscar winner for best song, a Golden Globe winner, and winner of numerous American Music Awards.

Smokey Robinson (1940–)
Singer, Songwriter, Producer

William Robinson Jr. was born in Detroit, Michigan, on February 19, 1940. After his mother died when he was ten years old, Robinson was raised by his sister. Nicknamed "Smokey" by his uncle, Robinson was a bright student who enjoyed reading books and poetry. A reluctant saxophone student, Robinson turned his creative energy to composing songs, which he collected in a dime store writing tablet. While attending Detroit's Northern High School in 1954, Robinson formed the vocal group the Matadors, which performed at battle-of-the-band contests and at recreation centers.

Robinson's introduction to Berry Gordy in 1957 resulted in the Matadors' first record contract with George Goldner's End label. Upon joining the newly formed Motown label in 1960, the group changed its name, upon the suggestion of Gordy, to the Miracles. Although the Miracles's debut album failed to attract notice, the group provided Motown with its first smash hit, "Shop Around" (1961), a song written and co-produced by Robinson.

In close collaboration with Gordy, Robinson spent the following decade as one of Motown's most integral singers and producers. With the Miracles he recorded such hits as "You Really Got a Hold on Me" (1963), "Tracks of My Tears" (1965), "I Second That Emotion" (1967), and "Tears of a Clown" (1970). As a writer, he provided the label with hits like "My Guy" for Mary Wells, "I'll Be Doggone" for Marvin Gaye, and "My Girl" for the Temptations.

In 1972 Robinson left the Miracles to launch a solo career. Despite the moderate success of his records during the disco craze of the 1970s, Robinson continued to perform and record. In 1979 Robinson experienced a comeback with the critically acclaimed hit "Cruisin." Three years later, Robinson appeared on the NBC–TV special *Motown 25: Yesterday, Today, and Tomorrow.* Between 1986 and 1991 Robinson released five more albums, including *Smoke Signals, One Heartbeat,* and *Love, Smokey.*

Robinson signed with a British company, Music by Design, in 1995 and released *Intimate* in 1999 while touring and making concert appearances. He was inducted into the Songwriters Hall of Fame, and the Rock and Roll Hall of Fame (1986) and received a Grammy Award for his vocal performance of the song "Just to See Her" (1987). He released a gospel record *Food for the Spirit* (2004) and a pop album *Timeless Love* (2006). Robinson has received numerous awards including an honorary doctorate from Howard University and Kennedy Center Honors in December 2006.

Proclaimed by Bob Dylan as one of America's greatest poets, Smokey Robinson is a pop music legend who has risen to fame as a brilliant songwriter, producer, and singer. His instantly recognizable falsetto voice continues to bring Robinson gold records and a legion of loyal fans.

Diana Ross (1944–)
Singer, Actress

One of six children, Diane Ernestine Earle Ross was born in Detroit, Michigan, on March 26, 1944. An extremely active child, Ross swam, ran track, and sang in church. In 1959 she joined the Primetes, a group composed of Mary Wilson, Florence Ballard, and Barbara Martin. After failing to attract notice on the Lupine label, the group auditioned for Berry Gordy Jr., who signed them to Motown. Upon the suggestion of Gordy, the group changed its name to the Supremes. Released in 1961, the group's song "I Want a Guy," featuring Ross on lead vocals, failed to attract notice. Not long afterward, following Martin's departure, the trio continued to record with Ross on lead vocal.

The Supremes did not find commercial success on the Motown label until 1964, when they were placed under the guidance of the Holland–Dozier–Holland production team. H–D–H turned out the Supremes's first smash hit, "Where Did Our Love Go?" (1964), followed by numerous others such as "Baby Love" (1964), "I Hear a Symphony" (1965), "You Can't Hurry Love" (1966), and "Reflections" (1967). With preferential treatment by Gordy, Ross became the dominant figure of the group. By the mid-1960s, Ross's emerging talent prompted Gordy to bill the group as Diana Ross and the Supremes.

In 1970 Ross left the Supremes to launch her solo career. Her debut album *Diana Ross* featured the writing and production talents of Ashford and Simpson, an effort that included the hit "Reach Out and Touch (Somebody's Hand)." A year later she made her film debut in the Motown-sponsored movie *Lady Sings the Blues,* for which she received an Oscar nomination for her biographical portrayal of jazz singer Billie Holiday. Her role in the 1975 Motown-backed film *Mahogany* brought her not only an Oscar nomination but the number-one selling single "Do You Know Where You're Going To." In 1978 Ross starred in the film version of *The Wiz,* the last full-scale motion picture to be backed by Motown.

After leaving Motown in 1981 Ross signed a $20 million contract with the RCA label. Her debut album, *Why Do Fools Fall in Love?* (1981), went platinum. This was followed by four more albums for RCA, including *Silk Electric* (1982), *Swept Away* (1984), and *Eaten Alive* (1985). Two years later, Ross left RCA to sign with the London-based EMI label, which produced the albums *Red Hot Rhythm 'n Blues* and *Working Overtime* (1987), and *Greatest Hits, Live* (1990). Ross continued to achieve tremendous success as the owner of her own multi-million-dollar corporation Diana Ross Enterprises.

In the 1990s Ross continued her popularity both nationally and internationally and returned to both film and the pop charts. Her later films include *Out of Darkness* (1994), *Double Platinum* (1999), and her record releases include "I Got a Crush on You," a duet with Rod Stewart, and the albums *Blue* and *I Love You* (2006).

Gil Scott-Heron (1949–2011)
Hip-Hop Artist, Poet, Writer

Born on April 1, 1949, in Chicago, Illinois, Gilbert "Gil" Scott-Heron was raised by his grandparents in Jackson, Tennessee, but later moved to New York City with his mother. Scott-

Heron's interests in language and literature began in high school and at nineteen resulted in his first novel *The Vulture,* a murder mystery. His first professional venture in music was an album with Flying Dutchman Records, *Small Talk at 125th & Lenox* (1970), and was followed by *Pieces of a Man* (1970), which had a version of his work "The Revolution Will Not Be Televised" on it. Scott-Heron's work focused on a celebration of blackness while offering a lyrical and poignant look at the social upheaval and media misrepresentation of the 1970s. The album *The Revolution Will Not Be Televised,* a spoken-word indictment of mass media and consumerism, was released in 1974. Scott-Heron was praised for his vivid depiction of urban life and a political assessment of racism and injustice in American culture.

In 1974 after a disagreement with Flying Dutchman Records, Scott-Heron signed with Arista Records, a new venture of record producer Clive Davis. He joined forces with an old friend, Brian Jackson, from his year spent at Lincoln University, and produced some of his most thoughtful work as a musician, poet, and social thinker with the album *From South Africa to South Carolina* (1975), which had the Top-40 hit "Johannesburg." He went on to produce the solo album *No Nukes Concert* (1979), and among his most noted singles were "Shut 'Em Down" (1979), "Let Me See Your I.D." (1975), and "Whitey on the Moon" (1970).

Arista released *The Best of Gil Scott-Heron* (1984) and *The Revolution Will Not Be Televised,* a re-release (1988) to a new generation. Scott-Heron and his group Amnesia Express began to make appearances and Scott-Heron's music, which he called bluesology—playing what it feels like—was embraced and the album *Spirits* (1994). Scott-Heron's work was sampled by many hip-hop artists.

Scott-Heron died on My 27, 2011, at New York City hospital after battling drug addiction and other health problems. Although he did not fully embrace how great his influence was as a revolutionary poet on the world of hip-hop and spoken word, other artists clearly saw the powerful, brutal, and lyrical honesty and truth that helped you to know "what it feels like."

Tupac Shakur (1971–1996)
Rapper

Tupac Amaru Shakur was born on June 16, 1971, in the East Harlem section of Manhattan, New York. Named after a Peruvian revolutionary, he was also known professionally as 2Pac (or Pac) and Makaveli. He made his entertainment debut in a production of the play *A Raisin in the Sun* at the Apollo Theater in 1984. His family had a history of resistance through his mother's involvement with the Black Panther Party, and with violence and authority, as Shakur's sister, stepfather and godfather were all in prison for various reasons. Due to these influences and being black in America, Shakur's view of the world, along with his talents, were formed.

After moving from Harlem to Baltimore, and attending the School for the Arts, Shakur's family moved to Marin City, California. Shakur worked as a back-up dancer and roadie for the group Digital Underground and earned himself a spot as a rapper in the show. In 1991 he signed with Interescope Records and released his debut album *2Pacalypse Now,* which contains profanity and descriptions of violence.

Shakur followed his first album with *Strictly 4 My N.I.G.G.A.Z* (1993), *Me against the World* (1995), and *All Eyez On Me* (1996). He had a hard-hitting, lyrical, free-flowing style in which he related the life experiences of a young black man in America who sometimes expressed his anger with a world of injustices. His music, like his life, reflected turmoil and violence as Shakur became immersed in numerous lawsuits, sexual and assault charges, as well as becoming the center of feuds and disagreements. His professional life was on a high note and he earned accolades for his rap music and his acting performances in *Juice* (1992), *Poetic Justice* (1993), *Above the Rim* (1994), and *Gang Related* (1997). He also wrote a book of poetry titled *The Rose that Grew from Concrete* that was published after his death.

Shakur had survived acts of violence, including an incident that involved being shot five times, but on September 7, 1996, he was shot in Las Vegas, Nevada, and died six days later due to complications. The persons responsible for his death were not found. The album *The Don Killuminati: The 7 Day Theory* (1996) was released posthumously and was followed by *Better Days* (2002), *Tupac Resurrection* (2003), *Loyal to the Game* (2004), and *Pac's Life* (2006), which were all collections of his unpublished works.

Sister Rosetta Tharpe (1915–1973)
Singer, Pianist, Guitarist

Rosetta Nubin was born on March 20, 1915, in Cotton Plant, Arkansas. She sang in the Holiness Church growing up, as set by the example of her mother, and she learned how to play the piano and the guitar. At the age of four she appeared as "Little Rosetta Nubin, the singing and guitar playing miracle" and played with her mother at tent revivals throughout the South. In 1934 she married preacher Thomas Thorpe (misspelled as Tharpe), and she became known as Sister Rosetta Tharpe. Throughout the 1930s she was making recordings and appearing in nightclubs. In an appearance at the Cotton Club, she performed accompanied by her guitar.

Tharpe's performances in the South helped to spread the news of her talents as a gospel singer and she became quite well known. She performed at Carnegie Hall as part of a gospel concert with John Hammond, and she sang with gospel groups like the Dixie Hummingbirds, blues musicians such as Muddy Waters, and popular musicians such as Benny Goodman. Tharpe settled down and made Philadelphia her home. She died on October 9, 1973.

Tina Turner (1939–)
Singer

Annie Mae Bullock was born on November 25, 1939, in Brownsville, Tennessee. She moved to Knoxville with her parents at age three and sang in church choirs and at local talent contests. After moving with her mother to St. Louis at age sixteen she met pianist Ike Turner, leader of the R&B group the Kings of Rhythm. Hired by the band to sing at weekend engagements, Annie Bullock married Ike Turner in 1958 and took the stage name Tina Turner. When the band's scheduled session singer failed to appear at a recording session in 1960, Tina stepped in to record the R&B song "Fool in Love," which became a million-seller.

 With a major hit behind them, the Turners formed the Ike and Tina Turner Revue, complete with the Iketes. Major international success came for the Turners in 1966 when producer Phil Spector combined his "wall of sound" approach with an R&B sound to record the hit "River Deep, Mountain High." Subjected to years of physical abuse by her husband, Turner divorced Ike in 1976 and set out on a solo career. That same year she co-starred in The Who's rock opera film *Tommy* as the Acid Queen.

In 1984 Turner's career skyrocketed with the commercial success of the album *Private Dancer,* which featured the hit singles "What's Love Got to Do With It?" and "Better Be Good." Turner's sensuously vibrant image soon appeared on high-budget videos, on magazine covers, and in films such as the 1985 release *Mad Max 3: Beyond the Thunderdome,* in which she played the tyrannical Aunty Entity. With the immense commercial success of her 1989 album *Foreign Affair,* Turner closed out the decade as one of the most popular singers on the international music scene.

Turner engaged in six major tours between 1984 and 2000 and was placed in the *Guinness Book of World Records* for the most concert tickets sold by a solo performer. Turner has received numerous awards, including induction into the Rock and Roll of Fame in 1991, eight Grammy Awards, and recipient of the Kennedy Center Honors. Her songs "River Deep, Mountain High" and "Proud Mary" have also been inducted into the Grammy Hall of Fame. With a music career that spans over fifty years, Tina Turner has come to be known as the "hardest-working woman in show business." From soul music star to rock goddess, Turner is revered for her show-stopping vocal style and energetic stage act.

Luther Vandross (1951–2005)
Singer, Composer, Producer

Born in Manhattan, New York, on April 20, 1951, Luther Ronzoni Vandross was the son of a gospel singer and a big band vocalist. Vandross received his musical education by listening to recordings of Aretha Franklin and the Supremes. At the age of fourteen while watching the performance of Dionne Warwick he decided to become a singer. In high school Vandross formed numerous singing groups. Throughout the 1970s he was great as a background singer, performing with such artists as Bette Midler, Diana Ross, Chaka Khan, David Bowie, Carly Simon, and Ringo Starr. He also sang advertising jingles, such as AT&T's theme "Reach Out and Touch."

Following the release of his first album, *Never Too Much* (1981), Vandross was called upon to sing duets with a number of pop artists, including Aretha Franklin and Dionne Warwick. As a successful writer and producer, Vandross released eight million-selling albums, including *Best of Love* (1991), which went multi-platinum, as well as *Never Let Me Go* (1993), *Your Secret Love* (1996), and *I Know* (1998).

As Vandross continued to tour and create music that enamored audiences with the sheer quality of his silky smooth voice and the expressiveness of the songs, his work was acknowledged with a 2001 American Music Award. His last album was *Dance with My Father* (2003). He suffered a heart attack and died on July 1, 2005. One of the premier pop artists of the 1980s, Luther Vandross was responsible for the emergence of a new school of modern soul singers.

Albertina Walker (1929–2010)
Gospel Singer

Albertina Walker was born on the south side of Chicago, Illinois, on August 29, 1929. She grew up in a hard working Baptist family who belonged to the West Point Baptist Church. Albertina and her sister sang in the church choir and occasional sang as a duo, the Walker Sisters. She was inspired by gospel singers such a Mahalia Jackson, Sally and Roberta Martin, and Tommy A. Dorsey.

Walker, along with keyboard player James Cleveland and members of another ensemble, created the group the Caravans. The group was highly successful and from 1952 to the late 1960s they dominated gospel performances and had tremendous influence on the genre. They performed all over the United States and Europe.

When the group disbanded in 1967 Walker launched a solo career and continued her successes. She was nominated for a Grammy (1993), received a Grammy for her album *Songs of the Church* (1995), and received a Dove Award for *Let's Go Back: Live in Chicago* (1997). Walker died in Chicago, Illinois, on October 8, 2010, from respiratory complications after a long battle with emphysema.

Jackie Wilson (1934–1984)
Singer

Jack Leroy Wilson was born on June 9, 1934, in Detroit, Michigan. Wilson's mother sang spirituals and gospel songs at Mother Bradley's Church. As a youngster he listened to the recordings of the Mills Brothers, Ink Spots, and Louis Jordan. In high school he became a boxer, and at age sixteen he won the American Amateur Golden Gloves Welterweight title. But upon the insistence of his mother, Wilson quit boxing and pursued a career in music. While a teenager Wilson sang with the Falcons in local clubs and at talent contests held at the Paradise Theater. He also worked in a spiritual group with later members of Hank Ballard's Midnighters.

In 1953 Wilson replaced Clyde McPhatter as lead singer of the Dominoes. Wilson's only hit with the Dominoes was the reworking of the religious standard "St. Theresa of the Roses" (1956). Upon the success of the recording, Wil-

son signed a contract as a solo artist with the Brunswick label. Wilson's debut album *Reet Petite* (1957) featured the hit title track song, which was written by songwriters Berry Gordy Jr. and Billy Taylor. The songwriting team of Gordy and Taylor also provided Wilson with the subsequent hits "To Be Loved" (1957), "Lonely Teardrops" (1958), and "That's Why I Love You So," and "I'll Be Satisfied" (1959).

During the early 1960s Wilson performed and recorded numerous adaptations of classical music compositions in a crooning ballad style. This material, however, failed to bring out the powerful talent of Wilson's R&B vocal style. Although Wilson's repertoire contained mostly supper-club standards, he did manage to produce the powerful pop classics "Dogging Around" (1960) and "Baby Workout" (1963). Teamed with writer/producer Carl Davis, Wilson also recorded the hit "Whispers" and the R&B masterpiece "Higher and Higher" (1967).

Following Wilson's last major hit, "I Get the Sweetest Feeling" (1968), he performed on the oldies circuit and on Dick Clark's *Good Ol' Rock 'n' Roll Revue*. In 1975 Wilson suffered a serious heart attack on stage at the Latin Casino in Cherry Hill, New Jersey. Forced into retirement, Wilson spent his last eight years in a nursing home until his death on January 21, 1984. Between 1958 and 1963 Wilson reigned as one of the most popular R&B singers in America. Dressed in sharkskin suits and sporting a process hairstyle, Wilson exhibited a dynamic stage presence and a singing range that equaled his contemporaries James Brown and Sam Cooke.

The Winans
Gospel Music Group

Detroit's first family of gospel music, the Winans have won a number of Grammy Awards for their infectious modern pop gospel sound. David Jr., Michael, and twins Marvin and Carvin first sang at their great-grandfather's Zion Congregational Church of Christ on Detroit's east side; their father, minister and singer David Winan Sr., first organized the quartet.

While attending Mumford High School, the group attracted large crowds at school talent contests. Originally called the Testimonials, the quartet released two locally produced albums, *Love Covers* (1977) and *Thy Will Be Done* (1978).

Upon being discovered by gospel singer Andraé Crouch, the group released its first national debut album *Introducing the Winans* (1981), which was nominated for a Grammy Award. The follow-up album *Long Time Coming* (1983) also received a Grammy nomination. After changing record companies two years later, the Winans released *Let My People Go* (1985) on Quincy Jones's Qwest label. Known to join secular pop artists in collaborative singing projects, the Winans featured Michael McDonald on their release *Decisions* (1987). They also sang back-up on Anita Baker's hit single "Ain't No Need to Worry," and provided vocal tracks for Michael Jackson's song "Man in the Mirror," featured on his *Bad* album.

In 1992 the Winans appeared at "Culturefest 92" in West Africa. A year later they were invited to sing at President Bill Clinton's inauguration festivities. Known as funky gospel, the Winans's music features electric keyboards, guitar, and bass, as well as saxophone accompaniment. "In today's world, you have to have some type of beat to draw people," related Carvin. "You catch the young people with that first. The words will seep in at one point." With their release *Heart & Soul* (1995), the group was listed among the top five on the gospel album charts.

The second generation of Winans, BeBe (Benjamin) born in 1962, and CeCe (Priscilla) born in 1964, began as the Winans Part 2, with older brother Daniel.

After singing as back up for Andraé Crouch and later as members of the PTL singers of Charlotte, North Carolina, BeBe and CeCe Winans had their first hit "Up Where We Belong" (1984). They signed with the Sparrow Records and released their debut album *BeBe & CeCe Winans* (1987). With success on both the R&B and

gospel charts the duo won Grammy nominations and Dove Awards. This was followed by *Different Lifestyles* (1991), and *First Christmas* (1993).

The duo earned numerous awards while following their individual interests. BeBe Winans's solo career includes the releases *BeBe Winans* (1997), *Live and Up Close* (2002), and *Cherch* (2007). He has been able to balance his music with acting in films such as *The Manchurian Candidate* (2004) and on Broadway with *The Color Purple* (2008), as he continues to increase his acting roles, and with entrepreneurship in a weekly radio show that is available on thirty-three radio stations. CeCe Winans's solo career debuted with *Alone in His Presence* (1996), which sold platinum, followed by *Everlasting Love* (1998), *Alabaster Box* (1999), and *CeCe Winans* (2001), which all went gold. CeCe started her own recording company Pure Springs Gospel and she has become a gospel superstar. She released the album *Songs of Emotional Healing* (2010).

BeBe and CeCe Winans and the Winans family continue to have a strong influence on the body of work that raises gospel music to new heights and brings young and old closer to a spiritual awareness. Individually and collectively the Winans have won numerous Grammy Awards, Dove Awards, Stellar and NAACP Awards, and Soul Train Music Awards.

Stevie Wonder (1950–)
Singer, Pianist, Composer

Stevland Hardaway Morris Judkins was born on May 13, 1950, in Saginaw, Michigan. Raised in Detroit, he first sang in the church choir. But the music that attracted him most was the sounds of Johnny Ace and B. B. King, which he heard on late-night radio programs. Blind from birth, he learned to play piano, harmonica, and bongos by the age of eight. Through the connections of Miracles member Ronnie White, he auditioned for Berry Gordy Jr., who immediately signed the thirteen-year-old prodigy and gave him the stage name of "Little Stevie Wonder." After releasing his first singles "Thank You (For Loving Me All the Way)" and "Contract of Love," Wonder scored a number-one hit with "Fingertips Part 2" in 1963. In the following year Wonder hit the charts with the song "Hey Harmonica Man."

With the success of his recording career, Wonder began to tour more frequently. Motown's arrangement to assign Wonder a tutor from the Michigan School for the Blind allowed him to continue his education while on the road. In 1964 he performed in London with the Motown Revue, a package featuring Martha and the Vandellas, the Supremes, and the Temptations. Wonder's subsequent recording of the punchy R&B single "Uptight (Everything's All Right)" became a smash hit in 1966. Wonder's growing commercial success at Motown brought him greater artistic freedom in the studio. In collaboration with Clarence Paul, Wonder produced a long succession of hits, including Bob Dylan's "Blowing in the Wind" (1966), "I Was Made to Love Her" (1967), and "For Once in My Life" (1968).

After recording the album *Signed, Sealed & Delivered* (1970), Wonder moved to New York, where he founded Tarus Production Company and Black Bull Publishing Company, both of which were licensed under Motown. With complete control over his musical career, Wonder began to write lyrics containing social and political issues. Through the use of over-dubbing, he played most of the instruments on his recordings, including the guitar, bass, horns, percussion, and brilliant chromatic harmonica solos. His three creative albums, *Music from My Mind, Talking Book,* and *Inversions* (1972), all feature Wonder's tasteful synthesizer accompaniment.

Wonder's Journey through the Secret Life of Plants (1979) was an exploratory musical soundtrack for a film documentary. Wonder's soundtrack for the film *Woman in Red* (1984) won him an Academy Award for best song for "I Just Called to Say I Love You." A year later, Wonder participated in the recording of "We Are the World" for USA for Africa, the famine relief project. Wonder's album *Square Circle* (1985) produced the hit singles "Part Time Lover" and "Overjoyed." He released *Characters* (1987), followed by *Conversation Piece* (1995), which contains songs like "Greenhouse" and "Legal Drug Dealer" that address social issues.

Wonder has contributed to the works of other artists such as Marvin Gaye's *Inner City Blues* and Quincy Jones's *Q's Jook Joint*. His list of awards and honors, as lengthy as his list of recordings, includes induction into the Rock and Roll Hall of Fame (1989), an Essence Award, Kennedy Center Honors (2000), and a lifetime achievement award from the Songwriters Hall of Fame in New York (2002). Wonder has received more than twenty-two Grammys, including a Grammy for lifetime achievement (2005). After a ten year period Wonder released the album *A Time to Love,* with Prince, EnVogue, and India Arie singing on the title track (2005). In 2008 the Library of Congress announced Wonder as the recipient of the Gershwin Prize for Popular Song. As popular music's genius composer and singer, Wonder has remained at the forefront of musical change. His colorful harmonic arrangements have drawn upon jazz, soul, pop, reggae, and rap-derived new jack rhythms. Wonder's gift to pop music is his ability to create serious music dealing with social and political issues while at the same time revealing the more deeply mysterious nature of the human experience.

SCIENCE,
TECHNOLOGY,
INVENTORS, AND
EXPLORERS

The earliest African American scientists and inventors are largely unknown, their contributions to America buried in anonymity. While Benjamin Banneker's eighteenth-century successes in timepieces and urban planning are known and applauded, numerous achievements of seventeenth and eighteenth-century blacks in architecture, agriculture, and masonry cannot be identified. While historians increasingly recognize that blacks had a significant impact on the design and construction of plantations and public buildings in the South, and that rice farming in the Carolinas might not have been possible without the efforts of blacks, the individuals who spearheaded these accomplishments remain unknown.

Prior to the Civil War, in one of history's most absurd bureaucratic fiats, slaves neither could be granted patents nor could they assign patents to their masters. The underlying theory was that since slaves were not citizens, they could not enter into contracts with their owners or the government. As a result the efforts of slaves were dismissed or, if accepted, credited entirely to their masters. One can only speculate on the part blacks actually played in significant inventions. One such area of speculation concerns the grain harvester of Cyrus McCormick. Jo Anderson, one of McCormick's slaves, is believed to have played a major role in

the creation of the McCormick harvester, but available records are insufficient to determine the degree of Anderson's importance in the invention.

The inventions of free blacks, however, were recorded. The first black granted a patent was probably Henry Blair in 1834 for a seed planter. But again, records fail the historian, for the race of patentseekers was rarely noted. Blair may well have had numerous predecessors. Many inventions by blacks, including Augustus Jackson's invention of ice cream in 1832, were not patented.

The Reconstruction era marked an unleashing of the creativity that had been suppressed in blacks during generations of slavery. Between 1870 and 1900, at a time when some eighty percent of African American adults in the United States were illiterate, blacks were awarded several hundred patents. Notable among these were the shoe last (Jan Matzeliger, 1883); a machine for making paper bags (William Purvis, 1884); assorted machinery-lubricating equipment (Elijah McCoy, beginning in 1872); an automatic railroad car coupler (Andrew Beard, 1897); and the synchronous multiplex railroad telegraph (Granville Woods, 1888).

The contributions of black scientists are better known than those of black inventors, partly

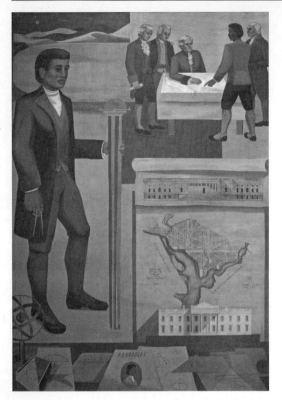

Astronomer and mathematician Benjamin Banneker is
depicted in a mural by Maxime Seelbinder.

because of the recognition awarded George
Washington Carver, an agricultural scientist who,
incidentally, refused to patent most of his inventions. African American scientists contributed
enormously to the knowledge of blood plasma,
open heart surgery, and cortisone, all vital aspects
of modern health care.

The achievements of black inventors and scientists of the mid-twentieth to twenty-first century has been obscured by reasons more complex
than blatant racial prejudice, among them the dis-
placement of the individual inventor by government and corporate research and development
teams; individuals, whatever their race, receive less
recognition under this system. The people behind
such modern inventions as the computer, television, heart pacer, and laser are relatively obscure
while such names as Bell, Edison, and Marconi are
taught to every schoolchild. In spite of this obscurity black scientists continue to contribute ex-

traordinary inventions specifically through the
work of Otis Boykin, who invented twenty-eight
electronic devices, including the control unit for
the pacemaker; Ben Carson, a neurosurgeon who
led a medical team that successfully separated con-
joined twins; and Emmett W. Chappelle, a bio-
chemist who discovered a method for detecting
bacteria in water, food, and body fluids.

An increasing number of black students have
demonstrated an interest in science—even more so
since the death of Major Robert H. Lawrence,
America's first black astronaut. African American
scientists and engineers are an integral part of the
National Aeronautics and Space Administration
(NASA). In the corporate world and academia
African American scientists and engineers are playing a substantial role in the development of solid
state devices, highpowered and ultra-fast lasers, hy-
personic flight, and elementary particle science.

Black inventors' contributions to the
progress of the twenty-first century has been invaluable and include many individuals with impressive credentials and numerous patents,
including Dr. James E. West, inventor of the Elec-
tret Microphone, which is used in everything that
requires a microphone; Dr. Mark Dean, one of the
most prominent inventors in the field of computers, who holds three of the original patents
for the personal computer; Valerie Thomas, the
inventor of the Illusion transmitter, which produces an optical illusion of three-dimensional
images; John Henry Thompson, who invented
Macromedia™, which combines computer programming language with visual arts to create
multimedia applications; Lonnie G. Johnson,
who has over forty patents, but is best known for
the Super Soaker, a squirt gun enjoyed by children and adults alike; Dr. Shirley Jackson, an inventor in telecommunications who has created
developments in fiber optics, portal fax, and
Caller ID; and George Alcorn, the inventor of the
imaging X-ray Spectrometer, a machine that
helps scientists determine the contents of material when they cannot be broken down.

The number of African American manufacturing and servicing firms in various computer and

engineering fields continues to grow. In academia today there are more African American science and technology faculty members, college presidents, and school of engineering deans than in the recent past. Many of these academicians are serving in the country's major educational institutions.

BIOGRAPHIES

George E. Alcorn (1940–)
Physicist

George E. Alcorn was born on March 22, 1940, in Miami, Florida. He received a college degree in 1962 from Occidental College, and an M.A. and Ph.D. from Howard University in 1963 and 1967, focusing on nuclear physics. He began his career at IBM but joined NASA in 1978.

At NASA Alcorn invented an imaging x-ray spectrometer, and developed a method of using laser drilling, which resulted in his work earning him the NASA/Goddard Space Flight Center Inventor of the Year Award in 1984. Alcorn served as deputy project director at NASA from 1992 to 1994, and he served as chief of Goddard's Office of Commercial programs. In 2005 he was named Assistant Director for Standards/Excellence in Applied Engineering and Technology at Goddard.

Alcorn received the Government Executive Magazine's Government Technology Leadership Award in 1999, and in 2001 he received a special congressional award for assisting the Virgin Island businesses in using NASA technology. Alcorn has over twenty inventions and eight patents and is recognized as the premier inventor in the area of fabrication of plasma semiconductor devices and techniques.

Archie Alexander (1888–1958)
Engineer

Born in Ottumwa, Iowa, on May 14, 1888, Archie Alfonso Alexander graduated from the University of Iowa in 1912 with a B.S. in civil engineering. After working for a bridge construction firm, he founded his own business in 1914, A. A. Alexander Inc. In the next eleven years he completed contracts amounting to $4,500,000. Alexander's firm was responsible for building the Tidal Basin Bridge in Washington, D.C., and the heating plant at the University of Iowa, his alma mater.

In 1925 Alexander was awarded the "Laurel Wreath" by his fraternity Kappa Alpha Psi, and in 1928 he was awarded the Spingarn Medal. He continued working with his alma mater and was named an outstanding alumnus, and one year as Governor of the Virgin Islands in 1954. He died in Des Moines, Iowa, in 1958.

Benjamin Banneker (1731–1806)
Astronomer, Mathematician

Benjamin Banneker was born on November 9, 1731, in Ellicott, Maryland. His mother was a free woman and his father was a slave who eventually purchased his own freedom.

At the age of twenty-one Banneker constructed a clock based on a pocket watch he had seen, calculating the ratio of the gears and wheels and carving them from wood. The clock operated for more than forty years.

Banneker's aptitude for mathematics and knowledge of astronomy enabled him to predict the solar eclipse of 1789. Within a few years, he began publishing an almanac that contained tide tables, data on future eclipses, and a listing of useful medicinal products and formulas. The almanac, which was the first scientific book published by an African American, appeared annually for more than a decade in Centralia, Illinois.

In 1771 Banneker served as a surveyor on the six-person team that helped lay out the base lines and initial boundaries for Washington, D.C. When the chairman of the committee, Major Pierre Charles L'Enfant, abruptly resigned and returned to France with his plans, Banneker was able to reproduce the plans in their entirety. He died on October 25, 1806.

Andrew Jackson Beard (1849–1910)
Inventor

Andrew Jackson Beard was a slave, born in 1849 in Eastlake, Alabama. While working in an Alabama railroad yard, Beard saw men lose hands and arms in accidents occurring during the manual coupling of railroad cars. The system involved the dropping of a metal pin into place when two cars came together. Men were often caught between cars and crushed to death during this split-second operation. Beard's invention, the "Jenny Coupler" (patent 594,059), was an automatic device that secured two cars by merely bumping them together. In 1897 Beard received $50,000 for an invention that has since prevented countless injuries and deaths.

Jim Beckwourth (1798–1866)
Explorer

James Pierson Beckwourth was born on April 6, 1798, near Fredericksburg, Virginia. His father was a landowner and member of a prominent Virginia family; his mother was an African American woman, possibly a slave.

The family moved to a farm near St. Charles, Missouri, in 1806 and Jim attended school in St. Louis from 1810 to 1814. He was apprenticed to a St. Louis blacksmith but soon decided to head west. In 1824 Beckwourth joined a westward-bound fur trapping and trading expedition under the leadership of William Henry Ashley. Beckwourth embodied the spirit of the legendary mountain men of the American West.

In 1827, while still engaged in the fur trade, he married a Blackfoot Indian. In 1829 he took refuge from a debt collector by hiding with the Crow Indians, where he married again. Beckwourth claims he was made a Crow chief in recognition of his fighting prowess against the Blackfoot Indians.

By 1837 Beckwourth was with the United States Army in Florida serving as a scout during the Seminole Wars. He soon returned to the Rocky Mountains, married a woman in New Mexico, and in 1842 opened a trading post near what is now Pueblo, Colorado. Between 1844 and 1850 he fought in the California uprising against Mexico and in the Mexican-American War.

In 1850 he joined the California gold rush and while in the Sierra Nevadas discovered a mountain pass that now bears his name. He made the gap more passable, opened an inn, and by 1851 was guiding wagon trains through the pass.

In 1856, with the help of ghostwriter T. D. Bonner, Beckwourth published his memoirs, *Life and Adventures of James P. Beckwourth, Mountaineer, Scout and Pioneer.* Beckwourth traveled to St. Louis and Kansas City, where the popularity of his book enhanced his reputation and he was regarded as a celebrity.

He returned to Denver, married again, opened a trading post, and was charged with and acquitted of manslaughter. Tiring of city life, he signed on with the Army as a scout and fought the Cheyenne Indians. Beckwourth probably died of food poisoning on or around September 25, 1866, while riding to a Crow encampment. Accounts of the Crow Indians intentionally poisoning him are generally dismissed as false.

David Blackwell (1919–2010)
Mathematician

David Harold Blackwell, an extraordinary African American mathematician, was born on April 24, 1919, in Centralia, Illinois. When he was sixteen years old Blackwell, who had a great love for mathematics, studied at the University of Illinois and graduated in 1938 with an A.B. degree. He went on to earn an M.A. in 1939, and in 1941 at the age of twenty-two, he completed his Ph.D. at the University of Illinois.

Although denied a second year appointment to a post-doctoral fellowship at Princeton's Institute for Advanced Study by Princeton University's president, racism did not deter Blackwell in his goal of scholarship in academia. He was named to the faculty at Howard University and went on to serve in key academic roles. After leaving Howard University for a short time Blackwell returned and remained there until 1954.

Blackwell, a prolific writer, published over eighty articles in the field of mathematics and was vice president of the Institute of Mathematical Sciences in 1955. In 1965 he was the first African American to be named to the American Academy of Sciences and later honorary fellow of the Royal Statistical Society. He has received numerous other awards and honorary degrees, and in 2002 Berkley and Cornell Universities established the Blackwell-Tapia Award to recognize those who have inspired and achieved great things in the area of mathematical sciences. Blackwell died on July 8, 2010.

Guy Bluford (1942–)

Astronaut

Guion Stewart "Guy" Bluford Jr. was born November 22, 1942, in Philadelphia, Pennsylvania. He graduated with a B.S. from Pennsylvania State University in 1964. He then enlisted in the U.S. Air Force and was assigned to pilot training at Williams Air Force Base in Arizona. Bluford served as a fighter pilot in Vietnam and flew 144 combat missions, sixty-five of them over North Vietnam. Attaining the rank of lieutenant colonel, Bluford received an M.S. from the Air Force Institute of Technology in 1974 and a Ph.D. in aeronautical engineering in 1978.

In 1979 Bluford was accepted in NASA's astronaut program as a mission specialist. On August 30, 1983, with the lift-off of the STS-8 Orbiter *Challenger,* Bluford became the first African American in space. He flew two other space shuttle missions—in 1985 and 1991—for a total of 314 hours in space. Bluford retired from NASA in 1993 to pursue a career in private industry.

Bluford has won numerous awards, including the Distinguished National Science Award given by the National Society of Black Engineers (1979), NASA Group Achievement Award (1980, 1981), NASA Space Flight Medal (1983), and the NAACP Image Award (1983). Some of his military honors include the National Defense Service Medal (1965), Vietnam Campaign Medal (1967), Air Force Commendation Medal (1972), Air Force Meritorious Service Award (1978), and the USAF Command Pilot Astronaut Wings (1983). Bluford was inducted into the International Space Hall of Fame in 1997.

Charlie Bolden (1946–)

Astronaut

Charles Frank Bolden Jr. was born on August 19, 1946, in Columbia, South Carolina. He is a graduate of the U.S. Naval Academy and the University of Southern California and has a B.S. in electrical science and an M.S. in systems management.

Bolden began his career as a second lieutenant in the U.S. Marine Corps, becoming a naval aviator by 1970. In 1973 he flew more than 100 sorties while assigned in Thailand. Upon his return to the United States, Bolden began a tour as a Marine Corps selection and recruiting officer. In 1979 he graduated from the U.S. Naval Test Pilot School and was assigned to the Naval Test Aircraft Directorates.

Bolden was selected as an astronaut candidate by NASA in May 1980, and in July 1981 he completed the training and evaluation program—making him eligible for assignment as a pilot on space shuttle flight crews. Bolden has served as pilot for the STS-31 Hubble Space Telescope mission and commander for the STS-45 mission. He has been awarded the Defense Superior Service Medal, the Defense Meritorious Service Medal, the Air Medal, and the Strike/Flight Medal. In 1994 he took a position at the Naval Academy, and in 1998 he was promoted major general. From 2000 to 2002 he was Commanding General, 3rd Marine Aircraft Wing. He retired from service in 2004.

Marjorie Lee Browne (1914–1979)
Mathematician

Browne was born September 9, 1914, in Memphis, Tennessee. She received a B.S. in mathematics from Howard University in 1935, an M.S. in 1939, and a Ph.D. in mathematics in 1949, both from the University of Michigan.

Browne taught at the University of Michigan in 1947 and 1948. She accepted the post of professor of mathematics at North Carolina Central University in 1949 and became department chairperson in 1951.

Browne's doctoral dissertation dealt with topological and matrix groups, and she has been published in the *American Mathematical Monthly*. She was a fellow of the National Science Foundation (1958–1959, and 1965–1966). Browne belongs to the American Mathematical Society, the Mathematical Association of America and the Society for Industrial and Applied Mathematics. Brown died on October 19, 1979.

Alexa I. Canady (1950–)
Neurosurgeon

Alexa Irene Canady, the first African American female neurosurgeon in the United States, was born on November 7, 1950, in Lansing, Michigan. After completing her education with a B.S. in 1971 and an M.D. in 1975 from the University of Michigan, Canady began her internship at the Yale-New Haven Hospital from 1975 to 1976. She later became the first African American female to get a residency in neurosurgery at the University of Minnesota from 1976 to 1981.

In 1983 Canady moved her internship to Children's Hospital in Michigan and became the director of the facility by 1987. She retired in 2001 as chief of neurosurgery at Children's Hospital in Michigan.

Canady's accomplishment have been recognized with numerous awards, including induction into the Michigan Women's Hall of Fame and being named Woman of the Year in 1993.

George E. Carruthers (1939–)
Physicist

George E. Carruthers was born on October 1, 1939, in Cincinnati, Ohio, and was raised in South Side, Chicago, Illinois. He built his first telescope at the age of ten. He received a bachelor's degree and a master's degree in aeronautical engineering in 1961 and 1962, and a Ph.D. in physics in 1964 from the University of Illinois. He started employment with the Navy in 1964. Carruthers is the recipient of the NASA Exceptional Scientific Achievement medal for his work on the ultraviolet camera/spectrograph.

Carruthers is one of two naval research laboratory scientists responsible for the Apollo 16 program's lunar surface ultraviolet camera/spectrograph, which was placed on the moon in April 1972. Carruthers designed the instrument, while William Conway adapted the camera for the lunar mission. The spectrographs, obtained from eleven targets, include the first photographs of the ultraviolet equatorial bands of atomic oxygen that girdle the earth.

Carruthers continued his work and became head of the Ultraviolet Measurements Group in the Space Science Division. He won the Arthur S. Fleming Award in 1971 and the Outstanding Scientist Award in 2000. Caruthers was inducted into the National Inventors Hall of Fame in 2004.

Ben Carson (1951–)
Neurosurgeon

Benjamin S. "Ben" Carson was born on September 18, 1951, in Detroit, Michigan. A child with a quick temper and a lack of interest in school, he later turned his life around. After earning a scholarship out of high school, Carson received a B.A. in psychology from Yale University and an M.D. in neurosurgery in 1977 from the University of.

In 1984 at the age of thirty-three Carson became the youngest chief of pediatric neurosurgery in the United States. In 1985 Johns Hopkins named him director of the Division of Pediatric Neurosurgery. In 1987 Carson received national and international acclaim when he successfully separated a pair of West German Siamese twins in an operation that lasted twenty-two hours and was supported by a surgical team of seventy doctors, nurses, and surgical technicians.

Carson survived his own personal health challenge in 2002 when he was diagnosed with prostate cancer but endured and continues to serve. He has authored three bestselling books, including *The Big Picture* (1999), and has received the 2008 Presidential Medal of Freedom and other awards. He established the Carson Scholarship Fund and co-founded the Benevolent Endowment Fund to assist with financial concerns of the uninsured. His own triumph over personal circumstances has also made him a sought-after speaker and inspiration for young people.

George Washington Carver (c. 1864–1943)

Agricultural Scientist

George Washington Carver was born a slave in Diamond Grove, Missouri, between 1861 and 1865. Carver was only an infant when he and his mother were abducted from his owner's plantation by a band of slave raiders. His mother was sold and shipped away, but Carver was ransomed by his master in exchange for a race horse.

While working as a farm hand, Carver managed to obtain a high school education. He was admitted as the first black student of Simpson College, Indianola, Iowa. He then attended Iowa Agricultural College (now Iowa State University) where, while working as the school janitor, he received a degree in agricultural science in 1894. Two years later he received a master's degree from the same school and became the first African American to serve on its faculty. Within a short time his fame spread, and Booker T. Washington offered him a post at the Tuskegee Institute.

Carver revolutionized the southern agricultural economy by showing that three hundred products could be derived from the peanut. By 1938 peanuts had become a $200-million industry and a chief product of Alabama. He also demonstrated that one hundred different products could be derived from the sweet potato.

Although he held three patents, Carver did not patent most of his many discoveries made while at Tuskegee, saying, "God gave them to me, how can I sell them to someone else?" In 1938 he donated over $30,000 of his life's savings to the George Washington Carver Foundation and willed the rest of his estate to the organization so his work might be carried on after his death.

George Washington Carver devoted his life to research projects connected primarily with southern agriculture. The products he derived from the peanut and the soybean revolutionized the economy of the South by liberating it from an excessive dependence on cotton. Carver died on January 5, 1943.

Jewell Plummer Cobb (1924–)

Cell Biologist

Jewell Plummer Cobb was born on January 17, 1924, in Chicago, Illinois. By 1950 she had completed her education by earning an M.S. and a Ph.D. in biology. As a cell biologist Cobb studied the effects of cancer on human cells and different issues regarding skin pigments such as melanoma and preventive techniques such as ultraviolet light.

Cobb has championed the cause of the women and minorities in science as well as being active in her community. She has received numerous honors and awards, including the National Science Foundation Lifetime Achievement Award for Contributions to the Advancement of

Women and Underrepresented Minorities presented in 1993. In 2001 Cobb was named principle investigator for the Science and Technology Engineering Program (STEP) Up for Youth at California State University, Los Angeles.

Price C. Cobb (1928–)
Psychiatrist, Writer

Price C. Cobb was born on November 2, 1928. Cobb, following in the footsteps of his father, who was a doctor, earned his B.A in 1954 from the University of California of Berkeley, and in 1958 he received his M.D. from Meharry Medical College in Nashville, Tennessee. Cobb established his own practice in psychiatry in San Francisco a few years after graduation.

Cobb's first book, co-authored with University of California colleague William H. Grier in 1968, was *Black Rage*. The book discusses the psychiatry associated with social and economic racism that was pervasive during that time. They also authored a second book on the role of religion in the African American community entitled *The Jesus Bag* in 1971.

Cobb founded the Pacific Management Systems in 1967 as a diversity training service. Cobb is a member of numerous organizations and community groups and continues to encourage people to reevaluate their impressions and misconceptions of others.

W. Montague Cobb (1904–1990)
Physician, Medical Editor

William Montague Cobb was born in Washington, D.C., on October 12, 1904. He earned a B.A. from Amherst College, an M.D. from Howard University and a Ph.D. from Case Western Reserve. For fifty-one years W. Montague Cobb was a member of the Howard University Medical School faculty, and thousands of medical and dental students have studied under his direction. At Howard, he built a collection of more than 600 documented skeletons and a comparative anatomy museum in the gross anatomy laboratory.

As editor of the *Journal of the National Medical Association* for twenty-eight years, he developed a wide range of scholarly interests evinced by the nearly 700 published works under his name in the fields of medical education, anatomy, physical anthropology, public health, and medical history.

He was the first African American elected to the presidency of the American Association of Physical Anthropologists, and he served as chairman of the anthropology section of the American Association for the Advancement of Science. Among his many scientific awards is the highest award given by the American Association of Anatomists. For thirty-one years he was a member of the board of directors of the NAACP, and served as the board's president from 1976 to 1982. He died on November 20, 1990.

Elbert Frank Cox (1895–1969)
Mathematician

Cox was born in Evansville, Indiana, on December 5, 1895. He received his B.A. from Indiana University in 1917, and his Ph.D. from Cornell University in 1925. His dissertation dealt with polynomial solutions and made Cox the first African American to be awarded a doctorate in pure mathematics.

Cox was an instructor at Shaw University from 1921 to 1923, a professor in physics and mathematics at West Virginia State College from 1925 to 1929, and an associate professor of mathematics at Howard University from 1929 to 1947. In 1947 he was made full professor.

Cox was a Brooks fellow and an Erastus Brooks fellow, and he belonged to the Mathematical Society and the Physical Society. Cox died on November 28, 1969.

Ulysses Grant Dailey (1885–1961)
Surgeon

Born in Donaldsonville, Louisiana, in 1885, Ulysses Grant Dailey graduated in 1906 from Northwestern University Medical School, where he was appointed a demonstrator in anatomy. He served as surgical assistant to heart surgeon Dr. Daniel Hale Williams, founder of Provident Hospital and noted heart surgeon, (1908–1912), and he later studied in London, Paris, and Vienna. In 1926 Dailey set up his own hospital and sanitarium in Chicago. His name soon became associated with some of the outstanding achievements being made in anatomy and surgery.

For many years an associate editor of the *Journal of the National Medical Association,* Dailey traveled around the world in 1933 under the sponsorship of the International College of Surgeons, of which he was a founder fellow.

In 1951 and again in 1953 the U.S. State Department sent him to Pakistan, India, Ceylon, and Africa. A year later he was named honorary consul to Haiti and retired there. Dailey died in 1961.

Charles R. Drew (1904–1950)
Physician, Blood Plasma Researcher

Born on June 3, 1904, in Washington, D.C., Charles Richard Drew graduated from Amherst College in Massachusetts, where he received the Messman Trophy for having brought the most honor to the school during his four years there. He was not only an outstanding scholar but the captain of the track team and a star halfback on the football team.

After receiving his medical degree from McGill University in 1933, Drew returned to Washington, D.C., to teach pathology at Howard University. In 1940, while taking his D.Sc. degree at Columbia University, he wrote a dissertation on "banked blood." Using techniques already developed for separating and preserving blood, Drew further explored the field of blood preservation and applied research procedures to clinical work. This led the British government to call upon him to set up the first blood banks just prior to World War II.

During World War II, Drew was appointed director of the American Red Cross blood donor project. Later, he served as chief surgeon at Freedmen's Hospital in Washington, D.C., as well as professor of surgery at Howard University Medical School from 1941 to 1950. He was killed in an automobile crash in 1950.

Joycelyn Elders (1933–)
Physician, Endocrinologist, Former U.S. Surgeon General

Joycelyn Elders, born Minnie Lee Jones on August 13, 1933, in Schaal, Arkansas, initially sought a career as a lab technician. After completing her B.S. degree in biology from Philander Smith College in Little Rock, Arkansas, Elders enrolled in the University of Arkansas School of Medicine. Elders also changed her name to Minnie Jocelyn Lee and later dropped the Minnie. Elders graduated in 1960 and did a residency at the University of Minnesota followed by a residency at the University of Arkansas Medical Center in 1961. It was here that she began a twenty-year career beginning as chief pediatric resident. She went on to specialize in pediatric endocrinology and publish over 100 articles and papers in this area. She became professor of pediatrics and maintained that position from 1976 to 1987 when she was named director of the Arkansas Department of Health.

Elders's public advocacy regarding teen pregnancy and sexual behavior opened the door for her nomination by President Bill Clinton in 1993 as Surgeon General. She was approved as U.S. Surgeon General on September 7, 1993. Elders' tenure was not lacking in controversy around her support of the use of marijuana and the discussion in schools about masturbation. Elders was forced to resign as Surgeon General in 1994.

Elders returned to teaching at the University of Arkansas in 1995, as a professor of pediatrics, and has continued to teach and lecture. In 1996 she wrote her autobiography, *Jocelyn Elders, MD: From Sharecropper's Daughter to Surgeon General of America.* Although she retired from medicine in 1999 she continues to lecture on heath related issues and to advocate for needed service and information for the public. In 2002 she became an expert on childhood sexual development and earned a degree from Bates College.

Philip Emeagwali (1954–)
Computer Scientist

Philip Chukwurah Emeagwali was born on August 23, 1954, in Akure, Nigeria. He completed a B.S in mathematics at Oregon State University in 1977 and an M.S. in civil engineering from George Washington University in 1981. Emeagwali became a U.S. citizen in 1981 when he married renowned scientist Dale Brown. He continued his education and earned an M.A. in applied mathematics from the University of Maryland in 1986, and a Ph.D. in scientific computing from the University of Michigan in 1993.

The creation of the world's fastest computer by Emeagwali in 1989 made possible the theoretical linking of computers to communicate with one another, which led to the creation of the Internet. For his work he received in 1989 the Gordon Bell Prize, the highest award in the computing world. He has done research for the U.S. Bureau of Reclamation in the area of engineering and the Minnesota Army High Performance Computing Research Center.

Emeagwali has received numerous awards and recognition for his work, including the 1998 Distinguished Scientist Award from the World Bank, and the Gallery of Prominent Refugees of the United Nations in 2001.

Helene D. Gayle (1955–)
Epidemiologist, AIDS Researcher

Born on August 16, 1955, in Buffalo, New York, Helene Doris Gayle began her career in medicine after graduating from Barnard College in 1976. She graduated from the University of Pennsylvania with an M.D. in 1981 with an interest in public health. In that same year she also earned an M.A. from Johns Hopkins in public health. In 1984 Gayle was selected to enter the epidemiol-

ogy training program at the Center for Disease Control (CDC) in Atlanta, Georgia. Gayle has been vocal in the effects of AIDS and HIV infection on the African American community. In 1992 Gayle was hired as a medical epidemiologist for the AIDS division of the U.S. Agency for International Development and her role as scientist and community advocate was clear.

In 2001 Gayle served as director of CDC's AIDS, HIV, and TB Prevention. She was also named Assistant Surgeon General and Rear Admiral in the U.S. Public Health Service, and in 2006 she was selected as president of the humanitarian organization CARE USA and program director for HIV/AIDS and TB for the Bill and Melinda Gates Foundation.

Gayle's service and advocacy has earned her many awards and honors, including the Women of Color Award, and the 2002 Medical Leadership in Industry Award.

Evelyn Boyd Granville (1924–)
Mathematician

Evelyn Boyd Granville was born on May 1, 1924, in Washington, D.C. She attended Smith College from 1941 to 1946 and earned a B.A. and an M.A. in mathematics. She received a Ph.D. from Yale University in 1949, thereby becoming the first African American woman to be awarded a Ph.D. in pure mathematics.

Granville's first teaching position was as an instructor at New York University from 1949 to 1950. She moved to Fisk University where she was an assistant professor, and then to the University of Southern California as a lecturer, where she remained from 1961 to 1973. Since then she has been an associate professor at California State University. Glanville is the author of *Theory of Applications of Math for Teachers*.

Frederick D. Gregory (1941–)
Astronaut

Frederick Drew Gregory was born January 7, 1941, in Washington, D.C. He is the nephew of the late Dr. Charles Drew, noted African American blood plasma specialist. Under the sponsorship of U.S. Representative Adam Clayton Powell, Gregory attended the United States Air Force Academy and graduated with a B.S. in 1964. In 1977 he received an M.S.A. from George Washington University.

Gregory was a helicopter and fighter pilot for the U.S. Air Force from 1965 to 1970 and a research and test pilot for the U.S. Air Force and NASA in 1971. In 1978 he was accepted into NASA's astronaut program. In 1985 he went into space aboard the Spacelab 3 *Challenger* space shuttle as a pilot.

Gregory belongs to the Society of Experimental Test Pilots, the Tuskegee Airmen, the American Helicopter Society, and the National Technical Association. He has won numerous medals and awards, including the Meritorious Service Medal, the Air Force Commendation Medal, two NASA Space Flight Medals, and the Distinguished Flying Cross (twice). He is also the recipient of George Washington University's Distinguished Alumni Award, NASA's Outstanding Leadership Award, and the National Society of Black Engineers' Distinguished National Scientist Award. In 2003 he was honored with the Presidential Rank Award for Distinguished Executives.

Lloyd Hall (1894–1971)
Chemist

Lloyd Augustus Hall was born on June 20, 1894, in Elgin, Illinois. An honor graduate in science from East High School of Aurora, Illinois, Hall went on to receive a B.S. in pharmaceutical chemistry from Northwestern University in 1916. He continued his training with graduate work at the University of Chicago and University of Illinois, then he embarked on his unique and fruitful career.

As the chief chemist and director of research for Griffith Laboratories of Chicago beginning in 1924, Lloyd Hall discovered curing salts for the preserving and processing of meats, thus revolutionizing the meatpacking industry. He has more than 100 patents registered for processes used in the manufacturing and packing of food, especially meat and bakery products.

In 1954 Hall became chairman of the Chicago chapter of the American Institute of Chemistry. In 1959 he retired. Hall served as a consultant for many state and local organizations and was appointed by President John F. Kennedy as a member of the American Food for Peace Council from 1962 to 1964. He died in 1971.

Matthew Henson (1866–1955)
Explorer

Matthew Alexander Henson was born August 8, 1866, in Charles County, Maryland, near Washington, D.C. He attended school in Washington for six years but at the age of thirteen signed on as a cabin boy on a ship headed for China. Henson worked his way up to seaman while he sailed on the world's oceans. Tiring of life at sea, Henson took a job in a Washington, D.C. clothing store. While there he met Nicaragua-bound U.S. Navy surveyor Robert Edward Peary. He was hired on the spot as Peary's valet. Henson was not pleased to be a personal servant, but he felt his new position offered future opportunities.

Peary eventually developed an interest in arctic exploration. After numerous trips to Greenland between 1893 and 1905, Peary became convinced that he could become the first man to stand at the North Pole. Henson accompanied Peary on these trips to Greenland and became an integral part of Peary's plans.

In 1906, along with a number of Inuit, Peary and Henson set out from Greenland on their first attempt to reach the North Pole. They came within 160 miles of their goal but were forced to turn back because unseasonably warm weather had created open sheets of water that could not be traversed by dogsled.

Undaunted, Peary and Henson tried again in 1909. Although Peary was undoubtedly the driving force of these expeditions, he was increasingly reliant on Henson. Henson's greatest asset was his knowledge of the Inuit language and his ability to readily adapt to their culture. He was also an excellent dog driver and possessed a physical stamina that Peary lacked due to leukemia. Henson believed that he was serving the black race by his example of loyalty, fortitude, and trustworthiness.

By the end of March 1909 they were within 150 miles of their goal. Henson, because of his strength, would break trail and set up camp for the night, while Peary followed. On April 6, Henson thought he had reached the pole. When Peary arrived later he asserted that they were three miles short. After a brief rest they both set out together and stopped when they thought they were in the area of the North Pole. There have been conflicting theories ever since as to who was the first man to reach the top of the world.

In 1912 Henson wrote *A Negro at the North Pole,* but the book aroused little interest. He took work as a porter and then as a customs official in New York. By the 1930s, however, Henson began receiving recognition for his contributions to arctic exploration. In 1937 he was the first African American elected to the Explorers Club in New York. In 1945 he and other surviving members of the expedition received the Navy Medal. In the early 1950s Henson also received public recognition from President Dwight D. Eisenhower.

Henson died in 1955 and was buried in New York. In 1988 his remains were exhumed and buried with full military honors at Arlington National Cemetery next to the grave of Robert Peary.

William A. Hinton (1883–1959)
Medical Researcher

Born on December 15, 1883, in Chicago, Illinois, William A. Hinton graduated from Harvard in 1905. He finished his medical studies at Harvard Medical School in three years, graduating in 1912. For three years after graduation he was a voluntary assistant in the pathological laboratory at Massachusetts General Hospital. This was followed by eight years of laboratory practice at the

Boston Dispensary and at the Massachusetts Department of Public Health. In 1919 Hinton was appointed lecturer in preventive medicine and hygiene at Harvard Medical School, where he served for thirty-four years while continuing to work at the Boston Dispensary. In 1949 he was the first person of color to be granted a professorship at Harvard.

In 1931 Hinton started a training school at the Boston Dispensary for poor girls so that they could become medical technicians. From these classes of volunteers grew one of the country's leading institutions for the training of technicians. Though he lost a leg in an automobile accident, Hinton remained active in teaching and at the Boston Dispensary Laboratory, which he directed from 1916 to 1952. He died in Canton, Massachusetts in 1959.

One of the world's foremost authorities on venereal disease Hinton is responsible for the development of the Hinton test, a reliable method for detecting syphilis. He also collaborated with Dr. J. A. V. Davies on what is now called the Davies-Hinton test for detection of this same disease.

Shirley Ann Jackson (1946–)
Physicist

Born in Washington, D.C., on August 5, 1946, Shirley Ann Jackson graduated as valedictorian of her class from Roosevelt High School in 1964. In 1968 she received a B.S. from Massachusetts Institute of Technology. She stayed at M.I.T. for her doctoral studies, and in 1973 she became the first African American woman in the United States to earn a Ph.D. in physics.

Jackson has worked as a member of the technical staff on theoretical physics at AT&T Bell Laboratories, as a visiting scientist at the European Organization for Nuclear Research in Geneva, and as a visiting lecturer at the NATO International Advanced Study Institute in Belgium. In 1995 Jackson was named by President

Bill Clinton as chair of the Nuclear Regulatory Commission. In 2001 Jackson was named both director of the AT&T Corporation and to the board of the Public Service Enterprise Corp. within days of each other.

Jackson has received numerous honorary degrees and awards. She was inducted in the National Women's Hall of Fame in 1998 and was one of seven fellows for the Association for Women in Science.

Mae Jemison (1956–)
Physician, Astronaut

Mae Carol Jemison was born October 17, 1956, in Decatur, Alabama; her family moved to Chicago when she was three. She attended Stanford University on a National Achievement Scholarship and received a B.S. in chemical engineering and a B.A. in Afro-American studies in 1977. She then enrolled in Cornell University's medical school and graduated in 1981. Her medical internship was at the Los Angeles County/University of Southern California Medical Center in 1982. She was a general practitioner with the INA/Ross Loos Medical Group in Los Angeles until 1983, followed by two years as a Peace Corps medical officer in Sierra Leone and Liberia. Returning to the United States in 1985, she began working for CIGNA Health Plans, a health maintenance organization in Los Angeles.

In 1987 Jemison was accepted in NASA's astronaut program. Her first assignment was representing the astronaut office at the Kennedy Space Center in Cape Canaveral, Florida. On September 12, 1992, when the space shuttle *Endeavor* lifted off, Jemison was aboard and became the first African American woman in space. She served aboard the *Endeavor* as a science specialist.

In 1988 Jemison won the Science and Technology Award given by *Essence* magazine, and in 1990 she was Gamma Sigma Gamma's Woman of the Year. In 1991 she earned a Ph.D. from Lincoln University.

Jemison resigned from NASA in 1993 to pursue personal goals related to science education and minorities. Jemison founded the Jemison Institute for Advanced Technology in Developing Countries, a consulting firm the Jemison Group, and in 1994 she founded the International Science Camp in Chicago to encourage youth interests in science.

Frederick McKinley Jones
(c. 1892–1961)
Technician

Frederick McKinley Jones was born on May 7, 1892 or 1893, in Cincinnati, Ohio. At the age of five Jones was left in the care of a priest by his father after the earlier departure by his mother. When he left the rectory at sixteen, Jones worked as a pin boy, mechanic's assistant, and finally, as chief mechanic on a Minnesota farm. He served in World War I, and in the late 1920s his fame as an adept mechanic spread when he developed a series of devices to adapt silent movie projectors into sound projectors.

Jones built the first automatic refrigeration system for long-haul trucks in 1935. Later, the system was adapted to various other carriers, including railway cars and ships. Previously, foods were packed in ice, a system whereby even slight delays led to spoilage. Jones's new method instigated a change in the eating habits and patterns of the entire nation and allowed for the development of food production facilities in almost any geographic location.

Jones also developed an air conditioning unit for military field hospitals, a portable X-ray machine, and a refrigerator for military field kitchens. During his lifetime, a total of sixty-one patents were issued in Jones's name. Jones died on February 21, 1961.

Percy Lavon Julian (1899–1975)
Chemist

Born in Montgomery, Alabama, on April 11, 1899, Percy Lavon Julian attended DePauw University in Greencastle, Indiana. He graduated Phi

Beta Kappa and was valedictorian of his class. Throughout college Julian lived in the attic of a fraternity house where he worked as a waiter. For several years, Julian taught at Fisk and Howard universities, as well as at West Virginia State College, before attending Harvard and the University of Vienna. He earned his Ph.D. in 1931.

In 1935 Julian synthesized the drug physostigmine, which is used today in the treatment of glaucoma. He later headed the soybean research department of the Glidden Company and then formed Julian Laboratories in order to specialize in the production of sterols, which he extracted from the oil of the soybean. The method perfected by Julian in 1950 eventually lowered the cost of sterols to less than twenty cents a gram, and ultimately enabled millions of people suffering from arthritis to obtain relief through the use of cortisone, a sterol derivative. Julian also discovered a means to produce progesterone and testosterone from soybeans, which helps to prevent miscarriages and assist men with low sex drives.

In 1947 Julian was awarded the Spingarn Medal, and in 1968 he was awarded the Chemical Pioneer Award by the American Institute of Chemists. Julian died on April 9, 1975.

Ernest Just (1883–1941)
Biologist

Born in Charleston, South Carolina, on August 14, 1883, Ernest Everett Just received his B.A. with high honors from Dartmouth in 1907, and his Ph.D. from the University of Chicago in 1916.

A member of Phi Beta Kappa, Just received the Spingarn Medal in 1914 and served as associate editor of *Physiological Zoology, the Biological Bulletin,* and the *Journal of Morphology.* Between 1912 and 1937 Just published more than fifty papers on fertilization, parthenogenesis, cell division, and mutation. In 1930 he was one of twelve zoologists to address the International Congress of Zoologists, and he was elected vice president

of the American Society of Zoologists. He died on October 28, 1941.

Samuel Kountz (1930–1981)
Surgeon

Born in Lexa, Arkansas, on October 30, 1930, Samuel L. Kountz graduated third in his class at the Agricultural, Mechanical and Normal College of Arkansas in 1952. He pursued graduate studies at the University of Arkansas, earning a degree in chemistry. Senator J. W. Fulbright, whom he met while a graduate student, advised Kountz to apply for a scholarship to medical school. Kountz won the scholarship on a competitive basis and was the first black to enroll at the University of Arkansas's Medical School in Little Rock. Through his research, Kountz discovered that large doses of the drug methylprednisolone could help reverse the acute rejection of a transplanted kidney. The drug was used for a number of years in the standard management of kidney transplant patients.

In 1964, working with Dr. Roy Cohn, one of the pioneers in the field of transplantation, Kountz made medical history by transplanting a kidney from a mother to a daughter—the first transplant between humans who were not identical twins. At the University of California in 1967 Kountz worked with other researchers to develop the prototype of a machine that is now able to preserve kidneys up to fifty hours from the time they are taken from the body of a donor. The machine, called the Belzer Kidney Perfusion Machine, was named for Dr. Folkert O. Belzer, who was Kountz's partner.

Kountz died on December 23, 1981, after a long illness contracted on a trip to South Africa in 1977.

Lewis Howard Latimer (1848–1928)
Inventor, Engineer

Born in Chelsea, Massachusetts, on September 4, 1848, Lewis Howard Latimer enlisted in the U.S. Navy at the age of fifteen, and began studying drafting upon completion of his military service.

Latimer was employed by Alexander Graham Bell in 1876 to make the patent drawings for the first telephone. In 1881 he invented a method of making carbon filaments for the Maxim electric incandescent lamp. He also supervised the installation of electric light in New York, Philadelphia, Montreal, and London for the Maxim-Weston Electric Company. In 1884, he joined the Edison Company. Latimer died on December 11, 1928, in New York City.

Robert H. Lawrence Jr. (1935–1967)
Astronaut

Robert Henry Lawrence Jr. was born on October 2, 1935, and was a native of Chicago, Illinois. While still in elementary school he became a model airplane hobbyist and a chess enthusiast. Lawrence became interested in biology while at Englewood High School in Chicago. As a student at Englewood, Lawrence excelled in chemistry and track. When he graduated, he placed in the top ten percent of the class.

Lawrence entered Bradley University, joining the Air Force Reserve Officers' Training Corps. There he attained the rank of lieutenant colonel, thus becoming the second highest ranking cadet at Bradley. Lawrence was commissioned a second lieutenant in the U.S. Air Force in 1956 and soon after received his bachelor's degree in chemistry. Following a stint at an air base in Germany, Lawrence entered Ohio State University through the Air Force Institute of Technology as a doctoral candidate and completed his degree in 1965. In June 1967 Lawrence successfully completed the Air Force's Manned Orbital Laboratory program and became the first African American astronaut. Lawrence died on December 8, 1967, when his F104D Starfighter jet crashed on a runway in a California desert. On December 8, 1997, his name was inscribed on the Space Mirror Memorial at the Kennedy Space Center in Florida.

Walter E. Massey (1938–)
Physicist

Walter Eugene Massey was born on April 5, 1938, in Hattiesburg, Mississippi. He graduated in 1958 with a B.S. from Morehouse College in Atlanta, Georgia, and completed his Ph.D. in physics from Washington University in St. Louis, Missouri, in 1966. As a result of Massey's research, which centered on solid state theory and theories of quantum liquids and solids, Massey was able to join the faculty of Brown University, achieve full professorship, and become dean of the college in 1975.

Massey was active in improving science instruction in urban schools. He developed the Inner City Teachers of Science Program while at Brown University. In 1990 President George H. W. Bush named Massey as head of the National Science Foundation, making him the second African American to hold the position. He served until 1993. Massey went on to serve as president of Morehouse College from 1995 to 2007. Beginning September 13, 2010, Massey was named the new president of the renowned School of the Art Institute of Chicago.

Jan Matzeliger (1852–1889)
Inventor

Jan Ernst Matzeliger was born on September 15, 1852, in Paramariboin, Dutch Guiana. Matzeliger found employment in the government machine works at the age of ten. Eight years later he immigrated to the United States, settling in Philadelphia, Pennsylvania, where he worked in a shoe factory. He later moved to New England and settled permanently in Lynn, Massachusetts.

The Industrial Revolution had by this time brought the invention of machines to cut, sew, and tack shoes, but none had been perfected to last a shoe. Matzeliger lost little time in designing and patenting just such a device, which he refined over the years so that it could adjust a shoe, arrange the leather over the sole, drive in the nails, and deliver the finished product—all in one minute's time.

Matzeliger's patent was subsequently bought by Sydney W. Winslow, who established the United Shoe Machine Company. The continued success of this business resulted in a fifty percent reduction in the price of shoes across the nation, doubled wages, and improved working conditions for millions of people dependent on the shoe industry for their livelihood.

Between 1883 and 1891 Matzeliger received five patents on his inventions, all of which contributed to the shoe-making revolution. His last patent was issued in September 1891, two years after his death.

Matzeliger died on August 24, 1889, at the age of thirty-seven of tuberculosis, long before he had the chance to realize a share of the enormous profit derived from his invention. In fact he never received any money for his patents. Instead he was issued stock in the United Shoe Machine Company that did not become valuable until after his death.

Elijah McCoy (1844–1929)
Inventor, Engineer

Elijah J. McCoy was born on May 2, 1844, in Colchester, Ontario, Canada. He spent his early years as an apprentice to a master mechanic in Scotland. At sixteen he moved back to the United States and settled in Ypsilanti, Michigan. For forty years after the Civil War, McCoy acquired some fifty-seven patents for devices designed to streamline his automatic lubrication process.

McCoy's inventions were primarily connected with the automatic lubrication of moving machinery. Perhaps his most valuable design was the "drip cup," a tiny container filled with oil that flowed to the moving parts of heavy-duty machinery and was regulated by means of a "stopcock." The drip cup was a key device in perfecting

the overall lubrication system used in the large-machine industry even today. McCoy received little money for his patents. He later formed the Eljah McCoy Manufacturing Company. He died in Detroit, Michigan, on October 10, 1929.

Ronald McNair (1950–1986)
Astronaut

Ronald Ervin McNair was born on October 21, 1950, in Lake City, South Carolina. He graduated from North Carolina A&T State University with a B.S. in physics. He also received a Ph.D. in physics from the Massachusetts Institute of Technology in 1976. He was presented an honorary doctorate of laws from North Carolina A&T in 1978.

McNair was working in optical physics when he was selected by NASA to train as an astronaut in 1978. In August 1979, he completed a one-year training and evaluation period that made him eligible for assignment as mission specialist on space shuttle flight crews. He presented papers in the areas of lasers and molecular spectroscopy and gave many presentations in the United States and Europe. He was the second African American to orbit the earth on a NASA mission.

McNair was aboard the flawed shuttle *Challenger,* which exploded shortly after liftoff from Cape Kennedy and plunged into the waters off the Florida coast in January 1986. The shuttle had a crew of seven persons, including two women, a mission specialist, and a teacher-in-space participant.

Garrett A. Morgan (1877–1963)
Inventor

Born in Paris, Kentucky, on March 4, 1877, Garrett Augustus Morgan moved to Cleveland, Ohio, at an early age. His first invention was an improvement on the sewing machine, which he sold for $150.

Morgan is best remembered for his "gas inhalator." Its value was first acknowledged during

Inventor Garrett Morgan was also a hero. As this photo from a newspaper shows, he rescued a man in 1917 in what became known as the Lake Erie Crib Disaster.

a successful rescue operation of several men trapped two hundred feet below the surface of Lake Erie after a tunnel explosion in the Cleveland Waterworks. During the emergency Morgan, his brother, and two other volunteers—all wearing inhalators—were the only men able to descend into the smoky, gas-filled tunnel to save several workers from asphyxiation.

Orders for the Morgan inhalator soon began to pour into Cleveland from fire companies all over the nation, but when Morgan's racial identity became known, many of them were canceled. In the South, it was necessary for Morgan to have a white man demonstrate his invention. During World War I the Morgan inhalator was transformed into a gas mask used by combat troops.

In 1923, having established his reputation with the gas inhalator, he was able to command a price of $40,000 from the General Electric Company for his automatic traffic signal. Morgan died on August 27, 1963, in Cleveland, the city that had awarded him a gold medal for his devotion to public safety.

Waverly J. Person (1927–)
Geophysicist, Seismologist

Waverly J. Person was born in Blackenridge, Virginia, on May 1, 1927. Person served as a technician at the National Information Earthquake Center before deciding to do graduate studies. Beginning in 1962, Person attended American

University and George Washington University while maintaining his job. Once he completed his studies in 1973 and was qualified as a geophysicist and seismologist, he was transferred to the United States Geological Survey's National Earthquake Information Center in Colorado.

In 1977 Person was named director of the Colorado National Earthquake Information Center, and in 1994 he was named director of the United States Geological Survey's National Earthquake Information Center. Person received numerous honors and awards for his professional and personal contributions to the earth sciences. He celebrated fifty years of service in 2005 and commented on how he still loves his job.

Norbert Rillieux (1806–1894)

Inventor

A native of New Orleans, Louisiana, Norbert Rillieux was born on March 17, 1806, the son of Vincent Rillieux, a wealthy engineer, and Constance Vivant, a slave on his plantation. Young Rillieux's higher education was obtained in Paris, France, where his extraordinary aptitude for engineering led to his appointment at the age of twenty-four to instructor of applied mechanics at L'Ecole Centrale. Rillieux moved to Paris permanently in 1854, securing a scholarship and working on the deciphering of hieroglyphics.

Rillieux's inventions were of great value to the sugar-refining industry. The method formerly used required gangs of slaves to ladle boiling sugarcane juice from one kettle to another—a primitive process known as "the Jamaica Train." In 1845 Rillieux invented a vacuum evaporating pan (a series of condensing coils in vacuum chambers) that reduced the industry's dependence on gang labor and helped manufacture a superior product at a greatly reduced cost. The first Rillieux evaporator was installed at Myrtle Grove Plantation, Louisiana, in 1845. In the following years, factories in Louisiana, Cuba, and Mexico converted to the Rillieux system.

When his evaporator process was finally adopted in Europe, he returned to inventing with renewed interest—applying his process to the sugar beet. In so doing, he cut production and refining costs in half.

Rillieux died in Paris on October 8, 1894, leaving behind a system that is universally used throughout the sugar industry and in the manufacture of soap, gelatin, glue, and many other products.

Mabel Staupers (1890–1989)

Nurse, Activist

Mabel Keaton Staupers was born in Barbados, West Indies, on February 27, 1890. She graduated with honors from the Freedmen's Hospital School of Nursing in 1917. She did some private nursing after graduation and later spent time at the Jefferson Hospital Medical College in Philadelphia, Pennsylvania. After moving to Harlem she discovered through survey's some of the needs of the community and helped to establish the Harlem Committee of the New York Tuberculosis and Health Association.

Staupers championed the cause of integrating African American nurses into mainstream medicine. Success finally came when the U.S. Army announced race was no longer a factor in the Army Nursing Corp in 1945, and in 1948 the American Nurses' Association's delegation opened the organization to African American nurses. Staupers's efforts were rewarded with the Spingarn Medal from the NAACP in 1951 among other awards and honors. Staupers recorded the journey of integrating the nursing profession in her book *No Time for Prejudice: A Story of the Integration of Negroes in the United States* (1961). Staupers died on November 29, 1989.

Lewis Temple (1800–1854)

Inventor

Little is known of Lewis Temple's early background, except that he was born in Richmond, Virginia, in 1800, and had no formal education. As a young man he moved to New Bedford, Massachusetts, then a major whaling port. Finding work as a metal smith, Temple modified the design of the whaler's harpoon, and in the 1840s manufactured a new version of the harpoon that allowed lines to be securely fastened to the whale. Using the "toggle harpoon," whalers soon entered a period of unprecedented prosperity, more than doubling the catch for this leading New England industry. Temple, who never patented his harpoon, died destitute in May 1854.

Vivien T. Thomas (1910–1985)
Surgical Research Technician

Vivien Theodore Thomas was born in Nashville, Tennessee, on August 29, 1910, and enrolled in the Tennessee Agricultural and Industrial College in 1929. He had to drop out of college because of the stock market crash, which wiped-out all of his savings for school. Thomas was able to get a position as trauma researcher and assistant to Vanderbilt professor Alfred Blalok.

Thomas worked long hours in the lab for Blalok, which resulted in major advances in the use of blood transfusions. This had a major impact on life-saving measures during World War II. When Blalok was hired by Johns Hopkins in 1940 he insisted that Thomas also be hired. Thomas and Blalcok also developed a procedure for reconstructing blood vessels when poor circulation impacted lung function in children. Thomas became well known for his work with Blalcok, even after Blalok died in 1964.

Thomas was presented with an honorary degree in 1976 and became a medical school faculty at Johns Hopkins in 1977. He retired in 1979. The story of Thomas's life was published in 1985 in *Pioneering Research in Surgical Shock and Cardiovascular Survey: Vivien Thomas and His Work with Alfred Blalock*. Thomas's life story was also made into a television movie. Vivien Thomas died on November 26, 1985.

Levi Watkins Jr. (1944–)
Surgeon

Levi Watkins was born in Parsons, Kansas, on June 13, 1944, and grew up in Montgomery, Alabama. Watkins graduated from Tennessee State University in 1966 and was accepted as the first African American student at Vanderbilt University and at the University's Medical School. Watkins graduated in 1970 and did his internship at Johns Hopkins Medical School in Baltimore, Maryland. His research both at Johns Hopkins and at Harvard Medical School led to the discovery of angiotensin blockers for patients susceptible to heart failure.

In 1980, two years after becoming a faculty member and the first African American chief resident of cardiac surgery at Johns Hopkins, Watkins successfully implanted an AID (automatic implantable defibrillator). This device has resulted in saving the life of numerous patients. Watkins became a full professor in 1991 and has continually sought to increase minority presence at Johns Hopkins.

Watkins has received numerous awards including recognition for his innovative work with the automatic defibrillator, as well as the Humanitarian Physician Award from the American Red Cross (1987) and the Guidant Corporation Achievement Award (2000). Watkins holds the position of professor and surgeon at the Johns Hopkins Hospital Division of Cardiac Surgery, associate dean at the School of Medicine and dean for the School of Medicine's postdoctoral programs and faculty development.

Daniel Hale Williams (1856–1931)
Surgeon

A pioneer in the field of open heart surgery, Daniel Hale Williams was born in Holidaysburg, Pennsylvania, on January 18, 1856. His father died when he was eleven, and his mother deserted him after apprenticing him to a cobbler. He later worked as a roustabout on a lake steamer and as a barber. He apprenticed with a prominent physician in 1878 which encouraged his enrollment in the Chicago Medical College in 1883.

Williams opened his office on the south side of Chicago at a time when Chicago hospitals did not allow African American doctors to use their facilities. In 1891 Williams founded Provident Hospital, which was open to patients of all races.

At Provident Hospital on July 10, 1893, Williams performed the operation that earned him renown in the medical field. A patient was admitted to the emergency ward with a knife wound in an artery, lying a fraction of an inch from the heart. With the aid of six staff surgeons, Williams made an incision in the patient's chest and operated successfully on the artery. The crisis period soon ended, and three weeks later, Williams performed minor surgery to remove fluid from the patient's pleural cavity. After recuperating for another month, the patient had fully recovered and was able to leave the hospital.

Williams was instrumental in the forming of the Medico-Chirurgical Society and the National Medical Association. In 1913 he was inducted into the American Board of Surgery at its first convention. Williams died on August 4, 1931, after a lifetime devoted to his two main interests—the NAACP and the construction of hospitals and training schools for black doctors and nurses.

O. S. Williams (1921–)
Aeronautical Engineer

Oswald S. Williams was born on September 2, 1921, in Washington, D.C. He grew up in New York City and later earned a degree in aeronautical engineering in 1943 and a master's in 1947. Williams was hired by Greer Hydraulics in 1950 but later was hired at Grumman International as a propulsion engineer in 1961.

At Grumman International, Williams managed the Apollo Lunar Module system for eight years, which entailed operating costs of over $42 million. The engines he devised enabled *Apollo 13* to return safely to earth after the ship's main rocket engine exploded. Williams became vice president at Grumman in 1974 and was a member of the American Institute of Aeronautics and Astronautics and associate fellow and chair of the institute's Liquid Rocket's Technical Committee.

Williams left Grumman and subsequently completed his M.B.A. in 1981. He also taught at

St. John's University in Queens, New York, where he received his MBA.

Granville T. Woods (1856–1910)
Inventor

Born in Columbus, Ohio, on April 23, 1856, Granville T. Woods attended school until he was ten. He was first employed in a machine shop, and he continued to improve his mechanical aptitude by working on a railroad in 1872, in a rolling mill in 1874, and later by studying mechanical engineering at college. In 1878 Woods became an engineer aboard the *Ironsides,* a British steamer, and within two years was handling a steam locomotive on the D&S Railroad.

In 1887 Woods patented the most advanced of his many inventions—the Synchronous Multiplex Railway Telegraph. This device, designed to avert accidents, kept each train informed of the whereabouts of the train immediately ahead of or behind it by enabling communication between stations from moving trains.

After winning a suit brought by Thomas Edison, claiming Edison was the first inventor of multiplex railway, Edison offered Woods a position in his company. Woods declined. Later Alexander Graham Bell purchased the rights to Woods' telegraph system. This gave Woods the capital to continue his inventions.

Woods marketed this product, and others that followed, through his own company. The patent files in Washington, D.C., show Woods to have been an extremely prolific inventor. In the twenty-year span between 1879 and 1899, no less than twenty-three separate inventions bear his name. In 1887 alone he registered seven separate inventions with the patent office, all of them connected with the ingenious railway communications system he devised. In later years Woods spent much of his time and money trying to keep control of his inventions. He died on January 30, 1910, in New York City.

SPORTS

African Americans in sports, particularly beginning in the twentieth century, are a key part of American culture from their athletic prowess, which often struck fear during the period of Jim Crow, such as Jack Johnson in boxing; to their place as role models and activists such as Arthur Ashe in tennis; to that of entrepreneur and moguls such as Michael Jordan in basketball. There are athletes who challenged segregation such as Jackie Robinson in baseball; challenged stereotypes and laws such as Muhammad Ali (also known as Cassius Clay) in boxing; broke barriers such as Althea Gibson in tennis, and Jim Thorpe and Alice Coachman in track and field. Athletics in the twenty-first century continue to raise the bar of achievement, from Tiger Woods in golf, to Venus and Serena Williams in tennis, to Kobe Bryant and LeBron James in basketball. These athletes are admired and beloved within the evolution of American culture. Despite the many achievements both on and off the field there still remain issues of access and opportunity, as well as the inequity in the roles of African Americans as players versus owners, that continue into the twenty-first century.

The black community saw a champion for social change in the athlete Arthur Ashe. The untimely AIDS-related death of Ashe in 1993 robbed the black community of a pioneering sports hero who was also one of the most passionate and articulate spokesmen for minority athletes. Ashe—the first Black American man to win Wimbledon, the U.S. Open, and the Grand Slam of tennis—spent his entire career protesting unjust racial practices in the sporting world. His outstanding accomplishments notwithstanding, Ashe was distressed by the discrimination he faced in his own career and by what he perceived as racist hiring and promotional tactics throughout collegiate and professional sports. As a tennis star, and later as an author and newspaper columnist, he called for equal opportunity in all aspects of athletic endeavor.

The concerns Ashe voiced have continued as American sports move forward. The dilemma is obvious: although black players predominate on the field in a number of professional and amateur sports, minorities are grossly underrepresented in the business of managing, owning, and running teams.

The 1990s witnessed the flowering of a grass-roots movement to spark more hiring of minorities in the vast sports industry. A 1992 *Sporting News* magazine poll identifying the 100 most important people in sports named only six blacks. Although seventy-five percent

Arthur Ashe Stadium in New York City is home to the U.S. Open tennis tournament.

of the players in the NBA were black in 1992, only two head coach positions belonged to minorities. The same scenario held true for football—sixty percent of the players in the NFL were black in 1992; two head coaches were black. PGA golf tournaments were still held at private clubs with all-white memberships. Hockey, tennis, and horse racing included only minimal numbers of blacks. In reviewing the progress of sports in 2000, minorities and particularly blacks had not seen any major shifts to change this trend. The black population of the United States in 2000 was more than twelve percent, determined by the U.S. Census Bureau. Blacks in sports continued to be disproportionately high in relationship to demographics. Based on 1999 statistics, participation by blacks in football was sixty-seven percent, basketball seventy-eight percent, and baseball thirteen percent. Top management held by white Americans in all three sports was between eighty-four and one hundred percent.

The situation is much the same at the amateur level. Black athletes have excelled at the Olympic Games, but a vast majority of collegiate coaches, trainers, and athletic directors are white. Blacks are also scarce among the ranks of referees, umpires, play-by-play announcers, and agents.

Interestingly, professional boxing—that most brutal of sports—has the best record for integration throughout its ranks. Not only are many of the fighters minorities, but many of the trainers, managers, and promoters are as well. The flamboyant Don King, long a fixture in the sport, was one of the members of the *Sporting News*'s list of the most important figures in organized athletics.

Gains were subsequently made. Professional basketball had four black general managers in 1992: Elgin Baylor of the Los Angeles Clippers, Bernie Bickerstaff of the Denver Nuggets, Wayne Embry of the Cleveland Cavaliers, and Willis Reed of the New Jersey Nets. Art Shell of the Los Angeles Raiders and Dennis Green of the Minnesota Vikings are the first two black head coaches in professional football since 1923. Track coach Bob Kersee had a hand in the Olympic medals won by his wife, Jackie Joyner-Kersee, and his sister-in-law, Florence Griffith Joyner. Agent W. Jerome Stanley negotiated a $16.5 million contract for Reggie Lewis of the Boston Celtics in 1990. Perhaps most important, Peter C. B. Bynoe and Bertram Lee became the first black managing partners of a major sports franchise—basketball's Denver Nuggets.

It is the athletes themselves who stand poised to transform not only organized sports, but society as well. Outside the entertainment industry, no other profession has supplied so many well-known and well-loved figures to the American public. No other industry could ever offer more opportunities for blacks to become role models, national heroes, or spokespersons for social causes. For instance, the discovery that basketball star Earvin "Magic" Johnson of the Los Angeles Lakers was infected with the AIDS virus did more to advance public knowledge of the disease than a decade of prior publicity had done.

Arthur Ashe was not prone to optimism about the future of blacks in the business sector of sports, but even he saw some chance of improvement by decade's end. In an *Ebony* essay published in August 1992, just a few months before his death, he wrote: "We as African-Americans will continue our cultural emphasis on sports participation, and we will make our mark in new areas." Ashe's words, like his life, should be inspiring for generations to come.

Prior to 1947 professional baseball was segregated, and blacks played in the Negro Leagues. These leagues provided the only opportunities for several generations of extremely talented and dedicated minority ball players. A surge in the popularity of baseball after World War II helped pave the way for black participation in the formerly all-white major leagues. Brooklyn Dodger second baseman Jackie Robinson broke the color barrier in 1947 and went on to be named rookie of the year.

Robinson and other early black major leaguers faced widespread hostility from fans and second-class treatment in the Jim Crow South. Nevertheless, blacks began to stream into professional baseball, breaking records that had previously been held by white superstars. By the 1970s, blacks were on the rosters of every team in the league and were joined in increasing numbers by talented players from all parts of Latin America. Today minority players—including those of color from the Caribbean and elsewhere—comprise some twenty percent of all major league positions.

A number of black athletes have risen to prominence in baseball. Hank Aaron holds the record for most career home runs. Ricky Henderson set a single-season record for stolen bases. Willie Mays is acclaimed as the game's greatest center fielder. Frank Robinson was the only player ever to win an MVP award in both the National and American leagues and was the first black named manager of a major league franchise. In 1993, two-time National League MVP Barry Bonds became the highest-paid baseball player of all time with a contract that paid more than $7 million per year.

Major league baseball has made modest strides toward equal opportunity employment in the many franchise front offices, despite declining black membership. Frank Robinson became the first black manager in 1974, and since then a half dozen other blacks have managed on the major league level. Bill White, a former All Star, was named president of the National League in 1988. From his office on Park Avenue in New York City, White negotiates labor agreements, oversees league expansion, dispenses fines and suspensions, and enforces league rules. Teams employing blacks in high executive positions include the Baltimore Orioles, the Boston Red Sox, the Atlanta Braves, the Los Angeles Dodgers, and the Houston Astros. Nevertheless, the percentage of black participation in baseball's business management lags behind the percentage of minority players in major league baseball.

Professional basketball began to integrate in 1951 when the Boston Celtics drafted Chuck Cooper and the New York Knicks hired Nat

The first "colored" world series pitted the Kansas City Monarchs against the Hilldale Athletic Club in October 1924.

"Sweetwater" Clifton. By the late 1960s, most of the sport's biggest stars were minorities—men like Bill Russell, Wilt Chamberlain, Kareem Abdul-Jabbar, Elvin Hayes, and Willis Reed. These and other talented athletes helped transform the game from a relatively polite and static affair to a fast-breaking, physical, high-speed contest.

Black players won more and more roster positions as the 1970s progressed. Athletes such as Kareem Abdul-Jabbar, Julius "Dr. J" Erving, Moses Malone, Bob McAdoo, and Wes Unseld helped further the evolution of the modern professional basketball game. By the 1980s, black dominance of the sport was assured with the arrival of Earvin "Magic" Johnson, Patrick Ewing, Michael Jordan, Clyde Drexler, Charles Barkley, and Shaquille O'Neal.

A full three-quarters of all NBA players are black. This reality was vividly reflected in the composition of the first American Olympic basketball team composed of professional players. Of the twelve men asked to represent the nation at the 1992 Olympic Games, only two were white. The celebrated "Dream Team" won the gold medal easily.

Basketball was also one of the first major sports to hire black head coaches. Bill Russell was the first in 1966. At one time as many as a half dozen NBA head coaches were black, but by 1992 the number had declined to two. As many as twenty-four head coaches were hired and fired between 1990 and 1992—not one of them black. In 1992 the Denver Nuggets were partially owned and fully run by a black man, Colorado businessman Bertram Lee. Basketball was the only sport in 1992 to feature a black general manager, with four in the position representing the

Los Angeles Clippers, the Denver Nuggets, the Cleveland Cavaliers, and the New Jersey Nets. Almost twenty years later there has been some progress, but the ratios are still low. In 2010 there were nine black coaches among the thirty who make up the NBA. Black coaches have become a common presence on the scene and are hired, fired, and served as mentors in ever-increasing numbers. Although the trend for hiring black coaches has improved, the length of tenure still adds a question of longevity in these positions. In 2005 it was reported that white coaches held their positions for nearly two and a half seasons compared to black coaches who hold their tenure for a little over one and a half years. Citing competitiveness as a focus that makes race a non-issue the Association must still address these unequal tenure trends, which can be seen in all aspects of coaching positions.

In 1997 two professional Basketball Leagues were established for women players, the WNBA and the ABL. The ABL folded after three seasons. The WNBA was successful and showcased the talents of Lisa Leslie, Sheryl Swoopes, Chamique Holdsclaw, and Cynthia Cooper. The WNBA continues to be successful into the twentieth-first century but still struggles with the lack of amateur ventures to locate talented female athletes and the economic support to create a greater viability of the sport as a career.

The vast popularity of basketball in America transcends any racial boundaries. The best players are not just black heroes, they are American heroes. As such they have an enormous power to shape public opinion, especially among the young. This power is displayed in everything from athletic shoe advertising to literacy programs and AIDS awareness, and it remains a vital force well into the twenty-first century.

Unlike the other major American sports, professional football began as an integrated entertainment. Blacks played alongside whites on the gridiron until 1930. Then for fifteen years the sport was all white. In 1945 a handful of black players were recruited, including Woodrow Strode of the Los Angeles Rams and Ben Willis of the Cleveland Browns.

Slowly the number of black roster players increased as the 1950s progressed. In 1957 the history of the NFL was forever changed by the arrival of Jim Brown. Brown, a superstar for the Cleveland Indians, led the league in rushing for eight of his nine years in football and established a new career rushing record. By the time his tenure on the field came to an end in 1966 other black players had emerged as stars, among them Chicago Bears running back Gale Sayers, and New York Giants safety Emlen Tunnell.

One stumbling block remained for black football players. Three key positions were quietly considered "white only": middle linebacker, center, and quarterback. In the interest of winning games, however, these artificial boundaries inevitably fell. Willie Lanier of the Kansas City Chiefs became the first in a long line of black All-Star middle linebackers. Quarterback James Harris of the Los Angeles Rams became the first black starter at his position in the 1970s. Centers Ray Donaldson of the Indianapolis Colts and Dwight Stephenson of the Miami Dolphins both turned in long careers as starters in the 1980s.

Black stars also redefined football's defensive game in the 1970s. The process began with the "Purple People Eaters" of the Minnesota Vikings defensive line—including Carl Eller, Allan Page, and Jim Marshall. It extended through the Los Angeles Rams's "Fearsome Foursome," which included Rosey Grier, David "Deacon" Jones, and Lamar Lundy. Possibly the best-known unit, however, is the Pittsburgh Steelers's "Steel Curtain," including "Mean" Joe Greene, L. C. Greenwood, and Dwight White, who helped the Steelers win four Super Bowls.

The 1980s witnessed an explosion of black talent. Chicago Bears running back Walter Payton did the unthinkable when he broke Jim Brown's rushing record in 1984. Jerry Rice grabbed an all-time record 101 touchdown receptions and helped the San Francisco 49ers win two Super Bowls. Doug Williams overcame injuries to quarterback the underdog Washington Redskins to a Super Bowl victory in 1988. Two teams featured black starting quarterbacks: Warren Moon of the Houston Oilers and Randall Cunningham of the Philadelphia Eagles. By 1990 blacks comprised a full sixty percent of the 1,316 players in the NFL.

The coaching ranks have been slow to integrate but are showing some progress. Art Shell of the Los Angeles Raiders became the first black head coach of the modern era in 1990. Dennis Green assumed the head-coaching duties for the Minnesota Vikings in 1992. Professional football has also added black coaches to the important positions of offensive and defensive coordinators. Although limited in numbers black coaches have had a strong impact on football in creating strong competitive teams. In Super Bowl 2007 two black head coaches battled for the win: NFL's Chicago Bears coach Lovie Smith and the AFC's Indiana Colts coach Tony Dungy. In the same year black head coach Mike Tomlin was hired as the youngest head coach for the Pittsburgh Steelers franchise at age thirty-four. In his second season Tomlin's team won the Super Bowl in 2009 and returned to the Super Bowl in 2011 only to lose to the Green Bay Packers. Through January 2011 the NFL has had nineteen black head coaches in its entire history with seven currently serving, which includes Smith and Tomlin as well as Jim Caldwell of the Indiana Colts, Raheem Morris of the Tampa Bay Buccaneers, Leslie Frazier of the Minnesota Vikings, and Hue Jackson of the Oakland Raiders.

Football has seen a continuation of blacks' presence on the field, with minor increases in leadership roles. In 1987 Doug Williams, quarterback for the Washington Redskins, was the first black to lead a team to the Super Bowl and win. Tennessean Titan's quarterback Steve Mc-

Nair, who suffered a tragic death in 2009, came within yards of leading his team to victory in the Super Bowl of 2000.

Basketball continues to see great players following in the footsteps of Michael Jordon, such as Kobe Bryant and LeBron James; golf has the phenomenal Tiger Woods who had over fourteen tournament wins in 2008 and after breaks for health and family issues returned to golf in 2010; Willy T. Ribbs Jr. who won five races in the SCCA [Sports Club Car of America] Trans-Am Series in 1982 and three top tens in the SCCA in 2000. Black-ownership roles for all professional sports is still minimal as demonstrated by the fact that in 2008 Robert Johnson was the only professional sports owner. He owns the Charlotte Bobcats.

As with basketball and football players, salaries have risen dramatically since the mid-1980s—a result of player-directed lawsuits and strikes. Front office personnel are more willing than ever to listen and respond to star players' demands, a fact that has lead to profound changes in management. At the same time players who break moral clauses are quick to be media sensations and suffer fines and public outcry. Players who commit such acts are subject to being cut from endorsement agreements. As a result of endorsements and the enormous income opportunities that come with roles as spokespersons, criticism suggests that athletics, and particularly African American athletes, have moved away from political and social commitments and have concentrated on making themselves acceptable for these economic roles.

Black athletes have been boxing professionally since colonial times. Joe Gans, a native of Baltimore, Maryland, was the first Black American to win a world boxing title in 1906 in the lightweight division, and Jack Johnson was the first heavyweight champion in 1908. Blacks have virtually dominated the sport since the 1930s, especially in the most popular heavyweight division. Joe Louis held the world heavyweight title for a record eleven years and eight months in the 1930s and 1940s, and the American public cheered for middleweight champion Sugar Ray

Robinson when he demolished German opponent Max Schmeling prior to World War II. Henry Armstrong held three world titles at once—featherweight, lightweight, and welterweight—during the Great Depression.

Louis, Robinson, and Armstrong were stars in what is considered the first Golden Age of blacks in boxing. A new Golden Age was ushered in on March 8, 1971, when Muhammad Ali and Joe Frazier drew the sport's first multimillion-dollar gate. Ali, a national figure since winning an Olympic gold medal in 1960, was one of the first athletes to exploit his position to comment on American political and social events. Almost single-handedly he transformed boxing from a second-rank endeavor to a top-drawing entertainment.

No serious white contender has risen in boxing's heavyweight division since the days of Ali. Other divisions have featured stellar black fighters also. During the 1970s and 1980s fans were thrilled by middleweight and welterweight match-ups between Sugar Ray Leonard, Marvin Hagler, and Thomas Hearns. When Ali was no longer able to defend his heavyweight crown, new challengers such as Larry Holmes and Leon Spinks ascended to the championship ranks.

As purses for major boxing events inched into the neighborhood of $100 million per match in the mid-1980s, a new generation of fighters arose. The advent of pay-per-view television and cable network sponsorship has led to soaring profits for the sport and its practitioners. Entrepreneur Don King became the most famous and the wealthiest boxing promoter of the modern era. His powerful position in the ranks of boxing and his ability to ingratiate himself with champion after champion, has continued his success in the field.

"Iron" Mike Tyson, a tough youngster from Brooklyn, became the best-known heavyweight champion since Ali and the wealthiest boxer of all time. His tumultuous reign ended with a knockout by Buster Douglas, who in turn lost to Evander Holyfield. Holyfield was unseated in 1992 by Riddick Bowe, another citizen of the same Brooklyn projects where Tyson had grown up. Unlike the combative Tyson, Bowe earned a reputation for professionalism and social activism as he spoke against apartheid policies in South Africa, and for the need for more sports programs in the nation's ghettos. In 1993 Holyfield defeated Bowe and once again became the heavyweight champion.

Boxing is a brutal and dangerous sport, but it demands years of specialized training, rigorous conditioning, and singular dedication. The public appetite for major boxing events will continue to provide ample opportunities for talented athletes from all over the world.

American sporting history has been greatly enriched by the activities of a number of talented black women athletes. From the championships won by tennis star Althea Gibson to the gold medals earned by Jackie Joyner-Kersee, women have achieved both fame and power from athletic endeavor.

One of the best-known black heroines in sports is Althea Gibson. During the crisis years of the civil rights era in the late 1950s, Gibson made her mark by winning a Grand Slam tennis tournament in 1956, two Wimbledon titles in 1957 and 1958, and the U.S. Lawn Tennis Association national singles championships in 1957 and 1958. Gibson was the first African American to gain top honors in professional tennis, and her performance paved the way for subsequent stars such as Arthur Ashe, Zina Garrison, and Venus and Serena Williams.

High jumper Alice Coachman became the first black woman to win an Olympic gold medal. She earned the gold at the 1948 Olympic Games in London, paving the way for generations of American athletes to come. Other Olympic medal winners include Wilma Rudolph, who overcame a serious disability to snatch three gold medals in the 1960 Olympics; Anita DeFrantz, who won a bronze medal for competitive rowing in the 1976 Olympics and became the first African American member of the International Olympic Committee; Florence Griffith Joyner, who won a phenomenal three gold medals and one silver medal for track events at the 1988 Olympics;

Debi Thomas, the first black woman to win an Olympic medal in figure skating with a bronze showing at the 1988 Olympics; and Jackie Joyner-Kersee, an Olympic champion in the grueling heptathlon competition and the long jump in the 1988 Olympics.

Women continue to excel in sports but the earning power of women in sports still lags behind that of men. Despite those inequities women athletes continue to excel such as Cheryl Miller, gold medal winner (1984) and Basketball Hall of Fame member; boxer Laila Ali, a Super Middleweight Champion (2002); Dominique Dawes, Best Gymnast at the U.S. National Championships (1994), and gold medal winner (1996); and champion tennis players Venus and Serena Williams—by 2010 Venus had earned seven Grand Slam Singles and won five titles at Wimbledon, and Serena had earned thirteen Grand Slam singles and won two titles at Wimbledon.

BIOGRAPHIES

Hank Aaron (1934–)
Baseball Player

Born in Mobile, Alabama, on February 5, 1934, Henry Louis "Hank" Aaron first played sandlot ball as a teenager. He later played for a team called the Black Bears, but soon thereafter signed a $200-per-month contract with the Indianapolis Clowns of the Negro American League.

In June 1952 Aaron was purchased by the Boston Braves. The following season, playing for Jacksonville, his .362 average led the South Atlantic League. This led to a promotion to the Braves, then based in Milwaukee, and the beginning of his brilliant major league career in 1954.

Aaron enjoyed perhaps his finest season in 1957, when he was named Most Valuable Player and led his team to a world championship. His stats that year included a .322 average, 44 homers, 132 runs batted in, and 118 runs scored.

Aaron hit more home runs than anyone else in the history of major league baseball. He attained this plateau with his second home run of the 1974 season, a shot that marked his 715th career roundtripper and thus broke the previous record of 714, which had been held by Babe Ruth. Aaron finished that season with 20 homers and brought his career mark to a total of 733. He completed his career with a total of 755 home runs.

Over his career, Aaron won a pair of batting titles and hit over .300 in twelve seasons. He won the home run and RBI crowns four times apiece, hit forty or more homers eight times, and hit at least twenty for twenty consecutive years—a National League record. In addition, he was named to twenty consecutive all-star teams.

In January 1982 Aaron received 406 of 415 votes from the Baseball Writers Association as he was elected into the Baseball Hall of Fame. Aaron, who was one of the first African Americans in major league baseball was awarded the Presidential Medal of Freedom, the nation's highest civilian award, in 2002.

Kareem Abdul-Jabbar (1947–)
Basketball Player

Kareem Abdul-Jabbar was born Ferdinand Lewis Alcindor Jr. on April 16, 1947. In high school, at seven and a half feet tall, he was easily the most sought after basketball player, particularly after he established a New York City record of 2,067 points and 2,002 rebounds, leading Power Memorial High School to three straight championships. Power won ninety-five and lost only six games during Lew Alcindor's years with the team; seventy-one of these victories were consecutive.

Abdul-Jabbar combined great height with catlike moves and a deft shooting touch to lead UCLA to three consecutive NCAA Champi-

onships. Twice, as a sophomore and a senior, he was chosen as the top collegiate player in the country. He finished his career at UCLA as the ninth all-time collegiate scorer, accumulating 2,325 points in eighty-eight games for an average of 26.4 points per game. After leading UCLA to its third consecutive NCAA title, Abdul-Jabbar signed a contract with the Milwaukee Bucks for $1.4 million.

In his rookie season (1969–1970) he led the Bucks, a recently established expansion club, to a second-place finish in the Eastern Division, only a few games behind the division winners, the New York Knickerbockers. After being voted Rookie of the Year, he went on to win the scoring championships in 1971 and 1972. At the end of the 1974–1975 season he was traded to the L.A. Lakers. Abdul-Jabbar enjoyed a very successful career with the Lakers, leading the team to NBA championships in 1980, 1982, 1985, 1987, and 1988.

A serious person both on and off the court, Abdul-Jabbar is a convert to the Hanafi Muslims. Greatly influenced by the life and struggles of Malcolm X, he believes that the Islamic religion (as distinct from the nationalistic Black Muslims) and a determined effort have much to offer for a good life.

Abdul-Jabbar announced his retirement after the 1988–1989 season, one year after the Lakers had won back-to-back World Championships. He was elected into the Basketball Hall of Fame in 1994. In 2005 Abdul-Jabbar served as special assistant to the Lakers coach, Phil Jackson.

Muhammad Ali (1942–)
Boxer

Born January 17, 1942, as Cassius Marcellus Clay Jr. in Louisville, Kentucky, Ali started boxing because he thought it was "the quickest way for black people to make it." After winning the 1960 Olympic gold medal as light-heavyweight, he turned professional. In 1963 he converted to

Islam, though the faith strongly disapproves of boxing, and changed his name. A year later, Ali won the world heavyweight championship by knocking out Sonny Liston.

Nine successful title defenses followed before Ali's famous war with the Army began. Refusing to serve in the armed forces during the Vietnam War, Ali maintained that it was contrary to Muslim tenets. Stripped of his title and banned from boxing in the United States, Ali faced prison, but he refused to back down and was finally vindicated by the U.S. Supreme Court in 1970.

Coming back to the ring after a three-and-a-half-year layoff, he worked his way up for another title shot. His biggest matches along the way were Superfights I and II against Joe Frazier, in which Ali suffered his first loss and evened the score in a return match.

Few fans gave Ali a chance against heavyweight champion George Foreman when they met in Zaire on October 30, 1974. A four-to-one underdog at ring time, Ali amazed the boxing world, knocking out his stronger, younger opponent. After regaining the crown, Ali knocked out Chuck Wepner and Ron Lyle, and decisioned Joe Bugner. In 1978, after fighting Frazier for the third time, Ali lost his title to Leon Spinks and briefly retired.

Ali fought well past his prime regaining his title briefly from Leon Spinks. In December 1981 Muhammad Ali entered the ring and lost a bout against Canadian heavyweight Trevor Berbick. It was a rare occasion and an inauspicious end to a career for a fighter who had won the heavyweight title three times. Ali retired in 1981 and in 1982 he was diagnosed with Parkinson's disease.

In 1996 Ali was selected to light the Olympic torch in Atlanta, Georgia. In 2001 the film *Ali* was produced starring Will Smith which earned an Academy Award nomination. In 2005 Ali opened the non-profit Muhammad Ali Center, which displays Ali memorabilia addresses issues of personal growth, peace, and social responsibility.

Ali has received numerous awards and recognition for his personal dedication to his faith and his uncompromising view on race and politics. He also has traveled extensively as an ambassador of good will. Because of his work in the civil rights movement Ali was awarded the Presidential Medal of Freedom and the Otto Hahn Peace Medal in Gold from the United Nations.

Henry Armstrong (1912–1988)
Boxer

Henry Armstrong was born Henry Jackson Jr. on December 12, 1912, in St. Louis, Missouri. In 1929, while fighting under the name of Melody Jackson, he was knocked out in his professional debut in Pittsburgh, Pennsylvania. Two weeks later, however, he won his first fight. For the next eight years he traveled from coast to coast, fighting all comers until he was finally given a shot at the featherweight title on October 20, 1937, when he defeated Petey Sarron.

Less than a year later, on May 31, 1938, Armstrong picked up his second title with a decision over welterweight champion Barney Ross. Within three months he had gained his own triple crown, winning a decision over lightweight champion Lou Ambers on August 17, 1938. Armstrong was the only fighter ever to hold three titles at the same time. Armstrong was inducted into the Black Athletes Hall of Fame in 1975 and died in 1988.

Arthur Ashe (1943–1993)
Tennis Player

Born on July 10, 1943, in Richmond, Virginia, Arthur Robert Ashe learned the game at the Richmond Racket Club, which had been formed by local black enthusiasts. Dr. R. W. Johnson, who had also served as an adviser and benefactor to Althea Gibson, sponsored Ashe's tennis career, spending thousands of dollars and a great deal of time with him.

By 1958 Ashe reached the semi-finals in the under-fifteen division of the National Junior Championships. In 1960 and 1961 he won the Junior Indoors Singles title. Even before he finished high school, he was ranked twenty-eighth in the country.

In 1961 Ashe entered UCLA on a tennis scholarship. He was on his way to winning the U.S. Amateur Tennis Championship and the U.S. Open Tennis Championship, in addition to becoming the first black man ever named to a Davis Cup Team.

In 1975 Ashe was recognized as one of the world's great tennis players, having defeated Jimmy Connors at Wimbledon as well as taking the World Championship Tennis (WCT) singles title over Björn Borg. At Wimbledon he defeated Connors 6–1, 5–7, 6–4.

In 1979, at the age of thirty-five, Ashe suffered a heart attack. Following quadruple bypass heart surgery, he retired from playing tennis. He began writing a nationally syndicated column and contributed monthly articles to *Tennis* magazine. He wrote the book *Advantage Ashe* (1967), a tennis diary, *Portrait in Motion* (1975), and his autobiography *Off the Court* (1981). In addition, he compiled the historical work *A Hard Road to Glory: A History of the African American Athlete* (1993).

Ashe was named captain of the U.S. Davis Cup team in 1981. He was a former president and active member of the board of directors of the Association of Tennis Professionals, and a co-founder of the National Junior Tennis League. Late in his career he also served as a television sports commentator.

In April 1992 Ashe announced that he had contracted AIDS as the result of a tainted blood transfusion during heart-bypass surgery. He died on February 6, 1993.

Ernie Banks (1931–)
Baseball Player

Ernest "Ernie" Banks was born in Dallas, Texas, on January 31, 1931. Banks moved to Chicago in 1953 to begin his professional career in baseball. He was the second African American to sign with the Chicago Cubs, preceded by Gene Baker, and was one of Chicago's most popular players.

Banks was selected as the most valuable player during the 1958–1959 Cubs season and had a career total of 512 home runs. After retiring in 1971 Banks briefly served as a coach for the Cubs. In 1977 he was inducted into the Baseball Hall of Fame. Banks is best known for his 1958 season of forty-four home runs and five grand slams, which stood as a record for over thirty years.

Elgin Baylor (1934–)
Basketball Player

Born on September 16, 1934, in Washington, D.C., Elgin Gay Baylor first became an All American while attending Spingarn High School. While at Seattle University he was a college All American. In 1959 Baylor made a sensational professional debut with the Minneapolis Lakers; he became the first rookie to be named most valuable player in the All-Star Game. That same year he was named to the All-League team, setting a scoring record of 64 points in a single game.

After five years as a superstar, Baylor injured his knee during a 1965 playoff game against the Bullets. Constant work brought him back to competitive form, but he never reached his former greatness. His career point total of 23,149 is fourth highest in NBA history, and his field goal average of 27.4 is second. His best season was 1961–1962, when he averaged 38.2 points a game. When he retired in 1968 Baylor had made the All-Pro first team nine times and had played eight consecutive All-Star games.

Baylor was inducted into the Black Athletes Hall of Fame in 1975, and the Basketball Hall of Fame in 1976.

Barry Bonds (1964–)
Baseball Player

Barry Lamar Bonds was born on July 24, 1964, in Riverside, California. He began his professional career with the Pittsburgh Pirates in 1986, and in 1993 he joined the San Francisco Giants. Bonds proved to be a strong hitter and began breaking records in 2001. By 2007 Bonds had won the National MVP Award for the seventh time, and had successfully broken Hank Aaron's home-run record of 762.

Bond's abilities were challenged in 2003 in a grand jury investigation of Bay Area Laboratory Co-operative and of Bonds's personal trainer, Greg Anderson. Bonds was accused of using steroids as administered by his trainer, but he denied the accusation. In spite of this, Bonds was convicted of four counts of perjury and one count of obstruction of justice in November 2007. Before the 2008 season, Bonds was released by San Francisco to be a free agent. As a result of the convictions, Bonds retired. In April 2011 Bonds was convicted of one count of obstruction of justice by the jury.

Lou Brock (1939–)
Baseball Player

Louis Clark "Lou" Brock was born June 18, 1939, in Eldorado, Arkansas. He began his professional career with the Chicago Cubs in September 1961. In 1964 Brock was traded to the St. Louis Cardinals and began breaking records. In 1966 Brock broke the record of Maury Wills of 104 stolen bases in a season. Brock lead the National League in stolen bases from 1966 to 1974. He set a record of 118 stolen bases in a single season. Brock also, in his 1977 season, broke Ty Cobb's career record of 892 stolen bases. Brock's career record was 938 stolen bases.

Brock had a slump early in the 1978 season but regained his focus and made a strong comeback. He retired from baseball in 1979. He received many awards, including the National League Comeback Player of the Year Award and the Hutch Award also in 1979. His jersey number 20 was retired by the St. Louis Cardinals. In 1978 the National League decided to name its annual stolen bases award after Lou Brock. In 1985 Brock was inducted into the Baseball Hall of Fame, and in May 1994 he was inducted into the St. Louis Walk of Fame. After retirement Brock went into business for himself and became a successful florist.

Jim Brown (1936–)
Football Player

James Nathaniel "Jim" Brown was born February 17, 1936, on St. Simon Island, Georgia, but his family moved to Manhasset, Long Island, New York, when he was seven. While at Manhasset High School he became an outstanding competitor in baseball, football, track and field, basketball, and lacrosse; following graduation he had a choice of forty-two college scholarships, as well as professional offers from both the New York Yankees and the Boston Braves. Brown chose Syracuse University, where he gained national recognition. An All-American performer in both football and lacrosse, he turned down the opportunity to compete in the decathlon at the 1956 Olympic Games, since it would have conflicted with his football schedule. He also spurned a three-year $150,000 offer to become a professional fighter.

Brown's 1957 entry into professional football with the Cleveland Browns was emblematic of the manner in which he would dominate the game in the decade to come. He led the league in rushing, paced Cleveland to a division championship, and was unanimously named rookie of the year. Brown broke rushing and scoring records in both single-season and lifetime totals, and he was All-League fullback virtually every season. His records include most yards gained (lifetime 12,312) and most touchdowns (lifetime 106). He was voted Football Back of the Decade for 1950 to 1960.

Brown announced his retirement in the summer of 1966, deciding to devote his time to a budding movie career and to the improvement of black business. He has made several films, including *Rio Conchos* (1964), *The Dirty Dozen* (1967), and *100 Rifles* (1969). In addition to his moviemaking activities, he is president and founder of Amer-I-Can.

Kobe Bryant (1978–)
Basketball Player

Kobe Bean Bryant was born on August 23, 1978, in Philadelphia, Pennsylvania, but spent time in Pistola, Italy, while his father continued his basketball career as an NBA journeyman player. When the family returned to Philadelphia Bryant continued to excel in basketball and was named the 1996 national high school player of the year by *USA Today*.

At six feet six inches tall and a high school guard, Bryant was confident that he could play in the NBA. He chose to skip college and was drafted in 1996 at seventeen years old by the Charlotte Hornets. He was traded almost immediately to the Los Angeles Lakers.

Bryant's points-per-game progressed from eight points to well over twenty-two points per game. In the 1999 and 2000 seasons the Lakers with Bryant and Shaquille O'Neal won the first of three consecutive championships. Bryant in 2002 was the youngest player to win three NBA championships. In 2003 Bryant was charged with sexual assault, which damaged his reputation and lost him numerous endorsements. His marriage suffered, and Bryant offered a public apology to his wife with an eight-carat purple diamond ring. In 2004 the charges were dismissed.

By 2006 O'Neal had been traded to the Miami Heat, partly because of rumors of a feud

between O'Neil and Bryant. In that same year Bryant broke the team record as the second highest scorer reaching eighty-one points in one game. In the summer of 2008 Bryant participated in the U.S. Olympic Men's Basketball competition and won a gold medal. The Lakers have since won the 2009 and the 2010 NBA championship with Bryant named as MVP in 2010.

Roy Campanella (1921–1993)
Baseball Player

Born on November 19, 1921, in Philadelphia, Pennsylvania, Campanella began playing semi-professional baseball at the age of fifteen with the Bacharach Giants. In 1945 Campanella turned down the opportunity to become the first black in the major leagues when he mistakenly understood Branch Rickey's offer to be a contract with a rumored black team in Brooklyn. A few days later he learned from Jackie Robinson that the offer had involved the possibility of playing with the Brooklyn Dodgers of the National League.

In 1946 Campanella was signed by the Dodgers. Before the year was out, however, Campanella was brought up to Brooklyn. Over the next eight years the Dodgers star played with five National League pennant winners and one world championship team. He played on seven consecutive National League All-Star teams (1949–1955).

In January 1958 Campanella's career was ended by an automobile accident, which left him paralyzed and confined to a wheelchair. In March 1969, he was inducted into the Baseball Hall of Fame, and in 1975 he was inducted into the Black Athletes Hall of Fame. Campanella died on June 26, 1993.

Wilt Chamberlain (1936–1999)
Basketball Player

Wilton Norman "Wilt" Chamberlain was born in Philadelphia, Pennsylvania, on August 21, 1936.

By the time he entered high school he was already six feet eleven inches tall. When he graduated from high school he had his choice of seventy-seven major colleges and 125 smaller schools. He chose Kansas University but left after his junior year with two years of All-American honors behind him.

Before joining the NBA in 1959 Chamberlain played with the Harlem Globetrotters. Although dominating the sport with the Philadelphia 76ers (1959–1967) and with the Los Angeles Lakers (1968–1972), Chamberlain was a member of only two championship teams, Philadelphia (1961) and Los Angeles (1972). For his gargantuan effort in defeating the Knicks in the latter series, including playing the final game with both hands painfully injured, he was voted MVP. At the start of the 1974 season, he left the Lakers to become player–coach of the San Diego Conquistadors (ABA) for a reported $500,000 contract.

Wilt Chamberlain holds most of the major basketball records: for single games, most points (100); most field goals made (36); most free throws (28); and most rebounds (55). His career records are: most rebounds (23,924); highest scoring average (30.1); most points (31,419); most field goals made (12,681); and most free throws attempted (11,862).

Chamberlain was inducted into the Basketball Hall of Fame in 1978 and later became involved in the entertainment industry performing in several movies. He also owned several businesses and wrote his autobiography, *View from Above* (1991), which discussed his sexual exploits and was considered controversial. On October 12, 1999, Chamberlain died of a heart attack in Los Angeles, California.

Alice Coachman (1923–)
Track and Field Athlete

Alice Marie Coachman was born on November 9, 1923, in Albany, Georgia, at a time when seg-regation was fully entrenched in American society. In spite of her family's desire for her to focus on more accepted and lady-like careers, her interest in sports remained strong. After breaking high school records in track and winning the Amateur Athletic Union Nationals in the high jump and the fifty-yard dash events, Coachman entered Tuskegee College and earned a trade degree in dressmaking in 1946.

Coachman continued to excel in sports while in college, winning national track and field championships. With the cancellation of the 1940 and 1944 Olympic Games because of World War II, Coachman was invited to participate in the 1948 Olympics and became the first black woman to win a gold medal in high jump and also in the Olympic Games for that year. Even though in 1948 she was past her prime years of competition, she out-jumped all of her competition creating a record that lasted eight years. After the Olympics, Coachman was welcomed home as a star, but due to racism and segregated audiences she was not permitted to speak at public events.

Coachman retired in 1949 with her Olympic gold medal and thirty-one national track titles. She completed her education and earned a B.A from Albany State College in 1949 and remained involved in academics and sports. In 1994 she established the Alice Coachman Track and Field Foundation. In 1975 Coachman was inducted into the National Track and Field Hall of Fame, and in 1996 she was honored at the Olympics in Atlanta, Georgia, as one of the 100 greatest athletes.

Leonard S. Coleman Jr. (1949–)
Baseball League President

Leonard S. Coleman Jr. was born on February 17, 1949, in Newark, New Jersey. At Montclair High School Coleman was a sports fan and played both baseball and football. After high school Coleman earned a B.S. in history from Princeton University in 1971, an M.P.A. in 1975 from John F. Kennedy School of Government, and an M.A. in education and social policy from Harvard University in 1976.

Between 1976 and 1991 Coleman worked for various community and financial institutions including the Greater Newark Urban Coalition, the New Jersey Department of Community, and as a finance banker for Kidder, Peabody & Co. In 1991 Coleman was hired as executive director of marketing development for Major League Baseball. In 1994 Coleman was selected as president of the National League, becoming the highest ranking African American executive in sports. He took on rebuilding the image of the league after a lengthy players' strike. He also was an advocate for African American baseball players. Coleman served as president until 1999. After leaving this position Coleman was named president of Newark Sports & Entertainment. In 2010 Coleman was named director of Omnicom Group Inc., an Advertising Agency.

Cynthia Cooper (1963–)
Basketball Player, Coach

Cynthia Lynne Cooper was born on April 14, 1963, in Chicago, Illinois. She was an avid player of basketball beginning at age sixteen. After winning a basketball scholarship to the University of Southern California at Los Angeles, she became part of the greatest women's basketball team in the history of women's college basketball. This stellar team included players such as Hall of Famer Cheryl Miller. With little opportunity for basketball beyond college Cooper took her skills overseas and played in Spain and Italy from 1986 to 1994. She also played on the Olympic women's basketball team in 1988 and 1992.

With the formation of the Women's National Basketball Association (WNBA) in 1997 Cooper was able to play in the United States with the Houston Comets. She made the highest scoring record for the organization twice in 1997 with thirty or more points. Cooper was also named MVP in 1997.

Cooper retired as a player in 2000 but took a position as coach of the Phoenix Mercury in 2001. In 2003 Cooper returned briefly as a player but retired again the next season in 2004. Cooper

became head coach of Prairie View A&M University's women's basketball team in 2005.

Dominique Dawes (1976–)
Gymnast

Dominique Margaux Dawes was born November 20, 1976, in Silver Springs, Maryland. Dawes was an active and athletic child who from the age of five was competing in gymnastic competitions. By 1991 at the age of fourteen she already ranked thirteenth nationally in compulsories and ninth overall. She was already determined to participate in the 1992 Olympics. Dawes was the first African American to excel in gymnastics. During the 1992 Olympics in Barcelona she won a bronze medal; in the 1996 Olympics in Atlanta she won two bronze medals and a gold medal as part of the Olympic team; and in 2000 she won a bronze medal in Sydney.

Dawes completed her education in 2002 earning a B.A. from the University of Maryland. She went on to serve as president of the Women's Sport Federation from 2004 to 2006. In June 2010 President Barack Obama appointed Dawes co-chair of the President's Council on Fitness, Sports, and Nutrition.

Lee Elder (1934–)
Golfer

Robert Lee Elder was born on July 14, 1934, in Washington, D.C. Elder first picked up golf as a caddie at the age of fifteen. After his father's death during World War II, Elder and his mother moved to Los Angeles, where he met the famed black golfer Ted Rhodes. He was later drafted by the U.S. Army, where he sharpened his skills as captain of the golf team.

Following his discharge from the Army he began to teach golf. In 1962 he debuted as a professional, winning the national title of the United Golf Association, a black organization. Elder played seventeen years with the United Golf Association prior to his joining the PGA, participating in close to fifty tournaments. He debuted with the PGA in November 1967 finishing one stroke out of the money. In thirty PGA tournaments Elder earned $38,000; he was the first black professional golfer to reach $1 million in earnings.

Elder was the first African American to play at the Masters. On the Seniors PGA Tour Elders has won eight tournaments and has since been inducted in the NCAA Hall of Fame for his work with HBCUs [Historically Black Colleges and Universities].

Julius "Dr. J." Erving (1950–)
Basketball Player

Julius Winfield Erving II (also known as "Dr. J") was born in Hempstead, Long Island, New York, on February 22, 1950. As a player at Roosevelt High School, Erving made the All-County and All–Long Island teams. He was awarded an athletic scholarship to the University of Massachusetts, but after completing his junior year he left college, hired the services of a management firm, and signed a $500,000 contract for four years with the Virginia Squires of the ABA. Voted rookie of the year in 1972, he renegotiated his contract and eventually signed with the New Jersey Nets for $2.8 million for four years.

In his first season with the Nets (1973), he led the league in scoring for the second consecutive year and paced his team to the ABA championship. After being traded to the Philadelphia 76ers, Erving became a favorite with the city's fans, leading the 76ers to the NBA championship in 1983. Between his combined seasons with the two teams, he became the thirteenth player to score 20,000 points. Erving retired following the 1986–1987 season. Known for the slam dunk Erving was elected to the National Basketball Hall of Fame in 1992. In 1997 he was named executive vice president of the Orlando Magic basketball organization.

George Foreman (1949–)
Boxer

George Edward Foreman was born January 10, 1949, in Marshall, Texas. Foreman grew up in Houston, Texas, and learned to box while in the U.S. Job Corps. At the 1968 Olympics, Foreman won a gold medal as a heavyweight boxer. He won the professional title as a heavyweight on January 22, 1973, after knocking out Joe Frazier. Foreman defended his title against Muhammad Ali on October 30, 1974, at the fight known as the "Rumble in the Jungle" where Ali won the fight. Foreman retired from boxing in 1977.

In 1994 after a career as a minister Foreman mounted a comeback, which resulted in a match on November 5 against Michael Moorer, the heavyweight title holder at the time. Foreman won and successfully became the oldest boxer to hold the International Boxing Federation (IBF) and World Boxing Association (WBA) heavyweight titles of the world. Foreman resigned from his IBF title and was stripped of his WBA title for refusing to fight the contenders for the title. Foreman again retired from boxing in 1997. In 2003 he was inducted into the International Boxing Hall of Fame.

In 1995 Foreman became spokesman for a grilling machine that promoted healthy eating, which has brought him continued recognition and economic prosperity.

Althea Gibson (1927–2003)
Tennis Player

Althea Gibson was born on August 25, 1927, in Silver, South Carolina, but was raised in Harlem, New York, where she learned to play paddle tennis. After her paddle tennis days, she entered and won the Department of Parks Manhattan

Girls' Tennis Championship. In 1942 she began to receive professional coaching at the interracial Cosmopolitan Tennis Club, and a year later won the New York State Negro Girls Singles title. In 1945 and 1946, she won the National Negro Girls Singles championship, and in 1948 she began a decade of domination of the same title in the women's division.

A year later Gibson entered Florida A&M University, where she played tennis and basketball for the next four years. In 1950 she was runner-up for the National Indoor Championship, and that same year became the first black to play at Forest Hills. The following year she became the first black to play at Wimbledon. In 1957 Gibson won the Wimbledon singles crown, which she won again in 1958, and she teamed with Darlene Hard to win the doubles championship as well. In 1957 and 1958, Gibson won the U.S. Open Women's Singles title.

Gibson has served as a recreation manager, a member of the New Jersey State Athletic Control Board and the Governor's Council on Physical Fitness, and as a sports consultant. She is also the author of *I Always Wanted to Be Somebody* (1958). In 1959 she recorded an album *Althea Gibson Sings* and appeared in the film *The Horse Soldiers*. At the U.S. Open Tournament in 2002 Gibson's career was celebrated along with the recognition of her seventieth birthday. On September 28, 2003, at the age of seventy-six Gibson died of respiratory failure.

Bob Gibson (1935–)
Baseball Player, Coach

Robert "Bob" Gibson (nicknamed "Hoot" and "Gibby") was born on November 9, 1935 in Omaha, Nebraska. He was able to play on the Omaha Technical High School track team but was barred from the baseball team because he was black. Having been rejected by the University of Indiana because of quota limits, Gibson attended

Creighton University in Omaha and became the first African American to play on the baseball and the track team at the university.

After spending time in the minor leagues, Gibson began his professional career in 1959 with the St. Louis Cardinals. Stepping into the role of pitcher from 1961 to 1975, Gibson successfully had thirteen consecutive winning seasons, and won seven of nine World Series games he pitched. In 1968 Gibson started thirty-four games, completed twenty-eight, and was the first pitcher to have a career total of 3,117 strike outs.

Gibson was awarded the league's Gold Glove as the best fielder for nine consecutive years from 1965 to 1973. He was elected to the Baseball Hall of Fame in 1981.

Josh Gibson (1911–1947)
Baseball Player

Joshua Gibson was born on December 21, 1911, in Buena Vista, Georgia. Gibson began playing baseball on an amateur team sponsored by Gimbels Department Store where he worked as an elevator operator. His career began in the Negro League in 1929 and he debuted with the Homestead Grays on July 31, 1930. Gibson played for the Grays on and off for sixteen years.

Gibson was known as a powerful hitter and one of the best catchers in any league. Gibson never played for the major leagues because the league was only for whites during his lifetime. He is known to have hit a 580-foot home run in Yankee Stadium over the bleachers and out of the stadium. He is also credited with hitting more than 800 home runs in his career and as many as eighty-four in one season. Gibson died on January 20, 1947, from a stroke. He was inducted into the Baseball Hall of Fame in 1972.

Ken Griffey Jr. (1969–)
Baseball Player

George Kenneth "Ken" Griffey Jr. was born November 21, 1969, in Donora, Pennsylvania, but the family moved to Cincinnati, Ohio. Griffey followed the role model of his athlete father, Ken Griffey, who played for the Cincinnati Reds. Griffey, while in high school in 1987, was drafted by the Seattle Mariners and began playing major league ball in 1989. He was such a popular player that he won ten Gold Gloves for center-field play, and was selected as MVP in 1997. In 1998 he hit fifty home runs in back-to-back years. Griffey was so respected by his teammates in the league that he was voted Player of the Decade for the 1990s.

In 2000 Griffey returned to his home town with the Cincinnati Reds, signing a nine-year, $112 million contract, one of the highest paying contracts at that time. In 2004 after being plagued with injuries from 2001 to 2004 Griffey hit his 500th home run and was named National League Comeback Player of the Year in 2005. Griffey continued to break records and hit home runs while dealing with injuries. On August 22, 2007, he was selected as an all-time Gold Glove winner as of the greatest defensive player in the last fifty years, and in 2008 he was named an American Public Diplomacy Envoy by then Secretary of State Condoleezza Rice. In 2009 Griffey hit his 621st home run in new Yankee Stadium.

In 2008 Griffey played for the Chicago White Sox and later returned to the Seattle Mariners for the 2009 and 2010 seasons. On June 2, 2010, Griffey announced his retirement. In February 2011, he was hired by the Seattle Mariners as a special consultant.

Florence Griffith-Joyner (1959–1998)
Track and Field Athlete

Born on December 21, 1959, in Los Angeles, California, Florence Delorez Griffith started in track at an early age. She first attended California State University at Northridge, but later transferred with her coach Bob Kersee when he moved to UCLA. She married 1984 Olympic gold medalist Al Joyner in 1987.

At the 1984 Olympic Games she won a silver medal. She returned to the Olympic Games in 1988, winning gold medals in the 100-meter, 200-meter, and 400-meter relay races, and a silver medal in the 1600-meter relay race. She also set the world record for the 100-meter and 200-meter races that year. Griffith Joyner nicknamed "Flo-Jo" was inducted into the Track and Field Hall of Fame in 1995. She died in her sleep of an epileptic seizure in 1998.

Chamique Holdsclaw (1977–)
Basketball Player

Chamique Shaunta Holdsclaw was born in Flushing, New York, on August 9, 1977. While in high school she lead the women's basketball team to four New York State championships. After high school she attended the University of Tennessee. As a member of the women's basketball team she excelled and became a three-time All-American, three-time Player of the Year, and three-time NCAA title winner. In 1998 she became the first African American female basketball player to receive the Sullivan Award as the top amateur athlete in America.

With the establishment of the WNBA, Holdsclaw was drafted for the Washington Mystics in 1999. During her first season she was named rookie of the year and averaged 16.9 points a game. In the 2000 Summer Olympics she led the women's basketball team to a gold medal. In 2005 she was traded to the Los Angeles Sparks and played with them until she announced her retirement on June 11, 2007. She came out of retirement in 2008 to play for the Atlanta Dream, and after being released in 2010 she signed with the San Antonio Silver Stars. Holdsclaw continues her outstanding career in the WNBA.

Larry Holmes (1949–)
Boxer

Larry Holmes was born in Cuthberth, Georgia, on November 3, 1949. At the age of twenty-four he became a professional boxer after serving as a sparring partner for Muhammad Ali. Holmes won the World Boxing Council heavyweight title from title holder Ken Norton on June 9, 1978. After defending and losing the title Holmes went on to defeat Ali in 1980 for the heavyweight title in a technical knockout in Las Vegas.

Holmes maintained the heavyweight title for seven years against twelve contenders and finally lost it to Michael Spinks on September 22, 1985. Holmes announced his retirement in 1986 but launched a comeback in 1988 and again in 1991. Holmes's final fight was in 2002 and he was inducted into the International Boxing Hall of Fame on June 8, 2008.

Evander Holyfield (1962–)
Boxer

Evander Holyfield was born in Atlanta, Georgia, on October 19, 1962. At twenty-two, he participated in the 1984 Olympics and won a bronze medal in the light heavyweight division. Holyfield became a professional boxer in 1986 and by 1989 had become the undisputed cruiserweight champion.

In 1990 Holyfield won the heavyweight title defeating Buster Douglas, but later lost the title to Riddick Bowe. In 1993, and by 1997, Holyfield had won both the IBF and WBF titles thus unifying the heavyweight titles. He lost them both in 1999 to fighter Lennox Lewis. Holyfield has won the world heavyweight title four times. In June 2008 legal notices were placed on Holyfield's property seeking payment for unpaid debt.

Holyfield who is known for his ability as a boxer and for his devout faith continues to fight in the heavyweight division. His record stands at forty-four wins, ten losses, and two draws.

Reggie Jackson (1946–)
Baseball Player

Reginald Martinez "Reggie" Jackson was born on May 18, 1946, in Wynecote, Pennsylvania. Jackson was encouraged by his father to become an all-around athlete while at Cheltenham High School, where he ran track, starred at halfback, and batted .550. An outstanding football and baseball collegian at Arizona State University, he left after his sophomore year to join the Athletics (then located in Kansas City).

In 1968, his first full season with the Athletics, he had the second worst seasonal totals in baseball history—home runs (29), RBIs (74), errors (18), and strike-outs (171). After playing a season of winter ball under Frank Robinson's direction, Jackson was back on track. His performance continued to improve, and in 1973 he batted .293, led the league in home runs (32), RBIs (117), and slugging average (.531), and was selected most valuable player.

The first of the big-money free agents, Jackson hit 144 homers, drove in 461 runs, and boosted his total career home runs to 425 while with the Yankees. In January 1982, after an often stormy tenure in New York, he signed with the California Angels. Jackson retired as an active player in 1987, and he has occasionally served as a commentator on baseball broadcasts. Because of his outstanding performance in post seasons, Jackson became known as "Mr. October." During his years with the Oakland Athletics and New York Yankees, Jackson captured or tied 13 World Series records to become baseball's greatest record holder. In 1993 Jackson was elected into the Baseball Hall of Fame, and on May 22, 2004, his number 9, was retired.

LeBron James (1984–)
Basketball Player

LeBron Raymone James, born in Akron, Ohio, on December 30, 1984, decided early on he would take his talents to the NBA when he graduated from high school in 2003. While in high school his phenomenal talents landed him a *Sports Illustrated* cover. At six feet six inches tall and 250 pounds, James was drafted by the Cleveland Cavaliers on a standard three-year contract.

James was selected in 2004 as Rookie of the Year, and in 2009 and 2010 as most Valuable Player in the NBA, and co-captain of the 2008 Olympic team that won a gold medal. James declared himself a free agent in 2010 and much to the dismay, anger, and outrage of his fans, he joined the Miami Heat. "King" James, as he is called, is a powerhouse on the court and is predicted to continue to have an outstanding career in basketball along with his goal of building his name into a billion-dollar brand, as he told CBS's *60 Minutes* in March 2009.

Earvin "Magic" Johnson (1959–)
Basketball Player

Earvin Johnson was born August 14, 1959, in Lansing, Michigan. He attended Everett High School and in 1974 made their varsity basketball team as a guard. It was while playing for Everett that he picked up the nickname "Magic" because of his ball-handling abilities. While in high school Johnson made the All-State team and for three years was named the United Press International Prep-Player of the Year in Michigan.

In 1977 Johnson enrolled at Michigan State University and played college ball until 1979, when he was selected by the L.A. Lakers in the National Basketball Association draft. Johnson played with the Lakers until his forced retirement in 1991 when he tested positive for HIV, the virus that is closely associated with acquired immunodeficiency syndrome (AIDS).

Throughout his college and professional career Johnson was an outstanding basketball player who brought much excitement, goodwill, and admiration to the game. He was the recipient of many awards and was chosen to play on many post-season All-Star teams, including All–Big Ten

team (1977), NCAA Tournament's Most Outstanding Player, NCAA All-Tournament team, Consensus All-American (1979), NBA Finals Most Valuable Player, NBA All-Star team, NBA All-Rookie team (1980), All-NBA team (1982–1989, 1991), Seagram Seven Crown of Sports Award, NBA Finals Most Valuable Player (1982), Schick Pivotal Player Award (1984), NBA Most Valuable Player (1987, 1989, 1990), Sporting News NBA Player of the Year, Allstate Good Hands Award, NBA Finals Most Valuable Player (1987), and NBA All-Star Game's Most Valuable Player (1990).

Upon retiring from professional basketball Johnson made appearances on the court, including playing on the U.S. Olympic basketball team in 1992 and playing in the 1992 NBA All-Star Game, where he won another most valuable player award. Johnson served in various roles with the Lakers from coach in 1994 to a brief time as a player again in 1995. In 2001 Johnson was honored with a star on the Hollywood Walk of Fame.

Johnson has become a successful entrepreneur in several enterprises that offer opportunities to urban communities and to those who otherwise might not have access to jobs or services. He has partnered with Starbucks to bring franchises to inner cities, Hewlett-Packard for on-line services, and Loew's Cineplex to build movie theaters in areas such as Houston, Atlanta, Harlem, and Cleveland, to name only a few of his ventures taken on by the Johnson Development Corporation.

Jack Johnson (1878–1946)
Boxer

John Arthur "Jack" Johnson was born in Galveston, Texas, on March 31, 1878, the son of a school janitor. He was so tiny as a boy that he was nicknamed "Li'l Arthur," a name that stuck with him throughout his career. As a young man, he "hoboed" around the country, making his way to Chicago,

Boston, and New York, and learning the fighting trade by working out with veteran professionals whenever he could. When he finally got his chance at the title, he had already been fighting for nine years and had lost only three of approximately 100 bouts.

Johnson became the first black heavyweight champion after winning the crown from Tommy Burns in Sydney, Australia, on December 26, 1908. With his victory over Burns, Johnson became the center of a bitter racial controversy, as the American public clamored for the former white champion, Jim Jeffries, to come out of retirement and recapture the crown. When the two fought on July 4, 1910, in Reno, Nevada, Johnson knocked out Jeffries in the fourteenth round.

In 1913 Johnson left the United States because of legal entanglements. Two years later he defended his title against Jess Willard in Havana, Cuba, and was knocked out in the twenty-sixth round. His career record was 107 wins and six losses. Johnson died in 1946 in an automobile crash in North Carolina. He was inducted into the Boxing Hall of Fame in 1954. Johnson's story became the basis for the play and film *The Great White Hope* (1970); Ken Burns focused on Johnson's life in his documentary *Unforgivable Blackness: The Rise and Fall of Jack Johnson* (2005).

Marion Jones (1975–)
Track and Field Athlete

Marion Lois Jones was born in Los Angeles, California, on October 12, 1975. Jones excelled in high school sports and won the California State Meet in the 100 meters sprint four years in a row culminating with her senior year. Jones, who only played basketball briefly in college at the University of North Carolina at Chapel Hill, set her sights on the 1996 Olympics track and field. Because of a broken foot Jones did not make the Olympics that year, but continued to win races and break records. By 1999 she had won thirty-seven consecutive races at national and international games including the World Cup and the USA Outdoor Championships. Jones was named *Track and Field News* top woman Athlete of the Year for three consecutive years.

Jones participated in the 2000 Summer Olympics in Sydney, Australia. She won three gold medals and two bronze medals. She also competed in the 2001 Goodwill Games winning a gold medal in the 100 meter. Jones was accused in 2004 of using performance enhancing drugs as a result of a drug investigation centering on the BALCO designer steroid drug case, but the charges were dismissed as she had never failed a drug test. In October 2007 Jones admitted to taking steroids before the 2000 Summer Olympics, and she admitted lying to two grand juries. She was subsequently suspended for two years and on October 5, 2007, she announced her retirement.

After the U.S Anti-Doping Agency's investigation, Jones was required to forfeit all of her medals, prizes and awards, and on January 11, 2008, she was sentenced to six months in jail for lying to the grand juries. On March 10, 2010, Marion Jones signed to play with the WNBA team the Tulsa Shock.

Michael Jordan (1963–)
Basketball Player

Michael Jeffrey Jordan was born in Brooklyn, New York, on February 17, 1963, and attended the University of North Carolina. As a rookie with the Chicago Bulls, Jordan was named to the All-Star team during the 1985 season. A skilled ball-handler and a slam-dunk artist, in 1986 he became the second NBA player in history to score more than 3,000 points in a single season.

Jordan was the NBA's individual scoring champ from 1987 through 1991. He was also named the NBA's most valuable player at the end of the 1987–1988 season. In 1991 Jordan led the Chicago Bulls to their first NBA Championship and was the league's most valuable player. Under Jordan's leadership, the Bulls experienced repeat NBA championships in 1992 and 1993. In the autumn of 1993, Jordan announced his retirement from basketball.

Jordan spent a season in the Minor Baseball League, but returned to the Chicago Bulls in 1995. His return added two more NBA Championships for the Bulls, and Jordan earned his fourth MVP award. On January 13, 1999, Jordan again announced his retirement. He proceeded to produce documentaries, films, and books on his iconic status and his drive for excellence. In 2000 Jordan became part owner of the Washington Wizards. He played for the Wizards briefly but retired for the final time in 2003. His overall game average was at its highest with 30.2 points per game.

In 1992 Jordan played for the United States Olympic basketball team, which captured the gold medal in Barcelona, Spain. He is the founder of the Michael Jordan Celebrity Golf Classic, which raises funds for the United Negro College Fund. Jordan was named Athlete of the Century by Sport Channel ESPN, and his abilities in marketing products from Jordan basketball shoes to Gatorade has made him a household name.

Jackie Joyner-Kersee (1962–)
Track and Field Athlete

Born on March 3, 1962, in East St. Louis, Illinois, Jacqueline "Jackie" Joyner-Kersee studied previous outstanding women athletes and soon teamed with her husband, coach Bob Kersee, to pursue her dreams of success in the field of competition. Prior to winning the 1988 gold medal, she participated in the 1984 Olympics and came away with a silver medal for the heptathlon despite a torn hamstring muscle.

The only woman to gain more than 7,000 points in the heptathlon four times, she set a world record for the grueling two-day event with 7,215 points at the 1988 Olympic trials prior to the competition itself. Often touted as the world's greatest female athlete, Joyner-Kersee won two gold medals at the 1988 Olympic games. She earned another gold medal in the heptathlon and a bronze medal in the long jump at the 1992 Olympic Games in Barcelona, Spain. In 1996 she became the first woman to win six medals in the history of U.S. Women's Track and Field when she won a bronze medal for the long jump. Joyner-Kersee briefly played basketball in the ABL before becoming a sports agent.

"Sugar" Ray Leonard (1956–)
Boxer, Television Analyst

Ray Charles Leonard, the most popular boxer of the modern era was born in Rocky Mount, North Carolina, on May 17, 1956. At the age of twenty he participated in the 1976 Montreal Olympics and won a gold medal in the boxing light welterweight division. By 1979 he had become a professional and won the welterweight title. His most famous fights were with Roberto Duran and Tommy Hearns. He used a taunting approach to frustrate Duran forcing him to quit in the second round, and came from behind with Hearns to win based on a technical knockout.

After retiring due to a detached retina, Leonard came back briefly in 1987 to fight "Marvelous" Marvin Hagler for the middleweight title, but again retired in 1991 with a brief return in 1997. He was inducted into the Boxing Hall of Fame in 1997.

Leonard went on to use his expertise as a boxing analyst for HBO and ESPN Classic Sports in 2001. In 2004 Leonard started the reality boxing show *The Contender,* which lasted for four seasons while Leonard served as executive producer. He also competed on the dance show *Dancing with the Stars* during their twelfth season.

Carl Lewis (1961–)
Track and Field Athlete

Frederick Carlton "Carl" Lewis was born on July 1, 1961, in Birmingham, Alabama. He attended

Willingboro High School in New Jersey, and the University of Houston. In the 1984 Olympic Games in Los Angeles, California, Carl Lewis became the first athlete since Jesse Owens in 1936 to win four gold medals in Olympic competition.

An often controversial track and field performer, the New Jersey native went into the 1984 competition with the burden of tremendous expectations as the result of intense pre-Olympic publicity. He did not set any Olympic records, even as a gold medalist, and found that his statements regarding training and drug use were often the subject of public concern.

Lewis went to the 1988 Olympics in Seoul, South Korea, hoping to duplicate his four gold-medal wins, and he was the subject of widespread interest as he faced off against his archrival, Canadian Ben Johnson.

Lewis won gold medals in the long jump and the 100-meter dash—though the latter prize came after Ben Johnson was disqualified following the race when he tested positive for steroid use—and

a silver medal in the 200-meter dash. At the 1992 Olympics in Barcelona, Spain, and the 1996 Olympics in Atlanta, Georgia, Lewis won a gold medal for the long jump. He was inducted into the Track and Field Hall of Fame in 2001.

Joe Louis (1914–1981)
Boxer

Born in a sharecropper's shack in Chambers County, Alabama, on May 13, 1914, Joseph Louis Barrow moved to Detroit as a small boy. Taking up boxing as an amateur, he won fifty out of fifty-nine bouts (forty-three by knockout), before turning professional in 1934. He quickly gained a reputation in the Midwest.

In 1935 Louis came east to meet Primo Carnera, a former boxing champion who was then staging a comeback. Louis knocked out Carnera in six rounds, earning his nickname "The Brown Bomber." After knocking out ex-champion Max Baer, Louis suffered his lone pre-championship

Joe Louis takes on Max Schmeling in the legendary 1935 boxing match.

defeat at the hands of Max Schmeling, the German title holder who knocked him out in the twelfth round. Less than a month later, Louis knocked out another former champion, Jack Sharkey, in three rounds. After defeating a number of other challengers, he was given a title fight with Jim Braddock on June 22, 1937. He stopped Braddock in the eighth round and began the long championship reign that would see him defend his crown as often as six times in six months. Louis held the heavyweight championship for more than eleven years, longer than anyone else, and defended the title more often than any other heavyweight champion. His twenty-five title fights were more than the combined total of the eight champions who preceded him.

One of Louis's greatest fights was his 1941 come-from-behind, thirteenth-round knockout of Billy Conn. After winning a disputed decision over Joe Walcott in 1947, Louis knocked out the Jersey challenger six months later and went into retirement. Joe Louis died April 12, 1981, at the age of sixty-seven.

Willie Mays (1931–)
Baseball Player

Born in Fairfield, Alabama, on May 6, 1931, Willie Howard Mays Jr. made his professional debut on July 4, 1948, with the Birmingham Black Barons. He was signed by the New York Giants in 1950 and reached the major leagues in 1951, in time to become the National League's Rookie of the Year with twenty home runs, sixty-eight RBIs, and the sensational fielding that contributed to his team's pennant victory.

After two years in the Army, Mays returned to lead the Giants to the World Championship in 1954, gaining recognition as the league's most valuable player for his forty-one homers, 110 RBIs, and .345 batting average.

When the Giants moved to San Francisco, Mays continued his phenomenal home-run hit-

ting and led his team to a 1962 pennant. A year later *Sport* magazine named him "the greatest player of the decade." He won the MVP award again in 1965, after hitting fifty-two home runs and batting .317.

Traded to the New York Mets before the 1972 season, he continued to play outfield and first base. At the end of the 1973 season, his records included 2,992 games (third on the all-time list), 3,283 hits (seventh), and 660 home runs (third). Willie Mays is one of only seven ballplayers to have hit four home runs in one game. After acting as a coach for the Mets, Mays left baseball to pursue a business career. He was elected to the Baseball Hall of Fame in 1979. In 2001 a statue and plaza outside the new stadium of the San Francisco Giants were dedicated to Mays. After twenty-one seasons with the San Francisco Giants, Mays was called the game's finest defensive outfielder and perhaps its best base runner as well.

Cheryl Miller (1964–)
Basketball Player, Analyst

Cheryl D. Miller was born in Riverside, California, on January 3, 1964. In high school her height of six feet three inches and her basketball abilities in scoring as much as 105 points a game brought many opportunities for college. Miller was also selected as the Street and Smith's National High School Player of the Year in 1981 and 1982. With over 250 scholarship offers, Miller decided to enroll at the University of Southern California (USC) and subsequently led them to two national titles. Miller was named All-American four times, and National Player of the Year three times.

In 1983 Miller participated in the World Championships, the Pan American Games in Venezuela, and in 1986 she participated in Goodwill Games in Moscow. In 1984 Miller won a gold medal at the Olympic Games. Miller was inducted into the Basketball Hall of Fame in 1994, and in 1999 she was among the first group of women players inducted into the Women's Basketball Hall of Fame. She served as coach for her alma mater, USC, from 1993 to 1995, and she served as head coach of the WNBA Phoenix Mercury from 1997 to 2000. She resigned in 2000 sighting fatigue as the reason.

Miller serves as a sideline reporter and analyst and makes appearances on NBA-TV. She was inducted in 2010 to the FIBA Hall of Fame for International Players.

Edwin Moses (1955–)
Track and Field Athlete

Edwin Corley Moses was born on August 31, 1955, in Dayton, Ohio. Moses attended Morehouse College on an engineering scholarship while training in local high schools for the 1976 Olympics. He excelled as a track star in hurdles, and by 1976 he had won a gold medal at the Olympic Games and was internationally known. Moses was awarded the Sullivan Award in 1983, which is given to the best amateur athlete, and in 1984 he was selected by *Sports Illustrated* as Athlete of the Year. Moses won a bronze medal at the 1988 Olympic Games for the 400-meter hurdles. In 1994 Moses was elected to the USA Track and Field Hall of Fame.

Moses earned an M.B.A. from Pepperdine University in 1994 and serves as a financial consultant. Moses has also served as chairperson of the U.S. Olympic Committee Substance Abuse Center and the International Olympic Committee Athletes Commission.

Shaquille O'Neal (1972–)
Basketball Player

Shaquille Rashaun O'Neal (nicknamed "Shaq") was born in Newark, New Jersey, on March 6, 1972. O'Neal's abilities as a basketball player were showcased in high school when he led his home team, Cole High School in San Antonio, Texas, to a state championship. With numerous college scholarships to choose from O'Neal enrolled at Louisiana State University (LSU) and led the LSU

Tigers to nation prominence. O'Neal was named during the 1990–1991 season All-American two times and was selected as the United Press International Player of the Year and the Associated Press Player of the Year.

O'Neal signed with the NBA team the Orlando Magic in 1992. During his first season seven feet one inch, 300-pound O'Neal, was selected as Rookie of the Year. His dominance on the court was undeniable. O'Neal played for the Los Angeles Lakers (1996–2004); the Miami Heat (2004–2008); the Phoenix Suns (2008–2009); the Cleveland Cavaliers (2009–2010); and the Boston Celtics (2010–2011). As a center in the NBA O'Neal has been named an All Star fourteen times, named World Champion four times, and league's MVP. He has also been part of four NBA championships.

O'Neal has also made his presence known in commercials, hip-hop recordings, as a rap artist, and other aspects of popular culture. He has been the focus of numerous books and articles and continues to excel on and off the court. In 2011 O'Neal announced his retirement.

Jesse Owens (1913–1980)
Track and Field Athlete

James Cleveland "Jesse" Owens was born on September 12, 1913, in Danville, Alabama, Jesse and his family moved to Ohio when he was still young; the name "Jesse" derived from the way a teacher pronounced his initials, "J. C."

In 1932, while attending East Technical High School in Cleveland, Owens gained national fame with a 10.3 clocking in the 100-meter dash. Two years later Owens entered Ohio State University, and for the next four years he made track history, becoming universally known as "The Ebony Antelope." While competing in the Big Ten Championships at Ann Arbor, Michigan, on May 25, 1935, Owens had what has been called "the greatest single day in the history of man's athletic achievements." In the space of about forty-five minutes, he tied the world record for the 100-yard dash and surpassed the world record for the broad jump, the 220-yard low hurdles, and the 220-yard dash.

At the Berlin Olympics in 1936 Owens won four gold medals—at that time the most universally acclaimed feat in the history of the Games. When Adolf Hitler refused to present him with the medals he had won in the various competitions, Owens's fame became even more widespread as a result of the publicity. Although the track and field records set by Owens have all been eclipsed, his reputation as one of the first great athletes with the combined talents of a sprinter, low hurdler, and broad jumper has hardly diminished with the passage of time.

"Satchel" Paige (1906–1982)
Baseball Player

Leroy Robert "Satchel" Paige was born in Mobile, Alabama, on July 7, 1906. He began playing semi-professional ball while working as an iceman and porter. In the mid-1920s he became a professional player with the Birmingham Black Barons, and while later playing at Chattanooga, he acquired the nickname "Satchel" because of his "satchel-sized feet."

For the next two decades Paige compiled a phenomenal record. In 1933 he won thirty-one games and lost four. Paige also dominated winter ball in Latin America during the 1930s. In 1942 Paige led the Kansas City Monarchs to victory in the Negro World Series, and four years later he helped them to the pennant by allowing only two runs in ninety-three innings, a performance that included a string of sixty-four straight scoreless innings.

In 1948, when he was brought up to the major leagues, Paige was well past his prime, but he still was able to contribute six victories in Cleveland's pennant drive. Four years later, while pitching for the St. Louis Browns, he was named to the American League All-Star squad.

Until the 1969 baseball season, Paige was primarily active on the barnstorming circuit with the Harlem Globetrotters and a host of other exhibition teams. In 1969 the Atlanta Braves, in an attempt to make Paige eligible for baseball's pension plan, signed him to a one-year contract as coach.

Long before Jackie Robinson broke the color barrier of "organized baseball," Paige was a name well known to the general sports public. As an outstanding performer in "Negro baseball," Paige had become a legendary figure whose encounters with major league players added considerable laurels to his athletic reputation. Paige died June 8, 1982.

Walter Payton (1954–1999)
Football Player

Born July 25, 1954, in Columbia, Mississippi, and a graduate of Jackson State University, Walter Payton played his entire football career for the Chicago Bears and received numerous awards for his performance. Nicknamed "Sweetness," he broke O. J. Simpson's single game rushing record after gaining 275 yards during a game with the Minnesota Vikings in 1977. When Payton retired as a running back for the Chicago Bears after the 1986 season, he was the National Football League's all-time leading rusher, having broken a record held for many years by Jim Brown. Payton retired in 1987 after a spectacular career. He went on to start a foundation to aid children and to own a race car business. He wrote two biographies and was appointed as an assistant to the NFL Commissioners Board. Payton was inducted into the Pro Football Hall of Fame in 1993. In 1998 he was diagnosed with liver disease and died on November 1, 1999.

Calvin Peete (1943–)
Golfer

Calvin Peete was born on July 18, 1943, in Detroit, Michigan, into a family of nineteen children. Peete spent time as a farm laborer and peddler and worked along the Eastern coast. He began playing golf at the age of twenty-three, and although some saw his inability to straighten his left arm as a handicap, Peete moved directly into a professional career in 1971.

Peete won his first tour victory in 1979 at the Greater Milwaukee Open. In 1982 he won the Greater Milwaukee Open for a second time and also won the Anheuser-Bush Classic, the BC Open, and the Pensacola Open. Hampered by the lack of a high school diploma Peete was not fully accredited by the PGA. With the support of his wife, in 1983 he passed the Michigan Equivalency Examination after leaving school twenty–four years earlier. His accomplishment earned him a Black Achievement Award from *Ebony* and a Jackie Robinson Award.

Also in 1983 Peete won two more PGA titles, he represented the United States as a member of the prestigious Ryder Cup team, and won the Ben Hogan Award. In 1984 Peete had the best score average on the PGA tour. He retired from professional golf in 2001, and in 2002 he was inducted into the African American Ethnic Sports Hall of Fame.

Jerry Rice (1962–)
Football Player

Jerry Lee Rice was born in Starkville, Mississippi, on October 13, 1962. Rice worked with his father in construction, and he attributes his superb catching abilities to those days when he had to catch bricks tossed to him. After setting eighteen division records while attending Mississippi Valley State, Rice was a first-round draft choice for the 49ers in 1985. His 1987 season was considered his best with twenty-two touchdowns.

In both 1987 and 1990 Rice was named the NFL Player of the Year by the *Sporting News,* and every season until 1997 Rice was named to the Pro Bowl. He also led the 49ers to three Super Bowl victories and was named the MVP in Super Bowl XXIII. Rice ended his career with the 49ers in 2001 and signed with the Oakland Raiders.

Between 2001 and 2005 Rice was instrumental in the Raiders reaching Super Bowl XXXVII. Rice later moved to the Seattle Seahawks and the Denver Broncos. When deciding to retire in 2005, Rice wanted to end with the team he began with.

Rice officially retired on August 24, 2005, on a one-day contract with the 49ers. In 2010 Rice was voted number one on the NFL Network's "Top 100 NFL Greatest Players" list.

Oscar Robertson (1938–)
Basketball Player, Executive

Oscar Palmer Robertson was born in Charlotte, Tennessee, on November 24, 1938. After moving to Indiana, he led his high school team to two state basketball titles. As the first African American to play at the University of Cincinnati, Robertson was named player of the year for three consecutive seasons. He also set fourteen major college records. In 1960 Robertson earned a gold medal at the Olympics as co-captain of the U.S. basketball team.

Robertson signed with the Cincinnati Royals in 1960. He was named rookie of the year in his first season, and he had his best season in 1964 when he averaged 31.4 points per game. He was also selected as the Most Valuable Player in 1964 and was named an NBA All-Star twelve times. Robertson played for the Milwaukee Bucks from 1970 to 1974 before retiring.

Robertson was elected into the executive role of president of the NBA Players Association. His leadership during the landmark NBA antitrust suit which bore his name as president, resulted in free agency and draft rules that have allowed higher salaries for all players. Robertson was elected into the Basketball Hall of Fame in 1979 and the Olympic Hall of Fame in 1984. He was also named as one of the 50 Greatest Players in NBA history. Robertson took on the role as president and CEO of Orchem in 1981, and he started the Oscar Robertson and Associates consulting firm in 1983. Since 1994 a nine-foot bronze statue honors Robertson outside the Cincinnati Bearcats Fifth Third Arena at Shoemaker Center.

Eddie G. Robinson (1919–2007)
College Football Coach

Edward Gay "Eddie" Robinson was born on February 13, 1919, in Jackson, Louisiana. He excelled as an athlete in high school and after earning a scholarship from Leland College he became their star quarterback. He went on to obtain a master's degree from the University of Iowa in 1954. His involvement in a coaching clinic while in college prepared him for his first job after earning his B.A. Robinson began coaching at Grambling State in 1941 and had a successful tenure of fifty-seven years.

Robinson coached numerous NFL stars and surpassed Bear Bryant's lead with the most victories for a head coach. He had an overall record of 408 wins, 165 losses and fifteen ties. Robinson retired in 1997. He died on April 3, 2007.

Frank Robinson (1935–)
Baseball Player, Manager

 Born in Beaumont, Texas, on August 31, 1935, Frank Robinson moved with his family to Oakland, California, at the age of five. During his teens he was a football and baseball star at McClyronds High School. After graduation in 1953 he signed with the Cincinnati Reds.

Frank Robinson was major league baseball's first black manager. Named to the head post of the Cleveland Indians in 1975, Robinson exhibited the same cool, confident demeanor that served him well during an eighteen-year career as a major league player.

In 1956 he made a smash debut in the major leagues, hitting thirty-eight homers and winning Rookie of the Year honors. In 1961 Robinson was named most valuable player for leading Cincinnati to the National League pennant. Five years later, Robinson won the American League's Triple Crown and became the first player to win the MVP in both leagues. By the end of the 1973 season he had hit .297 in 2,432 games with 2,614 hits, 1,639 runs, and 1,613 RBIs. Robinson left the Indians in 1977 and became the manager of the Rochester Red Wings, a minor league team, in 1978.

In 1981 Robinson was hired by the San Francisco Giants, which he managed until 1984. He also managed the Baltimore Orioles during the late 1980s. Robinson served three years as assistant general manager for the Orioles and later became manager for the Montreal Expos/Washington Nationals from 2002 to 2006. Robinson, elected to the National Baseball Hall of Fame in 1982, received the Presidential Medal of Freedom, the highest civilian award, in 2005.

Jackie Robinson (1919–1972)
Baseball Player

Jack Roosevelt "Jackie" Robinson was born in Cairo, Georgia, on January 31, 1919, and was raised in Pasadena, California. At UCLA he gained All-American honorable mention as a halfback, but he left college in his junior year to play professional football for the Los Angeles Bulldogs. After serving as an Army lieutenant during World War II, Robinson returned to civilian life with the hope of becoming a physical education coach. To achieve this, he felt he had to make a name for himself, and for this reason he decided to spend a few seasons in the Negro baseball league.

In 1945, while he was playing with the Kansas City Monarchs, Branch Rickey of the Brooklyn Dodgers assigned him to the Montreal Royals, the team's top farm club, where he was to be groomed for a career in the majors. On April 10, 1947, the Dodgers announced that they had purchased Robinson's contract, and the following day he began his major league career, thus breaking the league's "color barrier." During a ten-year career, he hit .311 in 1,382 games with 1,518 hits, 947 runs, 273 doubles, and 734 RBIs. He stole home nineteen times, once in World Series play. He won the National League's most valuable player award in 1949 and played on six National League pennant winners, as well as one world championship team. Robinson was inducted into the National Baseball Hall of Fame in 1962.

After his retirement from baseball Robinson became a bank official, president of a land development firm, and a director of programs to com-

The 1951 cover of issue #5 of the Jackie Robinson comic book. Robinson was a hero to many baseball fans across America.

bat drug addiction. He died on October 24, 1972, in Stamford, Connecticut.

"Sugar Ray" Robinson (1920–1989)
Boxer

Born Walker Smith Jr. in Detroit, Michigan, on May 3, 1920, "Sugar Ray" Robinson took the name Robinson from the certificate of an amateur boxer whose identity enabled him to meet the age requirements for getting a match in Michigan; the "Sugar" came from his having been dubbed "the sweetest fighter."

As a ten-year-old boy Robinson had watched a Detroit neighbor, Joe Louis, train for an ama-

teur boxing career. When Robinson moved to New York two years later, he began to spend most of his time at local gyms in preparation for his own amateur career. After winning all eighty-nine of his amateur bouts and the 1939 Golden Gloves featherweight championship, he turned professional in 1940 at Madison Square Garden, fighting for the first time on a card headlined by the Fritzie Zivic–Henry Armstrong fight.

After several years of being "the uncrowned king of the welterweights," Robinson beat Tommy Bell in an elimination title bout in December 1946. He successfully defended the title for five years and on February 14, 1951, took the middleweight crown from Jake LaMotta.

In July 1951 he lost the title to Randy Turpin only to win it back two months later. Retiring for a time, Robinson subsequently fought a series of exciting battles with Carl "Bobo" Olsen, Carmen Basilio, and Gene Fullmer before retiring permanently on December 10, 1965, with six victories in title bouts to his credit—more than any other fighter in history.

Suffering from diabetes, hypertension, and Alzheimer's disease, one month shy of his sixty-ninth birthday, Robinson died of apparent natural causes at the Brotman Medical Center in Culver City, California, on April 12, 1989. Over his career, he won 174 of 201 professional bouts, including titles in three weight classes.

Wilma Rudolph (1940–1994)
Track and Field Athlete

Wilma Glodene Rudolph was born on June 23, 1940, in St. Bethlehem, Tennessee, and moved with her family to Clarksville. At an early age, she survived polio and scarlet fever, and was left with the use of one leg. Through daily leg massages administered in turn by different members of her family, she progressed to the point where she was able to walk with the aid of a special shoe. Three years later, however, she discarded the shoe and began joining her brother in back-yard basketball games.

While a sophomore at Burt High School in Clarksville, Rudolph broke the state basketball record for girls. As a sprinter, she was undefeated in all her high school track meets.

In 1957 she enrolled at Tennessee State University and began to set her sights for the Olympic Games in Rome. In the interim she gained national recognition in collegiate meets, setting the world record for the 200-meter dash in July 1960.

In the Olympics she earned the title of the "World's Fastest Woman" by winning gold medals for the 100-meter dash, the 200-meter dash (Olympic record), and for anchoring the 400-meter relay (world record). At the time Rudolph was the only American woman runner to win three gold medals in the Olympic Games. She was named by the Associated Press as the U.S. Female Athlete of the Year for 1960, and also won United Press Athlete of the Year honors.

Rudolph has served as a track coach, an athletic consultant, and the assistant director of athletics for the Mayor's Youth Foundation in Chicago. She is also the founder of the Wilma Rudolph Foundation. Rudolph died on November 12, 1994, at her home in Brentwood, Tennessee, of a brain tumor.

Bill Russell (1934–)
Basketball Player

William Felton "Bill" Russell was born on February 12, 1934, in West Monroe, Louisiana. The family moved to Detroit, Michigan, when he was nine, but two years later the family continued on to Oakland, California. There, at McClyronds High School, Russell proved to be an awkward but determined basketball player who eventually received a scholarship to the nearby University of San Francisco.

In college Russell came into his own, becoming the most publicized athlete on the West Coast during his sophomore year. Over the next two years his fame spread across the nation as he led his team to sixty consecutive victories (a collegiate record) and two straight NCAA titles.

The Celtics had never won an NBA Championship before Russell's arrival in 1957. With the help of Russell's defensive capabilities, the Celtics became one of the most successful teams in the history of professional sports, winning the world championship eight years in a row. Russell himself was named most valuable player on five separate occasions (1958, 1961–1963, 1965). In 1966 Russell became the Celtics's player/coach.

After the 1968–1969 season, having led the Celtics to their eleventh NBA crown, Russell retired as both coach and player. A five-time NBA most valuable player, Russell is the NBA leader in career minutes (40,726) and second in career rebounds (21,721).

After retirement Russell was a color commentator on NBC–TV's *NBA Game of the Week*. In 1974 he accepted a lucrative contract to become head coach and general manager of the Seattle Supersonics. That year he was inducted into the Basketball Hall of Fame.

Russell left basketball for several years but returned once again to active coaching with the Sacramento Kings in 1987, and in 1988 he served as the team's director of player personnel.

Russell is regarded as the finest defensive basketball player in the game's history. The six feet ten inch star is also the first black to coach and play for a National Basketball Association team. His style of play is credited with revolutionizing basketball. In 1996 Russell was named one of the 50 Greatest Players in NBA History, in 2007 he was inducted into the FIBA Hall of Fame, and in 2011 he was awarded the Presidential Medal of Freedom for his accomplishment during the civil rights movement.

Deion Sanders (1967–)
Football and Baseball Player

Deion Luwynn Sanders was born in Fort Meyers, Florida, on August 9, 1967, and attended college at Florida State University. After graduating in 1989 Sanders pursued and did well in both football and baseball. He was drafted by the Atlanta Falcons but later signed with the Washington Redskins. Sanders was selected as All-Pro seven times. He aided his teams in winning the Super Bowl in 1994 with the San Francisco 49ers and with the Dallas Cowboys in 1995. Sanders retired from football in 2001.

Sanders was drafted and played with the New York Yankees baseball team, until 1991, when he was traded to the Atlanta Braves. He played in two World Series with the Atlanta Braves and also played with the San Francisco Giants and the Cincinnati Reds. Because of football injuries Sanders career lasted a short time. In 1998 Sanders rediscovered his Christian faith, in contrast with his notoriety as a flashy and often fun loving personality. In 2006 he became part owner of the Austin Wranglers an Arena football team in Austin, Texas. He was inducted into the Pro Football Hall of Fame in 2011.

Gale Sayers (1943–)
Football Player

Gale Eugene Sayers was born in Wichita, Kansas, on May 30, 1943. After high school he briefly enrolled at Kansas State but left when he was signed by the Chicago Bears in 1965. His career ended in 1971 due to a knee injury. Sayers's career includes fifty-six touchdowns, and thirty-nine rushes. His performance was so influential that he was inducted into the Pro Football Hall of Fame in 1977.

Sayers returned to Kansas State and completed his B.A. and also earned a master's degree. He served as assistant athletic director at Kansas State in 1981, later as athletic director for South-

ern Illinois University, and in 2000 Kansas State dedicated the School of Education's Gale Sayers Microcomputer Center.

Charlie Sifford (1922–)
Golfer

Charles "Charlie" Sifford was born in Charlotte, North Carolina, on June 2, 1922, when laws of segregation were fully enforced. Sifford became a caddie at the age of nine, and by thirteen he had won a caddie tournament. He continued to perfect his skill and later moved to Philadelphia. Sifford won the Negro National Golf title six times from 1952 to 1956.

In 1957 Sifford became the first African American to be allowed to play in a predominantly white golf event. In 1959, when the white–only requirement was removed from the PGA tours, he was the first to be awarded a card of approval. Sifford faced many racial challenges, as he discussed in his autobiography *Just Let Me Play: The Story of Charlie Sifford, the First Black PGA Golfer,* published in 1992. Sifford went on to win the Hartford Open in 1967, and on the Seniors Tour the Senior Open in 1975, and the Suntree Open in 1980. Sifford was inducted into the World Gold Hall of Fame in 2004.

O. J. Simpson (1947–)
Football Player

Orenthal James "O. J." Simpson was born in San Francisco on July 9, 1947. Nicknamed "The Juice", Simpson began his football stardom at the University of Southern California, winning the Heisman Trophy in 1968. A year prior to that, he was a member of the USC relay team, which set a world record of 38.6 seconds in the 440-yard run. A year after graduation, ABC Sports voted him College Player of the Decade. He signed with the Buffalo Bills in 1969, and three years later he achieved his first rushing title, gaining over 1,200 yards.

Simpson enjoyed his finest season in 1973. On opening day he rushed for 250 yards against the New England Patriots, breaking the record of 247 yards held by Willie Ellison. He gained an astonishing 2,003 yards for the entire season, surpassing the previous mark of 1,863 yards held by Jim Brown. In addition, he scored twelve touchdowns, averaged six yards per carry, and had more rushing yardage than fifteen of the other NFL clubs. He was named player of the year and won the Jim Thorpe Trophy.

Simpson, who may have been the finest running back in pro football, retired from football in 1978. He has appeared in several feature films and worked as a sports commentator for ABC–TV and co-host for NBC–TV's *NFL Live*. In 1995 Simpson was found not guilty of killing his ex-wife and her male friend in a highly publicized trial. The nation watched the case unfold and responded with outcries, both pro and con, regarding the decision. In 2007 after Simpson had been to court for civil suits regarding the case and the publication of a best seller entitled *If I Did It* in 1996, Simpson was incarcerated on armed robbery and kidnapping charges of sports memorabilia. Simpson is currently serving time for his offense.

Marshall Taylor (1878–1932)
Cyclist

Marshall W. "Major" Taylor became America's first black U.S. National Champion cyclist in 1899. Born on November 26, 1878, in Indianapolis, Indiana, the son of a coachman, he worked at a bicycle store part time as a teen. After attending his first race, his boss suggested that Major enter a couple of races. To their surprise, he won a ten-mile race and proceeded to compete as an amateur.

By the time he was sixteen, he went to work in a factory owned by a former champion, and with his new boss' encouragement, competed in races in Canada, Europe, Australia, and New Zealand. During nearly sixteen years of competition, he won numerous championships and set

Marshall Taylor racing in Paris, France, in 1908.

several world records. Years after he retired, he met President Theodore Roosevelt, who told him that he had followed his career with admiration. Taylor was a member of the Bicycle Hall of Fame. He died in 1932.

Debi Thomas (1967–)
Figure Skater

Debra Janine "Debi" Thomas was born on March 25, 1967, in Poughkeepsie, New York. In 1985 Thomas became the first African American to win a major championship, the National Sports Festival in Baton Rouge, Louisiana. In 1986 she won the U.S. World Figure Skating title, and in 1988 at the Olympic Games in Calgary she won a bronze medal and became the first African American to win an Olympic medal in a winter sport. Thomas retired from the sport in 1992 to pursue a career in medicine. She completed her medical studies at Northwestern University in 1997.

Gene Upshaw (1945–2008)
Football Player, Executive

Eugene Thurman Upshaw Jr. (known as "Uptown Gene") was born on August 15, 1945, in Robstown, Texas, and played football at Texas A&I University. During his career he was named All-Pro eight times and inducted into the Pro Football Hall of Fame in 1987.

In 1982 Upshaw became the executive director of the National Football League Players Association and later the president of the Federation of Professional Athletes AFL-CIO. Upshaw received the Byron White Humanitarian Award in 1980 and the A. Philip Randolph Award in 1982. Upshaw died on August 20, 2008, from pancreatic cancer.

Bill White (1934–)
Baseball Player,
National League President

William DeKova "Bill" White was born on January 28, 1934, in Lakewood, Florida. He began his major league career with the New York Giants in 1956 and spent thirteen years as a player with the San Francisco Giants, St. Louis Cardinals, and the Philadelphia Phillies. During his career White was named to the National League All-Star team six times and won seven Gold Gloves. He retired from baseball in 1969, and in 1971 he joined Phil Rizzuto as a television play-by-play announcer for the New York Yankees.

On April 1, 1989, Bill White became the first black president of the National League. He held the position until 1994.

Serena Williams (1981–)
Tennis Player

Serena Jameka Williams, the younger sister of the Williams Sisters tennis team, was born on September 26, 1981, in Saginaw, Michigan. Guided by her coach and father Richard Williams, Serena became so successful on the women's circuit that by June 1998 she was in the top twenty of the Women's Tennis Association. Known as the most influential and talented tennis players since Althea Gibson in the 1950s, Serena won her first Women's Tennis Association (WTA) tour title in 1999. She also won the Open de Gaz de France, her first Grand Slam single, as well as two other key titles.

In 2000 at the Sydney Olympic Games, Serena along with her sister Venus, won the Olympic gold medal for women's doubles. Serena continues to win titles in doubles competition, she won at Wimbledon in 2000 and again in 2002, and as of 2010 she has won thirteen Grand Slam singles titles. In 2009 Serena became the top money winner in women's sports history. Both Serena and Venus Williams have received numerous awards and recognition for their contribution and inspiration in not only tennis, but in women's sports.

Venus Williams (1980–)
Tennis Player

Venus Ebony Starr Williams was born on June 17, 1980, in Lynwood, California, and along with her sister Serena, became part of a powerful and successful African American tennis team. Their father Richard Williams served as their coach and manager.

 Venus Williams won her first singles title in 1998. She has since won over twenty single titles, a gold medal at the Sydney 2000 Olympics, and on February 2002 she became the top ranked player in the world. As of 2010 Venus has won Wimbledon's Center court five times, and the U.S. Open two times. Venus has also signed lucrative endorsements that far exceed compensation records for female athletes. Both Venus and Serena Williams have received numerous awards and recognition for their contribution to women's sports.

Tiger Woods (1975–)
Golfer

Eldrick Tont "Tiger" Woods was born on December 30, 1975, in Long Beach, California. He won his first competition before the age of four years old and made his first appearance at sixteen at the Los Angeles Open Professional Golf Association of America (PGA) tour. After graduating from Stanford University and majoring in economics, Woods decided to become a professional golfer in 1996. By 1997 he had won the Augusta National Invitation Tournament known as the Masters, which is held in Augusta, Georgia. Woods became the first African American to hold membership in this exclusive club through his winning of this auspicious tournament. Two other African Americans preceded Woods as members by invitation. Woods went on to win the Masters three more times—2001, 2002, 2005.

 In 2006 Woods had his fiftieth title win with the Buick Invitational victory. He was thirty years old at the time. In 2008 he won the U.S. Open in La Jolla, California, and took a hiatus for knee surgery. In 2009 Woods began mounting a comeback but suffered personal embarrassment when investigations showed he had committed infidelity in his marriage. Woods lost many of his endorsements due to the loss of his squeaky clean persona. After his divorce in 2010 Woods returned to golf in April at the Masters Tournament, but both his playing and the viewership of the tournament were in a slump.

MILITARY

As with other aspects of American society, the role of black people in the nation's armed forces has been evolutionary. It was shaped by the white majority of an infant republic that embraced and later rejected slavery. It was later affected by an adolescent "separate but equal" era of racial segregation. Finally, the United States has matured—as an increasingly multicultural society in its understanding of race and racism. Historically, it has been a short—but humanly painful evolution.

Sadly, a nation's history is often shaped by its wars. Insofar as blacks and the U.S. military are concerned, the historic linkage extends from the Revolutionary War to "Operation Desert Storm." A memorial to the 5,000 black soldiers of the Revolutionary War has been planned for the Mall in Washington, D.C. Ironically, that memorial of the eighteenth-century war comes after similar recognition of the nineteenth-century "Buffalo Soldiers" at Fort Leavenworth, Kansas, and of the twentieth-century Tuskegee Airmen at the United States Air Force Academy.

Based on European experiences, the early American colonists were wary of the military. Both the Declaration of Independence and the U.S. Constitution reflect the fear of a large and permanent military establishment. As a result, much of early U.S. military history revolves around the locally recruited militia—now the National Guard of the states and territories.

Grudgingly, America's founding fathers accepted free black men for service in the Continental Army. On January 16, 1776, the Congress authorized that "free Negroes who have served faithfully in the Army at Cambridge may be reenlisted therein." By 1778 the Continental Army was racially integrated.

Integration did not last, however. Exclusion of blacks from the military became law in 1792 when Congress restricted military service to "free able-bodied white males." Six years later, the Secretary of War reiterated this law when he issued an order to the Commandant of the Marine Corps that "no Negro, mulatto or Indian is to be enlisted."

The War of 1812 was mainly fought by naval forces, and black sailors made up approximately twenty percent of Navy crews. While the Army and Marine Corps continued to exclude blacks, the Louisiana legislature authorized enlistments of free black landowners in the militia. The black troops' bravery in combat was a key factor in the American victory at the Battle of New Orleans, though it was fought after the war had officially ended.

An 1890 photo of the Buffalo Soldiers taken by Chr. Barthelmess at Fort Knight, Montana.

At the outbreak of the Civil War the United States suffered a near-fatal blow. Led by Robert E. Lee, nearly half of the West Point–trained U.S. Army officer corps defected to the Confederacy. The nation had to recruit, train, and deploy an expanded military but lacked trained leaders. One result of this situation was the enactment of the Morrill Land Grant College Act, which mandated the inclusion of a course on military science—the forerunner of today's Reserve Officers' Training Corps (ROTC).

As soon as the war began, blacks outside the rebel territory volunteered for the Army. Expecting a short war, Secretary of War Cameron rebuffed the offers. Although some Army leaders such as Major General John C. Freemont sought to recruit blacks as soldiers, the Lincoln administration countermanded such actions. Meanwhile, the Confederacy relied on slave labor to construct fortifications and assist in related combat service support tasks. By 1862, after significant military setbacks, Congress lifted the ban on blacks in the military and approved their use as Union Army laborers.

Following the Emancipation Proclamation in September 1862, Massachusetts was permitted to organize two black regiments: the 54th and 55th Massachusetts Infantry. (The exploits of the 54th Massachusetts Infantry formed the basis of the motion picture *Glory*.) In May 1863 the severe manpower shortage forced the War Department to approve the organization of additional black regiments led by white officers. The units were designated as United States Colored Troops (USCT).

Following the establishment of USCT regiments, blacks fought and died in every major Civil War action. For a period they did so being paid $3.50 per month less than white troops. In some units black troops refused to accept the lower pay. After vigorous protests by both black and white citizens, the 1864 Army Appropriations Act approved identical pay scales for all soldiers.

The passions of the Civil War resulted in the violation of emerging doctrines of land warfare, particularly concerning the treatment of noncombatants and prisoners of war; these doctrines had arisen in Europe in the wake of the Napoleonic wars. The most serious documented breaches of land warfare law were committed by the Confederacy. In an infamous example, white Union prisoners of war at Andersonville Prison in Georgia were treated barbarically by Confederacy soldiers. Black soldiers who fell into Confederate hands were either re-enslaved or summarily killed. One of the bloodiest events orchestrated by the Confederacy is known as the "Fort Pillow Massacre." Tennessee Congressional Report No. 65, dated April 24, 1864, identified the rebel leader responsible as General Nathan Bedford Forrest; following the war, Forrest organized the Ku Klux Klan. According to the report:

> The rebels commenced an indiscriminate slaughter, sparing neither age nor sex, white or black, soldier or civilian. The officers and men seemed to vie with each other in the devilish work; men, women, and even children, wherever found, were deliberately shot down, beaten, and hacked with sabres; some of the children not more than ten years old were forced to stand up and face their murderers while being shot; the sick and wounded were butchered without mercy, the rebels even entering the hospital building and dragging them out to be shot or killing them as they lay there unable to offer the least resistance.

This nation's highest decoration for valor, the Medal of Honor, was established by Congress on December 21, 1861. Issuance was initially limited to enlisted men of the Navy and Marine Corps, but was expanded to include the Army on July 12, 1862. On March 3, 1863, commissioned officers also became eligible for the Medal of Honor. During the Civil War, 1,523 Medals of Honor were awarded, including twenty-three for black servicemen. The first black recipient was Sergeant William H. Carney, 54th Massachusetts Infantry, for combat valor on July 18, 1863, at Fort Wagner, South Carolina.

By the end of the Civil War, more than 35,000 black troops had died—approximately thirty-five percent of the blacks who had served in combat. United States Colored Troops had constituted thirteen percent of the Union Army.

Post–Civil War America had acquired a new appreciation of the importance of military power.

In 1866 the 39th Congress passed legislation to "increase and fix the Military Establishment of the United States." The peacetime army included five artillery regiments, ten cavalry regiments, and forty-five infantry regiments. This legislation also stipulated that "to the six regiments of cavalry now in service shall be added four regiments, two of which shall be composed of colored men."

With that new law, the nation gained its first all-black Regular Army regiments: the 9th and 10th Cavalry, and the 24th and 25th Infantry— the "Buffalo Soldiers." Although the term Buffalo Soldiers initially denoted these four post–Civil War regiments, it has been adopted with pride by veterans of all racially segregated black Army ground units of the 1866–1950 era.

A misconception perpetuated by Hollywood films involves the depiction of an all-white Army's post–Civil War westward expansion. In reality, approximately twenty percent of Army soldiers on duty in the West were black. According to Gary Donaldson in his *History of African-Americans in the Military,* "even today, few Americans realize that when the cavalry came to the rescue of white settlers in the Old West … the rescuers, those gallant soldiers in blue, might well have been black." The heroism of black soldiers is attested to by the eighteen Medals of Honor they earned during what historians term either "The Indian Campaigns" or "The Plains War."

Black participation in the war against Native American Indians was a situation fraught with irony, both in terms of fighting another race subjugated by Anglo-Americans, and in terms of anti-black sentiment within the U.S. military. One of many painful episodes for the original "Buffalo Soldiers" was the case of Second Lieutenant Henry Ossian Flipper. Born in Thomasville, Georgia, on March 21, 1856, Flipper was the first black to graduate from the United States Military Academy at West Point, New York. He ranked fiftieth among the seventy-six members of the Class of 1887, and became the only black commissioned officer in the Regular Army. Assigned initially to Fort Sill, Oklahoma Territory, Lieutenant Flipper was eventually sent to Fort Davis, Texas. He was assigned the duties routine to a newly commissioned officer, such as surveying and supervising construction projects. Flipper also acquired some combat experience fighting Apache Indians led by Chief Victorio.

In August 1881, Lieutenant Flipper was arrested and charged with failing to mail $3,700 in checks to the Army Chief of Commissary. The young lieutenant was tried by court-martial for embezzlement and conduct unbecoming an officer. He was acquitted of the first charge (the checks were found in his quarters), but convicted of the second. Upon confirmation of his sentence by President Chester Arthur, Flipper was dismissed from the service on June 30, 1882. Returning to civilian life, Flipper used his West Point education as a surveyor and engineer in working for mining companies. He also published his memoirs as well as technical books dealing with Mexican and Venezuelan laws.

Nearly a century after Flipper left West Point, a review of his record indicated that he had been framed by his fellow officers. His records were corrected and he was posthumously granted an honorable discharge from the Army. On the one hundredth anniversary of his graduation, his bust was unveiled and is now displayed in the Cadet Library at the United States Military Academy.

America's "Ten Week War" with Spain marked the nation's emergence as a global colonial power. Although the United States had just completed its own "Indian Campaigns," the tension between the two nations arose from Spain's treatment of Cuba's indigenous population, which increasingly resisted autocratic Spanish rule on the island. In 1885 open rebellion by the Cuban people resulted in brutal suppression by the Spanish. The battleship USS *Maine* was sent to Cuba to protect U.S. interests there and as a reminder of America's intention to enforce the Monroe Doctrine.

On the evening of February 15, 1898, a gigantic explosion rocked the warship. It sank rapidly in Havana's harbor, killing 266 American sailors—including twenty-two blacks. The cause of the *Maine's* sinking was undetermined, but inflamed American passions were represented by the slogan, "Remember the Maine, to hell with Spain."

On March 29, 1898, the United States issued an ultimatum to Spain, demanding the release of Cubans from brutal detention camps, a declaration of an armistice, and preparations for peace negotiations mediated by President McKinley. The Spanish government did not comply, and on April 19 the U.S. Congress proclaimed Cuba free and independent. In its proclamation, Congress authorized the president to use U.S. troops to remove Spanish forces from Cuba.

In the annals of U.S. military history, the Spanish-American War was of special significance for the black officer. It was the first time black men served in all Army grades below general officer. This opportunity arose because of a geographically determined national security strategy. Separated from Europe and Asia by oceans, the United States understood that those waters provided a mobilization time cushion. Any perceived threat from either direction had to overcome U.S. naval power before touching the United States. Thus, the Navy became "the first line of defense." The small Regular Army was really a cadre force in charge of the recruitment, training, and deployment of volunteers—or draftees. An additional mobilization asset was the various state militia composed of part-time citizen soldiers.

The war with Spain was an expeditionary campaign requiring maritime deployment to foreign soil. It was the nation's first large-scale exposure to the complex logistics of overseas operations, an experience that would evolve into occupation duty and counter-insurgency (COIN) warfare.

The Regular Army of only 28,000 men included the all-black 9th and 10th Cavalry regiments, and the 24th and 25th Infantry regiments. All four regiments distinguished themselves during combat in Cuba. A manpower augmentation of 175,000 troops came from the federalized state militia/national guard reservoir, designated United States Volunteer Infantry (USVI).

The 93rd Infantry Division, seen here in a 1942 photograph, was one of the first front line African American divisions.

The USVI included the nation's oldest all-black national guard unit, which had its organizational roots in Chicago, Illinois. Formed in the wake of the 1871 Chicago fire, it was originally known as the Hannibal Guards. It became the 9th Battalion, an Illinois militia unit, on May 5, 1890; the unit was commanded by Major Benjamin G. Johnson, a black man. When the war erupted, other all-black militia regiments were organized: the 3rd Alabama, the 23rd Kansas, the 3rd North Carolina, the 9th Ohio, and the 6th Virginia.

Until it was converted to artillery battalions in World War II, the 8th Illinois was a unit commanded by a black officer; Colonel John R. Marshall was the highest-ranking black officer of the Spanish-American War, and commanded the 8th Illinois until 1914. Marshall was born on March 15, 1859, in Alexandria, Virginia. After attending public schools in Alexandria and Washington, D.C., he became an apprentice bricklayer. He moved to Chicago and was appointed Deputy Clerk of Cook County. Marshall joined the Illinois National Guard, organized a battalion, and served in it as lieutenant and as major. In June 1892, he was commissioned as a colonel and assumed command of the 8th Illinois USVI Regiment. He led the regiment to Cuba, where it joined with the 23rd Kansas and 3rd North Carolina in occupation duty.

Although only ten weeks long, the Spanish-American War produced six black Medal of Honor recipients—five from the 10th Cavalry, an infantry unit in Cuba. A black sailor won the sixth medal for heroism aboard the USS *Iowa* in the waters off Santiago, Cuba. The Spanish-American War provided a small increase in the number of black Regular Army officers. Benjamin O. Davis served as a lieutenant in the 8th Illinois USVI. Upon his discharge, he enlisted on June 14, 1899, as a private in the 9th Cavalry. He was promoted to corporal, and then to sergeant major. Davis was commissioned a Regular Army second lieutenant of cavalry on February 2, 1901. Also commissioned as Regular Army officers that year were John R. Lynch and John E. Green. As the twentieth century began, the U.S. Army had four black commissioned officers (excluding chaplains): Captain Charles A. Young, and Lieutenants Davis, Green, and Lynch. In 1940 Davis became the nation's first black general officer.

The nation's entry into World War I again raised the question of how to utilize black troops. Of the more than 400,000 black soldiers who served during the war, only about ten percent were assigned to combat duty in two infantry divisions. The 92nd Infantry Division was composed mainly of draftees. Black men from the 8th Infantry of the Illinois National Guard and the 315th Infantry of the New York National Guard formed the 93rd Infantry Division (Provisional). The majority of black World War I soldiers were assigned to stevedore units at ports, or to labor units as quartermaster troops.

The most difficult question for the War Department was the demand that blacks be trained as commissioned officers. Initially, the idea was dismissed as ludicrous. It was said to be "common knowledge" that black men inherently lacked leadership qualities. Only through the persistence of the NAACP, the Urban League, and black newspapers like the *Chicago Defender* did the War Department policy eventually change. An all-black Officer Training School was established at Fort Dodge, near Des Moines, Iowa. On October 14, 1917, the school graduated and commissioned 639 black officers. The War Department, however, had an iron-clad rule: No black officer could command white officers or enlisted men. White supremacy was to remain ensconced in the nation's armed services.

One solution to the issue of utilizing black officers and soldiers was characteristic of military racism at this time: several black regiments were "attached" to the allied French Army. Colonel William Hayward, commander of New York's 369th Infantry criticized General John J. Pershing for this decision. According to Arthur W. Little in *From Harlem to the Rhine: The Story of New York's Colored Volunteers,* Colonel Hayward charged that Pershing "simply put the black orphan in a basket, set it on the doorstep of the French, pulled the bell, and went away."

Despite the imposed "orphan" status, it was the 369th Infantry Regiment (15th New York) that established the best World War I record of any U.S. Army infantry regiment. The 369th served for 191 consecutive days in the trenches and never lost a foot of ground to the Germans. The so-called "Harlem Hell Fighters" won their laurels while attached to the French 4th Army, using French weapons and wearing U.S. uniforms. In 1919 Columbia University President Nicholas Murray Butler gave *Harper's Weekly* his assessment of the 369th Infantry Regiment: "No American soldier saw harder or more constant fighting and none gave better accounts of themselves. When fighting was to be done, this regiment was there."

Black soldiers earned an impressive number of awards for combat bravery in defeating German troops. Sergeant Henry Johnson of New York's 369th Infantry Regiment was the first American, black or white, to receive the French Croix de guerre. France awarded its Croix de guerre to thirty-four black officers and eighty-nine black enlisted men during the war. In the 92nd Division, fourteen black officers and thirty-four black enlisted men earned the U.S. Army's Distinguished Flying Cross (DFC). Ten officers and thirty-four enlisted men of the 93rd Division were DFC recipients.

No Medal of Honor was awarded to a black serviceman during World War I. In 1988 the Department of the Army researched the National Archives to determine whether racial barriers had prevented the conferment of the nation's highest decoration for valor. The archives search produced evidence that Corporal Freddie Stowers of Anderson County, South Carolina, had been recommended for the award. For "unknown reasons," the recommendation had not been processed. Stowers was a squad leader in Company C, 371st Infantry Regiment, 93rd Division. On September 28, 1918, he led his squad through heavy machine gun fire and destroyed the gun position on Hill 188 in the Champagne Marne Sector, France. Mortally wounded, Stowers continued to lead his men through a second trench line.

On April 24, 1991, President George W. Bush belatedly presented Stowers's Medal of Honor to his surviving sisters in a White House ceremony.

With the end of the war, the nation generally returned to applying the "separate but equal" doctrine with a vengeance. Some senior white Army officers advocated barring enlistment or re-enlistment of blacks altogether, an action that would have eventually abolished the four black Regular Army regiments by attrition.

A focal point of the Army's anti-black sentiment was the black commissioned officer. Despite countless well-documented cases of superb combat leadership, most black officers were eliminated from active duty following World War I. Many opponents of black officers focused on their allegedly poor performance; specifically, critics attacked the black Officer Training School (OTS) class at Des Moines, Iowa. One of the severest critics was Major General Charles C. Ballou, commander of the World War I 93rd Infantry Division. Ballou emphasized in a 1920 letter that while white candidates were required to be college graduates, "only high school educations were required for … the colored … and in many cases these high school educations would have been a disgrace to any grammar school. For the parts of a machine requiring the finest steel, pot metal was provided."

However, there were combat-experienced white officers who held a decidedly different view of black officer training, such as Major Thomas A. Roberts. "As I understand the question," Roberts wrote in April 1920, "what the progressive Negro desires today is the removal of discrimination against him; that this can be accomplished in a military sense I believe to be largely possible, but not if men of the two races are segregated." Noting the "tremendous force of the prejudice against association between negroes and whites," Roberts declared, "my experience has made me believe that the better element among the negroes desires the removal of the restriction rather than the association itself."

As for commissioned officers, the Reserve Officers' Training Corps (ROTC) detachments at Howard and Wilberforce Universities provided the bulk of new black second lieutenants. With no allocations for black officers to attend service schools, the lack of opportunity to maintain proficiency caused considerable attrition in the number of black reserve officers. To retain their commissions, other officers took advantage of correspondence and specially organized lectures and seminars.

Less than two months after World War II began in Europe, the nation's preeminent black organizations, the NAACP and the Urban League, had mobilized to defeat American racial segregation as well as Axis fascism. The black community could clearly foresee that the United States would eventually ally itself with Britain and France in war against Germany, Italy, and Japan.

Military mobilization began on August 27, 1940, with the federalizing of the National Guard and activation of the Organized Reserve. On September 16, 1940, the nation began its first peacetime draft. When Japan attacked Pearl Harbor on December 7, 1941, there were 120,000 officers and 1,523,000 enlisted men on active duty in the Army and its Air Corps. By the end of World War II, the Selective Service System had inducted 10,110,104 men; 1,082,539 (almost eleven percent) were black.

America's war effort required rapid expansion of both military and industrial power. Victory depended on the constant provision of ammunition, guns, planes, tanks, naval vessels, and merchant ships. The nation would have to unite to survive. Essential to the desegregation activism of the NAACP and the Urban League was the influence of black-owned weekly newspapers such as Robert S. Abbott's *Chicago Defender* and Robert Vann's *Pittsburgh Courier*. The rallying slogan was the "Double V"—victory against fascism abroad and against racial discrimination in the United States. The goal was equal opportunity in both the armed services and civilian defense industries.

Soon, the NAACP and the Urban League were joined by the black activists of the March on Washington Movement led by A. Philip Randolph of the Brotherhood of Sleeping Car Porters and Maids. Randolph predicted that upwards of 100,000 blacks would march on Washington demanding equal employment opportunities in defense plants. On June 25, 1941, a week before the scheduled march, President Franklin D. Roosevelt forestalled the protest by issuing Executive Order 8802. The president's order established a Committee on Fair Employment Practice "to provide for the full and equitable participation of all workers in defense industries, without discrimination." Of course, the executive order did not apply to the armed services.

The necessity of winning the war opened the job market to millions of black men and women who surged into defense plants, earning the same wages as their white co-workers. The war years thus brought economic upward mobility for many black civilians. Furthermore, through the postwar benefits of the G.I. Bill of Rights, the number of black college graduates and homeowners increased dramatically.

A fact that has been largely ignored is that the U.S. Army took its first steps toward racial integration early in World War II. The obvious waste of duplicated facilities caused the Army to operate all of its twenty-four Officer Candidate Schools as racially integrated institutions, where the primary quality sought was proven leadership capacity. The so-called "ninety-day wonders" who survived the standard three-month course were commissioned as second lieutenants in one of the twenty-four Army branches ranging from the Army Air Forces Administrative School in Miami, Florida, to the Tank Destroyer School in Camp Hood, Texas. Of course, upon graduation, black officers were only assigned to black units.

The exception in racially integrated Army officer procurement was the Army Air Force Aviation Cadet program that trained pilots,

bombardiers, and navigators in a segregated environment. Ironically, black non-flying officers graduated from the integrated AAF Officer Candidates School at Miami Beach.

A total of 926 black pilots earned their commissions and wings at the segregated Tuskegee Army Air Field (TAAF) near Chehaw, Alabama. The 673 single-engine TAAF pilot graduates eventually formed the four squadrons of the 332nd Fighter Group.

Led by Lieutenant Colonel Benjamin O. Davis, Jr., a 1936 West Point graduate, the 99th Fighter Squadron was assigned to the 33rd Fighter Group commanded by Colonel William M. Meyer. The 99th's first operational mission was a June 2, 1943, strafing attack on the Italian island of Pantelleria. On this date, Captain Charles B. Hall scored the squadron's first air victory by shooting down an FW-190 and damaging an ME-109. The 99th then settled into normal operations—or so the men thought.

In September Colonel Davis was recalled to take command of the 332nd Fighter Group. That is when he and the black community discovered that the so-called "Tuskegee Experiment" was about to be declared a failure. To this effect, Colonel Meyer submitted an extremely negative letter appraising the 99th Fighter Squadron:

> Based on the performance of the 99th Fighter Squadron to date, it is my opinion that they are not of the fighting caliber of any squadron in this group. They have failed to display the aggressiveness and daring for combat that are necessary to a first class fighting organization. It may be expected that we will get less work and less operational time out of the 99th Fighter Squadron than any squadron in this group.

On October 16, 1943, squadron commander Davis appeared before the War Department's Committee on Special [Negro] Troop Policies to answer his group commander's allegations.

In his 1991 autobiography, written after his retirement as an Air Force lieutenant general,

A photo taken in 1945 in Ramitelli, Italy, of some of the members of the Tuskegee Airmen.

Davis describes the problem he faced at the Pentagon as a lieutenant colonel: "It would have been hopeless for me to stress the hostility and racism of whites as the motive behind the letter, although that was clearly the case. Instead, I had to adopt a quiet, reasoned approach, presenting the facts about the 99th in a way that would appeal to fairness and win out over ignorance and racism."

Davis presented such a convincing factual case that Army Chief of Staff General George C. Marshall ordered a G-3 (operations) study of the black squadron. The study's title, "Operations of the 99th Fighter Squadron Compared with Other P-40 Squadrons in the Mediterranean Theatre of Operations," precisely describes its contents. In his book, General Davis describes the G-3 study: "It rated the 99th according to readiness, squadron missions, friendly losses versus enemy losses, and sorties dispatched. The opening statement in the report was the clincher: 'An examination of the record of the 99th Fighter Squadron reveals no significant general difference between this squadron and the balance of the P-40 squadrons in the Mediterranean Theatre of Operations'."

On October 13, 1942, the Army activated the 100th, 301st, and 302nd Fighter Squadrons. Com-

bined with the 99th, the four squadrons would become the 332nd Fighter Group. Colonel Robert R. Selway Jr., a white pilot, was its initial commanding officer. With the 99th vindicated by the G-3 study, Davis assumed command of the Fighter Group at Selfridge Army Air Field in Michigan. The 332nd departed for Italy on January 3, 1944, and absorbed the 99th as its fourth squadron.

While the 99th was deployed and the 332nd was organizing, the TAAF program expanded to training two-engine B-25 pilots. While the fighter pilot fought alone, the B-25 "Mitchell" medium bomber required a five- to six-man crew that included two pilots and a bombardier-navigator. The 253 medium-bomber pilots who were trained at TAAF, as well as 393 black navigators and bombardiers from Hondo and Midland Fields in Texas, formed the nation's second black flying organization when the Army Air Force activated the four-squadron 477th Bombardment Group (Medium) in June 1943.

The 477th was plagued from the start by a shortage of enlisted aircrew members, ground technicians, and even airplanes. Fifteen months after activation, the 477th was still short twenty-six pilots, forty-three co-pilots, two bombardier-navigators, and all of its authorized 288 gunners. Moving from base to base for "operational training," the 477th logged 17,875 flying hours in one year without a major accident. Although finally earmarked for duty in the Pacific, the war ended before the 477th was deployed overseas.

As for the 332nd Fighter Group, it became famous for escorting heavy bombers. It was the only AAF fighter group that never lost an escorted bomber to enemy planes. The wartime record of the 332nd Fighter Group was 103 enemy aircraft destroyed during 1,578 combat missions. In addition to more than one hundred Distinguished Flying Crosses, the 332nd also earned three Distinguished Unit Citations.

The Tuskegee Experiment thus proved that black men could fly "state-of-the-art" aircraft, and could also conduct highly successful combat operations meeting AAF standards. The fruit of the Tuskegee Airmen's efforts would be harvested in less than three years with the 1948 racial desegregation of the U.S. military.

The World War II U.S. Army fielded two major black combat organizations: the 92nd Infantry Division in Europe, and the 93rd Infantry Division in the Pacific.

Both of the Divisions suffered from avoidable impediments. Just as in World War I, the 93rd Division was employed only in a fragmented manner. Major General Raymond G. Lehman's headquarters sailed from San Francisco, California, on January 11, 1944; the artillery and infantry battalions and division headquarters assembled on Guadalcanal at the end of February. As scholar Ulysses Lee observed in *The Employment of Negro Troops*, "This was the last time until the end of the war that all elements of the division were gathered in the same location." The division spent the rest of the war island-hopping, relieving units that had defeated Japanese troops. The 93rd Division World War II casualties were twelve killed in action, 121 wounded in action, and five who died later of wounds.

Elements of the 93rd Division, primarily the 24th Infantry Regiment, performed well during the 1944 Bougainville campaign. Generally, the division's performance was considered adequate and acceptable. The usual after-action comments were made concerning the lack of initiative by junior officers, but overall the 93rd Division was described as well-disciplined and having good morale.

The 92nd Infantry Division, in contrast, gained a reputation as a chaotic outfit. During its preparation for deployment overseas, elements of the 92nd Division were sprinkled across the United States. While the division headquarters were at Fort Huachuca, Arizona, subordinate units were stationed at Fort McClellan, Alabama; Camp Robinson, Arkansas; Camp Breckinridge, Kentucky; and Camp Atterbury, Indiana. The division's World War II casualty figures were vastly different than those of the 93rd Division: 548 killed in action; 2,187 wounded in action; and sixty-eight who died later of wounds. From its training in the United States through combat in Europe, the division's main problem seemed to

be its commander, Major General Edward M. Almond. Many veterans of the 92nd Division continue to blame General Almond for the division's reputation and casualties.

It appears that "Ned" Almond was openly racist. In a 1984 interview retired Lieutenant General William P. Ennis Jr. gave a "warts and all" description of Almond. As a World War II brigadier general, Ennis had commanded the corps artillery that supported the 92nd Division. According to Ennis in the *Journal of Military History*, Almond and many white Southern officers in the division were selected because "in theory, they knew more about handling Negroes than anybody else, though I can't imagine why because [Almond] just despised the ground they walked on."

The contrast of attitude at the division's various posts was amazing. While Almond denigrated the competence of black officers, Officer Candidate School (OCS) commandants generally held different views. For example, Brigadier General H. T. Mayberry, who commanded the Tank Destroyer OCS, observed in a 1945 interview that "a considerable number of young, potentially outstanding Negro officers were graduated. It was surprising—to me, at least—how high the Negroes (those who graduated) stood in the classes."

Lieutenant Colonel Robert C. Ross, a field artillery battalion commander in the 92nd Division, reported to Almond on five black officers who completed the basic artillery course. Three were made course instructors while two were selected "as outstanding students from the entire forty-eight officers, both white and colored, from the first Officers Basic School."

One black officer, Captain Hondon B. Hargrove, was a 1938 Wilberforce University ROTC graduate. After his wartime service in the division's 597th Field Artillery Battalion, he commented that Almond did not believe that "any black, no matter what his file showed, or how much training he had, was able in an officer's position.... He firmly believed only white officers could get the best out of [Negro troops] ... [and] just could not countenance black officers leading them."

General Almond established his headquarters at Viareggio, Italy, on October 5, 1944. Two days later, the division's 370th Infantry Regiment began its assault on Massa. Professor Lee described the 92nd Division's major weakness: "It was a problem in faith and lack of it—the wavering faith of commanders in the ability and determination of subordinates and enlisted men, and the continuation in the minds of enlisted men of training period convictions that they could not trust their leaders." Thus, the Massa attack degenerated into chaos. In what became a major charge against the division, the men began to "melt away" from the fighting. After Massa there were increasing cases of mutinous behavior toward both black and white officers.

In February 1945, the 92nd became the focus of serious Pentagon scrutiny. The man who examined the situation was Truman K. Gibson Jr., a black insurance company lawyer from Chicago, and civilian aide to Secretary of War Henry L. Stimpson. In his assessment, Gibson refused to blame the victim or to generalize about the capabilities of black soldiers based on the performance of General Almond's 92nd Division. In a March 14 news conference in Rome, Gibson maintained that "If the division proves anything, it does not prove that Negroes can't fight. There is no question in my mind about the courage of Negro officers or soldiers and any generalization on the basis of race is entirely unfounded."

On May 14, 1945, a week after Germany surrendered, Lieutenant Colonel Marcus H. Ray wrote a letter to Gibson. A fellow Chicagoan, Colonel Ray was a National Guard officer of the 8th Illinois when it was mobilized in 1940. He ended the war as commanding officer of the 600th Field Artillery Battalion of the 92nd Division. Colonel Ray closed his letter to Gibson by observing that "those who died in the proper performance of their assigned duties are our men of the decade and all honor should be paid them. They were Americans before all else. Racially, we have been the victims of an unfortunate chain of circumstances backgrounded by the unchanged American attitude as regards the proper 'place' of the Negro...."

The most highly acclaimed black ground combat unit of World War II was the 761st Tank Battalion. As an organization it enjoyed circumstances very different from the 92nd Division. Like the 92nd Division, commanding officers of the 761st Battalion influenced the unit's performance, but with a positive outcome. Before the United States entered World War II, some white U.S. Army officers favored opening opportunities for black soldiers. They rejected the dogma of their colleagues who declared that modern weaponry was "too technical" for blacks. Fortunately, one such officer became the Commanding General of Army Ground Forces.

In this post, Lieutenant General Lesley James McNair spent most of his time visiting the nationwide array of ground forces training camps. And when he visited the 761st at Camp Claiborne, Louisiana, he openly praised and encouraged the Army's first black tankers. When the 761st went ashore in France on October 10, 1944, the men believed that their outfit's existence was due mainly to McNair. (General McNair was killed by U.S. "friendly fire" on July 25, 1944, in France. The Joint Chiefs of Staff National Defense University is located at Fort Lesley J. McNair, named in his honor, in Washington, D.C.)

The 761st joined the 26th Division on October 31, 1944, and was welcomed by the division commander, Major General Willard S. Paul: "I am damned glad to have you with us. We have been expecting you for a long time, and I am sure you are going to give a good account of yourselves." Two days later, General George S. Patton visited and welcomed the 761st.

The 761st's initial combat was on November 8, 1944, at Athaniville, France—the first of 183 continuous days of combat for the battalion. During their advance through six European countries, the 761st proved to be a stellar combat organization. The battalion is credited with killing 6,266 enemy soldiers and capturing 15,818. Despite its outstanding combat record, the 761st did not receive its much-deserved Presidential Unit Citation until January 24, 1978.

The veterans of the 761st still pursue a World War II mission: a posthumous Medal of Honor for Staff Sergeant Ruben Rivers, of Tecumseh, Oklahoma. Sergeant Rivers was severely wounded on November 16, 1944, when his tank ran over two mines near Guebling, France. With his lower thigh torn and his kneebone protruding, Sergeant Rivers refused evacuation. Instead, he remained with his tank and crew for three days of continuous combat. When his company was taken under fire by German heavy weapons, the company commander ordered his tanks to pull back below the crest of a hill. Sergeant Rivers's tank opened fire at the enemy and continued firing until it was hit in the turret by an armor-piercing round that killed Sergeant Rivers.

The veterans of the 761st have been acknowledged—unfortunately, not without some controversy—by the Public Broadcasting System (PBS). On Nov. 11, 1992, PBS presented an hour-long documentary called *The Liberators,* focusing on the exploits of the 761st Tank Battalion. Moreover, the broadcast asserted that the 761st helped liberate the most infamous of all Nazi concentration camps—Buchenwald and Dachau. Unquestionably, the 761st did liberate some concentration camps, but the assertion that the battalion played a role in the liberation of those two specific camps has been challenged by some 761st veterans. The April 1945 after-action report of the 761st contains no entries concerning either of the two camps. Furthermore, the April 1945 location entries in the report place the 761st miles from either camp. PBS therefore withdrew *The Liberators* from further exhibition pending additional research.

Following a decade of excluding blacks from enlistment, the U.S. Navy in 1932 decided to accept blacks, but placed them in a separate branch of the Navy. The branch was known as the Stewards' Service, referred to in the black community as "sea-going bell hops." The 1940 Navy consisted of 170,000 men of whom 4,007 or 2.3 percent were blacks in the Stewards' Service. In addition to blacks, Navy stewards were also recruited from among Filipinos and other Asian-American populations.

The advent of World War II transformed this situation. President Franklin D. Roosevelt had served as assistant secretary of the Navy during World War I, and considered it "his branch" of the armed services. Therefore, his January 9, 1942, memo to the Navy had tremendous impact. The president noted to then-Secretary of the Navy Frank Knox: "I think that with all the Navy activities, Bureau of Navy might invent something that colored enlistees could do in addition to the rating of messman."

The Navy did relent on April 7, 1942, by announcing it would accept 14,000 black enlistees in all ratings and branches. The initial training of black sailors was conducted at the Great Lakes Naval Training Station, north of Chicago, Illinois.

It was at Great Lakes that the Navy finally made a breakthrough regarding black personnel. In January 1944, sixteen black petty officers began a special and intensive course of instruction that was conducted without public announcement. Three months later, the Navy announced the commissioning of twelve black ensigns and one warrant officer. These men are known as the Navy's "Golden Thirteen."

Shortly after the Golden Thirteen were commissioned, the Navy opened the V-12 officer training programs to black men. Among the V-12 graduates who became Navy officers in World War II were Samuel L. Gravely Jr. and Carl T. Rowan. Gravely became the Navy's first black admiral; Rowan is now a syndicated columnist and broadcaster.

By the end of World War II, 165,000 blacks had served in the Navy; 17,000 in the Marine Corps; 5,000 in the Coast Guard; 12,000 in Construction Battalions (Sea Bees); and 24,000 in the Merchant Marine.

As the Allied victory of World War II approached, the highest levels of the U.S. government recognized that a new domestic racial era had emerged. The war to defeat fascism had indeed involved the entire U.S. population.

One impetus for change of military policy toward blacks was an August 5, 1945, letter from

Colonel Noel F. Parrish, commander of Tuskegee Army Air Field, to Brigadier General William E. Hall, Headquarters Army Air Forces. Colonel Parrish recommended "that future policy, instead of retreating defensibly further and further, with more and more group concessions, openly progress by slow and reasonable but definite steps toward the employment and treatment of Negroes as individuals which law requires and military efficiency demands."

Although Secretary of War Henry L. Stimpson often revealed racist tendencies, his assistant, John R. McCloy, was considerably more liberal. Stimpson was succeeded by Robert P. Patterson, who adopted McCloy's suggestion for a study of future use of blacks in the military. The study was made by a board of three Army generals: Lieutenant General Alvan C. Gillem Jr., a former corps commander; Major General Lewis A. Pick, who built the Ledo Road in Burma; and Brigadier General Winslow C. Morse of the Army Air Force. During a six-week period, the so-called Gillem Board took testimony from more than fifty witnesses toward forming the Army's post-war racial policy. Two key individuals who worked with the Gillem Board were the two black Chicagoans who served sequentially as civilian aide to the Secretary of War: Truman K. Gibson Jr. and the recently discharged Lieutenant Colonel Marcus H. Ray. It is noteworthy that racial desegregation of the military was driven by the considerable political and economic influence of black Chicago.

The Gillem Board's findings leaned toward more "efficient" use of Negro manpower, but did not advocate actual desegregation. That vagueness reactivated the pre-war coalition of the NAACP, the National Urban League, and the grassroots labor forces led by A. Philip Randolph.

The advent of the Cold War led to the National Security Act of 1947. One of the major elements of the new law was the establishment of the Department of Defense (DOD), with the subordinate Departments of Army, Navy, and Air Force. The other new entity created was the Central Intelligence Agency (CIA).

In the continuing movement toward desegregation of the military, 1947 brought two important black personnel shifts within the Department of Defense: Lieutenant Colonel Marcus H. Ray returned to active duty as senior advisor on racial matters in Europe. In the Pentagon, Dr. James C. Evans, a Howard University professor and Department of Army official, moved to the new post of special assistant to the Secretary of Defense. As the highest-ranking black civilian in the Department of Defense, Evans served under ten secretaries of defense until his retirement in 1970.

The demand for desegregation of the military became a key political issue in black America. As preparations for the 1948 presidential election intensified, President Harry S. Truman faced a campaign against Republican Thomas E. Dewey, states' rights segregationist Strom Thurmond, and the Communist Party–supported Progressive Party of former Vice President Henry A. Wallace. In such a fragmented situation, the black vote became crucial.

By May 1948, President Truman had decided to desegregate the armed forces by an executive order. Evans guided the politically sensitive staff coordination effort through the Pentagon. In other executive branch and Capitol Hill offices, two political concessions were required. First, no deadlines would be imposed. Second, the order would not denounce racial segregation. With a final sign-off by the attorney general, President Truman issued Executive Order No. 9981, which signaled a policy to end segregation in the military.

As North Korean forces surged across the 38th parallel on June 25, 1950, only the Air Force had desegregated. The U.S. ground forces in Korea were savaged by the North Koreans and driven south.

The first U.S. victory of the Korean War was won by black soldiers of the 24th Infantry Regiment on July 20, 1950, at Yechon. Captain Charles M. Bussey, a World War II Tuskegee Airman, was the ground commander and earned a Silver Star at Yechon. Two black soldiers were awarded posthumous Medals of Honor during the Korean War: Private First Class William Thompson and Sergeant Cornelius H. Charlton, both of the 24th Infantry Regiment.

Private First Class Thompson distinguished himself by conspicuous gallantry and intrepidity above and beyond the call of duty in action against the enemy on August 6, 1950, near Haman, Korea. While his platoon was reorganizing under cover of darkness, enemy forces in overwhelming strength launched a surprise attack on the unit. PFC Thompson set up his machine gun in the path of the onslaught and swept the enemy with fire, momentarily pinning them down and thus permitting the remainder of his platoon to withdraw to a more tenable position. Although hit repeatedly by grenade fragments and small-arms fire, he resisted all efforts of his comrades to induce him to withdraw, steadfastly remaining at his machine gun and continuing to deliver fire until mortally wounded by an enemy grenade.

Sergeant Charlton, a member of Company C, distinguished himself in action against the enemy on June 2, 1931, near Chipo-Ri, Korea. His platoon was attacking heavily defended hostile positions on commanding ground when the leader was wounded and evacuated. Sergeant Charlton assumed command, rallied the men, and spearheaded the assault against the hill. Personally eliminating two hostile positions and killing six enemy soldiers with his rifle-fire and grenades, he continued up the slope until the unit suffered heavy casualties and was stalled. Regrouping the men, he led them forward, only to be again forced back by a shower of grenades. Despite a severe chest wound, Sergeant Charlton refused medical attention and led a third daring charge that would advance to the crest of the ridge. Observing that the remaining emplacement that had retarded the advance was situated on the reverse slope, he charged it alone and was hit again by a grenade, but raked the position with fire that eventually routed the enemy. The wounds inflicted during his daring exploits resulted in his death.

The early defeats American forces experienced in Korea prompted President Truman to replace his close friend, Secretary of Defense Louis A. Johnson, with retired General of the Army George C. Marshall, who had been Truman's secretary of state from 1947 to 1949.

One of Marshall's first acts as secretary of defense was the creation of a new entity: Office of Assistant Secretary of Defense for Manpower & Reserves, or OASD (MP&R). Marshall appointed Anna M. Rosenberg, a forty-eight-year-old New York City labor and public relations consultant, as head of this office. In 1944 she had persuaded President Franklin D. Roosevelt to have Congress enact the education provisions of the World War II G.I. Bill of Rights. Dr. James C. Evans's office of special assistant became a part of the OASD (MP&R), thereby bringing together two individuals familiar with discrimination—a Hungarian Jewish immigrant woman and a black male college professor. Known affectionately in the Pentagon as "Aunt Anna," Rosenberg and the OASD (MP&R) had responsibility for industrial and military manpower, including Selective Service System policies. Secretary Rosenberg viewed military desegregation as an impetus for civilian society reform, observing: "In the long run, I don't think a man can live and fight next to one of another race and share experiences where life is at stake, and not have a strong feeling of understanding when he comes home."

The effective implementation of Truman's Executive Order No. 9981 depended in part on black military personnel taking advantage of hard-won opportunities. The individual who was truly the mentor of the black military professional, especially black officers, was James Evans. During much of his tenure in the Pentagon, Evans's executive officer was Army Colonel John T. Martin, who later was director of the Selective Service System for the District of Columbia. Commenting in 1993, Colonel Martin reflected that "James C. Evans and his associates accomplished much behind the scenes—and with no fingerprints—to advance the careers of all [black] personnel in the military."

By the end of the Korean War, racial segregation had been eliminated from the U.S. armed services. In the years preceding the Vietnam War, increasing numbers of blacks entered the services and opted for full careers. Between 1953 and 1961, there was a slow but steady increase in the number of black career officers in each service. This became a sophisticated form of non-civilian affirmative action. More Blacks sought opportunities in the military once the selective service was eliminated and replaced with an all-volunteer military. With little economic and educational opportunities for blacks in the 1960s and 1970s the military became one of few options. This created a disproportionate number of African Americans who participated in the Vietnam War and further complicated the controversies about the reason for the war. With the continuous loss of lives the country saw many groups raising their voices in protest. It was not until 1973 that the United States withdrew from Vietnam.

By 1972 the presence of blacks in the military had increased by seventeen percent in the Army, and by 1981 it had doubled to one third. Other areas of the service also saw substantial increases as well. Also in the 1970s the military reviewed their court records for discriminatory rulings. As a result, in 1977 Henry O. Flipper an 1877 West Point graduate, and only the fifth black to attend West Point, was given an honorable discharge in lieu of a 1882 dishonorable discharge that Flipper vehemently denied. World War I, which had no black recipients of the Medal of Honor, awarded this honor to Corporal Freddie Stowers in 1991, and in 1977 seven African Americans who served in World War II were awarded the Medal of Honor.

The Persian Gulf War in 1991 was not only historic because of its military existence, but also because this war was the first to have an African American commander, General Colin Powell, chairman of the Joint Chiefs of Staff. There was also General Cal Waller as second-in command to General Norman Schwarzkopf in Operation Desert Storm. The Iraq war, which began in 2003, under the administration of President George W. Bush to topple Saddam Hussein was ended under the administration of President Barack Obama in 2010 after a period of over seven years. Many

Black Americans were not in agreement with the war while over twenty-five percent of the armed forces in the war were black. Black Americans continue to be disproportionately over-represented in the military as a whole while being only a little over twelve per cent of the population. Although the overall percentage is high, the areas that blacks often enlist in are in non-combat units, which offer training and further career paths after leaving service.

Blacks continue to be a large presence in the military due to social and economic conditions, which make military service a viable option not only for national service but also future opportunities. The military for Black Americans has always been a key barometer to claim and declare their right and their responsibility as citizens.

BIOGRAPHIES

Clara Adams-Ender (1939–)
Army General, Former Chief of the U.S. Army Nurse Corps

Clara Adams-Ender was born July 11, 1939, in Willow Springs, North Carolina. She graduated from high school in 1956 and attended nursing school at North Carolina Agricultural and Technical State University. She was a reservist while in college and upon graduation she entered the active U.S. Army Nurse Corps. Finding her calling in the area of teaching, Adams-Ender earned a master's degree in nursing in 1969 and became an instructor and then an assistant professor at Walter Reed Army Institute of Nursing Center of the University of Maryland in Washington, D.C. She later became chief of the department of nursing in 1984.

Adams-Edler went on to be appointed as the eighteenth chief of the U.S. Army Nurse Corps and brigadier general with responsibility for over 25,000 health professionals. In 1991 she became deputy commander of the military district of Washington and commanding general at Fort Belvoir, Virginia. She retired in 1993 and founded her own management company. Adam-Ender has received numerous awards for her distinguished service, including the Meritorious Service Medal with three oak leaf clusters.

Jesse L. Brown (1926–1950)
Naval Aviator

Jesse Leroy Brown was born October 13, 1926, in Hattiesburg, Mississippi. He graduated from Eureka High School in 1944 and studied engineering at Ohio State University from 1944 to 1947. In 1946 Brown joined the Naval Reserve and in 1947 became an aviation cadet.

Brown's flight training was at Pensacola, Florida, and in 1948 he became the first African American to earn the Navy Wings. In 1949 Brown was assigned to the USS *Leyte* and won the Air Medal and the Korean Service Medal for his twenty air combat missions. On December 4, 1950, he was shot down while flying air support for U.S. Marines at the Battle of the Chosin Reservoir. He was posthumously awarded the Purple Heart and the Distinguished Flying Cross for exceptional courage, airmanship, and devotion to duty.

In 1973 the USS *Jesse L. Brown,* a destroyer escort, was named in his honor and launched at the Avondale Shipyard at Westwege, Louisiana.

William H. Carney (1840–1908)
Army Infantry

William Harvey Carney was born a slave in Norfolk, Virginia, on February 29, 1840. Around 1856, Carney's father moved the family to New Bedford, Massachusetts. In 1863 Carney enlisted in the 54th Massachusetts Colored Infantry. On July 18, 1863, Carney and the 54th Massachusetts led an assault on Fort Wagner, South Carolina, during which Carney was severely wounded. On May 23, 1900, Carney was issued a Medal of Honor. He died on December 8, 1908.

Benjamin O. Davis Jr. (1912–2002)
Air Force General

Benjamin Oliver Davis Jr. was born in Washington, D.C., on December 18, 1912. Davis was educated in Alabama (his father taught military science at Tuskegee), and later in Cleveland, Ohio, where he graduated president of his class. Davis went on to attend Western Reserve University and the University of Chicago before accepting an appointment to the United States Military Academy in 1932. In 1936 Davis graduated thirty-fifth in his class of 276.

After serving in the infantry for five years, he transferred to the Army Air Corps in 1942 and was among the first six black air cadets to graduate from the Advanced Army Flying School.

As commander of the 99th Fighter Squadron (and later commander of the all black 332nd Fighter Group), Davis flew sixty missions in 224 combat hours during World War II, winning several medals, including the Silver Star.

In 1957 Davis was made chief of staff of the 12th Air Force of the United States Air Forces in Europe (USAFE). In 1961 he became director of Manpower and Organization, and in 1965 he became chief of staff for the United Nations Command and U.S. forces in Korea. Davis was assigned as deputy commander in chief, U.S. Strike Command, in 1968. He retired from active duty in 1970. He died on July 4, 2002.

Benjamin O. Davis Sr. (1877–1970)
Army General

Born on July 1, 1877, in Washington, D.C., Benjamin O. Davis Sr. graduated from Howard University and joined the army in 1898 during the Spanish-American War. At the end of that war, he re-enlisted in the 9th Cavalry and was made second lieutenant in 1901. Promotions of blacks were rare in those years, but Davis rose through the officers' ranks until he was made a full colonel in 1930. During that time, in addition to his military commands, he was a professor of military science and tactics at Wilberforce and Tuskegee Universities, military attaché to Liberia, and instructor of the 372nd Infantry of the Ohio National Guard. After his promotion to brigadier general and his service in World War II, he became an assistant to the inspector general in Washington, D.C., until his retirement in 1948.

Among General Davis's many awards and decorations are the Distinguished Service Medal, the Bronze Star Medal, the Grade of Commander of the Order of the Star of Africa from the Liberian government, and the French Croix de guerre with palm. General Davis died on November 26, 1970.

Charity Adams Earley (1918–2002)
WAC Officer

Charity Edna Adams Earley was born in 1918, in Kittrell, Vance County, North Carolina. She was awarded a B.A. in 1938 from Ohio's Wilberforce University. While pursing her master's at Ohio State University she joined the newly formed Women's Auxiliary Army Corps (WAAC) in 1942. Upon graduating from basic training she became the first African American woman to be commissioned in this new military unit. She was later promoted to captain and assigned to Fort Des Moines Planning and Training Section.

Adams, after serving overseas in 1944, later separated from the military unit renamed as the Women's Army Corps (WAC). In 1946 Adams completed her master's degree, and married Dr. Stanley Earley. Charity Adams Earley recounts her military service in the 1989 book *One Woman's Army: A Black Officer Remembers the WAC*. She died January 13, 2002.

Henry O. Flipper (1856–1940)
Army Officer, Engineer

Henry Ossian Flipper was born a slave on March 21, 1856, in Thomasville, Georgia; his father, a craftsman, bought his family's freedom. Flipper attended Atlanta University and in 1873 was appointed to the United States Military Academy.

Flipper graduated from the United States Military Academy in 1877 and was commissioned as second lieutenant and assigned to the all-black 10th Cavalry. In 1881, however, Flipper became the victim of a controversial court-martial proceeding, which cut short his career.

Flipper went on, as a civilian, to become a notable figure on the American frontier as a mining engineer and consultant and, later, as a translator of Spanish land grants. Flipper tried several times to vindicate himself, befriending such prominent Washington officials as Senator A. B. Fall of New Mexico. When Fall became secretary of the interior, Flipper became his assistant until the infamous Teapot Dome affair severed their relationship.

Flipper returned to Atlanta at the close of his mining career and lived with his brother, an AME bishop, until his death in 1940. His quest to remove the stain of "conduct unbecoming an officer and a gentleman" remained unfulfilled at the time of his death. Nearly a century after he left West Point, however, a review of his record indicated that he had been framed by his fellow officers. His records were corrected and he was posthumously granted an honorable discharge from the Army. On the one hundredth anniversary of his graduation, his bust was unveiled and is now displayed in the Cadet Library at the United States Military Academy.

Samuel L. Gravely Jr. (1922–2004)
Navy Admiral

Samuel L. Gravely Jr. was born in Richmond, Virginia, on June 4, 1922. He enrolled at Virginia Union University but quit school to enlist in the Navy. He received naval training at the Great Lakes facility in Great Lakes, Illinois, and the Midshipmen School at Columbia University in New York. During World War II, Gravely served aboard a submarine chaser. After the war he returned to school and received a B.A. in history in 1948.

Gravely was called back to duty in 1949 and decided to make a career of the Navy. During the Korean War he served aboard the cruiser USS *Toledo*.

Gravely was steadily promoted through the ranks, and in 1962 he accepted command of the destroyer escort USS *Falgout*. Stationed at Pearl Harbor as part of the Pacific Fleet, he became the first African American to assume command of a Navy combat ship. In 1971, while commanding the guided missile frigate USS *Jouett*, Gravely was promoted to admiral, the first African American to achieve that rank. In 1976 he was again promoted, this time to vice admiral, and placed in command of the U.S. Navy's 3rd Fleet, a position he held until 1978.

While in the navy Gravely received many medals, including the Legion of Merit, Bronze Star, Meritorious Service Medal, Joint Service Commendation Medal, and the Navy Commendation Medal, as well as medals for his service in three wars. Gravely also received numerous civilian awards, including the Distinguished Virginian Award presented by the Governor of Virginia. Gravely died on October 22, 2004, at Bethesda Naval Hospital.

Marcelite J. Harris (1943–)
Air Force General

Marcelite Jordan Harris was born in Houston, Texas, on January 16, 1943. Her interests began in the area of theater, but after earning a B.A from Spelman College in 1964 Harris decided to join the U.S. Air Force.

In 1965 Harris was commissioned as a second lieutenant and in 1967 she was promoted and transferred to Birburg Air Base in West Germany. Harris continued her education in her area of maintenance by successfully completing a

course in aircraft maintenance and a B.S. in business management from the University of Maryland University College Asian Division in Japan. Harris remained overseas until 1986 after creating an outstanding service record. Harris was named colonel in 1986, and major general for the U.S. Air Force Headquarters in Washington, D.C., in September of 1994. On May 25, 1995, Harris was promoted to the rank of major general and became the first African American woman to receive the rank. The position provided management of 125,000 persons and a budget in excess of $250 million.

Harris retired on February 22, 1997, after having served in the U.S. Air Force for thirty-one years and having the position of two-star general. Among her many awards are the Meritorious Service Medal with three oak leaf clusters, a Bronze Star, and Legion of Merit with oak leaf cluster.

Daniel "Chappie" James Jr. (1920–1978)
Air Force General

Daniel "Chappie" James Jr. was born on February 11, 1920, in Pensacola, Florida. He attended Tuskegee Institute, where he took part in the Army Air Corps program. He was commissioned a second lieutenant in 1943. During the Korean War James flew 101 combat missions in F51 and F80 aircraft. After the war he performed various staff assignments until 1957, when he graduated from the Air Command and Staff College at Maxwell Air Force Base, Alabama. In 1966 he became deputy commander for operations of the 8th Tactical Fighter Wing stationed in Thailand, before being promoted to commander of the 7272nd Flying Training Wing at Wheelus Air Force Base in Libya.

James became a brigadier general in 1970, and a lieutenant general in 1973. He has received numerous civilian awards as well as his military awards, which include the Legion of Merit with one oak leaf cluster, Distinguished Flying Cross, Air Medal with ten clusters, Distinguished Unit

Citation, Presidential Unit Citation, and Air Force Outstanding Unit Award. In 1975 James was appointed commander in chief of NORAD/ADCOM, and was promoted to four-star general, making him the first black four-star general in U.S. military history.

On February 25, 1978, James died of a heart attack at the age of fifty-eight in Colorado Springs.

Hazel W. Johnson (1927–2011)
Army General

Hazel W. Johnson-Brown was born on October 10, 1927, in Malvern, Pennsylvania, and received nurse's training at Harlem Hospital in New York. She enlisted in the U.S. Army in 1955 and in 1960 joined the Army's Nursing Corps as a first lieutenant. She then went on to earn a bachelor's degree in nursing from Villanova University, a master's degree in nursing education from Columbia University, and a doctorate in education administration from Catholic University in Washington, D.C.

In 1979 Johnson was promoted to brigadier general, the first African American woman to hold that rank, and was placed in command of the Army Nurse Corps. In 1983 she retired from the service and began working for the American Nursing Association as director of its government affairs division. In 1986 she joined the faculty of George Mason University in Virginia as a professor of nursing and in 1997 she was awarded an honorary degree from Long Island University's Brooklyn Campus.

Johnson is a recipient of the Army's Distinguished Service Medal, Legion of Merit, Meritorious Service Medal, and the Army Commendation Medal with oak leaf cluster. She died August 5, 2011.

Henry Johnson (1897–1929)
Army Infantry

Henry Lincoln Johnson was born in 1897, in Alexandria, Virginia, and later moved to Albany, New York. A member of the 15th National Guard of New York, which became the 369th Infantry, Johnson was probably the most famous black soldier to have fought in World War I.

The 369th was the first group of black combat troops to arrive in Europe. After a summer of training, the group saw action at Champagne and fought its way to the Rhine River in Germany, receiving the Croix de guerre from the French government. Johnson and another soldier (Needham Roberts) were the first Americans to receive this French medal for individual heroism in combat; Johnson was cited by the French as a "magnificent example of courage and energy." He was later promoted to sergeant. Johnson received no decoration for his efforts from the U.S. Army and when discharged on February 14, 1919, he received no disability for his injuries. Johnson died in poverty on July 2, 1929. He was buried with full military honors in Arlington National Cemetery.

Dorie Miller (1919–1943)
Navy Cook

Doris "Dorie" Miller was born on a farm near Waco, Texas, on October 12, 1919. He was the son of a sharecropper and grew up to become star fullback on the Moore High School football team in his native city. At nineteen, he enlisted in the U.S. Navy. Miller was nearing the end of his first hitch as a messman aboard the USS *Arizona* on December 7, 1941, when he had his first taste of combat and manned a machine gun during the Pearl Harbor attack and brought down four Japanese planes.

For his heroism Miller was awarded the Navy Cross, which was conferred by Admiral Chester W. Nimetz, the commander in chief of the Pacific Fleet.

He remained a messman during the hostilities, serving aboard the aircraft carrier *Liscome Bay* and was promoted to mess attendant third class.

He was killed in action in the South Pacific in December of 1943. Miller was commended for "distinguished devotion to duty, extreme courage, and disregard of his personal safety during attack."

Although efforts were defeated to posthumously award Miller the Congressional Medal of Honor, the Navy instead named the first U.S. destroyer after an African American when the USS *Miller* was subsequently named after Miller in 1973.

Frank E. Petersen (1932–)
Marine Corps General

Petersen was born March 2, 1932, in Topeka, Kansas. He attended Washington University in St. Louis and George Washington University in Washington, D.C., before entering the Naval Reserve in 1951 as an aviation cadet.

In 1952 Petersen was commissioned as a second lieutenant in the U.S. Marine Corps. He was a designated naval aviator and received flight training at the United States Air Station at Pensacola, Florida. He also received flight training at Corpus Christi, Texas, and the Marine Corps Air Station at Santa Ana, California.

Petersen flew thirty-one air combat missions during the Korean War. In 1953 and 1954 he was assigned to the 1st Marine Aircraft Wing as its liaison officer. From 1954 to 1960 he was assigned to the Marine Corps's Santa Ana facility, and in 1968 he commanded the Marine Aircraft Group in Vietnam. In 1979 Petersen was promoted to the rank of brigadier general.

As an African American Marine Corps officer, Petersen accomplished many firsts. He was the first African American to receive a commission as aviator, to attend the National War College, to command a tactical air squadron, and to be promoted to marine general.

Petersen is a recipient of more than twenty medals, including the Distinguished Flying Cross, the Air Medal with silver star, the Korean Service Medal, the Korean Presidential Citation, the National Defense Service Medal with bronze

star, the United Nations Service Medal, and a Purple Heart.

Colin L. Powell (1937–)
Army General, National Security Adviser, Chair of the Joint Chiefs of Staff, and Secretary of State

Colin Luther Powell was born in New York City, New York, on April 5, 1937, and graduated from Morris High School in 1954. In 1958 he received a B.S. in geology from City College of New York; while in college Powell was active in the ROTC program and attained the rank of cadet colonel.

Powell began his military career immediately after graduation by accepting a second lieutenant's commission in the U.S. Army. In 1962 he served as a military advisor in South Vietnam. Returning to the United States, Powell earned an M.B.A. from George Washington University in 1971, and in 1972 he accepted his first political appointment as White House Fellow. This led to his promotion to brigade commander in 1976 and assistant division commander in 1981.

In 1983 Powell was back in a political position, serving as military assistant to the secretary of defense. In 1987, after holding posts with the National Security Council, Powell was appointed by President Ronald Reagan to the position of national security adviser, head of the National Security Council. In 1989 Powell took the position of chairman of the Joint Chiefs of Staff, the highest military position in the United States. From this position, Powell received international recognition as one of the chief architects of the 1991 Persian Gulf War. In the autumn of 1993 Powell retired as chairman of the Joint Chiefs of Staff.

Powell stepped back into political life in December 2000, when President George W. Bush nominated Powell for the post of secretary of state. After a unanimous confirmation Powell served as the first African American in this post. His primary efforts were placed on the War on

Terror, which officially began in September 2001. Powell successfully brought other nations into this campaign and enforced the disarming of Iraq, as declared by the United Nations. Powell remained in this esteemed post until November 15, 2004, after the re-election of George Bush.

Powell continues as an active contributor in community-based organizations such as the Boys and Girls Club, and the Advisory Board of Children's Health Fund, and as a limited partner in Kleiner Perkins Culfied & Byers beginning in 2005.

Powell is a recipient of numerous awards, including the Purple Heart and the Bronze Star, Legion of Merit Award, Distinguished Service Medal, Soldier's Medal, the Secretary of State Distinguished Service Award, as well as numerous honorary degrees.

J. Paul Reason (1943–)
Navy General

Joseph Paul Reason was born on March 22, 1943, in Washington, D.C. He moved from high school to college at Howard University for three years before embarking on his life-long career. Once receiving a nomination to attend the United States Naval Academy, Reason applied to the nuclear propulsion program. He completed the program and took his first assignment in 1968. By 1970 he had earned a master's degree in computer systems management and after several posts and having served under President Gerald Ford, Reason was assigned to the USS *Mississippi* as the executive officer in 1979. Reason remained on this ship until 1985, when he became commander of his own ship, the nuclear missile cruiser USS *Bainbridge*.

Reason continued serving in the role of commander of operations from Alaska and Seattle to the Pacific and the Indian Oceans and the Persian Gulf. In May 1996 Reason became the first African American four-star general when he was appointed by President Bill Clinton as com-

mander in chief of the U.S. Atlantic Fleet based in Norfolk, Virginia. He retired in November 1999.

Reason received numerous awards, including the Distinguished Service Medal, a Legion of Merit, and a National Defense Service Medal.

Roscoe Robinson Jr. (1928–1993)
Army General

Roscoe Robinson Jr. was born on October 11, 1928, in St. Louis, Missouri. He graduated from the United States Military Academy with a bachelor's degree in military engineering. He also has a master's degree in international affairs from the University of Pittsburgh; he received further training at the National War College, the Army Command and General Staff College, and the Army's Infantry School.

After graduating from West Point, Robinson was commissioned a second lieutenant in the U.S. Army. He served as a personnel management officer from 1965 to 1967, and in 1968 he was promoted to commanding officer of the 82nd Airborne Division's 2nd Brigade at Fort Bragg, North Carolina. Robinson was promoted to general in 1973 and was placed in command of forces in Okinawa. In 1978 he was placed in command of the 7th Army. From 1982 to 1985 Robinson served as the U.S. representative to NATO. He has also held the position of executive chief of staff, United States Pacific Command. Robinson retired from active service in 1985.

Robinson was awarded the Silver Star with oak leaf cluster, Legion of Merit with oak leaf cluster, Bronze Star, Air Medal, Army Commendation Medal, Combat Infantryman Badge, Distinguished Flying Cross, Master Parachutist Badge, Defense Distinguished Service Medal, and Army Distinguished Medal with oak leaf cluster. Robinson died on July 22, 1993, of leukemia and is buried in Arlington National Cemetery.

Roderick Von Lipsey (1959–)
Air Force Colonel

Roderick K. Von Lipsey was born in Philadelphia, Pennsylvania, on January 13, 1959. His early years were spent in private schools, and after high school he attended the United States Naval Academy in Annapolis, Maryland, in 1976. Von Lipsey graduated in 1980 and entered the Marine Corp as a commissioned second lieutenant.

After training in aircraft maintenance, Von Lipsey took pilot training on the F/A 18 Hornet fighter jet in 1985. After missions in Europe, the Mediterranean, and other service locations state side, Von Lipsey led a squadron attack against Iraqi forces in Kuwait during Desert Storm in 1991. His mission was so successful, highlighted by the safe return of all his aircraft, that Von Lipsey was awarded the Distinguished Flying Cross.

Von Lipsey went on to serve as a junior and then senior aide to the Joint Chiefs of Staff general, Colin Powell. He served in this role until 1995 and later earned a promotion as lieutenant colonel. He also received a Strike/Flight Air Medal with Numeral 4, and a Defense Meritorious Service Medal, among other awards for his commendable service. After twenty years of service Von Lipsey retired in 1999.

Bibliography

Africans in America

Adeleke, Tunde. *UnAfrican American: Nineteenth-Century Black Nationalists and the Civilizing Mission.* Lexington KY: University Press, 2000.

"Africans in America." PBS.com. http://www.pbs.org/wgbh/aia/ (20 Sept., 2011.

Appiah, Kwame Anthony, and Henry Louis Gates Jr., eds. *Microsoft Encarta Africana 2000* [multimedia]. Redmond, WA: Microsoft, 1999.

Bennett, Lerone Jr. *Before the Mayflower: A History of Black America.* 7th ed. Chicago, IL: Johnson Publishing Co. 2000.

Berry, Mary Frances. *My Face Is Black Is True: Callie House and the Struggle for Ex-Slave Reparations.* New York, NY: Alfred K. Knopf. 2005

Collier-Thomas, Bettye, and V.P. Franklin, eds. *Sister in the Struggle: African American Women in the Civil Rights-Black Power Movement.* New York: New York University Press, 2001.

Curtin, Philip C. *Africa Remembered: Narratives by West Africans from the Era of the Slave Trade.* Madison: University of Wisconsin Press, 1967.

Franklin, John Hope, and Evelyn Brooks Higginbotham, eds. *From Slavery to Freedom: A History of African Americans.* Ninth Edition. New York: McGraw-Hill, 2010.

Gates, Henry Louis Jr., and Nellie Y. McKay, eds. *Norton Anthology of African- American Literature.* 2nd ed. New York: W.W. Norton, 2003.

Glaude, Eddie S., Jr. ed. *Is It Nation Time?: Contemporary Essays on Black Power and Black Nationalism.* Chicago, IL: University of Chicago Press, 2002.

Hine, Darlene Clark, William C. Hine, and Stanley Harrold, *The African-American Odyssey.* 2 vols. 2nd ed. Upper Saddle River, NJ: Prentice Hall, 2002.

Inikori, Joseph E., and Stanley Engerman, eds. *The Atlantic Slave Trade: Effects on Economics, Societies, and Peoples in Africa, the Americas, and Europe.* Durham: Duke University Press, 1992.

Kelly, Robin D., and Earl Lewis, eds. *To Make Our World Anew: A History of African Americans.* New York: Oxford University Press, 2000.

Larvester, Gaither. "Reparations." Oxford African American Studies Center. http://www.oxfordaasc.com/article/opr/t0005/e1026. (14 June, 2010).

Narins, Brigham, ed. *The African American Almanac*. 10th ed. New York: Thomson Gale, 2008.

Oxford African American Studies Center: The Online Authority on the African American Experience. http://www.oxfordaasc.com. 11 June, 2010).

Painter, Nell Irvin. *Creating Black Americans: African-American History and Its Meanings, 1619 to the Present*. New York: Oxford Press, 2007.

Robertson, Claire C., and Martin A. Klein. *Women and Slavery in Africa*. Portsmouth, NH: Heinemann, 1983.

Robinson, Randall. *The Debt: What America Owes Black People*. New York: E. P. Dutton, 2000.

"S. Con. Res. 26 Apology for Slavery—Presentation Transcript." Slideshare.net. http://www.slideshare.net/renewvipolitics/s-con-res-26-apology-for-slavery. (25 Aug., 2009).

Smith, Jessie Carney. *Black Firsts: 4,000 Ground-Breaking and Pioneering Events*. 2nd ed. Detroit, MI: Visible Ink Press, 2003.

Sweet, John Wood. *Bodies Politic: Negotiating Race and the American North, 1730–1830*. Baltimore: John Hopkins University Press, 2003.

White, Deborah Gray. Ar'n't I a Woman? Female Slaves in the Plantation South. *2nd ed. New York: W.W. Norton, 2000.*

Wilbert, *Jenkins L.* Climbing Up to Glory: A Short History of African Americans during the Civil War and Reconstruction. *Wilmington, DE: Scholarly Resources, 2002.*

Winbush, *Raymond A., ed.* Should America Pay? Slavery and the Raging Debate on Reparations. *New York: Amistad/HarperCollins, 2003.*

Civil Rights

Clar, D. *The Eyes on the Prize Civil Rights Reader: Documents, Speeches, and Firsthand Accounts from the Black Freedom Struggle*. Eds. David J. Garrow, Gerald Gill, Vincent Harding, and Claybourne Carson. New York: Penguin, 1991.

Dyson, Michael Eric. *I May Not Get There with You: The True Martin Luther King, Jr.* New York: Free Press, 2000.

Field, Ron. *Civil Rights in America, 1865—1980*. Cambridge: Cambridge University Press, 2002.

Goldsworthy, Joan. "Black History Month: Myrlie Evers-Williams." *Gale Cengage Learning*. http://www.gale.cengage.com/free_ resources/bhm/bio/everswilliams_m.htm. (3 Feb., 2010).

Graham, Herman III. *The Brothers' Vietnam War: Black Power, Manhood, and the Military Experience*. Gainsville: University Press of Florida, 2003.

Harris-Lacewell, Melissa. "New Era For Civil Rights." *Jet*. May 17/24, 2010. p. 28.

Iton, Richard. *In Search of the Black Fantastic: Politics & Popular Culture in the Post-Civil Rights Era*. New York: Oxford university Press, 2008.

Joseph, Peniel E., ed. *The Black Power Movement: Rethinking the Civil Rights-Black Power Era*. New York: Routledge, 2006.

Lewis, David L. *W.E.B. Du Bois: The Fight for Equality and the American Century 1919–1963*. New York: Holt, 2000.

Lovett, Bobby. *The Civil Rights Movement in Tennessee: A Narrative History*. Knoxville: University of Tennessee Press 2005.

Lowery, Charles D., and John F. Marszalek, eds. *Greenwood Encyclopedia of African American Civil Rights*. Vols. 1–2. Westport, CT: Greenwood Press, 2003.

Narins, Bringham, ed. *The African American Almanac*. 10th ed. New York: Thomson Gale, 2008.

National Civil Rights Museum. http://www .civil-rightsmuseum.org. (11 June, 2011).

Padgen, John B. "The Mississippi Writers Page: Myrlie Evers-Williams." Olemiss.edu. http://www.olemiss.edu/mwp/dir/eves_myrlie/. (3 Feb., 2010).

Smith, Jessie Carney, and Linda T. Wynn. *Freedom Facts and Firsts: 400 Years of the African American Civil Rights Experience.* Detroit: Visible Ink Press, 2009.

"Then & Now." CNN.com. Jan 10, 2005. www .cnn.com/2005/us/01/03/cnn25.tan.anita/index.html. (30 Dec., 2009).

Politics

"14 Exit Poll Statistics about Obama's Victory." *The Color Line.* Context.org. http://context.org/color/200811/06/14-exit-poll-stastics-about-obama%E2%80%99s. (12 Feb., 2010).

Ballance, Frank W. *Biographical Directory of the U.S. Congress, 1774-Present,* Bioguide.congress.gov. http://bioguide.congress .gov/scripts/biodisplay.pl?index=B001238. (11 Jun., 2011).

"Barack Obama." *Encyclopedia of World Biography.* http://www.notablebiographies .com/news/Li-Ou/Obama-Barack.html. 12 Feb., 2010).

"Biography of Mayor C. Ray Nagin." *City of New Orleans.* http://www.cityofno.com/pg-35-7-mayor-c-ray-nagin-biography.aspx. (10 May, 2010).

"Black Selected officials increased six-fold since 1970: study." *Jet.* April 15, 2002. Web. http://findarticles.com/p/articles/mi_m1355 /is_17_101/ai_84971343. (26 Jan., 2010).

Colburn, David R., and Jeffrey S. Adler, eds. *African-American Mayors: Race, Politics, and the American City,* Urbana, IL: University of Illinois Press, 2001.

"CRS Report for Congress: African American Members of the United States Congress: 1870–2008." Senate.gov.

www.senate.gov/reference/resources/pdf/RL 30378.pdf. (26 Jan., 2010).

"Dr. Regina Benjamin Is Surgeon General Choice." CNNhealth.com. http://www.cnn .com/2009/HEALTH/07/13/surgeon.general/index.html. (10 May, 2010).

"How He Did It: A Team of *Newsweek* Reporters Reveals the Secret Battles and Private Fears behind an Epic Election." *Newsweek.* November 17, 2008. Web. Newsweek.com. http://www.newsweek .com/id/167582/output/print. (17 Feb., 2010).

"John W. Thompson—Chairman of the Board." Symantec.com. http://www.symantec.com/about/profile/management/directors/bio/jsp ?bioid=john_thompson. (18 May, 2010.

Manning, Jennifer E. "Membership of the 11th Congress: A Profile." *Congressional Research Service.* June 21, 2010. Web. Senate.gov. http://www.senate.gov/CRSReports/crs-publish.cfm?pid. (12 July, 2010).

"Myrlie Evers-Williams." *Gale Cengage Learning.* Gale.Cengage.com. http://www.gale .cengage.com/fee/bhm/bio/everswilliams_m.html. (3 Feb., 2010).

Narins, Bringham, ed. *The African American Almanac* 10th ed. New York: Thomson Gale, 2008.

National Urban League. *The State of Black America.* Vols. 1979–2009. New York: National Urban League.

Obama, Barack. *Dreams from My Father: A Story of Race and Inheritance.* New York: Three Rives Press, 1995.

———. *The Audacity of Hope: Thoughts on Reclaiming the American Dream.* New York: Crown Publishers, 2006.

"Obama: Nobel Peace Prize Is 'Call to Action.'" CNN.com.

http://www.cnn.com/2009/WORLD/europe/10/0 9/nobel.peace.prize.index.html. (3 Feb., 2010).

"Office of History and Preservation, Office of the Clerk, U.S. House of Representatives."

Black Americans in Congress 1870–2007. Washington, DC: U.S. Government Printing Office, 2008.

Painter, Nell Irvin. *Creating Black Americans: African-American History and It Meaning 1619 to the Present.* New York: Oxford University Press, 2007.

"Rice, Condoleezza." *Encyclopedia of World Biography.* Notablebiographies.com. http://www.notablebiographies.com/news/Ow-Sh/Rice-Condoleezza.html. (10 May, 2010).

"Rice, Susan E." U.S. Department of State. State.gov. http://www.state.gov/r/pa/ei/biog/120486.htm. (10 May, 2010).

"Special Feature: Realizing the Dream". *Essence.* January 2009. pp. 67–135.

"The Times of His Life." *Essence.* January 2009. pp. 73–75.

"Walter White (1893–1955)." *The New Georgia Encyclopedia.* Web. Georgiaencyclopedia.org. http://www.georgiaencyclopedia.org/nge/Article.jsp?id=h-747. (3 Feb., 2010).

Education

"A Dream Fulfilled." *Jet.* July 26, 2010. pp. 20–21.

Anderson, James D. *The Education of Blacks in the South, 1860–1935.* Chapel Hill: University of North Carolina, 1988.

Braun, Henry, Frank Jenkins, and Wendy Grigg. "Comparing Private Schools and Public Schools Using Hierarchical Linear Modeling." *National Assessment of Educational Progress: The Nation's Report Card.* July 2006. Web. NCES.ed.gov. http://nces.ed.gov/nationsreportcard/pubs/studies/2006461.asp. (11 June, 2011).

Fairclough, Adam. *Teaching Equality: Black Schools in the Age of Jim Crow.* Athens, GA: University of Georgia Press, 2001.

Fischel, William A. "The Real Race to the Top: Since the Days of the Little Red Schoolhouse, Communities Have Successfully Pushed Local Officials for Better Public Schools." (2010) *Academic OneFile.* Web. 13 January, 2010.

Ford, Glen. "Radio BC: Black Children Left Behind—by Design." *The Black Commentator.* Issue 171 (February 16, 2006).

"How No Child Left Behind Benefits African Americans." *ED.gov*, U.S. Department of Education. Ed.gov. http://www2.ed.gov/nclb/accountability/achieve/nclb-aa.html. (13 July, 2010).

Marable, Manning, ed. *The New Black Renaissance: The Souls Anthology of Critical African-American Studies.* Boulder, CO: Paradigm Publisher, 2005.

Meier, Deborah, and George Woods, eds. *Many Children Left Behind: How the No Child Left Behind Act Is Damaging Our Children and Our Schools.* Boston: Beacon Press, 2006.

National Assessment of Educational Progress. *The Nations's Report Card.* Washington, DC: National Center for Education Statistics, May 2006.

Ross, E. Wayne, and Valerie Ooka Pang, eds. *Race, Ethnicity, and Education.* Vols. 1–4. Westport CT: Praeger, 2006.

Schorn, Daniel. "The Harlem Children's Zone: How One Man's Vision to Revitalize Harlem Starts with Children." *CBS News.* May 14, 2006. Web. CBSnews.com. http://www.cbsnews.com/stories/2006/05/11/60minutes/main1611936.shtml. (12 July, 2010).

Walker, Yvette, "No Child Left Behind." *Encyclopedia of African American History, 1896 to the Present: From the Age of Segregation to the Twenty-first Century.* Ed. Paul Finkelman. Web. Oxford African American Studies Center. Oxfordaasc.com. http://www.oxfordaasc.com/article/opr/t0005/e0914. (14 June, 2010).

Religion

Edwards, Robin T. "Religion Survey Holds Surprises: Catholic Blacks Graduate, Big

Church Boom." *National Catholic Reporter*. December 17, 1993.

Grant, Jacqueline. *White Women's Church and Black Women's Jesus: Feminist Christology & Womanist Response (American Academy of Religion Academy Series. No 64)*. New York: Oxford University Press, 2006.

Harris-Lacewell, Melissa V. "Righteous Politics: The Role of the Black Church in Contemporary Politics." *Cross Currents* 57 (Summer): 180–96.

HistoryMakers. http://www.thehistorymakers.com/ biography.

"MegaChurches: Large Congregations Spread across Black America." *Ebony*. December 2004.

Moon, Fletcher F. "Faith-Based Entrepreneurship." *Encyclopedia of African American Business*, Vol. 1. Ed. Jessie Carney Smith. Westport, CT: Greenwood Press 2006.

"The New Mega Churches: Huge Congregations with Spectacular Structures Spread across the U.S." *Ebony*. December 2001. p. 148.

Olupona, Jacob K., ed. *African Spirituality: Forms, Meanings, and Expressions*. New York: Crossroads, 2000.

Raboteau, Albert J. *Canaan Land: A Religious History of African Americans*. New York: Oxford University Press, 2001.

Reagon, Bernice Johnson. *If You Don't Go, Don't Hinder Me: The African America Sacred Song Tradition*. Lincoln: University of Nebraska Press, 2001.

Ross, Rosetta E. *Witnessing and Testifying: Black Women, Religion and Civil Rights*. Minneapolis, MN: Fortress Press, 2003.

Salvatore, Nick. *Singing in a Strange Land: C. L. Franklin and the Rise of the Black Church in America*. New York: Little, Brown, 2004.

Smith, Vern E. "Where Do We Go From Here?" *Crisis*. July/August 2006. Vol. 113, Issue 4. pp. 31–35.

Weems, Renita J. "Black America and Religion." *Ebony*. November 2005.

Literature

Bell, Bernard W. *The Contemporary African American Novel: Its Folk Roots and Modern Literary Branches*. Amherst: University of Massachusetts Press. 2004.

Bruce, Dickerson. *The Origins of African American Literature, 1680–1865*. Charlottesville, VA: University Press of Virginia, 2001.

Byerman, Keith. *Remembering the Past in Contemporary African American Fiction*. Chapel Hill: University of North Carolina Press, 2005.

Dickerson-Carr, Darryl. *The Columbia Guide to Contemporary African American Fiction*. New York: Columbia University Press, 2005.

Farrar, Hayward Woody. "Black Press" *Encyclopedia of African American History, 1896 to the Present: From the Age of Segregation to the Twenty-first Century*. Ed. Paul Finkelman. Web.Oxford African American Studies Center. http://oxfordassc.com/article/ opr/t005/e0017. (26 Jan., 2011).

Gabbin, Joanne V., ed. *The Furious Flowering of African American Poetry*. Charlottesville: University Press of Virginia 1999.

Gates, Henry Louis Jr., and Nellie Y. McKay, eds. *The Norton Anthology of African American Literature*. 2nd ed. New York: W.W. Norton, 2004.

Johnson, Vernon Damani, and Bill Lyne. *Walkin' the Talk: An Anthology of African American Studies*. Upper Saddle, NJ: Prentice Hall, 2003.

Marable, Manning, ed. *The New Black Renaissance: The Souls Anthology of Critical African-American Studies*. Boulder, CO: Paradigm Publishers, 2005.

Pride, Armistead S., and Clint C. Wilson II. *A History of the Black Press*. Washington, DC: Howard University Press, 1997.

Quashie, Kevin, Everod, R. Joyce Lausch, and Keith D. Miller. *New Bones: Contemporary Black Writers in America.* Upper Saddle, NJ: Prentice Hall, 2001.

Suggs, Jon-Christian. "Literature." *Encyclopedia of African American History, 1896 to the Present: From the Age of Segregation to the Twenty-first Century.* Ed. Paul Finkelman. Web. Oxford African American Studies Center. http://www.OxfordaascData.com/ article/opr/t0005/e0019. (13 Jan., 2011).

Tarver, Australia, and Paula Barnes, eds. *New Voices on the Harlem Renaissance: Race, Gender, and Literary Discourse.* Madison, NJ: Fairleigh Dickerson University Press, 2006.

Wirth, Thomas H. *Gay Rebel of the Harlem Renaissance: Richard Bruce Nugent.* Durham, NC: Duke University Press, 2002.

Wolseley, Roland E. *The Black Press, USA.* 2nd ed. Ames, IA: Iowa State University Press, 1990.

Business Entrepreneurs and Media

Acham, Christine. *Revolution Televised: Prime Time and the Struggle for Black Power.*Minneapolis: University of Minnesota Press, 2004.

Barber, John T., and Alice A. Tai, eds. *The Information Society and the Black Community.* Westport, CT: Praeger, 2001.

"Black Film Center/Archive: African American Oscar Winners." *Department of African American and African Diaspora Studies, Indiana University, Bloomington.* Web. Indiana.edu. http://www.indiana.edu/~bfca/feataures/Oscars.html. (26 Jan., 2011).

Burroughs, Todd Steven . "Television." *Encyclopedia of African American History, 1896 to the Present: From the Age of Segregation to the Twenty-first Century.* Ed. Paul Finkelman. Oxford African American Studies Center. Web. Oxfordaasc.com. http://www.Oxfordaasc.com/article/opr/t0005/e1161. (2 Jan., 2011).

Dawkins, Wayne. *Rugged Waters: Black Journalists Swim the Mainstream.* Newport News, VA: August Press, 2003.

"Economic Trends—Third Generation Black Entrepreneurs." *The African American Almanac.* 10th ed. Ed. Bringham Narins. New York: Thomson Gale, 2008. pp. 667–668.

Hooker, Cliff. "Black Business Stability: Strong Direction and Specialized Business Plans Increase the Chances of Surviving." *Black Enterprise.* July 2005.

Hunt , Martin K., and Jacqueline E. *History of Black Business: The Coming of America's Largest African-American-owned Business.* Chicago: Knowledge Express, 1998.

Mars, Errol I. "Richard Dean Parsons" *Black Profiles: Entrepreneurs—Executives.* Web. Blackentrepreneurprofile.com http://www.blackentrepreneurprofile.com/profile-full/rchive/2004/september/article/richarddeanpardons. (11 Nov., 2011).

Meeks, Kenneth. "The 75 Most Powerful African Americans in Corporate America: Meet 75 Executives Who Hold Tremendous Clout in the World of Business, Including the 18 Who Earned CEO Positions." *Black Enterprise.* February 2005.

"Revenues for Black-Owned Firms Near $89 Billion, Number of Businesses Up 45 Percent." *U.S. Census Bureau; Newsroom.* Web. Census.gov. http://www.census.gov/ PressRelease/www/realease/archives/business_ownership/006711. (10 May, 2010).

Sampson, Henry T. *Swing' on the Ether Waves: A Chronological History of African Americans in Radio and Television Broadcasting, 1925–1955.* Lanham, MD: Scarecrow Press, 2005.

Smith, Jessie Carney, ed. *Encyclopedia of African-American Business History.* Vols. 1–2. Westport, CT: Greenwood Press, 2006.

Walker, Juliet E. K. *The History of Black Business in America: Capitalism, Race, and Entrepreneurship.* New York: Macmillan Library Reference USA, 1998.

Zook, Kristal Brent. *Color by Fox: The Fox Network and the Revolution in Black Television*. New York: Oxford Press, 1999.

Arts—Performance and Visual

Asim, Jabari. "The Reel Deal: Independent Filmmakers Continue to Tell Our Stories on Their Own Terms." *Crisis*. Vol. 118/1. Winter 2011. pp. 16–20.

Collins, Lisa Gail. *The Art of History: African American Women Artists: Engaging the Past*. New Brunswick, NJ: Rutgers University Press, 2002.

Glass, Barbara. *African American Dance: An Illustrated History*. Jefferson, NC: McFarland, 2007.

Kirschke, Amy H. *Art in Crisis: W.E.B. Du Bois and the Struggle for African American Identity and Memory*. Bloomington: Indiana University Press, 2007.

Mapp, Edward. *African Americans and the Oscar: Seven Decades of Struggle and Achievement*. Lanham, MD.: Scarecrow Press, 2003.

Pencak, William. "Entertainment Industry and African Americans." *Encyclopedia of African American History, 1896 to the Present: From the Age of Segregation to the Twenty-first Century*. Ed. Paul Finkelman. Web. Oxford African American Studies Center. Oxfordaasc.com. http://www .oxfordaasc.com/article/opt/t0005/e0393. (25 Jan., 2011).

Powell, Richard J. *Black Art: A Cultural History*. 2nd ed. London: Thames & Hudson, 2003.

Romare, Bearden, and Harry Henderson. *A History of African-American Artists from 1792 to the Present*. New York: Pantheon, 1993.

Sandow, Greg. "The Classical Color Line." *Village Voice*. 42:14 April 8, 1997. pp. 71–72.

Wald, Elijah. *Escaping the Delta: Johnson and the Invention of the Blues*. New York: Amistad, 2004.

Ward, Geoffrey C. *Jazz: A History of America's Music*. New York: Alfred A. Knopf, 2000.

Music

Davis, Francis. *The History of the Blues: The Roots, The Music, the People*. Cambridge, MA: Da Capo Press, 1995.

Hodges, Graham Russell Gao. "Blues." *Encyclopedia of African American History 1896 to the Present: From the Age of Segregation to the Twenty-first Century*. Ed. Paul Finkelman. Oxford African American Studies Center. Web. http://www.Oxfordaasc.com/article/opr/t0005/e0154. (11 Feb., 2011).

Jackson, Buzzy. *A Bad Woman Feeling Good: Blues and the Women Who Sing Them*. New York: Norton Press, 2005.

"Michael Jackson Biography (1958–2009)." Biography.com. Web. http://www.biography .com/articles/Michael-Jackson-38211. (25 Feb., 2011).

Oakley, Giles, *The Devil's Music: A History of the Blues*. Cambridge MA: Da Capo Press, 1997.

Oja, Carol. *Making Music Modern: New York in the 1920s*. New York: Oxford University Press, 2000.

Oliver, Paul. *The Story of the Blues*. Boston, MA: Northeastern University Press, 1998.

Prahlad, Anand, ed. "Appropriation of Black Folklore." *The Greenwood Encyclopedia of African American Folklore*. Westport, CT: Greenwood Press, 2006.

Papillion-Posey, Erica. "The African-American Male and the Classical Color Line." Web. Operagasm.com. http://operagsm.com/ 2010/the-african-american-male-classic-color-line/. (10 Feb., 2010).

Sellman, James. *"Gospel Music."* Encyclopedia of African American History 1896 to the Present: From the Age of Segregation to the Twenty-first Century*. Ed. Paul Finkelman. Oxford African American Studies Center. Web. http://www.Oxfordaasc.com/ article/opr/t0002/e1692. (13 Jan., 2011).

Smith, Jessie Carney, Ed. *The Encyclopedia of African American Popular Culture*. Vols. 1-4. Santa Barbara, CA: Greenwood Press, 2011.

Ward, Geoffrey C., and Ken Burns. *Jazz: A History of America's Music*. New York: Alfred A. Knopf, 2000.

Science & Technology

"A Rich Heritage Gives Way to Modern Ingenuity." *Famous Black Inventors*. Black-inventor.com. Web. http://www.black-inventor.com/. (18 Feb., 2011).

Barber, John T., and Alice A. Tait, eds. *The Information Society and the Black Community*. Westport, CT: Praeger, 2001.

Hogue, Carol J. R., Martha A. Hargraves, and Karen Scott Collins, eds. *Minority Health in America: Findings and Policy Implications from the Commonwealth Fund Minority Health Survey*. Baltimore: Johns Hopkins University Press, 2000.

Mickens, Ronald E., ed. *Edward Bouchet: The First African-American Doctorate*. Hackensack, NJ: World Scientific, 2002.

Sinclair, Bruce. *Technology and the African American Experience: Needs and Opportunities for Study*. Cambridge, MA: MIT Press, 2004.

Sluby, Patricia Carter. *The Inventive Spirit of African Americans: Patented Ingenuity*. Westport, CT: Praeger, 2004.

Smelser, Neil J., William Julius Wilson, and Faith Mitchell, eds. *America Becoming: Racial Trends and Their Consequences*. 2 vols. Washington, DC: National Academy Press, 2001.

Ward, Thomas J., Jr. *Black Physicians in the Jim Crow South*. Fayetteville: University of Arkansas Press, 2003.

Warren, Wini. *Black Women Scientists in the United States*. Bloomington, IN: Indiana University Press, 1999.

Webster, Raymond B., ed. *African American Firsts in Science and Technology*. Detroit: Gale Research, 1999.

Sports

Ashe, Arthur R. Jr. *A Hard Road to Glory: A History of the American-American Athlete 1970–Present*. 4 vols. New York: John Wiley & Sons, 2005.

Bass, Amy. *Not the Triumph but the Struggle: The 1968 Olympics and the Making of the Black Athlete*. Minneapolis: University of Minnesota Press, 2002.

Chappell, Kevin, and Melody K, Hoffman. "Historic Super Bowl Is Latest Victory in Black's Long Struggle in the NFL." *Jet*, February 12, 2007. p. 59.

Edelson, Paula. *A to Z of American Women in Sports*. New York: Facts on File, 2002.

Kirsch, George B., Othello Harris, and Claire E. Nolte. "Track and Field." *Encyclopedia of Ethnicity and Sports in the United States*. Westport, CT: Greenwood Press, 2000.

LaFeber, Walter. *Michael Jordan and the New Global Capitalism*. New York: W.W. Norton, 2002.

Leonhardt, David, and Ford Fessenden. "Black Coaches in N.B.A. Have Shorter Tenures." *New York Times*. March 22, 2005. Web. NYTimes.com. http://www.nytimes.com/2005/03/22/sports/basketball/22coaches.html. (21 Feb., 2011).

Lumpkin, Angela. "Feature Articles on African Americans in Sports Illustrated in the 1990s." *Physical Educator*. 66.2 (2009): 58+.

Rhoden, William C. *Forty Million Dollar Slaves: The Rise, Fall, and Redemption of the Black Athlete*. New York: Crown, 2006.

Whitaker, Matthew C. *African American Icons of Sport: Triumphs, Courage and Excellence*. Westport, CT: Greenwood Press, 2008.

Wigginton, Russell Thomas. *The Strange Career of the Black Athlete: African Americans and Sports*. Westport, CT: Greenwood Press, 2006.

Military

Astor, Gerald. *The Right to Fight: A History of African American in the Military*. Novato, CA: Presidio, 1998.

Buckley, Gail L. *American Patriots: The Story of Blacks in the Military from the Revolution to Desert Storm*. New York: Random House, 2001.

Edgerton, Robert B. *Hidden Heroism: Black Soldiers in America's Wars*. Boulder, CO: Westview Press, 2001.

Haskins, James. *African American Military Heroes*. New York: John Wiley, 1998.

Lanning, Michael Lee. *The African American Soldier: From Crispus Attucks to Colin Powell*. Secaucus, NJ: Birch Lane Press, 1997.

Latty, Yvonne. *We Were There: Voices of African American Veterans, from World War II to the War in Iraq*. New York: HarperCollins, 2004.

Neely, Mark E., and Harold Holzer. "The Picture of Bravery." *American Legacy*. Fall, 2000.

Sellman, James. "Military, Blacks in the American." *Africana: The Encyclopedia of the African and African American Experience*. 2nd ed. Ed. Kwame Anthony Appiah. Web. Oxford African American Studies Center. Oxfordaasc.com. http://www.oxfordaasc.com/article/opr/t0002/e2653. (11 Feb., 2011).

Steward, T. G., *Buffalo Soldiers: The Colored Regulars in the United States Army*. New York: Humanity Books, 2003.

Trudeau, Noah Andre. *Like Men of War: Black Troops in the Civil War, 1862–1865*. Boston: Little, Brown, 1998.

Photo Credits

Photographs in The African American Almanac are reproduced from the following sources. Any photographs not included in the list below are in the public domain.

BIOGRAPHICAL PORTRAITS

Hank Aaron: Library of Congress

Ralph David Abernathy: Library of Congress

Adele Addison: Carl Van Vechten/Library of Congress

Ira Aldridge: Library of Congress

Archie A. Alexander: U.S. Office of War Information/Library of Congress

Debbie Allen: Helga Esteb / Shutterstock

Marian Anderson: Carl Van Vechten/Library of Congress

Louis Armstrong: Library of Congress

Crispus Attucks: Library of Congress

Pearl Bailey: Carl Van Vechten/Library of Congress

Ella Baker: The Ella Baker Center for Human Rights

Josephine Baker: Carl Van Vechten/Library of Congress

James Baldwin: MDC Archives

Ernie Banks: Scott R. Anselmo

Benjamin Banneker: Library of Congress

Amiri Baraka: David Sasaki

Ernie Barnes: DrPenfield

William "Count" Bassie: Heinrich Klaffs

Angela Bassett: Joe Seer / Shutterstock.com

Romare Bearden: Carl Van Vechten/Library of Congress

Harry Belafonte: Carl Van Vechten/Library of Congress

Chuck Berry: Roland Godefroy

Halle Berry: Vince Bucci for NAACP

Mary McLeod Bethune: U.S. Farm Security Administration/Office of War Information Black & White/Library of Congress

David Blackwell: Konrad Jacobs

Art Blakey: Heinrich Klaffs

Julian Bond: Sam Felder

Arna Bontemps: Carl Van Vechten/Library of Congress

Gwendolyn Brooks: MDC Archives

Ruth Brown: caviera

Kobe Bryant: Rico Shen

John W. Bubbles: Carl Van Vechten/Library of Congress

Ralph Bunche: Carl Van Vechten/Library of Congress

Nannie Helen Burroughs: Library of Congress

Octavia Butler: Nikolas Coukouma

Cab Calloway: Courtesy of Special Collections, Franklin Library, Fisk University

Diahann Carroll: Carl Van Vechten/Library of Congress

Betty Carver: Brian McMillen

George Washington Carver: Library of Congress

Wilt Chamberlain: New York World-Telegram & Sun/Library of Congress

Ray Charles: Victor Diaz Lamich

Cinqué: Portrait by Nathaniel Jocelyn, 1839. Public domain

Ornette Coleman: Davide Leonardi

Don Cornelius: Joe Seer / Shutterstock.com

Bill Cosby: Eugene Parciasepe / Shutterstock

Andraé Crouch: Jon Torger Salte

Paul Cuffee: Library of Congress

Countee Cullen: Carl Van Vechten/Library of Congress

Angela Davis: dielinke sachsen. Photo: Gerd Eiltzer

Ossie Davis: Carl Van Vechten/Library of Congress

Sammy Davis Jr.: Library of Congress

Ruby Dee: Carl Van Vechten/Library of Congress

Beauford Delaney: Carl Van Vechten/Library of Congress

Samuel Delany: Alex Lozupone.

Ayuba Suleiman Diallo: Portrait by William Hoare of Bath. Public domain

Dean Dixon: Carl Van Vechten/Library of Congress

Fats Domino: Klaus Hiltscher

Frederick Douglass: Courtesy of Special Collections, Franklin Library, Fisk University

W.E.B. DuBois: Library of Congress

Katherine Dunham: Library of Congress

Michael Eric Dyson: John Bracken

Laurence Fishburn: Joe Seer / Shutterstock

Roberta Flack: Roland Godefroy

George Foreman: Paul Dickover

Aretha Franklin: Ryan Arrowsmith

Morgan Freeman: Helga Esteb / Shutterstock

Marcus Garvey: George Grantham Bain collection/Library of Congress

Henry Louis Gates Jr.: Jon Irons

Marvin Gaye: Florence Lefranc

Dizzy Gillespie: Carl Van Vechten/Library of Congress

Nikki Giovanni: Brett Weinstein

Danny Glover: Vinicius Tupinamba / Shutterstock.com

Whoopi Goldberg: Miro Vrlik Photography LLC / Shutterstock.com

Ed Gordon: Eternal Concepts PR

Louis Gossett Jr.: Helga Esteb / Shutterstock.com

Al Green: Dwight McCann

Dick Gregory: Juliet Kaye / Shutterstock.com

Bryant Gumbel: Miro Vrlik Photography LLC / Shutterstock.com

Buddy Guy: Brian McMillen

Fanny Lou Hamer: *U.S. News & World Report*/ Library of Congress

Lionel Hampton: René Speur

William Christopher Handy: Carl Van Vechten/Library of Congress

Isaac Hayes: William Henderson

Roland Hayes: Courtesy of Special Collections, Franklin Library, Fisk University

Roy Haynes: Professor Bop

Josiah Henson: Bradshaw & Godart/Library of Congress

Chester Himes: Carl Van Vechten/Library of Congress

Geoffrey Holder: Carl Van Vechten/Library of Congress

Billie Holiday: Carl Van Vechten/Library of Congress

John Lee Hooker: Masahiro Sumori

Jesse Jackson: Library of Congress

Mahalia Jackson: Carl Van Vechten/Library of Congress

Reggie Jackson: Library of Congress

Shirley Ann Jackson: World Economic Forum (Qilai Shen)

Etta James: Roland Godefroy

J. Rosamond Johnson: Carl Van Vechten

Samuel L Jackson: Joe Seer / Shutterstock.com

Absolom Jones: Delaware Art Museum

Marion Jones: Thomas Faivre-Duboz

Michael Jordan: Joshua Massel

Coretta Scott King: Library of Congress

Martin Luther King Jr.: Library of Congress

James Armistead Lafayette: public domain

Jacob Lawrence: Carl Van Vechten/Library of Congress

Martin Lawrence: Helga Esteb / Shutterstock.com

Canada Lee: Carl Van Vechten/Library of Congress

Spike Lee: Miro Vrlik Photography LLC / Shutterstock

Abbey Lincoln: Roland Godefroy

Audrey Lorde: K. Kendall

Joseph Lowery: Richard Renner

Malcolm X: New York World-Telegram & Sun/ Library of Congress

Thurgood Marshall: Library of Congress

Curtis Mayfield: Algemene Vereniging Radio Omroep

Dorothy Maynor: Carl Van Vechten/Library of Congress

Robert McFerrin: Carl Van Vechten/Library of Congress

Terry McMillan: David Shankbone

Charles Mingus: Tom Marcello

Arthur Mitchell: Carl Van Vechten/Library of Congress

Monique: Derrick Salters / Shutterstock.com

Toni Morrison: Angela Radulescu

Archibald Motley: National Archives and Records Administration/Library of Congress

Elijah Muhammad: Library of Congress

Eddie Murphy: Natalia Yeromina / Shutterstock.com

C. Ray Naggin: Jeffery Schwartz, flickr user jeffschwartz

Frederick O'Neal: Carl Van Vechten/Library of Congress

Gordon Parks: Library of Congress

Calvin Peete: Ted Van Pelt

Tyler Perry: Helga Esteb / Shutterstock.com

Pearl Primus: Carl Van Vechten/Library of Congress

Richard Pryor: Alan Light

Sun Ra: Pandelis karayorgis at en.wikipedia

Phylicia Rashad: Helga Esteb / Shutterstock.com

Paul Robeson: Office of War Information

Chris Rock: Joe Seer / Shutterstock.com

Al Roker: DFree / Shutterstock.com

Sonny Rollins: Yves Moch

Richard Roundtree: Helga Esteb / Shutterstock.com

Edith Sampson: Carl Van Vechten/Library of Congress

Sonia Sanchez: MDC Archives

Gayle Sayers: Michael Tolzmann

Gil Scot-Heron: Mikael Altemark

Dred Scott: Library of Congress

Al Sharpton: David Shankbone

George Shirley: Carl Van Vechten/Library of Congress

Noble Sissle: Carl Van Vechten/Library of Congress

Bessie Smith: Carl Van Vechten/Library of Congress

Will Smith: cinemafestival / Shutterstock.com

William Grant Still: Carl Van Vechten/Library of Congress

Billy Strayhorn: Carl Van Vechten/Library of Congress

Wanda Sykes: Rena Schild / Shutterstock.com

Koko Taylor: Sumori

Sojourner Truth: public domain

Harriet Tubman: Library of Congress

Tina Turner: Helge Øverås

Cicely Tyson: Helga Esteb / Shutterstock.com

Alice Walker: MDC Archives

"T-Bone" Walker: Heinrich Klaffs

Fats Waller: Library of Congress

William Warfield: Carl Van Vechten/Library of Congress

Booker T. Washington: Library of Congress

Ethel Waters: Carl Van Vechten/Library of Congress

Muddy Waters: Greg Goode

Camilla Williams: Carl Van Vechten/Library of Congress

Juan Williams: Pete Wright

Montel Williams; Helga Esteb / Shutterstock.com

Oprah Winfrey: Joe Seer / Shutterstock.com

Richard Wright: Carl Van Vechten/Library of Congress

OTHER PHOTOS

Title page: *Black Belt* by Archibald Motley: National Archives and Records Administration

Page 2: Jamestown National Historic Site: iStock

Page 3: Africans on the slave bark *Wildfire*: Library of Congress

Page 5: *Burgoyne's Surrender at Saratoga* by Percy Moran: Library of Congress

Page 8: Illustration of Fugitive Slave Law: Library of Congress

Page 10: 1893 painting by Charles Webber of the Underground Railroad: Library of Congress

Page 11: President Andrew Jackson: Library of Congress

Page 13: President Abraham Lincoln: Library of Congress

Page 22: *Discovery of Nat Turner*, Bettman Archive

Page 32: Frederick Douglass. Library of Congress

Page 33: W.E.B. DuBois: Library of Congress

Page 35: March on Washington, 1963. Library of Congress

Page 62: Barack Obama, makes a campaign stop on Sept 21, 2008, in Charlotte, NC: Walter G Arce / Shutterstock.com

Page 93: Tuskegee Institute: Jeffrey M. Frank / Shutterstock.com

Page 95: iStock

Page 112: Martin Luther King III addresses a crowd at Ebenezer Baptist Church on what would have been his father's 82 birthday, January 15, 2011: L. Kragt Bakker / Shutterstock.com

Page 117: Easter procession, Chicago, IL. Library of Congress

Page 119: Rastafarian man. Klaus-J. Kahle

Page 132: Langston Hughes. U.S. Office of War Information

Page 134: Alice Walker. MDC Archives

Page 145: Alex Haley statue. Robert Pernell / Shutterstock.com

Page 164: Homer Plessy plaque, New Orleans. Deadwildcat at en.wikipedia.com

Page 167: Hampton Institute classroom. Library of Congress

Page 170: Editor Lerone Bennett in his office at *Ebony* magazine. U.S. National Archives and Records Administration

Page 173: *Oprah Winfrey Show* kick off in Chicago, IL: Kenneth Sponsler / Shutterstock.com

Page 198: Actor in blackface. Library of Congress

Page 200: New York City Theatre Guild production of *Porgy and Bess*. Library of Congress

Page 202: Ossie Davis as Gabriel in *The Green Pastures*. Carl Van Vechten/Library of Congress

Page 205: Samuel Roberts of the Alvin Ailey American Dance Theater: pjhpix / Shutterstock.com

Page 208: Promotional postcard of Charles Correll and Freeman Gosden as Amos and Andy. Public domain

Page 211: *Christ in the Home of Mary and Martha* by Henry Ossawa Tanner: Library of Congress

Page 263: *Africa Rising* by Barbara Chase-Riboud: Library of Congress

Page 266: Landscape by Robert Duncanson. Public domain

Page 268: *Color of Metals* by Sam Gilliam: Library of Congress

Page 271: *Black Belt* by Archibald Motley: National Archives and Records Administration

Page 280: *Savoy* by Richard Yarde: Library of Congress

Page 283: Metropolitan Opera House: SeanPavonePhoto / Shutterstock.com

Page 285: W.C. Handy House: Library of Congress

Page 286: New Orleans jazz musicians: Leon Ritter / Shutterstock.com

Page 294: Hitsville, U.S.A. Patricia Marks / Shutterstock.com

Page 296: British Rapper Tinie Tempah: Aija Lehtonen / Shutterstock.com

Page 325: Clifton Chenier on accordian, brother Cleveland on washboard. Jay's Lounge and Cockpit, Cankton, Louisiana, Mardi Gras 1975: Bozotexino

Page 394: *Benjamin Banneker: Surveyor-Inventor-Astronomer,* mural by Maxime Seelbinder. Library of Congress

Page 409: Garrett Morgan rescuing a man at the 1917 Lake Erie Crib Disaster: Public domain

Page 414: Arthur Ashe Stadium: Ffooter / Shutterstock.com

Page 416: Group portrait of players from the Monarchs and the Hilldale baseball teams in front of grandstands filled with spectators before the opening game of the 1924 World Series. Public domain

Page 434: Joe Louis looks for an opening during boxing match with Max Schmeling. Public domain

Page 440: Front cover of *Jackie Robinson* comic book, Issue #5. Public domain

Page 443: Marshall "Major" Taylor riding bicycle in Paris, 1908. Public domain

Page 448: Buffalo Soldiers. Public domain

Page 451: 93rd Infantry Division, 1942. National Archives and Records Division

Page 455: Tuskegee Airmen, 1945. Library of Congress

Index

Note: (ill.) indicates photos and illustrations.

and music, 385
and politics, 77
and science, 399
and the arts, 213
and the military, 464
photo, 93 (ill.)
Tutu, Desmond, 58
TV One Inc., 172, 184, 354
Twelve Million Black Voices (Wright),
161
Two Can Play at That Game, 242
Two Cities (Wideman), 160
Two Trains Running, 160, 203, 228
2Pac. See Shakur, Tupac
Tyler, John, 7
Tyler Perry's House of Payne, 208
Tyner, McCoy, 326, 349
The Tyra Banks Show, 180
Tyra's Beauty Inside and Out (Banks),
180
Tyree, Omar, 135
Tyson, Cicely, 144, 203, 252, 252 (ill.)
Tyson, Mike, 418–19

U

Uggams, Leslie, 200, 252–53
Ugly Betty, 258
Ulmer, Kenneth, 119
Un ballo in maschera, 298, 317
Un-American Activities Committee,
89
Unbossed & Unbought (Chisholm), 70
The Uncalled (Dunbar), 142
"Uncle Jack," 114
Uncle Jam Wants You, 359
Uncle Tom and Eva, 266
Uncle Tom's Cabin (Stowe), 18, 145
Uncle Tom's Children (Wright), 160
Under a Soprano Sky (Sanchez), 156
Under Construction, 364
Under Fire, 215
Under One Root, 238
Under the Cherry Moon, 384
Under the Gun, 257
Under the Virgin Moon, 243
Undercover Brother, 257
Underground, 341
*The Underground Rail Road: A Record of
Facts, Authentic Narratives, Letters,
etc., Narrating the Hardships, Hair-
breadth Escape, and Death Struggles
of the Slaves In their Efforts for
Freedom, as Related by Themselves
and Others, or Witnessed by the Au-
thor, Together with Sketches of Some
of the Largest Stockholders, and*

*Most Liberal Aiders and Advisers, of
the Road* (Still), 20
Underground Railroad, 9, 10 (ill.), 18,
20–21, 147
Undine Moore Day, 311
UNESCO (United Nations Educa-
tional Scientific and Cultural Or-
ganization), 104, 274
*Unforgivable Blackness: The Rise and
Fall of Jack Johnson*, 432
UNICEF, 53
Union Army, 13, 82, 128, 448–49
Union Memorial Methodist Church,
300
United African Movement (National
Youth Movement), 50
United Church of Christ, 88
United Golf Association, 426–27
United House of Prayer for All People,
124
United Methodist Church, 126
United Nations
and civil rights, 45
and music, 298
and politics, 65, 69, 85–86, 88
and religion, 129
and science, 402
and the arts, 216
and the media, 182
and the military, 467
history of Africans in America, 15
United Nations Educational Scientific
and Cultural Organization (UN-
ESCO), 104, 274
United Nations Service Medal, 466
United Nations World Conference, 15
United Negro College Fund, 55, 185–
87, 433
United Negro Improvement Associa-
tion, 109
United Press International, 431, 436
United Service Organizations (USO),
216, 218, 335
United Shoe Machine Company, 408
United States Air Forces in Europe
(USAFE), 462
United States Colored Troops (USCT),
448–49
United States Commission for the Re-
lief of the National Freedmen, 92
United States Geological Survey, 410
United States Information Agency, 190
United States Military Academy at
West Point, 448–50, 454, 461–63,
467
United States Pacific Command, 467

United States Volunteer Infantry
(USVI), 450–51
United Way of America, 101
Unity Fellowship Church, 121
Universal Foundation for Better Living
Inc., 122
Universal Music Group, 177
Universal Negro Improvement Associ-
ation, 26–27, 168
Universal Records, 333
University Democrats, 71
Unseld, Wes, 416
Unstoppable, 254
Untitled, 260
Up, Up, and Away, 251
Up From Slavery (Washington), 27
Uplift the Race (Lee), 239
the Upsetters, 385
Upshaw, Gene, 444
Uptight, 224
Uptown Records, 356, 360, 382
Uptown Saturday Night, 217, 222, 245
Urban Coalition, 60
Urban Institute, 60, 80
Urban Journal, 188
Urban League
and business, 168, 178
and civil rights, 35, 46, 55–57, 59–
60
and education, 98, 106, 109
and music, 284
and politics, 66, 68, 71, 86
and religion, 129
and the arts, 244, 270, 276
and the media, 186
and the military, 452–54, 459
Uridin, Jalal, 295
U.S. Anti-Doping Agency, 432
U.S. Census Bureau, 194
U.S. Information Service, 261
U.S. Lawn Tennis Association, 419
U.S. Marine Band, 329
U.S. National Championships, 419
U.S. Olympic Committee Substance
Abuse Center, 436
U.S. Open, 413, 422, 428, 445
Us Organization, 107
U.S. Strike Command, 462
USA for Africa, 374, 385, 392
USA Outdoor Championship, 432
USA Today, 424
USAF Command Pilot Astronaut
Wings, 397
USAFE (United States Air Forces in
Europe), 462